PENGUIN BOOKS

LADIES AND GENTLEMEN—
LENNY BRUCE!!

Albert Goldman was educated at the University of Chicago and Columbia University, where he taught on and off for the better part of his twenty-year career as a professor of English and comparative literature. Gradually, his interests shifted from the classics to the popular culture of the present day. Having served as a music critic and contributed to the leading intellectual journals, he left the university in 1972 to devote himself entirely to journalism and the composition of a series of pioneering studies of the popular arts, of which the first was this biography of Lenny Bruce. Subsequently, he published best-selling lives of Elvis Presley and John Lennon. Currently, he is at work on a book about Jim Morrison.

Lawrence Schiller is an Emmy Award winning motion picture producer and director, having produced and directed such award-winning films as *The Executioner's Song* and *Peter the Great*. In addition, in the late 1970s he collaborated with writers such as Norman Mailer and W. Eugene Smith in the publication of many bestsellers, including *Marilyn*, *The Executioner's Song*, and *Minamata*. In the 60s and early 70s Mr. Schiller was an award-winning photojournalist for *Life*, *Time*, *Newsweek*, *The Saturday Evening Post*, and *The London Sunday Times*.

OTHER WORKS BY ALBERT GOLDMAN

The Mine and the Mint: Sources for the Writings of Thomas DeQuincey
Wagner on Music and Drama (co-editor with Everett Sprinchorn)
Freakshow: The Rocksoulbluesjazzsickjewblackhumorsexpoppsych
  Gig and Other Scenes from the Counter-Culture
Carnival in Rio (with photographs by Douglas and Lena Villers)
Grass Roots: Marijuana in America Today
Disco
Elvis
The Lives of John Lennon
Elvis: The Last 24 Hours

OTHER WORKS BY LAWRENCE SCHILLER

Marilyn (text by Norman Mailer)
The Scavengers (with Richard Warren Lewis)
LSD (with Dr. Sidney Cohen and Richard Alpert, Ph.D.)

Ladies and Gentlemen
LENNY BRUCE!!

by Albert Goldman,
from the journalism of
Lawrence Schiller

PENGUIN BOOKS

PENGUIN BOOKS
Published by the Penguin Group
Viking Penguin, a division of Penguin Books USA Inc.,
375 Hudson Street, New York, New York 10014, U.S.A.
Penguin Books Ltd, 27 Wrights Lane, London W8 5TZ, England
Penguin Books Australia Ltd, Ringwood, Victoria, Australia
Penguin Books Canada Ltd, 2801 John Street,
Markham, Ontario, Canada L3R 1B4
Penguin Books (N.Z.) Ltd, 182–190 Wairau Road,
Auckland 10, New Zealand
Penguin Books Ltd, Registered Offices:
Harmondsworth, Middlesex, England

First published in the United States of America by
Random House, Inc. 1974
Published in Penguin Books 1991

10 9 8 7 6 5 4 3 2 1

Letters, personal files and additional records of Lenny Bruce
courtesy of Sally Marr and The Estate of Lenny Bruce

Photographs courtesy of the Lenny Bruce Estate; photograph of
Joe Ancis courtesy of Joe Ancis

LIBRARY OF CONGRESS CATALOGING-IN-PUBLICATION DATA
Goldman, Albert Harry, 1927–
    Ladies and gentlemen—Lenny Bruce!! / by Albert Goldman, from the
journalism of Lawrence Schiller.
        p.   cm.
    Reprint. Previously published: New York : Random House, 1974.
    ISBN 0-14-013362-3
    1. Bruce, Lenny.   2. Comedians—United States—Biography.
I. Schiller, Lawrence.   II. Title.
[PN2287.B726G6   1990]
792.7'028'092—dc20
[B]   90-7697

Printed in the United States of America
Set in Times Roman

For George DeLeon
　　　　—A.G.

For Judi and my mother
　　　　—L.S.

CONTENTS

One   A DAY IN THE LIFE: A   3
RECONSTRUCTION

Two   HONEYTIME   64

Three   JEW BOY   81

Four   THE MISSING MAN   90

Five   HOW SICK HUMOR CAME UP THE RIVER   119
FROM BROOKLYN TO MANHATTAN,
ALONG THE GOWANUS PARKWAY
(42ND STREET EXIT)

Six   DIRTY LENNY   146

Seven   OPEN UP THOSE GOLDEN GATES   214

Eight   THE SICKEST OF THE SICK   251

Nine   "AMERICA'S NO. 1 VOMIC" (WINCHELL)   299

Ten   "ZUG ME, ZEYDAH! ZUG ME! TAKE IT,   377
YOU LITVAK LOLITA!"

Eleven   PERSECUTION   413

Twelve   TRIALS AND ERRORS   464

Thirteen   PRIVATE PARTS   510

Fourteen   SHIT   576

HOW THIS BOOK WAS WRITTEN   643

INDEX   647

Ladies and Gentlemen—
LENNY BRUCE!!

Chapter One

A DAY IN THE LIFE:
A RECONSTRUCTION

February 1960. Times Square. A dirty gray morning. From the Camel's sign a giant smoke ring floats through the dun air like a frost-blown kiss. The plate-glass sides of the papaya stands are as steamy as shower stalls. The movie barkers, in greatcoats with epaulettes of greenish grime, stalk back and forth clapping their hands in frost-rimed gloves. Even the shabby pigeons are reluctant to perch atop the cold metal head of George M. Cohan.

Around ten, a yellow cab, somewhat unsteadily driven, pulls up before a narrow gray dilapidated building on one of the dreariest side streets off the Square. Above the spattered pavement an extinguished neon sign flaps patches of cold hard shadow across the stone steps: HOTEL AMERICA, FREE PARKING. The cab stops with a jolt, back doors flying open so that two bare-headed men dressed in identical black raincoats can begin to crawl out from the debris within.

From the street side emerges a small dark-haired crab-backed fellow. He is handsome in your raffish Broadway manner, like a cat burglar or double-dealing private eye: a nose that looks like it must have been fixed, smooth tan skin, tight curly hair, Arab eyes, and delicate virtuoso hands. Tonight Lenny Bruce will open at New York's most sophisticated supper club, the Blue Angel, for $3,500 a week; right now he's having trouble keeping himself from falling on his ass. It's so cold, so early; he hurts so much inside. He has his fists jammed in the pockets of that black raincoat as if he were cranking up his hips on a set of hand pulleys.

Lenny's companion has crawled out the other door into the traffic. Tall, lean, and loose, in the West Coast style, he has a surprisingly soft, sleepy, pussycat punim, with shifty voluptuous eyes. Bending nearly double to pay the cabdriver, he pulls out an enormous roll of bills. Carrying the money, he is Lenny's current sidekick, road manager, baby-sitter, amanuensis, and "go-fer," Terry Lane, a former burlesque drummer from Los Angeles.

Lenny is Terry's temporary benefactor.

Terry is Lenny's temporary custodian.

At the moment, they are both whacked out of their kugels.

The night before, they wound up a very successful three-week run in Chicago at the Cloisters with a visit to the home of a certain hip show-biz druggist—a house so closely associated with drugs that show people call it the "shooting gallery." Terry smoked a couple of joints, dropped two blue tabs of mescaline, and skin-popped some Dilaudid; at the airport bar he also downed a pair of double Scotches. Lenny did his usual number: twelve $\frac{1}{16}$th-grain Dilaudid pills counted out of a big brown bottle like saccharins, dissolved in a 1-cc. ampule of Methedrine, heated in a blackened old spoon over a shoe-struck lucifer, and the resulting soup ingested from the leffel into a disposable needle and then whammed into the mainline.

Lenny was also into mescaline that evening: not just Terry's two little old-maidish tabs, but a whole fistful, chewed up in his mouth like Gelusils, exposed with his tongue to the assembled company in the manner of a dyspeptic Seventh Avenue garment manufacturer, and then washed down with a chocolate Yoo-hoo.

A couple of hours later, when Lenny jammed himself inside the toilet closet on board the plane, he calmly observed his face in the mirror becoming the head of a bird. A hard pointed beak sprouted from his nose, whorls of brightly colored feathers were circling his small red eyes, and his ears had disappeared entirely inside the smooth lovely lines of his neck and head. In the darkened drowsy cabin he stumbled back to his seat again, talking like Donald Duck. In front of him sat a prominent Catholic bishop. Lenny began to skim his bald pate with a rolled-up copy of *Time* magazine, closer and closer, until the stewardess said, "Please, Mr. Bruce, not here . . . on my plane . . ."

Then, somewhere over eastern Ohio—or was it western Pennsylvania?—the beautiful high the boys had cultivated in Chicago turned into an epic downer that left them passive, helpless, strapped into those airplane seats, mumbling loudly, disturbingly, a split-screen nightmare.

All those bad scenes on those little pop-up screens behind their eyes! A miracle that they had gotten off the plane at Kennedy, held their gear together, fallen into a cab headed for New York, and had even come up with the right name for their hotel: *The America*. Lenny always says, "I'm not like Shelley Berman, a Reform rabbi. Why make it at the Waldorf or the Plaza when I can have the same suite here for only thirty-six dollars a week?"

All the way into town they had bugged their driver, who kept glancing over his shoulder anxiously, or through his rear-view mirror, watching them lolling back there with their arms sometimes flung over their heads, as if they were doing the Watusi with their eyes shut. But some primal trouper's instinct had alerted them to the need to straighten out when the guy leaned over and yelled back at them: "Hey, you two, this is it!"

Now just trying to walk straight and look straight and get the fucking bags out of the cab without any being copped is a tough performance. What a mess they're making of the job. A bag of fruit has lost its bottom; apples, oranges, and grapes are rolling into the gutter and dribbling back against the curb. Lenny keeps swinging his shaving kit by its tab; Terry is carrying their precious 8-mm. home-movie camera like a combat photographer at Tarawa. One suitcase has been dropped too hard; its locks have busted, flooding the sidewalk with old copies of *Time, Newsweek,* and *Playboy*.

Thank God, at this moment a black bellhop comes to the grimy portico of the America and peers outside. Just one look at that crap blizzard on the sidewalk and he screeches with delight—*Lennnn-nnnnny Bruce!*

Stopped in his tracks, Lenny whirls around, arms flying, to cast a crazy, glazed look in the direction of the voice. "Chester, you woolly-haired sonofabitch! Come here and help us!"

It's like a scene out of *My Old Kentucky Home* done to a time-step. Chester comes chuckling down the steps to grab the bags and scoop up all that fruit and save the day. He is rewarded with a pat on his head "for luck" and a five-dollar bill, a kiss, a hug, one pump of the ass—all the instant intimacies of show biz.

Meanwhile, Terry has stumbled into the narrow unfurnished lobby, with Lenny, on the lam, following close behind, and Chester shuffling up the rear. Across those tiled yellow floors, smeared with the sheen of bare fluorescence, Lenny walks bent from the waist like an old man with lumbago, while Terry floats on ahead with the stride of an underwater goose-stepper.

The America is one of the most bizarre hotels in the world: a combination whorehouse, opium den, and lunatic asylum. One set of rooms is kept permanently empty for the nighttime hooker trade. One set is occupied by broken-down vaudevillians, like the rouged and bangled old crone who was the second wife of Buster Keaton. (This old girl never leaves her room even though it is not provided with a toilet.) One whole wing is rented out to junkies, who require a peculiar form of room service. "Look, Chester, I'm gonna take a big blast tonight. You better come up in three hours and have a look at me. If I'm blue, for Chrissake get me under the shower!" By the standards of this snake pit, where every bellman carries a piece under his red jacket, Lenny and Terry are as unremarkable as Rotarians at the Taft.

"Hi! I'm Lenny Bruce." Casting his poached-egg face into the albuminous face of the expressionless desk clerk. "I open tonight at the Blue Angel. I wired ahead for the room with Dufy blue. Gimme the key."

Lenny has this thing that every room in which he camps overnight should be painted Dufy (rhymes with goofy) blue so he's wired ahead fifty dollars to cover the paint job. The room should be just so . . . 365 days in a year he's on the road and wiring ahead that fifty dollars.

The instant the clerk hands across the key, Lenny whirls around in an airplane spin and makes off for the back of the lobby, where there's an elevator crammed behind a brass accordion gate. He swings it wide open, enters, closes it again after shoving in Terry, presses heavily and repeatedly on button six, and then shuts his eyes, breathing in deeply, jaggedly, as the old lift bumps and shifts and trundles its way up the drafty shaft toward his floor.

They burst out of the car into a narrow twisting corridor, as tight as the companionway of a ship, heading in the wrong direction. They reverse field, pass rooms 6G, 6D, 6B to—at last—6A. Lunging through the door like movie dicks, they burst into the world's crappiest-looking apartment.

Ready for the comeback of Lillian Russell, it has a big carved wooden mantelpiece framing a fireplace that doesn't work; for thirty years it's been a junkie stash hole. There is a moth-eaten carpet that appears to have been dyed with bottles of cinnebar and India inks. Across the windows hang heavy old portieres in musty samite and gold brocades; you can see perma-creases all over them, as if they'd been stored for years in the basement. On the lurid blue walls ancient reproductions of *Blue Boy* in gummy oils and the bosomy, blond, infinitely spiritual *Blind Girl* stare sightlessly into some cramped middle distance. There's a dim old St. George spearing an ineffectual dragon inside a chipped gilt frame. The walls, though freshly painted, are peeling, and not exactly Dufy blue except in the enameled bathroom, where the tub rests on tiny claw-footed legs, as if awaiting the body of Marat.

The instant Lenny and Terry are in the room, they start bolting and locking and chaining up the entranceway, lined for the greater part of its length with heavy brass security devices. They have instant access to two large rolls of Reynolds Wrap inside one suitcase, and they start to spread it across all the grimy windows, to keep out the sunlight during the day and create at night a flashing shimmer of light where otherwise there would be only the throbbing neons and depressing blackness of 47th Street. Inside all this aluminum—like a Brighton Beach sunbather propped inside his reflector—Lenny tears off his coat, his jacket, his shirt. He unzips the black leatherette shaving bag. Out come the works in a tumble: a half-dozen bottles of Methedrine with pointed Man-from-Mars heads, shiny disposable cellophane syringes, a long red urocatheter.

Terry seizes the red garter and whips it around Lenny's right arm. Lenny cracks the wrappings on a fresh syringe and snaps the neck off a Meth ampule. He thrusts the needle inside the vial, drawing back the colorless fluid. Holding the syringe perpendicular, he watches raptly as the first drop glistens at the tip. Then he looks down at his arm. This once sinewy limb with the American eagle tattoo atop the bicep is now a ruined, festering crotch. At the crack inside the elbow is a big black golf ball of infestation. Shooting six, eight, ten times a day has produced a hematoma. Lenny will have to shoot a smaller vein.

"Come on, man, for Chrissake. Bind it tighter. Tighten that thing! Harder! Harder!" Lenny is opening and closing his hand, flexing his wrist and forearm, staring at the back of his hand, the hand of a pianist perhaps, a Toscanini, jerking and flapping, as the catheter tightens, like the death gasps of a halibut.

Finally he sees where it's possible to hit. The right hand is laid out flat on the table. He steadies his left arm, his shooting arm, by grounding his elbow on the scratchy, sticky maple surface. He starts to slide the needle into a vein about an inch behind his knuckles.

Lenny isn't very steady. The first time he jabs only skin. He pulls back, sucks the needle clean, and goes in again. This time he lances the vein, but when he starts to push the plunger, he feels this sharp burning pain: "Shit, I've gone through . . ."

Lenny has pushed the needle clean through his vein. His hand oozes blood; pain nags at him. His head lolls down toward the table. His left hand trembles. "Terry, hit me!" He looks up. "Come on, man . . ."

Terry gives Lenny the garter ends. He takes up the syringe. With his big capable male-nurse hands, he aims and barely penetrates the skin. *There* . . . ooh!

A hit. A delicate column of blood starts to back up inside the plastic syringe. Lenny's right. It looks just like the stem of a rose. And there, where it meets and melds with the Meth, is the flower.

When Lenny sees the blood, he drops the garter and snatches the syringe from Terry. Squeezing down on the plunger hard, he empties the chamber, then starts to jack it full. The syringe is engorged with blood like a giant thermometer. He jacks it another time, when suddenly the Meth stuns him, and his head bobs down against the tabletop.

A swooning faint overcomes him, but he instantly feels flooded with a sudden surge of great strength—a feeling of warmth fills his whole body. His heart pounds. His vision sharpens. In the aluminum glare he seems to take on a halo of shimmers. Now he has perfect control over the ups and downs of the syringe. Again blood is forced back into his vein. With another pumping flick of the wrist, he jacks it back into the tube again, pumps it out again and in again, and then, breathing out a sigh, removes the needle with a quick professional twist.

Slowly, gratefully, Lenny brings himself erect, his stigmataed arm falling limply to his side. He stares down at Terry. "O.K., man, you next."

"No, no. I've had enough . . ." Shaking his head emphatically, Terry explains: "That fucking mescaline is still working in my head. No more for me till I sleep . . ."

"Come on, man, try it . . ."

"Lenny, I'm not a fucking pig like you!"

Lenny's laugh is mirthless. "Funny . . . ha ha . . ." His back is beginning to tighten up on him again; his mouth flaps open a little too loosely. "O.K., if you're not gonna shoot, then get the other bags and let's stash all this shit."

Your obedient servant. After all, Terry lives off Lenny's largesse: the $250 a week, the free junk, the extra girls, the clothes and meals and tickets and deals. More important, though, is the way he loves Lenny, like some fondly indulgent mother, who can deny nothing to her brilliant but ailing child. So many people love Lenny Bruce like a mother.

Terry unbolts the door and schleps in the other bags from the hall. Lenny reaches inside his hip pocket and produces a long, shiny, mean-looking gravity blade. A snap of the wrist and he carves the switch plate off the wall. Stopped in his tracks, Terry gazes, astonished. He's only just begun this gig with Lenny. He's still not hip to all his business.

"Man, what's with the light switch?"

"*Dig!*" Lenny's deeply absorbed with unscrewing the plate.

Out comes one of the screws, around revolves the rectangular placard against the scabby blue wall, exposing a dirty sinister-looking hole crowded with fuzzy old cloth-wrapped wires. "Heat don't like sticking their hands in where there's juice!" crows Lenny as he removes a brown bottle from his pocket and carefully stashes it inside the cavity. He is smiling, a mischievous little boy, when he revolves the switch plate to cover the hole again and bites down the screw with the point of his blade.

Now Lenny is into the whole business of stashing, the exhilarating nonsense of concealment and grab-bagging. Picking up the nearest suitcase, he swings it onto the big double bed and springs open the lids. He reaches inside a jumble of clothes, shoes, magazines, and toys. He hauls out a pale-green pasteboard box. His daily bread: a factory-sealed carton of one hundred glossy ampules of Meth. Gloatingly, Lenny reads the label:

This will have to be carefully hidden.

Lenny continues to fish out stock from his portable drugstore, handing each item to Terry, who lines everything up on the table. Finally the inventory:

1 bottle Dilaudid, 200 pills.
1 box no. 26 ¾-inch Luer-lok needles.
2 no. 30 needles.
2 no. 15 transfer needles.
2 2-cc. hypodermic syringes.
1 3-cc hypodermic syringe.
100 Hypak disposable syringes.
1 bottle Tuinal sleeping tablets.

1 bottle Biphetamine spansules.
1 bottle Phisoderm antiseptic soap.
1 bottle Phisohex antiseptic solution.
1 box cotton batting.
2 white plastic baby bottles with black caps for carrying moonshine
    Methedrine made by mixing the powdered drug ("crystal") with
    distilled water.
1 cooking spoon.
1 box kitchen matches.
1 elastic belt.

With Scotch tape from a big roll, Lenny starts to stash the goodies
in his favorite hiding places. Some go on the ledge above and behind
the closet door. Other pieces are taped to the tops of the drawers inside
the dresser. Nothing goes inside the medicine cabinet except the sleeping pills, the baby bottles, and the antiseptic solution.

Lenny's doing a number at this point in his life. The police aren't
rousting him yet. There was that one bad scene in the parking lot of
the Crescendo; but Lenny cooled the beef so fast he actually got back
in time to make the second show. He learned his lesson.

From then on he has concentrated on getting *prescriptions* for his
drugs. Not that he doesn't like to run out and score in the street. *What
junkie isn't into scoring?* But when you've got a lot of prescription
stuff, you can play with the bottles and make it look like the illegal
stuff is the same shit for which some doctor wrote scripts.

Doctors are the keys to the medicine chest. Lenny is really a genius
at putting away docs. His greatest scores are made right in the clubs
where he works. Soon as he starts a gig, he asks, "Is there a doctor
who shows up here a lot?"

"Oh, yes. Dr. Schwartz is always here because he likes the music."
After the show Lenny goes over to the doctor's table (imagine how
flattering that is!) and introduces himself and sits down and orders a
drink (which he can barely stomach). He comes on very charming and
little-boyish and chatters on about how much he admires doctors and
the wonderful work they do and how it was too bad that he never
followed through with his early ambition to study medicine—what is
a poor boy to do?

Gradually, he maneuvers the conversation around to this medical
problem that's been bugging him—he suffers from terrible migraines.

"What do you take for your headaches?" Well, he's been taking
Cafragut, which doesn't seem to help. Once, though, somebody prescribed a wonderful little pill that was called Dilong, Dilode, Di . . .

"Dilaudid?"

"Yes, that's it!"

"Hmmmmmm." The doctor frowns. "That's a very powerful drug, generally prescribed for terminal cancer, deep knife wounds, or extensive burns. *But if it works* . . . here's a prescription for 100 pills."

Now it's just a step from a doctor who lays a hundred Dilaudids on you to a doctor who decides he has a calling to save you from all the bad-assed pushers in the world. After all, the whole English narco program—which makes Lenny slather with longing—is based on the idea that addiction is a disease and one of the medicines is dope.

Even in America, there are doctors who feel that it is better to write script than have their junkie patients fed strychnine from the end of a dirty spike. Lenny lucked into one of these good guys in L.A., a youthful orthopedic surgeon from some small town.

Lenny was the doctor's first celebrity; he could hardly get over the fact that such a famous person was sitting right across his desk earnestly imploring his help. At first he balked when Lenny demanded Demerol for his headache and Methedrine for his "lethargy" (or was it his "narcolepsy"?). After a couple of visits, however—and a lot of sensible and entertaining chats, with those big dark eyes playing over him and all that flattering attention and sub-faggot flirtation—he finally relented and wrote prescriptions and phoned Schwab's and gave Lenny everything he wanted. Then the final demand was presented. One afternoon, after a long, philosophic discussion of the "realities" of the drug problem in the United States, young Dr. Norman P. Rotenberg pulled out of his top drawer a sheet of stationery and wrote to Lenny's dictation—well, not exactly "dictation," but with many urgently tendered "suggestions"—the letter that Lenny craved as the ultimate shield against the heat.

Lenny has the letter in several different forms: as a precious manuscript reposing in his luggage; as a Xerox in his files back home in Hollywood; as a small photo reduction suitable for carrying around in his wallet. To have it sewn into his skin next to the hollow in his right arm is what he'd really like.

Second in importance to the letter is the book: Lenny's folio-size city-by-city gazetteer of drug labels and prescriptions. It's a loose-leaf album in a plastic binder, the pages covered with hundreds of quaintly engraved labels off bottles, vials, and boxes of drugs. Every time Lenny has a prescription filled, he peels off the label and pastes it into his book. "If they ever bust me," he says, "I'll show them this book, with all these prescriptions written by all these doctors and filled by all these druggies and I'll say: These bastards made me into a junkie. No wonder I take stuff when they prescribe it for me! Damn right, Jim. If they ever bust me, I'll bust the whole fuckin' A.M.A.!"

Lenny's drug album is great fun to read. The directions on the

NORMAN P. ROTENBERG M D
⋯⋯ ⋯ ⋯ ⋯ ⋯
BEVERLY H LLS CALIFORNIA

December 29, 1961

TO WHOM IT MAY CONCERN:

Mr. Lenny Bruce of 8825 Hollywood Blvd., Los Angeles, California,
has been under my professional care for the past two years for
various minor orthopedic conditions. In addition, Mr. Bruce
suffers from episodes of severe depression and lethargy. His response to oral amphetamine has not been particularly satisfactory,
so he has been instructed in the proper use of intravenous injections of Methedrine (Metamphetamine Hydrochloride). This has given
a satisfactory response.

Methedrine in ampules of 1cc. (20mg.) together with disposable
syringes, has been prescribed for intravenous use as needed.

Mr. Bruce has asked that I write this letter in order that any
peace officer observing fresh needle marks on Mr. Bruce's arm may
be assured that they are the result of Methedrine injections for
therapeutic reasons.

                    Very truly yours,

                    Norman P. Rotenberg, M.D.

                    Norman P. Rotenberg, M. D.

NPR:ss

labels are so cute, so coy. "Take one at bedtime." Isn't that darling? *Time for beddy, Lenny. Take your medicine, honey. Mummy will put it in chocolate milk. There, there, sweetheart! Make it allgone. Good boy!*

Just as funny are the ones that say, "Take one in the morning." For Lenny that's the same as "Take one at bedtime." He never sleeps; that's why he's got all those sleeping pills like Tuinal. He just goes and goes on Meth until he's dying from fatigue. Then a handful of Tuinals—Lenny never takes *one* of anything—and he knocks himself out. Then he wakes up so drugged that his friends have to schlep him out of bed and walk him around the room for an hour.

But those kinda scenes never happen now. Because he got hip to Methedrine. The Magic Vitamin! You can be whacked out of your kugel on downers and one good blast of Meth will clean out your whole system. Set you back on your feet. Make you wild to do things, go places, and talk your fucking head off. Ever since that miraculous day in Detroit when Lenny was turned on by an experimental dentist, he's had his life on a string. For every downer he's had an upper—a regular yin-yang chemical yo-yo.

Once his pharmacy is stashed, Lenny is ready to relax and enjoy life. He tells Terry to take the stuff they won't be using immediately down to the hotel safe—where no one would think of looking for it—and as Terry scoops everything into a laundry sack, Lenny takes off his pants. He's got this thing about running around naked—well, not really naked but like some coy housewife out in Mineola with her kimono. When he finally steps out of the bathroom with a towel knotted around his waist, you try to relate like guys in a gym—but there's always this leak of lubricity. Not like he wants to cop your joint, but there's this funny aura of soft white flesh and things falling out that aren't supposed to fall out and little grabs and giggles and—Christ! The whole fuckin' thing is a tease, man! He married a stripper and he's the tease!

Or is he queer? Buddy Hackett and the boys at Hanson's were always kidding about that. "Where's Lenny?" Buddy: "Off in Morocco suckin' some sailor's cock."

Forget it! It's not that simple. Like the man said: "polymorphous perverse." The tree before it forks. That soft sensuous sex schmaltz spread over the whole world. Over tits and asses, cocks and balls, ripe peaches and juicy nectarines, big rich quarts of ice cream and little girls' tooshies, pet dogs and old dishwashers' well-oiled skin, mescaline trips and soft raggy Levis lifting your bird and pink-nippled sweet-faced goyishe punims—you name it, Jim! Lenny can get off on anything! Like he used to say: "Put a guy in the joint and he'll shtup anything—*mud!*"

Lenny hots up the atmosphere. Just look in his luggage—what's the first thing you see? A whole layer of shiny bright girlie magazines. "Stroke books," he calls them. *Playboy, Rogue, Dude, Gent, Nugget, Cavalier.* But he relates less to the pornographic bodies than he does to the sweet, dumb faces. How he loves to sit and study those goyishe punims.

Sometimes he's mean to them; he writes bad-boy captions beneath their pictures. "Doris was fressed up by a dyke roller-rink champ before her first period."

Sometimes he speculates on what they're really like. "See this chick with the heavy, wavy hormone hair? Well, she's got a mustache. Oh, you can't *see* it. Some artist took it out with an air brush. But it's there. Definitely! All spick broads, guinea broads, Jew broads—even Elizabeth Taylor—got that little mussy."

You'll never see Lenny with a spade chick—though he's asshole tight with some black men. When he sees a white cat walking down a street with a black broad, he gets uptight. No, man, what Lenny wants is that nice pale blonde or redhead, that Rita Hayworth, Ann Sheridan, Marilyn Monroe pussy. That sweet, white silky stuff.

Apart from his stroke books, Lenny's got a lot of reading material valised: *Time, Newsweek, Life, Variety, Down Beat, Metronome, TV Guide,* the local papers, books on drugs and show business, novels, picture books, caption cuties—a whole library. Terry is the librarian. Tall, shy, a country boy from Modesto, San Joaquin Valley, he went to college and music school, broke into the business as a jazz drummer, and when times got bad for jazz in the late forties, drifted into burlesque. Lenny met him in L.A. at Strip City. A Sunday night. Ethnic night! The whole house was full of lisping, smiling Japanese gardeners from Gardena dying to get a look at some giant white titties. As Terry settled down behind his drum set, he noticed this new M.C. teaching the piano player the changes for his opening number. The tune was "Remember Pearl Harbor." That killed Terry. By the next night, they were friends.

What grabbed Lenny was that Terry was a reader. One night Lenny asked his friend to draw up a list of fifty books every educated man should know. Poor Lenny. Never got beyond the tenth grade. But he came from the sort of Jewish family that reverences learning. His father was always quoting Pearl Buck. Lenny would say, "Wouldn't it be great to just sit and read! Really get *down* with it!"

Lenny hadn't got the patience, the concentration, the sitzfleisch. When he pushed too hard, he got terrible headaches. But Terry would sit at the table between shows, riddling off titles like an English professor! Evelyn Waugh, Aldous Huxley, Christopher Isherwood, _Black Lamb and Grey Falcon._ Whew! Lenny was impressed.

That was five or six years ago. Now Lenny Bruce is famous. He's the hipster hero. Around his face, figure, and fast-talking mouth resonates the whole hip culture. He's the _Playboy_ playboy come to life, with a gorgeous girl in one hand and in the other a copy of Dr. Schweitzer. When he walks out on the floor with _The New York Times_ rolled up in his fist and a heavy furrow running down his forehead (which gets the girls horny), he looks like some New Wave writer figuring out an existential detective story that could run in _Esquire_ while they were filming it at St. Tropez.

When Lenny starts to shpritz, interspersed with the hip jargon, flying off the bops and beats of his Broadway-Brooklyn raps, are allusions to big sounds like Stravinsky, Picasso, Charlie Parker, José Limon, James Joyce, jazz, existentialism, analysis, peyote cults, and California. He's concerned about the racial scene, the man in the White House, the economy, the way the country is changing. He has a philosophy, an attitude, speaks from experience, _done an awful lot of reading._ "Yes," he muses onstage, a finger arched across his lip, "I like to read for a couple of hours every night before I go to bed."

Well, why shouldn't he say that? It's part of his act, his image. But the image is a bitch to sustain. Lenny isn't that knowledgeable about jazz. He saw Europe through the porthole on the S.S. _Brooklyn._ Most everything he knows, he picked up at the movies. Even so, there's a way of handling his problem. Mort Sahl found the solution. It's called _osmosis._

The way Sahl worked? Wherever he was, at home, on the road, he would have his room lined with magazines and books. A voracious skimmer, he never read anything. By flipping through this and staring at that, reading a sentence here and picking up a word there, he got an idea of where everything was at. When he went into his monologue, you'd swear he'd digested the whole world. Charles de Gaulle, Dwight Eisenhower, segregation, Shelley Berman, trade unions, _Marty,_ Dave Brubeck, New York, Berkeley, Beckett, newspapers, coffee-houses, sandals, J. D. Salinger, filter-tip cigarettes, the State Department, Dick Clark, German radios, birth control, Charles Van Doren, Adlai Stevenson, natural-shoulder suits, Cuba, Israel, Dave Garroway, the Diners' Club, Billy Graham, sports cars, the Strategic Air Command—wow! A barrage!

Lenny doesn't need all that crap. He's really funny, not just nervous, like Sahl. But the trick is the same. He sits a guy like Terry down and says: "Look, man, here's the gig. I need an intellectual seeing-eye dog. Somebody who can check out the papers every day, read *Time* and *Newsweek,* do a little research for me, just set me up nice so when I go out on the floor tonight, I'm the best-informed person in the city. Dig it?"

The system works fine. Terry, Richey, Benny, or whoever's traveling with Lenny is always a smart, studious sort of cat. After all, what is literacy? Words. How do you learn words? Hear them. If you got a good ear and a tongue that can mimic anything, you can learn whole languages by rote. Lenny is a mind-mouth man. His brain is located somewhere between his ears and his tongue. All he has to do is get the hang of a word, and he finds a place to slip it into his act. That night he walks out on the stage and drops the bomb right on their heads. FLAMBOYANT, RATIONALIZATION, HERCULEAN, PROPINQUITY, PELLAGRA. Bam! Bam! Bam! He's killing the people!

What's more, Lenny is like Tennessee Williams or Arthur Miller. Scenes, voices, jump shots, zooms, pans, one-liners, burlesque bits, childhood memories—every fuckin' thing you'd ever want for movies, books, plays is flyin' through his head. He just has to get it down on paper. Needs a guy who can bring him out and get it down. He doesn't have to sit at a typewriter. Bring in Miss Knurch, some plain chick in a brown wrapper, set her in a corner like a court stenographer, and let her take it all down. The important thing is who he's talking to, the guy's *face.* Some faces are magnets. Just one look—everything flies out of your mouth. Fuckin' face is making you a genius! You want to tell it what you got in your head. You want to shock it, choke it up, gross it out, fuck it around.

Like with this autobiography Lenny's doing: *How to Talk Dirty and Influence People.* Great title! A cat like Terry says, "Lenny, how about when you were on the farm in Long Island . . . how about the Navy . . . how about the time you met Honey in Baltimore?" You don't hit all of them on a given day, but there's bound to be one aspect you can relate to, one set of changes you can blow. That's your creative shpritz for the day, man. Where it's *at!*

Terry also helps with the unpacking of Lenny's wardrobe: a half-dozen Kleenex suits, flimsy but elegantly fashionable Continental models that sell for $49.99 on Sixth Avenue. (Press one every afternoon for a week, then when it's time for a cleaning, make a present of it to the bell captain.) For off-duty hours, he's got his treasured Levis, worn with white boots that give his feet a Mother Goose look. Lenny buys the Levis in Army-Navy stores and bleaches them with Clorox, just like he did in the service. Then he takes them to some little uptight Hebe tailor and floors the man with his exacting specs: every seam must be opened, every piece of cloth recut, and a whole fancy custom-tailoring job done on this two-bit work garment. The tailors always scream and gesticulate and dribble ashes down their vests. Button-holing Lenny like he's a judge sentencing them to death, they plead with him to forget this mishigaas. Lenny laughs and pushes them down behind their sewing machines. He offers them stunning bribes. When he slips into the finished product and appraises the work, posing casually before a pier glass, his flair for fashion is confirmed. The pants cling to his thighs and round his ass with irresistible effect. The crotch carries his bird light and tight. The rounded collars flow down into a center vent that reveals his delicate blue-black chest hairs. "Cute 'n' kissy!" exults Lenny in the mirror. The way he loves to look—*"Cute 'n' kissy!"*

Lenny carries a vast supply of white underwear because he has all the classic Jewish cleanliness phobias. He may bathe or shower three times a day, swill glass after glass of mineral water, and spend endless hours in the bathroom sitting on the can meditating deeply on his current plans and future dreams. Lenny comes from a lower-middle-class society that allows no one any privacy unless they are protected by the seal of the bathroom door. Going into the bathroom is the equivalent of saying, "I want to be alone."

In *Stamp Help Out,* the kooky picture and caption book sold at his concerts, Lenny printed a photo of himself sitting naked on the can, head lowered, hands folded, with a funny sort of reflective, pursed-lip expression on his face that spells out the Toilet Thinker, the latter-day Jewish version of the Rodin classic. Actually, his ultimate ideal of pleasure is to sit naked on the can and take out a syringe and pop a vein and shoot and jack and shoot and jack and then maybe have some chick come in and cop his joint or just kiss his mouth—and him all the while dreaming of Honey and how she first loved him—and then draw out the syringe loaded with blood and shpritz it on the wall where there hangs an Andrew Wyeth picture of a typical American boy, associated in Lenny's mind with his roadies, all the young, blond straight-looking cats with whom he travels from city to city. Yes,the bathroom means a lot to Lenny Bruce. Cleanliness. Privacy. Fantasy. Ecstasy.

Fifteen minutes later, as Terry comes striding back into the room, the phone rings. The telephone is Lenny's favorite instrument, but he considers it beneath his professional dignity to take the calls himself. Terry must screen the callers and weed out everyone but the people of importance. After a couple of quick words into the receiver, Terry turns and says: "It's Arnold, Arnold Levinson. He's down in the lobby." "Great!" shouts Lenny across the room, "tell him to get his fat ass up here on the double!"

Always polite and soft-spoken, Terry relays the message through the battered greasy Bakelite: "Lenny says 'Please come up.' "

Within two minutes, there is a discreet knock at the door. After the usual delay caused by the business of unbolting, unchaining, and turning lock handles, the door swings open and there stands Arnold Brandeis Levinson.

Thick, slab-chested, a man with large pores and tiny eyes, Arnold looks comical squeezed inside the latest-model thin-line Continental suit. He's a show-biz attorney, and he's also supposed to be Lenny's manager; yet, there is a lot of make-believe in everything he does in Lenny's name because Lenny never really trusts anyone to do anything for him. Often Arnold finds himself being undercut by his own client. He is one of the legion of Lenny Bruce admirers who pay the price of pointless, not very profitable service for the privilege of access to the fascinating one.

"Lenny, how are you?" Beaming, Arnold crosses the room and seizes the towel-draped hero in a clumsy bear hug. "How was Chicago?"

Terry stands outside this touching scene; he doesn't know from fat Jewish lawyers who look like song pluggers. Levinson has just shaved, but already his face is shadowed with a new growth.

Terry hangs up clothes and tries to put away suitcases. He stacks magazines and manuscripts. Better to be Lenny's valet than just gawk at these two grown men, one naked, one ill-dressed, embracing like a *Pietà*.

"No shit, Lenny, tell me about Chicago. How did it go?" If Arnold notices Terry at all, he doesn't bother to introduce himself.

Lenny is coy. Backs away. He'll shpritz a bit.

"Chicago is so corrupt it's *thrilling!* There's some stuff you can't put down over long distance. Dig? Like turning on with the fuzz . . . I'm not shitting you, the narco squad." Lenny grins, knowing he is also turning Arnold on. ". . . We're sitting upstairs in this private dining room of a Maf restaurant with the head narco on the Gold Coast blowing pot together . . . Feature that . . ."

Perfunctorily, Arnold says, "You're kidding . . ." Which means he has a hard-on to hear more, more, more!

Lenny's flea-skip mind is already somewhere else. ". . . Another time we're out on a raid with these cats—I'm not shitting you, man —we're all together cozy in the squad car and we stop at this spade joint, the Sutherland . . . wasn't that it, Terry?"

Terry breathes out, "Sutherland Lounge . . ."

"Never mind names," Arnold, almost breathless, puts in.

Lenny is coy again, a cocktease! "It was the Sutherland, yeah, and they hit on a couple of guys who were dealing backstage. So they grab 'em, line 'em up against the wall with their hands on the bricks . . . dig this! . . . the head narco comes up to this one spade cat, reaches inside his jacket, grabs the stuff, and barks into his ear: *'This better be dynamite or I'll come back here and kick your ass all over the floor!'* "

Arnold is having a really good time. He's beginning to sweat, his face is getting red.

"So then . . ."

"*Then* . . ." Terry starts to put in.

Lenny is all over the floor, acting, waving his hands at all that Dufy blue, talking like a spade, like a cop. Even Terry can't help but chuckle. Lenny sure can act.

"We're back in the squad car now and we're really turned on. We're snorting pure drugstore cocaine, that dumb red rooflight is flashing, the siren is going whah-whah-whah . . . How's that for corruption, baby?"

Abruptly, Arnold feels called upon to be outright motherly. "Lenny, they might be setting you up for an entrapment. You ought to be more cool, baby . . ."

"Man, it *was* cool!" his soft watery Arab eyes bulging. Then he goes into his Steve McQueen bit. Lenny admires Steve McQueen's cool. He's flea-skipped now to the club, the big date in Chicago. After all, Arnold is his lawyer. He's here to talk business.

"It was a straight Mafia-type joint with the money under the table and the boss running around in the kitchen and all the big hitters sitting at ringside talking business all through my show. Real shtarkers, dig! The kind that wear wool suits with no underwear . . ."

Arnold laughs. Lenny's delighted. The line is from a great new piece of material he's worked up during this last week in Chicago and is going to try out tonight at the Blue Angel.

It's a great *what if:* "What if Shelley Berman were to work a Chicago Maf club!"

First, the shtarkers at ringside: Lenny does them like the sound of tape playing backward, growling *ahooahaooererudh* down in the Satchmo register. Then he does Shelley—a nasal, high-pitched hornet voice shooting zingers into the hoods.

"O.K., you guys, your cage is clean, you can get back in now . . . Where'd you get those ties—in *Sicily*?"

The hoods don't even hear him. It's inconceivable to these killers that anyone would dare to put them on: to put *them* on is to stick your feet into concrete and sink to the bottom of Lake Michigan. Finally, though, one barb gets through. The enraged hood rears up from his table and does a real dinosaur take. Lenny suddenly snaps into profile and roars, claws, works his head up and down like a papier-mâché brontosaurus. Perfect! Says everything. These guys are right out of the Ur-muck, the primal schmutz. Arnold chokes with laughter. His many chins are working. He wants a show, to be entertained, to see and hear all the new bits and some of the old. "Lenny, do more! Do Bela Lugosi! The Lawrence Welk bit, one more time please! . . . please! . . ."

Lenny is prancing around the room. "Not now, Arnold. You know I don't do bits . . ." He wants to see how much Arnold will plead. He's dancing around Terry wagging his ass. He's ready for anything with either cat. He's turned on. So much love at one time.

Abruptly his mood changes. A set of tight crabbed muscles in his groin relaxes on him, and he sort of sinks down offstage. This is his lawyer. We're here to talk business like grown-up men, aren't we? "Arnold, how much is this date really worth tonight?"

"It's O.K, Lenny. The price may be a little low . . ."

"What do you mean *low?* I told you I don't work for less than thirty-five hundred . . ."

"You should go and speak to him, Lenny. The date is firm. They're happy to have you. But the price has to be negotiated . . ."

Lenny would like to know if Blue Angel owner Max Gordon will comply with all of his special requirements: the Shure mike for "shading," the no-serving rule while he works, the limit on how close the nearest ringside table can be set. He is even more interested in his price—and he would enjoy hassling about it. He's terrific with owners. If he doesn't get what he wants up front, whammo, he's in to see the head man, whoever he is. "I don't feel so good tonight. I think I'll make it a short show . . ."

"Whaddya mean a *short show?* You're advertised. We got a full house out there . . ."

Lenny then goes into his lethargy, his lumbago, the hip, the back, the aftereffects of hepatitis.

At last the owner gets the message: "You mean you want more money, right?"

"Yeah, man, more money, more *motivation* . . ."

Lenny can get bread, cash on the barrel head, from the worst Maf types. He loves doing people. There should be no problem with Gordon. So what else is new? There must be some business they have to conduct. What sort of business? The trust fund for Kitty, Lenny's daughter? Arranging an allowance for momma Sally? Trying to put some money away . . . That's not so easy if you're blowing six hundred dollars a week on drugs. . . .

Arnold says, "Leave it to me, Lenny," a futile remark to make and he knows it, but he wants to be entertained again. He dosen't want to talk business. There's one subject that always titillates him: Lenny's sex life.

"Tell me," he interjects suddenly, "you still making out with that actress, Faye Dunaway? Nice girl!"

Lenny stares back at his mouthpiece, appraisingly. Should he go along with Arnold and give him a little squeeze on that engorging pecker of imaginings and fantasies, or keep the conversation on business? Let the cat have his fun . . .

Arnold's eyes dim: "What about Betty?"

"Betty," Lenny laughs, "she was a solid swinger . . ."

Lenny is *bored* with ancient exploits recapitulated. He either needs more Meth or better company. To be turned on again . . .

Arnold says, "Tell about Tina Louise . . ."

"Tell about that Faye Dunaway chick, come on," Arnold insists. "What's it like to fuck all that starlet pussy . . ."

Lenny isn't relating. "Look, man, in all my life—I'm gonna tell you the *emmis*, Arnold—in my life I've fucked at a conservative estimate maybe three hundred broads, cunts, you know . . . some of them were hookers, some were strippers, some exotic dancers in the dressing room waiting for their nails to dry, and some were little shmucky fans who came dancing by after a show to tell me, *'Come up later and I'll be in my jammies.'* But I'm gonna tell you one thing, flat out. That with all the tits and ass, all the bullshit glamour, there's been just one lady in my life that ever really captured my cock and made me wanna come back for a second piece—and that's my old lady, Honey, man. She's the only woman who *always* gets me horny."

Arnold knows this only too well: Lenny's former wife, Honey, was the one he gave it all away to: his soul, his dick, his love; and Honey took it all and treated him like shit. He gave her $16,000 to open up a dress shop on the Sunset Strip, and she blew it in one week turning on every freak in Hollywood. She still calls Lenny at all sorts of crazy hours—as Terry must know—and says: *"Guess what I'm doing right now!"*

That bitch. That fucking hillbilly whorehouse junkie dyke bitch! Arnold is beginning to feel like the irate mother-in-law. He says, "Listen, Lenny, you know what I'm really dying for?"

"A hot pastrami sandwich?"

"No bullshit, listen! Do you still do that bit with Dracula? The

Bela Lugosi—just do it for a minute. Just let me hear it again. I love
it so. For me you can do it. . . ."

"Come on, stop with the bits already, Arnold, and the bullshit.
Look, man, now look! I wanna tell you something. You're my manager.
There's two ways this deal can work. O.K. 'Cause there's two kinds
of managers. There's one manager who's like a nice Jewish father
. . . says, 'Now look here, Sonny. This is a pretty shitty business and
I saved up a little money in my time and like, shit, why don't you take
this money and get out of this fucking business. What do you want it
for. It's no good for you.'

"The other kind is the way I'm gonna have it with you or we're
not gonna have nothing! And that's like the telephone company, dig
it? Any time of the day and night—provided I pay my bill—I can pick
up that fucking phone and say give me L.A., Miami, Bangkok—
whatever the fuck it is—and I'm *there!* They don't give me a lot of
bullshit and say: 'Sure, when the prick needed a phone he was all "Gee
whiz!"and "I'll never forget this," but now that he doesn't need us—
because he has a goiter—he leaves us no "Goodbye," no "Thank you."

"That's the way I want it should be with us, man. Because, I'm
gonna tell you flat out, I just can't make scenes where I'm guilty: I
gotta do this, I *gotta* do that, I gotta put you away and tickle your dick.
Man, my whole life I've always felt guilty about anyone working for
me. I've overpaid and overtipped and overcomplimented. Every time
I've wanted something from somebody, I've always gone into that 'Say,
I hate to bug you—Christ, I know you're swamped already' crap. If
you could follow me around in hotels—even fuckin' toilets like this—
I'm always writing notes: 'Dear Housekeeper (I'm afraid to say *maid*):
I am sorry the room is in such a mess. I will give you five dollars a
week for a flower' (so they should see the money as a gift and not
wages for the servile). I'm tired of that shit, man, tired of guilted-out
relations with everybody."

Poor Arnold looks like a wet rabbit under this downpour. He's a
very mediocre pathetic guy who isn't worth very much as a lawyer or
a representative, and he knows it; but he gets along with show people,
they get along with him, and there's never too much tension; he's one
of Lenny's most efficient cat's paws.

How they got together tells the whole story. One day this shlocky
show-biz attorney is sitting in his office when the phone rings. "This
is Lenny Bruce . . ."

Arnold starts to fumffer: "Blah blah blah you must be putting me
on . . ."

"No, man, this is Lenny Bruce and I wanna come over and see
you on business . . ."

Arnold has heard the records. He's really turned on but cautious. He says: "Oh yeah, man, I'll make an appointment, yeah . . ."

Lenny says: "No, man, it's got to be *right now*. It's very urgent . . ."

So right away Arnold was *had,* and he's been had ever since. That's the way Lenny comes on to everybody. Like the Japs at Pearl. You do this. Run over there. Boom . . . Lenny is always dictating . . . Like *right now!* . . .

Arnold suddenly says: "What are we going to do about the Angel thing? You open tonight! That's a little room, man. It only seats a hundred and fifty people. You're really going to have a hassle on thirty-five hundred. You should come down. Go for twenty-five hundred and a percentage of the gate. You made a fortune last year at the Den on percentage . . ."

"Fuck percentage! I used to do that when I could have my mother stand at the door with a clicker and check it all out. I'm through with all that. I'm *hot* now. It's hip to laugh at Lenny Bruce. We're going for straight numbers . . ."

The phone rings.

"Get that, Terry . . ."

There is a momentary hushed conversation. Lenny isn't paying any attention. His mood is deepening rapidly. He's about to fall down into a big chasm of need—the drug thing again. He tries to rally himself. "I can't talk business now, man; let's go downstairs and give Terry here a little tour of Times Square. He's only been to New York once before in his life and then he was traveling with some nitwit band. Come on, we'll hip him to some of the groovy spots . . ."

Arnold asks, "And then maybe we'll go over to see Gordon . . ."

Lenny whips off his towel and stands bare-assed naked near the closet to select a fresh Levi suit. "What's the hurry, man, it's only twelve, maybe twelve-thirty. We ought to make it to Hubert's first . . ."

Terry asks, "Lenny, you're not gonna fix again, are you?"

Belligerently: "What do you think?"

In a flash he's fished a hypodermic and a Meth ampule out of his stash and is flipping the catheter around his arm. "If we weren't in a hurry, I would sterilize one of those number 30 needles and do my hand with that," he remarks to Terry. The number 30 needle is so delicate that it will blow in the wind. Lenny has the idea that it should be used for shooting into parts of the body that are visible because it leaves such a tiny mark. Lenny's always thinking of different angles on the drug scene. He's got another kind of needle, a very thick number 15, which he uses to slurp up the solution fast, instead of slowly drawing it through a 26 or 30. Then, when the syringe is loaded, he screws off the transfer needle and screws on the shooting spike. Very clever.

This time the shot goes smoothly. Lenny's not bad with the needle when his nerves are calm. As Terry cleans up the rubbish from the shot, Lenny slips into a suit of cute 'n' kissy Levis. Next, he checks out the constant companion of all his walks and cab rides: his portable tape recorder—a midget Mohawk installed in a specially designed attaché case. One lock is the on/off switch, the other is a tiny mike. Soon, the room will be a Sargasso Sea of unstrung magnetic tapes as Lenny goes through the night playing reel after reel. He's got some incredible phone conversations and tapes of women moaning and screaming as he balls them and jazz from the hi-fi and a couple dozen tapes of his own shows. Sometimes, when you sit and talk with him, he'll reach over with an absent-minded gesture and press the button on the recorder. Out of the speaker will emerge his own voice from the night before onstage, and Lenny will sit there staring at you with big spooky eyes and that expression ventriloquists get when they listen to their dummies: that fixed, overly attentive, yet abstracted look that masks the secret workings of their throats.

The three men leave the room. Filing through the serpentine halls, Lenny gets some big hellos from the black chambermaids. This warm reception doesn't come from being lovable. From the moment he sets foot in a hotel, he starts piecing people off. The bellhops get five-dollar tips. The switchboard operator, who handles his dozens of calls, gets ten. Esther Cohen, the homely Jewish spinster in 11C who does his typing, gets her price, plus unexpected little presents like a candy heart with a little note: "Here's $5 to buy some powder for your toosh!" He even slips a couple of bucks to the old Jewish pensioner who hangs around the lobby and adores Lenny and always mumbles when he walks by: "Zug nisht!" ("Don't say anything!") Lenny loves that phrase and uses it in his act. Yes, Lenny never forgets the basic rule: *everybody wants a taste,* a little piece of the action. He's known poverty, now he's making money. He doesn't mind parting with it.

His money problems are not caused by his generosity but by his craziness. He likes to throw money away. Just a few months ago, in Hollywood, a struggling actor named Bobby Ball asked Lenny if he could borrow his car to drive to an important audition. "You like the car?" asked Lenny, pointing to his $1,600 imported sedan. "Here's the key. I don't need a car. I'm on the road all the time. The car is yours." Bam! The third car that year down the drain. The same thing goes on at a lower rate with all the strung-out jazz musicians and broken-down show people who are forever putting the touch on Lenny. He never fails to come across. Then a couple of months later, playing some grisly date in Toledo or Lima or Detroit, he starts bemoaning his lot: how hard he works and how little he has in the bank. He writes a long letter to his accountant, begging him to hide the money in some place where he can't find it: in a secret vault or in stocks and bonds —anywhere—so that next time Honey calls him and says, "Daddy, I got a beef!" he can't take his last thousand and give it to the bitch. Money and dope! Dope and money! There's never enough of either. But Lenny makes artificial shortages. He squanders his goodies. The day of reckoning will find him a pauper.

The moment Lenny hits the street, he shapes his hands around his mouth like a megaphone and starts pointing out the landmarks like a Gray Line Tour guide. DIRECTLY BEFORE YOU IS THE FIRE ESCAPE AND STAGE DOOR OF THE WORLD-FAMOUS PALACE THEATER, HOME OF SOPHIE TUCKER (MOTHERTUCKER), AL JOLSON, ED WYNN, EDDIE CANTOR, MAURICE CHEVALIER, AND OTHER FAMOUS VARIETY STARS.

TO YOUR LEFT YOU SEE, AS THIS TOUR PROCEEDS, THE NOTORIOUS HAUNT OF JUNKIES, WINOS, AND PIMPS, THE FLANDERS HOTEL, WITH ITS EXTENSIVE LOBBY RUNNING FROM 47TH TO 48TH STREET.

THE VIEW TO YOUR RIGHT IS OF DUFFY SQUARE AND THE HAND-SOME PIGEON SHIT STATUE OF GEORGE M. COHAN, THE GREAT GOY WITH THE JEWISH STAGE NAME.

Steamily they progress up the block to a papaya stand on the corner, where Lenny insists they enter and partake of its wonderful health foods. Living out in California for a decade has hipped him to grains and vitamins, minerals and strange-tasting vegetable concoctions. As relentlessly as he works with dope and dissipation to undermine his health, just as determinedly he labors with health foods and fads to build himself up. He's very inconsistent about eating. Generally, he lives on egg salad sandwiches with huge portions of ice cream and boxes of Baby Ruths. Sometimes, though, he goes through a Henry VIII phase with nine-course Chinese banquets served in the hotel room and masticated with epic messiness. Soft, sweet, liquidy baby foods are his favorites, and he's always thirsty. So this papaya stand is almost as good as Candyland.

Lenny immediately gets a flash looking at the Puerto Rican standing behind the counter. "Hey, how are you? You have a very nice haircomb. I like that big high pomp." This P.R. can barely understand English, but Lenny is smiling and putting him on so cheerfully that he smiles back. In a fast aside, he whispers to the boys that the inspiration for the haircomb came from a Charlie Chan movie; turning back to the counter, he goes right on with the bit. "Listen, Number One Son, we want number one papaya, Piña Colada, coconut champagne.

O.K.?" Glancing at the cat with the orange-slicing gig, he exclaims: "Did you ever see a fucking machete chop like that! Sock that board, brother! I'm gonna clap time while you cut oranges. Scatty-waa, skooby-doo, da-de-de. Yeah, tote that bale, lift that nigger, fuck that white woman!"

Everybody's turning around and looking like, *"What the hell is this? Is he crazy? On something?"* Lenny's flying high. The guys are between a chuckle and a flush. Laughing? They're embarrassed. That uncomfortable laugh that starts with ha! and ends in oy!

A minute later, they're out of the schvitzy fruit parlor into the cold grimy draft of Times Square. Terry and Arnold turtle-neck inside their coats; Lenny breathes deep like a vacationer in the Adirondacks. That Methedrine furnace is burning inside him and his head is humming with intoxicating memories. Everything he looks at is charged with nostalgia.

Next door is the Metropole, where the moldy fig Dixielanders blow above the bar to an audience of cornball out-of-towners, half of them standing in the street and gaping through the open doors of the saloon.

Across the street is the Copper Rail, 125th Street in midtown, with steamy metal pans offering black-eyed peas and collard greens, fatback and chili sauce, the only bar in town where the black cats can cock back their stingy brims and let their voices slide up into the jive talk of Harlem.

Up the block is Hanson's, the ultimate candy store, where all the young comics hang out or run upstairs to talk to their agents in 1650 Broadway or do shtick at the back tables till old man Hanson chases them off or an agent runs in with a hot booking.

A block beyond is 52nd Street and Birdland and the Colony and all the famous jazz clubs—the Onyx, Three Deuces, Famous Door, the Swing, and the Downbeat—all plastered over now with pictures of strippers.

Farther over on Seventh are the Stage and the Little Carnegie and the eating joints where the shinglemen get together late at night at—what's that dump, *The Bird and Bottle?*—to cut up the money from the swindle in Jersey. Canvassers and closers, mechanics and bosses, the whole crew that used to hang out at Kellogg's Cafeteria before they shut it down. Oh Jesus! What a hard-on Lenny Bruce has for this fashluganah Square! No shit, man! He could get down and kiss the schmutzy pavement, like an old Jew in the Holy Land.

Now he's hauling the other guys behind him as he heads downtown toward 42nd Street. They pass a candy store with big red hearts in the window. *Pop!* go his fingers as he shouts, "Valentine's Day is coming!"

Into the store. He stands for a moment in front of the big glass case, lips pressed together, head down between his shoulders, eyes racing back and forth across the goodies. How he loves to play the little boy! Then he's ordering a big frilly-laced red-ribboned heart for Kitty and another one for Sally and then—a genius idea! "Terry, let's send a candy heart to Ralph Gleason and sign the card, 'Love, Nat Hentoff.' "

Terry chuckles inwardly. Ralph and Nat are editors of rival jazz journals; Ralph is a diabetic.

Charging out of the shop, Lenny stops in front of an oriental rug store and tries out his Sabu accent, "I vant to go Bagh-dad!" Then he explains to Arnold how he once had his name up there in big black letters on the marquee of the Strand, back in 1949, after he won the "Arthur Godfrey Talent Scouts." Did a skimpy little good-looking-boy act: jump on, do eight minutes of nothing, and run off—pathetic! Then, it's past the recruiting island and around the corner into 42nd Street.

Lenny is growing more and more excited. Enthusiasm and Methedrine are the twin screws driving him like a bouncing, spuming speed-boat through the crowds on the congested sidewalks. Words are smoking out of his mouth like machine-gun bullets; he isn't bothering to see where they hit. He's lost contact with the other guys and is plowing straight ahead on his own course. When he gets this manic, he always goes for some freaky physical move. Sure enough, the first sight of the movie marquees on 42nd Street, lying back one behind the other like pages in a giant baby primer, sparks him into action. He breaks into a clumsy sidewalk dance—is he Ruby Keeler on top of the cab?—and sings "42nd Street! Broadway!" while making those old-fashioned Busby Berkeley arm motions, you know, with the elbow gloves going up at angles. Waving his arms and stomping his feet in that black raincoat, a dancing octopus. Actually, he's more like a back fracture case trying to break out of his body cast. He can flail his extremities to a froth, but that damn cement-stuck spine of his won't give an inch. He's rigid at the core, tight-assed.

Arnold and Terry come up to find Lenny gathering a crowd. He spots them and yells without dropping a beat: "Get the cameras over here—I can't keep this up much longer!" Then, suddenly, he reaches over and seizes Terry's arm and drags him across the street and plants him in front of a huge pinball arcade; its big battered sign reads HUBERT'S MUSEUM AND FLEA CIRCUS. Breathlessly, Lenny babbles, "Look, man, isn't this fantastic!"

Terry looks and sees the world's largest collection of fusty, feisty, filthy war-surplus fun machines: bell-flash pinball, ramp-thump skee-ball, see-saw rocking pony, racing car windshield LOOK OUT!

Ancient Gypsy fortune teller, blue-flash-green-curtain foto booth, Western Badman facedown, creaky-dopey candy crane, submarine torpedo kill-the-Japs, knuckle-white grip tester, and an old-fashioned shooting gallery, crammed with all those corny ducks and profile tanks and twerpy soldiers.

"Cack, cack, cack" go the .22s, as the three men turn to stare at the dozens of little hooky-playing black kids who are scampering around this debauched rumpus room, plying the machines with coins and getting their rocks off. Hubert's is a temple to the god Vicarious Violence.

After allowing Terry one good look at this fun jungle with its spider monkeys, Lenny hauls him and the perplexed Arnold through the uproar to the back of the arcade. In a little booth, filling it like a coil of sausages in a box, sits an enormous woman selling tickets off a roll. Lenny buys three, hula-hulas through a turnstile, and descends headlong down a very steep flight of stairs. It's like tumbling down a coal chute into another world.

Standing around this large subterranean chamber, elevated like statues on their tiny spotlit stages, are all your archetypal freaks. Sealo, the Seal Boy. Andy Potato Chips, the Midget. Estelline, the Sword Swallower. Congo, the Jungle Creep. Princess Wago and her Pet Pythons. Presto, the Magician. John Hailey, the Strong Man. Jean Carol, the Tattooed Lady. On linoleum-tiled platforms they pose, speaking earnestly to the gawks, the dumb tattoos. First they tell their story; then they turn gracefully to the right, like clockwork figures, and motion the crowd on to the next attraction.

Lenny is ecstatic at the sight of the freaks. This is his heaven, the place toward which his fantasies have streamed since that first time, twenty years ago, when he was brought here as a little boy by his mother. Lenny lived out in North Bellmore, Long Island, with his father, Myron, and his step-mother, Dorothy. She was a legal secretary and he a clerk in a shoe store. They were hard-working, hard-trying people—but they weren't much fun. The real fun was Lenny's real mother, Sally. Though she was just a bar-maid in Greenpoint, she paid her rare visits all dolled up in a coat with a fox collar and a big toothy grin. They would go to the Long Island Railroad station and stand in the waiting room, sort of shy at first and then later affectionate. Lenny would bury his face in his mother's fur collar. He would snuggle next to her on the train.

Always they would come to Times Square. To have lunch, see a double feature, and go to Hubert's. That was the best part of the trip. Seeing the lady with the enema tubes coming out of her and the lady who was half man and especially the flea circus. Lenny has a tenacious grip on these childhood experiences; he never tires of repeating them. They are somehow the key to his whole being: his sick humor and his grotesquerie and his own freakish and bizarre existence, alone, on the road, with his drugs and needles and his onstage mystery and fascination.

Now he's dragging his friends with him back into his childhood, making them the playmates he never had when he was a lonely and isolated kid. His head bobs from side to side, a silly-billy grin is on his face, and his tongue is fashioning the strangest, naïvest, put-on dialogue with the freaks. Looking up at the tattooed lady, who appears to have some monstrous, leprous skin disease, he exclaims: "*Boy, you really have groovy legs!*" Asking the sword swallower, a Chinese, how the sword tastes: the man replies, "Just like ice-y cream." Finally, he drags the boys down to see Professor Roy Heckler and his flea circus.

The Professor is a dried-out, middle-aged man with a bald kidney-bean head, heavy horn-rimmed glasses, and a Polident baritone voice. For twenty-five years he has been delivering the same spiel about his fleas: "And now here's Napol-ee-on Bon-ee-part dragging his cannon. And here is Bru-tus pulling a chariot. Brutus and Napol-ee-on Bon-ee-part are going to do a race. Brutus is ahead. No, the winner is Napol-ee-on Bon-ee-part." The man seems so spaced, so indifferent to whether anyone is listening, you instinctively look to see if he has a malfunctioning hearing aid.

With his chin right on the table only a foot away from the fleas, Lenny watches barely visible little mites dressed in ballerina costumes, kicking soccer balls, turning carousels, lying in their cotton wool "flea hotel," and feeding greedily off the Professor's arm: he's Sally's little malted-milk-face boy, utterly absorbed by teeny-weeny fleas. He even breaks up when the Professor cracks his one joke: "If a dog were to walk by, I'd lose my act!"

Just to the right of the flea circus is a platform that contains the sinister-looking electric chair, a heavy wooden frame chair looped with leather straps and pigtail wires, in which the audience is invited to sit and receive a token electric shock. Beside the chair is Lenny's other favorite act, Albertus Alberta—half man and half woman. This old closet queen, as Lenny calls him, is dressed in a schizzy costume: a 1930s tux on the right side and on the left a flapper's flounced and spangled dress. Displaying each side of his body in turn, he delivers his spiel with a heavy French accent: "*Ledies and Gennelmen, I wuz born of noble parents in Parees, Frawnce, but I em a freak of medical sci-ence. You can thank the cree-a-tor that you whare not born like me: on half ze wo-man, one half ze man. You notice, this left pahrt of my bodee, I wear a 2½-inch Kitty Kelly skyscreper heel. I hev no muscle here, jus like ze wo-man, and a small wrist and feet and backside of ze wo-man. But"*—abruptly shifting to display his other side and lowering his voice to a truck driver growl—*"ON THIS SIDE, I CAN KICK A SOCCER BALL FIFTY YARDS AND LIFT THIS DUMBBELL OF ONE HUNDRED POUNDS,"* and on and on with everybody either gasping in wonder or doubling over with laughter.

One whole freak-packed half-hour they watch. Then Arnold— who retains some sense of business even if he is on a joy ride—decides they have all had enough and starts to nag Lenny to go back upstairs, get in the cab, and go over to the Blue Angel, where Max Gordon is awaiting them. Lenny is hard to persuade. Finally, he comes puffing up the stairs to tell Terry that they will come back another day, after getting out of their minds on mescaline: "That's the only way to really enjoy Hubert's."

Flagging down a cab on 42nd Street, all three climb inside and Arnold gives an address on East 55th Street. Lenny casts Terry a broad, farcical wink, touches the switch on his attaché case, and then leans forward to start up a conversation with the cabbie, a gross-looking middle-aged man with heavy, shiny black hair parted down the middle like an old-time bartender. "Ugggh, see some pretty weird types on this Forty-second Street, don't ya?"

"Mister, what I've seen in this city, I couldn't even begin to tell you. What are you, from out of town?"

"We just came from out of town. We don't know too much about New York."

"Well, mister, I'll tell ya. You're better off that way."

"I bet there are some places where we could meet some girls and get laid."

"Well, every man to his own taste. You got your taste and I got my taste, right? But I'll tell you one thing, mister, the bigger the lady, the more beautiful she's dressed up, the more fancy she looks, the bigger cock she sucks in her mouth. That's what I say. I never fuck any woman, I make them suck that thing down there."

"Oh, yeah?"

"Yeah. I was going out with a beautiful schoolteacher and she never sucked no cock. And I said, I'm going to make her suck cock. You know how to make a woman suck cock? It's very simple, you *just don't fuck them!* You go out with them and you kiss them, and you're doing things to them, but you never take it out and stick it in them. Get it? And they get hotter and hotter until finally, this beautiful, dignified, fine-talking schoolteacher, she's eating it right out of my fly. And that's the trick with women. Who wants to sweat his ass off? Lay back and let 'em suck, that's what I say. And the bigger, the fancier the lady, the bigger the fucking cock she's gonna suck!"

Then, staring into the rear-view mirror: "You're a nice-looking young fella. I don't think you'd have any trouble . . . and that kid back there with you, he wouldn't have any trouble, too. What the hell are you going over to this place for at two in the afternoon?"

"Well, we're going to ask if we can have a job."

"There ain't no job. Shit, this town is dead. I remember years ago, the fucking johns and the hookers, and we had the clubs and theaters. Now it's bullshit. New York is bullshit. That's what I say."

They pull up to the curb, Terry hands the driver a couple of bills—very little for such a great performance—and Lenny, Terry, and Arnold tumble out of the cab snickering like little boys who have just planted a firecracker in the teacher's desk. Lenny can hardly contain himself. He's dying to run back to the hotel and play back the tape. The cat was funny in the cab, but on tape . . . *Are you kidding?* This is the greatest animal he ever caught. *Bring 'Em Back Alive.* That schmuck! If only he knew his dirty mouth was on tape. Why, Lenny might even clean it up and do it on the floor tonight. He could bill it as a switch on the crude but lovable cabbies in the movies. Or that schmaltzy Hebe that Eddie Cantor does on TV. The thought of Cantor triggers his mind to a gag.

"Hey, Arnold, do you know why Cantor's eyes bug out? Because he takes it in the keister! That's right, Eddie shtups him in tochas and all the money they raise at the B'nai B'rith benefits goes to cool out the beefs!" Arnold's face splits in a big pumpkin laugh and Terry smirks.

The Blue Angel has Lenny uptight. It's not his sort of joint. He made his name in offbeat places along San Francisco's Broadway and L.A.'s Strip. Worked a lot of Mafia clubs in Chicago, Miami, Detroit, Pittsburgh, and Atlantic City. But the Blue Angel is his first heavy "class" date. It's this dim little East Side *boîte,* where he pictures Hildegarde wringing her chiffon rag and going through those long verse intros while the fag piano player tinkles behind her tooshie. It's got to be a lot of rich hemophiliacs and polo faggots and geriatric Russian princesses with purple veins on the back of their hands standing as high as their diamonds. Through the whole show, he'll be hearing people whispering: "What's *shmuck?* What's *putz?* What's *shtick?* What's, vots, vus?" But he has to make this gig. Because he digs the prestige, the name, the fame. He'll be able to stomp the out-of-town owners. "What's that? You don't want to stop service during my act? Well, you've got to because I'm used to working chic supper clubs— like the Blue Angel."

Walking into the club's murky interior, he immediately recognizes the proprietor, Max Gordon, a little, bald-headed, round-shouldered, cigar-smoking man with moist, arteried eyes crowned with bushy gray triangular brows. Though very soft-spoken and gentle in appearance, Max has the hard heart of a survivor. Greeting Lenny with a sweet smile, as if he were his zeydah, Max schlumps down atop a bar stool and awaits the pitch. He knows what's coming.

Lenny goes straight to the point when he talks business. "Look, Max, I wanna work this room but you've got to meet my price. I'll do two a night, three on the weekend, work a seven-day week, sweep up after hours. But the number is thirty-five hundred in cash!"

Max's eyebrows fly up in practiced surprise. The cigar is withdrawn from his little mouth like a cork from a bottle. "You gotta be kidding! You're way out of line! Thirty-five hundred dollars! I never paid that to anyone! I had Eartha Kitt . . . Miles Davis . . . Harry Belafonte . . . I never heard such a price. How would I make that?"

Lenny's right back at him, big dark eyes reaching under those shaggy eyebrows. "You'll *make* it, Max. Look what I did last year in New York. Went into the Den at the Duane, a nothing cocktail lounge, a place nobody ever heard of. I worked there one week and they were famous. After six months they were rich. Man, I schlepped in half the city, copped all kinds of press, did two shots on Steve Allen, killed the people! I'll do the same job for you. Better!"

Max has played this game before. He lobs it back to Lenny. Looking down at the floor, he moans: "This year business is bad. Nobody goes out anymore. We don't get the after-the-theater crowd like we used to. I'm not sure I can blah, blah, blah."

Lenny's moving in for the kill now. He's got his face right into Max's face and he's writing and toting up columns of figures on the palm of his hand. "Look, Max, just break it down in dollars and cents. Seven days, thirty-five hundred, that means I have to do five hundred dollars a night to pay myself. You got a hundred and fifty people here, a three-fifty cover, nobody walks out without getting stuck for twice that. A hundred and fifty times seven—that's a grand a night. So when all's said and done, I pay my salary with the first show and the second show is yours! It's that simple."

"Lenny," sighs Max, "it's a lot of money any way you figure it. If you were the only act it would be different. But, we got a policy here—three, sometimes four acts on the bill. I'm putting you with Robert Clary; he doesn't come cheap!" Meanwhile Max is thinking: "Yes, Lenny's hot now. He did business at that dump, the Duane. But this is not a little cocktail place. Here is a very chic club for middle-aged people who live on Sutton Place and come by after the show to drink a Scotch and Perrier and see a couple of French or English acts, something witty, clever, sophisticated. Lenny Bruce is different. He's with obscenities and fast talking and inside humor and hostility. People will be offended. There'll be walk-outs. Some nice middle-aged businessman staying with his wife at the Waldorf, business and vacation combined, they'll come up and say, 'What the hell kinda place are you running here? I didn't think this was the kind of show you put on here!' No joke!"

Finally, Max slides very slowly off his stool, takes a little shuffling walk down the bar to where the black glass partition marks off the entrance to the main room. For a minute he runs his eyes over the satiny, quilted walls, the pink and black tables crowded together like pieces on a chessboard, the tiny velvet-draped stage at the back of the room. At last, he turns around and comes up to Lenny, rolling the cigar in his flat, tapered, dry, old man's fingers. "All right, Lenny, I'm going to give you your price. *For one week only!*"—this with an emphatic pumping motion of the soggy-tipped cigar. "If you don't do business, I'm going to cancel. Understand me?"

"If I don't do business, I'm going to *kill* myself! You can even charge admission. Does that satisfy you?" Laughing, Lenny gives Max a hard squeeze on his bent shoulders. Shouting "Ah be gezint!" over his shoulder, he walks out the front door with his funny knock-kneed gait.

On the way back to the hotel, he is jubilant. Nothing delights him more than getting his own way. He's doing V-for-Victory signs with his hands. He's got an arm around Terry, and he's indulging Arnold in all kinds of fast shtick. A funny incident occurred around Christmas, just before Terry joined him in Chicago.

Lenny had taken a week off to work on his autobiography with a cat named Art Steuer, a ghost writer. They were holed up in this nine-by-eleven garbage can on North Dearborn, right in the heart of the Tenderloin. A round-the-clock scene with the meals in from the Chinks and nobody even bothering to take off his clothes. Lenny is very uptight because this is his first book, and he's not sure he can write. Having his words taken down makes him terribly self-conscious. Every two minutes, he yells: "Hold it!" Then he veers off on a different tack. Even worse than being stuck with everything that comes out of your mouth is not knowing how you're going over. Normally, he has a hundred people our there telling him that he's the greatest. Here, he's got this tired, cynical, dead-pan hack who keeps saying, "Don't worry, I can fix it up."

One night Lenny flips: "Goddamit, Art, we can't go on this way. Gotta find out if this stuff is good or we're just jerkin' each other off.

Gotta put the book to the test!" He throws on his coat and runs out of the room.

Ten minutes later, he's back, all excited and breathless, with this sleazy, horrible, cunty-looking broad. He's gone out and got himself a hooker! When the whore sees Art, she turns around real tough and says: "Hey, Buster, you didn't tell me there wuz two of yiz. I charge more for a party." Lenny says: "Look, honey, for the third time, I don't want you to ball me or blow me or do any of that shit. I'm gonna pay you for the trick, but I just want you to *read*. Sit down here and read some of this book I wrote."

The chick is really suspicious, but she sits down at the table with her coat on and glares at the first page. Then she tries to read it with her finger tracing the words and her mouth shaping the syllables. Ten minutes pass while she crawls down the page. Meanwhile, Lenny is staring at her as if she were a gypsy with a crystal ball. Finally, the tart looks up with this pained expression on her face and says: "Listen, mister—I'd rather fuck."

On the punch line, Lenny screams with laughter. One of his most ingratiating mannerisms is that he laughs at his own jokes.

The boys in the back seat are in a real buddy-buddy mood. Lenny's always at his best with guys. Women he puts away, charming them, fascinating them, seducing and little-boying them. With guys he's completely himself: free to say anything or do anything or fall into any mood. His whole Broadway-Hollywood-Show-Biz-Hustlerville world is really just an extension of adolescence. All day long the guys hang out in his room or around his pool, they do business or play games, they kid each other and do bits, they eat together and travel together and sleep together in the same rooms. Sometimes they even ball the same chicks—or each other. Whatever they're doing, Lenny is the leader, the spunkiest, most daring kid on the block. Sometimes he bloodies his nose or breaks a leg, but he has a lot of fun leading the boys all over the neighborhood in search of adventure.

Getting out of the cab into the cold raw air, with the big red-and-green sign of the America flaring over their heads, they decide to go up to the room and continue their business discussion. The lobby is rank with odors of oriental food. The Pinoy Pinay, a Philippine restaurant, beckons from the left. Its goofy sign triggers Lenny into a bit. "Hey, Arnold, dig the concept of a Filipino—a guy with a gold tooth who comes quick and giggles!" Zap! There's abstraction for you. Arnold grunts his pleasure. The switchboard girl gets up from her chair and says, "Mr. Bruce, here's a list of the calls that have come in for you . . . there's a lot of them."

When Lenny Bruce comes into a hotel, the switchboard lights up like a Luftwaffe raid over London. Every junkie, hooker, shadow-comic, shingle-man, and jazz musician in the city is trying to get through. All the dope fiends want to lay a taste on Lenny so they can hang out together. You know, "Let's get Lenny high and dig his crazy head!"

Almost as bad as the junkies are the broads who crash his quarters. Every painted-up, garter-belt whore wants to crawl in the sack with him. Give him some free trim. Lenny can't stand these freebie chicks. He's got his mind on business these days. Chicks don't mean a damn to him. He could go for a month without getting laid. Or he could jump the next broad who comes through the door. Really doesn't matter. What counts now is writing material, playing dates, getting his price up, moving into TV and films, and just keeping the show on the road. Chicks are the preoccupation of the unemployed.

Back inside his Dufy-blue command post, Lenny starts to issue orders. A job for everyone. Arnold has to get on the phone and start negotiating a deal with *Rogue.* They want Lenny to do a monthly column: salty, funny, hip contemporary stuff like he does on the floor. Solid! He'll be the hipster Dorothy Kilgallen. Let them come up with a number.

Terry must prepare surgery for the next case: the famous star of night-clubs, TV, and film, Lenny Bruce—who will soon be needing another injection. Terry must put the needles into immersion antiseptics (plopping them into a jar where they look like gleaming little tadpoles) and prepare the regular hypodermic syringes. Disposables are great for a fast blast, but they aren't for everyday use. Less finely honed than regular needles, they have tiny burrs that hurt like hell and tear up your veins.

Lenny loves to play doctor. He busies himself with the utensils of cooking: the heavy kitchen matches and the spoon and the cotton batting. Actually, Dilaudid is highly potent by mouth. But Lenny is just as hooked on the spike as he is on the drug. He makes jokes about shooting aspirin and often inoculates himself with penicillin. Any drug that isn't soluble—like Dolophine—makes no sense to him. After all, what would shooting be if it weren't preceded by an elaborate ritual? The ancient medicine man standing before the hotel campfire mixing his potions and bringing them to a frothing boil over the white man's safety match!

Once Lenny has crossed the most powerful of downers with the most vigorous of uppers, he retreats to the bathroom to savor in private the joys of the needle. He has no compunctions about shooting up in front of friends. It's no more embarrassing than taking a leak with another man. But if he's really going to get into his head after the flash, he's got to have his favorite meditation chamber. As he sits there heavy-headed above the bowl, the voices in the next room fade to the edge of awareness. He sinks down into that core of semiconsciousness that contains his deepest and most secret thoughts. Every junkie has a few scenes that comprise his ultimate reality. These are the obsessions to which he returns over and over again while under the influence of the drug. For Lenny the flash always triggers the association of that first time with Honey, years ago in Miami.

What an experience that was! Here was this callow Jewish kid of twenty-five, trying to look much older, with this fantastically volup-tuous stripper right off an old Petty Girl calendar. A big heart-shaped face with full, rich lips and sultry staring eyes. Fantastic tits with pale blue veins and exquisite pink nipples. Ass and belly and thighs and legs a mile long down to that high-arched foot just made for a cham-pagne slipper and a hot wet kiss with his tongue. No wonder Lenny can't stick a needle in his arm without thinking back to all the hot and steamy times with Honey.

He comes out bleary-eyed from the bathroom. His crew is sitting in their armchairs, reading the morning papers. Looking at them, he has the strange sensation that he hasn't seen them for hours. He's been alone, way down on the bottom of the sea. Now he's surfacing, but nobody around him has the faintest idea of how far he ventured into the depths. Like a dog who scruffs up some dirt over his mess, Lenny is eager to bury his latest descent with some purposeful, businesslike activity. Let's face it. He *is* profoundly guilty about the pleasure he derives from narcotics. He balances his ethical books by suffering a lot of pain for his illicit pleasures. He suffers physically and emotionally; but most of all he compensates for the stolen hours of bliss with hard, compulsive work. He was brought up to work, and by God, he never stops working. He's always into projects and plans and letters and calls and trips and openings and closings and all sorts of ordeals that keep him out on the road month after month, working his ass off and living bad in cheap hotels and never once knowing what it is to lie back and just let the good vibes roll down his body like molasses.

Now he stirs up the exhausted Terry with the demand that they compile a list of tasks that must be accomplished in the next couple of days. Wearily, Terry takes a clipboard that he carries for such prolusions and marks "1" very firmly in the upper left-hand corner with a period anchoring it on the page. Lenny is parading up and down the room, marshaling his thoughts through the forms of restlessness that always accompany his mental processes.

"I want you to go up to Harlem tomorrow, Terry, to Cecil Greene at the St. Theresa Hotel, and buy a couple of cans of pot for Soulman [their Chicago drugstore host last week] plus a carton of Bambu papers to wrap it in. That'll really kill him, when he sees those Bambu papers!" Bambu papers are really rare in drab old Chicago.

When Arnold hears this talk of pot, he pipes up with the smile of a bright student who already knows the answer: "You don't dig pot for yourself, do you, Lenny?"

"No, man, I hate that shit. It's a dizzy, dopey high. A shluffy high. I got enough shit going around in my head. I don't need some dumb *schvacho* hallucinogen. And I sure as hell ain't gonna get busted for holding that smelly garbage!"

Eyeing Lenny attentively, with slightly raised chin, expecting the next dictate, Terry hears the phone ring. Lenny snatches it up with a sudden uncontrollable reflex that is the most habitual gesture of his life. He answers with his fakeout voice: a low indistinct murmur, like someone just roused from sleep or a mourner mumbling through a heavy black veil. "Hullo?"

One sentence from the other end of the line, and he's identified the caller and is modulating rapidly to the appropriate key. The voice is female, young, innocent—a friend, victim, and lover. His tone is low, warm, intimate, inviting. "Barbara! What are you doing here? This is really great! Come up here right away. Hmmmmmmp!" A big smacky kiss over the house phone.

Turning to face the curious Terry and Arnold, Lenny confides: "Now you're gonna see a really cute—and hot—little chick. Just got in from Florida." A hesitant knock at the door followed by the metallic noises of unbolting and the curtain rises on Miss Barbara Bernstein of Miami Beach.

One of those deeply tanned Jewish brunettes whose skin at forty will be brown leather, Barbara is pure Miami. At sixteen, she was running around to nightclubs in loud convertibles driven by hopped-up Hebes from New York with a fake I.D. in her purse and a girl friend named Judi for protection. She made all the swinging scenes for years without ever once putting out. (Oh, maybe *once!*) When she met Lenny Bruce, she saw him as a star, an image. Just looking at him, with that perfect nose and that beautiful mouth, she knew they could have a relationship. The first time she saw him work, at the Belaire Hotel, she stole his picture right out of the display case in the lobby. Then, the craziest thing happened—she actually met Lenny! Spent time with him. Had fun with him. Without ever going out on a real date, they became lovers. It's not a big romance. She isn't kidding herself. But they're such good friends. When she decides to move to New York, the first thing that comes into her mind is hanging out with Lenny at his hotel, just like in Miami.

Lenny's attitude toward Barbara is rather more complicated. He puts people in pigeonholes, and he doesn't like them popping out unexpectedly. If you're part of his L.A. scene and you turn up in Frisco, you may get a chilly reception. Why? Because Lenny feels— it's one of his basic convictions—that people are always crowding him, moving in closer and closer to take bigger and bigger bites.

Now Barbara here is perfect in Miami. On the beach in a white two-piecer, skimming over the water in a speedboat with a scarf around her hair, or tooling down Collins Avenue in a cool convertible, she's really a delight. And it's so cute how she takes out those little sandwiches on seeded rye and lays them on the beach blanket. But in New York? In this crummy hotel? With all the hookers and hustlers? Yet there's no sense getting uptight. She's a nice-looking girl with long black hair, zaftig figure, and soft but bold eyes. And she's a great suck. What the hell! Let her hang around. Maybe later on they'll have some fun.

As soon as Barbara steps through the door, he takes her in his arms and gives her a long sweet kiss—just as if they were alone. Keeping one arm around her while taking the bag she's carrying with the other, he introduces her to Arnold (who rises politely) and Terry, who offers her a pleasant smile and a gentle hello. Drawing out a chair and helping her off with her coat, Lenny does the honors of his blue dormitory like an English milord in a thirties movie.

"Don't you recognize that bag?" Barbara says to Lenny, with an expectant smile on her face. Lenny stares at the old white fake-leather suitcase and makes out the dim initials HB on the top. "Hey!" he exclaims in his high-pitched nasal voice, "this is the bag I gave you, right?"

"Yes it is, and you told me that when I came to see you, I should bring it back. So here I am, returning your rightful legal property."

It was an old bag of Honey's, and he had impulsively given it to this kid. He's always giving things to people on the spur of the moment, things that happen to be lying around. It's his way of saying, "I appreciate what you've done for me."

But his mind is rolling back to the business she interrupted. "Listen, hon," he says apologetically, "we were just finishing up some business, so if you could just excuse me for a few minutes, I could wind this up and then we could talk some more, O.K.?"

Yes, she's glad to just sit there and watch him work. She did that many nights in Miami. She would stay up all night, supposedly taking dictation but actually playing games and gossiping and eating Chinks and finally going out into the pink dawn half-exhausted and half-elated by spending a night with a genius. Sure, she can wait.

Whatever he's doing, Lenny loves an audience. Now he's really in the mood for his business correspondence. It's all done by dictation because Lenny is illiterate. Well, not exactly illiterate—but he can hardly write. It's some kind of physical-emotional hang-up. He can't seem to control the pen, and it wanders all over the page and makes these dumb-looking letters, with big loops and blob shapes that are hard to read and sort of embarrassing to send. Read back, it never says exactly what he meant. So he has to write another whole thing squeezed into the right-hand margin. Sometimes even *that* doesn't get it. So he has to print very hard and slow in block letters way down at the bottom of the page, where there's hardly any space.

Better than writing is to take pictures and paste them on a sheet of paper and write funny captions underneath. Or do dialogue. Or copy out a bit—but that's pretty tedious. Best, really, is to dictate, have it typed, and sign it.

So he paces the room now with his head in the air and his hands drawing pictures of what he means. "Now here's the bit, man. We're gonna write to Seymour Grush, 121 South Beverly Drive, Beverly Hills, California—this is my accountant, Barbara"—with an earnest explanatory look—"and we're gonna say: 'Dear Grush, I am . . .' Strike that . . . make it . . . 'Dear Grush . . . Seymour . . . It was good talking to you on the phone . . .' "

Involuntarily, Lenny glances over toward Barbara, who says, also involuntarily, "Don't let me interrupt."

He grunts back at her softly.

"Dear Seymour . . . About the house, a few points I want you to stress to the architect and builder . . . the first to you . . . and naturally you won't divulge this to the architect and builder . . ."

Lenny is stuck again. The house is his favorite toy, the first house he ever owned, a $50,000 mustard-colored two-story bunker with a kidney-shaped pool and a spectacular view down the Hollywood hills and far out across the Strip to Long Beach. Lenny has just bought the place and is having it remodeled. His dreams of what it should be like are strictly suburban: the right kind of garbage disposal, air conditioners in every room, heated bathroom floors.

Pacing back and forth with his hands clasped against the small of his spine, he resumes. "I want everything called for in my letter, Seymour. No matter how much it costs . . . Even if . . . let's say I could save five thousand dollars by not having that particular whim or fancy. In essence . . . let's see . . . by this letter . . ."

Lenny is beginning to make hand gestures. He glances up and is caught in Barbara's hot moist Jewish look of passion. With lips pursed she says, "I do hope you can concentrate and I'm not interrupting."

"Air conditioning," retorts Lenny, with a brisk nod of executive disdain toward Terry. "I want an air conditioning unit that will be a little heavier than the house needs. Room temperature to me is the most important part of our living . . ."

Terry says, "Hold it a minute, Lenny, the phone," just as it starts to tinkle. He answers in a low voice: "Who?"

"It's Joe Ancis. He wants to lay something on you . . ."

"Later. Later."

Terry says, "Later, baby, call him later."

He drops the phone back on the cradle.

"You were saying, Lenny . . ."

"About the air conditioning," Arnold puts in.

"Thank you, sweetie." Beginning to pace again. "So, in other words, Seymour, if this house would usually require a ten-ton unit I want a fifteen installed . . . The same applies for the heating. It would be nice if we could get the combination kind, that's in the pages that I ripped out of this book that I'm enclosing . . ."

Lenny nods. It's as if he had just completed one rubric and were about to launch on another. Raising his chin off his chest, he keeps his eyes closed to avoid Barbara's heady glance.

He's trying to visualize the house with all improvements in place: the rows of coach lamps, the control panel with red, green, blue, and orange lights, the kitchen with all the latest electric burners and see-through ovens, and the hi-fi in every room that Lenny can cut into from a central control—yes, even outside, blaring on the patios . . .

"The floors in the living room can be cheap," Lenny, open-eyed again, goes on, "because we intend to have wall-to-wall carpeting immediately, except the bathroom and kitchen . . ."

This time he nods at Barbara curtly, as if to anticipate another of her trembling shy looks or remarks.

"The thing now," Lenny dictates, "is to figure out which way the cars drive in . . . Will they drive in the front of the house or the back? Keeping in mind the overall picture . . ."

Ring.

Again the phone!

"Get that, will you, Arnold?" snaps Lenny, but Terry has already grabbed it.

"Hello? Hi . . . How are you?" Terry glances up guiltily like a sneak thief. "It's Jack Roy . . ."

Another very funny friend of Lenny's. Jack Roy, like Joe Ancis, a shingleman, will later bill himself as Rodney Dangerfield.

Terry is whispering, "Jack really wants to speak to you, Lenny," and Barbara is squirming in her chair and Arnold is all shlonked out with love and expectation and maternal curiosity, and Lenny is still three thousand miles away in Hollywood movieland refurbishing his dream house.

"Later!" he barks. "Later!"

As soon as Terry hangs up, Lenny rattles on: "Now I want the wide cement road . . . driving right up to the garage . . . with those lampposts alternatively spaced . . . *for attractiveness and safety* . . . I want the road to be nice and wide . . . the cliff on the right coming up . . ." He has again closed his eyes. ". . . just past the gate . . . it will have to be cut, graded, and planted . . . with an attractive foilage that will be unusual and need little watering and gardening . . ."

The rhetoric is a bit ladies-magazine-ish for Lenny, who recognizes his plagiarism and glances about the room mischievously.

"It sounds lovely," Barbara says soothingly, as if to encourage him to give out with more of the same.

Now Lenny really feels as if he is being crowded by this Miami chick, but all he says is, "Jesus, look at the time! I gotta go get straight and shaved. Why don't you two guys finish up this thing with the notes on your clipboard, Terry, and I'm going to run into the toilet and get shaved and I'll be right out . . ."

Lenny has already departed for the bathroom. Against the sudden gush of a faucet, he calls out, "Don't forget to mention the baby's bathrooom, Terry . . . it should be adjacent to the guest room . . . the guest room should be twelve by fourteen . . . get it . . . *no less* . . . and the master bathroom should have one whole wall a mirror . . ."

Terry is scribbling notes rapidly and furiously hoping to get it all down before there is another phone call.

Arnold is staring at Barbara, wondering what's with this chick and the stuff Lenny passes up . . .

Barbara is trying not to stare back at Arnold. She knows he wouldn't mind fucking her, *but she would;* she's hoping Lenny will at least try to relate to her alone for thirty seconds.

Making scrape-scrape noises, humming, rat-ta-too-do, clapping his hands under water, saying, "Don't forget the closets . . . I want good sliding doors."

Lenny is elsewhere, at toilet, thinking about fine wooden veneers and sliding doors . . . He'll end up wasting a fortune on this ugly little house.

The phone has begun to ring again. This time Arnold stabs for it and barks out, *"Busy,"* and hangs up. He returns to ogling Barbara.

"Lenny," she starts to say, a very frightened little Jewish mouse, "I . . ."

"Can't hear you," he yells back. "Why not come in here a minute so we can talk . . ."

The door closes on them embracing, his face covered with a froth of shaving foam, and a wicked glimmer in his eye as it winks shut.

Terry and Arnold sit alone opposite each other casting appraising glances toward the closed door.

Terry says, "You know, Lenny hasn't been in bed for two days. It worries me; someday he's just going to fall over. It worries me, what should I do?"

"He's out of his nut," Arnold says. "Eventually, he'll sleep. Don't worry about him, he's strong as an ox. He never sleeps."

Like the sleeve on an accordion, the door of the bathroom is slowly opening. As if somebody had given it a little nudge . . . a touch . . . in the middle of the sentence. Arnold and Terry look up, as if they were watching a curtain slowly rising. As the door slowly opens, they can peek inside the bathroom, where Lenny, bare-assed naked, stands in front of the mirror, his face covered with shaving foam and a razor working on his cheek and . . . there's this Barbara, down on her hands and knees, a slave, an animal, sucking his joint! Just then, Lenny leans around, gives them back a sort of appraising, "Hmmm, she's not bad, how do you think she's doing, fellas?" look. Meanwhile, he goes right on shaving. Mr. Cool.

Arnold and Terry are flabbergasted. This is really out of hand! They see Lenny reach up inside the medicine cabinet and pull out a syringe that he must have stashed there. A disposable. He takes it and says, "Honey, you don't mind if I relax a little while you're doing that, do you?"

And he makes with the syringe like he's going to put it in his arm, and for one second she looks up with the dick in her mouth, and her eyes sort of rolling up funny around the dick. She's trying to look and she's got this big bone hanging out of her mouth, the faithful dog there. She's looking up and she sees this needle, and the vein, the purple golf ball in his arm . . . and then she screams! Tries to get up but falls backward and bumps her head on the toilet bowl.

Then he kicks the door shut, but they hear. "Oh, honey! Here, let me help you. I'm sorry, sweet . . ."

The two guys are fumffering around in their chairs trying to look different ways and it's really sicknik time. Later on, they'll laugh their heads off at this whole scene; now it's not so fuckin' funny. Lenny's practical jokes often take a bad turn. It's like he starts with a fantasy, then goes crashing into reality.

Finally, Lenny and Barbara come out of the bathroom together.

Lenny's wearing his bathrobe now, and he's still got a little foam on his face. Very considerately, he says, "Where are you staying?"

"I told you, I have this aunt in Brooklyn."

Lenny takes her into the hall and sweet-talks her for five minutes, standing out there with his robe on. Arnold and Terry listen to the conversation like twin conspirators. Arnold's got big stains under his arms and Terry's starting to think about getting high. Everything has gotten bent out of shape.

Lenny comes back in the room, looking very mischievous, his head bobbing from side to side, his eyes rolling around in their sockets. "O.K., you lechers, I hope that satisfied you. Next exhibition I work, I'm gonna do it with a gorilla!"

For the first time all afternoon, Arnold fails to respond to the gag. He gets up heavily from the chair into which he was plotzed; he gathers up his coat and mumbles something about his wife waiting for dinner. A quick "See you tonight!" He's out the door and down the hall.

Terry, too, starts to get up. "I'm goin' down and pick up a paper," he says, making for the door. Hardly has he gotten the words out of his mouth than Lenny is crowding him with an anxious look on his face. "Man, you're gonna come right back up, aren'tcha?" Then, before Terry can answer, Lenny flips his fear of being alone into a bit: "Because," he whines, imitating the sound of a five-year-old, "Mommy said you shouldn't go out and leave me. I might play with matches and burn myself!" Terry smiles, but he thinks, "Lenny *is* just like a kid when it comes to being left alone."

It's the turn-around time of day. The old hotel is groaning its way back to life after the stuporous slumber of the long winter afternoon. Steamy-sweet odors are rising from the Filipino restaurant, the heavy-footed tramp of new arrivals is heard outside the door, a furniture leg screeches upstairs, muffled conversation and giggly laughter leak through the wall from the neighboring room. Down at the end of the hall, a black bellman can be heard shouting, "Get the fuck outta this room! You ain't supposin' to be in here. Now, git, you fuckin' ho!"

Lenny is beginning to feel the first distant tingles of opening night. All day his mind has been on everything but his craft. Now showtime is drawing near. He has to get himself tuned up. He wants his "ca-tharsis": a warm bath followed by a high colonic irrigation, which he gives himself with the big old-fashioned red enema bag hooked to the shower-curtain rail. He suffers from that classic junkie ailment, a paralyzed asshole. Dope so deadens the muscles of the rectum that most heavy users have to decide each day which is more important—to get high or take a shit? For Lenny it's an especially vexing problem because he was brought up to believe that "regularity" is the foundation of health and that all sorts of diseases can result from "letting that crap rot inside you."

Uggh! He's really obsessed with his asshole, this dirty comic. That's why he's always sitting on the can, praying for relief. That's why he never leaves his room without first going into the bathroom and carefully washing his ass. His speech constantly betrays this obsession. "Toilet" is one of his favorite words: cheap little clubs are "toilets" or "shithouses"; when you bomb, you go "into the toilet"; people who talk dirty have "toilet mouths." After his high colonic, America's fastest-rising young comedian has to prepare his big pre-show blast of Meth.

To get himself way up, he needs a double dose of his normal 1-cc. amp. Terry prepares a really mighty shot, while Lenny picks out a place right behind his knee. It's difficult and painful; he's got to twist and squirm. Once that rush hits him, it's all worthwhile. One second he's soft and lassitudinous. The next he's ready to walk through walls, leap high buildings with a single bound, and impale a whole chorus line, like shiksabab.

He's really in a marvelous mood, jabbering and singing and getting dressed in a brand-new Italian-cut Kleenex suit with sharp black boots that have cute little loops at their backs. He even considers eating for a moment; then he scotches the idea. No sense loading up his stomach when he has to work. Terry can eat at the club. Lenny will take a piece of fruit. He's a regular Jewish mama with that take-a-piece-of-fruit routine. Even Terry decides to taste a little Meth. He cracks an amp and drinks the stuff down like tequila. It will help him stay awake during the show.

Finally, they're ready to go. Lenny is moving in fast, jerky nervous movements. Lining up his props. The newspaper, which he may or may not use. The cigarettes that he smokes during the White-Collar Drunk bit. Trick matches . . .

Going down to the lobby, Lenny is telling Terry about the fantastic reception he got at the Den in the Duane last year. Only his first record was available and his reputation had just begun to spread from West to East; yet on opening night the turnout was tremendous. Oh sure, there were some spectacular walkouts. Henry Morgan, the old radio comic, ran out so fast that his date got stuck with the check. Martin Gabel walked during the *Palladium*, but he had to sit on the stairs for twenty minutes because his wife, Arlene Francis, was fascinated by Lenny. The club owner was crazy about him. Kept raising his salary every week. Couldn't do enough for him. Redecorated the dressing room and hung it with Andrew Wyeths. Engaged a lavish suite for him at the Tuscany that must have been worth $1,200 a month.

By the time they pick up a cab at Duffy Square, Lenny's doing *Mr. First-Nighter* . . . "Your cab, sir." . . . "The little theater off Times Square" . . . Les Tremayne and Barbara Luddy. "You know, Terry," he suddenly breaks into his own performance, "when I was a kid my favorite thing in the whole world was my little yellow-dialed Philco. I had it in my room next to my bed and every afternoon as soon as I got home from school, I would switch it on and get those fifteen-minute shows like Dick Tracy and Buck Rogers and Little Orphan Annie and Jack Armstrong. I really envied Jack Armstrong. Here's this putz running all over the world with a private tutor and a good-looking chick. People are always laying great things on him, like expensive skis, and he puts the damn skis on and goes down the hill like a champion! I was on the awkward squad in school. Couldn't do shit. Me and a kid with a rheumatic heart called Bruce. (Now there's a weird bit!) When I first went into the business, I worked under the name of Mickey Leonard—my father's nickname plus my first name. Then I switched to Lenny Bruce. I never knew why I picked the name. It just sounded right and looked good on the marquee. Then, one night I'm working at Ann's in Frisco and I'm doing free association. Suddenly, I come up with this kid named Bruce who had the bad heart! Now, don't you think *that* had something to do with my choosing the name? Everything is so weird, man. We never know what the hell we're doing. Jack Roy used to rib me. He'd say, 'All you guys who try to get away from being Jewish by changing your last name always give the secret away by forgetting to change your *first* name. What kinda goy has a first name Lenny?' "

Terry's lying back in the corner of the cab during this monologue, feeling pretty happy. That jigger of Meth has brightened his eyes, opened his ears, warmed his heart, and put an edge on his appetite. Something tells him this will be a great night. Yes, every day with Lenny is an adventure.

When they walk into the Blue Angel, one look tells them that opening night is a sellout. The joint is jammed to the doors. The bar is buried under people. Every table in the back room is filled. Clouds of smoke and noise and crackling tension are rising from crowded bodies and widely distended mouths. Lenny's people have come to see him.

He draws a very special kind of audience. Night people, inside people, hipsters, like that table full of shinglemen over there: Joe Ancis and Jack Roy and Moe the Roller (who rolls the neatest joint on Broadway). They're drinking pretty good and enjoying a night off.

They didn't make a single sit in Jersey. Gave up the whole swindle to dig Lenny. Beyond them are some strange-looking women with tough, ballsy voices. Diesel dykes with their femme friends; the Tiny Tim crowd from Fat Black Pussy Cat or Page Three. Along the side walls, sitting at the banquettes, are the comics: Buddy Hackett, Shecky Greene, Milt Kamen, and Mel Brooks. All the heavies shpritzing themselves blind. Talking and broadcasting to the room at the same time. Some wild-looking hookers are camped up front with their sharp little pimps. After the show, they'll work the bar. Spade celebrities have the ringside: Wilt Chamberlain, Sammy Davis Jr., and a couple of young Swedish models laughing with forced hilarity and enjoying all the attention they're getting from the rest of the room and from the waiters, who are always superpolite to names and mixed couples.

Hustlers and celebrities aren't the only people in the room. You can spot drab newspaper men with their really drab wives and Earl Wilson yentas in bow ties and schmucky agents and flacks and show-biz parasites. People, too, from the other side of the tracks: from the thee-ah-tah and the butcher-paper intellectual weeklies and even a pair of horn-rimmed Brooks Bros. Ivy League Yiddish-British English Professors with their heavy-talking spouses. A dynamite audience of a kind that assembles for no other performer. Some of these people never go to nightclubs. They're bringing fantastic expectations to this evening. Any other comic would be throwing up in his dressing room. Not Lenny. He digs a heavy audience, an audience of wigs and intellects, who don't scream like fractured Hadassah ladies but just sit there and gloat over his brilliance, the incisiveness of his mind, the daring of his confessions, the zingy pinball ricochet of his associations, the zap of his language drawn from every dialect of the underground: showman, jazzman, hipster, whore. He'll eat these people up tonight. Make them sweat through their deodorants. When he walks off that stage, they'll go into shock.

First, though, he has to go backstage and suffer through the other acts. Standing in the wings with his hand in his pocket and a cigarette in his mouth, giving off his coolest Steve McQueen hip detective look, he watches sardonically as the singer—one of those wispy weird acne-on-the-shoulders Little Girl Blues—clutches the mike and croons her spooky ballads.

Finally the M.C. goes into Lenny's introduction, saying all the dumb crap they always say: "Outrageous . . . Honest . . . Sick . . . Healthy." What bullshit! He'll straighten this cat out before tomorrow evening. Lenny's walking out and getting a nice hand before he opens his mouth.

He looks great up there in his dark, slim-line suit with those marks of intensity in his face and those pale flawless features and that Italo-Jew-New-York-just-the-way-you're-s'posed-to-look head on him. They dig his looks, too. Dying to hear him shpritz.

Surveying the room, he spots the looped and draped velours above the stage. He steps forward and cases them, like he was an appraiser from the City Marshal's office. Suddenly, he lowers his head and shoots a bold glance into the house—a real arched-brow zinger. "Looks like some faggot decorator went nuts in here with a staple gun!" Bam! He's in, they're tittering. Then he goes for the extension: "Whoo-who!" [High fag scream] "It's just got to flow like *this*!" [Big wrist flap and faggy, camp gestures as he dances around triggering off staples with his thumb] They're starting to laugh. Now for a quick change-up. Take them into his confidence. "You know when I was a kid, I always dreamed about going to a nightclub." Nice, easy mood, nostalgia. Then into the thirties movie bits with the George Raft takes and the Eugene Pallette club-owner pushing back the panel in the office to get a view of the stage and the little shaded lamps on the tables and the tuxes and the deep-cleft gowns and the hair on the guys bayed back at the temples and Lenny home from the movies standing in front of the bathroom mirror with a scissors cutting away the hair from his temples so he'd have a hairline like Brian Aherne or Robert Taylor and then his disillusionment years later when he went to the Copa for the first time and everything was so tacky and there wasn't even a men's room attendant and they had whisky bottles right on the tables like a Bay Parkway Jewish wedding and . . . and . . . and . . . By the balls! They're hanging on his words. Eating out of his hand! Kvelling because it's *their* experience—but exactly!

Time for another quick change-up. Whoops! He's got a cigarette but he needs a light. "Excuse me, sir. Would you be good enough to let me have your cigarette?" The spotlight falls on the giant black, Wilt Chamberlain, at the ringside table with the platinum blond models. He stands up with a big grin splitting his face and reaches up easily to Lenny's level onstage. Lenny takes the cigarette, touches it to his, puffs up a light. Suddenly, something catches his eye. He stares at Chamberlain's cigarette, examines the end of it closely. In an astonished tone, he confides to the audience: "He *nigger-lipped* it!" The audience is struck dumb, seized in a paroxysm of embarrassment. "Can he . . . Did he . . . How could he! Outrageous! . . . Disgusting! . . . Sick!" Suddenly, Wilt Chamberlain doubles over with laughter, slapping his big bony hand against his thigh. Sammy Davis throws his head back and screams with the loudest laugh in the world. Instantly the whole house untenses and starts to giggle. Now they realize that was a *bit*. A fantastically bold bit about racial prejudice, which is, of course, all stereotypes and stock reactions and people saying dreadful things like that, but really *meaning* it. Whew! What a shock! What a catharsis! This guy is a genius, a magician. The ballsiest cat on the stage today.

Next thing you know he's pinning a guy at the third table back. "You there, Mr. Roosevelt!" It's true, the man looks exactly like the dead President. "And you, Maurice Chevalier!" Perfect! The man, a foreigner, is a dead ringer for the old star. Wow! What an eye! Now Lenny's rapping about Chicago, where he worked last week. "It's so corrupt, it's thrilling!" Boom, then into the Shelley Berman bit with the premise and the complication and the wool suits, the dinosaur takes, and the final extension, with the waiter in the kitchen desperately writing. "Dear Toledo Teddy: I've always admired your work. Blah, blah, blah. Signed, Dominus Vobiscum." Now they're really laughing. The shinglemen are doubling over as if machine-gun bullets were ripping into their guts. Christ, they sell to hitters like that in Jersey!

With all the laughter, Lenny is getting walkouts. One middle-aged man, very red in the face, is hustling his wife into her mink stole as he glares disapprovingly around the room. He isn't going to pay his money to hear this filth! And a gray-haired Jewish lawyer with a bent back is getting up to leave, more in sorrow than in anger, slowly wagging his head. How can people who call themselves liberals listen to such terrible racial stereotypes? This is what he's fought all his life. Now he should treat it like a joke?

The walkouts make the people who remain feel even closer to Lenny. They're the insiders. They dig what he's putting down. Fuck the squares! Only, they're getting pretty thirsty listening to all this wild stuff. People at the back of the room are making signals to the waiters. Drinks are being discreetly passed to accessible tables. Rules about not serving are O.K., but when there's a buck to be made—are you kidding, Carlo? The waiters really dig Lenny. They can smell money in the air. Let him say whatever he wants to. After all, he's entitled to his opinions! And they'll pocket a little extra change.

Lenny is really getting into his rhythm. It takes him a while to warm up and get his curve breaking nice across the dinner plates. Now he's catching that inside corner with every line. His high-pitched nasal voice is shaping the hip words and phrases just like a jazzman bending a note or bopping a tune. Talking fast, fast, fast. A Charlie Parker tempo. Those hands of his flying all over the place, like a deaf-mute in a panic. Now he's going through a whole series of insane what-ifs, like the genie in the candy store. Old Jew: "Make me a malted." Genie: Zoom! "You're a malted!" Or Lawrence Welk auditioning a junkie spade jazzman. Spade: "Ah got a monkey on mah back." Welk: "Dot's nice. We luff animals in dis band." Or Dracula and the building

superintendent. Super: "I don't know where you people lived before
. . . you're always gonna have trouble . . . tell your kids to stop kissin'
my dog on the neck."

When he runs through these what-ifs, you get a crazy surrealistic
jumble, like a mad projectionist up in his booth tearing the film out
of a dozen different flicks and throwing it all on the screen at the same
time. Just when you're getting used to bizarrely mismatched people
talking at cross-purposes, he flea-skips to a heavyweight routine: *The
White-Collar Drunk.*

"Ladies and gentlemen, in our profession [Profession! There's
dignity!] there is a tradition [Another heavy word!] of impersonating
[Heavy!] drunks, alcoholics. Red Skelton's *Guzzler's Gin,* a masterpiece. [Can you dig him digging Skelton! Piety, man piety!] Today,
though, we see a different kind of drunk. I call him The White-Collar
Drunk." Now Lenny does the regular audience at the Blue Angel:
cool, sophisticated, buffed nails, and whacked out of their heads.
Funny! He's really got the goyim down. Now he's going into the bit.
Does the upstage walk. The impressionist's turn. Lights a cigarette
and confronts the audience. A perfect take! He's transformed himself
into an upper-East-Side-faggot-alcoholic-prick-WASP-snob! He's got
the art-director cigarette puff. The big long sucky drag—then the arcing
away of the arm and the pantingly erotic exhalation. Funny! He's
getting laughs without lines. The way he holds that cigarette cocked
up in his hand—between the *middle* fingers! The way he puts on
that New England lockjaw voice! Phew! When it comes to doing fags,
Lenny Bruce is Sir John Gielgud. Now he's playing the other guy at
the bar, the gross-out Blue-Collar Drunk, good Gallo-wine man with
a toiletbowl voice. "If you don't give me thirty-nine cents for a Thun-
derbird, I'm gonna have to take you downtown." Then they're insulting
each other, hate answering hate, Fag vs. Hard Hat. Bout after bout
of baffled rage.

Next he's into *Father Flotsky,* one of his classics, his take on the
1930s prison-break movies. Everybody knows this piece from the record. The moment he announces it, he gets all the good vibes that
come from recognition. People are like children. They want to hear
the same story in the same words over and over again. Lenny is always
trying to shove something new down their throats. It's a hassle. Tonight, he's being nice to them by doing his standards.

This prison-break bit is three or four layers of association operating
simultaneously. It's great nostalgia, with all the old mugs and clichés
flooding back through your memory: the tough, hard-boiled warden,
played by Hume Cronyn; the handsome but mixed-up prison doctor,
Warner Baxter; the coarsely sympathetic con, Bart MacLane; and the

"Woman Across the Bay," Ann Dvorak—"with her two hooker friends, Linda Darnell and Iris Adrian." That's another level in this humor: making the people recognize, now that they're adults and know the score, the perversions and vices and sick stereotypes in those good wholesome American movies. Then, as if that isn't enough, he kicks the whole thing up onto the level of travesty. He's got a Death Row that's a crazy fantasy on criminal "types." A spade prisoner singing "Waterboy" and talking like a Tom, who shouts: "When Ah die, Ah'm gwine to that big ribber boat up in the sky! First thing, Ah'm gonna find out what 'gwine' is!" A tough little New York Leo Gorcey killer sings songs from *West Side Story* with altered lyrics: "I'm gonna fry tonight!" Then the Pat O'Brien prison priest, Father Flotsky, has this ridiculous confrontation with the bust-out hoodlum, giving him this big long moral speech that finally breaks down in absolute nonsense —"When the good road leads to the bad road . . . and the bad road . . . the good road . . . then the bad road blah, blah, blah."

Finally, the day is saved by the sudden appearance of the male nurse, Kiki. With a dazzling burst of comedy, Kiki bargains with the warden on the prisoners' demands. Warden: "O.K. you fruit, what else?" Kiki: "A gay bar in the West Wing and *I* want to be the Avon Representative for the whole prithon!" Socko, boffo, bingo, *#+*!!! The whole club is screaming with laughter, like an enormous red-tonsiled throat. He's really faklamached them. Now, will he bow off, or try to break the bank?

Fanning down the waves of applause with his free hand, while clutching the Shure mike in his fist, Lenny races straight into *How to Relax Your Colored Friends at Parties*. Usually, Eric Miller, a black guitar player, appears in this bit, lean and interesting-looking, his instrument slung around his neck. Lenny plays a suburban American building contractor, drunk at a party and drawn irresistibly to the hired musician. He gets off this long speech about how much he likes colored people, really admires their achievements. Tonight, working as a single, he has to do the dialogue as monologue. No problem, because he's always got a score of voices whirling around in his act. The whole polyglot lingo of America resounds through Lenny Bruce like an Aeolian harp with a bent septum. Not only will he do the bit solo—he'll point it at tonight's audience by changing the name of the contractor from Mr. Anderson to Mr. *Ancis*. (That'll give Joe a kick!)

Now Lenny's holding a whisky glass and toasting and talking in a hearty drunken voice to an invisible but all too obvious black cat. "That Joe Louis was a helluva fighter . . . Credit to your race . . . Don't you ever forget it, you sonava gun . . . Here's to Henry Armstrong! . . . These Hebes here . . . You're not Jewish, are you? . . .

No offense . . . I don't care what a guy is, providing he keeps his place . . . You're awright! . . . Know a lotta people in show business? . . . Ever meet Aunt Jemima? That guy on the Cream of Wheat box . . . Here's to Paul Robeson! . . . You get anything to eat? . . . I'll see if there's any fried chicken or watermelon . . . You're awright, come over here! . . . I'd like to have you over to the house . . . Be dark soon . . . Only I gotta sister . . . You wouldn't want no sheeny plowin' your sister, I don't want no coon plowin' mine . . . Promise you won't?"

Lenny's got that ugly, down-twisted mouth, like the old shtarker goyim when they're trying to be friendly. He's got their hearty "har-har" laugh. That punch-in-the-shoulder, man-to-man delivery. Pissed to the ears! Loaded with hate! A bullshitter, a bigot, an anti-Semite —a real 100%, flag-waving, Fourth-of-July American.

Suddenly the needle skitters off the record. Everybody knows this bit down to the point where the spade is invited out to the house. Tonight there's more—

"You really like to do it to everybody's sister?"

"Well, no, you missed the vernacular. It's not everybody's sister —I do it to sisters."

"Whaddya mean 'sisters'?"

"Just that—sisters."

"Why, you don't mean *sister* sisters!"

"Yeah."

"Ah, that's *impossible*. I never knew *that*. Ah, that's a lotta horse-shit. You can't do that to the—to the sisters? No kidding! Do they put out, those sisters?"

"Well, I mean, if you're built the way we are, you know . . . We're built abnormally large. You know that, don't you?"

"I heard you guys got a wang on ya, ya sonuva gun ya."

"Yes, uh, to use the vernacular, uh, it's sort of like a baby's arm with an apple in its fist. I think that's what, uh, Tennessee Williams said."

"Well, uh, ya mind if I see it?"

"No, I couldn't do that. I'm just playing guitar at this party."

"What the hell! Just whip it out there. Let's see that roll of tar paper you got there, Chonga!"

Dirty Lenny! Dirty Lenny! Dirty Lenny! The comics are shaking their heads in disbelief. The shinglemen are in convulsions. The dykes are barking like mastiffs. And one Broadway columnist is slipping out the door to lodge a complaint with the police. When the fuzz arrive, they'll find a dark stage. As soon as he gets the last laugh, Lenny charges off, head down, hands jammed in pockets, shouldering through the tumultuous house like a grimly slicing ice plow.

Without a coat, he jumps into the getaway cab that Terry has waiting, its engine running, beside the curb. The driver takes off. Lenny crumbles in a corner. Crashing. Suffering emotional bends worse than the pains of kicking. It's the ghastly moment of parturition from the audience, the umbilical snip that every comic dreads. You've killed the people, wiped them out, realized your dream of *total power*. Every gag, every laugh has carried you higher and higher. But when you start to come down, you realize that you're a million miles from reality. You can't talk to anyone, reach out to anyone, touch anyone—you're excruciatingly alone.

The cab pulls up before the America, nosing in between two huge white Eldorados. Lenny takes one look out the window and screams: "Terry! Dig those spade pimps! Is this an album cover!" Big black men in $250 green silk mohair Continental-to-the-bone hustler's suits (fresh out of the pawnshop) swathed in high-yaller polo coats and topped with tiny stingy-brims set lightly atop patent-leather, permanent-wave hair conks. White-on-white shirts (stolen from the best) with flamboyant hand-painted ties and orbicular fake-diamond stickpins. Massive pinky rings, with the pimp's name spelled out in zircons—TEDDY. Brilliantly shined $75 French alligator dude shoes. And a whole lotta shuckin' and jivin' and laughin' and knee-bendin' yackety-yakkin' goin' down there as the cats cock up those long cigarettes into mouths outlined with Crayola mustaches and emphasized by heavy shades that make them look like insanely happy blind men.

Across from the pimps cluster—like girls at a square dance—the white hookers with their fox furs and towering lacquered beehives and pencil-thin skirts and scissory legs and 4½-inch skyscraper heels. Most of them are garish bleached blondes, with charm bracelets, painted up to the eyes and batting their fake double-row lashes like moths in the chill night air. They're doing $25-a-shot prostitution plus pushing smack and grass. Only it's not straight prostitution—not on 47th Street! This is the Murphy Game. The chump pays the pimp for the hooker. She goes upstairs to turn the trick and tells him to follow. When he gets there, she's split.

Lenny can't resist the temptation to play the fool. Flinging open the cab door, he jumps out and runs over to the pimps, who stop in mid-sentence and eye him for a moment with open-mouthed astonishment. "Boys, boys," he cries with the busy gestures of a junior-high teacher at an afternoon tea dance, "don't be shy! Come over to the girls and I'll introduce you. We only have this prom once a year and we spent so much money on the band and I just think you should get to know each other!" Grabbing one evil-looking spade, he starts to pull him over to the girls. As the others catch on to the bit and who he is and the whole shtick, they break up! "You crazy mother, what you doin' out here with no coat on?" They're all slapping their thighs.

Dissolve to Lenny in his room again. With his shirt off and his necktie around his arm and the pills and the spoon and the cooking and the spike and the shot and this time it's the heavy stuff, Dilaudid, and when he gets the hit, he sinks down into a chair, completely wrecked and saying over and over again: "It's good! It's good! It's good!" Then he's just a frog sitting on a lily pad, blinking his eyes.

Terry, hovering anxiously in the background, watches this performance with some apprehensiveness. You never know with this heavy stuff what will happen. Lenny has told him about the dangers of an overdose and instructed him in what to do. "For Chrissake, man, don't panic and run out on me. Work on me. Gimme mouth-to-mouth and a heart rub. Get me in the tub or shoot some saline into me. Don't be afraid to call the doctor. Better go to the can than die!" Terry searches for a white face and bent form, signs of an O.D. Satisfied that Lenny's safe, he drops his pants and pricks himself in the rear. Terry can't put the spike into the mainline, but he digs Dilaudid as a skin pop. Soon he gets a thing going that in ten minutes brings him within hailing distance of Lenny. Lighting a cigarette and settling back in a chair with those cat eyes opening and closing in a lazy rhythm, he begins to nod off. Just at that moment, Lenny starts to talk in a mumbling dialect: "Man, we oughta go out and play. Terry. I feel good, let's do something."

Brought upright by this suggestion of further activity, Terry tells what's uppermost in his mind. "Lenny, you gotta take a week off and kick. You're taking so much now, I'm afraid you're gonna O.D. Each time you go down, you go lower. Aren't you afraid it's going to stop your heart, your breathing?"

Lenny's head is heavy and his eyes are at half-mast. When he tries to talk, the sound rumbles in his throat before his lips part. "Yeah," he mumbles, "when this gig is over, we'll go down to Florida for a week and I'll kick. It's not hard to kick. I've done it a hundred times."

"Have you ever stayed off dope for a real long time?"

"Never more than a week, man. I used to think I could stop whenever I wanted. That I was stronger than dope. Now I have to say dope is stronger than me . . . you start off with one or two pills, then it's three or four, and pretty soon to get that flash, you gotta have a whole handful. An' shit! Who wants to shoot without the flash? You understand? It's like kissing God!"

Terry feels pretty cool himself; he can guess what Lenny means, even if he doesn't mainline. Yet he's worried about the end of all this joy popping. "Lenny, aren't you afraid of death?"

Lenny raises his head and smiles wanly. "No, man. There's nothing sadder than a middle-aged hipster!" The phone rings. Terry makes a move to answer but Lenny holds up his hand. He'll take this very late caller.

He uses his fake-out voice: "Hullo?" A deep vibratory voice hums into the instrument, and Lenny's distrustful expression swiftly changes to a big boyish grin. "Billy, you bad man! Get on up here before I call the police."

Lenny's very special connection, Billy James, is the greatest of the new jazz drummers: a funky, double-jointed, upper-cutting genius who took jazz drumming away from the elegant and aristocratic bop drummers and set it back in the soul groove. Billy isn't playing much these days, but he does a lot of "teaching" and has many "pupils." The principal lesson is how to score; the students are all junior junkies. Tuition is the money you're invariably beaten for when you deal with Billy.

A crisp be-bop tattoo resounds on the door; the vault opens on a tall, thin black man in a raggedy raincoat and Dizzy Gillespie beret. "My main man!" He lays a broad copper-skinned palm, flat open for Lenny to slap down upon in the greeting that all the brothers use— and the white cats can never make.

Lenny really digs this wild genius-type cat, digs him for what he is and for what they have been through together in the West Coast shithouses. Billy is a great talker, who likes to come on as a man of culture and refinement. Tonight, he's on a misson: "Lenny, I jes' run into a cat who's got some *dynamite* shit. I thought I ought to bring the good news to you before anyone else, seein's how you and me is old stone buddies and shit."

Amused, Lenny recognizes the familiar hustle. Before he parts with any bread, he's going to have some fun with Billy.

An indignant pose. A how-dare-you look and an oh-no-you-don't lift to his voice. "Listen, Billy, the last time I gave you money for shit, you burned me. Grabbed the money and ran!"

"Maaaaaaan!" Billy's voice glisses up into the soprano register, as he responds with astonishment to this startling and wholly unexpected accusation. His face a mass of expressive corrugations, his eyes bulging so far out you can see the yellow all the way around the pupils, he launches into a self-defensive tirade that has Lenny snickering around the edges of his stern facial mask. "I don't know what transaction you're making reference to—I ain't see'd you in nearly a year! What's the sense, though, in standin' bullshittin' here when I got the man that's got the item you dig, swiped right offna drugstore shelf. I'm

tellin' you, Lenny, the minute the cat said 'Dilaudid,' I thought of you.
You know you can't get off behind no other kinda shit!"

Lenny is enjoying his role as mark. He pretends to soften. To
nibble at the bait. "What's the number, Billy?"

"Eighty cent gits it."

"Eighty dollars for a bottle of pills, man! You must be outta your
nut! And how do I know that you won't burn me again?"

Billy, reaching into those depths of virgin sincerity that lie open
and accessible to every true con man: "Lenny, baby, I'm not gonna
burn *you*. You my man. You one o' the cats. Gimme the eighty, man;
I be back in twenty minutes with the shit."

Suddenly he opens his coat, unbuckles his belt, and starts to pull
the old ratty-looking thong off his pants. "Here, man. Jes' to show
you how quick I be back, I'm gonna let you hold my belt. You *know*
I'm not gonna go runnin' with my pants fallin' down!" This line, delivered with a sincerity and spontaneity never rivaled in the Actors
Studio, sends Lenny reeling back in a mock gesture of overwhelmed
conviction. Shaking his head like the man who's now seen everything,
he takes the proffered belt and nods to Terry. Out comes the roll of
bills, off the top come four twenties. Into Billy's big bony hand goes
the money and the scene is played out. A fast burst of jivey amicability
covers the retreat of the drummer as he virtually runs out the door
shouting assurances that he'll be back in twenty minutes to deliver the
shit and recover his indispensable belt.

Lenny doubles over with choking laughter. Terry smiles his enigmatic smile. Finally: "Some day, man, I'm gonna have a trophy room
in my house and one whole wall is gonna be covered with all the pledges
I've gotten from the fuckin' Billy: belts and newspapers and little hats.
That'll be my Billy Hold-This-I'll-Be-Back-in-a-Minute Wall. Meanwhile, maybe we can get high sniffing this belt!"

Nighttime is also thinking-about-home time. With Billy gone, Lenny
starts to brood about Kitty, Sally, and Honey, the three women in his
life, the feminine constellation that revolves around this eternal son.
Kitty was only about a year old when Lenny and Honey were separated
and divorced. He got custody of the kid because her mother was doing
time at Terminal Island. At first he tried to get by with the help of a
nursemaid and a housekeeper. Then he copped out and said it would
be better if Kitty lived with his mother; that way she would have a
relative around her and Lenny could support both of them in the same
house. Hmmmm.

Now he decides to call Sally and find out what's happening. He

gets the long-distance operator on the line and gives her a number in
Hollywood. After the usual beeps and tweets, the phone rings twice
and a voice comes on. It's a troubled, suspicious, middle-aged voice
—not so different in its distrustful intonation from his own. He moves
in fast, "Ma, it's me—how's Kitty?"

LENNY, SWEETHEART, IS THAT YOU? WHAT A GREAT SURPRISE!
He doesn't call her very often; that's a fact.

DID YOU OPEN TONIGHT, HONEY? HOW DID IT GO? TELL ME
EVERYTHING THAT HAPPENED.

The voice is strong now, warm and urgent. Sally's whole life is her
Lenny, but the cord that connects them is often three thousand miles
long and a lot thinner than a telephone cable. She never knows from
one day to the next whether Lenny will dig her or put her down.

He's annoyed that he has to give a book report when all he wants
is the word that Kitty is O.K. So he offers a few telegraphic comments.
"Show went good . . . got my number . . . did a new piece of material
. . . Ma, how's Kitty?"

YOUR KID HAS EVERYTHING, LENNY, A MILLION-DOLLAR PER-
SONALITY AND YOUR MOTHER'S SENSE OF HUMOR. A loud self-
congratulatroy laugh follows this modest statement. Sally's an old
trouper and she's always onstage, always trying to put the people away.
Her most difficult audience is her son.

"That's great, Ma, but what is she really doing?"

SHE IMITATES HER DADDY AND THE FUNNY WAY HE WALKS! CAN
YOU BELIEVE THAT? FOUR YEARS OLD AND SHE'S DOING PEOPLE!

Lenny is not keen on the idea of his kid growing up to be a gypsy
like her mother.

"Ma, don't always be cuing her. I want my kid to grow up straight.
Is she listening to you?"

LENNY, I DON'T LET HER GET AWAY WITH A THING. I KNOW
LITTLE GIRLS. AFTER ALL, I WAS ONE MYSELF. KITTY CAN'T FOOL
HER GRANDMA. LISTEN, LENNY, WHERE ARE YOU STAYING?

Christ! Here it comes. The lecture on "How to live on the road."

"I'm at the America, like always, Ma."

LENNY! YOU'RE CRAZY TO STAY IN A PLACE LIKE THAT. YOU'LL
GET SOME DISEASE THERE. WHY DON'T YOU GO TO THE PARK SHERA-
TON LIKE ALL THE OTHER ACTS? WHEN I WAS IN THE BUSINESS, I
ALWAYS STAYED IN THE BEST HOTELS IN TOWN. YOU OWE IT TO
YOURSELF.

Lenny takes a deep breath. She's starting to get to him.

"Ma, you always stayed in the best and look how much money
you got today."

Getting a soft, husky Barbara Stanwyck bleat in her voice, Sally cops a plea.

LENNY, I'M JUST A JEWISH MOTHER WHO CAN'T HELP WORRYING ABOUT HER SON.

Some Jewish mother! At forty-nine she married a nineteen-year-old Chicano named Tony Viscarra whom she tried to mold into another Lenny Bruce. Boy, did he run her ass off! Now, she's torching for him.

"Ma, I gotta sleep now. I'm tired. I just wanted to see how everything was with you and Kitty."

Whoops! He's cutting her off again and there's one very important matter that must be brought up. With a sudden soberness and flatness of tone, she asks:

LENNY, DID YOU DECIDE WHAT TO DO ABOUT MY ALLOWANCE? I'VE GOT TERRIFIC EXPENSES WITH THIS KID AND I'M NOT WORKING.

"Call Seymour Grush tomorrow. He's got instructions to give you money and pay the rent and the pediatrician and the maid and the whole shtick. Don't worry about anything. The house will soon be done and you'll be living in a mansion. Don't stop working, though. It's the only thing that will keep your mind off Tony."

Sally doesn't want any discussion of her wayward husband. After chasing around Europe with him and going broke in Paris, the whole subject is much too touchy. She jumps back to Lenny's favorite theme.

THE DOCTOR SAYS THAT KITTY IS MUCH MORE INTELLIGENT THAN MOST KIDS HER AGE. ON THE I.Q. SHE GOT 138!

138 I.Q.? His was a lousy 112.

Lenny digs that. He'd love to raise Kitty like a fairy princess, cut off from all the ugliness of the world and surrounded by flowers and poetry and love.

"*De techter will be kluger den de tatta!* You dig it, Ma?" (Jesus, he spoke a whole line in Yiddish! He oughta take a bow!)

"Ma, I really gotta go now. Take care . . . don't worry about bread . . . and don't encourage Kitty to show off. I don't want any kid of mine running away to join the circus. Fashtayt?"

The phone clatters to rest. Lenny feels a momentary wave of depression. Talking to his mother is really a downer. He used to forget her for weeks when he was on the road. Now that she's Kitty's keeper, he can't lose her. What a drag!

Turning to the beat-up pay TV, he slips a quarter in the slot and watches the tube go into blue-white paroxysms. He's almost too weary to rest. Can't seem to sidestep himself, to fall down dead, relax, doze off. It's 3 A.M. As he clicks through the last desperate channels to stay on, staring dumbly at a kaleidoscope of dreary old ghosts, the alu-

minum crinkles against the windows and reflects back at him distorted
miniature replicas of his exhausted self.

Terry says, "Boy, you really do seem restless tonight." He is falling
asleep in his clothes, as if his whole body could evaporate through the
stitches with each stretch, each yawn. If only Lenny could try to get
some rest, then maybe he could too. "You still didn't get offstage,"
Terry tells him, "did you?"

Lenny is frog-eyed, croaking: "Think I gotta fix again . . ."

Again? Terry wants him to go out entirely, not just further up or
down. "Listen, baby, why don't you go see that chick I told you about?
The one who is always sending you those postcards . . ."

"What is this shit with chicks? You know I got no eyes for chicks."

If Terry can sell Lenny on going to see that chick, he can maybe
be alone, crap out, get off his feet. He's trying to seem enthusiastic
yet matter-of-fact. He doesn't want to tout Lenny.

"Matter of fact," he announces abruptly, "I was with an agent in
the club tonight who says this Gloria number is dynamite. Aces . . .
This gorgeous Southern hot-box model. And she must really dig your
ass, Lenny, to be sending you all those things. I bet you could have
some fun with her tonight. Why not? Instead of running around here
in my way doing bits like a caged animal, you could really get it off,
and then maybe I'd get some sleep. Because I've just got to lay out.
I really need it, Lenny . . ."

"Lemme see that nitwit postcard again."

Lenny is being compassionate. He doesn't really know if he is that
horny—though maybe—if she's the right sort of chick. "Just let me
look at that card again because I don't really know, Terry . . ."

Already his roommate is poking and sorting inside that makeshift
archive of magazines and manuscripts until, at last, he is able to produce this large, frilly, old-fashioned turn-of-the-century item purchased, obviously, from some faggoty Third Avenue camp supply
store.

"Dig this fella," says Terry, as he hands Lenny the ultimate billet-
doux, a come-on that mixes sentiments with their antithesis so cunningly and knowingly that both sender and receiver must, momentarily,
pulse within the same time loop.

On one side of the card, fading just a bit, a plumb little boy in
old-fashioned sailor suit and ribboned boater sits on a swing beside a
little girl with golden Orphan Annie curls. His bulky legs are encased
inside high-button shoes. She wears billowy skirts, white stockings,
slippers. They kiss ever so coyly, like hummingbirds. Captioned beneath their bottoms is: "This is better than swinging."

As if that weren't too much, Terry has found a second card: in faded tints of orange and yellow, an old biplane with elegantly strutted wings and butterfly fins soars beneath the line "Flying to you from————." The blank of this 1925 airmail card was for scribbling in Atlantic City, Myrtle Beach, Daytona . . .

The sender has obviously followed Lenny's moves from city to city in the trades. Always she encloses the same simple straight message: "If you're ever in New York and you have nothing to do please call me—TE 8-7076 . . . Gloria Stavers."

By Lenny's standards such a message implies sensibility, refined, charming, straight, not tacky, sensual. He takes note of the firm, clear, shapely feminine hand, the light faint whiff of an expensively funky cologne. "Pretty heavy . . . a pretty heavy hand. This chick must be pretty much together," Lenny muses. "Let me take a shot here."

He goes to the phone, connects the tape recorder, dials the number. Just then the television commences to broadcast the 3:30 station break between late-night horror movies—a series of public service announcements for various diseases. On the third ring he gets an answer: "Hello . . ." A deep voice, throbbing, thrilling, though somewhat blurred with the fatiguing lateness of the hour: *"Hello . . ."*

"Hi. This is Lenny Bruce."

The voice crispens, freshens: "Oh come on. You've got to be kidding . . ."

"No, this is me. I've got all your cards and I want to thank you. Could I come over?"

"Sure." She doesn't even hesitate. "It's really crazy you called tonight. I just came in from a party. I'm feeling great. Yes, do come over."

"I'll be a few minutes."

Lenny puts down the phone. His adrenaline is really pumping again, only not quite enough to make the date. So now there is other work to be done: sleeves to be rolled, syringes to be refilled with old reliable Dilaudid.

Terry cautions him. "Listen, man, two downers in a row; I don't know how you're gonna get it up."

"You know me, man, one thing about me," Lenny says. "I'm not like out of the junkie casebook. If I want to shtup I'll do it on Dilaudid or Meth. In fact, I'm gonna make myself a speedball with Dilaudid *and* Meth."

"That's not true, Lenny, and you know it. Remember that hooker in Chicago? That druggist sent her as a freebie and even so you couldn't get it up . . ."

"Man, she was an awful pig. If I had wanted to I could have . . . but not with that . . ."

"Come on, Lenny," Terry insists.

"Shut up and give me a hand. Now don't argue with me, baby. I'm tired and I just want to get it off good . . ."

Terry has already begun to obey orders again. He has found that red garter and wrapped it tight around Lenny's ruined arm. Now they are trying to get the vein up again, but it's in a terrible state, virtually destroyed. Terry says: "This thing with your veins, man, how much longer can you go on this way? That arm is really dangerous-looking. Isn't there some other place you can shoot?"

"I could do my hands again, or the back of my leg, if you want to do it for me."

Professionally, Terry says: "I think we'd better try it someplace else, because this is turning into a problem. Take your pants off and lie down on the couch. I'll shoot just behind the knee."

Lenny lies with his pants beneath his knees like a patient etherized on the proctologist's table, and as they work the leg back and forth, finally Terry is able to lay it in there—very painfully, though that doesn't seem to bother Lenny at all. He is very unresponsive to pain. He feels what other people feel, but he doesn't scream and carry on like other people. Every time he has a horrible operation or disease or falls out of a building, or some incredible suffering descends on him, he bears it with an odd stoic fortitude, and maybe even gets funny and crazy and hysterical about it all. Every down in his life is an up, so that now, when they get through, he is able to doze like a child on the sofa for about half an hour, and gets up again, feeling better.

This second shot has cooled him down. Now he's dry ice melting. He doesn't have the wheels spinning in his head, the shreck, the tension. That manic movement of his head has stopped. He feels very cool, collected, indifferent, totally into himself. Lenny isn't even talking very much, which, for him, is unthinkable. He gets into one of his sets of tailor-made jeans outfits.

"Man, you got to look cool tonight," he says, when he glances at himself in the mirror, and musses his hair. It's smooth, wavy, oily hair, quite nice-looking, though Lenny always complains that it's much too flat. He says he's a real Flat Top, like in Dick Tracy. He'd like it higher on top, maybe with long sideburns.

"No, come on, you don't want long sideburns," Terry always objects. "You're doing a dirty act, so you better look clean."

Always they argue about Lenny's hair, like women. Nothing is ever decided. Now, as Lenny starts out the door without so much as a "Later," it's no sweat with Terry. He's dying to sack out.

A night feeling, funny, almost uncanny, overtakes Lenny as he drifts down through the hotel; he feels like a moth fluttering out into some velvety softness beyond oblivion, so calm, smooth, self-contained, so very breezy yet somehow dusty. Lenny has a little invisible whistle in his mouth. He's whistling.

He gives a small wave to the cashier at the lobby desk. No words. Just two fingers up in the air. It's four o'clock. The large black minute hand corroding like a bloody needle against the giant clock chatters up to the perpendicular and then seems to stop.

Outside the hookers have taken sanctuary and the pimp cars are stashed along the Upper West Side. Sheets of windblown newsprint are the only moving thing, or perhaps a cop, an occasional drunk. Lenny hails a cab for the silent submerged run uptown to the East Side. He rides in sodden, sudden, unbecoming silence, as if inside a goldfish bowl, a sort of lumpen semi-hard-on against his thigh.

Every time he makes one of these blind dates, he always thinks how great it would be if he could fall in love again and forget about Honey. Drive one nail out with another. That's his only hope. Otherwise all his success will be spoiled by that nagging feeling that he's all alone in the world with no old lady to kiss and hug in bed at night, no sweet soft relaxed womanly body to draw the pins and needles out of his body and give him the solace of the breast. Where, though, is he going to find another Honey? A face like a kindergarten teacher and a body like a $100-a-night hooker. Wow! How he'd like to conk out now with all that sugar in his arms!

His cab pulls up, at last, in front of a modern white brick building in the East Fifties. Behind the plate-glass monogrammed entranceway, a uniformed doorman, dozing inside an armchair, is jolted awake by Lenny's slamming of the cab door. He comes to attention and then insists upon announcing him over the house phone.

A low throbbing well-modulated buzz is his open sesame. He enters another lobby, furnished like a decorator's sketch. All in all, this is a very chic address, a very chic pad. If she's young, single, a good-looking chick, Lenny thinks, she's got something good going because this is not the sort of place where airline stewardesses shack up.

He enters through the smoothly gliding doors of the automatic elevator. Something about automation always has gotten Lenny hot: a dim, efficient, gliding sensuality.

When the car lets him off again, he goes out into a hallway so very different from the squalid entrails of the America that it's like wiping yourself with fur. The paper on the walls is tactful, discreeet. There's a beautiful clean strip of carpet along the floor. No peeling paint here, or weird smells, or fifteen bolts and locks on every door with dents from the crowbars where the heisters tried to get in.

Lenny presses the small white ivory apartment button—*ding dong.*

The door swings open, and here's this beautiful girl. Not stunning and not gorgeous and not acres of hooker ass, and not like your uptight streamlined model, impossible paste-on bitch, but like a really lovely girl, very elegant and thin and delicate with a tiny waist. She's wearing this peasant blouse from Tibet that must have cost three old women their eyesight. Tight, tight pants, sealed in. A lovely face, nice eyes, no fake makeup, heavy eyeliner. A really beautiful shiksa. Such nice skin. But what's really heavy about this scene is that he can see beyond her into the pad and it's really too much, like out of a magazine. A big studio apartment with this gleaming polished wooden floor you could eat off, the walls lined with books, records, magazines. There's music on the hi-fi. Beautiful drapes, corduroy bolsters, milk-glass tables, tropical plants, a giant authentic bullfight poster from Spain. Everything is just a groove. And there are two cats walking slowly across the floor—one a blue, the other a Siamese—looking up at him. "Now, Chou-chou, be nice to our visitor," the girl says to the Siamese, as she lets Lenny through the door.

He's pretty banged out of his nut. In a different chemical condition, he might have been high-strung, even had an impulse to shake her hand; in this mood, he feels groovy and sexy and playful. So he gives her a long hot look and she's staring at him with her mouth slightly parted. And he walks in the room and he doesn't say anything and she doesn't say anything. He goes to the first bookcase and starts looking at the book titles. He really looks at them, man, reads them, like a second-hand bookstore: Stendhal, Plato, Nietzsche, Jewish persecution books . . . Heavy . . .

She closes the door and looks at him. What's he doing? He goes and looks through the next case of books: Hemingway, André Gide, *hmm,* what's this, a book on dope.

There's a hi-fi with records underneath, and he actually gets down and reads the covers: Miles Davis, The Staple Singers, Bach, Vivaldi, Billie Holiday. The chick wonders what's with him, he's weird, like a cat who came in out of the cold. But then she figures: "This is the way he has to do it. I'm cool. I'll stay cool. I'm just going to sit down and dig it."

She sits down, trying to compose herself with all her model cool.

Lenny's really into it now. He's actually into examining some of the books, the literary and philosophic titles, the Schopenhauer and Kierkegaard and especially the book on drugs done by doctors showing you all those pictures of pills. Dostoevsky—that's heavy. And Sartre. Genet . . . And such very hip jazz albums—Horace Silver and Charlie Parker; some soul sounds, some gospel, too—an autographed Ray Charles . . .

Next, he goes inside the little kitchen. Lenny's heavy on kitchens. He does a bit onstage about a hooker's icebox. Never anything in it: a split of champagne and maybe a parsley leaf stuck on the door, one dried-out olive, some tired lettuce. That's hookers—nothing to offer but dried cunts and empty iceboxes.

But when he opens this icebox, he sees she's into cooking. There are all these green leafy vegetables, fruits and milk, juices and eggs and bottled spring water—even Yoo-hoo chocolate pop!

After the kitchen, it's into the glossy clean white bathroom for Lenny. He examines all the colognes on display, and then the labels on the bottles in the medicine cabinet. He flushes the toilet once. Nice classy action there. No pipes groaning, like at the America, and through the open door he has a view of a reproduction of a Modigliani; a big deep bathroom, cool, a recess . . .

When he emerges again, Lenny is standing at the end of this big studio room before this lovely, slim short-haired brunette and he's into a bit now with his hands.

Like he's standing there, sizing it up with his hands. His beautiful hands are moving, shaping, framing the room with shutters, all different angles and shots and getting Gloria into the picture, too, and dropping down on one knee and focusing it and he's really got it all in there: that beautiful milk-glass coffee table, a swatch of glossy bare floor, all the nice furniture, copies of *Commentary, The Reporter,* the plants and flowers and leaves.

On the walls are neat frames around Marboro bookstore reproductions from the Picasso blue period. That big Spanish bullfight poster must have been schlepped back all the way from Spain. Lenny is so gassed and gratified and grooved by the whole scene that he finally just walks over there to her, sits down in front of her on the floor, crosses his legs, and he looks just adorable in his little tailor-made jeans with cute turned little round collars and all that nice little smoothed hair on him, and the cute little plastic surgery masterpiece of a nose, those beautiful swimming swami eyes.

He looks up at Gloria.

He gives her the longest, hottest, coolest, sexiest, sweetest, dirtiest look, the kind of frank adoring I-want-to-eat-your-pussy look that you can only give to somebody when you are so high that you don't even have to blink.

It's 5 A.M. The night is yawning.

Lenny sighs. "I *love* you . . ."

Then it was evening well into the next day.

Chapter Two

HONEYTIME

My father's name was Merle Gaston Jollis. I never saw him except once late at night when I was about six. My mother brought him to the room where my sister and I were sleeping. She switched on the light: "You two have been wanting to see your father. Well, here he is."

I must have been five or six. He smiled at us and asked which was which before she turned out the light again. I think they looked very nice together. Like a couple . . .

That was in Detroit. I was born in Manilla, Arkansas. The first thing I remember is not being allowed to talk to my sister. She's two years younger than I am. She was with my father's people. I was with my mother's people. My mother's people were like hillybilly people. My father's people were like city style.

My mother left after my sister was born and went to Detroit. That was in the thirties. I was born in 1927. Mom was very young and very beautiful. She had long red hair, just like me. I won't say what she did there. Pretty soon she remarried, a Canadian named Lloyd. They raided our house once when we were all in the tub. Cops with axes. I remember because we were all getting dressed for Thanksgiving Day. We were screaming and crying because we were in the tub and the police came crashing in the bathroom without knocking. I thought they were pretty out of line. It was exciting, but they could have knocked first.

The police said Lloyd was a bookie. I never liked Lloyd. He'd get jealous and hit Mom and used a lot of rank words. I guess I resented him a lot. Mom used to slip away and leave us with him. Then she'd come back and tell me about being in New York. I was like her confidante. Still, I got stuck with his name.

My name was Harriet Lloyd, but I've used a lot of other names. We all do. Lenny Bruce was really Leonard Alfred Schneider. Before I married him I was married twice. Once to Sekolian, an Armenian. He worked in a carnival. There wasn't very much between us. I liked to dance and so did he. The other guy came first. He was in prison. We'd done a job together. He was my friend. He said if we got married he would be paroled. I would have to say I was pregnant. I was very young. When it was all over I was still a virgin.

Until age nineteen I was always a virgin. I'd been in prison in Florida and seen lesbians and everything. I was the youngest white girl there, and I almost killed another woman in the kitchen. Beat her nearly to death with a poker. They gave me solitary. Ten days in the hole with bread and water . . .

My mother came to see me once and then I went home to be with her. We were almost like sisters sometimes. I knew about her other boyfriend: he was a sailor. I think she loved him more than Lloyd. I thought some of those people she hung around with were nice. You know, they liked to have fun.

The only thing Mom ever got uptight with me about was sex. Whenever I ran away and they found me and sent me back home again, I had to go to the doctor to be examined that I was still a virgin. She always said if I ever come up pregnant, she would kill me. But that was only until I went to prison that first time. Afterwards I was on my own.

I think I was sort of in love at fifteen. His name was Bob. We didn't do much except neck and pet and lift things. He was a sailor, too. They blew him up on the S.S. *Yosemite* during the war.

Then, let's see, I was born in 1927 and Lenny and I got together in Baltimore in 1951, when I was twenty-four. Honestly that seems so long ago but that was my first real love. I fell madly in love with Lenny. It was almost like love at first sight. That was in Baltimore in 1951. Later I had six abortions with him, in L.A., in Tijuana. That was before we had Kitty. We really planned Kitty. Honestly, I was so in love . . .

It's not true we were ever into drugs when Kitty was around. We made sure not to fix in front of her. Lenny was very strict about that. He could be that way. He would turn you on and then call you "junkie" . . .

But things get hazy sometimes, and I'm still a little blurry about
names and dates. Lenny and I called each other Momma and Daddy
and baby and honey before any of our L.A. friends started imitating
us. But when we met in Baltimore, I was stripping. My mother
didn't object. She was proud of me. The way I looked. I was the
headline stripper at a burlesque club. I can't remember the name of
the place. Lenny was at the Club Charles headlining. We met
because we were staying at the same hotel.

I can't even remember the name of the hotel, that was so long
ago. I had a woman lover then, a very nice, intelligent older person;
she was away in New York. In Baltimore, most people stayed at
this hotel. It had a twenty-four-hour coffee shop, with everybody's
picture on the walls, and the night people would congregate there.

I sort of remember this: we were both doing four-week
engagements. This was Lenny's first week and my last. I was bi; I
guess I always have been, women can be a lot softer, but I was also
a very good looker, striking, with long red hair and nice boobies.
Lenny used to say: "Sweet, freckled, shiksa punim." That was much
later, I think . . .

In those days I was calling myself Honey Harlowe. I'd never
seen Lenny Bruce before. It was his first week in Baltimore. He'd
already won the *Arthur Godfrey Talent Scouts.* He was on the way
up, but he was going through a lot of changes. You know, he was
going to sign up on this ship to Turkey as a regular deckhand, to do
the kind of job men do on ships. I don't know why. I'm hazy on
some things. I guess he just wanted to get himself together, you
know, straightened up, so for three months he was signed on to this
ship. Anyhow the first time I saw him in Baltimore I fell for him
hard, just by his appearance, the way he looked physically. Sexy
. . . I didn't even know about his head. That he could be so damn
funny . . .

I hadn't had that much fun with men yet, if you know what I
mean. That warm good feeling. I was more intimate with my friend,
this woman, but she was away in New York, and I was alone in the
coffee shop of the hotel on Lenny's opening night when all the clubs
had closed. Lenny didn't know anybody yet; I could tell that, you
know, that he didn't even know who was in town. The comic from
my club was Tommy Moe Raft, a short little guy, strictly burlesque,
slapstick. I was sitting with him. Lenny always said he was very
funny. All that kind of shtick with shoes ten times his size, big
shoulders and baggy pants. Like I already said, I was very
impressed in a dreamy sort of way with Lenny when he walked in.
He was with these two chorus girls from the Club Charles.

"Who's that?" I asked Tommy.

"Oh," he said, "he's a new comic, Lenny Bruce."

Tommy also knew the two girls. I asked him couldn't we have a little get-together party, you know, so I'd get a chance to meet Lenny. It went like this: he invited the chicks, and Lenny, I don't know, a couple of more types that were in the coffee shop, and then we all went up to Tommy's room because he had this little tape recorder and had been taping some bits, you know, to be done onstage.

Pretty soon we all started doing crazy little bits into the microphone, and Lenny, he got the Baltimore telephone book and would just pick any name at random. By now it was three-thirty or four in the morning, but Lenny started making calls, just to anybody in the book. He could be so crazy. You know, he really got the people shook up. Like if it was a guy, Lenny would more or less imply he'd been making it with the guy's old lady, even when he didn't know if the guy was married.

He wound up in a terrific argument with one dude. On purpose, Lenny told him: "O.K., mister, is that your final word on the matter? Because I love her and that's all there is to it. And we're both not gonna have the same woman because I'm coming right over there to get you so you might as well haul ass out of bed because I'm just around the corner right now . . ."

We're all laughing and grooving and Lenny's going on and on. He's really putting people on. Pretty soon I'm hysterical. It's almost daylight and everybody else has left except Lenny and me and Tommy, who is passed out in the corner, and then Lenny says we're splitting and he takes me up to my room.

It so happened, he had the room right above me. If I tapped like this he could hear me. Outside my room we stood in the hall talking and talking some more, you know, until you could see people starting in to leave for work, you know, the daytime people.

I still had on all this heavy makeup and stuff and Lenny had on his makeup too. In those days he was sort of Mr. Show Business, with the Max Factor pancake tan No. 2, and the tuxedo, and the tuxedo shirt, and one of those bows that tie beneath the collar. Cute . . .

That night we didn't even go to sleep. We went to our rooms and changed our clothes, and then we just went ahead and stayed up. We really made it together.

Anyhow, we fell madly in love, and we spent that week together like almost in each other's company entirely, because my friend was still away, and, as I say, we really made it together and fell madly in love. You know, I just knew I was crazy in love with Lenny and I could feel his love for me. He didn't mind about my friend. He was always pretty cool about things like that, especially other women. He would say: "Just so long as she's not here when I'm around." I guess he felt it was a need I had at the time. I mean he loved me so much, too.

But pretty soon Lenny had to go back to New York to catch his ship. He would be gone three months shipping out. I didn't know what to do. My friend was coming back. I was supposed to be in Miami. Lenny seemed pretty uptight. Before leaving he gave me his mother's address at 54 Livingstone Street in Brooklyn on a little key chain, and I gave him my mother's address in Detroit. I told him a letter could always reach me through her.

Anyhow, by the time I finished my Baltimore engagement, I was set to do the Paddock Club in South Beach, Miami. I flew down there. It was a treat, the wintertime. I had a real thing about Florida. When I was a kid I always used to run away from home and head down there. Once I got as far as St. Augustine in a stolen car . . . Did I tell you I was the youngest white girl in Raiford State Penitentiary? . . . I'm sorry . . . I'm drifting again . . .

It's 1951:

Lenny is in Spain already. I'm living off the 5th Street Causeway with my friend. He called me long distance from Spain. Seems he'd gotten in touch with my mother. Lenny was pretty crazy about some things. He really came on strong. Because he said he just couldn't make it without me. He was so madly in love with me he was flying back to Miami just to see me . . .

Now, Lenny was very romantic in those days. Crazy about flowers and poetry and all that stuff. So when he came back, he decided to surprise me with a real fairy-tale treat. He found out I was staying at the Floridian, and he got a room right above me like he had when we met in Baltimore. Then he goes to this nursery, some wholesale flower place, and he must have bought all the gladiolas in the whole store. Then he went around to different restaurants and got a bunch of those large potato-chip cans, you know, maybe a foot-and-a-half tall and maybe a foot around, and he covered them with that Reynolds Wrap paper, the silvery stuff, you know, and filled them up with gladiolas. Then he bribed the bellhop to open my room . . .

Well, when I opened the door to that room, there were beautiful big flowers everywhere. There must have been thousands of those glads, just beautiful; they were all over the place. He had

them on the dresser, the floor, the window sill—and two beautiful
crossed flowers on the bed!

He left a cute little note that said, "Call me and I'll come
running!" So I called and he came flying down from upstairs, and it
was just like, well, Paradise all over again . . .

Lenny really was my first love, my first and only love, and I fell
head over heels in love with him. I mean he swept me off my feet. I
was just so tired of holding my breath with people. With Lenny I
really felt something. Like, with a lot of guys it seemed like a big
triumph for them to make me. It was never that way with Lenny.

That was in 1951. We got married June 15. I had to get the
thing cleared up with Sekolian. Technically, I was still his wife. We
got married in Detroit. I was a June bride. As I say, my mother was
still living there, but not with Lloyd, and she was having this serious
operation. She wanted me with her before she went on the
operating table. That was in 1951. We weren't into drugs yet.
Maybe a little weed or hash. I had this millionaire friend, a very
righteous millionaire-type person, and I guess with my friend we
were all planning to go to Cuba together before I'd heard about
Mom and that Lenny was coming back. I had my passport and
everything. There were four of us. It was just going to be sort of
friendly. You know, we were planning to go around the world. Now
when my mother called, I had to drop everything and then they
went ahead and made plans to go to Europe. I went back to
Detroit. I flew. I called Lenny. He was working a few club dates in
Miami. Because I asked him to he said he would drive my car to
Detroit . . .

You see, I had a 1949 Chevy convertible, my very first car. It
was yellow and it had leopard-skin upholstery, a very wild-looking
car. It had whitewall tires and it was all bright yellow with that
leopard-skin upholstery. I guess I was kind of flashy in those days.
On the side of the car, I had my name in silver letters: Honey, and
then it was quotation marks around "Hot" Harlowe . . . Honey
"Hot" Harlowe . . .

Can you imagine something like that? Silver letters . . . how
corny! With HONEY, but, in the middle, quotes around Hot. It was
on the driver's side and underneath I had this little queen that was
an artist paint my caricature with long red hair, but the hair was
accentuated down to my feet, you know, and I had tassels on my
boobies and a G-string on . . . and it was painted right on the side
of the car. Right on the side of this yellow car, which Lenny took
and drove straight to Detroit to my mother's house. And because

she could tell he worshiped the ground I stood on, Mom told
Lenny, "Instead of getting a hotel room for yourself you can have
the other bedroom," because she was already in the hospital by
then. It was a two-bedroom place. I guess it was about three days
before Lenny proposed to me.

That happened in the hospital. We had gone to see my mother and
Lenny was pretty unsure of himself, you know, boyish. He asked me
and my mother both at the same time could we get married? And I said,
"Sure. Since we're both in love with each other."

Lenny was booked into the Elmwood Club, *the* club in Windsor,
Ontario, that's right across the river from Detroit. He was
headlining. When we got married, we didn't even take off work!
Lenny had on casual clothes and I had on a little suit and high
heels, and that's what we got married in. Judge Liddy was the
judge. That night when we went to work, Lenny wouldn't tell
anybody at the club we had gotten married, and we didn't have any
wedding pictures taken. Then I came in with my mother and a
bunch of people, I guess my sister and her husband and then just
some friends of Mother's. I guess we took up about three tables.
And my mother wrote a note to the bandleader with a little tip to
play—oh, you know—some song when people get married. I don't
remember which . . . and to play it for her new son-in-law, Lenny
Bruce. That's how the bandleader knew to announce our marriage.
Poor Lenny, he was so embarrassed, like he always was at his
birthday if somebody wished him a happy birthday. It just
embarrassed him, and then we had our pictures taken together.

We didn't have any honeymoon. Lenny had a three-week
engagement at the Elmwood. He followed Dorothy Shay, I think,
and then I got myself booked into the Club 509 in Detroit. We
didn't want to be apart and, you know, he was working strictly
legitimate clubs and I was working burlesque. So in order for us to
be together, I would have to give up stripping and start doing
something. Lenny thought I should sing. I never did have much of a
voice, but everything worked out beautiful. He started working with
me as a singer, and he really played Mr. Ziegfeld with my act.
You'd think he was producing a fantastic show the way he rehearsed
me. He always picked out the tunes I would sing. He had a certain
arranger in New York that did all the arrangements. We rehearsed
at my mother's house.

I had sung once before with two girls in a trio, the Honey King
Trio, with Toni and Nancy King, but now Lenny and I were going
to be an act together. He wrote little things to say between each

song. We worked hard. He would write all kinds of bits for me. I couldn't really sing but I was in love. We went to New York to meet his mother.

Sally was living on Livingston Street. She was using the name Sally Marr. No, Sally Marsalle. She was using that name then. Her real name was Sadie Kitchenberg and then, let me see, Sally Marr, and then she changed it to Boots Malloy. She'd been in show business too, vaudeville, clubs, won Charleston contests: she'd work as a crazy-leg dancer. She had nice legs. From Sadie Kitchenberg to Boots Malloy you better have nice legs. That's quite a switch, huh? We all have these show-business names: Lenny Bruce, Boots Malloy, and Honey Harlowe. But I changed it to Honey Michelle when I started singing. That was my singing name.

In that five-floor walk-up on Livingston Street in Brooklyn, we all lived together, Sally, Lenny, and me. A one-bedroom apartment, no elevator, it just had a living room and a bedroom, and the kitchen was about the size of a bathroom. Lenny had redecorated the place himself. He was on a tear, a kick, everything had to be black. He painted everything in the place black and gold, the walls, the ceilings . . . You've seen those great big huge natural sponges? About the size of a man's hand . . . Lenny would dip one of them in gold paint and then just, like, splatter it on the walls and different places, the gold and the black. He even painted the tub in the bathroom inside and out and the sink and the commode, everything black, even the kitchen. In the bedroom a window was broken. Like I said it was five floors up. *Right?* Well, the way our apartment was, it was right next to the fire escape and there was, oh what's the name of that kind of tree, a wisteria? . . . Sometimes we rehearsed there too . . .

That summer we worked the mountains . . . the Catskills. A place called Kramer's. He was the comic, I was the singer. Actually, in those days he was more an impressionist than a comic. He would do fifteen minutes of Leo Gorcey, Jimmy Cagney, and Peter Lorre: then he'd go to his singing impressions—Vaughn Monroe, Billy Eckstein, and Maurice Chevalier, complete with the straw hat! Bit by bit he built an act for us, a double, so we could work the places that already had singers but needed comedy talent. We would do like a satire on a handyman and, say, the Negro maid that had worked the season in the Catskills. Like, we were making the ride back to the city and talking over the Jewish people we worked for. He sounded like one of the guys on *Amos 'n' Andy*, and I did a voice like Butterfly McQueen.

Later on, he wrote me a really cute act. It was called "The Singing Southern Belle, Honey Michelle."

I had these big hoop skirts. You know what I mean. They were huge. I had this wardrobe made for stripping with hoop skirts, you see, but when I started singing we couldn't afford more than a couple of gowns and you needed at least three, one for every show, so I made a one-piece gown out of a hoop skirt and Lenny had this song written for me called "Hillbilly Lilly," which was my special material, and in the song this little Southern chick from the hills went to the big city and met this city slicker.

I sang, "Hillbilly Lilly learned to tease with the greatest of ease but she always managed to keep on her calico drawers," and, in about the third verse, I'd stop singing and do like a satire of a stripper to maybe one chorus of music, maybe walking around on the stage because this was my last song, you see, and underneath the hoop skirts I'd have on these real pretty bright plaid-taffeta tights, you know, with the big ruffles on them.

Then, let me see, in June we got married and went to New York to Sally's place and worked mostly the Catskills the first season from June until Labor Day, September. That's where we really tightened up the act and he wrote our whole act because we lived right there, you know, at Kramer's, as the social directors of the resort. And we just had one or two shows a week to do at the hotel. We could free-lance at other hotels too. Our room and board was paid. We had a chance to write our act together.

Say we'd have to do an hour between the two of us. Lenny would open up and do maybe ten minutes or so, warm the audience up is what it's referred to, and then he would introduce me. I'd sing maybe twenty-five minutes and then he would do his comedy time, maybe forty minutes, and during that time, a half-hour, I would change from my singing wardrobe into a cocktail-length dress. Then he'd call me back out, and we had about twenty minutes of special material that he wrote for us as a comedy team.

He wrote some funny things. One skit was called "The Bride of Frankenstein." And that *was* funny. I was supposed to be the bride of Frankenstein and he's Frankenstein. He's got his suitcoat backwards, you know, he'd push his arms through and stick them way out, make his legs real stiff and walk the way Frankenstein walks.

Lenny would come walking down the stage and I would be talking. Everybody asks me how I met Frankenstein. Well, it just so happens I was working as a waitress in this little Pizza-a-ole parlor in Pomona when in walks Frankenstein, and he was eating everything, including the waitresses . . .

Once we even did that on a TV show and the censors passed it. They didn't even realize what he was saying . . . Well, Frankenstein's supposeᵤ to be a ghoul anyhow, right?

In those days I would do anything for Lenny. I'd never met anybody like him. He was so nice and funny. If he said, "Be a comic"—I was a comic. He said, "Sing!"—I'd sing. He was into jazz. I learned how to play vibes. I even went to Berlitz School to study languages because Lenny thought it would give my singing a lot of class, and someday we could work in sophisticated East Side rooms.

We even sang together and did a soft-shoe number. There was this little colored dancer in New York, Henry Latangé, a wild dancer, and Lenny hired him to teach us both how to dance. Lenny always wanted to be a dancer, but he had the hardest time learning how. He was just very clumsy with his feet and his excuse was he was left-handed. He couldn't do the mambo or the cha-cha. He was going to learn the Pony and all that kind of stuff, and this little Latangé—with one of those little French marks above the *e*—was teaching him knee drops and falls and all that kind of stuff. Lenny about killed his poor self . . .

By then we had our act tightened up pretty good. We both had Maurice Chevalier hats and we both had canes, real cute little canes that we made ourselves.

Like I say, too, our funds were limited and Lenny was always what you would call a "shmooker" [*schnorer*] or something, somebody who saves the money and counts the money all the time. He always handled our money and I let him because that was not my department at all. He always took care of that. Like I wouldn't even get to see my paycheck, voluntarily. We always put all our money together, and regardless of how much we made, we would always save my salary, or else save his and live on mine. And we bought a bond almost every week and put money in the bank.

It was beautiful. Nothing seemed to change. We were so close. We shared everything. Lenny was always up to something. Before we were married, when we were living in adjoining rooms in Miami, he had this scam with Sally and some other show people. They called it the Brother Matthias Foundation for Lepers. Lenny was the founder. He'd visited a leper colony in British Guiana when he was in the Navy. He had a lot of feelings about these people and wanted to help them. They needed certain things, like sunglassses,

because the disease weakens their eyes. So he organized this
foundation and got it chartered by the state of New York. He got
some very nice contributions from different people and was even
written up in the papers. After a while, though, he began to ask
himself, "Why should I work so hard without getting paid?" So he
was in Miami that time, he decided to make a few bucks for
himself.

The way he worked the scam was really funny. He'd leave the
hotel with a sport shirt on and sandals and he'd have a little black
shopping bag with him, and inside was the black suit, the black hat,
and the thing that priests wore, you know, the complete outfit. So
he would drive to a secluded section and make the change, and then
he would be a priest. Can you imagine him getting out of that
yellow convertible with the leopard skins and all that painting on
the side dressed as a priest?

Lenny used to say that when he walked down the street like
that even the dogs would stop barking. He said even a dog wouldn't
bark at him . . . and that was the first time he got busted, for
panhandling . . . We had these adjoining rooms with a bath in
between and I had such a lot of wardrobe that I was sharing
Lenny's closet to keep my stuff from getting wrinkled, and when he
got busted, he brought the cops back to the Floridian to get proof
who he was. You see, Lenny was continually talking to them like
they couldn't understand what was going on. I think even when they
released him, they still didn't know what was going on, you know,
because he showed them all of his identification was for Leonard
Alfred Schneider and he said he was representing the Brother
Matthias Foundation and was getting donations for that leper colony
in British Guiana and then he also said he had another name of
Lenny Bruce and that he worked as a comedian . . .

Well, you know how it was with Lenny. When he first started
out with that Brother Matthias thing, it was strictly legitimate. They
even had a charter. Then I think Lenny got kind of carried away
with it in Miami. I guess the reaction was so startling to him.

Let me see. We got married in June, went to New York,
worked the mountains the first summer. Then Lenny got us our first
really big engagement in Pittsburgh, and it was a club owned by the
man who made Clark Candy Bars. Six hundred dollars a week, and
the day after opening we had this serious accident.

I can't remember the name of the club right now. I'm a bit hazy
about that. But it was our first big date. We were booked there for
six hundred dollars a week. Lenny also got us this one-night stand
to do at the Elks or Shriners, something like that, and we had to go

back to the club to get my music and the music for our double . . .
this was in the late afternoon between five and six. You know how
the weather is back East that time of day in September. You don't
really need your headlights on and the traffic was extra thick. Our
car was parked in a wrong zone, and we had to get it out of there. I
had all the music on my lap and was getting all the songs and music
in order for the show we were going to do when this other car, it
looked like one of those old-time gangster cars, went plowing right
through this stop sign and it hit us on the side I was sitting. The
impact threw me out of the car and I went sliding across the street
and a truck ran over the lower part of my body.

They all thought I was going to die. Did you know that? It was
so dramatic, like all the music sheets flew out with me, you know,
and it was all surrounding me and it had blood all over it. I was
unconscious, in shock, I guess, for about four weeks, had my pelvic
bones broken in four places, my bladder punctured, and my face
was all cut up and also my arms and legs. The doctors at the St.
Francis Hospital thought I'd probably die, so they didn't even
bother to get me cleaned up. My mother flew down and when she
saw me, she got angry. My hair was all matted with blood. She
asked the nun why, and she said since I was going to die anyway
. . . But my mother stayed with my aunt all day, washing and
setting and combing my hair. I was in the hospital seven weeks.

The breaks, I guess. A lot of dumb things have happened to me
like that. I don't have good luck. Like when I was living with that
fence over in Crenshaw and I really did need a fix and I thought I
would do anything, even turn a trick for blue-chip stamps, which I
could trade for money, the very first John I spoke to was a cop and
I got busted. I didn't suspect anything. He was driving a truck, and
I only wanted 150 stamps.

I guess I'm just a very unlucky person, and that's why I've
wasted my life. But that time in Pittsburgh I was lucky. It looked
much worse than it ended up. I had four good doctors. They did
plastic surgery on my forehead, over my eye, and on part of my
nose. But I had to wear a cast for a long, long time, you know,
underneath my breasts to the top of my hips and then after that a
brace. I really had to learn how to walk all over again.

And that's when we went back to Detroit. We'd already given
up my yellow Chevy because now that I was married and no longer
stripping I wanted to be a little more reserved and that black Chevy
we bought in place of it and were driving during the accident got
totally totaled. With the insurance money we bought a brand-new
1951 Cadillac, a four-door Cadillac, and Lenny said it was so safe it

was like one of the President's cars, black with white-wall tires and
all that chrome on it.

Oh, we did all kinds of bits inside that car. Lenny just loved it.
Nobody else was allowed to drive it. Even I wasn't allowed to drive
it for a while. In Detroit Lenny's father and stepmother flew out to
meet me, and they invited us to California and that's the car we
drove out here in. Lenny just idolized that car. You know, we
would stay in hotels, ridiculous Milner Hotels where it's $1 or $1.50
a night and the car would be staying in one of the top hotels where
they had a subterranean garage so that snow or rain or whatever
wouldn't get on it. We were paying more a night for the car than
for us. Can you believe it?

We really had a good time driving out here too. You know, we
would stop on the side of the road and set up one of those little
barbecue deals and maybe cook hamburgers and pork and beans.
Sometimes we camped out. And once we found this deserted shack
in Oklahoma and went inside. There wasn't any furniture, but you
could see that bums or somebody had gotten in there and put leaves
in there and made it comfortable to rest and they had made a
broom out of twigs all tied together around a piece of branch. We
camped out there but we didn't really sleep or anything. Not
Lenny . . .

Lenny's father was a podiatrist and made corrective shoes. His
wife's name was Dorothy. They lived at that time in Arcadia in one
of those little houses with the picket fence and rose bushes and that
kind of furniture—what do you call that kind of furniture?—maple!
With the big ruffle stuff. Their big thing was traveling and going to
all those kind of tourist places they take you on the Gray Line
tours. The old man wanted always to go and live in Australia,
where everything is clean and cheap. Never been in a nightclub. He
was so tight he would let out Lenny's old clothes and wear them.
He was bigger than Lenny, too, about five-eleven, maybe 185, with
salt-and-pepper hair.

The father liked me and he even wanted us to move
permanently. He said he would build Lenny a house on his property
where they had some chicken houses. It was "This is your home"
and "You feel free" and "Don't think twice," until finally we
believed it. Sunday, we went ahead and invited out a musician
friend of ours that we had worked with in the mountains. A really
great guy who was out here with his wife working the Million Dollar
Theater. That night, though, when we got talking, the father says,
"Is your friend Jewish?" So we laughed and said, "No. He's a
Puerto Rican conga player named Hector Rivera!" When Dorothy

heard "Puerto Rican," she had a fit. She was really prejudiced—and so was the old man. He starts talking real serious, and he says, "You can't have this Puerto Rican out here. What will the neighbors think?" Lenny and I couldn't believe our ears at first. When Lenny saw he was serious, though, he got very upset and told me to start packing.

We left and rented a place in West Hollywood. That was our first real home. We bought pots and pans and dishes and stuff like that and set up housekeeping. It was the first time in our marriage we'd done a thing like that. I suppose we could have gone out on the road again and made more money, but we decided to stay here and make less because we'd be happier. Sure we blew pot in those days but not that much . . .

It was that way with us. When it was good we didn't need dope. We really wanted to be together all the time, even after Lenny was working Strip City and I was at the Colony Club stripping; we felt very close to each other.

I mean, we'd both kicked around. We were in our late twenties. It was that way with us now because we wanted it that way.

Like most couples, the men usually go out with the men and the women with the women, but Lenny and I were almost always together, you know, twenty-four hours a day, you know, sometimes, even before we were into any heavy drugs. The only time we were ever apart was when we had to work. Wherever he went I went with him, and vice versa. Lenny was that way about having a kid, too. That's why I had to have all those abortions. He would say: "Why should we give up any of our love, you know, to a stranger?" It seemed like he always wanted to be, you know, playing with me, or making love, or just whatever, and he said we might have to give that time we'd been giving to each other to a stranger.

Lenny took the break with his father very hard. He wouldn't speak to him for years. At first we weren't doing too well. We would make the rounds and there was nothing. I think there was maybe one local TV appearance. We started dipping into our bonds. Lenny spent a lot of time brushing up our act. I learned how to sing "Granada" in Spanish. We weren't into Meth or drugs at the time. We weren't *that* depressed. I mean the first five years were gloriously happy. We took our first vacation together, seven weeks, to Ensenada. It seemed like when one was feeling down the other was able to bring the other one out of it. No matter how tough things got, we were happy.

Then, as I started to say, this agent that had booked me before for two weeks in San Jose, offered me Vegas for $300 a week.

Lenny said he didn't want me to start stripping again, but I wanted to go and make the money to tide us over.

In Gardena, which is mostly a Japanese community, they had a strip gig at the Colony Club; it was only one show a night. They called it "The Battle of the Burlesque Queens." I worked there for about a year and Lenny, meanwhile, was offered a job as M.C. at Strip City on Pico and Western. I think it was only $125 a week. That's when he started getting away from the act to ad-lib.

Up until then Lenny was just a stand-up comic with routines that he did over and over again, but that's when he started with the audience participation. He would buy the local newspaper and discuss it. He would always be able to satirize something he's seen in the paper. He could do little bits on the funny papers, too, the comics, like Little Orphan Annie.

If it wasn't the daily papers, it was the weeklies. Lenny would find somebody's picture that he could associate with somebody in the audience where the resemblance would be strong. Every day he would do that, find somebody like that, and the audience would begin to see it, too.

Also, that's when Leny started commenting on the surroundings in the club. He would do a little bit on a waitress, or the bartender, or the owner. There was this glass partition between the bar and the rest of the club at Strip City, and you could see through it and hear but it was still separated. Lenny called that the TB ward. Different little things like that until pretty soon the ad-libbing replaced the bits he used to do. It seemed he could hold the audience better, and it made him feel freer also. People came back to see him because they knew they weren't going to be listening to the same jokes night after night. They'd tell each other: "Come down and listen to this guy. He's always got something funny to say. Just listen to what he has to say about so and so . . ."

I think I had six abortions in three years. Lenny always made me. He would have the nerve up until the critical moment and then he'd start getting depressed. I had one in New York, one in Detroit, and four down there in Tijuana. Lenny would just say, "Oh, baby, I don't know how we're going to do it." Or, "Don't you think we ought to wait awhile?" It was always happening that way. I'd get pregnant and Lenny would be depressed. The only time he didn't was with Kitty. We took time off and planned her. Fortunately, I've always been very healthy. In that respect it worked out all right.

In the time I'm talking about, Sally Marr came out here to live, too, and we worked a burlesque show together out in the Valley, out on Lankershim. I'm a little hazy about the name. We'd worked together before in Detroit, and Lenny and she were always very tight. Sally was a comedienne; but since there wasn't any work in the legitimate clubs, she came out here to do burlesque. She got a room someplace, an apartment. She wasn't married yet. She did that out here, to a nineteen-year-old guy, Tony, a Pachuco. He worked at Lockheed. He was even younger than Lenny. Sally tried to make him just like Lenny, but he ran away. That's another story.

Lenny was sniffing a little, I think, and he was working on a script for a local TV show called *Honeytime*. We were going to sing and do comedy together. But nothing much came of that. Then Buddy Hackett came out to work Billy Gray's Bandbox and he was supposed to do a movie at one of the big studios with the Firehouse Five and he told this executive about what a great writer Lenny was and he had Lenny come down to the studio and they asked if he could punch it up, you know, the script . . . spice it up . . .

Lenny was paid $750 a week. He got full credit for the script. They said they were very pleased, but they changed it all around when he wasn't looking. They liked Lenny's ideas, but changed it overnight. I think they added a parrot.

I remember a lot about that time. I was just learning how to sew. We had a nice clean place with a picket fence. No big drug scene yet. I made a lot of Lenny's clothing. He would wear black Levis with black boots, and I made him a black and silver brocade vest that he'd wear without any shirt. That was also the time we made *Dance Hall Racket*. Lenny wrote the script for that movie, too, and he was one of the stars of the picture. I was in it, too. He even got Sally a role. He also wrote in the owner of Strip City. Lenny made him into a gangster.

A funny thing happened on the set of *Dance Hall Racket.* Lenny was playing a New York–Chicago gangster named Scallo, I believe; he carried a switchblade knife and was the type who talked tough to chicks. Always flicking that gravity knife, you know. Well, a couple of our New York musician friends were also in that film. Anyway, Lenny was supposed to have this little blond girl and she was smuggling diamonds without cutting him in. They owned a dime-a-dance place. O.K., so this little chick, a short little blonde, she had on a evening gown, just the way a chick's supposed to dress in those dime-a-dance places, and she had exceptionally large boobies under her strapless gown. The camera's rolling. The chick strolls in. Lenny takes his switchblade and sticks it under her chin. "Gimme the jewels." She doesn't know what's going on. "I don't have any jewels."

He sees her breasts. He's got a knife. He slits the front of her

gown, right between the cleavage of the bust, and her two falsies
jump out and go hopping across the floor. That wasn't written in.
Lenny didn't know she wore falsies. He just suspected it. I mean he
would always do little things like that. But the blonde insisted they
cut it out of the film.

That was the way he was in those days. We were married five
years now. I'd learned to cook and sew. I was twenty-eight. Lenny
was thirty. I wanted to have a family, a baby, at least one. I'd
already had six abortions. When I told Lenny, he still didn't want to
have a child. I told him, "You know I don't want to be childless the
rest of my life," but he said he definitely didn't want a kid. So I
packed and left . . .

I don't remember where I moved. I took all the money I had
and left. Take that back. It wasn't that way, now that I remember.
It so happens Lenny was working. I stayed home, packed his clothes
for him, and when he came home I told him he couldn't come back.
About a week later we divided up our things. I don't know where
he stayed. It's all so long ago and it didn't last for very long. He
kept the Cadillac and he gave me money to buy a little yellow MG.

About a week later we saw each other again. I don't know
where he was staying. Maybe with some other guy. I was hearing all
kinds of stories. He'd been in this place with this chick and another
girl had bought them twin bathing suits. I was hearing all kinds of
rumors. I was beginning to have a fit. You know, I was still madly
in love, and I could be pretty jealous sometimes. Whenever Lenny
worked somewhere I tried to know what was going on.

I think Lenny only hit me two times in all the years we were
married and, you know, I could really get somebody mad. I guess
he was pretty mad when I told him to leave, but he didn't say
anything, and then I started hearing all these stories. Anyway, we
had dinner together a few times and decided to get together again.
We found some property off Laurel Canyon with a view. We were
going to save and plan to have a baby. I can remember we went to
Palm Springs for a week and made love. I threw away my
diaphragm. I was always very easy to get pregnant.

Chapter Three

JEW BOY

Was there ever a comic before Lenny Bruce who made such a *tsimis* out of being Jewish? I mean—*what for?* What was he trying to prove with all that shit about the super who painted over the *mezuzah*? About the Faye Bainter mother vs. the Jewish mother? All that crap about *tuchuses* and *nay-nays*? How he had *rach'monis* for this guy and that guy was a *putz*, a *schmuck*? Do you remember how he would divide everything in the world into Jew and Gentile? Starting out with obvious things, like Spam is goyish and rye bread is Jewish? Then getting more abstract with mouths are Jewish and knees are gentile. Finally, like God with a wet pencil stub in his mouth, he'd be ticking off the entire universe into Js and Gs:—

All Drake's Cakes are goyish. Instant potatoes are goyish. TV dinners are goyish. Fruit salad is Jewish. Black cherry soda's very Jewish! Macaroons are very, very Jewish! Lime Jello is goyish. Lime soda is *very* goyish. Underwear is definitely goyish. Balls are goyish. Titties are Jewish. Trailer parks are so goyish that Jews won't even go near them. Chicks that iron your shirts for you are goyish (even Polish!). Body and fender men are goyish. Cat boxes are goyish. Ray Charles is Jewish.

Funny? Yeah, sorta cute. Makes a point. But why so compulsive, so obsessive, so nutsy? And, is it good for the Jews?

Because, let's face it, every other comic since Ben Blue has been a Hebe. *Jew* and *comic* are words that slot together like *Irish* and *cop, Chinese* and *laundryman, Italian* and *tenor.* Going back to the earliest years, to Webber and Fields, Dutch jokes, slapstick, and silent movies; to the first radio shows with Ed Wynne, and later, Eddie Cantor and Jack Benny; the talkies with the Marx Brothers, the Ritz Brothers, and Danny Kaye; burlesque with Phil Silvers and Red Buttons; Broadway reviews with Bert Lahr and Willy Howard; nightclubs with Joe E. Lewis, Henny Youngman, Buddy Hackett; the great days of TV with Milton Berle and Sid Caesar; the cabaret theater with Nichols and May; the sick comics, Mort Sahl and Shelley Berman; the modern film comics, Mel Brooks and Woody Allen—they've all been Jews. Jews, Jews, Jews, Jews, Jews! Yet not one of them ever made an issue of their Jewishness until Lenny Bruce came along.

Made an issue of it! Christ, they broke their asses to hide the fact! Look at the way they changed their names from David Kaminsky to Danny Kaye, from Joey Gottlieb to Joey Bishop, from Jerome Levitch to Jerry Lewis, from Murray Janofsky to Jan Murray. Look at how they tacked that cute little-boy ending on their first names: Joe-y, Dann-y, Sand-y, Lenn-y, Henn-y, Benn-y. And it didn't stop with just a name change. Everything they studied, everything they grabbed that would help them pass. Radio announcer's diction, so they shouldn't nasalize and dentalize and glottal stop and fall into that sing-song like a yeshivah bocher. Nose jobs because people wanted to see a nice goyische punim—no more beaks and pop eyes. Quiet, tasty clothes. Cigarettes instead of cigars. Flat-finished tuxedos instead of shiny mohairs. Why some of those Jewish comics studied so hard to be goyim, rubbed out so many Jewish features from their faces, cosmeticized their voices and speech so totally, that they wound up looking like they had been molded in the same plant that makes Barbie Dolls. "Ladies and gentlemen, the networks are proud to present Bob Blank. He isn't Jewish—but then he isn't human either."

Oh sure, at a meeting of The Friars or The Lambs, at a big B'nai B'rith dinner or UJA banquet, these comics might let down a little and do some Jewish material. Not much—just enough to say, "*Ich bin ech a Yid.*" ("I'm a Jew, too.") After all, a little of that home-rolled lochshin went a long way. *Unless you were working the Mountains.* Now that was a different situation. Up in the Catskills, you got a lot of people from the old country, people who hadn't ever mastered English and liked to be entertained in the language they grew up with in Warsaw or Odessa. These were people who, when they heard a young comic who spoke no Yiddish, would boo and hiss and go, "Phooey, *English!*"

So up there you got a special type of performer, who worked in dialect and did Jewish stereotypes and played the "Chicken Flicker Skit." This is that classic piece of material about the old Yittel who steals a chicken in the Mountains so he can *schlug kapouris* (a ritual in which the father swings a chicken around his children's heads while pronouncing a blessing). Arrested and haled before a gentile judge, he has to speak through an interpreter. All the humor arises from the confusions of language and meaning produced by this intermediary. The biggest laughs are gotten by outrageous Yiddish-English puns: "six months of hard labor" translating into *"sechs monaten harte leber."* When the old Jew hears this dreadful sentence, he exclaims, with many eloquent gestures pointing to his kishke: "Six months of hard *liver*, Your Honor! Better you should give me, with my stomach, a nice soft brisket of beef!" That was the real Jewish humor, but it stayed in the cupboard all year long, until everybody ran up to Grossinger's or the Concord for the High Holidays.

Now, what Lenny Bruce was into was something entirely different from either the Jewish-American comics, who were intent on passing, or the Yiddish-English comics, who were reflecting their audience's predicament as half-assimilated immigrants. Lenny was projecting an image, defining an identity, telling the audience that he had roots. "I'm a New York Jew boy," he was saying, "and I'm not ashamed. I'm proud, in fact, because ghetto Jews like me have lots of soul and salt and juice. We're intensely alive—which is more then the goyim can say!—and we're on the make. So dig me—a good-looking Hebe who could pass better than any sheeny in America, but who's too damn proud and ornery and gutsy ever to deny his own essence!" That was Lenny's message, and if you were sort of hip—you dug it! Oh yeah, you loved him for that honesty, and you could just imagine what he must have been like as a kid back there in—what would you say?— Brooklyn? the Bronx? Sure! He was a neighborhood type, one of the "element." You could just see him as a kid standing outside a candy store, cracking up in the booths of a luncheonette, digging jazz on 52nd Street, cruising a corner, or jouncing down the boardwalk at Coney Island—three giggly guys passing a skinny joint from hand to hand. No two ways about it, babe, Lenny Bruce was one of the boys. One of those smart little, fast little, crazy little Jew boys. A brightie, a smartie, a hippie!

That was the ringside impression. But if you walked out of the club and picked a copy of *Playboy* off the newsstand with Lenny's serialized autobiography, *How to Talk Dirty and Influence People*, you'd have to start touching up your mental picture. Though you heard him say with your own ears, "I grew up in New York, and I was hip as a kid, I was corrupt and the mayor was corrupt. I have no illusions,'' the fact of the matter was that Lenny Bruce had grown up in a little town on Long Island, called North Bellmore, and he had had more than his share of illusions. In fact, like many members of his generation, he had been brainwashed by the movies. His youthful idea of happiness was pure back-lot Americana:

> I dreamed of living over a barn, seeing the stars through a cracked-board room, smelling the cows and horses as they snuggle and nuzzle in a shed below, seeing the steam come up from the hay in the stable on a frosty morning, sitting at a table rich with home-canned goods with seven other farm hands, eating home fries, pickled beets, fresh bacon, drinking raw milk, laughing, having company in the morning, having a family, eating and working and hanging out with the big guys, learning to use Bull Durham.

How's that for your smart-assed little Jew boy from Brooklyn?

Still, you could hold on to your original idea if you concentrated on the fact that behind everything Lenny said about his early years, there was the image of his Jewish mother, bringing him up against all odds—against the fuck-off father who deserted the family, against the Depression that reduced them to living on relief checks and bottle deposits, and against the world, so cold, so hard, so full of miserable mischief-making people. Sally Marr was the lady's name, and she was quite a character in her own right. After Lenny's death, she went on with the show, giving interviews, angling for TV shots, standing out front of the Brooks Atkinson on the opening night of the musical *Lenny*, handing out tickets and hugs to all her old Broadway cronies. For Sally had never left the business. She was a comic, an MC, a burlesque banana. She'd gone from Sadie Kitchenberg to Sadie Schneider to Sally Marsalle to Sally Marr to Boots Molloy. She'd worked all kinds of joints with all kinds of people and wound up running a school for strippers at the Pink Pussy Cat in Hollywood. Or so the story read in *Newsweek*. What could be more natural than to think that this mother shaped this son, brought him up inside a trunk, taught him how to think funny and talk funny, and then followed him through his career like a stage mother with a sixteen-year-old daughter, until Lenny died and Sally began to mourn him and celebrate his memory in long, raucous interviews, where every sentence began ''Lenny'' and ended ''Sally''?

"Yes, of course, my son had a father, but oh God! What a loser! He was hopeless. The truth is I raised Lenny single-handed. Raised him the hard way, a million heartaches, a million laughs." A regular

Patsy Kelly movie she sketched for you, about a plucky, perky lady in a little hat with a flip brim working as a waitress, a barmaid, taking her little boy to the picture show on her day off, taking him to Coney Island or Hubert's Flea Circus. A mother scuffling to bring up her son and holding off the make-out guys and doing menial jobs and feeling very close with the kid. So close that when they got in the train or the subway, they would huddle together as one and Lenny would look out with those big beautiful eyes of his and he would see some strange character and he was curious, but he was shy and he would plead softly: "Ma, talk to that man over there." And Sally, the extrovert, Sally with the ready smile, would strike up a conversation with this complete stranger, get his story, draw him out, make him talk, and little cuddlefish Lenny would sit next to her and dig the whole scene with big round saucer eyes.

It was a charming, idyllic, poignant sort of story that she told about herself and her Lenny: how he came back on leave after he joined the Navy and walked into her boarding house with a duffel bag on his back and demanded in a big deep voice to talk with Sally Marr. The landlady started to give him a hard time because she ran a respectable house and she didn't want any sailors coming in to mess around with her tenants. So she calls up to Sally and Sally looks over the banister and there's this big sailor boy with a deep voice and a mustache and for a second she didn't recognize her Lenny. That was the greatest time of all, the war years, when Lenny suddenly became a man and Sally was still a young woman. Nobody could believe that they were mother and son. Like that time when Sally was working at the Serviceman's Canteen and Lenny came in with a shipmate looking for girls. Sally spots him but he doesn't see her. So she walks up to him real saucy and taps him on the shoulder and swings her hips and smiles and says: "Hi, Sailor—wanna dance?" Then they stepped right out on the floor and went into a fast Lindy with a boogie break and everybody stood around and watched then just like they were a professional dance team sent to entertain the troops. That was great fun—just like living in a movie!

So that's where Lenny got his Jewishness, from his mother who raised him, from the mother who in Jewish law is the most important parent, the parent that really makes you a Jew. What does it matter that he grew up in Bellmore or Shmellmore, just so he grew up Jewish? Jews grow up in South Africa, in Asia, in Australia; there are Jews in South America and in the American South; there isn't a place on this earth where you can't find some Jewish people—so what's a big deal that Lenny Bruce was a Yiddel from Lung Island? He was Jewish, he grew up Jewish, he was raised by his Jewish mother. Right?

WRONG!!!

Oi! What lies! What fantasies! What bullshit! Lenny Bruce had a Jewish mother, all right, and a Jewish father, too, for that matter; but any resemblance these two might bear to those familiar figures of Jewish life, the Tatah and the Mama, was purely coincidental. Sadie Kitchenberg and Myron Schneider were not characters out of a Jewish soap opera. Nor, when you got down to it, were they even close to the depictions in Lenny's biography. In the book, for example, he has the father leave the family to return only on infrequent visits. That is a precise description not of his father but of his *mother*. Sally, or Sadie, as she was originally called, divorced Myron when Lenny was eight years old. She went to Reno, got her decree, gave custody of the child to her husband, and then disappeared from Lenny's life—save for two brief periods and rare weekend visits—for the next *ten years*. Lenny didn't get tight with his mother again until he was a sailor in the wartime Navy, coming out of the Brooklyn Navy Yard on liberty and visiting this unfamiliar but interesting lady in her dance studio on Atlantic Avenue. Though the mother certainly influenced him in early childhood, afflicting him with her own high-strung, exhibitionistic temperament, she was not nearly as decisive an influence on his character, mind, and acculturation as was his father.

Mickey Schneider totally dominated Lenny's life from his eighth to his seventeenth year. He played both mother and father to the boy, and he played both roles heavily. While one might label his influence "Jewish," employing the word in its most extended and metaphysical sense, there certainly wasn't anything explicitly Jewish about Mickey Schneider. An English Jew, who didn't know a word of Yiddish and considered himself an "agnostic," Mickey reared his son in exactly the same manner as all the other children were reared in the 100 percent gentile town of North Bellmore. Lenny was never bar mitzvahed, never sent to Sunday school, never instructed in Jewish history, customs, law, or religion. He was never admonished with homely proverbial phrases, never hushed on the holidays or taken to synagogue, and he certainly never sat down to a Friday night supper table loaded with chopped liver, chicken soup, tsimis, cholent, brust deckel, or kishke. When the Christmas holidays rolled around, Lenny sang carols with the rest of the children, played in the Christmas pageant, and received his gifts without any talk of "Chanukah bushes." On Easter, he joined the school choir to sing "Up from the Grave He Arose." There never was a seder in his home nor a Papa asking him the *fere kashe* (the four questions). The notion that this child of the American Assimilation came from the *pruste Yidden*, the common gutsy soulful Jews of the ghetto, is simply ludicrous. Lenny Bruce was reared in goyville to be a perfect little goy.

Which is precisely what he was until he was a grown man, a veteran of years of service in the Navy, and an apprentice entertainer hanging around in the show-biz bullpens of Broadway. Then, for the first time in his life, he suddenly became aware of the positive aspects of Jewishness. The curse of differentness that had dogged him since his earliest years in Bellmore Elementary School abruptly lifted, and he found himself blessed with the gift of uniqueness. Instead of being an outsider enshrouded in a mist of prejudice, he was now an insider spotlighted with the flattering attention and confidences of his fellow Jew boys. Imagine! After a whole lifetime of feeling alone, he suddenly belonged to a whole "people"! No wonder that he went overboard and put himself through a crash course in Jewishness. Look what a payoff you got! For the first time in your life, you were with people who couldn't reject you *even if they wanted to*! Unlike the townsfolk of North Bellmore or his shipmates in the Navy—who had to be charmed and entertained and placated because fundamentally you knew they didn't regard you as one of them—the Jews were obligated by their own laws to accept anybody who could prove that he was Jewish. So why not Jew it up to the hilt? Use Jewish words and dig Jewish life and come on like you'd been brought up in a pushcart on Blake Avenue. It was fun. It was like playing a game. You could even hold on to your old goyishe self by remaining a little anti-Semitic. It turned out that nothing titillated Jews more than hearing all sorts of horrible things said about "mockies" and "Hebes" and "kikes." Leave it to the Jews to find some way to eat their cake and have it too.

Being licensed to make fun of Jews was actually the least important part of Lenny Bruce's Jewish identification. He was far less anti-Semitic than most of the guys around him, who were always doing bits on Garment Center types that would have made Julius Streicher roll over in his grave laughing. What Lenny dug was the "thrill of belonging," as it was called back in the fifties, when a lot of Americans were suffering "identity crises" and discovering long-lost connections with their roots and beginning to experiment with ethnic pride as an antidote to the grayness and deadness and invisibility of assimilation. This was the age when being Jewish began to be fashionable, when Jewish writers and Jewish thinkers and Jewish psychoanalysts were culture heroes in America. It was the age when Israel, the "State," began stiffening the backbone of American Jewry, making even the most bleached-out suburbanite proud of what had once seemed a cause of shame.

On a deeper level, being Jewish meant to Lenny Bruce having a retaliatory force at his disposal: a means of hitting back at all the people whom he felt had rejected him or scorned him or treated him

at a lower evaluation than that at which he pegged himself. Just iden-
tifying yourself as a Jew got these people uptight, put them on the
defensive, put them on notice that you knew your rights and weren't
going to take any more crap. "Jew" was a magical word, almost a
magic bullet. Depending on how you said it, how you inflected it, the
word could be derogatory, laudatory, dignified, ignominious, serious,
funny, shocking—damn near anything you pleased! The word, the
idea, the thing—it didn't matter—any manifestation or embodiment
of that mysterious essence *Jewishness* was susceptible to the most extraordinary modeling and shadings, ironies and put-ons; it was psychological Silly Putty, stuff you could play with until you damn near
went crazy with the sheer malleability and expressiveness of it. That
was a great thing for an artist with a very confused sense of identity
—and Lenny made the most of it.

At the same time, as an entertainer, as a public pleaser, he recognized that there was a tremendous schmaltz value in Jewishness.
Not that you would want to lay it on like the old-timers, the Harry
Goldens and the ghetto nostalgists—that was preposterous for a contemporary cat. Yet there was another kind of schmaltz, a modern, pre-
hippie warmth around the idea of "roots" and "soul" and "salt." You
could be a pretty sophisticated contemporary writer, like Herb Gold,
for example, and get some nice vibes going with those stories about
hard times in the Depression and how the Jews had to punch it out,
right down there in the gutter, where all the real people live. There
was a great swinging, rhetorical uppercut that could knock a nightclub
audience right on its ass in some cat coming out looking like one of
them with the Italian Continental suit and the Italian boots and the
sideburns and eye-bags and finger pops—and getting very *Jewish*.
Going into all kinds of shtick about kissing tooshies and hahhhing over
bowls of hot soup and singing in a phlegmy old voice, "*Shicker ist a
goy!*" ("Drunk is the gentile!") I mean, there was this incredible
change-up you could do out on the floor: just when they were getting
you into their sights as a hip, pot-smoking, jive-talking, café sophisticate, you could suddenly come on with that Brooklyn candy store
stuff and fahklamich them! Not just kill them, you dig, but bury
them—where they'll never be found!

The funny thing about it was that the further you got into that
Jewish bag, the further you wanted to go: which sort of suggested that
maybe it wasn't an act at all but one of those pre-existence identity
things. Like maybe you had been a real Hebe the first time around
and that was your tantric destiny or your karma or some shit like that.
Maybe it meant you were home, baby. You made it home! Isn't that
a possibility, for chrissake? That you just found what you were sup-

posed to be in the first place? That your first twenty years were a
mistake, a wandering in the desert, a complete and ridiculous fuck-up
because the people you were with didn't know who the hell *they* were?
Sure, come to think of it, it all made perfect sense. Everybody you
really dug was some cat with soul, some nigger or junkie or jazzman
who had his story written all over him. What was this shit with *identity*,
man? You just walked out there with the biggest fuckin' sign you could
find, like those cats walkin' on 42nd Street with the sandwich boards
in front and back—"Eat at Joe's." Beautiful! That's the way everybody
should be! We all ought to have signs, flags, uniforms, tattoos,
circumcisions—some shit to say who we are so there wouldn't be a
doubt about it. Is you *is* or is you *ain't*? That shouldn't ever again be
a question. Never, ever! *Fashtaat?*

   Yes, it was terribly important to Lenny Bruce that he settle once
and for all this nagging doubt about who he was. Because he had been
born the child of violently antagonistic parents, people who couldn't
get together on anything. From his earliest years, his earliest memories,
he was a child of discord. Can you understand what that means? To
be the shuttlecock, the ping-pong ball, the ricochet kid, kicked around
from one home to another, coming in one door and getting thrown
right out another, until you don't know where the hell you belong or
who you are with or what you will ever do with the terrible feelings
you have about all those bastards!

Chapter Four

THE MISSING MAN

Mickey Schneider has never been on television. He's a very retiring person. A sad-eyed, solemn man, he ushers you into his home, a tiny, fussed-over bungalow in Pasadena, planted at the end of a street, like a Dead End sign. Seating you at the dining-room table, neatly covered with flowered plastic, he plies you with coffee and cake, reminding you for all the world of some old Jewish woman who has lost her husband and her children and is reduced now to holding her world together with the formatlities of hospitality. There is something heavy and lugubrious about this man, even when he smiles: something that bespeaks a lifetime of tsuris that only another Jew could understand. There is a striking physical resemblance to Lenny. He has Lenny's eyes, those beautiful almond-shaped eyes, so soulful and hypnotic. Lenny's hair curls thick, threatening to turn kinky on his head. His leonine cast of features reminds you of the pictures of Lenny after the fall from the hotel window in San Francisco, when he got heavy from wearing the casts and he glared balefully into Bill Claxton's camera, impersonating a wounded colonel commanding the world from a wheelchair.

Nobody goes to interview Mickey because they don't know he exists. In the Lenny Bruce story, he's the missing man. Lenny slighted him in his book, and Sally always dismisses him as "prejudiced." She even tries to stipulate in her contracts that people who work with her won't go near him. Between the two of them, Lenny and Sally, they pretty well killed off the old man. So he's sensitive and sore. When you dial his number, you get a very slow, dignified "Hel-lo?" The slightly starchy speech of a man who was born sixty-odd years ago in Kent, England. Incredible as it seems, this old man, with his nearly Victorian scruples and manners and dignities, has been forced more than once to deal with those rip-off artists, those high-binders and jive-assed bullshitters who gathered around Lenny like ju-ju birds picking the teeth of a crocodile. He tells absolutely incredible stories of his dealings with Honey. How she came to see him once with some crazy scheme to put out a line of frozen foods. Instead of frozen strawberries or frozen blintzes or frozen chow mein, Honey's brainstorm was *frozen soul food*. Dig it! You walk into the supermarket, reach down in the freezer, and pull out an ice block full of chitlings or fatback-and-mustard-greens or deep-dish-Georgia-peach-cobbler-with-optional-á-la-modes-in-six-flavors! So while Mickey is sorting it out, trying to explain to this crazy broad that he can't sink his last penny in her harebrained scheme, there's suddenly this long angry ring at his door. BRRRRRRRRRRRR! Mickey answers the summons like some old-world butler and boom! In comes this big drunken nigger, with eyes red as fire, weaving across the room and yelling out to Honey—"Hey, bitch! You get any money out of the old muthahfukah yet?"

Mickey doesn't look favorably on long-hair writers who come asking him for the emmis on his late-lamented son, the Crown Prince of Schmutz and Dope. His first impulse is to decline comment. He never thinks about Lenny anymore; he detests what Lenny came to represent and wants no part of his posthumous fame or notoriety. When he doesn't show you the door, you sense some very tremulous feelings under that exterior of somber reserve. Gradually, as you sit there in that doll-house dining room, stacked with curio racks, drinking the coffee he fetches off the stove, he opens up. The sore spots. The damaged feelings. Bit by bit the story comes out. The story of Lenny Penny and Father and the Zoorks and Orrocks and the secret language they used to talk in the back of the shoe store in Freeport.

Way back at the turn of the century in the year 1905 the Schneiders came to America from England. They were English Jews, the *crème de la crème* of the late immigrants, people who spoke English as their native tongue and were damn proud of the fact. The family, nonetheless, was as typically Jewish in its pattern as if it had come from the Polish Pale or from Russia, Rumania, or Hungary. There was, first of all, the grandmother, a powerful matriarch who ran the show from her kitchen and posed for her photograph enthroned in a carved antique wooden chair next to one of those old curvy glass-and-gilt curio cabinets, the ancestor of all the bric-a-brac shelves in Mickey's little house. Antiques had been, in fact, the family business when they lived on

Wardour Street in Soho. The grandmother had run the business and brought up the children because the grandfather was a weak ne'er-do-well whom the family referred to euphemistically as a "world traveler."

It was a normal-sized family for those days: five children, commencing with the oldest boy, Mark, and coming down through two younger brothers (one of whom went to school with Charlie Chaplin) to the twins: Lenny's father, Myron, and his aunt. Grandma Schneider had a good head for business, and when the family moved to New York, they lived very comfortably in a brownstone on 72nd Street. Then they moved down the Jersey Shore to Asbury Park; back to Brooklyn on President Street; and eventually out to Long Island, to Freeport on the South Shore.

Freeport in the twenties was a clam-digging town with an active Ku Klux Klan and the German-American Bund in nearby Lindenhurst. Not exactly the sort of place in which most Jews would choose to settle. When you ask the surviving Schneiders (who still live in Freeport in charming, flower-ringed houses) why they picked such an unlikely neighborhood, they give you the craziest answers. Typical was Mickey's sister's reply, "My brother-in-law loved fishing." What they won't say is that they moved to Freeport—as many Jewish families moved to similar towns—simply to get away from the last vestiges of the ghetto. In the twenties, there was nothing fashionable about being Jewish; if you could put it behind you, you were much better off and more likely to become a hundred percent American.

Mickey Schneider, who came to this country when he was one and a half and moved to Freeport when he was a schoolboy, grew up at a great distance from Jewry, doubly removed by his British ancestry and his rural residence. In the twenties, Freeport was way out in the sticks. Just think about that automobile trip in *The Great Gatsby* from Long Island to New York. My God, it reads like they're journeying across the deserts of the Southwest—and they're just motoring in from Great Neck. Freeport, Bellmore, Roosevelt, Lindenhurst, Riverhead, and Lawrence—the towns that figure in the history of the Schneider family—are a lot farther out on the Island than Great Neck.

Bellmore, where Lenny grew up, was a whistle stop on the Long Island Railroad. If you wanted to get off there, you had to tell the conductor, and he would signal the engineer; when the train came to a stop, you had to go all the way down the steps and jump off on a mud landing. If for some extraordinary reason—like your mother suddenly dying—you had to go into the city at night, your only recourse was to flag down the train with a kerosene lantern. Bellmore was full of people who had been to New York only five or six times in a lifetime. The town was just as rural as if it had been up in Vermont or out in

Illinois. All along the roads into the village were little stands where people sold the produce they raised in their gardens. Some residents even owned horses and livestock. These were old-timers who proudly traced their families back to the beginnings of the republic. Right across the street from the house where Lenny Bruce grew up were foundations of houses built during the Revolutionary War.

Though Bellmore was an authentic American town, exploding with fireworks on the Fourth of July and quiet as a church on Thanksgiving, it wasn't a pretty place in which to live. It had evolved as a backwater, if not a dumping ground, for Freeport. The townspeople, Germans, Poles, and early Americans, were not only poor, they were boors. The kind of people who really vote for Miss Rheingold. The village, about a mile from the Schneiders' house, was just a row of one-story asbestos-shingle stores strung along the railroad tracks. There was an ancient movie house called The Itch, a few local taverns, and the VFW hall. The one big public place was an old-time beer garden known at various times as the Bavarian Inn, the Bavarian Village, or the Sunrise Village. A real heinie place with pitchers of beer on red-checked tables and oafs in lederhosen slapping their thighs, the Bavarian Inn always had the kind of comedian who threw a spotlight on every woman who went to the toilet. "Vee know vhere you're goingk! Ha! Ha! Ha! Ho! Ho! Ho!"

> *Oh, du Schönheit an der Wand,*
> *Ist das nicht ein Schnitzelbank?*

Mickey Schneider embodies many of the interests and aptitudes of small-town America. He is very good with his hands, the sort of man who doesn't hesitate to take on the job of building a whole house from scratch. He loves gardening, as do all his English relatives. He aspired always to be a professional man, studying at one time to be a lawyer, another time to be a pharmacist—but something always happened that interrupted his education. It wasn't until he was forty and a veteran of World War II that he was able, thanks to the GI Bill, to complete his education and qualify himself in California as a physiotherapist. Combining his new training with his long-standing vocation for fitting orthopedic shoes, he opened a so-called laboratory where he treated and outfitted patients with crippled feet. A hard-working, tightly disciplined man, he experienced a deep satisfaction in attaining this modest degree of professional status after more than twenty years of shoe-clerking.

Mickey met Sadie Kitchenberg when he was eighteen at a leap-year dance in Lynbrook. Sadie was never a very pretty girl, and she hadn't yet gotten her nose bobbed; but she was extremely vivacious, a terrific dancer, a great Charleston kicker. Those hot legs of hers roused Mickey's phlegmatic blood. He began to "keep company" with her, to seek "self-gratification." He was no more serous about Sadie than he was about several other girls. From the very beginning of their relationship, he realized that she wouldn't make him a suitable wife and that she wouldn't be acceptable to his family. He wasn't in love with her. Yet from the first night he paid a call at her house, he began to submit to a strange subliminal impulse that made him eventually consent to a marriage that nearly ruined his life.

Just prior to his meeting with Sadie, Mickey had been shopping with his mother in Freeport, and they had gone into a grocery store. Standing in one corner of the store was a pathetic-looking boy peddling ties and belts. He appeared feeble-minded, but what was really strange about him was the way he kept his head twisted, like a pigeon seeking its wing. Instantly, Mickey divined that the kid was trying to hide one side of his face. Irresistibly, he was drawn to where he could see that averted face. Horrible. Some hideous accident had befallen the boy; his face was all discolored and deformed. He looked like a soldier who had taken a shell blast right in the face.

Weeks, months, maybe even a year later, on the night that Mickey first entered the Kitchenberg house in Jamaica, he suddenly found himself once more confronting that mangled face. The boy was Carman Kitchenberg, Sadie's younger brother. Some years before, he had been playing with a group of children near a highway that was being surfaced with asphalt. Running clumsily along the side of the road, he had slipped and fallen, burying one side of his face in scalding tar. When they dragged him out, he was a case for the greatest plastic surgeon who ever lived. Nothing was done for him, terrible to say, and he grew toward maturity with one side of his face burned off.

The more Mickey saw of Sadie, the more absorbed he became with Carman. The boy was treated terribly by his family. He was the idiot boy, the scapegoat, the shame of the Kitchenbergs. Mickey's heart went out to Carman. He treated him as if he were the boy's mother, always hovering protectively over him and talking to him and trying to bring him out. Even today, listening to Mickey tell the story, it's not hard to imagine how this curiously maternal man, with his large, sad eyes, elegiac voice, and air of solicitousness, of sympathy, of almost funereal solemnity, might become fixated on the wretched Carman. Because there's a certain kind of Jewish man who is really a Jewish mother. He can do a man's work and shoulder a man's responsibilities, but his soul, his sensibilities, his eyes—the mist in his eyes—all testify to the overwhelming influence of his mother. Being his mother all over again, this kind of man experiences his mother's emotions, talks his mother's language, reflects back onto other people precisely the emotions and attitudes that his mother projected onto him.

The most important of these emotions is *Jewish love*. Gentiles don't understand about Jewish love. They can't grasp a positive, affectionate emotion that is so crossed with negative impulses, so qualified with antagonistic feelings that it teeters at every second on a fulcrum of ambivalence. Jewish love is love, all right, but it's love mingled with such a big slug of pity, cut with so much condescension, embittered with so much tacit disapproval, disapprobation, even disgust, that when you are the object of this love, you might as well be the object of hate. Jewish love made Kafka feel like a cockroach. Jewish love is really the final distillate of the twisted and contorted feelings of a people who have been the most hated race in history. A people who have lived so many hundreds and thousands of years amidst the hate of other peoples that they have absorbed much of that hate, assimilated it to the core of their being, where it exists wound around the powerful stem of pride that has supported the Jews through all their misfortunes. Like a sign in the flesh, like a genetic code, this fusion of self-love and self-hate is transmitted from one generation to another. The mother gives it to the son and the son gives it back to the woman he marries and she gives it in turn to his son, or failing that, he plays mother and gives it to the son, so that eventually the whole genealogy of the family is patterned by this ambivalence, like iron particles in a magnetic field.

In Jewish families like the Schneiders, you often have a grandmother who is an all-powerful matriarch, a domineering old lady who has a weak husband, or no husband at all, and rules her sons and daughters with unquestioned authority. The girls suffer the worst because they are destined to have their mother's desire to rule without their mother's strength and to have, like her, weak men or no men at all. Almost as bad, though, is the lot of the sons, who are never allowed to rise to their full masculine stature lest they jeopardize the authority of their mother. Brought up in the crossed rays of the most intense Jewish love, they develop into twisted personalities, loving where they should hate and hating where they should love. They attach themselves to women who hurt them and treat with contempt the women who offer them real love. They often display great talents in their work, but as men they have curiously ineffective characters. They've all got a cross going through them, like checks that have been through a cancelation machine.

Mickey Schneider is just such a canceled man. His true love object was never someone he could lust after or envy or admire, always

someone he could pity and bathe in the dubious light of Jewish love.
First, it was Carman, that poor creature. Mickey's greatest inducement
to marry Sadie was simply the anticipated pleasure of providing Carman with a good home. He wanted to take the poor boy as his ward,
and eventually he did exactly that.

Meanwhile he had to contend with the objections of his family.
They viewed the Kitchenbergs as a disgrace. The rag-peddler father
was, they kept insisting, a bootlegger, an embezzler, a charlatan. The
mother was a nice person, poor woman, but periodically insane. Insanity, they believed, ran in the Kitchenberg family.

Mickey's family recalls him acting pretty crazy himself during this
period. They didn't know that he was suffering from the most intense
feelings of guilt. One afternoon, he and Sadie had gone up into his
attic and indulged in "the sweet sin of love"—the phrase is from Pearl
Buck, whom Mickey has read with admiration. Not long after this
physical intimacy, Sadie announced to him that she was pregnant. It
was a lie, but he had no way of knowing it. At the tender age of
eighteen, he was not one to doubt a woman's word. He concentrated
on his duty, his responsibility, his sense of honor. He decided to marry
her, to make an honest woman of her, and later—who knows?—
perhaps to escape from her through divorce.

The announcement of his intentions precipitated an explosion of
angry emotions among the Schneiders. The family was unanimous in
opposing the union. The most decisive vote, however, belonged to his
sainted mother; she decided neither to condone the match nor to firmly
oppose it. She had feelings about Sadie. She felt sorry for the girl,
who had been forced to grow up without the steady presence of a
mother. Old Mrs. Schneider became Sadie's second mother, and the
marriage was celebrated. Unfortunately, the bride's family were
obliged to make the wedding arrangements. They did so in the worst
possible taste with a barbaric barbecue over an open pit in the ground.
For the *pièce de résistance*, they offered a huge stem of bananas hanging
down like a jungle picnic. On the wedding night, the family still maintains, Sadie smeared the sheets with lipstick.

Bride and groom went to live in a little town near Freeport.

The key to Sadie/Sally's personality is in the phrase "stagestruck." She
can never sit two minutes with you that she isn't up on her feet working
the room. She has to charm you, disarm you, tickle you, and make
you laugh. She's never had a true friend in her whole life because she
sees everybody as an audience to be flattered, cajoled, and seduced.
Ultimately, an audience is also someone from whom you walk away.

That's why nobody knows Sally's story, why she has always been a loner.

Her earliest memory is of a beauty contest back in 1919, when she was twelve, which was judged by the great Rudolph Valentino. One of Sadie's brothers schlepped her into New York that day and got her up onstage, telling everyone: "My sister can really dance, she's great!" That was the period of American orientalism: the sheik and his tents were on the silent screen, the pastel-colored houses going up in the suburbs were of Spanish-Moorish design, and the latest dance style was the shimmy. The instant Sally got onstage, the orchestra struck up "Hindoostan." Nothing daunted Sally: she went right into the latest kooch steps.

Next day, there was a write-up in the newspapers, and Sally's father, Cheil Kitchenberg, read the story. One minute he's sitting in the kitchen with a glass of tea, the next he's seeing his daughter turning into a nafkah. "Vot's dis?" Striking the paper with the back of his hand. "You were on stage?" He glares at Sally. "You were in New York City with Rudolph Valentino?" The thought of his daughter with the famous movie star sends the old man into a fit of rage. "*Never! Never* will you go on that stage again. Never will you be a bum. My daughter will not be a bum. I know these people. I deal with these people. I go in the Jamaica Theater to buy their schmutzig, schvitzig clothes. I'm with them there in the dressing room, and bigger bums, more terrible people I didn't see! This is what you want? To be a bum like them? To be on stage and show everything? No! This you wouldn't do."

So, Sally has to tell Jack Blue—or whatever that highbinder was called who came out to the house to sign her up—she can't go into any shows because her father disapproves. What a drag! Because she really loved the stage. The next best thing was local amateur affairs. Amateur beauty contests, amateur dance marathons, amateur theatricals, amateur Charleston contests. Then she meets Mickey.

Mickey's very serious and she sort of likes that. He's got a little ham in him and she figures to bring that out in time. He's good-looking, which is nice. The important thing, though, is that he admires her and stares at her with those heavy eyes of his and makes her feel like she's appreciated. Sally is destined always to have these wallpaper guys, who just sit and listen and stare and dig her. That's what she likes—a good audience. Somebody she can put away with her vivacity and charm. In later years, it was always a younger guy who wasn't too hip but was kinda sexy and not too hard to handle. That was her type.

What really pushed her into marriage was Mickey's mother, the matriarch. Sally was drawn to that woman. She was, after all, a very young girl. Barely eighteen when she married. Her own mother was committed to a mental institution on Sally's wedding day. Sally hadn't really had a mother. In Mrs. Schneider, she found the woman who could give her what she craved as a daughter: the wisdom, strength, affection. So she told Mickey this lie about being pregnant. That was one of her problems—as it was to be one of her son's—she was a person who would lie about anything. And suddenly she was married and a mother and a prisoner in a tiny little house in a tiny little town on Long Island. A long, long way from Broadway. So she kept punching with her amateur nights and amateur shows, and when Mickey turned dour and moralistic, she took a lover to keep her heart warm. The truth was that she didn't want to be a wife or a mother or anything that pinned you down to a dull routine away from the excitement of the stage. She had dancing feet.

When she went out to Reno in 1933 to get the divorce, the Hollywood people were there shooting *Gold Diggers of 1933*. One of those guys with an ascot and a pair of sunglasses spotted her in the casino, dancing. He gave her the line that they laid on all the girls in those days: "You oughta be in pictures." She knew he was right. She knew she had the spark. Anywhere she was, any time of day or night, she could always jump up and do her stuff. Wasn't that the magic they were always seeking? The oomph! Sex appeal? Razzamatazz? Then the guy made her an offer. She backed off, scared. There wasn't any Papa Kitchenberg threatening her this time, no uptight husband or nagging kid. She was a gay divorcee, ripe for the scene; but she couldn't find it in her heart to take the plunge. Copped out like a lady. Told the guy with the mustache and the permanent tan: "No, no thank you. I appreciate your interest, but I'm a mother. I have a little boy back home and he needs me."

The truth was she had this terrible ambivalence toward show business, an ambivalence that she passed along to her son. Lenny expressed it for both of them in later years every time he opened his mouth about the business. He was absolutely stagestruck, just like his mother—and much less affected by stage fright. But he was always very critical, censorious, and condescending toward anybody who made his living by doing an act. His favorite posture toward the business was that of Jehovah, who looks down on earth and sees every human act down to the tiniest detail. Then seeing all, divining everything, he pronounces judgment, like a stern father who is especially hard on his own children. That was the attitude that came out in bits like *The Tribunal*, where Lenny set himself up in a black robe to demand of each of a half-dozen famous performers what they did that could justify the enormous salaries they were making.

> JUDGE: . . . And you, Sammy Davis, Jr. . . . What do you do, Mr. Junior, to deserve forty thousand a week?
> DEFENDANT: [Sings] Racing to the moon . . . That old black magic . . . Hey Dean! I gotta booboo!
> JUDGE: [Interrupting] Strip him of his Jewish star, his stocking cap, his religious statue of Elizabeth Taylor—thirty years in Biloxi!

Jehovah on the mountain and the children of Israel dancing around the golden calf—that was Lenny Bruce's attitude toward the profession of entertainment.

The one great difference between mother and child, apart from talent, was that Lenny possessed a self-destructive instinct that was totally alien to Sally, a woman who could survive any number of disasters because she always recognized the cardinal importance of simply taking care of yourself. Sally was always out for Sally. When she came back from Reno, a young divorcee, she lit out on her own and led her life with a remarkable freedom from the guilt and anguish that most women of that period would have felt in a comparable situation. Though she loved her child, she loved herself better. She was perfectly willing to take care of the boy and do for the boy—on her terms. She was not willing to sacrifice her life to him. It all came clear when some months after the divorce Mickey decided to go up to Boston College to study pharmacy. He had been living with Lenny in his mother's house and incurring the wrath of his twin sister, who didn't like Lenny at all. Now he found himself in a position to kill two birds with one stone. A nephew was about to give up a candy store in Bellmore that Mickey could pick up for a few dollars. He decided to buy the store, stock it, install Sally as its proprietor, and lodge Lenny with her while he went off to study pharmacy at Boston College. He made all the necessary arrangements, dividing his meager income with moral rigor—ten dollars a week for child support and fifteen dollars for himself.

It wasn't two months from his departure that Mickey received a pathetic little note from Lenny, now about nine, who wrote: "Dear Father, I'm very unhappy. I want you to come back." Mickey gets in to his second-hand Essex and drives down along the old two-lane highway from Boston. Arriving about three in the morning, he walks into the candy store and finds Lenny asleep in the back room—alone. The child is perfectly safe. Sally is gone for the night. Mickey breaks off his education, takes back Lenny, and stops looking to Sally to help with the child.

Sally's subsequent history is a string of dreary jobs. She runs dancing classes for kids in Riverhead; works as a maid in the home of Tony and Rita DeMarco, the famous dance team; she even works in the home of an old Jewish publisher, who dresses her up and takes her dancing at the Roosevelt Grill because he needs exercise for his heart. Whenever she gets a chance, she still enters the amateur dance contests. Invariably, she meets someone who urges her to go into show business. One guy is a retired spotlight man, who owns a couple of little joints in Jamaica and South Brooklyn. He teaches her to be a barmaid and installs her in his place in Greenpoint. It's a rough dockyard district full of merchant seamen who come off their ships and get roaring drunk and battle each other in the bars. Sally holds the sailors' wallets for them while they drink, and the next day they always give her a big tip for saving their money. It's a long way from the respectability of Long Island, but Sally loves the rough-and-tumble of the place. Like Lenny after her, she gets a big kick out of watching the "types."

Once in a while, she gets a yen to see Lenny. Maybe months have gone by, maybe longer. Suddenly she's on the phone talking to Mickey. She comes out to the house in a cab or her boyfriend's car, picks up the kid in front of the house, and takes him off for a whirl of good times. She's a delinquent mother, but she's a great date. She takes Lenny to all kinds of shows, drags him up to the spotlight booth of the theater, and once, when he is fourteen, she even takes him to a burlesque show. After hassling with the guy at the gate, she gets her little "malted-milk face" into the theater and stashes him in a seat with a pair of binoculars. The kid stares his eyes out, and when they leave, Sally starts prodding him for his response. "Those women are gorgeous!" he gushes to his smiling mother. "And I loved that comedian, Red Buttons, singing 'Sam, You Made the Pants Too Long'!" Sally chuckles.

When Lenny got back to Long Island, things must have seemed pretty gray. The Depression had reached its worst moment: as you drove by the public dumps, you saw them crawling with raggedy men who lived right on top of the heaps of refuse in battered old packing crates. You couldn't go into a picture show without passing some poor veteran standing in the cold selling apples from the top of an orange crate. Even a child knew that things were bad, and things were especially bad for Mickey Schneider. After he took Lenny back, he found he had no place to put the boy. Neither his sister nor his sister-in-law would allow him to live in her home. Lenny, they insisted, was a troublemaker, a cheat, a liar, a two-faced flatterer. When you ask

Mickey why his relatives were so set against the child, why even today they get angry thinking about him, Mickey insists their charges are false.

"Was the boy a mischief-maker?"

"No, he was sweet and lovable."

"How is it your sister wouldn't allow him in the house?"

"I've never understood that. I've never forgiven her."

So Mickey's got the kid. There's no turning to anyone for help. What is he to do? He puts himself on a Spartan regime, moves into a room at the back of his brother's shoe store in Freeport, sleeps on an Army cot, spends all the money he saves through these economies on his beloved Lenny Penny. In the depths of the Depression, with thousands of people starving, he sends the boy to a private school in Lawrence. How's that? A private school for the son of a shoe clerk in the year 1935!

During this same period, Mickey meets Dorothy Cohen. She is the antithesis of Sadie Kitchenberg. Sadie's a meshugana, Dorothy's a legal stenographer; Sadie is always running; Dorothy sits all day beside a desk taking dictation. She's a person of character, a woman of her word, someone who is always on time for appointments. It's just too bad that she reminds so many people of a spinster librarian. No matter. To Myron she is an oasis in a desert. What a relief to find a woman who can help! Who can hold up her end of the bargain. Even so, he's being very careful this time. Their courtship is rather prolonged. Their discussions are deep. She knows everything, understands everything. Myron begins to feel very tender toward her. In a moment of incredible naïveté, he calls Sally, tells her that he is about to marry again, and implores her to take Lenny for a couple of months while he makes the necessary preparations to install himself and his bride in a new home.

Sadie agrees to this imposition. She is determined to show Mickey that she is above any feeling of rancor or jealousy. Lenny is dispatched to his mother's house—but not for long. Two weeks haven't passed, when Sadie calls one night and demands that Mickey come at once and take Lenny off her hands. She's worked up to fever pitch, and she's shouting into the phone: "I can't have this child here any longer. I can't take care of him. I don't want him here. You must come immediately, right this minute, and take him out of here!"

There's no mistaking or ignoring the urgency of her voice. Mickey and Dorothy look at each other. What can they do? They aren't even married, and already they're deep in domestic embroilments. No matter. They get in the car and drive to Valley Stream. As they come down the street where Sally lives, there's Lenny, standing out on the curb, a forlorn little figure, with all his clothes, clean, soiled—God knows what—tied up in a sheet, not even properly tied but falling out on the ground! A waif. When he sees the car, he gets this funny little smile on his face.

On July 5, 1936, Mickey Schneider and Dorothy Cohen are married in Lawrence, Long Island. Mickey's financial position has improved to the point that he can again, for the third time in his short life, invest in a new house. Obviously, he can't spend a lot of money, but with his skills and plodding persistence, he can take a place that is pretty dilapidated and renovate it into a comfortable home. The house they buy is at 710 Hughes Street, on the corner of Newbridge Road. It is a very quiet area, with closely planted maple trees. The white frame colonial house is in atrocious condition. No matter. Mickey can set it straight. He goes to work at once: a fresh coat of paint, a new garage, rose bushes under the windows and sweet vines climbing up the walls, and a flagpole on the lawn. This is the house in which Lenny lives from age eleven to seventeen. The house still stands, tight and white, a tribute to Mickey's craftsmanship. The first time you see it, you want to burst out laughing. Can this prim dwelling really be the home of *Lenny Bruce*? Why, it's every shingleman's dream to see this house coming up in his windshield. This is the house of the American Everyman. The Little Man. It looks like the birthplace of Richard Nixon.

Standing there in the leafy street, you ask yourself: "What went on behind these clapboard walls that could produce so extraordinary a creature as Lenny Bruce?" Was he really deprived of toys and compelled, as he says in his book, to steal his lunch every day from the green lockers of Bellmore Elementary? Did he hassle endlessly with the local storekeeper over the penny deposits on the soda bottles? Was he simply a victim of the Depression? No. That was all part of the myth he concocted in later years when he converted himself into a John Garfield Jew boy. The truth is—he was spoiled, spoiled rotten. Mickey and Dorothy made between them a pretty good living in the late thirties. As Lenny grew from childhood into adolescence, he was given everything a boy could desire. Lenny had his own room, his own little radio, his own little typewriter, and a pair of crossed foils on the wall. Down in the basement, he had a jukebox. Imagine a child of that period with a great big Wurlitzer in his rumpus room? Lenny wasn't shy about demanding things. When he was younger, he used to sleep with Father in the same bed. Once Father brought home some little chicks and Lenny insisted that when they went to bed the chicks sleep with them. Father explained that the chicks would suffocate. Lenny insisted that they wouldn't. Mickey gave in, as usual; the next morning the chicks were dead.

Mickey was always acting against his better judgment to make Lenny happy. Lenny liked his father to drive fast. "Father," he would urge, "go faster, faster!" Mickey would explain in his patient, schoolmasterish tone that he would get a ticket. It was the same thing with the airplane ride. Lenny was always begging to be taken up in a plane. Now, you know that in the thirties people didn't go flying about in planes. There were a few planes out on little grassy fields. Two wings, a lot of struts, a loud motor. You could go up for a dollar, if you had the nerve. Lenny couldn't be talked out of it. Every time they drove past one of those fields, he would put up such a clamor that one day, Father climbed into the front seat of an old two-cockpit job, held Lenny firmly in his arms, and roared up into the air over Long Island. Can you imagine it? Father and Lenny Penny flying!

In those days, Lenny and Father were always playing together. Once the divorce ended the daily quarrels in the house, Father returned to his true nature and became a very gentle and loving man. Even before they had the house on Hughes Street, they had their own little home in the back of Uncle Mark's shoe store. Lenny would come for the weekend, and they would play mumblety-peg with a shoe box. Sometimes they would make up secret words and have long conversations about those fascinating creatures, the Zoorks and the Orrocks. Mickey loved words, loved language, loved books. He bought Lenny encyclopedias and encouraged him to read. He spoke about the wonders of literature, of art and culture. When Lenny first started school, he surprised the teacher by the extent of his vocabulary. He spoke beautifully as a child. The only problem was that he was always chattering when he should have been silent. He had to be put in a special little seat away from the other children to learn discipline.

One of the reasons why he talked so much in school and disrupted the other children was simply that he was lonely. All day long and well into the evening, Father would be working in the store and Dorothy would be working at the office. Lenny would come home from school and find nobody to play with. He'd go out in the street and kick the leaves around. He'd make up stories to tell himself and listen endlessly to the radio. He loved his Philco radio with its cathedral-like wooden scrolls covering the coarsely woven speaker cloth. After school, on a gray winter afternoon, he would rush home and settle down beside the radio to follow the adventures of those fascinating people: Jack Armstrong, Dick Tracy, Little Orphan Annie, and Buck Rogers "IN THE TWENTY-FIFTH CEN-TU-RY!" The Lone Ranger was Lenny's favorite. He made him the subject of his last great routine, *The Masked Man*. When you listen to that bit, you begin to get a very strange notion of the Lone Ranger, the sort of vision of him that a lonely and love-hungry child might develop. What the routine really turns on is the fact that the masked man will never accept a thank-you. Every time he performs a good deed, he rides off in a cloud of dust without allowing the slightest expression of emotion to emerge from either his tightly compressed lips or from the grateful hearts of the townspeople. The Lone Ranger is, therefore, like a bad father: he does everything for you—even saves your life—but when you want to reach out with gratitude and love, he shows a stern face and rides away. Oh sure, his swift departure is meant to convey a heroic self-lessness, a sense of duty so compelling that it doesn't require even the smallest reward—even a "Thank you!" To Lenny, as a child, and later as a comic who worked as a false naïf, the message of the Lone Ranger's selfless withdrawals was coldness, narcissism, and arrogance—*fear of emotional involvement!* When the enraged townspeople finally stop the Ranger and compel him at gunpoint to accept a thank-you, he confesses that he always runs away from thank-yous because he's afraid he might get *hooked* on them. What if someday the people started crying for help, and he was too busy getting thank-yous to come to their aid?

It's so hard to know today what Lenny really made of his father. He complained in his book that when his father gave him things, like a set of encyclopedias, he made him feel guilty about the self-sacrifice entailed in making such a gift. Probably true. Like so many Jewish parents, Mickey Schneider sacrificed too much for his chidren and thereby induced guilt by his generosity. "Was Lenny loved as well as spoiled?" you finally ask Mickey.

"He received an abundance of love." That is the phrase he uses over and over again to describe his relationship with Lenny. "An abundance of love." What does it mean? How can it be if Lenny later denied his father and denounced his father and complained bitterly of his father's anger and brutality? Twenty-five years later, Lenny was still acting out for friends scenes with his father that had occurred when he was just a little boy. How his father would come home from work and inquire in a very calm voice whether Lenny had done as he had been told and mowed the lawn. When Lenny said, "No," Father would swell up like an ogre, look down at him with rage, and yell in a voice like a cannon, *"No!!!"* The effect was terrifying when Lenny would tell the story. Mickey let his anger build to the bursting point, like many quiet, mild-mannered men. Yet can such isolated incidents, disturbing as they are, produce the kind of psychological trauma that must have occurred in Lenny Bruce's childhood? Can a child develop such a set and unremitting antagonism toward a once-loved parent, as Lenny later evinced toward Mickey, as a consequence of an angry scene here and a guilt-inspiring sigh there?

Look at how Lenny was treated by his mother—and how readily he forgave her. Lenny always forgave everyone for the injuries they inflicted on him. If you gave him dope that made him jump out a window, or you arrested him time after time, or you cheated on him and tortured his masculine pride—he would forgive you! He was forgiving to a fault. The only person he never forgave was Father.

Sometimes, when you sit with Mickey Schneider and toy with the empty coffee cup on the plastic-covered table, when you look up at this poor man and see the tears standing in his eyes, hear his voice trembling, threatening to break as he talks about his poor dead Lenny, you get a very strange impression. You recognize how he saw Lenny from his earliest years; you realize that he saw Lenny much as he saw Carman Kitchenberg—as a poor, doomed, afflicted child, carrying within him the seeds of hereditary insanity. Mickey *did* give Lenny an abundance of love, but it was Jewish love. Full of alien emotions: pity, fear, and scorn. These poisons destroyed the wholesomeness of that love. They made the loved one reject his costly gifts. Eventually, they made him reject the giver.

Love is often likened to a beam, a light that shines down on the beloved from the lover. Not a pure white light illuminating its object, love is like the beam that comes from a movie or slide projector, a beam that carries a vividly colored image. Where this love light falls, it paints its image. It may even *implant* that image—especially if the loved one is a tender, impressionable child. Mickey Schneider implanted the image of the helpless, damaged, but lovable fool in Lenny Bruce. He planted that image so deeply that it became Lenny's essential character. Though Lenny might imagine himself in many other guises, as a handsome stud or a suave sophisticate or a brilliant legal mind, he knew—or feared—deep down inside himself that he was just an idiot boy, a cripple, a pariah—another Carman Kitchenberg. When the pain of this awareness became too much to bear, he deadened it with drugs.

Fifteen years after Lenny left Bellmore and turned his back on his father, he made a movie out in California that was supposed to be his masterpiece. Coming at the end of a period of filmmaking, when he had come to think of himself as primarily a movie, not a nightclub, artist, the film was an all-out effort to bring up from the depths of his soul an image and a story that would rival those of the greatest filmmakers. Lenny's hero among the comics had always been Chaplin; now he set out to make a modern film in the Chaplin tradition. The picture was called *Black Leather Jacket*. It was about a young boy with a hearing aid stuck in his ear, who is sort of charming and silly and simple-minded and poor and outcast. This kid works as a paperboy and lives in a rooming house run by a horrible mean-faced landlady —played by Sally Marr. His only companion is a tiny turtle, which he keeps in a bird cage. He's terrified of the landlady, and his efforts to hide things from her produce grotesque scenes, as when he hides some soup he cooked by pouring it in a bureau drawer. Most of the time, he lives in the street, where he stands waving his newspapers at the windshields of passing cars, getting a lot of rejection and shrugging it off with the classic Chaplin shoulder hitch. When things get glum, he strolls past a haberdashery window and stares with longing at a black leather motorcycle jacket, the acme of his desires.

One day, this poor lad is sitting by a wall with a thermos jug in one hand and a sandwich in the other, eating his lunch in the street because he's too poor to go into a luncheonette. On the other side of the wall two criminals appear, fleeing from the police. They're dope dealers and they've got to get rid of their stuff. So they toss it over the wall and continue running. Naturally, the dope falls plop into Lenny's thermos, as he looks the other way. Giving, like Chaplin, one of those dopey, ho-hum stares dead into the center of the camera, he takes a long swig from the thermos. Once he blinks, twice he blinks —his face is a painting of surprise. Suddenly, the screen flames from black and white into Technicolor.

Now Lenny is sitting astride the biggest, ballsiest motorcycle in the world, surrounded by fawning, flirting girls and wearing with button-bursting pride the cherished black leather jacket. Planting a cigar in his mouth, he adjusts his goggles, lays his leather-gloved mitts on the handlebars, and prepares to blast off into ecstasyville. At this point, the film breaks off. It was shot and reshot but never completed. There was no need to complete it. Lenny had bared his soul.

One other document deserves to stand with that film as testimony to Lenny's true self-image and as evidence of the nature of his relationship with his father. This is a remarkable letter written a year and a half before he died, at a moment when it appeared that he would be forced to go to jail for a narcotics conviction. Turning to his father, as he always did when he wanted someone he could rely on, someone who could be counted on to take realistic action in an emergency, he set out to write a request that his house be properly cared for during his absence. When he fixed his mind on his father, however, he was reminded of their early years and how these years connected with his later life.

Dear Father,
    This is the story of a boy and his father who spoiled him. He would want a bike, and his father would bring one home: and if

it wasn't to the boy's liking, he would throw it down on the ground and say, "I don't want that cheap old bike." And he would kick its spokes and jump on it: and the poor father would say, "Alright, my son, I'll work 24 hours a day and get you a nicer one." The more the son got, the more vicious he got. He ate the father's deserts and took the only pillow. When he got older, he had no more money, and he spent his last pension penny making a birthday party for the son. It was a lovely party with cake and everything; and as the son spit out the cake on the floor, he said, "I'm not eating this cheap crap!" And he ran out and slammed the door on his father's head. He started to rob banks and gas stations to get what he wanted; and finally he killed somebody and was on the way to the electric chair. On the way to the chair, the poor father was standing and crying: "Oh, my son! My son! Where have I failed you?" And the son said, "Come here father. I want to whisper something to you." The old man leaned to the son to listen and the son bit his ear off. I'm going to jail tomorrow because you spoiled me.

> I love you,
> Lenny

Lenny Bruce enlisted in the Navy six days after his seventeenth birthday on October 19, 1942. The country was in a frenzy of wartime activity. Any kid who wasn't doing well in school, or who got caught knocking off a gas station for ration stamps, or who just wanted to get away from home, could run down to a recruiting office, get a form, have it signed by his parents, and take off into the night. Lenny was dying to get away from home. He had dropped out of Wellington C. Mepham High School the previous spring because his life was going to pieces, and he couldn't keep his mind on his studies. Father, who was thirty-six and subject to the draft, was about to go into the Army. Dorothy wanted to sell the house and do war work in Washington. Lenny was planning to enlist in the Navy—so why force himself through one last semester? There was no hope of graduating in any case. As a result of the disruptions of earlier years, he was still in the tenth grade. He would have to come back and finish up after the war. Who thought about such things at that time?

Lenny couldn't bear Father's discipline any longer. Mickey had become more and more strict. He was really a martinet. All the Schneiders were great believers in "the rules." You were supposed to "police your quarters," and do well in school every day, and be a perfect host when guests arrived in the house. Meanwhile, the biggest war in history was going on right out there in the ocean, just a few miles from his doorstep! So Lenny told everyone that he was enlisting in the Navy. That was the prestige service, the better deal. He was especially proud to tell the Denglers. He was sure they would approve. What a shock when they said he should wait another year. If you read his life, you know the Denglers as the people who ran the chicken farm that Lenny ran away to and worked on for two years. The truth was, in his ramblings around Bellmore, Lenny had found his way out to the next and even more rural town of Wantagh. Here people did real dirt farming. One such family was that of Mr. and Mrs. Fred Dengler.

The Dengler farm was located on Wantagh Avenue (a dirt road at the time) and comprised seventy-two acres of vegetables, fruits, flowers, pastures, and farm buildings. There were cows, horses, chickens, ducks—a regular spread. Lenny had walked in one day, when he was thirteen or fourteen, and asked if he could help out. He was a sweet boy, recalls Mrs. Dengler, very polite but also very nervous. There wasn't much a kid like that could do, but they let him dig potatoes and drive a little truck they had through the fields. He would work there every day during the summer and after school hours in the spring and fall. He ate with the family, but nobody could ever remember his talking about his friends or any teachers or adults he liked. Mrs. Dengler thinks he didn't have any friends and that he thought he knew more than the teachers. He was very unhappy about his stepmother, who constantly rebuked him for being sloppy. He didn't say much about his father. Nobody ever heard a word about his real mother. When Lenny told the Denglers that he wanted to enlist but his father was against the move, they sided with the father. He was not only too young but too babyish to go into the service. It was just like that crazy idea he had had a couple years before, when he wanted them to adopt him as their natural son. The Denglers were so shocked, they didn't know what to say. They didn't want him living with them, and they certainly weren't about to adopt him. What was wrong with that boy that he couldn't see that his place was to stay with his rightful mother and father?

At that age, Lenny probably couldn't have explained his desires even if he tried. All he knew was that he was increasingly unhappy at home and doing worse all the time in school—where his grades had slipped from "excellent" during elementary school to "poor" during junior high—and eager to get away from this unhappy world. When his father received his draft notice, Lenny made up his mind. He would enlist to help his country. Thousands were doing the same. It was the moment of the Great Effort. The Germans occupied all of Europe, the Japs all of the Far East; yet American "know-how" would defeat them. But it would take a long time. You wouldn't be a youngster when you came back from this war.

The shock of going into the service was something that no real man ever discussed. You did it and kept your mouth shut. From that first morning at 90 Church Street when the doctor forced his finger up your tightly clenched balls and told you to "Cough!" you felt like you were on a bobsled you couldn't stop. It was go there and come here, and fill this out and take this slip with you, until you found yourself standing naked again, in a receiving building at Newport, Rhode Island, with all your worldly possessions packed in a box at your feet, to be followed, perhaps, another day, by a longer box wrapped in a flag. Lying in your bunk at night, you could hear the *thump-thump* of antiaircraft guns blasting away at spooky-looking sleeve targets. All around you were your "shipmates," a hundred and twenty strangers sleeping in your bedroom. Instead of the familiar objects, the crossed foils on the wall, the radio, the books, the calendar from the local bank, there was nothing but blank walls and windows and a big iron rail where your sea bag hung. At night it was even stranger. The boys slept deep but they were uneasy. This one moaned in his sleep, that one was always grinding his teeth.

Suddenly, after the shortest sleep of your life, a hand would be tugging at your shoulder and some ghostly figure in a white cap and a pea coat would be whispering, "Hey, mate, time for guard duty!" A kid who had never been up later than midnight, you would roll out of your bunk, slip down your sea bag from the rail, pull out your uniform, your warm jacket and gloves, and go to stand for hours in the dim half-light of the washroom or the boiler room or the front door of the barracks. Struggling to keep your eyes open, you would be full of anxiety lest the officer of the watch come by and find you napping—a deadly offense leading straight to the nightmare of the training film you had just seen, the one in which a sleepy lookout was responsible for the sinking of a ship and the loss of the whole crew. Sure enough, just before dawn, you'd hear the crunch of boots on gravel, and a burly, athletic-looking officer with a big pistol strapped to his web belt would loom up before you like the high school football coach. You'd struggle to salute while rapping out the words: "Rear door guard, Company C, reporting on duty, sir!" It was like reciting "Pick a peck of pickled peppers."

The Navy was supposed to make you a man, but in boot camp you were treated exactly like a child. You got up at dawn and ran out on the grinder to do calisthenics in your dungarees and sneakers. You "secured" the barracks and marched to breakfast. Ate a big square of dehydrated eggs with bread and marmalade. Marched back again to continue the endless scrubbing, scraping, and scouring of what must have been the cleanest building in the world. Went to classes that were nothing like any classes you had ever attended before. One day it was ship and plane identification: a dark room, a bright screen with flashing slides, and everybody shouting "Jap BB! German CV!" Then BONG! A Petty Girl would stretch voluptuously across the screen, and the guys would shout from shock. Another day, they marched you to the sail loft, where some old geezer with bosun's anchors on his sleeve would show you how to make some complicated, useless-looking rope knot. Next day, it was the firing range or the drill hall or the swimming pool, where you climbed a high wooden tower and leaped off, one hand pinching your nose, the other locked with a death grip around your balls.

At night you would sit in the dimly lit barracks and scratch out some pathetic little letter back home:

Dear Father,
    I would truly give all my worldly possessions to spend a few hours with you now. I know you'll say, "I told you so," but I'm kicking my rear section for not continuing my education. How is Dorothy? You know. Father, as young, chronologically speaking, as I am, I feel mentally superior to most of my associates. I don't say this boastfully, but I attribute the fact to the rather strained but intelligent surroundings I had. . . .

                                          Your loving son,
                                          Lenny

When the smoking lamp is lit, practice inhaling a cigarette. When the milk truck pulls onto the grinder, go out and buy a quart of chocolate milk. You are always hungry; they stop you if you try the chow line twice during dinner. If you're lucky, you have some close buddy who will talk to you and tell you about himself and listen to your dreams of what you are going to do when the war is over.

In the winter of 1942–43, Lenny was assigned to the cruiser *Brooklyn*, on which he served for the next two years. The ship was a big modern 10,000-ton vessel designed to hold 800 men but stuffed to the gunnels with 1,300 officers and men. Employed at first as a convoy escort and later as the flagship of a much-decorated Mediterranean task force, the *Brooklyn* won four battle stars in Algeria, Sicily, Anzio, and Southern France. Lenny was assigned to a forward turret as a shell passer. When a strident, raucous, blood-curdling klaxon would sound deep in the bowels of the ship, he would run up ladders and across decks, until he jackknifed through the door of a forward turret and jumped into his battle gear. Wearing a big helmet lined with foam rubber and a flotation jacket, he would stand by the shell hoist, open the hatch, haul out the shell, and push it into the breech, where another guy would shove it home. The firing of the ship's five-inch guns went on day and night because the vessel was used as a floating fort. Every couple of days, she would steam out of Palermo or Naples with a fresh load of shells and go to work pounding the German and Italian positions along the coast at Anzio. Close enough to shore to actually see the Germans jumping into foxholes, the ship presented a tempting target to the enemy 88s and to Field Marshal Kesselring's bombers. The air attacks would generally occur at night, and the whole sea would be illuminated by flares as the Germans lit up their targets before plastering them with bombs. Though the *Brooklyn* escaped damage from either shore batteries or bombs, she witnessed plenty of carnage. Lenny saw dead bodies floating in the water and noted how the mixture of green sea and red blood produced a sinister shade of blue.

On board ship, Lenny soon earned himself a reputation as a "kook." No one believed he was old enough to join the Navy; in the pictures from that period, he looks less like a sailor than a sea scout. Five foot six and weighing only 127 pounds, he was a little pipsqueak, with a head like a rosy apple. The crew laughed at his Little Lord Fauntleroy manners. After all, here they were in the middle of the North Atlantic, sailing through submarine-infested waters aboard a 10,000-ton attack cruiser keyed up for instant action, and here was this little twerp, traipsing off to the showers dressed like Freddie Bartholomew, with a suit of striped pajamas, a fancy belted bathrobe, and leather slippers on his feet! What's more, the kid was a goof-off: always reporting sick or making excuses or goldbricking his way out of some rough duty. To hold down the razzing, Lenny told jokes and clowned around and put on an act like he was queer. He wasn't queer—or was he? Who the hell knew! All you could say about Lenny Schneider, seaman first class, Second Division, U.S.S. *Brooklyn* (CL 40), was he was the damndest little weirdo in the fleet.

During the two-year period Lenny was aboard, the ship made port frequently at her home base, the Brooklyn Navy Yard. No sooner was she into her berth than the watch with liberty passes would be swarming ashore heading for the lights of Times Square. Lenny Bruce joined many of those liberty parties, but he also got into the habit of visiting his mother over on Atlantic Avenue, a couple of miles from the Yard. Sally had been running a dance studio across the street from the Atlantic Avenue Station of the Long Island Railroad since 1937. Imposingly titled The Marsalle School of Dance, it was just another

neighborhood dance studio, run by Sally and a partner named Mary
—the two of them known professionally as the Marsalle Duo.

The school was the outgrowth of Sally's efforts to teach young kids
how to dance out on Long Island. Two hard-trying women coaching
young girls in the latest steps and pushing clumsy businessmen around
the room to the strains of a portable phonograph. When business got
bad, Sally worked as as taxi dancer in Times Square. She always had
a boyfriend, some silent Joe, to pick her up after work, drive her in
his "machine," take her to dinner or dancing, and listen to her endless
supply of stories, all turning on her own cleverness and brightness and
irresistible charm. Not exactly an erotic personality, Sally appealed to
a certain kind of man. She came on like a star, like a celebrity, and
that got a lot of guys interested.

When the war came along there was a sudden demand for entertainers. Thousands of performers went into the service, and there was
no one to take their places but old-timers and amateurs. Anybody who
could sing a little or dance a little or toot a horn could get a job. After
all, what could people do with their money but blow it on booze and
entertainment? You couldn't buy a new car or a decent suit or build
a new house. Food was rationed and gas was rationed and even candy
bars were scarce. Meantime, you were working the swing shift and
making time-and-a-half and feeling that strange sense of wartime abandon. So every other night and all weekend long, you hung out in bars
and joints where they still had decent whisky and you dipped your bill
and had a few laughs and sang a few old songs and came home at
some crazy hour in the morning wondering what was happening to
your son in North Africa. Those were years when any kind of entertainment was prized.

Sally started working professionally in 1942, the same year her ex-
husband went into the Army and her son into the Navy. She began in
the neighborhood bars of Flatbush, working as an M.C.; then she
started telling jokes and doing bits and working herself up as a comic.
She developed some of her own material, and she bought some routines
from a writer named Burton Milton. Whenever she saw that she was
losing the people, she would do a fast dance step and grab them right
back again. Her best bit was based on her experiences at the dance
school. She would do a Jewish mother schlepping her daughter to
school and sitting there and urging the kid on with threats and promises
and ultimately the vow to get up on the floor and do the steps herself.
It was an amusing and authentic piece of material, and Sally used it
for years as she gradually worked her way into a better class of joints
in Manhattan.

Eventually, she got a job at a place called the Club 78, on 78th

Street and Broadway. She was the M.C. comic and by now she had
her act down. One of those performers who always keep the audience
off balance, she'd do a bit, take a bow, come back with a couple of
dirty stories, sing a few phrases of a song, do a fast spin or a Charleston
step, tell another dirty story, and then repeat the conversation she had
had with the cabdriver when she went home the night before at 4 A.M.
The driver had been a real crude-o, complaining: "My old lady's a real
pain-in-the-ass. She's always leaving her pants drying over the fuckin'
sink. I can't go in to wash without running my face into those wet
bloomers!" Just cutting out and quoting a conversation like that could
get you laughs, Sally discovered. Later, she passed the trick along to
Lenny, who liked nothing better than to open up his show with an
excerpt from some conversation that had just ended when he walked
out on the floor.

Working right along with her at the Club 78 was another and much
younger woman: Sandy Barton, a singer and a vocal comedienne.
Sandy would take a tune, like "Jim never brings me pretty flowers,"
and stuff it with gags—"I'm just lucky he doesn't give me the clap!"
—switching the song back and forth between a straight performance
and put-on. Sandy was one of those plain but hot-looking chicks who
can make you fall in love with her as she stands out there under the
lights. One of her conquests was Sally's kid. Sandy was seven years
older and married, but with her husband in the service, she was lonely
and Lenny was so cute. So she became Lenny's first real love, the
chick, as he used to say in later years, who "taught me everything."
Sandy was pretty sexy, and it's not hard to imagine what she taught
Lenny. The funny part of the relationship was that it all involved his
mother. He and Sandy and Sally would go out to dinner together, go
home together, sleep in the same pad together. In the morning, when
he had to get up early to go back to the base, Sally and Sandy teased
him. "If you bother me one more time," the sleepy boy threatened,
"I'm gonna say something you won't like to hear!" Sally asked Sandy,
"Now, what can he have in mind?" She'd rouse Lenny again, and he'd
get up on one elbow and cry like a cross baby—"Ma, go fuck yourself!"
The women laughed uproariously.

That "Fuck you!" stuff with Sally was really the keynote of their
whole relationship. Lenny never treated her as a mother. Why should
he? She wasn't really his "mother." She was his pal, older sister,
playmate. Far from being the Jewish mother with the chicken soup,
Sally was the no-bullshit buddy, who could set him up with a chick,
listen to his troubles like a shipmate, and then break him up with a
couple of great bits that he would take back with him to the ship and
do aft in the enlisted men's mess hall. A Falstaffian mentor, Sally was

the furthest thing in the world from a mother. In later years, after her own career had pretty well run down and Lenny was coming up fast, Sally began to play the Jewish-mother role to the hilt; but back in the war years, when she was still in her thirties, Sally Marr was like all those wisecracking, men-matching ladies in the thirties movies: a live wire, a pep girl, a barrel of fun, lots of laughs, a regular guy and great old pal. Just about anything you could imagine—except a Jewish mother.

In 1945, when the *Brooklyn* tied up in the Brooklyn Navy Yard for over six months to undergo a complete refitting, Lenny's romance with Sandy Barton began to get a little more serious. The war in Europe was virtually over; Lenny was growing restless in the service. Night after night he got liberty and went into Manhattan, where he watched his mother work in the clubs while he mooned over Sandy. One night he walked into the club and stood in front of the stage while she sang a really heavy, torchy ballad right in his face. Suddenly, Sandy's husband appeared out of the shadows and said, "What's going on here?" In the confrontation that followed, Lenny, Sally, Sandy, and the husband all got into an argument that wound up with the husband getting off dumb lines like, "If I was to divorce her, would you marry her?" Lenny answered, "Oh, mister, I'm not marrying anyone." And Sandy weepily protested, "I don't care if he loves me or not—I love him!"

Though Lenny didn't have any intention of marrying Sandy, he no longer could see why he shouldn't be with her whenever he pleased. His patriotic impulses had exhausted themselves through nearly two and a half years of heavy duty. The prospect of repeating everything he had done in the Atlantic theater in the Pacific was enough to drive him crazy. To his new pal, Flip (for Filipino) Reyes, a steward's mate, he complained of anti-Semitism and other abuses that made him desperately eager to get out of the Navy, no matter what the cost. Lenny brooded on his escape for months until he came up with a scheme that would set him free. The plot, as he explained it to Flip, was this: one day soon, Lenny was going to go into the crew's shower when it was filled with men and start grabbing the guys' cocks. He was always impersonating fags; there were even men who thought he was a fag— great! He would use that prejudice to get himself a discharge. When the men complained to their officer, he would confess that he was queer and longed to have homosexual relations with men. He would stick with this story until they gave him a discharge. It would probably be a dishonorable discharge—he didn't give a damn. He had to get out of the Navy immediately. Flip, an alienated minority type, a swinger who hated the Navy as much as Lenny, told his friend to go ahead and give the fag game a try.

Sometime in the summer of 1945, while the *Brooklyn* was in port, Lenny made a terrible scene aboard the ship and was brought before the medical officers. They examined him carefully and repeatedly, but he stuck to his story. Though he didn't actually engage in homosexual relations, he said, he was obsessed with the idea; the other day in the shower he had simply given way to an impulse that was always at the back of his mind. He was sure that as time went on he would have to indulge in more behavior of this kind—or do something even more flagrant. The ship's doctors recommended a dishonorable discharge, and in the fall of 1945, Gunner's Mate Second Class Leonard Alfred Schneider walked out of the Brooklyn Navy Yard a free—if somewhat tarnished—man.

That night, Sandy recalls, he walked into his mother's flat on Livingston Street wearing a brand-new suit with his uniforms under his arm and a big grin on his face. He was really turned on and swept the ladies up into his mood. He took them out to a Chinese restaurant for dinner, cut up in the subway train, and spoke about his desire to go on the stage. He wanted to become a singer and a dancer. That made the women laugh. Sandy said that Lenny danced like a sailor—from the knees down. Sally said that he'd never make it as a comic—he wasn't tough enough to stand the rejection. The only thing that troubled Sally that night was Lenny's sudden desire to marry Sandy, as soon as she could obtain a divorce. Sally was very fond of Sandy, they were best friends; but she had no intention of seeing her little "malted-milk face" marrying a mature woman. She put her foot down for once, and objected vehemently to the idea. The night ended with Sandy in tears.

Lenny's impatience to be discharged spared him only a couple months of service. With the dropping of the Bomb, the war in the Pacific came to a sudden, startling halt and within a year everybody who had been drafted into the services had been discharged. Mickey Schneider was among this horde of returning veterans; like many men at that time, he decided to use his mustering-out pay and his GI Bill benefits to set himself up in a new career and in a new home in California. Bellmore was full of painful memories—why revive them? California was the golden land of opportunity. Mickey moved to Arcadia in the L.A. area and built a house on a good-sized property, including enough land to build another house for Lenny. Sometime late in 1945 or early in 1946, he received his son in this new home.

Father could hardly recognize Lenny Penny. The Navy years had added inches to Lenny's stature and pounds to his skinny, boyish frame. He was developing into a surprisingly handsome young man. He drove a car and smoked cigarettes and spoke in a voice that had acquired some very deep tones.

Father was delighted to be reunited with Lenny, and he made him a businesslike offer. He suggested that Lenny go to a training school, perferably in physiotherapy; then the two of them could go into business together, running a clinic for people with diseased or deformed feet. Lenny found the suggestion repellent. He had his heart set on the glamour of the stage, not the security of a podiatrist's schedule book. What was more, he found himself utterly unable to stand his father's benevolent authoritarianism. When Father counseled Lenny against buying a worthless old prewar Chevy, Lenny went right ahead and laid out his money for the car. Other disagreements followed and soon Lenny left the house. His days with Father were now over. He belonged to his mother's world.

Before returning to New York, however, he tried to make a go of it in Hollywood. After all, if his goal was the stage or screen, why not begin right on the turf? Why go East so you can come back West? Availing himself of his GI Bill privileges, Lenny enrolled in the Geller Dramatic Workshop, a well-known Hollywood acting school that offered eight-week courses in speech and technique, as well as a chance to be seen in Workshop productions. The school was a good one, and some of its trainees became highly successful. Lenny himself appears to have shown talent, while at the same time refusing to take the training as seriously as the other students. He told Sally that when he was playing the Death Row scene in *The Last Mile*, he broke up the audience by approaching the electric chair with a Charlie Chaplin walk. He also claimed to have won the attention of Joe Pasternak and the attentions of his wife, though neither of them has any recollection of Lenny today. In the spring of 1946, Sandy Barton went to work in Hollywood, and she recalls Lenny at this time as being entirely caught up in the intoxication of the movie capital. He wore the typical clothes and hung out in the famous haunts and spent all his time dreaming of stardom. No opportunities came his way, however, and eventually he had to make a decision about his future. He decided to go back to New York and take a shot at the Broadway stage. Selling his now decrepit Chevy to Sandy—without telling her that the only way to drive it on a rainy day was to sit in the driver's seat with the wheel in one hand and an umbrella in the other—he journeyed back to New York and Sally.

On Broadway the success that had eluded him in Hollywood seemed to fall right in his lap. Trying out with hundreds of other young men in a John Golden drama contest, Lenny won a prize and a cash award for a comical rendering of a Hamlet soliloquy. Burlesquing the

Bard, he did the same sort of switch that he pulled in *The Last Mile* —playing Hamlet drunk as Barrymore. Nothing came of this precocious success; soon Lenny was driven to working at all sorts of odd jobs just to survive. He was a stock boy at Loeser's Department Store, an usher at the Roxy. After kicking around for several months, he finally abandoned his dreams of the theater and told Sally that he wanted to follow in her footsteps and go into show business. Sally still didn't believe that Lenny could survive the hardships of the business, nor did she have any confidence in his talent, but she introduced him to an agent named Buddy Friar, who booked "amateur" shows. Lenny's account of these shows and the work of the crazy "ringers" who entertained at them demands to be quoted; like everything he ever said about show business, it has a perfect balance of perception and humor:

There were 15 or 20 clubs—such as Squires in Long Island, the Clay Theater in New Jersey, George's Corners in Greenwich Village, the Blue Haven in Jackson Heights—that would put on amateur shows to fill in on slow nights. Supposedly, people from the audience would be called on as contestants. Actually, we were the forerunners of the rigged quiz shows.

The prizes were $100, $50 and $25. We "amateurs" would sit around the club, and when they called for volunteers we would get up. We were paid $2 apiece, carfare and, if we won, an empty envelope.

One of the other "amateurs" was a waiter from the Bronx who always sang "Sorrento." When he reached the last four bars, his face used to get red and his neck blue. I think he got a hand from the audience just for the fact that he lived through the number.

There was also some nut from Rye, New York, whose act consisted of standing on a chair, jumping straight up into the air, and then diving and landing square on his head. Not on his hands, mind you; they were held tight to his sides. No, he would land smack on his goddam head. It was a short act but it certainly was a hell of an opener.

There was another guy who played the sweet potato, doing a medley of patriotic songs like "The Caissons Go Rolling Along." Then there was a performer known as "Al Jolson, Jr."—he was about 65 years old. And there was a girl acrobatic dancer who used to come to the club with all her lights, costumes, props, and her mother. I always wondered why no one ever caught on. Did they think that she just happened to drop in that night lugging all

her paraphernalia? Sometimes legitimate amateurs would try to
get on, but they would be told that there wasn't enough time.

The winner was selected by holding a hand over the contestant's
head and asking for applause. I never won. The sweet potato
usually did. He had a limp and wore a doublesize ruptured duck
[a veteran's button] he had made especially for himself: you could
see it from anywhere in the house. This gave me an idea for the
first bit of material I ever did that caused controversy.

My agent had a pro date to fill on a Saturday night in Staten
Island, at a place called The Melody Club. Since it had struck me
funny that anyone who had been in the service would use that fact
to gain rapport with the audience, I had a picture taken of all my
campaign ribbons and medals (including a Presidential Unit Citation), had it enlarged, and put it on. I had the band play a big
fanfare and "Anchors Aweigh." Then I came out and said, "I stole
this routine from Dick Powell and Ruby Keeler."

Right away one guy wanted to punch me in the nose for making
fun of the ribbons. It was the first time I felt real hostility from
an audience. And they'd missed the point.

The owner asked me to take the bit out for the second show. I
tried to explain that I was trying to make fun of a guy who would
do such a thing, not of the ribbons. He replied, "When in Rome
do as the Romans do."

"O.K., but I'll never play Rome again."

After four or five months of these amateur gigs, including an appearance on the "Major Bowes Hour," Lenny took the next step in
his career by joining AGVA, The American Guild of Variety Artists.
On May 22, 1947, he was issued membership card no. 64227. Henceforth, he was a professional entertainer.

Chapter Five

HOW SICK HUMOR
CAME UP THE RIVER
FROM BROOKLYN
TO MANHATTAN, ALONG
THE GOWANUS PARKWAY
(42ND STREET EXIT)

A ll the witnesses agree: Lenny Bruce was adorable but essentially just another weak, no-talent schmuck when he started hanging around Hanson's luncheonette in the late forties.

Lenny's first (and only) writer, a certain Burton Milton, says: "A nice boy. He had a little talent for mimicry and . . . a little nerve. He could do a little Chevalier dialect, an impression, also . . . funny voices." Basically, just a "nice boy," insists Milton—though nice-boy Lenny never got around to paying Milton for the stuff he wrote.

That was in 1947–48, when Hanson's was a regular show-biz scene, like Lindy's or Chandler's or Reuben's—only sleazier, for the losers, the schleppers, all the bottom dogs. A nothing place. A small Midwestern drugstore that had wandered onto Broadway and squatted down directly opposite the Taft Hotel. Lenny certainly belonged in that world. He had just gotten back from Hollywood. His image was straight out of *Screen Gems*: a yellow polo coat with a tie belt, blue suede shoes, a Warner Baxter mustache, Reginald Gardiner hair. In the smarmy pub shot in the window of the A. S. Beck shoe store on Broadway, he appeared in three-quarters profile, the knuckles of a fleshy hand laid lightly against the roundness of a zaftig cheek, brooding with heavy-lidded eyes.

He affected the matinee-idol look, but he was more Yiddish than British. When he opened his mouth, the voice that emerged was so breathy and adenoidal, every head shook in amused condescension.

His Aunt Mema said he looked like "a Spanish pimp." His best friend quipped he looked like "a barber dressed up for a Saturday night date." A jelly-doughnut handshake. A giggle like a girl and a lisp, too, like a hipster with a head cold: "Crathee, man!" A MAMA'S BOY!

Hanson's was the hangout of the lox-jocks and the bagel-benders. It specialized in Max Factor No. 5 pancake makeups, BT-Downs, burgers, seltzer, and formaldehyde green pickles that set the teeth on edge. It was one of those places with a lunch counter up front, a tobacco and toiletry stand to one side, and a one-step-up gallery in the back with tables, booths, and phones. The grilled cheese tasted like Duco Cement, the cream always turned your coffee gray. Looking cold, hard, and crusty, the customers seemed turned up at the edges, too—like dried-out English muffins.

Once you stepped inside this glassed-in food and drug shop—with its display cases piled on top of one another in steadily rising walls that threatened some day to topple over and bury the comics under an avalanche of combs, scissors, clocks, cosmetics, perfumes, electric shavers, and boxes upon boxes of cigars, stashed up the walls like a tobacco library—you felt you were right in the heart of showland. Running around the ceiling, like a black-and-white frieze, were dozens of 8 × 10 glossies of old dance acts—the guy with his leg up on a chair, the chick corkscrewed into his arms, smiling—all taken by Boris Bachey. The air was full of bad music blasting from the jukebox in the rear, which was filled with terrible records by the lady singers who hung out in the joint all day, listening to the sound of their own voices. Up front, Hanson's did a brisk business in tampons, douche bags, and orthogynol jellies with the chorus girls of the nearby Latin Quarter. In the rear, beyond the Bromo poster, where the sizzle of the griddle could not penetrate—and where there was always just a faint stench of scorched onion rolls, the clatter of plates, and the hiss of soda siphons—the comics nodded grayly, with sagging faces, over their cups of battleship-gray coffee.

Sometimes Hanson's was electrified by the appearance of a "staahhr." Milton Berle would come in to kibbitz, while his chauffeur double-parked the tail-finned Caddy out on Seventh Avenue. Or Jerry Lewis, a graduate returning in triumph to his alma mater, would burst through the door to tummul in the back booths. (Legend had it that Jerry once balled a chick in the tiny space between the phones and the entrance to 1650 Broadway.) There were even times when Bob Hope came in, or Victor Borge would take old Hans's place (they were both Danish) to collect the boys' checks with funny bits and gags.

Normally, though, Hanson's was the 25¢ Minimum Club. A refuge from your lonely stifling room in the Edison or the Belvedere; a place where you could while away the hours talking to your cronies in the booths. Always there was this endless chatter about the *business*: about clubs and dates and managers and agents; who would be hot in the Mountains that summer; what was the percentage in working a cruise ship; would television ever amount to anything—or would they always have to wear blue makeup and practically lay their heads up against the camera? These were the comics who, when they worked, may have earned $175 a week to play a burlesque house in Montreal—where all the customers spoke only French. Naturally, there was much bemoaning of bad breaks and lousy gigs. Plenty of envy takes on those who were making it a little.

Hanson's was also a proving ground for new material. One of the boys in the back booths would suddenly get hot and in would come running a dozen or twenty guys keen to grab the lines and do the bit the next time they got out onstage. Or it would be two cats slugging toe to toe, trying to cut each other like Kansas City jazzmen at a breakfast dance. Or it would be a real quiet scene: two guys sitting at the counter drinking coffee, the one gently enunciating one-liners to the other with flawless timing while he looks at him from the side of his face. The really professional style was to treat the jokes without much excitement, as if they could be best appreciated divested of performance values, savored in the abstract like mathematical formulas.

Eventually, old Hans would squawk: *"Vill you qvit hangin' around here? Vill you qvit hangin' around?"* Then all the comics would whip out their 25¢ checks to cool the beef. Or the more hot-tempered guys would stalk out and take their business to the B & G next door. Down the street was the LaSalle Cafeteria, and you could always hang out on the corner, especially in summer when the place was buzzing with entertainers trying to get weekend bookings in the Mountains. Or you could show up at Hanson's for a second go-round with a friend you'd picked up who was willing to stand you that quarter. Or maybe you'd go home, upstairs, to that filthy crawling hotel room, with all the garbage on the bedspread, to shower and sprinkle cologne on your face and change for the night shift.

Nights in the Gardens of Show Biz: if you didn't have a gig, that meant a 42nd Street double feature—*Charge of the Light Brigade* and *They Died with Their Boots On* or *She Wore a Yellow Ribbon* and *Gunga Din*. Then you had to ready yourself for the mandatory appearance at Lindy's. Into the men's room of the theater, smear your face with makeup, open up your tie, as if you were struggling for air, sprinkle a couple of drops of water on your hairline to simulate sweat, and stroll up Broadway, just like you were coming home after playing a taxing but triumphant date. When you walk into Lindy's, all the heavies will be staked out at the center-front table: Henny Youngman, Milton Berle, Fat Jack E. Leonard. They look at you, nod gruffly, say, "How's it goin', kid?"; then you slip to a side table, grateful to have been "seen." The cheapest item on the huge menu is the Fruit Compote, 75¢, which, with the tip, allows you to make Lindy's for a buck. Or, if you've saved up all day for one real meal, order the special Lindy's Delicatessen Sandwich, $1.25, which includes pickles, mustard, and relish.

Other hangouts were the Stage and Little Carnegie delis, a couple of dismal chow mein gardens, and Kellogg's Cafeteria, but that was mostly for the older generation. The young comics and mimics, or "impressionists," as they preferred to style themselves, had their hiring hall at Hanson's. All the Catskill agents were in the back building, 1650 Broadway; a rear door connected you to that lobby; so you could go up in the elevator, be rejected, and drop back down again, without ever once seeing daylight.

Agents are notoriously rude to acts.

"Who dere?"

"Hello there!" Smile, wedging your face through the smallest possible opening in the door. "Remember me?"

"Nuhding doing today!"

On a lucky day you are growled into the room. Then he will consult his big book, looking for open dates. In those days both the RKO and Loew's chains were still playing one-night vaudeville, a different show every night. Studying the book he mumbles, "I got Tuesday and Thursday at the Jamaica Theater."

"O.K., Abe!" Another twenty-five dollars in your pocket. Boy, if you could get two of those a week, you'd be rolling!

When you figured you had your act together, you'd say to the agent, "Put me into the Jefferson!" The RKO Jefferson on 14th Street was the showcase for all the new acts. On Tuesday night the big bookers would go down there, sit in the first couple of rows, and focus their beady eyes on the boys. If you put them away at the Jefferson, you were O.K. You'd get the Olympia in Miami, the Capitol in Washington, the Loew's State and the Paramount in New York. It was the big time! Otherwise, back to Pottsville . . .

The impressionists were hot in this period. They were novelty acts, not headliners. They never knocked the comics out of the cherished next-to-closing slot. But they were popular with audiences. Even comics had to learn a few voices: Joey Bishop did Charles Laughton and Bette Davis. But comics looked down on impressionists, calling them "mimics." "Now, here comes a clever little mimic, Mr. Russell Dreck!"

Actually, the impressionists were in the van of the whole modern nostalgia for the great movie stars and the glamorous Hollywood of the thirties.

Lenny Bruce started out as an impressionist because there wasn't anything else he could do. To work as a comic, you had to have material and delivery, an attitude and a comic personality. Unless you were an absolute natural, like Buddy Hackett, it took years to work up such an act. Traditionally, comics were old guys. They started out in show business as hoofers, jugglers, musicians, or singers. Then one day—to liven up a dull act—they told a joke. Getting a good reaction, they told more jokes. Finally, they ended up carrying the fiddle onstage as a prop.

After the war, the comedy business began to change. You began to see young, good-looking comics: the Jan Murray type. These men weren't much older than Lenny, but they were "polished." They had their acts down to the last breath, gesture, and intonation. Lenny didn't because Lenny couldn't. Such mechanical perfectionism stood in total contradiction to his spoiled, self-indulgent temperament. About the only thing Lenny did have was an agent at 1650 Broadway, Marvin Worth, a Brooklyn boy from Borough Park who represented Sally, and as a special favor to his client, had auditioned Lenny and had even driven him to his first gig in Connecticut, where the kid solemnly bombed. "He was just too inhibited and stiff," remembers Marvin, "sort of *Shakespearean*—anybody ever tell you that?"

It took two years till Lenny got his big break—on the *Arthur Godfrey Talent Scouts*. Some would say it wasn't a break but a curse. The show was notorious for picking losers and rejecting performers of genius. Among the rejects of that time were Jonathan Winters, Wally Cox, Dick Shawn, and Carol Burnett. The winners included such subsequently famous names as Bernie George, Sonny Howard, and Leon DeLion. The format called for some ordinary citizen, a "talent scout," to recount to Godfrey the circumstances of his "discovery." Then the "talent" came on camera and did a three-minute bit. The night of Lenny's appearance, in October 1948, Sally Marr walked onstage at the CBS studio in Manhattan and told the network audience with great feeling that she was just a Brooklyn housewife, but she was convinced that someday her only son would become a big star. Lenny then jittered on camera to do his one professional bit, *The Bavarian Mimic*. The *Mimic* consisted of three standard impressions—Cagney, Bogart, and Edward G. Robinson—but done as a "switch": all three stars were depicted in a German nightclub—*talking in German!* Most of the gags have been forgotten, but New York comics still laugh over Lenny's punch line. Concluding the routine with Bogart, he paraphrased the standard line, "All right, Louis, drop the gun!": "All right, Schmeagah, drop the Yeagah!" That killed the boys at Hanson's.

Actually, the bit was a variation on a variation, adapted from Red Buttons's routine called *The Jewish Mimic*. Red actually complained to mimic Will Jordan that Lenny's German was *his* Yiddish—but he conceded that it didn't really matter because Lenny was no threat to anyone. How right Buttons was became instantly apparent when Lenny had to follow up his Monday-night victory with appearances on Godfrey's daytime radio show on Tuesday, Wednesday, and Thursday. Tuesday was merely a repetition of Monday night's winning performance, but for each of the next two days, Lenny had to come up with two additional five-minute routines—and he didn't have them. Determined to save her boy, Sally appealed to a friend, gag writer Burton Milton. This old joke tailor fitted out the boy on the spot with a couple of off-the-rack jokes. His parody of Chevalier singing "Louise" was capped with this immortal patter and punch: "Ah, Louise! You are so beeootiful! I see you now sitting on the George Washington Bridge— dangling your feet in the water!"

If Lenny had trouble getting through five minutes of radio, you can imagine what happened to him when he was engaged for $750 a week to work the Strand Theater on a bill headlined by Alan Dale. Wearing a rented tux, he stood in the wings on opening night, nervously wringing his hands and touching up his hair. Wobbling onstage, virtually paralyzed with fear, he clutched a floor mike for support and began babbling at an incomprehensible clip. It was the day of Harry Truman impersonations; mimics like George DeWitt and Tommy Ford had caricatured Truman into a handful of gestures and sounds that anybody could copy. Lenny sawed the air into square shapes with outstretched hands, did the usual lines about Margaret and Bess, struggled to get the Truman sound—but didn't come close. Another bit with a portable radio—a big fad at that time—fared no better. Winding up with *The Bavarian Mimic*, he laid a heavy German egg. Between shows he dashed over to the China Doll, a sleazy oriental club across the street from Hanson's owned by columnist Lee Mortimer. Lenny's booking in a "real nightclub" made him look sensational in the trade papers. "Just Concluded—5 Smash Weeks, CHINA DOLL," ran the ad in *Variety*. But after his moment of glory on Broadway, the only booking he would get was the Tick Tock Club in Milwaukee, where an audience of real Germans found nothing funny in his German double-talk impressions. What a terrible comedown!

Lenny was washed up before he began. For one bright, hectic moment it looked as though the cute, high-assed pretty boy with the wobbly walk and the loxy vibrato might really fool all the street-corner reviewers and feinschmeckers. Not to be. Lenny wasn't ready. He couldn't build on his success. He became so depressed he decided to get out of the business.

But he didn't.

He struggled on, working the Mountains, working Brooklyn, Long Island, and a few out-of-town houses. He'd go up to Montreal and take a shot at the French burlesque and write pathetic little schoolboy notes on blue-lined paper to Burton Milton. In that round, childish hand you learned in the third grade, he would complain that the audiences couldn't understand him, his room was expensive, his nut was enormous—$35 a week. With all the experience he had accumulated in nearly three years of working around the city, he still couldn't do the impressions like the really good mimics. His act was the copy of a copy, an attempt to do something he didn't really believe. Harry Truman with those dumb squared-off hand gestures. The bit about the kid with the portable radio. Even the shtick about Cagney, Robinson, and Bogart in the German nightclub, doing their stuff with Nazi accents—how funny was it? Christ, there were guys on the corner at Hanson's who were far more talented.

Will Jordan was one. Will had the real knack of impersonation. He could find the "key" to any public personality, the one little mannerism or sound or look around which you could structure a whole take. Performing inside Hanson's, he'd have the guys lined up out into the street—until he realized that they were all ripping him off. Then he got so worried about plagiarists that whenever he had a new "voice," he'd grab a comic or a dancer (but certainly not another mimic) and take him around the corner into the privacy of 47th Street. The regulars in the booths would watch his lips moving, the other guy breaking up—but they could never hear Will's tongue turning the key.

A few guys at Hanson's already had the knack of making money. Buddy Hackett was a good earner, doing as much as eight hundred dollars a week at Ben Macsic's Town & Country club in Brooklyn. Larry Storch was playing in *The Littlest Review*. Arnie Sultan had a couple of steady gigs that kept him yo-yoing back and forth between Miami and Wilmington. Jack De Leon made a living. Jack Marlin, Lenny Gaines, Jackie Gayle scratched along. But it was easy to crash when you were flying so low. Jack Roy dropped out to become a shingleman; then, many years later, he made a great comeback as Rodney Dangerfield. Still others survived only on the margins of the business, as oddballs, weirdos, warps, and crazies.

Davey Harris was one of the most grotesque. An old guy who often came down to Hanson's without his teeth, he always claimed his dental plates had been locked up inside his unpaid hotel room. Or if he had the teeth in his mouth, he would pop them out on his tongue while he entertained the boys with his crazy stories. He claimed he knew every famous person in the business. If you would listen to him, he would mouth through toothless gums long geschichtes meant to be the real inside dope about the big stars. Actually, it was all bullshit. Many guys would say, "Fuck off, Dave!" Lenny would listen. Really groove on Davey's nutty stories, dig them for hours and then come back to the tables saying, "Whew! I love that cat. He's so sick!"

Lenny's special favorite at Hanson's was Joe Ancis, the original sick comic. Joe was never a professional performer; he was too terrified of rejection to risk the flak from the ringsiders. Yet he was so heavy that guys like Buddy Hackett and Lenny Bruce sat for hours listening to Joe's rap without ever sticking in a word of their own. Sort of a sacred cow to these guys, a real kamicrazy go-for-broke style comic, Joe was a young man made of the fragile glass of genius.

Lenny met Joe one afternoon when he was sitting in the B & G's, next-door to Hanson's, with Marvin Worth and Whitey Martin. Joe came in, a tall, skinny Ichabod Crane–style cat, and sized up Lenny with a fast paranoid once-over. "Hmmm. Here's a guy with two agents and no work. O.K. I got nothing to worry about, no competition here, so into the shpritz!"

Pinning the chick at the counter, he starts to run her down for the boys. "Oi, is this a fucking grape-jelly job! Varicosities on the legs. Sweat stains under the arms. Cotton panties from Kresge's with the days of the week. Always wears the wrong day. Schleps home to Canarsie every night. Her old man beats her up while the mother listens to the radio in a wheelchair. Supper is ham and eggs and grits and all that Southern-dummy-cheapo-drecky-dumbbell shit . . .."

He talks like you'd squeeze the trigger on a machine gun. Words like bullets. Joe jams them together in fugues of impatience. Never bothers to make sentences, paragraphs, pauses.

He's right in there with every line. Knows just where to get you. Takes those words and runs them like a platinum wire into your pores and tear ducts. Wiggles them around like a celluloid in a latch. But again and again and again! Acupuncture. In no time, he has these guys paralyzed with laughter. Everybody has turned on his stool to look. He's making them beg. Making them scream—"Please, Joe, babe, stop, please, I'll get a rupture, a coronary!"

The Germans have a word—*Todlachen*. Laugh till it kills you. That's the way Joe likes to make them laugh. Demonic! The Marquis de Shpritz. He gets this mad glint in his eye and starts working like a Jewish rhythm 'n' blues act. A seizure, a paroxysm. Such restless ticking, twitching, hair patting, collar pulling, throat clearing, finger popping, hand slapping, knee bending, with elbows into the gut, shoulders up around the ears, bent from the waist.

You're caught in this terrible double bind. You're loving it! It's killing you! You can't bear to miss a single word. When he sees you're on the ropes, going down, he works twice as hard to kill you. Zooms in close to your face, locks onto the rhythms of your body, lasers and razors you till finally you tear yourself away. Then he stands up straight and laughs. He wants to laugh you out of existence.

Soon Lenny was looking forward to Joe's strafing runs. You have to imagine this schlepped-out, late-afternoon scene, with all these guys hanging around, killing time. They're standing on the corner bullshitting and talking, trying to make a few jokes. It's all low-key, there's no energy flowing. Suddenly, somebody spots Joe coming up Seventh Avenue. It's like "Steamboat round the bend!" From a block away you can feel the waves coming off this guy. An aura, a sonic boom of hysteria, his face is coming in like the head on a rocket. Then he walks up within two inches of each face and gives it a quick verbal chop. "You, schmuck, you look like a fuckin' fire sale at Sears and Roebuck! That tie is chalooshus! And you, putzo, look like an exhibitionist in a subway station. Those long coats are for guys who like to flash their peckers. 'Yoohoo, lady! Dig this!' Wham! And who do we have here under this big-brimmed Borsalino? Why it's old Mr. Hacker's boy, Leonard, with his cute little putty-ball nose. Mr. Hacker, why did you change your name to Hackett? Hacker wasn't your real name to begin with—so now you're a second-generation falso!"

Each cat gets a little shpritz of eau de poison. Then when he's got them all stunned, he does a quick change of pace. Some crazy sex fantasy. That's his major obsession. While he was riding in from Brooklyn on the BMT . . .

"Man, those trains are so crowded, you're squeezed into the most obscene postures. Like, I was holding onto the strap and looked down and pinned this chick, sitting in front of me, just on the level with my dick. I began to have this fantasy . . ." He's very earnest as he's telling you this. *What if*—that's the whole basis of his humor. "What if, sometime in the rush hour, you get on the train. They're all pushing and screaming. Finally, it gets going. It's a long fucking run, rocking along, and all the people are uptight, keeping their papers around them. You're standing there trying to read, and there's this chick in front of you. She's got this tremendous fix on your fly. You begin to feel like she's burning a hole in your crotch. It starts to make you uncomfortable. You don't know what to do, because it's not even like a lookaway job. Where is there to look? Bit by bit you're starting to get a hard-on. What can you do? You can't even reach down to put your hand in your pocket. You're stuck. It's getting bigger and bigger, and this chick is staring harder and harder. All of a sudden, she reaches up and gives it a little tap—like on a dog's nose. The thing shoots up some more. Now you're going crazy. 'Please! Please!' you're trying to whisper down out of your mouth. But this crazy chick gives it another little tap. You don't know what to do! All of a sudden, she reaches up and peels your banana. Takes it out and begins to gobble it up!"

And when he says "gobble it up," he makes this psychotic gesture, this caricature of his favorite sex act. He doubles up his fist and sticks out the thumb. His fist becomes the balls, the thumb is the prick. He sticks the prick in his mouth and does this mad tongue-wag, while, with his other hand, he reaches up and seizes the balls.

"So she's wailing away on your joint, man, the fucking newspapers are going down, the glasses are going down, the veins are popping out on heads, and I'm hanging on the strap and screaming—*'Go baby, go! Eat my meat, you popeyed cunt!'* "

Soon as he ends one bit, he starts in on the next. Or maybe one of the guys says, "Hey, Joe, do the one about the marine" . . . "Do the gym teacher" . . . "Do Miss Brown." Joe is the most totally inspired, totally freewheeling guy in the world. He can go for hours at a time, cutting this stuff out of whole cloth. But he does have some "standards," stories he's told many times. He's very freaky around these stories because actually he doesn't remember them too well. He's so out of his nut when he's shpritzing that he has no recollection of what he says. What's more, he can't cut the effort, the tedium involved in repeating something. It's much easier for him to make up a new story than to try to go back and recapture an old bit. He might fail to remember, to "relate" to the material. Let the professionals worry about getting their acts down; let them worry about what listeners expect. He doesn't want that—he just wants to be free, to play.

So, he's very coy, very shy of requests. Maybe that day he's in the mood—or maybe he isn't. "No, forget it, man. I'm not doing an act. You're the comic. I'm just the shpritzer."

Joe has one bit (that Lenny later copied) about a gym coach who's really a fag, a gym coach who talks in this hardy-har-har voice, and is really ballsy with the leather windbreaker, jock strap, and sweat pants, the college emblem and the patent-leather hair plastered back. A real he-man—a he-fag. "Hey, sonny, you got a cute pair of legs on you, strong legs, come over here, let me see them!" He gives a little touch there, a little slap here and finally he cracks the kid across the ass. All the while, Coach is talking: "Listen, sonny, I bet when you go out with the girls, I bet you got a real log on you, a real schlong there, eh kid? I bet you give it to them pretty good." Has all these horny obsessions about the kid and his cock and his ass and his legs and his thighs. Lusting after him. That bit ends, too, with Joe slobbering over his thumb.

Then he's got one about Miss Brown. This bit finds him in the hospital. He's lying in bed with a terrible fever. He feels very weak, helpless. Does the whole bit with his eyes practically closed and his voice down to a whisper. Twisting and turning in the bed. Cranky. There's this nurse swishing around the room, swish, swish—a stiff starched sound from white uniform. She wears white stockings and a white cap, with a little sweater over her white uniform blouse. All around the room is this swish, swish. She's got a cute ass on her, and her uniform is just slightly unbuttoned, just enough to get a little inkling of tits. Every once in a while she comes over and tidies around the bed, plumps up the pillow, tucks in the sheets. She's flirting with him, coming on with him. Again, he's begging her in the softest, feeblest voice not to molest him. "Please, Miss Brown, don't touch me. Please don't touch the bed. Please . . ."

Lenny loved anyone who was crazy, sick, and funny, so, of course, he was a great digger of Joe. He, in turn, was the kind of guy who only felt alive when he had got himself into alignment with some very good listener. Joe's whole life, his soul, was in those moments when he was doing his shpritz. That was his only release, his only satisfaction. His idea of heaven was to have a cat who'll sit there for hours, laughing and reacting and digging—*with no competition!* No one's allowed to interject one fucking word. "Laugh, O.K., but don't laugh too much, you interrupt my flow. Don't fuck up my rhythm. Laugh more to yourself."

In a few months Lenny and Joe are very tight. They are always hanging out together. The guys at Hanson's make fun of them: "Here comes the fruit market." Not so, though there was a kind of love between them. Once they were sitting in Lindy's together having a meal. Joe was always a gluttonous eater. He had a racing metabolism that just burned up food. When dessert was served, the waiter put a large piece of cheesecake in front of Lenny and a slightly smaller piece before Joe. The instant Joe looked at the cake, his face sank. He couldn't bring himself to say, "Give me the big piece." But it was written all over his face. Lenny smiled and, without saying a word, slid his piece of cake across to Joe.

They started out on the street corner with the gang at Hanson's, and that was too public. Too many dumb squares. They went to Lenny's place, the fifth-floor walk-up he shared with Sally on Livingston Street. A crazy little pad where mother and son lived like college roommates.

Sally had guys in and Lenny had girls. Sometimes they'd all be yelling and doing bits at the same time, Sally hanging in there and punching with the boys. Again, the same problem—no privacy. Eventually, they settled on Joe's room in his parents' apartment in Bensonhurst. A nothing little room in a nothing little apartment in a nothing-with-nothing neighborhood, way the hell out in South Brooklyn—but it offered a sanctuary from the world. A place where they could really be together. If Lenny didn't have a gig or he was getting bored with the gang on Seventh Avenue or his mother's narratives of how she knocked out a Shriners' convention in Albany, he'd skip downstairs, hop over to the IND subway station, and sail out across the rooftops of Brooklyn on the old Culver Line.

Past the dingy houses and empty streets, past the old Jewish cemetery jammed with headstones—a tenement for the dead—out along MacDonald Avenue with the wheels sounding on the elevated tracks. "Gevalt! Gevalt! Gevalt! Gevalt!" Finally, he'd reach the Avenue N station, run down the long flight of rusty iron stairs, and race the couple of blocks to Joe's pad in a scabrous three-story brick building facing an empty lot.

Joe lived in the second-floor rear of this six-family house. His father was a laundryman, who had to get up at six in the morning; when Lenny arrived the old people were already sound asleep in their bedroom. In Joe's room, though, the night was young. Poor Joe! He had spent his whole life locked in that room, a prisoner of love. Like many Jewish boys in Brooklyn, he had an unspoken deal with his parents to remain at home long past the age when he should leave, on condition that the parents allow him to carry on exactly as if he were living away from home.

It was a standard arrangement in that neighborhood, where Jewish parents counted their blessings in terms of how many children still remained with them in the house. In Bensonhurst, nothing was more common than to walk into a dreary old apartment, where nothing had been changed in twenty years, and find Ma and Pa watching TV in the living room, wholly oblivious of the fact that just six inches away— through that insubstantial wall of plaster, lath, and floral wallpaper— there was a "kid" of twenty-five blowing pot and digging bebop and maybe even balling the colored maid—or giving her head because the little Jew boys of Brooklyn were notoriously leckers and fressers.

Ducking into Joe's darkened apartment, Lenny would take a sharp left and push the door open to step suddenly into hipster heaven. Blue lights would be burning in the lamps, cool jazz purring on the "pick."

Soon Joe would be pacing the room as nervously as *der Führer* in his bunker, doing his famous shpritz with the absolute freedom and self-indulgent craziness that you can only get into when you have a listener who is practically another part of your own head. Interior monologue, free association, stream of consciousness—these are the fancy words for the shpritz. When Lenny did it in the clubs years later, critics would be amazed at his performance strategy—how he took the audience into his confidence as if he were talking to a room full of friends or just a single bosom buddy. What they didn't realize was that the shpritz had originated in exactly the circumstances they found so bizarrely inappropriate to a public stage.

Out there in the Bensonhurst–Boro Park Delta of Jewish humor, the Basin Street of Jewish jazz, the Beale Street of Jewish blues, Lenny first learned to be funny—to see funny, think funny, talk funny. To believe that being funny was the very greatest quality a human being could have, that once a person possessed this precious gift, he would find everything in the whole world was funny—funny being equivalent to vital, strong, ethnic, honest, and soulful. Funny guys were the guys who told the truth. Guys with an original point of view, a private language, a sound. The Jewish equivalent of the black jazzman. A hero.

Like all basic street words, "funny" was an enormously elastic term that could be inflected through a dozen different intonations to yield a dozen distinct meanings. It could range from the eye-sparkling, head-wagging, wish-I'd-said-that of "Funny!," virtually a one-syllable word signifying "Great!," to the long, imploring, interrogatively curved yet beseeching call for approval after a joke—"Funnnny?" It could be a curt, disgusted, alum-in-the-mouth "Funny," ironically bent to mean stupid, unfunny, corny. Or "funny" was a colorless little filler word constantly slipped into the sentence when the speaker's mind was intent on something else, when he was telling a story about this funny scene that occurred last week when he met this funny character and had the funniest experience with him which, in a funny way, really wasn't funny at all because it ended up real serious and not a joke— isn't that funny? The best way to use the word, though, was as a long crowing scream of wonderment, a high schrei of tremendously excited enthusiasm as you triumphantly wound up some great shtick, some genius-stroke narrative that had the boys groveling on the floor, down on their knees doubled over like victims of the firing squad. Raising your head up like a brave who has just taken a scalp, as delighted by your own genius as anybody around you, you would look up into that Mosaic heaven of funny faces, funny lines, funny flashes and shout out from the bottom of your soul—"FAAAAAAAAHHHHHNNN-EEEEEE!!!"

Joe Ancis was legendary, even as a kid, for being the funniest person in the borough. For one thing, he looked so "odd": tall, tubular, and thin, with a big, long nose and close-set, squinty eyes. His dusky complexion and the black hair plastered down on his skull did give him a sort of Sephardic look, but his family were simply Russian Jews from near St. Petersburg, who spelled their name a little differently from their relatives who spelled it A-n-z-i-s.

Saul and Sylvia, the tatah and the momma, were typical of all those old Jewish couples who spend their entire lives like two poor oxen harnessed to a plow pulling along some little neighborhood store or working in the garment center as "operators." The kind that went every Sunday night for the big treat of eating "dairy"—blintzes and sour cream—at The Famous on 86th Street and Bay Parkway. They were like working people anywhere, only with lots of sour cream.

In their longing to protect their precious son, to shield him against the terrors of the world, they had crippled the boy with the very same cautionary wisdom that was intended to keep him forever strong and wise. They had warned him, for example, that if anything ever falls on the floor, never touch it. It's poison! Also never eat without washing your hands. The more you wash your hands, the better off you'll be. If you go out, never eat meat. Chopped meat is poison: they grind up all kinds of crap and put it in there. If you eat that, you'll just fall over in the restaurant and die. If you have to eat out of the house, if you must go into a restaurant, order something like American cheese on white bread with lettuce and tomato. Tops, that's it! It doesn't matter if the other guys are eating a big steak or a ten-course meal, you just go for the cheese. Say, "No thank you, I'm really not hungry, I ate before." Never mix whisky and wine—that's in the books! And if you're walking along the street at night, you should get a white raincoat so the cars will see you. God forbid, a car might get out of control, jump up on the sidewalk, and kill you!

Also be very careful with girls. They're bad, crazy, vicious. They hold grudges forever. If you go out with a girl, be very careful; don't get involved; don't go home with her; don't take her out again. If you have to break up with a girl, be extra careful she don't get angry. She might take out of her purse a little bottle of acid and throw it in your eyes! The rest of your life you're blind.

Not surprisingly, Joe had become a rather cautious person. In fact, he was an emotional basket case. He had insane cleanliness phobias. When he would leave the house, he would take a bar of soap with him in his pocket, so that if he had to go in the men's room somewhere, he could scrub up. (Naturally you can't urinate without washing your hands immediately!) Using the men's room soap was absolutely out of the question. Just looking at that bar of soap, he could see it lying in the water with a big oyster, a big phlegm ball on it. Sure, the guy before him had hocked up some filth out of his throat and spit on the soap. Disgusting! Liquid soap was all right. This he would look for, pray for; but if there was no liquid soap, you would have to go for your own bar of emergency soap. Take that Ivory out, wash the hands good, then paper towels; if no paper towels, go for toilet paper. When you're finally through with this surgical scrub-up job, clean, immaculate, not a germ crawling on your hands, don't turn around and open that dirty door with all the filth on the knob. Men have just taken their hands off their peckers and put them straight on the knob. You'll blow the whole job! So, you reach in your pocket, glove your hand in the lining of the pocket, then with a practiced little twist, pop the door open and slip out. Safe!

Again, Joe has a complete lethargy thing. The poor little boy should never exhaust himself. He should sleep late. Lie around half the day in pajamas. Never think about working—time enough for that when you're old and your mother and father are dead and you're married. Sleep, wake late, come in the kitchen like a rumpled baby and yell at your little old mother: "Where's my orange juice? Is this the way you made the egg? What's the matter with the toast? You burnt it again! Leave me alone. Can't you see I'm reading? No, I don't want to talk to you." A cranky, lazy little domestic tyrant, carrying on in the house.

In high school, Joe began playing the alto saxophone. In those years lots of kids, especially in the Jewish-Italian neighborhoods, were into jazz. This was the period of the swing bands. Every kid wanted to be Benny Goodman or Gene Krupa. The latest furniture for an American living room was a big shiny set of Slingersland drums. Like a lot of local boys, Joe got himself a job up in the Catskills as a member of a band. You can't imagine how little and crummy were these hotels in the Mountains. But they all insisted on carrying on as if they were resorts. Which means they had a little patch of pool, some muddy tennis courts, and a skimpy staff—golf pro, social director, and the boys in the band: literally boys, sixteen or seventeen years old, living behind the dining hall in tiny slave cabins. They worked for thirty-five dollars a week plus meals, but they could pretend they were professional musicians.

In the Catskills Joe got his first lessons in being a hipster: he saw cats blowing pot and digging spade jazz. He was a terrible player but a great digger. In no time he had mastered the ins and outs of the jazz scene. He dug Coleman Hawkins burbling through "Body and Soul," Lester Young slipping through the cracks of the Basie Band on "Tickletoe," and Charlie Parker scorching around the track on "Ko Ko."

Dug all the hip bands, like Boyd Raeburn and Woody Herman. Billie
Holiday was his favorite singer.

Joe got Lenny into jazz. He hipped him to the whole cult as an
exercise in knowingness, which Lenny mastered beautifully without
ever developing a good ear or a true taste for the music. Like many
of the things that Joe loved for their own sake and tried to teach Lenny,
such as contemporary classical music and painting and certain books
and writers, jazz was something Lenny prized for the status it conferred
on its initiates, for the steep and complicated hierarchy of snob values
that could be contemplated apart from the actual music as the ultimate
pattern of hipness—Lenny's supreme goal and state of grace. Joe was
much more intelligent than Lenny, much better educated, gifted with
esthetic sensibilities and instinctively sophisticated. He was an inspiration and a model for Lenny in countless ways apart from his
shpritz—but it was the shpritz that fascinated Lenny and made him
pay attention to all the offbeat things that Joe was always rapping
about.

The shpritz was a mixture of many things. It entailed serious rapping about intellectual themes, taking off into wild way-out travesties
and extravaganzas. All the tricks of stand-up comedy—the timing,
mugging, dialects, and sound effects—plus physical clowning and practical jokes and crazy bust-out gags. Joe would start with words, but
then get so turned on he had to finish his statement by acting it out in
the most bizarre style. Only through the spotlight of comedy could he
gain the attention he was accustomed to from his doting parents, while
behaving in the tantrumlike style that was also his manner in the house.
Through the shpritz, the poison of emotional frustration and charac-
terological deformity was converted into joy, freedom, and, at least,
a local fame.

Most of the famous stories about Joe concerned less what he said
than what he did and the potent effects his humor had on other people.
He would get in a cab with a couple of other kids and start chanting
Italian names, bending the syllables outrageously and practically tearing his face off in the effort to shape the sounds. VEEEEETTTOH
FFFOOOCCHHYYAAHHTOH! EEEENOHCHYENTAY DEE
PAHLMEEEAIRREEEE! By the sixth or seventh name, the syllables
stretching like salt-water taffy all over the roof of the cab, the hackie
would be laughing as hard as the kids—so hard that he had to pull the
cab over to the curb lest he smash them all up.

Then there were the times when Joe was in a bus or a subway,
traveling back to Brooklyn with one of the neighborhood girls after
digging some jazz at the Royal Roost on Broadway. Looking at the
late-night commuters and schluffers and the dumb dating couples, he

would suddenly get an inspiration. Jumping to his feet in the speeding, swaying, racketing train— an uptight place where people always got unreal, like they'd been laid on ice—Joe would suddenly go into a tantrum. "EEElaine! I've had it! The next time your goddamned sister puts that can of tuna fish on the table, I'm getting up and walking out of the house! The nerve of that woman! After schlepping on *two trains* from Avenue J and bringing a present, to see a twenty-five-cent can of Bumble Bee on the table. I tell you, I can't take it anymore!"

On Pesach or Yom Kippur or Rosh Hashanah, while everybody is walking around in his best clothes and talking in a low voice and wearing a hat, here comes this meshugana, walking along Bay Parkway with his EEElaine, one of those girls who run with the boys and set up the other girls and play "chickie" or lookout while six guys make out with the same broad. A really nice girl, EEElaine is a skinny, pretty redhead with chorus-girl legs; she's all dolled up in a green silk dress with her sister's white fox stole and fancy ankle-strap shoes. She and Joe are walking by the Jewish Center, the Jewish synagogue, when suddenly he makes a scene.

Out of nowhere, he opens up a mouth and starts waving those spaghetti-finger hands and turns on his heel and comes back and shoves his face into EEElaine's face and screams: "What do you mean I have to pay twenty-five dollars to go into the shul? My father died this year. I have to go in there and say Kaddish for him. I never heard of such a thing! Selling tickets to a funeral! I'm a Jew. That's my synagogue. How dare they charge admission? What is it, Loew's Pitkin in there? I'm embarrassed. How could I ever explain *that* to the goyim—'This is my most serious religious holiday and I want to pray for my dead father but I can't go in the synagogue because I don't have twenty-five dollars for a ticket!' "

The more he tummuls this way in the street, the more people gather around him, shaking their heads and clucking their tongues. EEElaine is going into hysterics. She can't *stand* it! So she pulls Joe around the corner, and gasps: "Cool it, man, for Chrissake, if you don't stop, I'm gonna piss in my pants!" "Go ahead, I dare you," he snaps back, and lowering his face into hers, he gives her two or three more zingers until she squats down on the curb there and lets go—in the green silk dress with the fox fur and the ankle straps! When she's finished, Joe picks her up in his arms, walks up the block to where she lives, carries her up the stairs of the two-family house, and throws her down on the sofa in front of Momma.

"My God! What happened to my EEElaine? She's sopping wet!"
"Gussy . . . Gussy, you got a problem!"
After getting out of St. John's College, Joe had become a siding

salesman (today, he's the greatest closer in the business) and had gotten in with a flying circus of pot-smoking, shtick-trading, hooker-balling scam men, who drifted from one poor home-owning part of the country to another, taking the local suckers for all they were worth. One hot night, while Joe and his two canvassers are working the ghetto in Camden, he gets this wild idea. Ordering Eddie to drive his red convertible through the heaviest bar and taproom section, Joe mounts the back seat of the car, drops his trousers, pulls down his jockey shorts, and starts slapping his ass, screaming at the astonished black men in front of the bars, "Hey, baby, dig this white ass! Look at this white meat! Potchey, potchey, am tuchus!" Zoom! The great red potchmobile is an instantaneous legend.

All Joe's crazy scenes corresponded exactly with Lenny's own life-long yearning to bust out and go crazy and really give all the squares and assholes a taste of their own crap. Lenny had already busted out once when he got out of the Navy by pretending to be a fag. The Jew boys in Brooklyn never even went into the service because they had mastered all the techniques of draft dodging. Some of them came into their physicals wrecked from smoking pot and dropping bennies and staying up for days on end, without shaving or bathing or cutting their hair. The examining psychiatrists would inquire irritably, "What are we doing with nuts like this?" Instead of the customary 4F deferment, some of these neighborhood hipsters had letters way down in the alphabet, like O, Q, X—classifications usually reserved for men with one leg missing.

In many ways Lenny was much more temperamentally suited to be a bust-out guy than an uptight neurotic like Joe, whose greatest freedom zone was his mouth. Lenny always seemed like an absolute nut to Joe, a beautiful nut—"a unique blend of compassion, warmth, cuteness, laughter, and looseness"—but, for all that, a nut. Because Lenny would report incredible scenes to Joe. How he went to the shvitz, the Luxor Steam Baths, and as he was lying on the table, he let some faggot cop his joint. Or how he was baby-sitting for a friend one night and he finger-fucked his five-year-old daughter. Those stories sent chills of alarm up Joe's spine. "Oi, this guy is really sick!" he thought, because where Joe was all fantasy, with just an occasional spill into reality, Lenny was the kind of guy who would do anything he could imagine. To think it and do it were very much the same for Lenny Bruce. And not just Lenny got swept up in Joe's craziness. Hadn't Rodney Dangerfield, certainly a lot straighter cat than either Lenny or Joe, taken off his pants, folded them neatly across his arm, and run around the Confucious on 52nd Street one famous night?

Baring your ass, that much-pinched, much-kissed, much-bitten, gnawed, coveted, and obsessed-over tusch, toosh, tuschie of the Jewish nursery was not, when you get right down to it, a particularly strange thing for a little Jewish boy-man to do when he felt the infantile pleasures of exhibitionism and attention-grabbing and showing-off come cooking up his spine like a shot of the most powerful drug ever compounded in the Jewish pharmacies of America.

Joe's influence on Lenny wasn't confined simply to making him a zany. It worked equally strongly in the opposite direction—toward making him an almost intolerably pedantic lecturer on matters that inspired him with enormous enthusiasm but hardly belonged to his area of special knowledge. What Lenny later became in relation to the law, Joe was years before in relation to painting, art, sociology, all the academic subjects that captured his interest. He'd go to see a Van Gogh show at the Museum of Modern Art and then give a streetcorner lecture at Hanson's that sounded like something you'd hear in an art-history course. While the dummies stood there rapt in nitwit admiration and the hip guys frowned with impatience, Joe would hack through a barbed-wire fence of Greco-Latin abstractions: ". . . the spurts and articulations of these kinetic strokes . . . the basic concept of the whole aspect . . . the heavy densities of the pigmentation . . ." A dose! As this laboring verbal freight train hauls its way up the steep grades of INTELLECT Joe's native intelligence would suddenly assert itself, and abruptly the pedanticisms would be crossed by a fast, obscene, telegraphic speech that squirts the meaning in your eye like a spoon-stabbed grapefruit—". . . the people involved in the immediate observation of this *fuckin' squeeze-out* were . . ."

These street-corner gallery talks demonstrated to Lenny that being a hipster meant being smart, being knowledgeable, even being erudite. Far from being a cult of "soul"—like the hippies' "beautiful person"—the hipster ideal was extensive knowledge and refined taste. The hipster was the street intellectual. A jazzman like Charlie Parker dug Bartok and Stravinsky. A superfine rapper, like Joe, grooved on Shakespeare—"twixt incestuous sheets." The hipster didn't really know a great deal about the arts, but the aspiration was there, an enthusiasm for higher things, the desire to lift the street culture up to meet the serious arts. This was certainly the ideal Lenny espoused in his great years. He never wanted to be stuck with the label "comic." Philosopher, poet, satirist, filmmaker—those were the titles he coveted. When he got out onstage for one of his prestigious concerts, his favorite dates, he would do a few bits here and there, when he felt the audience needed a piece of candy; basically, he rapped like Joe

Ancis about serious steak-and-potato matters, like religion, politics, Jewishness, drugs, the Catholic Church, the Negro, the theory of comedy—all heavy stuff.

Joe was also the first to mix in one phrase languages of totally different provenances, totally distinct levels of usage. Big intellectual words would rub shoulders in his shpritz with old-country Yiddishisms and hipster jazz slang, underworld argot and baby talk. It was a crazy potpourri of language with the most astonishing riptides and undercuttings, one-uppings and incongruities. A pedant or a high school teacher might have been horrified, but anyone with a real sense of language applauded. Eventually you recognized that this gibberish of ill-assorted phrases operated according to an instinctive principle of balance. Hopping from one level of diction to another, like parakeets sporting in their cages, Joe's words were endlessly surprising and fascinating. There was a nimbleness, a dexterity, a witty metaphysical flibbertigibbet quality in his speech that impressed you as being just right for the world in which he lived.

"Hyperbolic" is the word for this style. It was loud, violent, strained, and forced up to the highest pitch of expression. Words were jammed together like nests of jackstraws. Single phrases were thrust out at you like slogans on billboards or commercials on the radio. Syntax, word order, the whole decorum of prose was short-circuited impatiently. Bang, bang, bang! That was the rhythm. Underscored with alliteration and pounded home with sledge hammer accents, a verbal rock 'n' roll. Boys felt the language was constantly failing them, cracking, breaking, sinking under the enormous weight of their demands. Like crazies they were tearing the books off the shelves, ransacking the files, schlepping up words and images from unterem drerd. The ideal conclusion for any of their shticks would have been a cerebral hemorrhage.

Lenny rarely captured this frantic, overpowering, rock-talk sound. He suffered from verbal disabilities: a tendency to singsong, a habit of mumbling, a coy and uncomfortable relation with the mike. Only late at night, when he was working to a very hip crowd and the Methedrine was scalding through his veins, could he attain the energy of the parent style. When he did, he produced the most dazzling poetry of his entire career.

Apart from the surrealistic poeticizing of speech, the other characteristic way of patterning language for the guys who hung around Joe Ancis was to turn words into music. Since so much of their humor was directed against those loved-hated, hated-loved Jewish parents, whom the kids regarded as virtual cliché machines, endlessly spouting phrases like "You made your bed, now lie in it!," the parental speech

patterns became as familiar as radio jingles. Not meaningful statements, not even distinct words after the one-thousandth repetition,
they were just riffs that demanded to be performed with suitable instrumental accompaniment. So one of the favorite forms of parlor
humor was orchestrating these Hebrew melodies. "You, George, play
drums," the star of the moment would command; "You, Jerry, be on
bass, and I'll do the heavy mockie momma telling the kid to come in
off the street. Ready?" Then the guy would put on his thickest, funniest
Molly Goldberg voice and start hollering, while the other two kids
improvised fills and socks on their real or imaginary instruments. "Yus-
sele! [drum roll]. Come in this house! [fast traveling music]. It's *kalt*
in street. Did you hear me? It's [crash] *kalt* [ca-rash] in street [thump].
Kumahame! [death march]."

Years later, Lenny used the same technique in one of his most
original bits, the routine called *To Is a Preposition: Come Is a Verb*.
Lenny's bit was based on the phrases people utter while fucking—as
he would say, "the real American folk music." These were the songs
he had heard as a child when he was supposed to be sound asleep.

Joe Ancis was always too bright, too sensitive to claim any part
in Lenny's success story. I chased him for seven years before he would
give me an interview. The only thing that hurt him, it turned out, was
reading the conclusion of *How to Talk Dirty*, where Lenny poses the
question: "What have been your influences?" The answer is a rhapsodic
piece of bullshit in which Lenny insists that everything he has ever
seen or heard or read has been an influence: a truth, no doubt, but
also an evasive if not a downright dishonest answer. At any rate, in
the long list of things he lists as examples of influences—everything
from Little Annie Rooney to smelling burnt shell powder at Anzio to
torching for his wife—he does not mention the name of Joe Ancis.

Joe's lack of celebrity should not make his influence seem less
credible. There is an enormous difference between being funny and
being a comedian. Many of the funniest people in America are just as
unknown as Joe Ancis. Or, they may enjoy public reputations as writers, teachers, musicians, or celebrities of one sort or another—but
nobody thinks of them, apart from their friends, as comedians. Philip
Roth, for instance, was a very funny man years before *Portnoy's Complaint* was published. He broke up his friends at parties, flew off in
conversation into marvelous fantasies, did all sorts of voices and dialects, rehearsed old radio shows, exhibited exactly the same sense of
timing, meter, and delivery as any professional comedian. Not until
Portnoy, however, did anyone have any true idea of Roth's comic
genius; and even now, after two consecutive books of nearly pure
comedy, there are features of his private humor, especially those that

depend on oral delivery, that are not familiar to the public. The same could be said about a number of men, some famous, some utterly unknown, who happen to possess the gift of seeing things in their ridiculous aspects.

A talent for comedy is a very different thing from a talent for public performance because to get out in front of the public, you have to have a special kind of nerve that is given to very few men. Comedians are, of all performers, the most vulnerable. Unlike every other species of entertainer, they do not appear to have a craft, a mystery. "Who is he, after all, this guy in the tuxedo, showing off and trying to be funny? Lots of people are funnier than he is—*I'm* sometimes funnier than he is! Am I right, Myrna?" Even the greatest comedians draw a certain amount of antagonism, a certain amount of static with which they must deal. Deal with it they do. The very first step in becoming a comic is learning how to handle rejection—a problem that has nothing essentially to do with being funny.

Indeed, if there *is* any connection between the fear of rejection and the gift for comedy, it is likely to be an inverse relationship, with the sensitive, high-strung, nearly hysterical funnyman being the last person in the world who could bear the hostility of the gross-outs at ringside. Joe Ancis, for example, once took a shot at performing for strangers. It was very early in his comic period, when he was still a high school kid:

> One of the guys in the class dug me because I was the psychological counterpart of the shtarke in the neighborhood who everyone wants to manage to go into the Golden Gloves. I had it with the humor thing. It was 52nd Street, some dumpy little club left over from the glad days: the real real bop joint with the dummy fuckin' wigged hookers. A semistrip joint with a half-assed singer. I think it was called the Swing Club. I was seventeen and a half, and he took me over there one night. "All right, man," he says, "it's O.K. to go on. The owner knows my dad." In other words, "Let the dummy go on, nobody gives a shit, anyway." If Chaplin or a fucking truckdriver did the bit, it would have the same effect with this audience. I got up, and I'd memorized some routine type of thing—and it was terrible. It was a freeze-up, a fumfer, a blank-out, whatever, man. It just wasn't my fuckin' thing—gags and all that shit.

One exposure to an unloving audience and Joe Ancis was dead. He wasn't a comic. Lenny Bruce went through the same scene countless times, without even sharing the conviction that Joe possessed that he was the funniest man on earth. But Lenny had the basic courage of the show-biz soldier.

Another and even greater distinction between Lenny and Joe was the fact that Joe had no way of improving his material. He was like the actor who goes to an audition and does a first reading that turns out to be his best performance of the part. Joe couldn't revise. He was one of those people who can throw their thoughts together on the spur of the moment but can never get them together any better, even when they're granted all the time in the world.

Lenny Bruce, by contrast, was an artist. He looked at Joe's spontaneous performances and saw a whole comic continent rising before his eyes. But it took Lenny ten years to map that continent. He had to translate a purely private, highly subjective, in-group humor to the public stage. First he had to work up his own material in the style that Joe had developed. Then he had to give a show night after night that was substantially the same and yet somehow preserve the air of pure off-the-top spontaneity. It took a mind that was capable of Dutch Master detailing, adding one little stroke to another for weeks, sometimes months, until a masterpiece was produced. Though Lenny may not have appeared the type for such incremental labors, they were the key to his success. They were also the reason why today, more than a decade after they were first inscribed in vinyl, his routines still continue to make people laugh, preserving a freshness and spontaneity that no real freshness or spontaneity can ever have after the passage of years.

Joe Ancis regrets now that not one of the thousands of hours of heedless shpritzing that he poured out in his creative period was captured on tape. It is a pity that none of his numerous admirers cared enough to secrete a tape recorder under a sofa or in the back seat of a car or in an attaché case planted opportunely right under Joe's endlessly wagging tongue. Yet if the sneak copy had been made and the screamed-out hysteria of the moment had been captured, it is more than doubtful that the tape would have much value for anyone who was not actually present at the session. The tightness, the scansion, the perfection of Lenny's patiently developed work still sounds pretty rough on records; how much rougher, rawer, nearly incoherent would Joe's stuff sound were we able to go back and hear it. The purest humor is that which is cooked up like a soufflé to stand perfectly for a few moments and then be consumed past the possibility of recollection. Joe cooked up endless feasts for his friends; whereas Lenny was like a painter of culinary still-lifes.

There was one other vital matter in which Joe furnished Lenny instruction. Re: Jewishness. Lenny had come to Broadway a veritable goy, without the slightest genuine knowledge of Jewish life, Jewish customs, beliefs, values, words, or mannerisms. He was this pretty little shaygitz from Long Island with an absolutely adorable nose. (Joe had one of those noses that are not only long but sort of take off for an extra little leap at the end. For years he longed for a nose job—not a heavy bob but just a "tipsky," a little bit chopped of the end. Alas! Hypochondriacs cannot afford the luxury of cosmetic surgery.)

It was from Joe that Lenny got the flavor of the Jewish lower classes. Joe came from that old-country Yidden. His family spoke Yiddish. He knew *all* the words—not just the phrases found in novels written by highly assimilated Jewish writers up at Yaddo. He didn't say "balls," he said "*baitsim.*" He didn't say "This pot is good stuff," he said it was "*richtige waare.*" He called a clumsy person a *leahman a getch*; a scandalous matter, a *schande an a chappah*! He spoke the kind of Yiddish that readers of the *Daily Forward* or *Der Tag* or the *Morgen Freiheit* recognized. Hanging around with Joe, you also got precious insights into Jewish life. Joe was the direct descendant of generations of Jewish uncles, wise in the lore of grandsons and grandmothers, cousins and stepdaughters, sons-in-law and relatives by marriage. The Jews have always been students, and their greatest study is themselves. Joe Ancis was the heir to all that knowledge.

Most important, he was that great Jewish character, the mishigoner. When he would lure all the children from his building into his car, and then, leaning out the window and talking to the terrified mothers, threaten to kidnap the little dahlinks unless they were better treated by their parents, he was enacting a Jewish psychodrama that cut a lot deeper than the schmaltzy crap that drips from the feder of Harry Golden. When he would take the children's shoes and sell them back to them or bang on the wall of Marvin Worth's apartment in Beach Haven, crying, "I know what you're doing in there!" When he would tell the neighbors that Marvin and his wife, Judy, were not married but were really living together. Or he would come across the hall in bathrobe and slippers to Buddy Hackett's pad, and getting uptight at being introduced to Tony Curtis and Janet Leigh, whip open his bathrobe and do a potchy tuchus shtick with the movie stars—Joe was instancing something that went down to the very core of Jewish life. He was the perfect naar, the fool, who is recognized in the Jewish world as a necessary companion to the rov or wiseman. Bizarre as Joe Ancis must appear to any goy, he always made perfect sense to Jews.

Lenny and Joe were tight from 1947 to 1951. When Lenny married Honey in the latter year, the friendship suddenly ended. Even though Lenny and Honey lived in New York for two winters and worked summers in the Mountains, Lenny never made any move to introduce Joe to his wife or even to hang out with Joe in their old haunts. In one sense, it was natural that this should happen: men always grow more distant from their friends after marriage and Lenny's relationship with Joe had been so close, so emotionally charged. Nor was Joe the only old friend whom Lenny rejected at this time. Buddy Hackett came up to Nemerson's one summer and started teasing Honey about some chick Lenny had balled. Buddy always disliked and distrusted Honey; he probably got pretty offensive with his so-called joke. Lenny was deeply aggrieved. He sat down and wrote Buddy a letter in which he said that nobody who claimed to be his friend could have behaved that way with his wife. Lenny didn't see Buddy again for years. Nothing of that sort happened with Joe; yet the break was just as complete. Why?

Joe had to wait many years until he got the answer. Meantime Lenny went out to the West Coast in 1953 and dropped completely from sight. Once in a long while, some wild story would come floating back: that Lenny had taken off his clothes in a strip joint or that he was working as a movie writer or something equally fantastic. No one really knew what had become of him, least of all Joe Ancis. Then in February 1959 Lenny suddenly showed up in New York, working at the Den in the Duane Hotel in Murray Hill. Immediately, the word flashed around town, "Lenny's back and he's working wild." All the guys ran down to the Den and they were shocked by what they saw. From his opening lines about the fag decorator who had gone nuts in the club with his staple gun, through the what-ifs, the raps on Jews, the bits on sex, even the film take-offs—the whole style, slant, language, and atmosphere of the show were directly taken from Joe Ancis. A guy came up to Joe in the street one day and said, "Man, he's doing you! Doesn't that bug you?"

Joe insisted it didn't matter; he wasn't a professional performer and wasn't even very funny anymore. It was important only that Lenny was back and making good. He went down to see Lenny and found him in a lavish suite at the Tuscany Hotel, a $2,000-a-month layout that the Den had offered Lenny in gratitude for the fantastic job he was doing at the club. The suite looked, of course, like a race riot had hit it: papers, clothes, tapes were lying all over the place. No sooner had the old friends begun to talk than the phone rang. It was Honey, fresh out of prison in California, calling from the airport to say that she was on her way into town. The moment Lenny hung up the phone, he began racing around the room trying to clean up the mess. Joe was miffed and amused. "Man, why stop here? Go vacuum the lobby.

Wash a couple of cars in the street. If she's so fuckin' observant, she'll find some schmutz somewhere." Sensing he really wasn't wanted, Joe left again without saying more than hello to Honey.

A couple of years later, when Lenny was playing Basin Street and living at the Hotel America, Joe spent another evening with his old friend. This time they got together in the wee hours of the morning, after the last show, and closeted themselves in Lenny's room, where they had a long, emotionally charged conversation.

"Man, there's somethin' been buggin' me for a long time," said Lenny. "When I'm out there on the floor, I'm doin' *you*. O.K., it's not *all* you, it's maybe twenty, thirty percent you—still, I feel I gotta skeleton in my closet."

"Hey, man, what difference does it make?" replied Joe. "I can't do it. I'm not in the business. Man, you're doing it and I'm *not* doing it. Besides, you have the voice, the looks. Man, you got a beautiful face."

"You motherfucker!" snapped Lenny, hurt by the reference to his looks, when what he prided himself upon was his mind.

"Come on," Joe coaxed, "you're using it to make a social comment. It's your ideas, your point-of-view—so why worry?"

"Well, man," countered Lenny, "I do worry and that's why in the old days I never introduced you to Honey. She's very perceptive. I figured to myself, here's this chick who thinks I'm a genius. If I introduce her to the guy who gave me a lot of my stuff, she'll dig right away that I'm not as creative as I look. So that's why you never met her."

Poor Joe thought of the letter he had gotten only a couple of months before from Victor Lownes III, vice-president of the Playboy Club:

Dear Mr. Ancis:

Buddy Hackett tells me that you are the original version of Lenny Bruce and, in his words, "the funniest man in the world." Have you ever thought of taking a swing at being a regular night-club performer?

We would certainly be interested in any thoughts that you have along this line with the thought in mind of possibly introducing you at one or another of the Playboy Clubs.

At any rate, we would be very interested in hearing about the relationship with Lenny that led Buddy Hackett to describe you as the source of Lenny's "whole way of thinking about things."

At that point, feeling the lateness of the hour and looking for an excuse to end an embarrassing conversation, Joe says, "Come on, man, let's go downstairs and get a taste. You know me, babe, I'm always looking to scarf."

Down they go in the narrow elevator, out past the desk in the lobby, and are just about to go into the street, when suddenly a shingleman with a hooker spots Lenny and says, "Hey! You're Lenny Bruce!" Polite as always, Lenny says, "Yeah, and this is my pal, Joe Ancis." "JOE ANCIS!" the guy virtually shouts. "I heard about you. I heard you were the *funniest man in New York City*!"

Chapter Six

DIRTY LENNY

Purple. Everywhere you look, purple. Purple walls and purple ceiling. Purple bar and purple floor. Strip City, "Home of Big-Name Burlesk" looks like the inside of a vintner's vat.

Within its venereal gloom a tiny three-piece bump-and-grind band is always hammering out dusky, sexy night songs. Low, raunchy music. A hard, mean, fuck-you! sound. Kenny Hume is the drummer. He sits up there behind the curtain during the fifteen-minute warm-up, zonked behind his sunglasses but holding himself proudly erect, a stripper riding either knee, caressing him and running her hands across his body, giggling, trying to make him miss a beat.

Lots of that dressing-room grab-ass in these strip bars. The broads can't dance. They can't even count. If you say hello, they're stuck for an answer. The musicians abuse them. Put them on in every key. Call them "baby" and "honey" in the tone that means "stupid."

On some ego trip unknown to man, these girls live for that moment when they can get out on the floor and show it. Some of them act shy when you catch them backstage. Out under the lights, they're all exhibitionists. And prima donnas! Just let the drummer ease off a little with his rolls and rim shots, and this little girl is running up to the office. Banging on the door and bursting in, practically in tears, complaining that the band is "swinging" on her—playing in jazz time, not the cock-stroking back-beat. The manager and part-owner of the club, Maynard Sloate, is unsympathetic. A former musician himself, he gives the girl an owl-like stare, pulls the cigar out of his mouth, and drawls,

"Make the best of it, honey. That band will be here a lot longer than you."

Most of the customers couldn't care less what the band plays or how the girl makes her turns. On Sunday night, ethnic night, they're spades from Watts, Japs from Gardena, beaners from downtown and East Los Angeles. They sit at the tiny tables with knees spread wide, heads hung low, lips parted, faces frowning, watching—one hand on the glass, the other on the bulge—those long white legs, those full white tits, that white ass split up the middle with a silver G-string as they knurl their private vision into perfect mental focus.

The moment the M.C. comic appears, a dapper little cat in a dark suit, the spell is broken. The concentration that lay across the stripper like the cigarette smoke layered over the tables is suddenly dispelled. As the guy begins to talk, in a bright, chirruping voice, he's practically drowned out by the murmur of thick, hoarse throats, the scrape of moving chairs, and the heavy harumphs! and harrars! of men clearing their phlegm. The appearance of the M.C. means intermission. A chance to order a drink, shift your balls, or get up from the table and take a piss.

Working these flesh joints is enough to drive any comic crazy. You feel like a faggot window dresser schlepping the manikins in and out of the display lights. Yet some pretty hip guys work at Strip City. Eddie Ryder became a Hollywood actor and made a lot of Toyota commercials. Joey Carter, Beryl Williams, and Danny Bishop all made out in later years. Even the musicians were into writing: Kenny Hume worked on Lily Tomlin's first album and Bill Richmond wrote about a hundred Jerry Lewis films.

What are they doing here? They're making a living while the café business is going down the shitter. In fact, since the war the whole live entertainment business has dropped dead. All the big bands have been forced to disband. The jazz joints have become the loneliest rooms in town. The strip club business is one of the few pockets of prosperity. It's a new hustle that sprang up toward the end of the war. Its basis is impatience.

Nowadays nobody has any time for the old theater burlesque. Who wants to see a line of broads in leopard-skin leotards hoofing around a papier-mâché jungle while the band plays "Jungle Drums"? Or two baggy-pants bananas standing in front of a drop supposed to represent Paris, saying: "This must be the place—the Rue de *Prix*!" Or even those featured strippers who take a half-hour just to get their clothes off? No, the strokers in the first row, the raincoat-in-the-lap guys, want to get turned on fast—and stay turned on until they get off. So the new idea is to sweat burlesque down to its essence. Get the show under a cheap roof and turn over the house on a tight schedule. That's Strip City.

Maynard Sloate bought this place in 1950 at auction. It was an old nightclub that had failed. He rechristened it, painted it in purple passion, and runs it now like an assembly line. A large room with a long mirrored bar on your right, tables on your left, and a big U-shaped stage at the rear, the club can hold two hundred and fifty sit-down patrons. The location on the corner of Pico and Western is ideal because the joint can draw business from both sides of the tracks.

During the week, you get a lot of Hollywood celebrities, slumming. Michael Wilding, Elizabeth Taylor's husband, comes in. So do Marlon Brando, Joan Collins—and Michael Rennie. This guy haunts all the strip joints. He's got himself a rep. One night one of Honey's friends, a chick named Dina Prince, walked up to him at the bar and said, "Hey, I understand you're a pussy hound!" She could have said that to every guy in the room. Actually, not many of them are geting laid out of this club. Maynard runs the place very strict. He's got the P.D. coming in every night, and he isn't about to get busted for procuring. There are no B-girls pushing drinks at the bar, no hookers looking for Johns, and no bust-out chicks trying to grab the customers' money and run. At most you could say there is a certain amount of "mixing."

Promptly at nine every night, the band plays the overture, the M.C. steps out onstage, and the first of four regular strippers does her stuff. The show runs one hour, with the feature girl coming on two or three times a night. The M.C.s (the union requires two men) do a few jokes between acts and then a fifteen-minute stand-up routine at the end of the hour, while the band breathes. Twice every night you have show time, with all the girls onstage and the band playing highlights from Broadway musicals and the comics doing cabaret blackout skits. Everything shuts down at 2 A.M., and rehearsal call is for two the next afternoon.

How did Lenny get here? When he and Honey walked out on Father in the spring of 1953, right after they got to the Coast, they found themselves in trouble. They were unknowns in a strange town with nothing going for them except their looks. Lenny got so worried about money that he started taking day jobs, mowing lawns and canvassing with shingle crews. Finally, Honey got her offer of three weeks in Vegas.

A month later, they were back together again after their first separation. They even got a chance to work as a double in a little joint called the Cup and Saucer out in Downey. Maynard Sloate found Lenny there: "Doing an act that didn't quite work. Still, I thought he was good enough so I offered him a ten-dollar increase over the

seventy-five dollars a week he was making so he would work my place."
That ten dollars tipped the balance and sent Lenny and Honey back
into burlesque: he to Strip City and she to the Colony Club in Gardena.
That was, in fact, the route they traveled for the next year and a half.
Every night they would leave the little bungalow they had rented in
West Hollywood, their little dream house with the white picket fence,
and get into that big black Caddy, Honey with a scarf around her hair
and a big round hat box, and Lenny in a shirt and slacks, carrying his
freshly pressed suit on a hanger. Down Wilshire Boulevard they would
drive to Western Avenue and along Western to Pico; there Lenny
would hop out, and Honey would take the wheel to drive all the way
out to Gardena.

The Colony Club was the best burlesque house in L.A. Owned
and operated by a washed-up comic named Irv, it was a supper club,
where the audience of prosperous, middle-aged businessmen, doctors,
lawyers and their wives dined comfortably and then sat back to watch
an old-time burlesque show in which the girls alternated with the baggy-
pants comics. The show was so archaic that it even had the traditional
straight girl—à la Claire Bloom being feather-dusted and yum-yum
tasted by Charlie Chaplin in *Limelight*. Decorously operated, the Colony kept its strippers behind the scenes, with no mixing at the bar and
no offbeat action—except that provided by Irv, who had every room
in the place wired to his intercom and would tell the ladies in the john:
"We can hear you—can you hear us?"

Honey did a classic strip act, with a lot of "parading." She never
stooped to the vulgar jouncing and jiggling that got to be such a big
thing in later years at the go-go clubs. Walking out demurely, dressed
in her Southern-belle costume, with the big festooned hoop skirt and
a bonnet and silk parasol, she would flounce around on the stage apron
close enough for a ringsider to reach out and touch her. Then she
retreated upstage, blinking her eyes coyly, and perched herself on an
old-fashioned settee. While the band began to stoke a fire under the
audience, she removed her hat and a pair of golden slippers. She took
great care in rolling down her stockings, removing each one from a
carefully arched foot. Next, she stepped out of a cumbersome hoop
skirt, revealing a pair of lacy pantaloons, which she modestly hid with
the parasol. After a lot of teasing and strolling around the stage, she
finally got down to the nude body, revealed with back lights through
the film of her parasol, which she twirled impudently as she exited into
the wings.

When the night was over, Honey would drive back to Strip City
and pick up Lenny at Scrivener's, the drive-in eatery across the street
from the club. He'd always be pacing restlessly back and forth, reading

the newspaper, searching for bits that he could do from the stage. After a long ride along the eerily deserted streets, they would pull up before the little house at four in the morning. Sometimes he had the hots for her before they even got out of the car. She would laugh, a deep throaty laugh, and push his hand away; but he wanted to make it—right there in the street. That was the hot and steamy time of their marriage, when they lived in that little dream house. Honey looked so great as she leaned against the sink doing the dishes. Lenny would stare at her from behind, and it was like a fantasy: something he had always imagined but never figured to really have. She was so gorgeous in those days. High, wide Ukrainian cheekbones, big voluptuous eyes, creamy skin—and that body! She wasn't a perfect figure by any means: too long in the torso and short in the legs. What she had, though, was that glamorous aura of *flesh*. The Alice Faye, Ann Sheridan, Rita Hayworth thing, with the big, heavy breasts and the massive curves and the sheer generosity of her body, yards of silken red hair, acres of creamy ass—and *it's all mine!* That was how he felt when he'd look up from the vacuum cleaner (good boy that he was!) and stare intently at the outlines of that body laid up against the sink.

Honey was jealous of him—no wonder, with all those strippers around that club. But he was just as jealous of her, although he always denied it and pretended that he didn't care and was oh-so-breezy around the house. There came a time—it wasn't many years later— when Honey would say, "Lenny, why don't you take a walk around the block? Jack is here and I'd like to ball him." And *Lenny would go!* Pinch his lower lip and lower his head and walk! Yes, he walked! *Let* her get away with it. Never wanted to fight—was *terrified* of fights and scenes! Let anybody get away with anything—just so there shouldn't be a *scene*. In five years of marriage he didn't hit her but *twice*. No, he wouldn't fight—but he could make you feel *guiltier* than any man on earth. Made her feel like a tramp, a whore. She hated him for that. She didn't trust him either, the little mamma's boy! Of course, he was getting his cock sucked in that club. She could tell. Why was he so hot some nights when they came home and so dead other nights, when she would have liked a little action? Some fuckin' cunt had sucked the life out of his prick—that's what it was! If she got her hands on that bitch—look out! She'd rip her face to ribbons. Just like the time in New York when she heard there was a girl in the line that wanted to make it with him. She had her spies. She heard the story. One night she came backstage kinda early. And she got hold of him, that greasy little bastard! And she told him: "Look, Prick! If I ever catch you fuckin' any of these cunts in this dressing room, I'll take a Gem blade and cut that little worm right off your body!" She meant it, too; and the girls in that club had a hands-off policy toward Mr. Lenny Bruce.

They had a lot of fights in that little dream house, a lot of jealous quarrels. She would smell him or pull his shirt out or give him an angry look. She scared the hell out of you, that broad! Had that fuckin' goyishe hand—always goin' on the muscle. Layin' up in the sack and this bitch arguing with you and suddenly WHOMP!—a fuckin' fist right in your eye!

Once he started working the strip bars, Lenny had to punch up his material with dirty jokes, a new departure for a kid who had enjoyed a reputation for being a clean young act. "Anybody can get a laugh with dirty toilet jokes; it takes talent to get laughs with clean stuff. You'll go a long way, Lenny, you're funny and clean." That was how Lenny characterized his reputation in the business before he entered burlesque. Actually, Lenny was a dirty comic from the day he bombed at the Strand in 1949. That experience embittered him. He tried to place the blame on his manager, Marvin Worth, insisting it was Marvin's fault that he had been pushed in beyond his depth. He also began to look for ways of getting laughs that he wouldn't have considered in his apprentice years. By the time of Honey's nearly fatal accident in Pittsburgh, in the fall of 1951, Lenny had adopted a pretty cynical viewpoint with regard to dirty jokes. "What the people really want is dirt," he confided to Mickey Deems, a more successful young comic, when the two got together in a Pittsburgh hotel room. "I do, 'Does your son eat lettuce? Does he eat like a rabbit too?' and I get laughs with this material!" Mickey, who was working at the Copa, directly across the street from the Carrousel, where Lenny was appearing, had heard him do these gags; he concluded that Lenny was a "third-rate comic who dealt in smut and had nowhere to go." He also noticed when Lenny smoked pot and started rapping, he slowly metamorphosed from a rather sweet, idealistic young man into a tough, acid-tongued hipster, putting down the whole world. Honey was in the St. Francis Hospital at the time and Lenny was upset. It was always his way when he was hurt of frightened to turn bitter, cynical, and dirty. Whatever else dirt represented for him, it was certainly a weapon, a defiling missile that he could hurl at audiences who ignored him or critics who taunted him or judges who condemned him.

In the strip joints, Lenny was often hurt. He was ignored, upstaged, heckled, and whipped into line. Degraded by his surroundings, another guy would have erected a barrier between his professional self—out there on the stage smiling and shouting, "A big hand of welcome for Melba, the Toast of the Town!"—and his private self, at home with his pretty wife in the house with the white picket fence. Lenny couldn't. He always had to show his emotions, display his attitude, and punish everybody he felt was accountable for his predicament. From the very beginning of his years in burlesque, he began to define a special role for himself: he chipped away the decorum of show biz, ridiculing the people around him and poking fun at the part he was compelled to play. Taking the audience into his confidence, he would spill the beans: "See that waitress over there in the butch haircut—she's a diesel dyke! That bartender? A muff diver! You know what the owner of this club said to a stripper this afternoon when she wouldn't dance at rehearsal: 'Turn in your cunt—you're through!' "

The restless, indifferent audiences began to listen. He was leveling with them. Telling them something they knew was true. They were angry because they couldn't make out with the strippers whose bodies they gloated over. They got their revenge when Lenny would ridicule the girls, bringing them on with sarcastic, insulting introductions: "And now, a little girl who shouldn't be in the business at all—Busty Brown!" They really cracked up when Lenny would explain the slogan of the club: " 'The Home of Big-Name Burlesk'? That means all the girls are *Polish*!"

Lenny's fraternal attitude toward the audience contrasted sharply with that of his colleagues. If an ordinary M.C. was attacked by a heckler, he would instantly retaliate from a well-stocked arsenal of anti-heckler shpritzes. When a heckler attacked Lenny Bruce, he always got a very polite response. Lenny insisted that everybody had a right to free speech and that the performer was entitled to attention only because he was trying to communicate something of interest. One night, though, this forbearing philosophy failed him.

The house was full of newspapermen, and Lenny was hoping for a write-up in the papers. But a heckler kept lousing up his act. Suddenly, Lenny got an idea. During intermission, he ran across the street to Scrivener's and had them pile up a plate with whipped cream. Then he secreted this weapon in the wings. Next time the heckler started to razz him, Lenny said to the man: "You'd be surprised at the number of comics who got their start by hollering lines up out of an audience. You might just belong in show biz, but you're going about it all wrong. What you need is a manager." Then he got solicitous about the schmuck's upcoming career and invited him onstage so they could do a double. Up comes the drunk. Into the wings goes Lenny. Slosh! goes the whipped cream into the heckler's besotted face. As the man was helped back to his seat, an ominous silence filled the club.

Another practical joke that got out of hand was the jibe Lenny aimed at Danny Bishop, who used to do a parody on "Pennies from

Heaven" called "Bennies from Heaven." Lenny hated the number. One night he decided to zap Bishop. Lenny had noticed that there was a very narrow crawl space between the roof of the club and the false ceiling that extended out over the stage. Squeezing into this dark narrow hole, he worked himself across the false ceiling to an air vent that was directly above center stage. When Bishop went into his song, Lenny began raining down aspirins through the air vent. The audience laughed at the gag, but suddenly the pitch of their laughter rose. The plaster ceiling began to crack! Down came chunk after chunk on the hapless Bishop. Then Lenny's foot slipped through! Next, his whole leg! Finally, a great big chunk fell out, and the ringsiders could see Lenny struggling desperately to hold onto an iron brace.

Lenny's year and a half at Strip City was one of the busiest periods of his life. Not only was he working at the club every night and lending a hand with the domestic chores during the day, but it was in this period that he first got involved in the movie business and made his first feature-length film. It all began with Buddy Hackett, who hadn't seen Lenny for a couple of years, and who was out on the Coast working at Billy Gray's Band Box, while preparing his first film for Twentieth Century-Fox. Hearing that his old friend was working in the city, Buddy went over to Strip City one night and caught Lenny's act. When the show was over, he walked upstairs and knocked on the dressing-room door. Without saying a word, the two men threw their arms around each other and began crying. In that instant, they were reconciled.

Over a drink at the bar, Lenny recapped everything that had occurred since he left New York. He spoke of his relationship with Honey in rhapsodic tones, insisting that it was as great spiritually as it was physically, saying that Honey was very bright and "perceptive" and had all sorts of unsuspected talents. By marrying her, Lenny had made the greatest move of his life. Listening to his bright report, Buddy began to feel guilty for the terrible things he had said about Honey before the marriage—how she was a head and a hooker and a dyke —and for the cruel way he had teased her after the marriage, when he told her about Lenny's affairs. Impelled to make amends, Buddy apologized for the past and complimented Lenny on his happy marriage and the quality of his act. Lenny waved away his work in burlesque and said that his real work was preparing the script of a TV series called *Honeytime*, which was a translation to the small screen of their nightclub act. Nightclubs were just a stepping stone in his career, Lenny insisted; his real goal was to become a writer.

The very next day, still feeling guilty, Hackett brought up Lenny's name in a conversation with Leonard Goldstein, Twentieth Century's golden boy. Goldstein and Darryl Zanuck had decided that one of the ways to mend the company's damaged finances was to return to the old practice of making B movies. They had set up a company called Regal Pictures, which was designed to produce a cheap but marketable product, while providing a training ground for the company's next super-executive, Zanuck's son, Richard. As it happened, Goldstein was troubled at that very moment by a picture he was making with child star Georgie "Foghorn" Winslow. Georgie, Charles Coburn, and Spring Byington had been cast in a picture titled *McCluskey Strikes a Blow* that had struck a snag. The movie couldn't be completed until some changes were made in the script; Goldstein was looking for ideas. Hackett told Goldstein he knew a young writer who was full of ideas; he even offered to take him over to Strip City to meet Lenny. Goldstein, who loved the street scene and knew all "the boys from Vegas," jumped at the chance to spend an evening on the town.

When he sketched the outline of the picture for Lenny, he was surprised at how quickly this unknown burlesque banana jumped in with all sorts of suggestions for improving the story. Determined to give Lenny a chance, Goldstein hired him on the spot as a writer of additional dialogue for $750 a week. First day on the job, Lenny proved his worth. He knocked out seventeen pages of perfectly acceptable dialogue—earning the enmity of the other writers, who told him to slow down to two or three. Lenny also came up with so many plots and visual ideas that eventually the whole concept of the movie was turned around, and the picture was retitled *Rocket Boy*. Goldstein was delighted and Lenny was proud. He boasted of having a special place in the parking lot and a table in the commissary. He called Sally and told her she should fly at once to the Coast: "It would give me so much pleasure for you to see me on the set."

Then, just as suddenly as the bubble had been blown, it burst. Leonard Goldstein died of a heart attack, and Lenny was dismissed from the studio. The loss of money and prestige was severe. Even more serious, though, was the difficulty he now experienced in getting another film-writing job. It was just as if he had never written for the movies. Nobody else would give him a tumble. Yet he had to get another such job because he was now convinced that his future lay not on the stage but in writing, directing, producing, and starring in films.

The next important person in Lenny's film career was a young friend named Richard Shackleton. Shack was a movie actor, a player of semi-feature roles—not a star or even a talent but one of those people whose names casting directors recognized and considered for parts. A one-time ballet dancer, he had tired of fags coming on to him and had given up dancing for acting. At twenty-one he was a rather fey and charming figure, small, wiry, blond, and absolutely goyish-looking. In later years, when they went on the road together, Lenny liked Shack to dress in tattered denims and sneakers broken out at the toe. He dug him as the All-American Boy. Shack met Honey first, then Lenny, under conditions that were pretty typical of the Bruces' stormy marriage. One night, when Shack was hanging out at his girl friend's pad in West Hollywood (he was involved with an actress named Ann Staunton), she told him a friend of hers was coming over with a new chick. The chick was Honey, who made a spectacular appearance with her red hair and white fox stole slung across her shoulders. Honey told Shack she was married but not living with her husband, who had a house in the very same area.

A few days later, Shack gets another call from Honey; this time she says she wants to bring her old man along. Lenny always had the knack of instant intimacy. He could meet a person, and within an hour be deep into his life, his problems, desires, ambitions, the works. Both Lenny and Shack were broke and both were on the make. Their only problem was how to score some bread so that they could launch an independent movie project.

Lenny came up with a scam. He put an ad in the *Los Angeles Times*: "Lenny, The Gardener, will clean, mow, and edge your lawn for $6." At that time the standard price for the same job was $15; soon he had a lot of people calling his number in the ad. He'd take a call and go roaring out to the address. Arriving rather breathlessly at the front door, he'd say, "Look, my truck just broke down. Do you have any equipment?" Then he'd take the equipment out and spread it all over the yard, maybe turn up a couple of spades of dirt. Then he'd say, "Look, I've got to go down to the store. I haven't eaten all day. Could you pay me now, and then I'll come back and finish?" When the people came across with the six bucks, Lenny, The Gardner, would split. According to Lenny, "I could do ten a day."

With this money and some more raised from other similar schemes, Lenny and Shack made *Dream Follies*, a film that has disappeared. It was a story about a Caspar Milquetoast husband, always dreaming about going to burlesque shows, but frustrated by his sour-faced wife. The casting in this little opus was curious. Lenny played the husband and Sally Marr his wife. In the one surviving sequence Lenny, in the guise of the busy, preoccupied business executive, arrives at the office, nods brusquely to his typist-secretary and opens his attaché case. Inside he finds a pair of Magic Glasses, which he slips over his eyes. Looking at the girl through these lenses, he sees her in the nude; she sits there busily typing, her boobs bouncing merrily in time with the keys.

Nobody remembers what happend to *Dream Follies*. The only thing clear is that it led straight on to another picture filmed in the same cheap style: *Dance Hall Racket*. This picture was bankrolled by Joe Abrams, one of the owners of Strip City. It was destined for cheap burlesque houses. The screenplay was another Lenny Bruce original and the director was Phil Tucker, who probably also directed *Dream Follies*. Tucker understood about camera angles and cutting, but was naïve about everything else. Lenny made use of this guy—just as he later used mediocre managers, lawyers, and writers—as an instrument of his will. He was sure he could compensate for any deficiency with his own brilliance, and in return enjoy the sort of control over the project that might be hard to obtain with a more gifted and therefore more independent-minded individual. The result of this collaboration, shot in a chintzy little studio on Santa Monica Boulevard behind the Harvey Hotel, is preserved in a single print.

A dingy tintype, shot with the camera stuck in cement and the light flat as a ceiling fixture, *Dance Hall* is an unconscious parody of all the sinsiter, sexy nightclub-gangster movies of Lenny's childhood. It's just the sort of movie that later in his career Lenny would ridicule in one of his marvelous travesties—killing everybody with his minute knowledge of all the clichés of the genre. Here, though, he was deadly serious, piously fulfilling the most nonsensical formulas.

The film opens with one of those Sturm und Drang movie scores that have the violins working themselves up into apoplectic fits followed by sudden attacks of the falling sickness that are relieved, in turn, by long passages of treacly lyricism. As this ranting, raving music—purloined doubtless from some other sound track—pours through the back-screen speakers, the camera stares stupidly, doltishly, in a creaky sequence of cuts, at a dockside customs inspection, a sailor buying tickets off a roll, and a scene inside a taxi dance hall, where some incredibly ordinary people are schlepping through a Lindy. Then we get the framing device: a journalist sitting in the office of the chief customs inspector, asking for stories that will spice up his article on the customs service. The inspector leans into his intercom: "Send in that file on the dance hall racket, Martin." In comes the file and off goes the story of the diamond smuggler who brought the gems into the country sewed into the ear of a puppy and then sold them to the evil Mr. Scally, the proprietor of Scally's Dance Emporium, a tough, raunchy joint down on the docks, which looks in Lenny's film transcription something like a high school gym decorated for a tea dance.

As the characters are introduced, you practically fall off your chair laughing. There's Sally as a cynical, wisecracking hostess named Maxine, talking turkey to the younger girls, boozing with the goofy customers, and finally getting up to do a flabby Charleston, with beads flying and eyes popping and hands going crisscross back and forth from knee to knee. There's Honey, in a deep-cleft gown, her hair up on her head in two scrolls, playing the girl friend of that stupid, cruel, psychotically giggling killer, Vinnie—played by Lenny Bruce in a black one-button roll with a white tie and French cuffs and a neat trick of snapping open a switchblade with one hand. (Lenny was always obsessed with knives.) Vinnie is Mr. Scally's chief goon. When a seaman gets paid off for smuggling in diamonds, Vinnie goes out in the dance hall and stabs him to death—because he was flirting with his girl! "You didn't have to kill him!" whines Honey. "Get him out of here, you dummy!" barks the boss. Poor stupid Vinnie, nobody digs him.

Between murders and sinister gangster conversations in Mr. Scally's office, the dance hall operates with all the atmosphere of a cardboard stage set. Trying for realism now and then, as in a scene where Lenny goes through a clothes rack looking for something suitable for a new girl, the film contains only one scene that has the slightest resonance of a human voice. This is a wholly extraneous episode in which Sally confronts the same new girl in the dressing room and unloads on her an older woman's philosophy of life. The gags, the tone of forced cynicism, the phony supercilious laugh, all suggest Sally as the author of the bit, as does the "philosophy," which contains surprising echoes of things she still says in private conversation.

Sally plays herself and makes some sort of mark in *Dance Hall Racket*. Lenny is totally forgettable because he insists on acting. His notion of film performance was strangely lethargic; most of the time he just stands there as if we were waiting for somebody else to make a move. His characterization consists almost entirely of the way he is dressed and the way he says the word "boss," giving it the Silly Putty vowel that New Yorkers once put into "walk" and "talk." "Yeah, bowhss." "O.K., bowhss."

Lenny dies finally in an elaborate ballet of staggers, turns, and falls. Then the camera jumps back to reel one, the chief inspector's office. The journalist slaps shut his notebook with an exclamation of wonder. And the film concludes with a last upsurge of Hollywood rhapsody.

The seat-shifting strokers in the cheap burlesque houses never saw the film because it was frozen out by the agents who controlled this market. Only one theater in L.A. would play the picture: a dirty dive down on Main Street. The "premiere" took place in this itchy joint about three one morning, after the strip clubs had closed: Lenny, Honey, Sally, Shack, and Joe Abrams sat watching their work breathlessly, while all around them snored the bums and the winos.

About the time he started making *Dance Hall Racket*, in the latter part of 1954, Lenny left Strip City. The club had provided him with a

secure base of operations while he got his bearings on the West Coast.
It had also given him an exhaustive introduction into the world of the
strip bars and even permitted him to define his characteristic onstage
attitude of amused condescension mingled with scorn. But it was a
repressive milieu. Every time Lenny started to get into something new
and unexpected, Maynard the Machine would check him with undis-
guised anxiety. After the bit, when Lenny was coming offstage, Sloate
would owl out of the shadows, his cigar blazing angrily in his mouth,
and testily remark: "Lenny, you're working to the band again."

It was true. The musicians were the only people in the club who
dug fantasy and abstraction and alliteration and the comedy of crazy
non sequiturs. They'd heard dozens of comics and thousands of lines.
They would get a guy down and chant his lines in unison with him as
he worked. If you could break up the boys in the band, you were
cooking!

It wasn't, though, until Lenny had left the sleazy but civilized strip
bars of the city for the raunchy ranch houses of the Valley that he
started to come on like Lenny Bruce: which is to say, like Joe Ancis
standing on the corner in front of Hanson's or shpritzing his face off
in Brooklyn. Why? Because it took an extraordinary license, a privileged position, a whole concatenation of incentives and permissions to
get that private backstage sense of humor out into the public arena.
It wasn't enough that Lenny had Joe's voice permanently recorded on
the grooves of his brain or that he could, whenever he wished, look
out at the world along the zingy lines of Joe's personal vision. These
faculties were already well developed by the time he got to California.
What he really needed was the combination of incitement and security
provided by the dirtier sort of strip bars. That incitement you got
working constantly in conditions of unspeakable dirtiness and sloppi-
ness and moral grunginess—and the security was provided by feeling
that you were already down as far as you could fall—so why fear falling
any lower?

In those years the deeper Lenny sank into the schmutz, the higher
he rose as an artist. The grosser and cruder the environment, the more
ironic, imaginative, and brilliant became the art. Creativity for him,
as for so many people, was a kind of licentiousness. Now he suddenly
broke free of all the restraints, inhibitions, and disabilities that had
formerly made him mediocre and began to blow with a spontaneous
freedom that suggested the style of his new friends and fans, the jazz
musicians of the modernist school. It was out in the Valley that this
whole process began, particularly at an upholstered sewer called the
Cobblestone Club, which by all accounts deserves to be reckoned
among the worst dives on the West Coast.

One of the reasons why things were allowed to slip to such a depth of degeneracy at the Cobblestone was simply the club's remote location. Situated an hour's drive from Beverly Hills, way out at the end of Lankershim Boulevard near San Fernando Road, the joint was practically in another part of the country. Desolate, ramshackle, with its nearest neighbors a power plant and a gravel yard, the Cobblestone could have been a roadhouse out in the middle of Kansas. The crowd that gathered there was usually just a bunch of Okies—truck drivers, Lockheed workers, shoddy small-time business types. The girls were mostly semi-pro strippers, who were either breaking into the business or were all washed up—though occasionally you did find a good dancer there. The whole tone of the place was that down-on-its-luck, honky-tonk atmosphere that is vastly more depressing than any form of honest suffering.

A big dirty beehive covered with cobblestones and plopped down in a huge parking lot (where everybody turned on in the evening during and after work), the club had its entrance around the far side, like an old-time speakeasy. The interior was funky wagon-wheel Western. The most conspicuous feature was a garish ski-ball machine located near the bar at the opposite end of the room from the stage. All night long, no matter what was happening onstage, this ski-ball machine would toll its scores. First, you'd hear a *whomp!* as the ball hit the rubbery alley; then a *CLANG!* as the ball shot into the center ring. Every stripper came offstage cursing and fuming about this attention-shattering noise. The comics suffered the worst because the noise was always throwing unexpected punch lines into their routines. They'd be up there doing a bit, and suddenly they'd find themselves in an animated cartoon. "So this little queer walks over to me and says *WHOMP! CLANG!* and I says to him *WHOMP! CLANG!*" Meantime, the audience is laughing its ass off, not at the bit but at the funny noises coming from the back of the room.

Honey and Sally played the club first. Sally had started working the strip joints when she came out to California to watch Lenny shoot *Rocket Boy*. The first night she turned up at Strip City, she knocked Lenny out by suddenly appearing onstage. It was a blackout skit in which a magician is tied up and covered by a screen. The M.C. counts to ten and removes the screen, supposedly revealing the magician miraculously untied. The gag is that each time the screen is removed, the magician is still struggling furiously with his bonds. The punch line comes on the third take, when the screen is removed and a pretty girl steps out and takes a bow. On this night when Lenny removed the screen for the third time, out came Sally with a big smile to take the bow—and hug her darling son.

Sally lived at the Elaine Apartments across from the Hollywood Ranch Market. Gregarious as ever, she quickly made friends among the show people and started to do a little partying. One night, while at a party for some Persian exchange students, she met Tony Viscarra. It wasn't love at first sight. It wasn't much of anything. She was this strange-looking lady with a crew cut; he was this low-rider Mexican kid in loud clothes with a Pachuco tattoo on his thumb, only two years out of Preston, a California Youth Authority reform school. She was forty-nine and he was nineteen. There was no physical attraction— but she made an impression. Bored at first by the dullness of the party, she finally got up on her feet and started working the room. She told jokes and did shtick and broke everybody up. Tony, who had come with a girl, got so involved watching Sally that he let his cigarette burn down to his fingertips.

"Ouch! Goddam," he cried. "What shall I do with this cigarette!"

"Put it at the end of a bobbypin!" she snapped back, transforming the cigarette with a word into a wicked roach. Tony broke up and the pair met laughing.

Laughing, they started dating. Laughing, they would go out on the floor and dance. Sally taught Tony the tango. She told him all about her life. She charmed him and entertained him and always left him laughing. At that time, he was a draftsman at the Lockheed plant in Burbank. Working late hours, he was out on the town every night. When Sally began gigging at the Cobblestone, not far from Lockheed, Tony got in the habit of coming in to see her at the club.

Sally would sit all evening with Honey at a table, eagerly awaiting Tony's appearance. Guys were always coming on to the girls, offering to buy them drinks. Sally would always order Tony's drink, Scotch, and then take the glass back to the dressing room, where she kept an empty bottle. Pouring drink after drink into the bottle, she would collect enough booze in the course of an evening so that Tony didn't even have to stand the price of his load. It was at the Cobblestone that Sally and Tony had their wedding party. Lenny was working up the road at the Bamboo Room; he came to his mother's party after the show. He had been rather stand-offish with Tony at first, saying to Honey, "What's that guy's story?" Tony, on the other hand, was enormously impressed with Lenny, and began to imitate his sharp, hip attitude and speech. Eventually, he asked Lenny what he thought about the marriage: did he harbor any resentment? "No," Lenny said, "it's my mother's life. If she's happy, I'm happy."

He wasn't really happy. He hated to see his mother making a fool of herself by marrying a kid who was ten years younger than her son. Lenny would greet Tony's appearance at the Cobblestone by shpritzing: "There's my father—but don't ask him for his I.D. Don't ask him for his ideas—you might embarrass him! He lies a lot—probably his Catholic background. The confessional teaches you to lie. He lied when they got married—said he was twenty. He was only twelve." Then Lenny would turn to the ringsiders and exclaim in his best David Copperfield voice: "Mother's very hot-blooded!" Mother was, in fact, a sucker—that's what he really feared. "You know, Ma," he warned one night, "you're married to a young guy, and a young guy could think different ten days from now. A year from now, he could be completely different." "Lenny, I know that." Sally smiled back. "O.K., Ma," he continued, apprehensively, "as long as you know that."

What must have bugged Lenny was the way this strange marriage underscored his own relationship with Sally. Lenny and Tony looked very much alike: their foreheads were identical, insisted Sally, and their curly, oily hair, small neat features, general body build, and stance were remarkably similar. Girls would see Tony and exclaim, "He's just adorable!" using exactly the same expression they had used for Lenny when he was Tony's age. Tony was—everybody said it—a substitute for Lenny in Sally's life: another naïve but cute little boy-man waiting and wanting to be molded by an older, wiser, and more experienced woman. Who knows? Maybe Lenny was a little jealous.

To their credit, Sally and Tony were perfectly clear about what they were doing. "I think there was a great mother image on her part to direct me," Tony said in later years, "and I think she saw a lot of Lenny in me. I saw a lot of mother in her." Eventually, Tony and Lenny became very close friends. They played together, talked together, and Lenny fell into the habit of calling Tony "Dad."

After Lenny became famous, he would often talk about the years when he worked the "toilets." Most people thought the word was just another colorful expression with no literal truth. The fact is that at the Cobblestone the ladies' room opened right off the stage, and as you worked on that stage, you could smell the odor of the nearby toilet. That toilet got to be an important station in Lenny's nightly passion. Any woman who had to go to the toilet was obliged to brave Lenny's remarks as she made her way onstage and through the door. As likely as not, when she got in the toilet, she would discover that she had been followed by a man—the club's M.C. What Lenny would do or say to these ladies has never been revealed. The audience saw the woman going into the toilet followed by Lenny, who would remain inside for long stretches, while the male patrons buzzed and chuckled and entertained themselves with obscene remarks.

The left side of the stage contained another door: this one leading to the dressing room. This was a door without a catch, and Lenny used to lay his back against it as he offered his cock to some kneeling stripper. As he leaned back, having his joint copped, feeling the sensations rise and spread from the tip of his prick, he could hear the din of the onstage band, the murmur and noises of the audience, the *WHOMP! CLANG!* of the ski-ball machine—he was practically being sucked off in public! Which is pretty much what his humor was tending toward in this period. Lenny Bruce was becoming a dirty comic. Not just a comic who says dirty words or tells dirty jokes or makes dirty gestures—that was old stuff in burlesque. That wouldn't have brought any heat on him—or made him a legend. Or gotten him a sobriquet like Dirty Lenny. You had to go much further than "Get a little behind, Fanny!" to earn yourself the kind of rep that Lenny Bruce enjoyed. What Lenny was getting into at this point in his career was not so much dirt as it was sexual fantasy. Under the influence of the dressing-room orgies and the endless incitements of the strip dancers and the licentious atmosphere of these gamey joints out in the Valley, he was beginning to boil up sexually and spill over onstage.

He had a routine, for example, about a monster. He would stand at one side of the stage where in every strip bar there were maroon-velour drapes, and he would put his hand around behind the curtain as if someone—or some *thing*—were moving behind the veil. Then, he would feign terror of this mysterious creature and cry out—"Oh, a *monster*! How terrible! What shall I do?" The whole Fay Wray rape fantasy. Then, the fluttering, the fumbling on the other side of the drape would begin to move down his body, until it was right at the level of his cock. Lenny's tone would change: his voice would swoon and he'd moan, "Oh, monster, monster! Please, not so fast, not so hard!" And it would appear that the creature was sucking him off and making him come right at the edge of the curtain. It was a perfect Joe Ancis–style sex fantasy, with the speaker in a passive, feminine posture, submitting with breathy hot-book protests to an incredibly satisfying rape. Yet it wasn't all that fantastic—when you think that a couple of feet away, on the other side of that curtain, he often lay back in exactly the same swoon, perhaps with the same words ringing in his head, being gobbled up by some monster of a stripper.

As the gap between Lenny's fantasies and Lenny's sex life—between how he was living in the dressing room and how he was living onstage—steadily narrowed, his whole definition of his role as a strip-club comic and M.C. began to change. Instead of just making fun of himself stuck in this shlocky club bringing on these shlocky broads and trying to entertain this audience of shlocky perverts, Lenny began to compete with the girls. He tried to shock the audience and ignite the whole depressing atmosphere. If the Okie assholes out front got too loud or obstreperous, he would silence them with a "scene." He might fake a fit. Fall down screaming on the stage, twitch his body spasmodically, foam at the mouth, and bang his heels on the floorboards. Suddenly, instead of a slim, handsome M.C. in a black suit, he was a three-year-old child throwing a tantrum. *"I'm the boss's son!"* he would scream. *"You've got to pay attention to me!"*

Usually, the only attention available was that leering, ogling attention paid to the strippers. So, Lenny began to fight these broads. He sharpened his introductions to whiplash intensity. He sneered at the girls and mimicked their motions. He practically declared war. The strippers were a grotesque-looking crew. They appeared to have been formed in front of fun-house mirrors. But it wasn't their ugliness or lack of talent or failure to appreciate jazz that was infuriating Lenny Bruce. It was simply the fact that the audience stared at them and ignored him. One night, he decided to teach them a lesson they would never forget.

It was a quiet night at the club: no heat in sight, very few women, mostly just the help and the band. Lenny had put on two or three strippers without event, when something happened that brought his smoldering anger to flame. When he introduced the next girl, he retreated to the dressing room and remained there during her act. She taunted and teased, paraded and jounced, slowly removing her clothes. When she finally reached her fleshy epiphany, she turned to exit through the dressing-room door. Just at that moment, the door swung open and out came that talented, handsome, witty, and vivacious M.C., Mr. Lenny Bruce—*bare-assed naked!* Walking slowly across the stage toward the mike, a painfully bored expression on his face, Lenny called out—barely stifling a yawn—*"Let's give the little girl a big hand!"* Then he demonstrated what he meant by plopping his hands together exactly twice! When the gasps from the house reached snake-pit intensity, he seized the mike and stared down with an earnest expression on his face. "What are you all staring at? You see nudity on this stage every night. What's the big deal if I get naked?"

The big deal was that he had finally stepped over the line. Galled beyond endurance by all those irritants that comics find most unbearable—inattentive audiences, offstage noises, unbeatable rival attractions—he had flipped out in his quiet, fell way and begun to behave not like a nice Arthur Godfrey amateur, but like a bad, crazy, attention-grabbing little Jew boy out on the pavements of Brooklyn. It had taken years to happen. The provocations had been enormous. Yet there was no mistaking the fact that Lenny Bruce had changed.

His latest bit was not so much shtick as statement—which is exactly how it was received in the business.

Overnight the story became a show-biz legend. Word traveled all over the country that Lenny Bruce had appeared onstage naked. Lou Levy, who had been subbing on piano, told the other musicians, and they told the comics and the comics told the singers and the singers told the personalities and the personalities told the celebrities and the celebrities told the columnists—and soon there were as many versions of this event as there are of the myths of antiquity or the legends of the world's great religions. Even Lenny Bruce changed the story and made it much funnier when he got around to telling it to Honey.

Lenny was beginning now to fall under the spell of the jazz life. Starting at Strip City and continuing at the Bamboo Room and Cobblestone, he began to spend all his spare time with the musicians. His favorite playmate—the guy he loved better than anybody since Joe Ancis—was an extraordinary character named Joe Maini. Maini was probably the greatest natural jazzman working on the Coast. Though he was only twenty-two when Lenny met him, he had been playing professionally since he was fourteen and had toured all over the country with various bands and combos. Joe was a disciple of Charlie Parker—and not just a distant admirer. He had palled around with Bird in New York, jammed with him many nights, both men playing the same instrument, the alto sax. Bird loved Joe, recognizing him as one of his own sons. He had even given Joe a hot alto and at another time, a hot tenor. Yet Joe Maini was not a finicky, supercilious bebopper, too proud to get on a stand with lesser musicians. He was a man of the people, who dug—like Charlie Parker—every kind of music when it was good of its kind.

He could work as a section man in a jazz band or play behind strippers, honking rock 'n' roll, or fill in on record dates with slick commercial singers. In later years he became a mainstay of the Hollywood studio business, the guy the leaders always called when something a little out of the ordinary was demanded. Joe could always be relied on to blow some kooky phrase, honk some nutty shout, that would cut through the shit and really set things down right where they belonged. Joe was a natural, some would say a genius. He embodied the pure ideal of the jazz musician in that last heady period before the whole business blew up and fell apart.

Being a great jazz cat in those days meant being a junkie. Every bopper was supposed to be as good with his needle as he was with his horn. Joe Maini was one of the best with both. Joe got busted for drugs when he was just a kid, but got off through the influence of an uncle. Then at the age of nineteen he left his hometown of Newport, and went to New York with his tight buddy, the trombone player Jimmy Knepper. Both men were worshipers of Charlie Parker; they imagined themselves hanging out with Bird and learning the secrets of his art. Arriving desperately poor at the moment of New York's worst housing crisis, they staked out an illegal rental in the basement of the William Henry Apartments at 139th Street and Broadway, down the hill from City College. An unfinished basement, really nothing more than a bed, a couple of chairs, and a beat-up old piano, this pad soon became one of the favorite hangouts, shooting galleries, and jam session sites of the New York jazz world. Charlie Parker came in one night and said, "I was playin' down in Florida and I heard about your place way down there."

Bird had heard the joint was jumpin'; he'd also heard—and consistently profited from the fact—that Joe was dealing junk. Unable to get work as a musician—Joe later recalled that he gigged exactly one night during a whole year—he became part of the distribution network of the big uptown pushers. He had no choice because he was hooked and needed desperately a source of supply. As he recalled:

> The first time I didn't even know I was hooked. It was New York and I'd been shooting for a month. We had this scam when we were broke of going from door to door with one arm hid, like it had been cut off. We were supposed to be Veterans of Foreign Wars, and I'd give this spiel and ask for a buck. We'd get $10 and then go score. I remember we got $5 off Carl Sandburg. The first night I didn't get any. I tossed and turned. Just thought it was a restless night, didn't think I was hooked. Then I went over to this house the next day, it was real warm—stick ball in the street— and I had a fucking overcoat pulled around my neck. It still didn't dawn on me there was something wrong. I just felt chilly. The cat fixed me—and I just got warm. Like someone turned the sun on me. Oh—Oh! I knew I was hooked. I tried to stop for two or three days. Then I got right back on. If I got through the physical sickness, I'd really get high the very next day after.

Offering the New York cats the two greatest things in life—dope and Bird—Joe ran for a year and a half the hottest little nightspot in the city. Musicians would come and line up out in the alley waiting for a chance to get inside and play. The piano, lacking a number of keys, was the most sought-after keyboard in Manhattan. Sometimes the jam sessions would go on for days without a break. When Joe or Jimmy got too whipped to continue playing, they would say, "O.K., you cats, don't bother about us!" and they'd crawl into the sack right in the middle of the room. Meanwhile, the heaviest players of that period were drinking and blowing and cutting each other like they used to do back at the old spook breakfasts in Kansas City.

One night the party ended. Some famous jazzman, whose name Joe was too generous to disclose, was busted down on 52nd Street. Offered the choice of naming his seller or going to the can, he snitched on Joe. When the narcs arrived at the basement, the place was jammed with about twenty-five musicians. Joe had just taken a shower and was standing on a chair—so his feet wouldn't get dirty on the filthy floor—drying himself. Suddenly, the feds burst through the door with their guns drawn. One of them ran up to Joe and yelled, "Hold it!" Joe had an enormous cock on him, the biggest cock in the music business, the object of a hundred jokes and funny stories. When the narc said, "Hold it!" Joe looked down at his cock with a funny expression on his face, the gun-pointing narc looked too, and both of them burst out laughing! Then the party resumed in a grim parody of its former life, with one narc answering the phone and talking like a hipster and inviting every caller to come up and blow. "Joe just went out, man. He be back directly. We's up here wailin' like fools. Come on up, baby!"

The penalties for dope in those days were stiff. Joe got a two-and-a-half-year bit—and there was no plea bargaining. He was shipped down to Lexington, Kentucky, where he found one of the best jazz bands in the world. At that time, Lexington held so many musicians and entertainers that the annual Christmas show was widely regarded as the best seasonal entertainment in America—right up there with Radio City Music Hall. The governor of the state and his lady, the top political bosses of Kentucky, the big-shot businessmen—anybody who was anybody—would bargain and pull strings to get an invitation.

After doing a one-and-a-half-year stretch, Joe was allowed to go free. Enrolling in Los Angeles's City College, he tried studying for a while; soon he was cutting all his classes except swimming. At last he dropped out, and like all the jazz musicians in L.A., he found work in burlesque. He met Lenny while working as a substitute at Strip City. From that first night, theirs was a runaway affair.

"My junkie lover" was Lenny's phrase for Joe; and he could have spoken for Honey, too, who thought Joe was one of the greatest people she had ever met. He was certainly a fascinating man, and no small part of his fascination lay in the fact that he was a mainlining drug addict. Up to that time, Lenny and Honey had steered clear of the heavy junk scene. They had snorted heroin a few times in New York, and since their meeting with Richey Shackleton, they had horned a lot more stuff in California. Lenny had even begun to experiment with the needle. Hung up about the experience of mainlining, he obsessed about it night and day. Somebody suggested that Lenny go in a drug-store and buy an insulin needle. This was a perfectly legitimate move, although, even then, there was a little heat around it. Lenny was still in his strict law-abiding phase; he couldn't work up the nerve to make the purchase. Finally, a lady friend bought a needle at the Farmer's Market and gave it to Lenny. He rigged up an eyedropper outfit, cooked the stuff according to the magazine articles, and started stab-bing his arm. Even in later years, after he'd fixed thousands of times, Lenny had trouble hitting himself. Now, at the beginning of his career, he couldn't even come close. He butchered his arm and never got the thrill he was seeking. Then, about a week later, he met Joe. "Here's how to do it, sweetheart!" murmured old junkie devil Joe as he slipped the geezer into Lenny's tattooed left arm. And a star was born!

Scoring soon became Lenny and Honey's biggest obsession. Scor-ing meant that they had to go into the black neighborhoods and meet the pushers on the street. It was a scary, tricky business, and it intro-duced an element of danger and criminality into their lives. It also changed their whole perspective on life. Banged out of your nut on horse, the little dream house with the white picket fence didn't look so satisfying. In fact, it looked sort of corny. When you were good 'n' high, your mind tended to go toward different, much wilder scenes. You wanted to get naked and do crazy things and really freak out. You lost all your fears and inhibitions. Life seemed much more beau-tiful and attractive—it was this great big plum tree standing there with all the fruit hanging down waiting to be plucked. Why shouldn't they go and have their fun?

Lenny was twenty-eight years old at this time. "Look," he'd say to Joe or Tony or whoever was listening, "you only have sixty-five years to live. Before you're twenty, you can't enjoy anything because you don't know what's going on. After you're fifty, you can't enjoy it either, because you don't have the physical energies. So you only have around twenty-five years to swing. In those twenty-five years, *I'm going to swing!*" Lenny was always careful to justify his actions in ethical or psychologial terms. "If you're not hung up about fixing, if it doesn't make you guilty," he would explain to Honey, "then it can't hurt you. It's the guilty ones that suffer," he would lecture, never bothering to ask whether it made her guilty or just how it made her feel.

Paling around with the cats, Lenny began to look for places where they could all work together. He'd never had an honest-to-God family, and he was really high on the tightness he had achieved with all his new friends. He wanted to cement their relationship in work and creativity—not just after-hours monkey business. One day he met a girl from a very good family back East who had come into an inheritance. She was living in Pasadena and looking for opportunities in filmland. Lenny was her latest obsession. He went to work on her with all the charm and class and salesmanship that he could command; pretty soon he scammed her out of seven thousand dollars, which he claimed he needed to finance "a very important TV pilot." Though the girl was a perfect victim for Lenny's wiles, she wasn't completely stupid: she demanded that Lenny show her something on paper and introduce her to the other people who were going to work on the project. A frantic scuffle to come up with a treatment and shooting staff followed upon these demands, and Lenny the Con Man ended up by conning himself into carrying out the project that had been hatched simply as a scam.

Fleetfoot was to be a children's program about the adventures of a little pioneer boy whose family is killed in the massacre of a wagon train. The boy is saved by the Indians and reared by five braves, each of whom is an expert in some manly art, like riding, shooting, tracking, or sending smoke signals. Convinced that he was on to something big, Lenny threw himself into the project. His choice for director was obvious: the same old hack he always used, Phil Tucker.

At this same time, Lenny met through Richey Shackleton and Ann Staunton a couple of other professional filmmakers named Frank Murphy and Bill Himes, whom he also conned into joining the project, the one as associate producer, the other as cinematographer. Neither man was to receive any money for his work, but both were to own a share of the film and were to have the same jobs on the series—once it was sold—as they had on the pilot. Similar deals were offered to several professional actors: Bob Swan, who played the leading Indian; Steve Peck, another Indian; and Mel Welles, the heavy villain. Richey Shackleton played Fleetfoot as a youth; as a child, the character was played by the young son of some Hollywood saxophonist. The rest of the parts were filled by Lenny's junkie friends, the foremost of whom was that perfect cigar-store Indian, Joe Miani.

Persuading all these people to work without pay was no small feat, even for a practiced con artist like Lenny Bruce; but by this time, he had really hit his peak as a hustler. He boasted publicly of his adventures in Florida, where he impersonated Brother Matthias; he frankly admitted to anyone interested that he was on the make, had scammed the money for the film, and was happiest when he could promote capital, equipment, and personnel through the use of his wits rather than his pocketbook. Frank Murphy—a year older than Lenny and an experienced moviemaker, who had done films about missiles for Douglas Aviation, worked in animation and later was associated with the

Peter Gunn TV series—recalls Lenny at this time as being "totally motivated, obviously talented, and thoroughly manipulative of people. He was a remarkable combination of a con artist and a person who had genuine empathy with people. It was always a question what would take over. His ability to scam people gave him his major thrill. If he could find someone who in his mind was slightly villainous and he could get his money, he would be in heaven." For the rest, Murphy recalls somewhat ruefully, "I was the square guy. I didn't know everything that was going on." Of one thing he was sure: Lenny had "a lot of respect for the idea of the series—we were all sure he would sell it."

So they set to work, filming in color because Murphy said that color would help them make a sale. What had to be filmed for the initial twenty-five-minute episode was, first, the massacre scene, with the villain killing Fleetfoot's parents. Then, the scenes of the little boy learning Indian arts. Initially, he would be a child playing games with the Indian children; then, a dissolve would bring him into adolescence, where the games would give way to tests of bravery. Richey Shackleton would have to leap over a field of upturned knives—rubber knives painted silver. He would also have to get into a terrific fight with the villain at the very end of the episode, avenging his parents by pushing the heavy off a cliff. Murphy tried to talk Lenny out of that last scene, arguing that it was just too corny. Lenny insisted that the episode appear, arguing, in turn, that it was just the sort of action that thrilled children.

Strictly speaking, they should have gone on location in Indian country; part of the appeal of the series was supposed to be the nature footage. Money for such an expensive safari was lacking, however; so they fell back on that ancient Hollywood adage (first uttered by some harried MGM official in the twenties): "A tree's a tree, a rock's a rock." The Indian country filmed in *Fleetfoot* was all within the city limits of Los Angeles; it was, in fact, Griffith Park, especially the caves at Old Bronson. Every day they purchased a permit to shoot in the park, and almost every day Lenny would get into a hassle with the park officials, who complained about the way his company was abusing the terrain with their digging and rigging and littering. Somehow, Lenny cooled all the beefs.

The shooting for the first couple of days went smoothly enough. The junkie musicians, several of whom bedded down on the floor of Lenny's living room, complained about getting up before late afternoon. They also groused about the extraordinary physical exertion involved in running up and down the hills with tomahawks in their hands. They got plenty of chances to cool out in the caves, however; virtually anywhere you turned on this location, you could find somebody shooting up. Murphy, a good Roman Catholic, hadn't the faintest idea of what was going on; he assumed that Lenny was vigorously opposed to drugs because one day he heard some actor express the wish to try dope, and Lenny gave the guy a lecture on the dangers of narcotics. Joe Maini, who was usually so stoned that he could barely stand, Murphy recalls as a "sweet, gentle guy." Bill Himes and Bob Swan were also completely out of the drug action.

As planned, Lenny found a job for everyone. Anne Staunton and Honey, who in the summer of 1955 was just beginning to show signs of pregnancy, were acting as "wardrobe" for the picture. They had plenty of work, shaving the men's bodies and sponge-dyeing them with Indian color and fussing over their scanty costumes and kook hair-pieces. Honey was always great with food, so she provided lunches for the whole crew. Everybody sat there in war paint munching on a ham and American cheese sandwich and drinking beer from a can. On a shooting schedule of seven days, there wasn't time for anything but work.

On the third day of shooting, Tucker and Lenny got into a quarrel so violent that the director walked off the scene and never again reappeared. The burden of the direction was now assumed by Frank Murphy, with Bill Himes and Lenny throwing in their suggestions. Lenny was good at communicating with the actors: he would tell them the story exactly and do the dialect they were to use. Everything seemed to be moving beautifully.

Then, one morning, a couple of officials from the teamsters union rolled up the hill in their Cadillac and demanded that Lenny hire a completely union crew or stop shooting. Lenny bribed them to leave, but it was obvious that the shooting would have to be wound up quickly because the union men were certain to return in a couple of days. Nervously fidgeting in the crisis, he remarked to one of the two grips on the job—square union workers who carried lights and equipment and hadn't the faintest idea of what the junkie actors were doing back in the caves—"Jeez! I wish I had some uppers to get myself into high gear!" One of the grips said, "You mean bennies? I got about two hundred bennies I keep hidden in my mailbox at the house. I just use them on weekends." "Man! Please! Jump in your car and get them! You'll save my life!" Soon as the cat returned with the bennies, Lenny had a second genius-stroke. Sending down to Goldblatt's for a huge container of coffee—a metal urn containing about ten gallons—he dumped all the bennies in the brew. Soon the crew was working at top speed, the junkie actors were running nimbly up and down the hills, and the squares like Murphy and Himes were laboring tirelessly through the night. In a tremendous 48-hour burst, *Fleetfoot* was brought to completion. Lenny and Richey chuckled for years over the dumb lines they kept hearing during those last two days: "Say! I've been working since dawn, and I've still got so much energy! How is it possible?"

When the shooting was completed, there still remained the tedious job of editing the footage into the final cut and dubbing in the sound track. Lenny knew nothing of these techniques; the whole job fell on Murphy and Himes, who worked around the clock for a couple of days until everything was completed except for the final dubbing session. The studio bill for this session was five hundred dollars; Lenny persuaded Murphy to lay out the money, offering him a mortgage on his now almost worthless black Cadillac. At the same time, a large sum was lavished on the preparation of a press book, with the script and color stills and a lot of copy designed to impress potential buyers. At the last moment, Lenny realized that one of the professional actors had not signed a contract committing him to continue in the same role during the projected series. The actor was confident that he was about to take off in some big parts, and he didn't want to tie himself down. Lenny got him into the kitchen of his house one afternoon and, according to Murphy, "threw the greatest temper tantrum I have ever seen. He screamed and pleaded for a quarter of an hour, threw himself all over the kitchen, gave a performance that should have been captured on film. The only comparable fits I've ever seen were a four-year-old girl and a famous Hollywood producer. Lenny was better than either."

The upshot of all these labors and scenes was a complete washout. The finished product looked professional, but it was, according to Murphy, "a lousy film. The tale was told too naïvely and some of the acting was bad." What was even more infuriating than the failure to sell the pilot was the fact that only a year later one of the networks launched a series on roughly the same idea. Had *Fleetfoot* been plagiarized? Lenny swore it had; he threatened legal action. Eventually, he lost interest in the project and failed to even retain a print of the film. (The only surviving copy is in the hands of Bill Himes.) About all that Lenny preserved was a handful of stills. Most of them were printed in *Stamp Help Out*. Only one picture was withheld. It showed Big Brave Bruce bending a little white boy across a log in preparation for the ancient ceremony of buggery.

Not only did Lenny plow on through one exhausting and futile film project after another, he gained strength and enthusiasm as he advanced! The stories of his psychological state during the filming of *Leather Jacket* suggest that he was swinging on the most powerful upper of his whole billowy career. He began, as usual, by sweeping everybody

off his feet. Running around Canter's—the Jewish deli that attracted
more characters than Damon Runyon's Lindy's—he got more promises
of work, equipment, and film than anyone would have thought possible. He got so carried away with his vision of success that he even
made an approach to one of the toughest guys in Hollywood, the
notorious mobster Mickey Cohen.

There he is in Cohen's kitchen one afternoon, pitching, pleading,
framing pictures with his nervous hands and selling his ass off for this
new movie. All the while Lenny is shpritzing himself blind, Mickey
Cohen is sitting there eating ice cream. He's got this big spoon in his
hairy fist, and he's gouging the rock-solid ice cream out of a pint
container. Down goes the spoon, bending under the thrust of his hand,
up comes another scoop, down goes the spoon, up comes the scoop,
like a steam shovel eating away at a mountain. Finally, Cohen has
shoveled the carton clean. He burps, lays down his tool, and looks
Lenny straight in the eye. "Kid," he says, "I'd like to invest. But I
gotta be honest with you. *I don't have it!*" Beautiful! Mickey Cohen,
at that time the boss of all the organized crime in L.A. and taking
maybe half a million a year in skimmings off the tables of Vegas, tells
Lenny Bruce, "I don't have it!" That was the end of the interview—
but not of Mickey Cohen.

Next day they've got the camera hidden in a newspaper box on
the corner of Santa Monica and Fairfax. Lenny snaps, "Action!"
and walks out into the middle of the street with the paper held up
in his hand. First car that pulls up for the light is Mickey
Cohen's! Can you imagine what he must have thought? "Here's this
nut," he must have said to himself. "He tells me he wants to make a
picture and he's out in the street selling newspapers!" Lenny whispers
to Mickey, "*Zug nisht, zug nisht*, Mickey—we're making a movie!"
When Mickey Cohen hears that, he almost plotzes. He gets the
weirdest expression on his face! Starts looking all over for cameras.
When the light changes, he guns up his engine and damn near runs
over Lenny.

The next day the whole crew runs up to Bunker Hill, where Lenny
cons the director of an old-age home into letting him use the entire
building for the rooming-house sequences in the picture. Sally is playing
the landlady, and it's a sick joke how all the old pensioners start coming
on with her. Lenny finally has to scream, "Ma, come on, already,
you're the star of the picture!" The same con he lays on society chicks
and Jewish gangsters, he lays on a Catholic priest who has a statue of
Jesus that he wants to use in the picture. But it doesn't work on the
priest—which really gets Lenny mad. They have to sneak-shoot the
statue, and Lenny claimed later that the priest's rejection of his request

was the germ for all the stuff he said about the Catholic Church in
Religions, Inc.

After they shot about a third of the film, everything came to a
stop. Lenny began to complain that they were barking up the wrong
tree with a 16-mm film: they should have shot on 35. At that point,
the Thalians (a charity organization of show-biz wives) asked Lenny
to write them a show. They offered to pay him off with a lot of raw
35-mm film stock. He wrote the show—which never ran—and began
to reshoot everything he had done on 16 on 35. Sally was no longer
available, having run off to Paris after Tony. Lenny had to replace her
with Buddy Shaffron, a landlord instead of a landlady. During the first
shooting, Lenny had been really hot. He would tear the camera off its
mount and whirl it around to catch some fleeting scene—a passing fire
truck, an ambulance—sometimes falling over into the street clutching
the precious box. Whatever you said about his work, he threw heart
and soul into it. Now he was cooling off. His second takes weren't as
good as the first. The whole remake was a mistake. When they got as
far as they had gone the first time, Lenny called a halt—and the project
was never again revived. For years after, Lenny spoke about his unfinished film. The big tin cans with the reels inside were shipped from
coast to coast, run off many times in offices and living rooms, used to
raise money or raise the morale of the exhausted comic. He even
commissioned a composer named Jack Weeks to write a sound track
for the portion he had shot—a score that he didn't much like. But it
was all over with Lenny and the movies. Once his club career got
going, he could never get back before the camera, unless it was the
TV camera, or once, at the very end, the movie camera, catching him
blinking into the lights on a nightclub stage in Frisco, an unrecognizable
figure, fat, fumffering, scarecrowish, tipping forward from the neck
and whirling around from the waist like some rag doll, not the handsome, nervous young man who had sat with his back to the wall and
eaten a sandwich and taken a gulp from a thermos and seen the whole
world go up in Technicolor as he bestrode his mighty bike and lowered
his goggles and prepared to blast off into ecstasyville.

During the period of *Fleetfoot*, Lenny began to run his habit up very
fast. His ascent to the highest heavens of narcotic addiction was aided
and abetted by an old friend who turned up unexpectedly at this time
and promptly blew Lenny's mind. Chic Eder had first met Lenny in
Miami in 1951. Writing from San Quentin, over twenty years later,
chic (he affects the lower case) recalled the beginnings of his relationship with Lenny in Miami, and the moment in Los Angeles when they
both began to live like crazy junkies.

I was working as a beach-boy at the Vanderbilt, between 20th and 21st on Collins, and picking up extra bread doing comedy sketches in water shows. But those gags were just a front for my major activities: I'd scored the master keys to more than 40 of the largest hotels and was into burgling—strictly cash, jewels and furs. I'd delivered a mink stole to a stripper in a club, and went over to a table to see if I could interest the comic B.S Pully in a few nice stones I'd recently "acquired." Seated at the table were H. S. Gump, the dwarf comic who sometimes worked with Pully (their initials stood for "Bull-Shit" and "Horse-Shit"—which sounds so corny today—and Pully once pissed on Gump right onstage), and this wild dude who turned out to be Lenny Bruce. Not only did he seem like a great potential customer, but I instantly dug him for the interesting cat that he was. We talked about the possibility of my stinging a particular type of stole that he wanted to get for Honey. When I learned that he was a comic and told him that I was doing water-show comedy, we decided to get together.

He'd come over and goof at the pool where I worked—and I'd treat him like royalty: a cabana, the whole red-carpet treatment. He caught my act a couple of times, and gave me some workable criticism on how to improve the dialogue in the skits. Our original relationship was based on a mutual admiration thing. Lenny was about five or six years older than me, and I saw him as the epitome of the sophistication I was trying to emulate at that time. Despite the age difference—which is strong when one guy is 20 and the other is 26—we discovered we had much in common . . . There were so many similarities in our younger lives: we'd both been "farmed-out" as kids; both lived in Riverhead, way out in Suffolk County; both Sally and my mother had worked as maids in wealthy homes (who ever heard of a Jewish *maid* on Long Island!?); Lenny'd been to sea, and I'd shipped out on yachts—having worked my way up from mess-boy to deckhand on the Sea Cloud, the last of the squareriggers. To me the ballsiest guy in the world was a stand-up comic. Lenny was awed by the guts it took to "cat" into people's rooms and relieve them of their valuables while they slept. It was only years later, when he was describing my double life of that period to my ex-old lady, that I realized how impressed he'd been by the Hollywood romanticism inherent in my life style.

The following years were frantic. I tried marriage and holding down a steady gig. Both sucked!—I got in the wind. I gradually got into burgling less and hustling more (although, in retrospect,

I can see where the outright stealing was a more honorable way of life). I crisscrossed the nation many times involved in various scams. In '54 I switched my base of operations to the more lucrative West Coast.

I'd learned that the easiest marks to hustle were the hustlers; and that nightclubs—particularly strip joints—were always good for a score. I was working Los Angeles one night when I spotted a club on Western Avenue, just off Pico Boulevard. The name— "Strip City"—spelled buck, so I pocketed a few flyers and "dropped in for a drink."

It was the middle of the week so there wasn't much action in the club. I'd spotted Lenny while clocking the house, but didn't recognize him until he got up to introduce the next bump-and-grinder. I picked up my drink, walked toward one of the empty ringside tables, and caught Lenny's eye. He snapped to who I was, and slid right into a dual-voiced shtick: "Wanna buy a hot?" "A hot what?" "A hot anything; I had a helluva week!"

I'd been on the periphery of the junk scene for years—snorting a few times, while retaining a healthy fear of the spike. Suddenly I met a guy [jazzman Art Pepper] who turned me on. Not being one to fuck around, I mainlined from the jump!

I was psychologically hooked from that initial geeze. It was as though nature had inadvertently neglected to supply my system with the required ingredients. Heroin was the missing chemical that made me a complete human being. Suddenly, all the soul-pain was gone. I felt right and light and aware and calm. There was an inner peace at the very core of my being. I was *alive!* All I wanted to know was: "Where and how do we score quantity?" Ten days later I was dealing: within a month I'd cut into the main-bag coming up out of Mexico. My entire life style flipped—every-thing I did revolved around the smack scene.

I'd known that Lenny was chippieing, but didn't realize how many others in his immediate circle were also fixing. Although almost everyone in that tip was a talented musician or entertainer, few of them were hip to the huckly-buck world of scoring. Finding the "source' is the secret of being a successful hustler, so I'd un-knowingly been preparing for years to become "the connection." That was my entrée into that tribe of brilliant, talented people.

Lenny consistently maintained that he could kick any time he chose, but I refused to even consider doing so. All I wanted to do was shoot as much smack as possible and still function.

Although some of those in the tip had formerly geezed other kinds of opiates, the only thing we were into at that time was heroin. All that changed, though, with the arrival of a character with whom I'd grown up in New York.

"Fast Harry," a chemist, was a short, skinny, wiry guy, with thick glasses and more complexes than a Bellevue back-ward. Harry was a couple of years older than me, and I was in awe of his genius. He had the fastest head for numbers of any kid in Hell's Kitchen. When he invited me out burgling with him, I was honored. Harry went to the New School for Social Research down in Greenwich Village, while I made the reformatory at the age of 12.

One winter in Miami Beach, I got a call from my pal: "I'm in trouble, chic. If I can get down there, can you put me up for a few weeks?" Harry was in the middle of his senior year, and was hooked like a dog on smack . . .

It took Harry almost a week to kick and, watching him, I vowed never to mess with heroin. Harry completed college, but also dove back into the dipper. Although in his mid-twenties, he was still living with his folks, which made it simple to locate him whenever I hit New York. Right after I began geezing, I phoned him to explain that *now* I could understand his diving into the spike-end of an eyedropper.

Harry had my phone number and I was overjoyed when he called to tell me to pick him up at L.A.'s Union Station the following day. When I saw the size of his steamer-trunk, I dug his need to travel by rail. His only comment was a railroad slogan of the day: "Next time take the train; it's *cooler*."

We schlepped that wardrobe trunk up the stairs, and barely got it through the door to my little flat. Harry opened it with a flourish, and blew my mind! It was filled with *drugs*! My myopic buddy had brought to fruition the dream of every junkie. Singlehandedly, he'd ripped off the narcotics vault of a wholesale drug firm's warehouse . . .

When I phoned Lenny he heard the excitement in my voice, and immediately bopped over with Joe Maini. I introduced them: "Sir John Falstaff, John Philip Sousa; meet Eli Lily!" Despite his having grown up in "The Apple," having a college education, and being a confirmed hype, Harry's naïeté in many areas of "the life" was such that Lenny and Joe, more than any of the others in our tip, wigged him with their hiptitude.

For openers, though, it was all Harry's show. He began removing different bottles from the trunk, explaining the properties of each as he laid them out on the bed. Then he unstashed different sized syringes, a small box of spikes, a bottle of alcohol, a rubber hospital tourniquet and a box of cotton.

"With your assistance, I'd like to prepare for you a heavenly cocktail from some of these ingredients." He took out a sort of portable Bunsen-burner with a metal container that fit over the flame . . . Lenny, who was immaculate in his personal-hygiene habits, was fascinated by the manner in which Harry sterilized everything in alcohol poured into a soup bowl. Harry's precise movements were reminiscent of a vaudeville magician's, which prompted Lenny to remark, "He's Merlin incarnate!" Swift Joe's immediate comeback was: "Yeah, but this alchemist's compounds are far more interesting than gold!" Harry was obviously delighted by the recognition of his talents; from there on out he was righteously "on."

"For a soluble solution, we will use morphine sulphate. Voila!" Using a horse needle inserted into a syringe big enough to baste a turkey, he withdrew an enormous quantity of liquid morphine from the tiny bottle by taking a second spike and inserting it next to the one in the syringe to allow a sufficient amount of air to enter the bottle through the rubber seal. "Here we have some Pantopon" [essence of opium, five times stronger than morphine], which he plopped into the container, "and although we have many different strengths of Dilaudid—64th, 32nd, 20th, 16th, and 'footballs' [a half-grain, used only by veterinarians and junkies]—we will use the strongest there is: *powdered* Dilaudid! That should round out the mixture nicely."

Noticing our rising anxiety to get it on, Harry lit the burner and quickly fitted four needles to syringes. Continuing his monologue—"We heat the morphine only enough to dissolve the Pantopon, since the powdered Dilaudid dissolved on contact with the liquid"—Harry completed his duties as "chef" and with swift dexterity drew up what seemed to be an unusually small quantity of the liquid in three of the outfits . . . "I think you'll find that each contains a grand sufficiency. Pig-junkies are soon dead junkies."

Having veins so huge that I don't even have to tie off to get a hit, I picked up a syringe, geezed and walked to the sink to rinse out the outfit. I never made it. Harry's "cocktail" reached my heart and I flopped into an armchair. It was only days later, when I got hip to the individual drugs, that I began to understand the potency of that mixture. Harry walked over, checked my eyes, clocked my pulse, then calmly took the syringe from my hand to clean it.

Joe, too, still had pretty good ropes, but Lenny'd had trouble getting a hit from the jump. He tied Lenny off about three inches below the elbow, hit him in the cephalic vein [inside the wrist] and, much to Lenny's amazement and delight, got an immediate register. The three of us were in awe of Harry's smooth and professional movements. He was so *sure* of himself that the rest of us felt like rank novices.

Looking around to ensure that each of us was comfortably nodding and scratching, Harry began preparing his own taste. It was Lenny who first noticed, and called to our attention, the fact that Harry had drawn up almost as much as he'd prepared for the three of us combined! He very calmly hit in the *back* of his forearm, then returned to straightening up his paraphernalia. There we were, so torn out of our gourds that we could barely move, and Harry wasn't even slowed down by his monumental jolt. He just went right on functioning, occasionally flipping us a supercilious grin.

Silence reigned as each of us kicked back to dig our high. I finally broached the subject of locating a permanent stash for Harry's "drugstore." When I got up to go to the corner market for some cardboard cartons, Joe decided to stumble along. Upon our return, Lenny had Harry hung-up in the first of many brain-picking sessions. Listening to their conversation, we learned that heroin was originally a German chemist's trademark for what he believed was the most sophisticated derivative of opium. Harry explained that science had advanced so rapidly in recent years that they now had substances twenty and thirty times as potent as the morphine we'd just fixed.

We made arrangements to meet later and introduce our chemist to others in the tip. Asking them to wait a moment, Harry poured the remainder of his concoction into two plastic vials. He laid them on Joe and Lenny with the advice to use it with prudence. The contents of each of those vials was easily worth well over $100 at street prices. Lenny and Joe were truly impressed by Harry's complete lack of avarice . . .

The only payment he asked of any of us was that we conscientiously assist him by giving a description of how the drug (or combination of drugs) affected us. He gloried in the fact that he was surrounded by a group of talented and articulate hypes. Being required to externalize physical and psychological sensations of this nature forced us to make analyses that we'd never have considered otherwise. It wasn't enough to talk about the heroin "surge," or morphine's "tingle," or the "flash" and "drive" of Dilaudid—Harry wanted much more detail. We learned that attempting to describe the sensations and reactions to those opiates was as difficult as, say, describing a toothache.

As Harry's "research" became a daily ritual with us, we grew progressively more introspective for his benefit. To varying degrees we were all educated by his scientific method of approaching the entire concept of drug-use. Although it's doubtful that any of us realized it at the time, we were engaged in a series of experiments that were destined to shape our preferences for future use; drastically changing our lives—and deaths.

Surprisingly—considering his intensive use of the drug a few years later—Lenny didn't dig Dilaudid by itself at that time. While he dug the "flash," he was bugged that it didn't "hold" him. (Dilaudid doesn't have the staying power of smack, the high only lasting for a couple of hours.)

Harry had tone to school in New York with a guy who was doing graduate work at UCLA at that time and who got him permission to use the school's Chemistry Department laboratory. I was still dealing smack, particularly to three connections in San Francisco, and Harry suggested a method by which we could both pick up a nice taste of bread. With his jaded tastes, he was only interested in the "cream" of the narcotics he'd scored; so he mixed up a batch of his lesser drugs and we added it to the next shipment of heroin that I copped from Mexico. Harry cut the mixture with so much milk-sugar that I became concerned about losing my best customers behind a burn. I needn't have worried. I made the deliveries, and the San Francisco dealers were burning up the wires wanting to reorder before my plane even got back to Los Angeles.

Lenny's curiosity about drugs complemented Harry's, and Harry—weakening under Lenny's persuasive manner of playing up to his ability as a teacher—agreed to take Lenny and me out to the lab with him while he processed another batch of our "heroin-fortifier." All Harry's instructions about being cool in school were wasted. Once he'd agreed to take us, it was only a matter of time before it became an "expedition."

Lenny had a black, four-door, 1951 Cadillac "gangstermobile" —which seemed the ideal vehicle for a trip to upper-class Westwood. When Lenny showed up, he already had two passengers: a talented young drummer named Gary Fromer and Joe Maini. Harry couldn't handle that. Lenny cooled him out by telling him that Joe and Gary just wanted to see the campus, and wouldn't even come near the chemistry building if he thought they might attract heat. With the four of us working on him, Harry, of course,

had relented by the time we got to the university; and the five of
us trooped into one of the older buildings that housed the lab.

There were a couple of other cats in the lab, but they were deep
off into whatever they were hung-up in on the other side of the
room. By the time we'd donned white smocks, we felt very professional. Lenny started to do a bit about the uniforms making us
invisible, only to be shushed by Harry. It was the first time Lenny'd
seen Harry nervous or flustered about anything, and he started
shooting whispered zingers at "Mr. Super-Cool."

Harry'd brought along a carpet-bag full of bottles and vials, and
a half-dozen of those big, green desk-blotters. He unrolled the
blotters and immediately put Gary and me to work. We had
hundreds of small tablets which he instructed us to place on the
blotters—leaving about an inch between each. He explained that
they were morphine tablets, but also contained atropine; that they
were used as a pre-operative medication, and that the atropine
dehydrated the user and also fucked up his vision. He gave us each
an eyedropper, and instructions on how to carefully place one drop
of water on each tablet. He explained how the water, going through
the tabs and being soaked up by the blotters, would draw out most
of the atropine without affecting the morphine itself; and, while
we wouldn't want to shoot any of it, it would become profitably
marketable when mixed with heroin.

As soon as he got us started, he put Joe to work pulling the
tinfoil off what we learned were individually wrapped opium suppositories. The pecking-order being what it was, Lenny became
Harry's "assistant"—and retained his prime gig of shpritzing.
("Don't let us bust you stashing them up your keister, Joe!") Harry
pulled out a number of large bottles labelled "tincture of opium."
While Joe, Gary and I continued our repetitious tasks, he and
Lenny went through a series of elaborate steps to extract the opium
base from the liquid. Joe was the first one done with his job, so
he came over to help us with the "Chinese-Torture" gig.

The two genuine students completed whatever experiments they
were conducting, and got in the wind. We could tell by their
friendly gestures upon departing that they'd bought-in with us
being fellow "professionals." The moment the door shut behind
them, pandemonium reigned. Cats like us could retain a facade
of reserved decorum for just so long, and we were way overdue
to get "loose."

Joe kicked it off. He jumped up on the long work-table, pulled
out his super-whang, and began pissing in the sink. Harry got

uptight: "Somebody could walk in at any moment!" Lenny told him: "Be cool, baby. Joe can't stand rejection. He gets angry, he's subject to shit in your centrifuge." With that, Lenny grabbed a couple of the opium suppositories, dropped his drawers, and began sticking them up his ass. To Harry's protestations that they wouldn't get him high, he answered: "I don't care; I just dig shoving stuff up my ass! Tried a peyote enema because the taste of it made me sick. That didn't get me high either, but I dug it. I think I'm very anal." We all started to get manic.

Gary bugged Harry to concoct something that would bubble and steam like a Jekyll/Hyde solution, and that got the rest of us into doing bits based on the mad-scientist flicks that had played such a major role in our childhoods. Harry filled Gary's request and put together some blend of chemicals in a flask that would have put to shame the work of any Hollywood propman. One problem, though, it wasn't safely drinkable.

Gary, who could do some wild feats with drum-sticks, started flip-juggling three long test-tubes. When Harry cautioned him about being careful, Gary just left all three of them up in the air, and turned to innocently ask: "Whadya say, Harry?" The different looks on Gary and Harry's faces when they crashed to the floor brought boffos that had us holding our sides.

Harry began to get visions of us totalling-out that lab, so he dove for his carpetbag. Before we'd started stepping on my last bag of heroin, we'd pinched a big hunk for our personal stash. Harry'd mixed in some powdered Dilaudid and a few other opiates, and he upped this and a box full of outfits. "Medication time at the funny-farm. You guys get that glass swept up while I chef this." Lenny started screaming: "Yenta-mother-bribe-time you mean! 'Make a nice potty and Mommy will give you a piece of candy.' 'I don't want a piece of candy; I want some titty!' " Harry was blowing in the key we could all hear, though, so we got the ex-test-tubes swept up.

Before leaving the lab, Harry cautioned: "They've got campus cops who get particularly inquisitive on weekend evenings, so be cool on the way to the car. We'd play hell trying to explain the contents of this satchel." Lenny had Harry hung-up rapping, while Joe, Gary and I walked a little ways behind them. We'd just hit the parking-lot when Harry glanced around at us. What he saw made him decide to never again take *any*body from our tip to that college. Joe had really dug his white smock, so he'd boosted and re-donned it. Once in the car, Joe met Harry's hostile stares with his great logic: "If they didn't want cats to boost them, then why did they stamp 'UCLA' on them? It's good advertising; like hotel towels."

As we piled out of the car to cop cigarettes at Westwood Village, there's this obviously snobbish matron holding a leash—attached to which was a large, standard-sized poodle taking a shit. As quick as the dog got done, the biddy leaned over and wiped its ass with a piece of Kleenex. That stretched our practiced credulity to the point where all we could do was gawk in open-mouthed awe. Lenny, who hated everything for which clipped and groomed French poodles stood, couldn't resist engaging the snob in a put-on. He began rapping poodle-talk, and had her enchanted, when Joe moved in. Joe put his face less than a foot from the woman's, and loudly asked: "Lick your leg for a quarter, lady?" You know how you can laugh and whoop until the tears run down your cheeks? Joe's line, and this haughty woman's reaction to it—lips pursed, dragging her dog away in a huff—brought on that kind of laughter . . .

We got into singing on the trip back to Hollywood. We parodied pop-tunes and, of course, the lyrics reflected our life-style. Lenny started it with a brand new take-off: "It's delicious, it's delightful, it's Dilaudid!" We pulled into our neighborhood doing four-part harmony on a standard that most of us knew: "Mona Lisa, Mona Lisa, pass the reefer / Caught a whiff of what you're smoking, let's get high / Is it ganja, is it hashish that you're toking / 'Cause a good joint never fails to catch my eye. / Do you still push reds and bennies, Mona Lisa? / Yes, a pill or two is still the right approach / Many weed-heads have been to your doorstep / Not to cry there, just get high there. / Thanks a lot, for the pot, Mona Lisa / So baby light a new one, while I kill this roach! / Mona Liiiiisa . . . Pass the reeeeefer!"

This was the spirit in which Lenny Bruce and his gang encountered the dread specter of narcotics addiction. Lenny obviously didn't give a shit. But being a scion of the double-dealing middle class, he couldn't allow the same freedom to Honey. Lenny felt he could kick whenever he wanted to. Honey was another story. She was not the kind to take bows for will power. She was also disliked by the other strippers. All she had to do was pass a joint around the dressing room at the Colony Club, and the police were in the office complaining to Irv that Honey was a bad influence on the girls. This accusation stung Lenny to the quick. Reacting instantly with that self-righteousness that always came out in his brushes with the law, he went right over to the police station and bawled out the cops for harassing his wife. Returning from this heated encounter, he had a long conversation about drugs with May-nard Sloate: "I would never think of doing anything like that," he declared, "because the thought of staying behind bars for even ten minutes just kills me!" Lenny was always disposed to substitute fantasy for truth, but in no other area of his life—with the important exception of his early years with Father—did he so consistently say the thing that is not, as when he spoke about drugs. He couldn't blink the fact, however, that Honey was becoming hopelessly strung out; and when they decided to have a baby, he began to put pressure on her to clean up. It wasn't, though, until she was well along in her pregnancy that she was finally brought up short by a magazine article on the danger of addicted mothers giving birth to addicted babies. Confiding in her obstetrician, Dr. Bruce Stern, Honey received assurances that if she stopped using drugs immediately, her baby would be normal. Mean-while, Dr. Stern made preparations lest the baby die of withdrawal symptoms immediately after birth.

While Honey was getting big with the baby, Lenny was extending his family in other, more characteristic directions by getting tight with the musicians at the Cobblestone. Several of these players became not only friends but members of the group, the gang, the family that he was unconsciously assembling at this time. Herb Geller, the house alto man, was one of the most respected players on the West Coast: a cool, sophisticated, inventive jazz soloist, touched by the influence of Art Pepper; a skillful studio musician, who was reputed to know the chord changes of every tune ever written; and a strip-club player who blew the bump-and-grind charts with the same attention to detail as he would lavish on some prestigious and money-making studio date. A tall, prematurely balding cat, wearing always an expression of bemused diffidence, Herb was a little freakier than he looked. Herb's wife, Lorraine, was another quiet one—an extremely tall, rather plain girl, who wore glasses and the same air of absent-minded reflectiveness that characterized her husband. Lorraine had the distinction of being one of the very few women to achieve acceptance in the almost totally male world of instrumental jazz. She was a good piano player, who worked the strip joints, just like the men; and, when the mood hit her, she would go off by herself, up the beach—as jazz musicians were supposed to do in those moody existential years—to drink and muse and get her head together. Being a professional musician didn't stop her from having children, any more than having children stopped her from touring and doing all the things that musicians are required to do. Lorraine was a remarkable woman, and her sudden and mysterious death, about a year after this time, left everybody feeling just a little spooky about the Family.

Jack Sheldon was another short, muscley, deeply tanned All-American-Boy type, like Richey Shackleton. Jack had a taste for female flesh. He was a one-a-day man, who regarded women as receptacles for his poisons and publicly bragged of being a lousy lay. One helluva trumpet player, he was a stylist with an individual sound, and lots of other things as well: a good singer, on the order of Mose Allison; a natural comedian; and a professional actor, who starred eventually on TV in *Run, Buddy, Run!* He was also an excellent swimmer and a teacher at the swimming school for children run by his mother and his wife, Patty, to whom he remained married through thick and thin and four thriving children.

The other important member of the Family was Sandra Maini. She wasn't actually married yet to Joe; that would come a couple of years later, after a wild wedding party at Duffy's, with the bride pregnant and the guests divided evenly between Joe's Old World Italian relatives—who believed every woman should go to the altar a virgin in a white dress—and Joe's junkie jazz friends, who couldn't understand why anyone ever bothered to get married. At this point (as she later described it herself in a tape-recorded interview with an L.A. journalist), "the world's dirtiest love affair" was still in its initial phases, with Sandra out in the street turning tricks for Joe, and Joe offering Sandra to his friends one minute and the next beating her up for chippieing.

No slatternly, ugly street trim, Sandra was a dead ringer for Sophia Loren. A high-line hooker, she had the furs, ankle bracelets, and flashy sports cars to set off her lip-smacking sex appeal. When Sandra first met Joe, he frightened and repelled her. He'd been drunk for a week, his hair was long and filthy, and his denim worksuit looked like it had been spot-welded to his skin. Driving home with him in his car, she found she was speechless. (She was also alarmed by the police car that tailed him for the whole trip.) When they arrived at her house, she flung open the car door and ducked into the house.

A year later, when she bumped into him again at the Tailspin Club, a rock 'n' roll joint, she behaved very differently. Now she was a topflight hooker, all dolled up in silk dress and mink stole. When she saw Joe up on the bandstand, she decided that she had to have him. "What are you doing after work?" she asked. "I'm going to ball the bass player" was his no less direct reply. (The bass player was Vivian Gary.) "What are you going to do tomorrow?" persisted Sandra, not easily turned off by a mere rival. "Nothing," drawled Joe.

Next afternoon, he arrived with Lenny Bruce, and the whole gang went up to Herb Geller's house. As Sandra tells it:

> I couldn't stop looking at Joe when he picked me up. Then Lenny started talking, and I really didn't know what was happening. What a combination! I was real rebellious at that time [she was eighteen and divorced], and I wanted to get really far out. With those two guys it wasn't really hard to do. They started just directing me, and I started going every way they told me to go—it really was pretty wild. Herb was on his way to New York, Lorraine to follow, Joe to take care of the house with Lynn Holiday, Gary Fromer, Russ Vrieland, Lenny and Don Payne—one big happy group. And me. We stayed up there for four months, never fed the cats, never cleaned the house, never did nothing for four months. There was a big swimming pool near Herbie's where we would have big parties, go swimming in the nude, get really high. Up on Lookout Mountain Drive.
>
> All the guys were trying to see who could draw the most, and I was the big chick up there. I would try and get the other guys chicks. Lenny used to see me in a club and he'd say, "See that chick, I really like her." I'd follow her in the bathroom and tell her, "Hey, that guy out there, Lenny Bruce he really . . ." I'd try to fix a date up and get her to come home with us. I was sort of one of the guys, only I wasn't. I was always with them all the time. Even when they went to jobs, I went around with them and got loaded with them. That time I didn't use junk. Pot, pills, booze. All the other guys were using stuff—Lenny, Gary, Lynn Holiday, Joe, the four of them used junk. They would go in the bathroom, and I used to wonder, "What are they doing in there for so long?" Then they would act real strange. Finally, they'd talk about it, and I got the idea. I got mad! I wanted to do it too! Wanted to do everything they wanted to do. When I first met Joe, I said, "I want to do everything you do and go everywhere you go." He said, "Can you shoot pool, baby?"

Sandra ended up shooting everything in sight, including her happiness, health, and sanity.

Once Joe and Lenny got into the swing of things, they had a different scam going every day. They both loved boosting. Lenny used to say that Joe had frostbitten armpits from stealing steaks in supermarkets. Joe just couldn't keep his hands off good food. He'd called up the Gellers and say, "Hey, I got this chicken and no place to cook it. Could I come up?" He was also deadly in drugstores. He'd come out to the car, empty his pockets, and get Lenny so turned on that they'd have to drive to another drugstore so Lenny could outdo Joe at stealing. Once they boosted a lot of lumber out of a yard. Sometimes, though, the thefts were more practical, like the time one of the guys got the clap.

They decided to visit Dr. Zucchini, on Highland Avenue, who was the bennie doctor. You'd go to him and say you had to go on a diet. For five dollars, he would give you a big box of old-fashioned bennies with crosses on them. On this visit, while the doctor was shooting the patient full of penicillin, Lenny was poking around in the physician's pharmaceutical refrigerator. Suddenly, he spotted a bottle labeled "methamphetamine hydrochloride." *Ding!* Just the day before, he had been reading an article in the paper about Bela Lugosi—how he had been hooked on this very same drug! It was too great a chance to pass up. Imagine! Shooting the same shit that made Lugosi such a freak. It was like sucking the vampire's blood! Lenny practically flew the car home in his eagerness to get this strange new drug out of the bottle and into his veins.

Late in '55, as Honey's pregnancy came to term, the whole drug scene began to get Lenny and Honey uptight. She was clean at the time, just taking a few tranquilizers and sleeping pills; yet the anxiety about giving birth to an addicted baby hovered over what was otherwise a happy time. Honey was always a big, strong, healthy woman, and except for a tendency to gain too much weight, her pregnancy had run a perfectly normal course. Lenny took off from work a couple of weeks before the estimated time, and their apartment began to fill with all sorts of new gadgets and bits of furniture for the baby. Richey Shackleton had suggested that if it was a girl, it be named Brandie Kathleen. Lenny objected that these sounded like strippper names. Nevertheless, when Kitty was born, those were the names that were typed upon the birth certificate. It wasn't until after the divorce that Lenny changed the first name to remove the hated connotations.

On November 7, 1955, Kitty was born at Cedars of Lebanon Hospital, after a labor of sixteen hours. She weighed five pounds, nine ounces and was absolutely normal. The moment Honey got the baby home, Lenny started taking over as if he were the mother. He diapered Kitty a dozen times a day. He suddenly became a clock watcher, yelling out in the middle of a phone conversation: "Honey! The baby has to go to sleep now, four o'clock!" When it was time for a feeding, this crazy junkie—who would cold-cook his stuff in a syringe and shoot it into his ass or leg right through his trousers—would suddenly become a fanatic about sterilization. "Not those bottles, Honey! These bottles! Those aren't sterilized enough. The temperature has to be exactly what the doctor said!'' Lenny read all the baby books. He read Dr. Spock. No man could have taken his paternal responsibilities more seriously. Honey was delighted by the way Lenny responded. She had wondered if his fear of having children, his jealousy and possessiveness, might make problems after the baby was born. Nothing of the kind ever revealed itself. Lenny Bruce was a model father.

Indeed, this whole period of his life seemed to be passing under the sign of paterfamilias. Lenny had gradually brought together a large extended family, among whom he was not only the oldest and brightest, but the most concerned for the welfare of the group. He wanted to help everybody and hire everybody, so they could always be together. As the idea of ''the group'' began to work its way to the forefront of his mind, he started combing the city for some club where they could all work—Honey, Sally, Tony, Joe, Jack, the Gellers, and even Sandra. None of the regular clubs would hire such a crew; but, he reasoned, there might be some offbeat place, some dark joint without a show, that could be conned into adopting an entertainment policy. That was how Lenny met Rocky.

Rocky Lo Fusello was an authentic tough guy, a retired sixty-year-old pharmacist from Chicago, who was soon to glory in the fact that his bust-out joint, Duffy's Gayeties, was the most infamous spot in the hucklebuck district west of Vine that was Los Angeles's equivalent to Times Square. A legion of scam artists and hustlers, pimps and whores, thieves and pushers from all over the country had settled in this area, intent on profiting from the booming economy and the endless stream of suckers that was pouring into Southern California. Sherman the Shutter was typical of the breed. He had one of those big old-fashioned tripod cameras with a hood and a shutter that made a loud click. He would catch a mark in his lens, swiftly rap him into nine poses in two minutes, separate him from as much buck as the traffic would bear, and then blow him off with a form card on which the victim would carefully print his address. In all the years he worked that district, Sherman never bought a roll of film.

Scams of this kind were just side-shows for the main attraction— the meat market. There were pros, semi-pros, and notch-joint veterans working through cabbies and bartenders; but L.A. is the land of the automobile and the telephone: the typical hooker was a call girl whose pimp was Ma Bell. The turnover among these working girls was prodigious because every week brought a fresh crop of hopeful naïfs who had come to Hollywood to be ''discovered.'' A month of carhopping or waiting on tables put them in the perfect frame of mind for a turnout. In fact, many of them hit the turf on their first day in town.

Greyhound had recently built a new terminal on Vine, and it

harbored a chrome-and-plastic gin mill called the DeVine Room. This was the hangout for some of the coldest pimps who ever stepped into a pair of alligators. A sharp mack would always have a swift old lady to help him keep his stable full, and they would both be togged out like fashion models. A bus would pull in from way down yonder and out would step Miss Sugar Beet, who had been the leading lady in the class play. "Hi there!" the pimp would greet her with a dazzling smile. "We're from Starlit House. You must be Miss Knish. The director asked me to . . ." When it turned out that there had been a mistake, Miss Sugar Beet would get a ride in a Cadillac not much shorter than the bus—a ride that would take her straight into the life.

Late at night, when the hustlers figured it was time to hang it up and get loose, their favorite resort was Duffy's—but that was only after Lenny Bruce had brought his gang into the place and transformed it into the craziest club in America. When Lenny first met Rocky, he appeared to be just another short, squat, cliché Italian, with a pinky ring, a guinea stinker, and white socks. Though he was a secret worshipper of the hoodlum cult, he looked like any old padrone going around before opening time gloating over his white linen tables and his drippy candles stuck in wine bottles and his corny wall paintings of the Grotta Azzurra and the bay at Capri. That's all there was to Duffy's Gaieties the night Lenny walked in there off Cahuenga Boulevard and stood at the little elevated bar in the front and ordered a Coke and looked down through the hole in the wall behind the cash register into the dining room, up the stairs onto the raised terrace, and then around to the side wall where he pinned a solid, practical-looking stage. That stage gave Lenny ideas, and when he dug the joint wasn't doing business, he struck up a conversation with the boss and told him he was an entertainer. "You oughta get a show in here," he urged, "get yourself some girls, a good band, and a comic. That's what people want out here—girls, laughs, some good sounds. Nobody goes out to eat in L.A."

Rocky listened and he thought and he talked it over with his wife, that blowzy peroxide blonde who sounded like a Ronzoni commercial. Rocky even tried to use his brains. He drove out to the Cobblestone, ordered a whisky at the bar, and watched Lenny work. Rocky had the real southern Italian sense of humor: he loved stories about pissing, shitting, and insulting people with long complicated curses about their anatomy and their ancestors. So when Lenny introduced the first stripper with one of his typical put-ons—"Now, Rita Ginch! Whoops! Has she shaved yet? Oh, she'll be right out, folks, soon as she finishes with her customer!"—Rocky started guffawing and hacking and doubling over at the bar as if he were having a bad asthma attack. This fuckin' little Jew boy was *funny*! He was O.K., this kid. He'd do business. Rocky just knew he'd do business.

So the pact with the devil was drawn and sealed with a glass of Bardolino. Lenny would come into the club on New Year's Eve, and start Duffy's Gaieties off on a new entertainment policy for the year 1956. They would have a band and strippers and a singer—and Lenny would be the boss over all the entertainment. He would hire the talent, tell them how to work, and be a boss. O.K.? Solid, Rocky!

Now Lenny really goes into overdrive. Sitting there at the phone by the bed, he starts lining up everybody in the Family. They're gonna have the greatest little club in the business. First of all, they'll have a dynamite jazz band. Joe Maini will be the leader and Lorraine Geller the piano player and Gary Fromer the drummer. Right away, though, they hit a snag. Joe says that he can't swing in a band that doesn't have a bass player. That three-piece shit is bad enough when you're playing honky-tonk for strippers. But if they're gonna swing and really blow some jazz, they gotta have the fuckin' bass, the foundation of the whole fuckin' band! So Lenny goes back to Rocky and gets him up front by the bar one afternoon and starts explaining to him that the sound would be so much richer and fuller-bodied with a bass instrument—just like when you cook the sauce! You could put in fewer ingredients, right?—make a thin, cheap sauce. Or you could cook rich! Make a real honest-to-God sauce that's a pleasure to take in your mouth! Understand? So Rocky says O.K., let's have the bass and do things right. It should be a rich sound. But then Joe makes a face when Lenny tells him it's a quartet because that's a dumb scene—three rhythm and only one solo horn. All bop bands have five pieces, man, you know that? Charlie Parker never worked with any dumb four-piece band. There has to be a trumpet to play off against the alto and get the interplay like Bird got with Miles or Red or Fats on all those dates Joe caught in New York back in '49 and '50. Five pieces is the classic combo—so why shouldn't they have five pieces at this new joint? Especially since they have Jack Sheldon, the coolest little trumpet since Chet Baker! So Lenny has to go back again to Rocky, to the heavy, hairy arms, the gray matted chest, the guinea stinker in the mouth, and that dumb corrugated face staring into his face as he tries to explain that no musician can blow so long by himself without a relief man. There has to be a relief man. Like Rocky is relief man at the bar, right? Like the bartender has to take a piss or make a phone call or —God forbid!—he gets sick! Rocky steps in and makes the gin 'n' tonics. So Joe, this Italian fella, who's the leader of the band? He has to have a trumpet relief man. You unnerstan'? Yeah, Rocky understands— but this whole fuckin' deal is startin' in to cost a lotta money. He's gonna say *yes*—but these guys better produce! You unnerstan'! If they don't produce—out the fuck they go and he puts a jukebox in the joint!

So Lenny broke up on the phone that night telling Joe how he conned this ape into letting them have an extra man. Now all he needs are the strippers. Honey and Lenny make lists of broads they know. The important thing is to have a good feature girl. If two or three times a night some fantastic fuckin' piece of ass walks out on the stage—the strokers are happy. After all, what are they payin' the money for? To get it off, right? Now, what really excites these overcoats? Something *strange*! Some freaky fuckin' cuntological phenomenon that they can't imagine without seeing it right up there at arm's length. So who should they hire? Some fuckin' prop dancer with a stage bed that licks flames up her cunt? A snatch that works Fay Wray style with a gorilla? No, it shouldn't be theatrical. It should just be righteous natural fuckin' hot-box steam. That's what everybody wants. A chick like the Eiffel Tower girl. What's her name? Jeanine France. That's it! Those long legs! Those legs that just don't stop! Christ! What's hotter than a tall chick? That's what everybody whacks off to! Some chick who has a problem with stockings! Fantastically long legs that go up and up and up to snatch heaven! Beautiful! Get her on the phone! She'll give head to the whole band!

So the recruiting goes on. Lenny hires half a dozen bust-out chicks at eighty-five dollars a week. Girls that aren't even dancers: they're just broads that flash onstage and go back to the bar and mix with the customers. He hires Sally as second banana. Honey he doesn't want stripping after the baby, so she will be the singer. Even Tony can work at the club. He's studying to be a hairbender during the day? O.K. This will be his night job. He can work behind the bar or show people to their seats. That's it—the whole Family will be together, play together, have happiness together. No more orphans when Lenny Bruce is boss!

Now, the important thing is that they shouldn't just go in there and do the usual dumb things. Go through the usual routines and bore the shit out of everybody. This is a new club, a new gig; they should have all new material. Lenny should write some great new bits and rehearse the cats in his pad and really get the show together before they even go in the club. So that was the scene during the month of December. Lenny and Honey moved into a brand-new, white-walled apartment building on Cahuenga Boulevard, just a few blocks from the club. They rehearsed every afternoon with the cats. Lenny started writing his ass off. Every day, he would get out of that bed, see that the baby had its bottle. Then when Brandie was sleeping in her crib,

Lenny sat down at the kitchenette table and started to write acts. Sit there with a stubby pencil and talk to himself and scratch out the greatest shit you ever saw. Whole fuckin' routines, right off the top. What a creative wig he got on at this time! It wasn't junk—though he shot plenty of that! It wasn't happiness—though he was very happy with the baby and Honey. It was just having some place to put his ideas. Being able to sit down and think: "Now Joe will say this line and Honey will do this bit." It was the *reality* of their whole situation that turned him on and made him so fuckin' creative. When you could see where the stuff would go, you could really settle down and write. Then when the cats got up, maybe about five in the afternoon, they would all come over to the pad and rehearse.

Since the whole crew was on junk, Lenny's bits all took the line of inside dope jokes, at that time a virtually unheard-of form of humor. He wrote a takeoff on *Man with the Golden Arm* that featured himself and Joe Maini. He did another bit about a jazz musician called Karl Spansule, who spoke nothing but the purest, coolest jive talk—to the point of utter incomprehensibility. Yet another dope bit was about a kid caught smoking pot in the bathroom. After he throws the joint away, he wonders how he'll get high. From afar comes the immortal answer: *"Smoke the toilet!"*

By opening night, Lenny is in a frenzy of activity. Reaching that manic state that always precedes his most bizarre outbursts, he races around the club, skating on the sawdust-strewn floor, fluttering the red-and-silver paper decorations, barking orders right and left. Cracking all sorts of hysterical jokes, he's building up a head of steam that signals—*look out!* When the freaky musicians meet the freaky girls in the dressing room, they go right into their freaky scenes. Suddenly, just as the first customers are starting to arrive, Rocky comes yelling through the club.

"Lenny! Lenny! Lenny!"

"What is it, Rocky?" Lenny gasps, suddenly serious.

"Whadkinda queers you bring in my club?" explodes Rocky, hurling his arms up to the ceiling and then turning to gesture frantically toward the dressing room. "I come inna room—and dere's dah star! The star ahdah show! This beautiful girl down on her knees widah drummer's cock in her moud!"

Lenny breaks up! "That's show business, Rocky!" he quips in his cheeriest nasality, as he resumes his obsessive preparations for opening night.

The joint is starting to fill up now, and the band is out onstage, Joe Maini with his strap around his neck blowing Horace Silver's "Doodlin'." Then, they suddenly break off and blow a fanfare. Bright lights go up onstage, and from the red double curtains on the right comes the M.C.—"Ladies and gentlemen, Lenny Bruce!"—a nice-looking young guy with his hair slicked back and wearing a drab understated tux. He screws the mike off the stand and starts to talk and smile about the new movies and how many of them deal with the theme of narcotics—and "where can we get some?" Ha, ha! That was a little joke, he threw in. Now, they're doing a pantomime, a couple of musicians and Honey, of *Man with the Golden Arm,* while Lenny stands off to one side with the mike in his hand narrating the action as it unfolds. The Italian guy with the long nose, the leader, he's funny, and so is the trumpet player, with the faces they make and the funny postures they get into with the needle and the stuff and the cops and the whole big crisis they hit in the bathroom. It's a very funny little skit, and the people are applauding while the M.C. is laughing and dismissing the hand and talking on to the next bit and the next—it's really a good show and it's going great! Meanwhile, the hour is getting later, and Honey is standing out under the lights in a sumptuous low-cut white gown—her figure is back again!—and she's opening those big painted chops of hers and singing "Granada." Joe is playing and conducting over his shoulder. He's cool, only his eyes look like they're gonna close at any minute. Then Lenny is back and he's gonna sing, and there he is into "How Are Things in Glocca Morra?" Well, he's not a great singer, but he's a nice-looking, funny guy.

Now there's some kinda huddle on the bandstand, and Lenny is real excited, breathless like, and he's making an announcement—he's calling for Rocky from the bar. He's explaining to the people what a wonderful guy is the owner of this club and how he put in a whole new show just to make everybody happy and now the band has this special song they wrote for the occasion, it's what they call a blues, and it was written specially by the leader, *The Wonderful Joe Maini!* —ha-ha—that's the kinda stuff they always say but still he is wonderful—whatever that means—and now the blues he wrote special for Rocky, titled "Dago Balls." The whole band stands up and they start to play-sing this tune, with Lenny conducting:

> There are tennis balls and there are basketballs,
> There are knitting balls and there are Christmas balls,
> But of all balls the best balls of all—are *Dago balls!*

Rocky is standing behind his bar staring down at the stage, and when the boys hit the punch line, he goes into such an uncontrollable fit of laughing-coughing that everybody thinks he'll die on the spot!

No sooner has he recovered and begun to load his waitresses' trays, than he sees the sight that does put him into an ambulance. At the stroke of midnight, with everybody out of his mind with excitement—throwing confetti, blowing goofy horns and kissing, kissing, kissing—Lenny Bruce comes clomping out onstage. He's *naked*—except for the mink stole around his neck and the silk stockings rolled down around his ankles which are wobbling badly as he tries to walk in Lorraine's high heels. With his cock jiggling between his legs like the tip of a fox stole, he stumbles hysterically to the mike, screams WHOOPEE! and stumbles back offstage—to a tumultuous round of applause!

Meanwhile, Rocky takes one look at Lenny's Jewish balls, and he bursts into a renewed fit of laughing and coughing that soon has him desperately beating the air and gasping for breath. Somebody picks up a phone and calls for an ambulance. In no time, the street is filled with the sound of sirens. The white-jacketed medical team rush into the bar, grab Rocky under either arm, and carry him out of the club. In the back of the ambulance, they administer oxygen, still his racing heart, and finally release him to return to the club—the soberest bartender in Los Angeles that New Year's Eve.

Life at Duffy's wasn't always so frantic, but there was something in the licentious atmosphere of the club that encouraged strange outbursts. One night Lenny found himself being heckled by a drunken woman, who was later identified as the mother of a famous movie star. With the encouragement of the audience, he coaxed the woman up onstage and began his counterattack by insisting that her voluptuous figure was padded. She answered proudly that her body was better than any of the strippers' on the bill. "Then go on, dear," Lenny urged, "take off your dress and show us!" Without waiting to be asked twice, she started taking off her clothes and didn't stop until she was naked except for her underpants. She wasn't jiving, as it turned out —her figure was dynamite! Lenny began singing the opening notes of "Night Train." As the woman began to sway her hips and go into a strip routine, Lenny seized her clumsily and began doing a raunchy dance. Between steps, he tore off his jacket, tie, shirt and was going for his pants, when the two stumbled and fell, rolling across the stage. The audience gave them both a big hand.

Another night, Honey starred in a scene that nearly ended Joe Maini's playing career. Honey, drinking heavily, had gotten very angry with Jack Sheldon. Sitting back in the dressing room, while Sheldon and the boys were onstage, she decided that she was going to have it out with Jack, once and for all. Just then, she heard voices approaching through the double set of drapes that covered the dressing-room entrance. She made sure that Jack Sheldon was the one who was loudest, the one who was leading the others offstage and into the dressing room. Overcome by a sudden surge of uncontrollable rage, she seized a quart whisky bottle off the counter and swung it with all her might at the figure ducking through the drapes. *Crash!* went the bottle on the head of—*Joe Maini!* Honey had goofed. Poor Joe! He was dazed, hurt, bleeding—and *confused!* "What did I do?" he cried. "What did I do?" She couldn't stand the look of woe on his face. Again, she felt that rush of emotion and started screaming bloody murder. Lenny came running. Taking one look at the shambles in the dressing room—the bleeding Maini and his hysterical wife—Lenny seized Honey by the hair and dragged her by brute force right out of the room and into the club, where he threw her into a chair and started slapping her face. The punch line to the story was typical of Joe. After complaining of nothing more serious than the spots of blood that had stained his instrument strap, he turned up next night with a maroon-colored strap. Too poor to buy a new one, he had gotten his mother to dip his old strap in red dye.

     The action at Duffy's was so wild that it could never be contained in words or restricted to the stage. It kept spilling over in every direction, sometimes implicating the whole city. Like that Saturday night when Lenny did his put-on of *Rocket to Stardom*. A late-night TV amateur contest sandwiched between old movies, the show was watched by every junkie and hipster in L.A., who found it hysterical. Sponsored by Bob Yaekel, a local Oldsmobile dealer, it was hosted by his sister-in-law Betty Yaekel, one of those klutzy broads with the platform shoes and lipstick on her teeth, always bubbling, bubbling, bubbling—until you're tempted to take a gun and shoot out her lights. Lenny was stimulated to perverse intensities by this really stupid program, always taking it off from the stage of Duffy's. He loved to imitate Bob Yaekel's hostile raps about cars with viewers who called in:

What are you driving around now? . . . '36 Terraplane? They're real bombs, those cars, aren't they? Good roadability, but when they turn over, they really stay there. You ought to trade that in on a new Olds . . . Well, let's see—how about six dollars? . . . Well, same to you, fella! . . . Thank you, sweetheart! Same to your mommy, too! Yes, and I bet you could take eight inches. Thanksalot, sir! And to your church, too! . . . Yes, yes, and a schvartzer up you, too!

One night Lenny alerted everybody at Duffy's, plus a score of friends watching in his apartment. Then, taking along Jack Sheldon to aid him in the adventure, he went down to the studio to appear on camera.

What every cacked-out Saturday-night loafer in L.A. spied from his easy chair or bed was, first, the spectacle of Lenny Bruce and Jack Sheldon being introduced as Herb Geller and Jerry Mandel (a well-known jazz pianist); then, the equally startling appearance of these two: Jack in a sweat suit suitable for jogging the mile and holding his trumpet, and Lenny, a maniacal speed-freak's grin on his face, decked out in a zoot suit that must have come out of the attic of some aging Lockheed worker who last donned its vast lapels and pagoda shoulders in 1944. Asked what they wanted to do, Lenny announced he would sing and "Herb" would accompany him, the tune being "Lonesome Road."

"Look down, look down that lonesome road," began Lenny, deliberately singing off key. Sheldon followed him wth some terribly blatted and broken arpeggios.

"Look, Mac," said Lenny, stopping in mid-chorus and glaring at Sheldon, "can't you get my key?"

Mrs. Yaekel walked on camera, offering to help them resolve their dilemma.

"Get away from here, dopey," Lenny snapped, pushing her aside.

"Look down, look down that lonesome road," Lenny resumed, even more out of tune than before.

The infuriated Mrs. Yaekel, realizing that she was being put on, returned to camera range and gave the signal for the hook.

Lenny refused to leave. "Look here, dummy," he snarled at Mrs. Yaekel. "Go away!"

Three ushers finally gave the boys the bum's rush, and the fun ended with Lenny and Jack racing up the aisle of the studio screaming, *"H. J. Caruso is innocent!"*—a reference to a used-car dealer who had just made headlines.

Not content with blowing Mrs. Yaekel's mind on camera, Lenny had arranged for all his friends to dial the program's vote-casting number and vote for the team who sang "Lonesome Road." The calls came pouring in with such volume that Mrs. Yaekel was reduced virtually to tears. "I can't understand why anyone would want to do this to me," she lamented. "I have always kept the door open to young talent on *Rocket to Stardom!*"

The put-on was always one of Lenny's favorite tricks, and the best medium for it was the telephone. By the time he reached Duffy's, Lenny had reached the point where he was willing to bring all of his secret games right out in the open for the general audience. Night after night, he would appear onstage with a telephone in his hand attached to a long cord. Dialing up some rival club, he would engage in long and elaborate dialogue with the owner, the maître d', or whoever was willing to talk to him. He loved to call Ciro's.

Hello? Is this Ciro's? Yeah? Well, we're from out of town. It's our last night in Los Angeles. The Andersons from Cedar Rapids told us to be sure and stop in and see your show. But me and the wife have only $1.75. Would that be enough, do you think?
. . .
Well, suppose I stand up at the bar and let Minnie, that's my wife, sit down and order some coffee?
. . . .
Well, wait a minute! Would it be all right if I came in the doorway and let Minnie sit in the car? Then I could tell her later all about the show.

Before the exasperated maître d' could answer, Lenny would bang down the phone and the whole club would erupt in laughter.

Crazy as the show was onstage or in the club—where there were often police raids and fistfights and bottles crashing off upturned tables—it was nothing to the scenes in the dressing rooms. Philly Joe Jones—who took over the drumming chores after Lawrence Marable got so bombed he spent one whole night prostrate on the stage working the drum pedal with his hands—recalls Lenny racing around during the show like a demonic little Puck. As Philly Joe, a figure of sardonic elegance behind his drum set, swung through the tricky bebop jazz numbers called by Joe Maini, he'd suddenly hear Lenny's voice buzzing at his ear like the tongue of the serpent. "Listen, man, when you finish this set come straight back in the dressing room—*and have your cock out!* If you can make it hard, great! But have it out when you come through the door!" "Lenny!" Philly Joe would murmur, cracking a big toothy grin, "I can't do something like that!" But when the last *ker-plunk* had sounded from his drums, he'd be advancing on the dressing room with his fly unzipped. Whipping out his shlong, he'd stand breathless before the maroon drapes. Then he'd enter the dressing room in precisely the condition Lenny desired. There before him is a sight to make a man ship over. A big naked stripper is kneeling in the middle of the floor, a bandage over her eyes, her hands bound behind her back, her mouth wide open, waiting to receive the first cock that comes through the door. As Philly Joe dips his wick, he hears Lenny giggling hysterically in the closet.

The closet got to be one of the favorite settings for Lenny's humor. As he plunged deeper and deeper into his schmutz bag, his humor took on a voyeuristic cast. Typically, he'd pin some member of the audience whom he knew and identify the man by name. Then he'd take the audience into his confidence by telling them how he had fucked the man's wife. Just as he was getting into the broad, the husband had come home. Lenny had run to the closet, which he described with hallucinatory vividness. "It must have happened!" everyone began to reflect, as he went into the most minute detail about what it feels like to be standing among the clothes, feeling the roughness of their textures on your cheek and the odors and sweat and grease in your nose. Meanwhile, your heart and breathing have been virtually suspended as you listen to the muffled voices on the other side of the door. Invariably, he would throw in a lot of crazy puns about being a "closet queen." Then he would burst out of the closet and do something insane before the husband—like jumping on the bureau and taking a shit in the pin tray! The punch line would be the husband calling Lenny some name that had never been heard before on a public stage.

When the last show ended, around 2 A.M., and the broken bottles had been swept up and the old strokers and lonesome Lockheed workers had been cleared out of the club, Rocky liked to treat his employees and regular customers to a "feast." Everybody would scarf to a bust-out on stuffed mushrooms, clams casino, and chicken cacciatore. Then, about 3 A.M., the whole gang would tumble out on Cahuenga, pile into a couple of cars, and take off for the Gellers' pad. If Lenny and Honey were planning to make the party that night, they'd have Kitty in a car crib which they loaded in the back of their old Cadillac. Zooming up the hills and around the curves and finally into the house's driveway, they would be getting high in their minds before they actually sank the spike in their arms.

The party wasn't long in beginning. Joe would have convinced a couple of the "new" girls that they should come along. Honey would be put to work convincing them that there was nothing wrong with getting naked and making it with the boys, who were really nice guys and had been a little too shy at first to invite them to the parties. The cool sounds would be playing on the box, the spike would be circulating from one cat to another, the bedroom door would be opening and closing, offering glimpses of chicks squatting over guys or guys with their heads buried in girls' bushes.

Lenny and Joe were always the instigators and stars of the freak parties. They were the first to get naked and the ones who thought up all the crazy orgy scenes. "Lenny was a devil," Joe mused just before his death. "He was really into fucking people. Girls would never think for a moment that they would do anything to anybody, and he would have them on the floor fucking ten guys. He had a magic to him." Joe wasn't any slouch himself. He had picked up on Lenny's exhibitionism, and at least once at every party, he would have to run through the whole house naked. He also got into the habit of using his cock as a comedy prop. Even when he was on the stand, he was always looking for a chance to sneak it out. When he worked with the Terry Gibbs band, he'd have to stand up and turn around to give the band the downbeat at the end of Terry's vibraphone cadenza. While old hard-trying Terry would be bent over the silver bars malleting his brains out, Joe would ease his long dong over the edge of his low-slung hipster trousers. Then he would turn to the band, one hand raised dramatically in the air, the other holding his horn, his head twisted clear around to watch the flying sticks—and the whole band would double over in convulsions of laughter as they caught sight of Joe's cock head peeking over his belt like a baby kangaroo from its pouch.

Probably the greatest of all Joe's public airings of his bird was the time he was asked to do a publicity picture for Selmer saxes. Posed dramatically by the photographer with his mighty horn gleaming out of the deep portrait shadows, Joe took advantage of the murky lighting to slip out his tool and lay it in the bell of the instrument. Amazingly, the picture was taken, processed, laid out, and printed in all the jazz magazines without anyone ever noticing the strange wormlike object sneaking into the horn. The jazz cats saw it though—and it killed them! They pinned it up in bandrooms, pasted it inside instrument cases. That picture became one of the greatest inside jokes in the history of the business.

Joe and Lenny could never take sex seriously. They loved to ball but they loved to play even more. Lenny was going after ginch night after night, but he could never resist the temptation of the bizarre. One night, Herb Geller recalls, he picked up the gang in front of Duffy's; as soon as Joe and Lenny got into the car, they began telling him of the great party they planned for that evening up at the house. "We got a great old lady," they enthused; "she's really a great old score." Herb drove them up the hill, and when he came in the house after parking the car—sure enough—he found the old lady sitting in a chair completely naked. She was an old, old lady with glasses. She was very sophisticated, smoking with a long cigarette holder and drinking out of a martini glass. Naked, she was talking about politics and movie stars. There was nothing vulgar about her appearance, and no one sought to take advantage of her. It was just another of Lenny's fantasies, and this old girl had made it come true.

Nudity was not usually such a decorous condition at the Gellers'. It was the strip-down before you swung into action. The swinging scene has in recent years received a thick coat of whitewash from the Love Generation. The orgy—pronounced in California with a hard *g*—has been billed as a pagan love feast, a celebration of nature, or a pledge of communal solidarity. As those who have tried it can testify, it is often a trigger for the most violent forms of sexual insanity. Many a swinger has found himself turning to stone as some crazy chick dances over his recumbent body brandishing a butcher knife or threatening to plunge out a window. Lenny and Joe had their share of psycho-style orgies.

One night they brought a chick up to the house who got in bed with Lenny, Joe, and Sandra; then she decided that all she really wanted was Sandra. "Get out of here, you two guys!" she yelled as she slammed the door on the retreating boys. That closed door had a sinister effect on Joe. It transformed him instantly from the lovable guy you normally saw—so loose, so tolerant, so everything-goes—into the guinea hitter whose pride has been stung. He threw his shoulder into the door and sprung it open. Then he pulled Sandra out of the bed and began beating her unmercifully. She ran screaming into the bathroom, slammed and locked the door, and began cutting her wrists—describing the whole process through the locked door. Again Joe threw himself against the door, and again it sprang open to reveal a disheveled and bloody Sandra standing there with a razor in her hand. At this point, the other chick got off a line that for years afterward was a favorite among the boys. Looking at the battered doors, the bloody Sandra, and the maniacal Joe, she cried, "This is more than I bargained for!" Next night, when he stepped on the stand, Joe described the whole incident to Herb Geller in these telegraphic words: "Man, last night we had the greatest sex, dope, and suicide orgy."

Honey's line with the girls at the parties was that she couldn't participate because she had just had a baby. But, she claimed, she got her kicks by watching, and she knew if the situation were reversed, blah, blah, blah. One big, tall girl who often turned up at the parties had the same scam going for her that Honey was practicing on the other chicks. She was a bisexual nymph crazy to get Honey into the sack. Every time she would come to a party, she would work on Honey, bringing first one guy and then another—all different types—a big basketball stud or a groovy-looking Tony Curtis–style actor. She was trying everything to make Honey bend. Finally, one night, Honey said, "O.K., just this one time."

The four of them got into bed and started swapping. Lying there in the half-light, giving head to this strange cat, Honey could see Lenny's face as he was giving his dick to the other chick—*and the expression on his face was identical with the one he got when they were making love!* Suddenly inflamed with rage, Honey leaped out of bed, grabbed a stiletto-heeled slipper, and began wildly beating all of them.

Cursing and slugging and hollering, she drove them all out of the apartment and ended the parties forever.

That little scene was the beginning of the end for Lenny and Honey. Both of them had always been terribly jealous of the other. Neither of them had ever fully accepted the swinging scene. Lenny wanted to fuck and suck and freak out at orgies, while Honey sat there pimping off the chicks for him. He was crazy as hell! Honey thought she could detach herself from the scene because Lenny was in love with her and she had his baby. She wasn't being honest either. If the problem had simply been one of sexual promiscuity, they might have solved it. What was really fatal to their relationship was not so much their mutual infidelities as their complementary histories of discord and divorce. Each had grown up in a home where husband and wife were constantly fighting, splitting, reuniting, and then repeating the whole process over again. Arguments, shouts, screams, blows, slammed doors, revved-up motors, disappearing cars constituted their emotional heredity.

The other thing that was against them was the history of their own relationship. They had quarreled and split up so many times that divorce—on a temporary if not a permanent basis—had become part of their marriage. They were impulse spouses. They had to be love birds or shrikes. There was no emotional middle ground. In sentimental moments in later years, both Lenny and Honey would look back at some period of their marriage and pine for its warmth. Lenny was particularly adroit at editing the past into pretty pronged-heart valentines. The truth was that there had always been something unreal, something fantastic and insubstantial about this marriage between a wide-eyed, baby-cheeked, momma's boy and a tough, experienced, and emotionally explosive strip queen. "Shitty Honey" was the phrase Lenny used for his beloved when she turned tough and goyish, when she started cursing like a whore, throwing dishes like a virago, grabbing guys—and girls—like a tramp. "Shitty Honey" was what aroused his deep Jewish contempt. To love someone as much as Lenny loved Honey, and to hate that person as profoundly as he sometimes hated her, proclaims an ambivalence, a fundamental emotional confusion that can probably never be resolved but must always be acted out in devastating psychodramas that exhaust the spirit and fill it eventually with emptiness and bitterness.

Dope broke the back of this already moribund marriage. The dope honeymoon ended, in fact, almost at the same moment as the sex honeymoon. In February 1956, Lenny began to turn yellow and sickly.

He was weak as a cat and virtually unable to work. The doctor took one look at him and diagnosed hepatitis. Confined to the West Los Angeles Veterans Hospital, Lenny began to sober up and take stock of the situation. He had been on a tremendous emotional bender ever since the birth of the baby. It was one of the deepest patterns of his life. He would go up like a rocket and then drop down like a stick. Now he was deeply depressed. Honey never came to visit him. When Frankie Ray, a friend of Sally's, came to sit with him, he told stories of going into the little apartment on Cahuenga and finding the baby neglected and sopping wet. Honey was becoming a fuck-off mother. When she finally turned up one afternoon, Lenny warned her sternly against drugs: "You'll end up lying here, just like me," he admonished, assuming the moralistic tone he had inherited from his father. Honey was embarrassed. She had just scored across the street from the hospital. "Why should I stop just because it makes *you* sick?" she argued. "If it don't make *me* sick, why should I stop using it?" Lenny brought up the child, reminding her of her maternal responsibilities, warning about the possibility of divorce. Bombarding her with arguments, he drove her from the room. She didn't come back again.

Released after less than a month in bed, still feeling weak and woozy, Lenny came back to the apartment on Cahuenga. What he discovered there disturbed him deeply. Honey had been running for weeks with Joe Maini and Jack Sheldon. She had built up a nice little oil burner of a habit. Increasingly indifferent to the baby, she neglected the routine Lenny had established for Kitty's care. When he reproached her and insisted she kick, Honey flew into a rage and counterattacked. "It's your fault I'm using this damn stuff to begin with!" she cried. "You shouldn't have turned me on in the first place!" Lenny was horrified by Honey's accusation. Vainly, he struggled to deny it. What had he done? Why couldn't she be just a social user? Why did she have to get strung out? Honey countered with more arguments. She blamed Lenny for all the freaky sex scenes into which he had inveigled her. Those parties were disgusting. They were perverted. What a hypocrite he was, demanding that she be straight while he wallowed in filth. Whatever happened was all *his* fault!

Day after day, the arguments flamed up and subsided. One night backstage at Duffy's, they had a terrible row. Honey had invited some of her friends back to the apartment after the show. She hadn't asked Lenny, and he wanted to be alone. He was still sick and weak. Honey refused to call off her friends. Lenny sank into a deep sulk. Later that night, after Honey had left the club, he took his revenge. He came onstage and began distributing little slips of paper bearing his home address. "You people are such a wonderful audience," he said, with mock solemnity. "Listen, my wife and I are having a little party after the show. You're all invited!"

Nearly two hundred strangers turned up for the promised party. Finding no place to park, they drove up on the front lawn, slicing deep ruts in the soggy turf. Once they entered the flat, they ran head-on into a frantic red-headed woman, screaming and shoving, trying to drive the people out of the room. "Who are you?" she shouted, in a menacing voice. "Get the hell out of here!" Watching the scene quietly from the sidelines, Lenny sniggered like Vinnie the gangster.

On the afternoon of March 8, 1956, Tony Viscarra got a call from Lenny. Would he come over and help Lenny move all his stuff out of the apartment? Honey and he were breaking up for good. Arriving shortly afterward with Sally, Tony found Lenny alone in the torn-up apartment. They loaded the boxes and bags into the car. When Tony returned for the last time, he found Lenny seated on a carton laboriously lettering a message in red lipstick on the new white wall.

IS THE PERSON WHO GIVES YOU YOUR FIRST DRINK
RESPONSIBLE FOR MAKING YOU AN ALCOHOLIC?

The next day, Lenny filed for divorce, alleging mental and physical suffering and humiliation. He sought permanent custody of Kitty, who was then four months old.

In mid-June, Lenny left the country to fulfill a six-week engagement at the Orchid Room in Honolulu, which had been postponed because of his hospitalization. Honey remained at home with Kitty. But only two days after checking into a Waikiki Beach motel, Lenny raced back to Los Angeles and went directly to his apartment. In an emotional scene, he threw himself sobbing at Honey's feet, swearing that he needed her and she needed him. He told her that his illness had left him too weak to endure the mental and physical strain of a separation. He pleaded with her to come with him to Hawaii, where they could not only be together but could find a way to get her off drugs. They were both crying as they agreed to reconcile. They flew back to Hawaii, taking Kitty along but leaving their stash behind them. When they checked into a suite at the Privateer Motel, they were fifteen hundred miles from their nearest pusher.

The original deal at the Orchid Room called for Honey to appear with Lenny. But when she failed to report on schedule, the owner, Tom Melody, booked another singer. In two days, however, Honey found a singing job eighteen miles away at the Pearl City Tavern in Pearl Harbor. Lenny insisted on supervising a rehearsal of the house band, a group called The Panamaniacs. But the bitterness between them surfaced once again while he was driving Honey back to the motel following the music rehearsal.

"I betcha I know which one of the five musicians you'd have eyes to ball," he said, trying to provoke her.

"Are you kidding?" Honey replied. "None of 'em are even as tall as me. I've hardly even looked at them."

An uneasy silence ensued.

"OH, YEAH?" Honey continued. "Which one?"

"The piano player," he answered, indifferently.

Honey remembers: "That night, when I went to work, I made it a point to take another look at the piano player. I had to see what could have put that swack in his mind." What she saw couldn't have been so bad because she shacked up with the guy till dawn in a secluded motel room that she paid for herself. Soon after she returned to her own room at the Privateer Motel, the telephone rang. A female voice, the wife of the piano player—who was not only married but the father of seven children—asked for Lenny. Honey could hear the screaming at the other end of the line: "Your wife kept my husband out until daybreak . . . He had lipstick all over his shirt."

"I was out of line completely," Honey admits. "But I wanted Lenny to tell me, 'You don't do those things. You don't stay out until six in the morning with one of the musicians.' But he didn't even say that. He said, 'Okay baby.' Didn't even complain. I found out I was doing stuff that I didn't even want to do, just to see how far I could go. I always just idolized Lenny. [Now] he wasn't my idol anymore."

Lenny hung up the receiver and went back to sleep without saying a word. He was disgusted with Honey. But he was still unable to act, even to express his anger. Probably he feared that a firm stand would make her walk. In any event, his goading prediction made earlier in the day had come true.

On the evening of June 30, 1956, their fifth day in Hawaii, Lenny stood under a bathroom shower, shaving with a safety razor. The steaming water coursed down his back as Honey, dressed in evening clothes, gathered up her belongings prior to leaving for the night's show at the Pearl City Tavern.

Among the sunglasses, lipstick, and mascara in her straw tote bag, she was surprised to find a tube of Sea and Ski suntan lotion. It seemed unusually light when she picked it up, as if there was nothing inside. Holding the plastic tube in front of a light bulb, she noted the outline of something that resembled toothpicks. The contents rattled when she shook the tube.

"Hey, baby," she shouted to Lenny. "Listen. There's something in here. Let me have your razor."

While Lenny watched, she sliced open the end of the tube with a razor blade, spread the plastic aside with her long fingernails, and discovered half a dozen sticks of marijuana.

"Wow!" she said. "How about that! Six joints! What do you think I should do with it?"

"Throw it away," Lenny advised.

"Why should I throw it away?" she snapped, remembering one of the musicians at the club who had been driving her back and forth to work. "Derek's been asking for some all week."

"Well, don't throw it away then," Lenny replied, perfunctorily.

Honey carefully extracted six joints from the tube, gently wrapped them in a Kleenex tissue, and laid the package inside her purse. She reminded Lenny to drop Kitty at the baby-sitter's house. Then she kissed him goodbye and left for work in a car supplied by the club and driven by the same guy, Derek Olwin, who had been trying to score for grass. He and Honey had been way down in the dives of downtown Honolulu—joints like the Swing Club, where they have arcades and tattoo parlors and cross-color bars—searching for a couple of reefers. Hawaii was so clean, they couldn't find a seed. Now she jumped in the car, all smiles, and crowed, "I've got us some weed!"

It was a dumb move. Just the night before, she had been rousted by the narcos. It was an experience that would have made anybody else run for the cellar. She had just driven into the parking lot of the Pearl City Tavern in Tom Melody's car, and four plainclothesmen had jumped out in front of the T-Bird, thrown open the doors, and started pulling her out while the car was still in motion! Right down to the police station they ran her, where a lady cop was waiting with a rubber glove on her hand to reach up her snatch and search her for stuff. What a going-over they gave her! Every pin curl had to be unrolled, every pore examined, not just her cunt but her asshole poked with hard, straight, accusing fingers. They didn't find a thing—but they did confiscate her address book. It was full of friends, club owners, baby-sitters, talent agents, merchants, and relatives. It also contained the name and number of an L.A. connection.

Next day, when she goes down to the federal building to pick up her confiscated book, she finds the head federal man sitting behind his desk going through her little book. "Well, Harriet," he says, "who's Joe Maini? Who's Sally Marr? Who's . . ." Finally, he pronounces the name of the connection. "Where do you know this party from?" he says real cool, as if it were just another name. "Well," Honey says, "when you work in a club, if somebody's a good customer, you take their name and phone number, and if you rework the club, you call and let him know you're opening there—because the more business you do for the club, the better it is for you." Snap! The guy shuts the book. Looks at her real stern and says, "You're a hard head! You're gonna end up doing five years!" Then he dismisses her.

Well, someone had it in for Honey, because that very afternoon an unidentified caller had phoned the Federal Narcotics Bureau office. This informant said: *"Harriet Bruce will be leaving the Privateer Motel at seven-thirty tonight. If you search her, she will be carrying marijuana cigarettes."*

That night, at seven-thirty sharp, Derek swings the car to the curb, Honey jumps in, chuckling about the grass, and they start down a one-way street heading for Kalakaua, the main road running out to Pearl Harbor. There's one stop sign before they reach the road, and just as they're slowing down, they notice two cars parked on either side of the intersection—facing in the wrong direction! Suddenly, the cars lunge forward to meet them, sandwiching them to a stop. As Honey stares in astonishment through the windshield, the doors of the two cars swing open, and there are the same federal men who tried to bust her the night before. "Oh, my God! That weed!" she flashes, as she stabs her hand down into her purse. "I'll take that, Harriet," purrs the narco, as he lays his hand, palm up, before her face.

Bail was high because they were not residents of Hawaii. Lenny raised $2,500 by pooling all their savings with an advance on his salary from the club. Fortunately, Tom Melody, an old comic, was a personal friend. Lenny consoled Honey by telling her that she wouldn't have to serve time; she would be allowed to go free on probation—*if they didn't break up!* The court and the judge, he assured her, weren't going to separate a happily married couple with a new baby just on account of six joints.

Nothing Lenny said or did, though, could stop the disintegration of their marriage. Three or four days later, Honey was going out with other guys and Lenny was on the verge of suicide. He moved out of the motel and into the Waikiki Biltmore. Locking himself in his room, he failed to make his scheduled appearance at the club. Tom Melody called Honey. "I don't know where he is," she answered. "He's not living here anymore. He's staying at the Biltmore."

For twenty-four hours Lenny locked himself in his room. Everybody went to the door—Tom Melody, the hotel manager, the house dick. They pleaded, they warned, they threatened. Finally, they tried to force the door, but he had it bolted and barricaded. He wouldn't answer, but they knew he was alive in there. Finally, they got Honey to talk to him through the door. "Please come out!" she begged. "We'll talk, we'll go for a ride, we'll go to some drive-in and eat and talk!" At last he emerged, pale and mysteriously silent. He told her that he had planned to kill himself if they didn't get back together.

After a drive and a talk, he felt well enough to go to work. Then they got into a pattern: he would come to visit her and then leave. They were in limbo. It was that weird moment when the wheel is at the tipping point. Will it turn one more time? Or will it stall and fall back? This was the situation, a few weeks later, when he made a dramatic decision.

On the afternoon of July 15th, Lenny asked Honey if he could take Kitty and spend the day alone with the baby beside the pool at the Biltmore. He said he just wanted to have her for a couple of hours. So Honey gave him one bottle of formula and a couple of diapers and off he went. When Lenny failed to return at five o'clock, Honey became uneasy, restless. By six o'clock, she was on the phone, speaking to the desk clerk at the Biltmore.

"Why, Mr. Bruce checked out," he informed her.

"You gotta be mistaken," gasped Honey.

"No, he checked out," came the flat reply.

Honey was frantic. She called their regular baby-sitter, but the woman had not seen Kitty or Lenny. Just before show time at the Orchid Room, she called the club. Lenny was not on the premises. Fearing the worst, she called the airport, inquiring if a Mr. Lenny Bruce had left that day. There was no record of a Lenny Bruce. Honey then described Lenny, adding that he might have been carrying an infant. The airline agent confirmed that a man and a baby conforming to that description had flown out earlier in the afternoon, using different names. Desperate, Honey tried to call their apartment in L.A. The phone had been disconnected.

Next day, she was able to reach Sally, who maintained she had not heard from Lenny in weeks. Honey didn't believe her. She phoned Duffy's that night and could hear Lenny's amplified voice talking over a microphone in the background. The voice on the other end of the line insisted Lenny was working in Hawaii.

The terms of Honey's bail forbade her to leave the Islands until her trial. Totally frustrated and alone, realizing her husband had kidnapped her daughter, she attempted to cut her wrists with a razor blade. She bungled the job. Bandaging the wounds herself, she spent the rest of the night drinking from a bottle of gin before she passed out on her bed.

As soon as Lenny had landed in Los Angeles with his romper-suited child, he had taken a taxicab directly to Sally's apartment.

"Why did you grab the baby?" she asked. "What made you do that?"

"Are you kiddin'?" he snapped. "You know where the baby was? In a pusher's house! For two days! She hadn't even eaten!"

The story was a lie—but it was also a truth. It was an incident that had occurred while Lenny was in the V.A. hospital, something he had learned about later. Now he used it to rationalize the cruelty of kidnapping Kitty. Honey was an unfit mother and he was protecting the child. Actually the important question wasn't whether Honey was fit or unfit, *but whether Lenny was the man who informed on Honey, set her up for that bust.*

That Lenny Bruce was a snitch, a police informer, is a well-authenticated fact. Three years after the arrest of Honey in Hawaii, Lenny himself was arrested for drugs and made his peace with the L.A. police by helping to entrap a number of local pushers. Would he have done such a thing to Honey? Especially at this time, when he was not deeply into drugs, not threatened with imprisonment himself—when he was motivated purely by vindictive feelings? Honey says, "Yes!" She believes to this day that Lenny framed her. She never confronted him with her suspicions, but after years of brooding over the events, taking every little scrap of evidence into consideration, she finds that her earliest suspicions have continued to grow and solidify. Who else could have made that call? Who would have had the motive that Lenny had to frame her? Who could have known what she would be holding that night? That at seven-thirty, she would be driving away from the motel with six joints wrapped up in her purse?

As for the intensity of Lenny's feelings, the extremity of his behavior—think of his hysterical pleadings, his threats of suicide! Think of the cruelty and calculation involved in kidnapping Kitty, cruelty and calculation that characterized all his behavior toward Honey for the next year as he deliberately withheld from her all news of himself and Kitty.

Lenny Bruce's special sensitivity was focused on the wife-mother figure who offered him his greatest happiness. He feared, above all things, abandonment. As a child, he had suffered terribly by being abandoned by his mother. Thirty years later he published that pain to the world at the emotionally charged climax of what has been called his greatest public performance: the Curran Theater Concert. Explaining why show-biz people fear solitude, he spilled the whole secret of his being in one desperately articulated paragraph:

Nobody wants to go back to that room alone unless they can say, "Ma! Gimme a glass o' water" . . . 'cause I don' want the water

—all I want is the water with your *hand* attached to the glass and your *arm* attached to your hand and [Frantic tone] *stay here!* When I go to sleep—*don't sneak out!* 'Cause when I wake up, I wanna *see* you there all the time.

That was Lenny's recollection of the primal scene, and like all real primal scenes, it wasn't any one incident or moment. It was like cancer—an endlessly repeated and prolonged sequence of irritations on the most sensitive tissue of the soul until there forms a lesion: a protective coating that becomes in time a deadly tumor destroying the life it is supposed to shield.

Honey was Sally all over again. Another sexy, exciting dancer, another possessing, enfolding female to whom he offered up his life. When Honey started to betray Lenny—a betrayal at which he connived like the cuckold husband in the old farces—he was shocked to a depth that even he couldn't comprehend. He sickened, he raged, he argued, protested, threatened, implored, humiliated himself and finally settled on the thought of suicide. At the same time, he grew murderously angry.

Again, it was years later until he could own up to the anger and the act that it inspired: this time the confession was no more than a strong intimation offered in a late-night conversation with Joe Maini and chic Eder. Lenny raised the question—just for speculation, you understand—of what these men would do if they found their old ladies were chippieing on them, betraying them with other men. The conversation as recollected by Eder ran something like this:

Joe, after some thought, felt that he'd either split from Sandra or somehow learn to live with it. My response was straight gut: "Whip her ass—and his, too!" Lenny laughed about what he considered a reversal of stereotyped ethnic roles. Didn't we realize that Jews are the ones who are supposed to take the cerebral approach? That Italians are notorious for clobbering their women—unfaithful or not? He shpritzed me about my "pimp mentality" and how "there's something weird about a Jewish hitter." Then, he lugged Joe with a lengthy diatribe about how full of shit his reasonable approach really was. He spoke of the killings and maimings so numerous in our society that we've placed them in the definable category of "crimes of passion." He told us about Honey making it with a tough-guy Italian connection who had something to do with a club she'd worked in Hawaii, and how anyone who's really hurt like that will go to *any* lengths to "get even." He was so vehement that I got to wondering about the particulars of Honey's bust. There

was a vague something in what he said—or the way he said it—
that gave the impression he was trying to justify something within
himself. During this period, I married Marcia . . . she busted me
balling two chicks . . . prudence dictated that I split Vegas. I spent
the day after Christmas, '63, through January 1st with Lenny . . .
A couple of days after my arrival, Marcia followed me to L.A.
. . . She said that she'd fucked one of my friends . . . "Cock-eyed
Nino Cha Cha Cha." . . . She told me he was a bum fuck—as
though that automatically mitigated the act! When I hipped Lenny
to what'd transpired, he looked me dead in the eye and asked:
"Come on, chic, the truth! The way you feel right now—*would
you set her up? Would you snitch on her?*" That plea to understand
myself is the capper in my belief that he was instrumental in Honey's Hawaii scene.

Whatever the truth may be about Lenny's innocence or culpability in
Honey's bust, the fact is that from that moment he was a different man.
As soon as he returned to Los Angeles, he placed an ad in the
paper for a housekeeper to take care of his motherless daughter. Then
he rented an apartment above a brake shop at 531 North La Brea
Avenue, and installed Kitty there with a lady named Lucille, who
watched over her for the next few years. On the wall of the apartment,
he lettered a sign indicating where he was to be reached at all times,
printing at the bottom: "In the event of emergency: call Myron Schneider." Returning to work at Duffy's, he immediately impressed everyone who knew him as being a changed man. "He got bitter after
Honey," Sally recalls. "As soon as Honey put him down, I saw a
different man. He used to say, 'You see here a lovely lady. Too bad
she's diseased.' This is how he used to introduce the strippers onstage.
He just went a different way completely." Lenny's close friends knew
what he meant by his attacks on the strippers, which soon became so
ruthless that some of the girls fled from the stage crying. Lenny was
enraged at Honey and nothing shows better the vindictive nature of
his anger than the crazy chase that began when Honey announced that
she was coming on a visit to L.A.
Unable to leave Hawaii because she was awaiting trial, Honey had
gone for six weeks without word of her husband or daughter; then she
obtained a court order permitting her to visit the Mainland on August
24. Accompanied by her mother, Mabel, she set out to find Kitty and
bring her back to Hawaii. Frankie Ray—a comic who was tight with
Sally and Lenny—who had received word that Honey would be arriving
in Los Angeles, was charged with the job of keeping Kitty out of
Honey's hands. He carried her from house to house for a week, always

just one step ahead of Honey. Once on a tip from a friend, he shuttled the child from Sally's apartment to the home of his former partner, Shecky Greene, out in the Valley. Shecky had just departed with the child in his car when Honey and Mabel appeared at the door demanding the baby.

"Where's the kid?" Honey shouted.

"What kid?" replied Ray. "There's no kid."

"What's the goddam kiddie car doing here then?" screamed Mabel. "I'm going to get you in a lot of trouble for this!"

On September 1st, a week after Honey had returned to Hawaii empty-handed, Lenny moved to dismiss the divorce complaint he had filed on March 9th, the day after he had put his handwriting on the apartment wall. But within ten days he submitted an amended complaint in Los Angeles Superior Court. It stated that Honey was not a fit or proper person to have custody of Kitty, then ten months old. It also alleged that Honey had disregarded her duties as a wife and mother because of habitual intemperance for more than one year prior to their July 15th separation.

The suit also charged that Honey used "intoxicating drinks" to such an extent that it caused Lenny great mental anguish as well as disqualifying her from properly attending to her duties as a wife and mother.

She received a copy of the suit in the mail from Seymour Fried, Lenny's attorney. She was relieved because it was the first contact she had had with Lenny or Kitty since they had left the islands. Honey's cross complaint, filed on October 29th, alleged "grievous mental and physical suffering." She claimed that she enjoyed custody of Kitty, until Lenny removed the child by deception and misrepresentation.

Lenny, meanwhile, had hired a private investigator to keep close tabs on Honey in Hawaii. Since the headlines accompanying her narcotics-possession arrest, she had found it difficult to obtain regular work, other than a few engagements at army service clubs and a brief stint replacing the ailing singer, Frances Faye, at the Clouds.

In order to support herself and pay her future legal bills, she turned to the one craft she knew besides stripping, working as a seamstress. She rented a sewing machine for five dollars a week and made outfits for the strippers who worked in the local clubs. Next, she hired a sewing expert, who taught her more intricate stitches and designs, while helping to turn out dozens of items of theatrical wardrobe. Honey was kept so busy that there was no time for narcotics. She had kicked her habit and had stayed clean since September. The money that formerly went for the purchase of drugs gradually accumulated in a savings account. For the first time since Lenny converted her from a stripper in the Catskills, she was showing evidence of intense ambition. Eventually, she was able to rent a boutique at the Waikiki Biltmore Hotel and employ four full-time seamstresses to produce a custom-made line of apparel.

Then, Honey branched out into theatrical management. Her first client was a local singer, who had just completed a two-year prison sentence; she possessed a powerful voice, but her foreign accent was holding her back. After signing her to a long-term contract (in return for 25 percent of her earnings), Honey began grooming her to perform, mimicking the way Lenny had worked with her years before. She improved her client's diction, put her on a diet, and taught her how to wear makeup. She designed and made her a wardrobe, had her hair straightened and styled, and arranged for a talented pianist to accompany her. Finally she arranged her first booking at a salary of $250 a week—an unusually high price for a local singer.

By the time Honey left for the mainland, on January 3, 1957, to show cause in her divorce action, a Honolulu court had convicted her of narcotics possession and sentenced her to three years' probation. Her probation officer, whom she shared in common with her client, granted her twenty-four days to return to California in order to appear in Los Angeles Superior Court. She was exceedingly nervous the day she arrived in court. She hadn't seen Kitty since she was six months old. Now she could anticipate being locked in a struggle for her custody.

A preliminary hearing the month before had awarded Lenny temporary custody of the child, subject to visitation rights, pending the divorce action. Even in such preliminary proceedings, the wife is usually awarded custody. Honey was shocked when Lenny won temporary custody. Now she was fearful that he might gain permanent custody.

Facing the prospect of a knock-down, drag-out battle, she sat in the courtroom nervously wringing her hands. Also present was Joe Maini. As either party needed a third party to testify in his or her behalf, Lenny said, "Well, baby, do you want to use him or do you want me to use him?" In view of the close relationship between the two men, she agreed to allow Maini to testify for Lenny.

Lenny informed the court that Honey objected to his being on the road constantly; Maini took the stand and corroborated his statement. But he didn't stop there: responding to pointed questions posed by Seymour Fried, Lenny's lawyer, Maini testified that Honey was an unfit mother. He said that she would become unconscious from excessive drinking at all-night parties and that she would neglect to change Kitty's diapers or feed the child. He also recalled that the baby was crying constantly.

Honey could not believe what she was hearing. She had always considered herself an attentive mother. What's more, she was enraged by the way Lenny had misled her in regard to Maini's testimony.

Honey's attorneys, Horton and Foote, called for a recess. Seated in an anteroom, Honey told them that Maini had served time in Fort Worth for drug addiction and that his word could not be valid. She threatened to identify Lenny as a drug addict before the court.

The lawyers went into a huddle with Fried. Through Fried, Lenny indicated that if Honey tried to impeach Maini's testimony, he would supply evidence of her close association with lesbians and her illegal use of drugs, as well as bringing her narcotics-possession conviction to the attention of the court.

Honey's conviction had received scant attention in the American press. Inevitably, if it was noted in court, it would be picked up in the local papers. This possibility alarmed Honey; she didn't want to be destroyed as an entertainer. The damaging testimony of Maini, therefore, went unimpeached. His comments were just as crucial in the case against Honey as was her past criminal record. Her attorneys advised her that she would probably lose custody; that ultimately it would be made clear that the best interests of Kitty would be served by awarding custody to Lenny. Shrugging her shoulders, she advised them to go ahead and do the best they could.

A subsequent stipulation between Fried and Horton and Foote awarded Lenny custody of Kitty for nine months annually, while Honey was granted custody for the remaining three months. Honey settled for $1 a year token alimony and waived child-support payments. "Why would I want his money?" she later observed. "I always believed that if I wasn't with him, I didn't want any part of him."

The brief divorce trial, conducted on January 21, 1957, awarded an interlocutory decree to Lenny and custody pursuant to the previous stipulation. The courts ordered Lenny to pay the salary and board of a nurse to accompany Kitty to Hawaii and transportation to and from Hawaii in lieu of child support during the three-month period beginning the same day.

Honey felt like a complete stranger to Kitty as she sadly shepherded her child and the nurse back to Hawaii. Her discomfort changed to rage when she discovered that her singer had become involved with an ex-convict. Soon after Honey returned, the con informed her that she would no longer be receiving her 25 percent commission and that her relationship with the singer was at an end.

"Oh, no, it isn't," Honey screamed. "We have a written contract."

"Well," he replied, "either we're going to do it legally or otherwise."

Cunning and cruel, the con informed the probation officer that

Honey had been present in his company on numerous occasions. On March 27th, Honey's three years' federal probation was revoked by the United States District Court of Hawaii for violating one of its conditions: associating with a known felon.

Kitty was returned to Lenny. Soon after Honey's probation had been revoked, Seymour Fried filed an order, on behalf of Lenny, to show cause for modification of the interlocutory judgment concerning the custody of Kitty. Lenny was granted sole custody and control.

On June 23rd, the same day, Honey was sentenced for a term of two years in the Federal Correctional Institution on the island of Oahu. Following a brief stay in the local territorial prison, she was transferred to Terminal Island, California, a medium-security prison located thirty miles from Los Angeles.

During her first six months in prison, Honey received no word from Lenny.

Chapter Seven

OPEN UP THOSE
GOLDEN GATES

After being Lenny's wife, Honey became his muse. No Euterpe, Melpomene, or Thalia, she was *Ira*—the muse of wrath. Arousing in Lenny the deepest rage he ever felt, she inspired in him the most brilliant humor he ever created. At the same time she charged his mind with the energy to imagine his famous bits, she also doused his pleasure in the old carefree life of the strip bars and filled him with a grim determination to achieve success in the big time. 1957 proved to be his most creative year and the turning point in his career.

Basic to his big breakthrough was the conviction that he didn't have to resort to the lowest sort of humor to command the attention of an audience. He had the faith that if he insisted on doing only those things that he thought were funny, he would eventually attract an audience that shared his point of view. Often the shlubs in the strip joints walked out on him, which brought heavy threats from the location operators, but Lenny refused to lighten up. He didn't give a damn where he worked or how little the gig paid: all he wanted was acceptance on his own terms. At the same time, he exercised all his skills as a craftsman. He bought a tape recorder—in those days a relatively uncommon instrument—and started to analyze his shows. He saw where he could prune excess verbiage, where a routine went astray, or where a good fragment could be inserted. He would discard a bit and then bring it back in a new form. When the show was over, he would quiz his friends about their reactions to his material. Never again would he work so hard at getting his act tight.

He also made good use of his great powers as a salesman. His first big customers were his old boss, Maynard Sloate, and Maynard's partner in a new club on the Strip, Gene Norman. The club was called the Crescendo, and it offered two decks of entertainment. Downstairs, in the big room, were the featured entertainers: topflight cabaret stars and supporting acts. Upstairs, in a small, intimate room called the Interlude, were the newcomers and the coterie performers. Lenny felt he was ready to work in either room—as a warm-up act for the stars or as an in-group entertainer upstairs; his big job was convincing the owners. Maynard was no great problem: he had known Lenny for years; he was willing to give him his chance. The hang-up was the other guy, Gene Norman: a big, deep-voiced, Ronald Reagan–style disk jockey, who made his living by exploiting the talents of black musicians and Jewish comics whom he secretly—or not so secretly—despised.

Gene didn't dig Lenny, and as the years went on, he dug him even less. The running battle between the two was one of the standing jokes of the Hollywood night crowd. Lenny would talk about Gene and his giant boxer, Boris, confiding: "They have sexual relations out in the alley." Gene would stand at the back of the room burning. The feud got so heavy that eventually Lenny had a clause inserted in his contract forbidding Gene Norman from setting foot inside the room while Lenny was onstage.

Back at the beginning, Lenny couldn't be so sassy. He needed a showcase for his talents, and the Crescendo was the hot room on the Strip. So he hired on as a warm-up comic for "big"names like June Christie, the Four Freshmen, Murray the K, and the Mills Brothers. The arrangement worked beautifully for the first five weeks; two or three times a night, Lenny would break up a stone-cold house. Then, the Mary Kaye Trio came along.

The night before they opened, they sat out front and watched Lenny work. What they saw made them panic. As their manager explained to Gene Norman, Lenny was certain to "clash" with the Trio's own comic, Frank Ross, "The Japanese Gardener." So Norman summoned Lenny to his office and informed him, in his most pompous and authoritarian tones, that the "club could not afford to take chances with a five-thousand-dollar-a-week act." If the Mary Kaye Trio thought that Lenny ought to lay out for three weeks, then he, Gene Norman, thought so, too. Lenny needn't worry, though, Norman generously added: his salary would be paid to him during the entire layoff. In return, Lenny would be expected to make himself useful around the club; for example, he could put on his tux every night and show people to their seats. That would be easy work and it would make the management feel better about paying him $175 a week for doing nothing.

"Absolutely *no!*" was Lenny's irate answer. Which took balls—because he had no savings, and he was supporting a whole domestic establishment around Kitty.

Eventually, he let some agent book him into a little joint in Anaheim called the South Seas. The first night, he was surprised to discover the room was virtually empty. The bartender, the waitresses, the manager—the whole staff—were on duty, but there were no customers. It was just as empty the second night and the third! Finally, Lenny asked the boss whether he wanted him to get up on the stage and perform. The man replied, "Take it easy, kid!" When Lenny pressed the point, asking would he ever get to work, the imperturbable boss responded: "That's entirely up to you." Pressing the point one step further, he finally asked: "Can I leave?" "*No!*" was the firm and by no means kindly answer. So for three wretched weeks, he hung around an empty nightclub, obviously a front for something but so carefully guarded that even that arch-snooper, Lenny Bruce, couldn't sniff out the secret. Weird!

Back at the Crescendo, he was grateful to find an audience. The audience was no less grateful when he started unpacking his head of all the funny ideas that had accumulated during those frustrating weeks in cold storage. At this time his impact on a straight audience was absolutely pulverizing. Instead of working out of phony show-biz "charm" and cuteness and carefully rehearsed topicality, Lenny Bruce was hitting the late fifties' mainline—the sense of smothered rage.

Everybody was pissed off in those days, but there were no socially acceptable outlets for hostility. "Hostile" was a word you heard constantly—but it was a scolding word, like "bad," "naughty," or "no-no!" All over the heavily psychoanalyzed USA, people were saying to other people, "Why are you being so hostile? . . . That's a hostile remark! . . . There's a lot of hostility behind something like that!" It was an incredible age, the fifties. An age of stifled violence obsessing about the BOMB!

The Bomb was right inside the guts and brains of every American man, woman, and child. People were burning with repressed sexuality, anger, fear. They were making incredible sacrifices to pay their mortgages, educate their children, and keep everything cool at the office. Eating crow every day for lunch. Lying low. Trying to "adjust," to "conform," to be "mature." Being taught by the analysts—whose wisdom and authority extended far beyond the tiny number of patients they treated—that the first rule of life was: "you have only yourself to blame!" No matter what happened to you—whether you were fired from your job, cheated on by your husband, fucked over by your kids, afflicted with disease, or riddled with anxiety—*all your own fault!* If you hadn't taken that job, married that man, given birth to that kid, inhaled those germs, built up those worries, *none of this would have happened!* You could have had a wonderful job, a doting husband, beautiful, darling children, perfect health, the nerves of a brain surgeon—if you had just acted *normal*! There was the wisdom, the comfort, the faith, hope, and charity of the "mature" fifties! Now, wouldn't you be angry, schmuck?

Nature had designed Lenny Bruce to be the kamikaze of the angry comics. He had an inexhaustible fountain of rage frothing up inside him. He also had the sort of spirit that exults in shaming people and turning them bottomside up. At the Crescendo, he developed a cruel variation on his old telephone act. He'd come out on the floor with the long-tailed phone, but instead of dialing up the maître d' of the Mocambo, he would lean down to a nicely tanned suburban couple and ask them—most politely, you can be sure!—whether they had a baby-sitter back home. If the answer was yes, he would bubble, "Wouldn't it be fun to give her a ring?" Naturally, the couple were delighted: eagerly they supplied him with their phone number and the girl's name. Dialing up the poor innocent, with a slightly malicious grin, Lenny would say: "Hello? Is this the Parker residence? Is this Betty Bird? Oh, Miss Bird, I have some bad news for you. The Parkers were in a three-car collision on the San Bernardino Freeway. I'm afraid they're both dead. Is there anything I can do for you?" As the poor fourteen-year-old screamed through the receiver, the club went into shock and Lenny would burst into a hacking laugh. Quickly he'd inform the girl that the call was just a prank. The Parkers were safe and sound seated right before him at the Crescendo. Would she like to speak with them? Ha, ha—pretty funny! Right?

Lenny's hostility was purely verbal. Physically, he had always been a coward, although he was fascinated with violence and forever seeking information about how to fight with your fists or with a knife. Then one night after the show, he suddenly became a hitter!

Leaving the Crescendo with Maynard Sloate and his partner in Strip City, Al Warner, and Frankie Ray, Lenny took off for Googie's, a late-night coffee shop on the Strip, next door to Schwab's. Every table was occupied, so they sat down on a bench by the door. Suddenly, a huge guy in a black crew-neck sweater looms up in front of them, drunk, enraged, and brandishing a catsup bottle. Nobody could believe what came out of this crazy's mouth when he shouted: *"Is there a Jew in the house? I'm gonna kill me a Jew tonight!"* To show he meant business, he smashed the catsup bottle on the floor.

Instantly, the noisy buzz of conversation hushed to an ominous silence. Then, without warning, the drunk lunged at Al Warner, shoving him off the bench. At that moment, Lenny leaped up and hollered: *"Let my people go!"* Wham! He plants his fist in the guy's face. Before he can crank up for another punch, the ape picks Lenny up by the seat of his pants and hurls him through the shop's plate-glass window. The crash is terrifying. Even more alarming is the sight of Lenny lying inert on the sidewalk covered with shards of broken glass. When the ambulance arrives, Lenny is still out cold. They have to put him on a litter to get him aboard the vehicle.

When Frankie Ray arrives at the receiving station on Santa Monica Boulevard, he finds Lenny still lying rigid on the stretcher, his eyes glassy. Suddenly, Lenny sits bolt upright and pulls Frankie close to him. Frankie is prepared to hear his friend's last words. What Lenny actually says is—"Call the papers!"

He had not been badly hurt. The raincoat he had been wearing had saved him from lacerations. He had played dead deliberately, wanting to capitalize on the publicity the incident was bound to create.

No sooner does Lenny finish touting Frankie than into the room walks their attacker, the huge drunk, whose face is now a mass of cuts and bruises. Without a moment's hesitation, Lenny leaps off his litter and belts the guy right in the bloody kisser! Instead of committing mayhem, the drunk turns chicken. He runs out of the building and disappears into the night.

By 4 A.M., the police have arrested the bully, who turns out to be a merchant seaman. Meantime, a crowd of photographers has arrived at the receiving station with Seymour Fried, Lenny's attorney. "That's not my good side," quips Lenny as the strobes flash; "if you don't shoot my good side, I'll never let you take my picture again!"

By the time Lenny wound up his long stay at the Crescendo, he had earned himself a neat little reputation as the new "in" comic in L.A. He had been picked up by an NBC-TV remote from the club, mentioned in the columns, and patted on the back by a lot of celebrities. But his career wasn't really moving. He did a couple of weeks at a place called Peacock Lane, and then started drifting back into the joints, the Zamboanga, the Mandalay, the Cobblestone, Duffy's . . . a few weeks out in the Valley . . . Same old crap! Yet his name was in the air. When a couple of old vaudevillians named the Slate Brothers got ready to open a new club on La Cienega Boulevard, they offered to bring in Lenny Bruce—as a headliner. It was his big chance. Opening night he's thrilled to see a celebrity crowd pouring into the club. Standing by the bar, Lenny recognizes Georgie Jessel, the Ritz Brothers, the Three Stooges, Bert Gordon (The Mad Russian of the Eddie Cantor show). Dynamite!

Speaking over a distracting buzz of conversation, Henry Slate introduces Lenny to the packed house. Instead of the babble sinking to a hush, however, the noise continues unabated. Lenny taps on the microphone, testing it. Then he launches into his opening routine. It's no go. His concentraiton is destroyed by the pockets of conversation all over the room. His audience is full of show-off celebrities!

Indifference was something Lenny could never brook. Out-and-out hostility, with bar glasses whizzing past his ears, would not bug him half so much as an audience that wouldn't listen. What was worse, this rudeness was being perpetrated by people whom Lenny despised: those awful Lindy's front-table types with their fake bonhomie and their vulgar clothes and their infuriating air of guys who've got it made. Painfully aware that all his carefully laid plans are being shot to hell, Lenny stalks off the stage after doing a scant ten minutes. Encountering Frankie Ray at the bar, he hisses out his rage, insisting that the older comics are deliberately ignoring him because he's a threat to them.

"Forget about it," advises Frankie. Just then, Buddy Hackett walks up. Sensing Lenny's anger and frustration, Buddy tries to cheer him up by telling a sick joke.

"Kid looks up at his father," Hackett begins, in his Kewpie-doll voice, "and says, 'Daddy, what's a degenerate?' The father answers, 'Shut up, kid, and *keep sucking*!' " The dirty punch line convulses all three of them.

Taking the stage for the second show, Lenny realizes that the noise is even worse than it was earlier in the evening.

"President Eisenhower . . ." Lenny begins, vainly. Nobody is listening.

"Please, will you be quiet for one minute?" he pleads, banging on the microphone. The crowd ignores him.

"Shut up for a moment!" he shouts. "It's important. An *emergency*! I just want to say one thing, and then you can all go back to talking to each other."

As the noise momentarily subsides, a sinister glint appears in Lenny's eyes. "I just heard a funny joke that I thought you'd appreciate, folks," he snorts, clutching the microphone. "A kid looks up at his father and he says, 'What's a degenerate?' The father says, 'Shut up, kid, and keep sucking!' *And that's what I say to you people out there!*"

Wham! An embarrassed hush settles over the room. Nobody can believe what they've heard. Casting his eyes toward the bar, Lenny sees all the painted-up broads doing their I've-never-been-so-shocked number. "Oh, look at that!" he mocks. "Hooker's Row is embarrassed. How shocked they are! They don't know what *sucking* is! That's *ridiculous*! Every one of you is in George Raft's little black book!"

With that blast, he turns his back, wiggles his ass at the customers, and makes two universally known Italian gestures with his fingers. "Goodbye," he screams, leaping from the stage, "and *fangoola-da-moma!*" Barely eluding the grasp of the enraged owners, he races out the front door.

Replaced by Don Rickles (a then unknown commodity, who, ironically, used the Slate Brothers stage to launch himself on a career of insulting celebrities), Lenny appeared to have blown his big break. Yet what initially appeared a suicidal display of temperament soon proved to be a great public relations stunt. The Slate Brothers were besieged with inquiries about Lenny's next appearance. Despite the pleadings of Henry Slate, Lenny refused to return. "I don't want to work there," he told Frankie. "It's not my type of place. It could really hold me back."

It was shortly afterward, in the fall of 1957, that Lenny Bruce was finally discovered. His patron was a lady named Ann Dee, who ran a joint called Ann's 440, in San Francisco. Ann didn't think of her club as a joint: she saw it as a super-chic boîte, featuring classy European acts. At the time she met and engaged Lenny Bruce, her big draw was Gilda, a beautiful French boy, who wore gorgeous gowns and sang risqué songs and pranced around in front of a chorus line. What inspired Ann to replace Gilda with Lenny Bruce is unclear. Perhaps she scented a new trend or anticipated trouble with her old policy. She was a strictly-business lady, who also ran a cabaret theater and managed a dozen Vegas lounge acts on the side. Whatever she did, it would have had to check out by some sort of calculation.

Ann's discovery of Lenny owed a lot to her new husband, Richard, a one-time bartender and bar manager in Long Beach. He had suggested that Ann go talent shopping on his old turf. The first act he presented to her was a comedienne named Boots Malloy. Boots worked loose and rough and Ann loved her act. Backstage after the show, she waxed effusive. "You've got so much going for you!" she exclaimed to the middle-aged lady in the butch haircut, pixie nose job, and Instamatic smile. "You should come to San Francisco and work for me!" It was a nice offer. A nice compliment. But at that point in her career, Sally Marr had decided that all the talent in the family belonged to her beloved Lenny. Lenny had wiped out everybody, so far as she was concerned. So when Sally heard, "You should come and work for me," she answered, "You should come and see my *son*!" Richard had already seen Lenny. He agreed, right off the bat, that Lenny was one of the most talented and interesting men he had ever met in the business. So there was no problem. Next night they set off to see Sally's boy at Duffy's.

Lenny was having a bad night when Ann walked into the joint. Despite the fact that he was Rocky's pet and the object of an underground cult among the jazz musicians, Hollywood celebs, and weirdo-warpo night people, Lenny could still have a terrible time in this dump because the customers were predominantly dumb schlubs who came to drink, watch the strippers, and get their cocks sucked later by slatternly B-girls. So what the fuck did they care what this kid said onstage with his fast nervous patter that you could hardly understand, for Chrissake! When Lenny was ignored, he would reach back for the oldest, corniest, dumbest attention-grabbers in the history of the business. On the night that Ann caught his act, he actually dropped his pants! When the breeches came down, he was discovered in an oversize pair of white shorts spotted with giant red polka dots.

Another, less astute scout would have backed away from Lenny Bruce. Most women would have figured him for hopelessly vulgar, a little crazy, definitely not a "class" act. Ann was different. Shrewd. She knew this business from the bottom up. She looked and she saw a fascinatingly handsome man. A young, thin, dapper performer with coal-black eyes and signs of dissipation etched into his face, a fascinating face that sometimes lit up with a little boy's enthusiasm and cuteness and sometimes froze into a sinister mask of hipster allurement. Hypnotic! You couldn't take your eyes off him. What did it matter if these animals at the bar, or elbowed over the tables, didn't dig him? Johns, marks they were. She knew the type. Never had them in her club. Hated them.

Ann started talking to Lenny, and everything she had imagined about him proved true. He *was* fascinating and brilliant and totally dedicated to his career. He was into filmmaking and writing; he also had a head for business. He told her that he had an act and she believed him absolutely. The question was simply one of money. How much would she offer? Ann was so confident he'd do business, so eager to have him at her club, that she offered him more money than any performer had ever received at her place: $750 a week plus a percentage of the gate. If he packed them in, he would be earning $1,000 a week. Not bad for a strip-bar M.C. whose usual take was $175. What's more, Ann promised to advertise his appearance in the papers and on the radio. She even offered to give him money to buy gifts for all the columnists. What more could you do for an unknown?

If Lenny Bruce was primed and ready to fire when he left for San Francisco, the city of Beatniks, poetry and jazz, Mort Sahl and cabaret theater was just as primed and ready to pop at the first touch of his talent. January of 1958 was the high season of the so-called San Francisco Renaissance, the city's brief apotheosis as a cultural hot spot. Looking back on that moment today through the haze of marijuana and incense that cloaks the second Renaissance, the vast hippie immigration in the summer of 1967, you can see more clearly than ever what a unique position San Francisco holds in American life. The promised land of all the beat, disaffected, whacked-out, or simply restless young men and women who in former times would have settled in Greenwich Village or in South Chicago or in one of the old Bohemias abroad, San Francisco is an American Paris. Lawrence Ferlinghetti said that the reason he settled in San Francisco after spending five years in France was that "it was the only place in America where you could get good wine." That sums it up very neatly—as does the analogy that has been drawn more than once between the North Beach area in San Francisco and the old Greenwich Village in New York. Like the old Village, North Beach was a traditional Italian enclave, redolent of good food and wine, tightly closed in on itself in the manner of a Sicilian village, yet wide open for tourist business and for daily commerce with the high-rise business district on its doorstep.

Until the mid-fifties, North Beach was a pretty quiet place compared with its neighbor, the International Settlement (the original Barbary Coast). Then, the colorful cootch joints of the Settlement, with their loud-mouthed sidewalk pitchmen, began to decline and the action shifted up the hill to Broadway. A sweet little tonk strip—nothing like the nightmare of 42nd Street or the raunchy swinging-door atmosphere of Bourbon Street or the futuristic madness of Miami and Vegas—Broadway still possesses its charming provincial quality. It reminds you of all the descriptions you've read of Beale Street in Memphis. Too small, too cheery, and too clean to be really bad, it's just about right for a couple of Holden Caulfield college boys off on a wild weekend.

In the mid-fifties, Broadway aspired even to a certain cultural sophistication. That was always the idea of Enrico's, the famous sidewalk café, whose essence is nostalgia for Jean-Paul Sartre, Les Deux Magots, and Existentialism. Sitting out on the pavement—under infrared heaters when the nights get chilly—you can play dominoes, wear a beret, and sip *café filtre* just as if you were on the Left Bank. Your meditations, though, will be disturbed from time to time by the racket of Finocchio's upstairs, where the transvestite show is identical with the Jewel Box Revue. But the disturbance is welcome because it reminds you that the real formula for San Francisco is precisely this intermingling of Old World charm and *Gemütlichkeit* with some of the most bizarre and freaky features of the West Coast.

Even as the café calm of Enrico's is crowned with the camp-it-up hysteria of a drag-queen show—Male West and John Harlowe, flaunting their fans and sucking their impossibly long cigarette holders and shrieking out the lyrics of old show tunes in piercing falsettos—so the rich wholesome fare of the traditional North Beach Italian restaurant is balanced down the block by an "erotic ice cream parlor," featuring treats like "Montana Banana" and "Pineapple Thunderpussy." As if this were not enough crazy-quilt diversity, you have to throw in a good handful of jazz joints and clip joints and gin mills and, in the year 1958, a whole new culture squatting down at one end of the street and up along the intersecting Grant Avenue—the Beats.

Larry Ferlinghetti's and Pete Martin's City Lights Bookstore (open till 3 A.M.) was one stronghold of the new Beat scene; another was the Co-Existence Bagel Shop, with its neighboring establishments, the Coffee Gallery and the Cellar, the former a stage for Lord Buckley, the latter a jazz joint. The Bagel Shop was a notorious hangout for the new Bohemians, and consequently the object of close scrutiny by the police; for though San Francisco rightfully enjoys a reputation for being one of the most hospitable and sophisticated cities in America, local opinion was sharply divided over the "Beatniks." As Eldridge Cleaver said, the Beats were basically just a clutch of middle-class white kids adopting the life-style of "niggers." The *ne plus ultra* of this life-style, dedicated to hanging loose and blowing pot and digging "sounds," was the interracial romance—working only one way, of course, with the man black and the woman white. It was these "mixed couples" that really got the locals hopping mad, thereby defining the true tolerances of San Francisco.

For two years the North Beach police harassed the Beats and sought to drive them out of the area. Two notorious North Beach police officers—William Bigarani and his sidekick, Officer Cuneo—patrolled Grant Avenue, handing out tickets and rousting "loiterers." When the cops spotted an interracial couple on the streets, they would pull up and shout: "I want *you* to go that way and *her* to go this way—and don't let me catch you together again!" Finally, things got out of hand when Bigarani entered the Bagel Shop one day and ripped from the wall a long poem denouncing the police written by a Beat bard named Bob "Bomkauf" Kaufman, author of the *Abominist Man-*

ifesto. At this point, the ACLU stepped in and the scene cooled. The Beats had felt the heat, however. They moved on to other havens.

It was not, therefore, an altogether permissive milieu into which Lenny Bruce was moving with his highly provocative comedy; and it's easier to understand Lenny's subsequent prosecution by the city fathers if you associate it with the long-strained hospitality of San Francisco's North Beach—an account heavily overdrawn by the time Lenny turned up at Ann's—than if you see it as the sudden arbitrary persecution of an isolated artist.

The San Francisco Renaissance is usually described in textbooks as if it were primarily a literary phenomenon growing out of a revolution in modern life-styles. Actually, the heroes of the movement were not writers like Allen Ginsberg and Jack Kerouac but the canonized saints of jazz, Lester Young and Charlie Parker. Ironically, as the Jazz Age ended with the exhaustion of its innovative energies and the death of some of its greatest players, the exaltation of jazz among the white American middle class reached its final apogee. Every white-bucked college boy was expected to dig jazz and every well-dated college girl whiled away her evenings impatiently tapping her foot under the table while this strange ritual was being enacted. So widespread was the jazz cult that even *Time* broke down and put the fuzzy face of Thelonius Monk on its cover.

The pale, pot-smoking Beats of San Francisco, with their sexless-looking black-stockinged women, were hardly unique in their worship of the great black Priapus. The most you could say for them was that they were a little more into the myth and mystique of jazz than was the average college boy or girl. Having passed beyond fascination to emulation, they now wanted to stand up and blow like a black jazz cat. Thousands of people in America wanted to make that same move. The image of the madly inspired, recklessly self-destructive jazz genius, blowing chorus after chorus on a glittering gold horn, before hurling himself into a quagmire of drugs, booze, women, and kamikaze hatred for the American social system—this myth-mash of true and fancy, Harlem and Hollywood—completely captured and held in thrall the imaginations of all sorts of Americans during those dull days.

In the arts, particularly, the inspiration of jazz was paramount. Abstract Expressionist painters, like Jackson Pollock, were imitating jazz by spattering their canvases with random-looking drips and squirts and by deploying these canvases in long impulsively unwound strips that could start and stop anywhere. These same long strips—reflecting the chorus-after-chorus, indefinitely extended jazz solo—turned up inside Jack Kerouac's typewriter, adapted to accommodate a whole roll of paper. Jazz novels were written by the dozen in this period. Jazz movies were made from the jazz novels, and jazz ballets, jazz symphonies, and jazz concertos were made by the makers of the jazz films' jazz scores.

Perhaps the most deliberate approximation to the jazz esthetic in another medium was the characteristic art of the North Beach Beats —poetry and jazz. This was San Francisco's special contribution to the anthology of American art forms. It was practiced by the city's most distinguished local poet, Kenneth Rexroth, and essayed by dozens of poetasters of every degree of talent and commitment, who got up in bars, coffee houses, and private pads, while the sounds came pouring out of a live or recorded jazz band, and tried to match the fervor of their words to the driving beat and elliptical phrasing of the jazz soloist. A hybrid form, like a steamboat with sails, poetry and jazz betrayed its transiency by its failure to commit itself to either one art or the other. Nothing like a song, a cantata, an oratorio, opera, operetta, musical comedy, or any other workable combination of words and music, poetry and jazz was radically incoherent. The poetry was written without the music; the music was played exactly as it would have been if the musicians had never heard the poetry. The most you could say for the experiment was that it pointed vaguely toward the day when pop music would abandon the witty, finely crafted lyrics of the Broadway show tune for the rhapsodic, surrealistic verbal pastiche of Bob Dylan. It's no accident, though, that when poetry really made a bid to compete with music for American ears, it did so in company not with jazz but with a much more obvious and elementary kind of music filched off the racks of blue-grass fiddlers and out of the carpetbags of hillbilly singers. Jazz could have no truck with white middle-class poetry, however rebellious or avant-garde. Jazz was one world. Poetry another.

Comedy was something in between. From the time that Lord Buckley had started breaking up speakeasy gangsters with imitations of the lingo of Negro jazz musicians, there had always been a thin though vigorous line of jazz comics in American nightclubs. Sometimes they were clowns like Harry "The Hipster" Gibson, who would run amok in the audience before he got onstage, passing out Benzedrine inhalers. Leaping on the platform, he would raise his inhaler to his nose, shout "Skoal!" and sniff mightily. Slappy White had a great reefer bit. There were also jive-talking black musicians, like Slim Gaillard or Babs Gonzalez: the former, coiner of nonsense songs like "Flat Foot Floogie (With the Floy Floy)" and "Cement Mixer, Puttee-Puttee"; the latter, author of some very amusing talking blues, peppered with pungent jazz slang. The jazz influence was also strong in Mort Sahl, the hero of the college generation, who had established the hip monologue as a popular contemporary entertainment.

A wise guy, a grad-school loudmouth, a spoiled little Jew boy who, as a child, used to stand behind the radio and shout through the dusty tubes like Gabriel Heatter; a hi-fi and sports-car nut; a Stan Kenton fan (Stan's musical demagoguery being the perfect objective correlative for Mort's brassy ego); a compulsive moviegoer; girl-crazy; status-conscious; and a classic consumer, who eased the burden of existence by buying each day some expensive foreign-manufactured watch, Mort Sahl was a supremely contemporary figure. His big breakthrough had occurred way back in 1953. Since that time he had so revolutionized the role of the comic that professional comedians viewed him with the same mixture of alarm and envy with which professional singers regarded Elvis Presley.

Born, but not reared, in L.A., with its muscle beaches, car cults, and Pachuco teen culture, always ambitious to be a star of the media—radio, journalism, movies, what did it matter?—Mort returned after the war from the deep-freeze tank of the Aleutians to fall in love with a pretty, charming, and extremely intelligent high school girl named Sue Babour. When Sue enrolled as a freshman at Berkeley, Mort followed her, experiencing a terrible winter in which he slept in holes and corners, lived off canned tuna, and got laid up in the hospital with appendicitis. Eventually, he conned his way into an all-night luncheonette near the main gate of the university, a place called the White Log, where he was discovered by Hube the Cube (Hubert Leslie), a central figure of the Beat movement, who made his living as a pincushion for the drug testers at the U.C. Hospital. Hube persuaded Enrico Banducci to install Mort in the original hungry i (variously interpreted as "hungry id" or "hungry intellectual"), a candlelit *cave* for Beats and students who would buy a drink in order to feast off the free lunch.

According to legend, on his first night in the joint, Sahl trotted onstage, took sharp aim, and fired a series of dead hits at politics. His best line was the suggestion that someone ought to invent a new type of Eisenhower jacket—a McCarthy jacket—its distinguishing feature being an extra zipper to go across the mouth. The seventy-odd patrons of the i rocked with laughter. It was the first time they'd ever heard McCarthy ridiculed—at least publicly. Sahl next convulsed his audience by quipping, "For a while, every time the Russians threw an American in jail, the Un-American Activities Committee would retaliate by throwing an American in jail too." Wildly applauded—more for his courage than his wit—Sahl became an overnight sensation.

Having smashed with a single blow the long-standing taboo against introducing political themes into nightclub comedy, Sahl went on to radically alter the public image of the stand-up comic by introducing a whole new rhetoric of relations between performer and audience. Instead of walking out on the stage of a nightclub nattily dressed, with a big smile, an ingratiating manner, and a bagful of carefully rehearsed routines, Sahl loped out on the floor dressed as if he weren't onstage at all, wearing slacks and a loose sweater over a shirt with an unbuttoned collar. He treated the audience with a mixture of friendliness and hostility that enabled him simultaneously to ridicule them—putting them on in their own half-hip, half-psychoanalytic jargon—while at the same time winning their confidence by making it plain that he was one of them. Shooting only part of the time at politics and the rest of the time at the foibles of young folk in the fifties—their fads (stereo equipment and Pogo), their mating hang-ups, their cynicism and apathy—Sahl created his own material by haranguing this audience as if it were his own family. Instead of disguising his private opinions, his angry attitudes, his scathing awareness of the current scene, as conventional show-biz comics had always done, Sahl actually capitalized on his intolerance, his opinionatedness, his mania for rash and brash generalizations. For the first time in the history of the cabaret business, a comic repudiated his responsibility to be funny, becoming instead the spokesman for a special group: the students, intellectuals, and bohemians Sahl called "my people."

Sahl was never a great comic. His nervous, jabbing, keep-them-off-balance delivery was the strategy of a man who was not comfortable in front of an audience. His creative method—a rapid scanning of the day's output of newspapers, magazines, and radio broadcasts—was a recipe for superficiality or, at best, the kind of quick, shallow laugh triggered by a topical allusion. Sahl was always devoid of the two basic ingredients of great humor: imagination and soul. He could make fun of the latest Hollywood movies. He could stab at the pieties of his own class. He could take an abrupt insight into politics or world events and phrase it neatly into a gag. What he could never do was suggest a world of living, breathing people behaving in ridiculous yet recognizably human patterns. Mr. Mort, like Jules Feiffer, succeeded best at one-upping the schmucks who make and report the news. He was a master of the art of taking a current idea or trend and giving it that slight little future twist, that logical extension that makes it turn up like a brilliant stroke of insight. A convenient compendium of his most successful gags was provided in the cover story which *Time* ran in 1960.

A SAHL'S EYE VIEW
THE UNFABULOUS FIFTIES

Publication of Yalta Papers: They should come in a loose-leaf binder so you can add new betrayals as they come along.

Korea: The turncoats were steadfast. They refused to give anything except their name, rank and exact position of their unit.

Ike's First Election: We need a man on a white horse. Well, we got the horse, but there's nobody on him. . . .

Neil McElroy, Appointed Secretary of Defense: A great blow to daytime radio.

Lung-Cancer Tests: There is a moral question here—whether or not mice should smoke.

Nixon in Russia: If he doesn't get along with them, he'll be in trouble, because over there he can't call anyone a Communist and hurt their career.

Missile Gap: Maybe the Russians will steal all our secrets. Then they'll be two years behind. . . .

In retrospect they sound very slick. Neatness, economy, and point. You can't imagine any man who really loves humor relishing this stuff. Sahl's best audience was always a little square. Ideally, it was composed of politically minded young middle-class couples out for a rare fling in a nightclub and eager to laugh at any jibe flung at one of their pet peeves.

It always enraged Lenny Bruce when people compared him with Mort Sahl. No two men in the same profession could have been further apart from the standpoint either of their work or their personalities. Mort was so puritanical that he neither smoked nor drank. A dirty word never passed his lips, and he would have been horrified at the thought of sticking a needle in his arm. When Mort would come into a club where Lenny was working, the moral shock was so great that Lenny would end up doing a perfectly clean show. There was no other person in the world who had such an effect on Lenny Bruce. Similarly, when the reporters would ask Lenny his opinion of Sahl, instead of coming out with one of his customary zingers, Lenny would hedge and dodge and come up with some dumb remark, like "I think he's great." Mort's political audacity and sophistication meant absolutely nothing to Lenny, who was given to making statements like the following: "I can't get worked up about politics. I grew up in New York, and I was hip as a kid that I was corrupt and that the mayor was corrupt. I have no illusions." The two men were poles apart. Mort Sahl was hip; Lenny Bruce was a hipster.

Lenny Bruce stood at the exact focal point of that great myth of the fifties: the Underground Man. In that age of universal comformity, it was believed, there lurked beneath the familiar surface of life an anachronistic underworld of ruthlessly appetitive and amoral beings who achieved heroic intensities through the violence of their rebellion against the middle-class norms. Norman Mailer used the hipster as a peg for his purely personal fantasies of violence and existentialism in pieces like "The White Negro." Hardworking novelists, like John Clellon Holmes, were painting the type, as in his fictionalization of Lester Young's life: *The Horn*. The young sociologist Ned Polsky was writing about hipsters and Beats in Greenwich Village. (Somehow, hipsters and Beats were always getting mixed up by those who knew very little about either. The difference was drastic: the hipster was your typical lower-class urban dandy, dressed up like a pimp, affecting a very cool, cerebral tone—to distinguish him from the gross impulsive types that surrounded him in the ghetto—and aspiring to the finer things in life, like very good "tea," the finest of sounds—jazz or Afro-Cuban—and maybe, once in a while, a crazy sex scene, laying up in bed for a weekend with two steaming foxes. The Beat was originally some earnest middle-class college boy, like Kerouac, who was stifled by the cities and the culture he had inherited, and who wanted to cut out for distant and exotic places, where he could live like "the people," write, smoke, and meditate for weeks in virtual isolation while rhapsodizing about this great land of ours.)

The hipster was also, like all nonconformists, a great theme of comedy. Even *Life* magazine—God bless its glossy heart!—printed bop jokes and cartoons, illustrating the new Cool Culture. Example: Two cats in zoot suits schlumped out on a corner, while a motorcycle roars by them at about ninety miles an hour. "Man," drawls one hipster to the other, "I thought that cat would *never* leave!" *Life* saw the hipster as irresistibly funny—and so did America.

All an actor in a chic little Broadway review, like *New Faces*, had to do was walk out onstage in a zoot suit, long since made familiar through *Li'l Abner* (and long since abandoned by real hipsters, who favored, after the war, lapel-less camel's hair jackets, with giant brass buttons: then, in the fifties, narrow, bottle-shouldered, four-button Continentals, with high choke collars and ribbon-wide ties) and the audience broke up! Even the dumbest nightclub comics did routines like the one Lenny called "Hep Smoke a Reefer." They thought that if you said "Man" and "dig" and "hep" (a word musicians never used), you were coming on like a Bopper. You were coming on—to tell the truth—like a kikey little fart who would have fainted if a real Bopper hit on him for two cents!

Lenny was different. Lenny aimed to be a real hipster. He hung out with the heavy cats—got right down with them. When he took off some okey-doke spook, he had the sound. He could get his voice up in that high falsetto jive range. D↷ those long, boxed-out junkie pauses—those four-bar rests. Come ↷p with the kind of words that

you couldn't find in any *Hiptionary*. Lenny's earliest demonstration of
his command of the nigger hipster jazz idiom was an imaginary interview he used to do in this period between Lawrence Welk and a strung-
out, stoned-blind spade Be-Bopper. Welk, auditioning the cat for his
band, talks in a high, shrill, tight-clenched Tcherman accent, like a
heinie Poll Parrot. When the spade mumbles some drowsy jive, Welk
gets crazy and screams: "WHAT THE HELL ARE YOU TALKING
ABOUT?" The Be-Bopper drawls: "I'm, ah . . . I dunno, sweetie,
that's my trouble . . . that's my scene, you know, like *no one comes
through to me*, you know . . . well, you know, sweetie, like everyone's
got their own scene, like you got your bubbles, Jim, I got my thing."
You got your bubbles! To Lawrence Welk, yet!

Even funnier is the exchange that begins when the irritable, half-
crazy Welk cries, "WHAT ARE YOU SCRATCHING YOUR
GODDAM FACE FOR?" " 'Cause I'm *allergic*, baby," comes the
well-practiced reply. Then, reacting with a junkie time-lag, the spade
finally repays Welk's hostility with a little of his own rancor: "What
the hell are you yellin' at me for, motherfucker? What's all this
screechin' here?" The relapsing into his drowsy singsong, he patiently
explains: "Look, I wanna tell ya, I jus' wanna get a taste . . . can I
get some bread in front?" Welk squawks: "You hungry? Wanna sandwich?" Lenny's spade-takes on this line were enough to qualify him
as the greatest reactor since Sid Caesar. At first, he'd do a real slow
take, a gradual, groping laugh—"Ahaha . . . haha!"—as the musician
slowly takes in what he must regard as a joke. "Do I wanna sandwich?
. . . Haha . . . Ssssssssshit! You're really somethin' else, baby . . . Do
I wanna sandwich?" The long sibilant hiss on "shit," the broken,
fumbling pauses, as the half-paralyzed mind of the musician struggles
to decide whether the bandleader is putting him on, are perfect. Finally,
the musician rouses himself: "You kiddin', baby? . . . You're a *freak*!
You know that?" *Freak*. The word, like "motherfucker," "bread,"
and "in front," is so common today that the impact of such language
in 1958 is hard to imagine. To the average listener it must have sounded
like code.

Actually, the ghetto idiom was far more than a badge of hipness
to Lenny Bruce: it was a paradigm of his art. For what the language
of the slums teaches a born talker is, first, the power of extreme
linguistic compression; second, the knack of reducing things to their
vital essences. Jazz slang is pure abstraction. It consists of tight, monosyllabic expressions that suggest cons in the "big house" mumbling
surreptitiously out of the corners of their mouths. Words like "dig,"
"groove," and "hip" are atomic compactions of meaning. They're as
hard and tight and tamped down as any idiom this side of the Rosetta

Stone. If any new expression comes along that can't be compressed into such a brief little bark, jazz slang starts digesting it, shearing off a word here, a syllable there, until the original phrase has been cut down to a ghetto short.

The same impatient process of short-circuiting the obvious and capping on the conventional was obvious in jazz itself. The simplest way to view the Be-Bop revolution was to see it in terms of a sudden, startling one-upping of traditional jazz. "Be-Bop," the word itself, was onomatopoeia for an abrupt, two-note, flatted-fifth motto that had replaced, in the playing of Charlie Parker and Dizzy Gillespie, the more loquacious and obvious cadences of Swing.

Yet as the compacting process got everything down to minimal forms—two-note cadences, monosyllabic metaphors, and caricatured impressions—it also opened up a lot of fresh space in which the new performers could elaborate their ideas in far-fetched fantasies or brilliant asides. Listening to Be-Bop, you'd be hard put to say whether it was the most laconic or the most prolix of jazz styles. At the very same time that it was brooming out of jazz all the old clichés, it was floridly embellishing the new language with breathtaking runs and ornaments and arabesques. Hipster language was equally florid at times, delighting in far-fetched conceits and taxing circumlocutions. You didn't say a man was over forty: you said he was "on the Jersey side of the snatch play."

Whether jazz was compressing or distending its themes, it was always treating them abstractly. Lenny saw this abstraction as common to all the hip arts whether they were jazz, abstract painting, avant-garde poetry, fiction, or music. In every art, he would explain, there comes a moment when people grow too familiar with the old outline to even bother to complete it. Instinctively, they adopt an abbreviation, a shorthand, some sign or symbol that will convey the gist of what they have to say without spelling the thing out letter by letter. This was, in fact, precisely how Lenny had hit upon abstraction during the course of his own career.

When he was an apprentice entertainer, working the neighborhood movie houses in the late forties, his ideal had been to impersonate famous movie celebrities with the utmost verisimilitude. He would go on the job with a bagful of wigs, glasses, cigars, pipes, and punched-up hats, which he would arrange neatly on a table where he could snatch them between takes. When he did Barry Fitzgerald in *The Long Voyage Home*, he would turn his back on the audience, slip on wire-rimmed spectacles, jut out his chin, fix his face into a mask, and then turn into the lights to talk in a strong Irish brogue. For Groucho Marx, he had a paste-on mustache, heavy horn-rims, and a big black cigar.

Humphrey Bogart was a turned-up coat collar and a hat with a snap-down brim—and so on through the impressionist's wardrobe. Gradually, though, as Lenny expanded his repertoire and increased his freedom of delivery, he began to grow impatient with props and costumes. They were always getting in the way. For example, he liked to do two characters conversing—dialogue was always an important feature of his work. Now, if you had to do one whole get-up for Ronald Colman and another for H. B. Warner, the scene from *Lost Horizon* wouldn't play. So Lenny began to rely more and more on what he could do with his voice, hands, and facial expressions. He discovered that if he captured Ronald Colman's heady singsong and mimicked H. B. Warner's palsied hands and husky, strangled voice, the illusion was just as satisfactory as if he'd sat in a dressing room for half an hour applying makeup. That discovery was the first step in the direction of abstraction.

The next step was to junk speech in favor of double-talk. Here he was following the lead of Sid Caesar, the greatest double-talk artist in the history of comedy. Sid was a genius with sounds and accents. He couldn't speak two words of any foreign language, but he would converse for hours in double-talk versions of German, French, Italian, Spanish, Russian, Polish, Japanese—and even more exotic tongues—with such passion and conviction and such a flair for the characteristic sounds of these languages that people would swear he was actually speaking the language.

Now, as Lenny realized eventually from his prolonged study of Sid's stage act, when you make a character speak in double-talk, you are actually abstracting the essence of his vocal mannerisms. Once the words are reduced to gibberish, the whole characterization resides in the inflections and tonal peculiarities of the character's speech. This was the discovery that Lenny put to such good use in his first successful bit: the German nightclub routine that earned him victory on the *Arthur Godfrey's Talent Scouts*. In later years, he abandoned the use of double-talk as an extended device, employing it only in little bursts, like a dab of color; but the basic aural-oral technique that enabled him to make Peter Lorre, Humphrey Bogart, and Barry Fitzgerald talk like "Baron Munchausen" enabled him also to make his junkie-spade-jazzman talk in a language of lisps and glissandos, pauses, and husky back-of-the-throat sounds that was actually an acoustic abstraction from the speech of dozens of hip-talking black musicians and street cats.

To say that Lenny had an essentially musical imagination—that he could lift a tune out of any random collection of sounds the way certain composers have lifted melodies out of the racket of industrial noise or the warblings of birds—is not at all the same thing as saying that Lenny was a great mimic. The truth is that he was a mediocre impressionist. Judged by the simple, crude, and irrefragable standard employed in such evaluations—does his take really sound like the star?—Lenny failed. Not only were his voices very crude copies of their originals: they were not even honest efforts at original mimicry. Like all second-rate impersonators, Lenny acquired his impressions at second hand. If Will Jordan did Sabu, Lenny did Will's Sabu. If Jack DeLeon did Lugosi, Lenny copied Jack's copy. The result was that Lenny's work was scorned by other mimics. They knew that he didn't have the ear or the facility they possessed; so they assumed that he was devoid of talent. In a narrow, technical sense, they were absolutely right. Lenny was not a mimic. He was a comic. He was less concerned about the voice—its accuracy, difficulty, rarity—than he was about the laugh.

He had observed that there were two ways of doing impressions. One was the crude, popular caricature—about half right and half wrong—which everybody in show business could do and raise a laugh. Then there was the painstaking, feinschmecker approach employed by the great mimics, who would play one record a hundred times or see the same movie over and over as they groped their way into the grooves of another man's voice and speech. That was the way that Larry Storch and Jack DeLeon and Will Jordan achieved their spooky likenesses. That was the kind of effort it took to do an act like Will Jordan's, where, like a college professor lecturing a class in phonetics, the impressionist demonstrated the essential vocal similarity between, say, Clark Gable, President Eisenhower, and Robert Mitchum. Discovering occult resemblances nobody else had ever noticed and voyaging out into the uncharted seas of voices heard but never "done"—second-rank movie stars, offbeat radio personalities, old-time vaudeville acts—these were the glories of the true impressionist, the vocal card tricks with which they would amaze each other when they got together in a dressing room or a recording studio or out on the corner at Hanson's. The only trouble with these little triumphs was—they weren't funny.

Consider the case of Will Jordan's classic take on Ed Sullivan. Here you have one of the universally acknowledged masterpieces of the art of mimicry. When Will makes the turn and presents you with that incredibly funny face—the lantern jaw, the huge protruding teeth, the eyes that bulge like marbles—when, standing there with his hands on his hips and his back arched into that hunched bend, he starts to talk in that harsh, nasal, stammering voice (stammering so badly at times that he has to press the tip of his nose with his finger), you're suddenly hit with a laser beam of laughter. That terrible paroxysmal laughter that hits you like an anxiety attack thrilling up from your diaphragm! So wonderful is the impression that everybody in the business, from Jack Carter to Jackie Mason, has stolen it. But far greater and more wondrous is the tribute that has been paid to it by its subject, Ed Sullivan. Not only has Sullivan had Will do Sullivan repeatedly over the years on his show, not only has he posed for pictures with Will—in which they resemble weird twins—not only has he publicly endorsed Will repeatedly, but—and this is really scary!—Sullivan has gradually acquired over the years all sorts of mannerisms that he didn't have originally but that Will stuck into the bit to make it funnier.

For when Will first did the take, nobody thought it was funny. Sullivan was—like most celebrities—a rather colorless man. He had enough mannerisms for an impressionist to do about sixty seconds. So, poor sad Will was forced to conclude, like any other hard-working but often unsuccessful experimentalist, that when you got Ed Sullivan down perfectly you got nothing perfect.

At that point, he began to tinker with the take. He raised the voice to a more metallic pitch. He exaggerated Sullivan's neck-brace posture and made him pivot like a doll in a Christmas window. He cracked his knuckles backward, whistled through his teeth, added a stammer-stopper nose buzzer. He also gave Sullivan a lot of lines that he never said on the air, like "Really big shoe!" The result was an instant success, a knockout. To this day Will bills himself as "The man who made Ed Sullivan laugh."

Now, the moral of this sort of thing was not lost on Lenny Bruce. Unless you were some kind of a nut about accuracy, a Tussaud wax worker, a Greek antique faker, you had nothing to gain by capturing every nuance of Peter Lorre's voice. In fact, you stood to lose a great deal with the average audience, which couldn't hear the difference between an accurate and a misleading impression but simply preferred an imitation with a few coarse strokes that made them laugh. Comedy, after all, was the name of the game.

So in Lenny's wonderful fantasy on the Lone Ranger, he makes no serious effort to duplicate the masked man's real voice. In fact, Lenny's Ranger doesn't sound even remotely like the famous radio hero. The real Ranger's voice was husky, low and murmurous, chosen to complement his handsome features and mysterious mask. Lenny's Ranger speaks in a high, tense voice—exactly the same voice Lenny once used to ridicule the cowboy baritones in musicals like *Oklahoma*. The reason for the shift is perfectly obvious: Lenny gives his Ranger the voice that matches his character as an uptight priggish moralist, a man too proud to stop for a "thank you." As the routine unfolds, we learn that the Ranger is really a fag, a Jew, and a sentimental old vaudevillian. To give this character a low sexy masculine voice would have completely destroyed the point. Actually, his Ranger's voice is not even an abstraction or caricature—it's a pure projection of fantasy—like the voices the animals have in animated cartoons.

The trick of matching voices to ideas obviously demands far fewer voices than the attempt to mimic every new star or celebrity. Even in the days when he was doing movie parodies and dramatic skits, Lenny got by with a very limited palette of impressions. He had his lispy spade voice, his screaming faggot voice, his gravel-throated Mafia voice, his hardy har-har Long Island contractor (or building super), his old Jewish storekeeper, his Deep South shitkicker, his babbling Pachuco—and a few standard show-biz types, like Bela Lugosi, H. B. Warner, Sabu, and Barry Fitzgerald. Compared with the hundred or two hundred voices that a great mimic can summon up, Lenny's bag was virtually empty. It contained mostly regional and ethnic accents, which are a lot easier to sustain than the speech of famous individuals. Limited as it was, however, this little stock of vocal disguises was perfectly adequate for Lenny's purposes. With these few dabs, he colored the most brilliant caricatures in contemporary comedy—and won himself, ironically, a reputation as a brilliant mimic with a flawless ear.

The vocal impression was not only the basic building block of Lenny's act; it became eventually his model for any sort of artistic statement: an instant shock of recognition, precipitating in a few highly charged seconds a whole wealth of accumulated associations and lending itself readily to dramatic manipulation in skits, bits, and movie parodies. As Lenny came to see, you could treat any subject the same way you did a movie star's accent. You could drop back, narrow your eyes, pick out the salient details, and roll them up in a tight little verbal spitball that would hit like a bullet. "A Filipino is a guy with a gold tooth, who balls a whore, comes quick—and giggles!" Wham! That took care of that subject. Now how about midgets?—"Little men with Buster Brown shoes: they use soap on their hair and have a crotch-eyed view of reality!" Boom! Again: flamenco dancer. "A guy who's always trying to get a look at his own ass." And so on through a thousand and one things until everything became an impression.

When Lenny got into his hot creative period at Duffy's and, later, at the Crescendo, he parlayed all his monologist's tricks into a series of classic movie parodies that were direct descendants of Sid Caesar's movie takeoffs. These movie parodies, Lenny's true masterpieces, are really nothing more than large-scale impressions. Instead of doing one character or two characters in a famous scene from some current picture, he does a whole film. He takes off a whole cast of characters and does all the incidental sounds, ranging from airplane engines, door clicks, and radio voices to the movie sound track with its violins, brasses, and tympani. (Lenny especially loved tympani—so much so that Kenny Hume always said that Lenny should have had a personal tympanist, the way other comics have a personal accompanist.) The great difference between Lenny and Sid was simply one of sohistication.

Sid was both perceptive and imaginative: if he had allowed himself the license that Lenny assumed, he might easily have become the greatest of all sick comics or black humorists. Violence was his basic medium and his deepest identifications were with hoodlums, badmen, and giant appetitive oafs who were constantly flying into insane rages and shooting everybody dead, including themselves. Anyone who runs over the plots of a dozen famous bits from *Your Show of Shows* will instantly perceive that the basis of Sid's humor was practically psychotic. If the bit didn't involve a gun or a Mafia character or a screaming German lunatic, it didn't mean a thing to Sid Caesar. Despite his penchant for the homicidal and the psychotic, however, Sid was dedicated to working within the commercial guidelines. He was, personally, very puritanical—objecting vehemently to dirty language and nudity on the stage—and like every performer who works on TV, he was terrified about giving offense to his vast and highly variegated audience. Even his strange fear of language could have been connected with anxiety about coming out in the open and really saying what he thought and felt. Sid's work, therefore, was always held down to a broad popular style that could not offend the proprieties of the television public. Though it developed some strange quirks in later years, when Sid became his own producer and was free to indulge his whims, the Caesar movie parodies never got very far out. Indeed, their basic tendency was to get more and more minutely realistic. When Sid remade his classic thirties gangster movie on his own show, for example, he went to fantastic lengths to make the TV cameras behave like movie cameras and to get the sets as convincing as movie sets and to achieve marvels of camp costuming, makeup, and musical scoring.

Lenny, by contrast, was always drawn to fantasy. Though he had begun his career by copying Sid's airplane bit, it's a safe guess that the parts he most enjoyed doing were not the incredibly accurate imitations of airplane engines (though Lenny did an acoustically impressive takeoff) or the chatter of machine guns and the whistle of bombs: the stuff that Lenny would have flipped for were the moments of madness—as when after an enormously prolonged and fantastically tense enginegunning sequence, Sid finally grows impatient with the balky, coughing machine and simply rips the throttle off the control panel, examining it for a moment with cocked-head curiosity, then carelessly tossing it out of the cockpit. That was the sort of craziness that would have appealed to Lenny Bruce.

Not being tied down to the pace of realism, Lenny made his routines move much faster than Sid's (a paradoxical feat in view of the fact that Lenny actually *worked* much slower than the apoplectic, brainstorming Sid). To take a famous example from the Ann's 440 period, *Father Flotsky's Triumph*, Lenny's take on the standard prison-break picture: the whole pace of this bit is drastically different from a Sid Caesar skit. The first thing that strikes you as characteristic of Lenny is how quickly he gets to the good part. Instead of mucking around in the prison yard, like Sid Caesar (who did a prison skit) giving a Method performance as a hood in striped pajamas, Lenny jumps in at the crisis of the film, at the final showdown between the warden and the hood —and stays there until the crisis has been resolved. What is equally characteristic is that instead of presenting the break as a desperate bid by stir-crazy prisoners seeking "freedom"—that noble-sounding virtue—Lenny interprets the *Riot in Cell Block 9* (the piece's original title) as an eruption of gross animals seeking sensual gratification. "We'll meet any reasonable demands," crows the Warden (played by Hume Cronyn) from his lofty moralistic perch in the machine-gun tower—"except the vibrators!" *The vibrators!* With that single, startling word, the whole bit suddenly comes to mad comic life! You laugh with that sock-in-the-solar-plexus gasp that Lenny got so often. The *vibrators*! In 1957 only the hippest of the hip were hip to electric vibrators. Like that legendary shingleman, what's-his-name, whom Lenny had met at Hanson's who used to run around the city all day long with a nice-looking attaché case in which he carried nothing but devices for sexual gratification: rubbers, ticklers, jellies, a whip, a pair of handcuffs, and, of course, a primitive electric vibrator designed to relax sore muscles and other working parts. Ah, it was incredible the punch that Lenny could pack into one of his throw-away lines. A word like "vibrators" would ring out in the house like a pistol-shot rap on a jazz drum!

The sexual theme of *Father Flotsky* provides not only the piece's startling opening shot but its thunderous closing cannonade. The situation is taut with the drama of confrontation. Dutch won't surrender to the boozy blandishments of Father Flotsky (who curses under his breath, "Give me the goddamned gun . . . *the rabbi is watching!*") Nor will he be intimidated by the Warden, who has ordered the tower guards to shoot "about three hundred to set an example." Just at the moment when the hail of bullets is about to rain down, a totally unfamiliar voice, a startlingly clear and urgent voice, cuts through the air: *"Don't scrub your good time, bubby! It's Kiki, the hospital atten-dant! You know—the one who gave you the bed baths!"*

That voice, so hard, so clear, so zingy—like Dame May Witty in high gear—is Lenny's greatest vocal caricature: the voice of Superfag. It would be a naïve Lenny Bruce fan who thought so much projection, such a deep and exactly detailed impression, could be attained without a great deal of emotional empathy. Lenny was obsessed with faggots all his life and this voice—which he employed in later years for his ultimate legal threat, the threat to hire an outrageously gay attorney! —was his abstraction of the whole gay world. No wonder it came slicing into this bit with the power of a Beethoven trumpet call. It is the wildest and most defiant gesture Lenny could muster, and it carries the day triumphantly.

Wonderful as is the comedy of *Father Flotsky*, it falls short of what Lenny achieved in his greatest routines. Comedy—like everything else in this world—divides ultimately into serious and frivolous, real or jive. Sid Caesar, zum beispiel, was a commercial comic working in a commercial medium; yet, as everybody realized looking at Big Sid tearing out his guts on the home screen, the cat was for real. When Sid did a classic bit, like *A Drunk There Was*, his forty-three-minute travesty of a silent movie, he not only made the people laugh—he achieved the authentic pathos of a man who is a drunkard and cannot bear the stigma of his disease. *The Drunkard* was serious comedy of the sort that Chaplin, Keaton, and Langdon had done in the twenties and thirties. It was funny and grotesque, camp and crazy, but it bore down on cetain conclusive images, real knockout punches like that passage at the end where Sid's daughter is marrying the boss's son and the poor old drunken father is out in the street trying to catch a glimpse of the wedding through an iron railing. Suddenly, a woman comes to the window, looks at him, and pulls down the blind. Sid casts a horrible glance of pain into the camera as the nickelodeon piano comes raving up behind him—a terrible tragic mask flashing through the camp the-atrics of the piece. That was serious modern comedy, and Lenny couldn't match it in his early years. Yet he knew where to find it. It was only a question of time till he made his own comedy that came to grips with suffering.

What Lenny did achieve during his first fame in Frisco was a single comprehensive metaphor for human experience that grew out of his profound ambivalence toward show business and especially the char-acter of the comedian. You find this basic metaphor in all his greatest work, which invariably poses the question: What if all the great people of this world—heroes of legend, leaders of nations, powers, potentates, principalities, the mighty God Himself—are simply the sort of crude, cynical shyster businessmen and degenerate hustlers that you find on Broadway, the New Jersey shingle business, or out on the road pushing baby pictures, Swiss watches, and fancy white Leatherette Bibles? What if, when we get behind the scenes at the White House or St. Patrick's or the Vatican at Rome, we were to find precisely the same mixture of petty cunning and crass exploitation that you find when you walk into a theatrical agent's office in the Brill Building or 1590 Broadway?

The first, and in some ways the greatest, application of this new satiric metaphor is a famous routine called *Religions, Inc.*

This bit snapped into focus after Lenny attended a vast religious rally run by Oral Roberts or Billy Graham (more likely the former) and instantly perceived how close the preacher was to pure show business. Next night at the club, he started working up the piece and within a couple of months it was complete. It was first recorded a year later, when Lenny came back to San Francisco to work at the hungry i. By that time it may have been losing some of its interest for Lenny; at least, one hears from fans in that area that the recorded version is shorter than the original version. (Actually, there is a tape I found in Lenny's private stash after his death that offers a much longer and superior version of the opening passage.)

As the piece began originally, Lenny would announce that the religious leaders of the world were holding a sales conference in San Francisco. Then he would roll off a list of names: Oral Roberts, Billy Graham, Patamunzo Yogananda, Danny Thomas, Pat O'Brien, Rabbi Wise, and General Sarnoff. Each of these great sales producers rises then to address "the men of the industry," commencing with H. A. Allen, who drawls in a Southern accent: "Good evening, gennelmen. Nice to see so many boys heah tonight. Most yew religious leaders ah haven't seen in many yeuhs. Ah jus' was talkin' to Billi this aftuhnoon. Ah said, 'Billi, yew come a lawng way, sweetie, lawng way. Who woulda thawt back in '31' . . . We were hustlin' baby pictures then, an' shingles and siding. We didn't know whatdehell we doin'. Sittin' one night in that Milner Hotel with nuthin' to do, watchin' that ole black sock under the bed gatherin' dust, ah picks up the Gideon, what was sittin' by the bed, an' ah says: 'Billi, there's gotta be a *buck* heah!' "

After a fast pointer talk on the religious sales chart—"The Big P, the Pentacostal, is stahtina move!"—and a quick rundown of the new religious novelty items—"gen-yew-ine Jewish-star-lucky-cross cigarette lighter combined with kiss-me-in-the-dark mezoozoo . . . wawkme-tawk-me camel . . . cocktail napkins printed, 'Anothuh mahtini for Muthuh Cabrini' "—the softspoken Southern con man introduces the hard-sell pitchman, Oral Roberts. Splitting the listeners' eardrums with his raucous blast, Roberts starts to rave it up in a spiel that is all suspenseful build-ups capped by screaming climaxes. Suddenly, there is an interruption, a long-distance call from the boss at Rome.

The angle of satire shifts slightly and the whole conversation be- tween the newly elected Pope John and Oral Roberts (who takes the call collect) is cast in the lingo of a Broadway theatrical agent talking to this act out on the road. *"Hello, Johnny! What's shakin', baby!* . . . Yeah, the puff of smoke knocked me out . . . Got an eight-page layout with Viceroy . . . 'The New Pope Is a Thinking Man' . . . Lissen, they're buggin' us again with that dumb integration . . . (Pope) *Dom- inus vobiscum populus succubus* . . . Lissen, hold on a minute . . . Hey, Billi wants to know if you can get him a deal on one of them Dago sports cars . . . Whenya comin' to the Coast? . . . I can get ya the Steve Allen Show the nineteenth . . . Wear the big ring . . . Yeah, O.K., sweetie, yew cool it tew . . . *No, nobody knows you're Jewish!"*

In this most familiar of all Lenny Bruce bits, it's obvious that he has not only expanded the premise—"organized religion is big business"—to Rabelaisian proportions, but he has also rendered with extraordinary accuracy and insight the little worlds of the Bible sales- man and the redneck preacher and the telephone-cradled-on-the-neck theatrical agent talking through the night to his "act" out on the road. Even today—after the record has been played a hundred times and the routine is imprinted on the mind like an old Pepsi-Cola commercial—the exhilarating impiety, the comical obscenity of that last conversation fills the mind with silent laughter. What a way to address the Pope—"HEY, JOHNNY! WHAT'S SHAKIN', BABY!"

Ann's 440, where Lenny opened in January of 1958, was a typical dyke club in every detail save one—the club's name did not wink the code word, "Three." Four-forty was the actual street address, smack in the heart of Broadway, slotted into the stretch of three-story houses across from the Jazz Workshop and down the block from Finocchio's. Ann's was a dark, clammy rendezvous for the femmes and butches. Aban- doning all hope as you threaded the carefully guarded door, you en- tered a long, dark chamber lined with plate-glass mirrors. To your left worked a bustling service bar; dead-ahead loomed a full-blown pro- scenium stage festooned and flounced with maroon velours. The girls were crammed together—a hundred odd couples—at wristwatch-sized tables, straddling chrome-and-red Leatherette chairs. The expensive drinks they were clutching couldn't get you high, and the bull-dyke waitresses who were hustling them were not shy about picking up empty—or not so empty—glasses. Norma, the manager of the room, bore a striking resemblance to Bruce Cabot. Ann Dee, the proprietor, looked like a fat Edith Piaf. Ann would stand behind the bar all night ringing up checks. (The chime of her cash register is clearly audible on Lenny's early records.) But if she saw that business was dragging, she would hustle up onstage, where she suddenly became a chanteuse, singing in a low husky voice, "My Funny Valentine."

Among the first people to pick up on Lenny were two influential columnists: Herb Caen and Ralph J. Gleason. A city of column readers, San Francisco rushed to hear the new find. Among the tide of listeners were people of intelligence and culture, Bay Area intellectuals, like Pauline Kael and Lou Gottlieb. Der Lou, who enjoyed a considerable following as a guru, was absolutely overwhelmed. He called up all the members of his informal ashram and cried: "This is the Leader!" Immediately, the local hipsters poured into the club. Wes Montgomery's brothers, Monk and Buddy, came. The singer Ernestine Anderson came. And all the jazzmen playing on the street came in to dig the word blower. Eventually, the Beat poets from Grant Avenue moseyed in: Larry Ferlinghetti and his gang. After them came the college professors and grad students from Berkeley, the Mort Sahl audience. Mark Shorer was a great fan, as were a number of other professors, some of whom later testified on Lenny's behalf when he got in trouble with the law. By the time Lenny got deep into *Religions, Inc.*, this assembly of oddly assorted people was given the final fillip of incongruity by being enlarged to include a number of seminarians and clerics, who wanted to hear the satire on organized religion. Sitting in the one-time dyke bar, assailed by an unprecedented barrage of filth, the padres were impressed. When reporters asked them what they thought of Lenny Bruce, the pale-faced religious invariably remarked, "Mr. Bruce is our favorite comedian."

Such success could not be ignored by the local record company; almost as soon as Lenny's engagement began at Ann's, the owner and the chief executive of Fantasy Records, Max Weiss, and Saul Zaentz, came in to see the show. Max and Saul had accompanied the Sahls and Paul Desmond to see Lenny once before at the Cobblestone, where he raved for twenty minutes about enemas; so they weren't exactly enthusiastic about the prospects of recording his extravagances and violations of good taste. When they got into the club and heard all the bright, fresh ideas Lenny had developed during the past two or three years, they decided instantly to get him on record. A West Coast jazz label, with a few spoken-word, folk, and Latin American albums, Fantasy had made the first recording of Mort Sahl at the Carmel Sunset Auditorium back in 1955, but Sahl had copped out of the contract and signed with RCA Victor. Now the Berkeley-based label would score a greater comic.

Lenny, for his part, was delighted to make any deal with a record company because this was the age of the comedy album. No longer a dumb "party record"—a couple of little bits squeezed onto a ten-inch 78—the new comedy LPs were heavy-selling home entertainment. Served up on hi-fi platters, Jonathan Winters, Nichols and May, Tom Lehrer, and Shelley Berman had found a vast new living-room audience. Shelley Berman actually had a record that climbed the charts to No. 1. Records were great because they got comics into places that they could never reach, like the college dorm or the Bohemian-Beatnik pad. People played the discs over and over again, until they really *heard* what the comic said. Records were also the greatest advance publicity and audience-building device ever invented. Naturally, Lenny was dying to make a deal with a record company.

There were problems, of course. Weiss and Zaentz recognized from the jump that they would have to record Lenny in a club because he couldn't work in a dead studio. That was a basic problem in all comedy recording—the laugh timing. The problem had first become obvious when talkies came in. For the first time in the history of the business, the funnymen had to set their gags once and forever so they would fit audiences all over the world. Often, they tried out the film somewhere around Hollywood for a couple of weeks; then they adjusted the sound track so the laughs wouldn't bury the jokes. That's why Laurel and Hardy movies play so slowly today: they were timed for audiences that didn't react as fast as we do now.

In Lenny's case, the whole problem of timing and audience interaction was complicated by the fact that he never did his material the same way twice. One night he would ad-lib a whole new extension; the next night he'd short-circuit the bit to a premature conclusion. Generally speaking, his delivery was very uneven: he wandered off mike and often spoke so rapidly that it was hard to know exactly what he had said. Editing the records was not an easy job; the results were technically rough. Typically, the effort to splice together several different tapes in order to present the routine in its fullest extension produced jumps in volume and changes in vocal quality that destroyed the illusion of a single, straight-through performance. A certain amount of censorship was also exercised over the language: individual words and sometimes whole lines were deleted. The choice of material may also have been partially determined by what was least likely to offend the code of that day.

By June 1958 there were two LPs in the works. *Interviews of Our Times* was a composite of pieces by Lenny and a couple of other comics, Henry Jacobs and Woody Leifer. The latter had made an EP (extended play—a seven-inch 45) with two routines on it: an interview with a hopelessly inarticulate jazzman who talks in nothing but shapeless monosyllables; and another interview with "Dr. Sholem Stein," a pretentious psychiatrist who speaks in meaningless psychoanalytical jargon. Fantasy wanted to put these two bits on a twelve-inch record, so they made a deal with Lenny to supply seven additional tracks. One piece, *The March of High Fidelity*, was a studio production number (with a lot of sound effects) about a guy who gets hooked on hi-fi equipment. Lenny used the classic dope-story pattern—the casual experiment with marijuana leading on to a devastating heroin habit—to portray the deepening involvement of hi-fi addicts with increasingly expensive equipment. The other routines were out of Lenny's club performances, the audience clearly audible. One of them is *Father Flotsky*, but in an early version, lacking much of the detail of the fully developed sketch issued later on Lenny's fourth album and labeled "unexpurgated." The most successful pieces on the first album are Lenny's Dracula bit and the interview between Lawrence Welk and the lisping, jive-talking jazzman.

By the time *Interviews* appeared, in the late summer of '58, plans were well advanced for a second, all-Bruce album, which was to contain Lenny's heaviest material, like *Religions, Inc.* Not very happy about the quality of the first album—and the fact that it had two tracks by a couple of mediocre comics—Lenny demanded that Fantasy take his name off *Interviews*. One month after the album was released and had begun to get air-play, Lenny changed his mind and demanded that his name be restored to the cover, itself a masterpiece of irrelevance. It shows Max Weiss, a heavy, balding, bearded man in horn-rimmed glasses, sitting in a flimsy-looking house furnished, evidently, by Goodwill Industries, reading aloud from a book titled *Pigs Ate My Roses*. At his knees sits one rather butchy lady, with bare feet and rolled-up trousers, and directly across from him another lady, very attractive and poised, in a striped leotard, smoking a cigarette with a holder. (The two ladies are Peggy Tolk Watkins, the author of *Pigs Ate*, as well as other collections of verse, and her partner, Irmine Droeger.) How this enigmatic trio happened onto the face of Lenny's debut album is a question that could be answered only by Max Weiss, who evidently had a penchant for putting his picture on comedy albums because he turns up as a Toulouse-Lautrec dwarf on the back

of Lenny's next album, posing on his knees next to the very distingué
Count Bruce.

During the whole period of Lenny's initial success, Honey was in
prison. Though he hadn't seen her in more than a year, she was constantly in his thoughts. He wondered what her life was like behind
bars: whether, for example, she had to put out for the prison matrons.
Sometimes, he alluded to her in his act. One day he decided to write
her a letter. He was still pretty bitter about her infidelities; so he gave
her a taste of her own medicine. "Since you've been in there," he
wrote, "I must have made it with 400 different chicks, and I never
made it with the same one twice." The letter was delivered to Honey
four weeks after the date on its postmark, partially censored by a
psychiatrist, who appended a four-page analysis of Lenny's juvenile
boast. The psychiatrist explained to Honey, in his best Dr. Franzblau
manner, that Lenny was suffering from "insecurity" as a result of
Honey's behavior, and that he was driven "to prove himself" over and
over again by balling hundreds of women. The shrink could have saved
himself a lot of trouble by simply talking to Honey. She knew very
well what Lenny's braggadocio meant—and she knew also that if he
couldn't sleep with any girl more than once, he was still pretty hung
on her.

   Actually, Lenny had gotten very compulsive in this period about
scoring chicks. One-a-day was his professed goal, and there were certainly lots of days when he made his quota. Lenny had always preferred
quickie, one-shot relationships. There was nothing new in this pattern.
Nor was it surprising that these quick stabs sometimes developed into
whirlwind romances. Despite the cynicism and sordidness of the world
he had long inhabited, Lenny Bruce still preserved a potent strain of
adolescent romanticism. The longing to be deeply in love with "a
wonderful girl" was always stirring at the back of his brain. Sometimes
he even thought for a few days or weeks that he had found the right
girl. That was obviously what was passing through his mind when he
met Sheryl Carson and swept her off her feet.

   Sheryl had actually met Lenny years before, back in 1955, when
he was working at the Cobblestone. He hardly noticed her at the time,
but she was overwhelmed by the experience. She had gone out to the
Valley with a carload of people to see the show. The instant she laid
eyes on Lenny, she was fascinated by him. His good looks, his powerful
personality, his no-bullshit raps from the stage—he was just "too
much." "I immediately fell in love with him," she recalled after his
death. "He could have sent a truck over the next day, and I would
have given him all my furniture." At the same time that she fell in

love with Lenny, Sheryl also recognized how threatening he might be to her peace of mind: "He scared me because I realized the power he had over me. I knew he was balling a lot of chicks, and I knew he dug great-looking shiksa-type girls with nice figures, and I felt I just wasn't his type." So when she saw Lenny in the clubs, she never came on to him, never tried to attract his attention, just smiled or nodded or let it go with a vague hello. That was the way it went until Lenny started working Ann's; then matters suddenly took another turn.

I was up there with a couple of hairdresser friends of mine. I had red hair at the time and Lenny dug redheads. So he noticed me that night, and I noticed him as if it were for the first time. He was walking across Broadway, going to work in the club. We had eye contact.

Later we went into the club, and after the show he came over to our table and sat down with us and said, "I'd like to go to sleep with you!" I said, "I'm looking for someone to stay awake with me." And he just cracked up, and he shook me and said, "Did you just say that?" He used to do that: I'd say something funny to him on the spur of the moment, and he'd say to me, "Did you just make that up?" He'd really get turned on by something funny because very few people made him laugh.

After we laughed it up, Lenny asked me to meet him later after I had gotten rid of my two hairdresser friends. So I drove them back to this nice motel where we were staying. Both of these boys were faggots, and they were kind of jealous of my going to see Lenny. One said to me, "This is terrible—you're going to see him and you just got your period." I said, "I didn't sign a contract. I can't help it if I've got my period!" Actually, it made me feel a lot safer about meeting Lenny that night.

Well, we went to some after-hours place downstairs, and Eric Miller was playing there. There were some cops out front, and I thought it was kind of wild, because how come you can drink after two o'clock in San Francisco and you can't in Los Angeles? I had been smoking pot, and I had sprayed, and I didn't want him to know that I smoked pot. I'm very cool about it. I'm a very good citizen. I even belong to the Auto Club. Yet the minute he got in the car, he sniffs and says, "You've been smoking pot!" His hipness! He just knew everything! You couldn't deceive him!

We had a very strange night. It was like we were in high school. He was very romantic. He sang in my ear at the club. All we did was neck and pet that night—he didn't even *want* anything else.

We were just very turned on. It was very crazy and very light and we were back in high school again.

Then we went to a cafeteria, the two of us. There was practically nobody there and he got some food. Some stewed fruit and bran muffins. We ate and then he said he had to leave. It was about eight o'clock in the morning. He came right out and told me where he was going. "I use narcotics," he said. "I'm going to meet my connection." I knew why he was telling me. He was saying: "This is me. I do all these things. If you dig me, you dig me. If you don't, I might as well tell you so you won't have any problem." Still, it devastated me to learn that he was a junkie. I was scared to death of being his girlfriend because he was too much to cope with. I knew he would do me in.

I left for Los Angeles the next day. He flew down a week later to see me on a Monday. The beauty shop where I worked was closed and he couldn't find me. He asked everybody around the shop but it didn't help. He left me a little note saying that he'd come down to find me. It had a little drawing of tears dropping down. Imagine! He didn't even know my last name! Then he flew down here again because he was really hot for me. Here was something that he was really trying to get, and he couldn't quite get it. He was really turned on now.

One day he walks into the shop. He's gorgeous! I'm just having my hair done, so I can't leave. "When can I see you?" he said. "I've got to see you!" I said I had to go to group therapy that night. I didn't really have to go, but I was dangling him. He even called me at group therapy that night. Finally, he came over to my house, and, well . . . he just wanted to make it. He practically attacked me, and I just kept holding him off because I knew I had this power over him at this particular time. This was my romantic period with Lenny, and we slept together many nights. It was strange, people used to tell me, "There's something about you that's like Sally." The first time I told Lenny, he said, "Well, that probably means I want to ball my old lady." Lenny used to say to Sally, "Ma, don't Sheryl and I look alike?" Like, they really took me into the family.

Honey never entered Lenny's mind at that time. I knew that it bothered him very much that Honey had slept with other guys—and even girls. Lenny had this double standard. A lot of guys do. They can do whatever *they* want, but they don't want their wives doing the same thing. He'd make cracks about "My wife's a die-girl [diesel dyke] lesbian."

His other problem was Kitty. He always bemoaned the fact that he was a father because he wasn't meant to be a father. He just realized that he wasn't capable of being a good father, and he had this darling child, and here he was being a father and he wasn't.

Eventually, Lenny and I became just friends, but my relationship with him was very important to me because I loved him and he let me love him. He let me be in on his scene—a part of his life.

Lenny's womanizing in San Francisco was ultimately a lot less important than his cultivation of a whole new series of interesting and sometimes influential male friends.

Two of the first people he met in Frisco were Herb Caen and Ralph J. Gleason. Caen was Mr. San Francisco: the creator of the Fisherman's Wharf mystique, the self-appointed ombudsman for every matter of civic concern and the city's leading wit and manufacturer of bons mots, his most celebrated coinage being the word "Beatnik." A highly influential molder of public opinion, Caen was the first writer to take the line that Lenny Bruce was not so much "sick" as he was the anatomist of a sick world. Writing in the *Chronicle* (whose editor had hailed his recent return as "the most important single event" in the *Chronicle*'s winning a sixty-five-year circulation war with the *Examiner*), Caen said:

> They call Lenny Bruce a sick comic—and sick he is. Sick of the pretentious phoniness of a generation that makes his vicious humor meaningful. He is a rebel, but not without a cause, for there are shirts that need unstuffing, egos that need deflating and precious few people to do the sticky job with talent and style. Sometimes you feel a twinge of guilt for laughing at one of Lenny's mordant jabs—but that disappears a second later when your inner voice tells you, with pleased surprise, "But that's true." The kind of truth that might not have dawned on you if there weren't a few Lenny Bruces around to hammer it home.

Lenny, for his part, was very impressed by Caen's sophisticated tastes and lavish life-style. The little beak-nosed newspaper writer was married at this time to Sally Gilbert, a handsome honey-blonde with a sharp, incisive mind. He lived in an impressive three-story, eight-room home in fashionable Pacific Heights and boasted that he was only the third occupant since the house was built in 1887. The mansion was opulently appointed with Louis XVI furniture, fifteenth-century French tapestries, Chinese silk screens, pre-Columbian pottery, and an imposing collection of books and old recordings. Paintings by modern artists hung on the walls and intellectual journals were scattered on the reading chairs and coffee tables. Much of the closet space was taken up by Caen's wardrobe, perhaps the most meticulous and extensive to be found in the entire city. It included nearly one hundred pairs of shoes.

This was precisely the style to which Lenny aspired and which he was later to emulate in a crudely caricatured way when he bought his "House on the Hill" and installed a Filipino houseboy and carried on for a season like a sophisticated man of the world. Lenny's authentic tastes, however, always ran in precisely the opposite direction: toward shabby hotels and cafeteria snacks and hanging out with weirdos and jazz musicians. Ralph J. Gleason was a little closer to Lenny's world —being a well-known jazz critic who had instantly identified Lenny with the jazz scene. Writing anonymously in *Variety*, in April, he described Lenny's humor as being "right out of a roadband sideman's perspective"—an association he was to explore in many subsequent pieces. Gleason himself, however, was much closer to a college professor or an Irish literary-pub type than he was to a jazz musician. A diabetic condition prohibited him from drinking, and drug use was a feature of the jazz life which he usually discounted as a figment of the Hollywood movie writer's imagination. Lenny assured Gleason in later years that he was not an addict, and Gleason believed him absolutely. He still denies that Lenny was ever hooked.

Another intellectual friend of this period was the celebrated Lou Gottlieb, Professor Aberrant of Music, Comedy, and, eventually, Eastern Cults and Offbeat Religions. Gottlieb possessed a Ph.D. in musicology and had studied composition with Arnold Schoenberg. The upshot of this formidable preparation was that he became the music director of the Limeliters. That, however, was a few years after he met Lenny. In 1958, Gottlieb was trying to become a stand-up comic in the Mort Sahl style and was working at the hungry i, a block and a half away from Ann's on Kearny. Getting friendly with Lenny after losing "sphincter control" watching his act, Lou asked the Schoenberg of the new-wave comics if he would help him develop his act. Lenny thought the problem over carefully and finally said, "Lou, you look like a bird. You should come on carrying a stuffed bird." "What would I say, Lenny?" asked the puzzled student. "Get me a bird book, man," snapped Lenny. Next night, poring over a volume of richly colored ornithological plates, Lenny finally found what he was seeking. Pointing to a picture, he said: "See this picture, man? Get yourself one of these birds stuffed. Then, walk on and say: 'This is a blue heron. It is a long-legged wader that subsists entirely on fish. This diet gives it its beautiful blue sheen, its keen eyes, its tireless energy but *lousy breath*!" Again, the slightly hysterical Gottlieb despaired of his sphincter.

Perhaps the most devoted and admiring of all of Lenny's new friends was the P.R. agent for Ann's (and several other clubs along Broadway), the ever-smiling Grover Sales. Grover, a great digger of comics, was blessed with a phonographic memory. To this day, he can sit for hours riddling off entire Lenny Bruce routines by heart: routines that he has memorized as you remember a record, with all the vocal intonations and pauses and speech mannerisms exactly duplicated. As Grover knew Lenny's material by heart, he often got a bigger kick out of watching the audience. He introduced Lenny to many of the night haunts along Broadway, like the City Lights Bookstore, where he would point out choice items that might make good takeoff points for Lenny's raps. When the hour got really late, however, and it was junkie time down south, Lenny and Grover would always split.

For the late, late show, Lenny had another new buddy, who was destined to play a small but important role in his life until practically the day he died. This was Eric Miller, the jazz guitarist at Ann's, a thin, quiet, engaging chap of no particular age and rather mediocre ability. Eric's great appeal to Lenny lay in the fact that he was an extremely pliable and tolerant sort of person, who could adapt himself to any and all of Lenny's whims. If Eric got hacked with something Lenny was into, he wouldn't mess up the game with complaints—he would just fade away and disappear. One other attraction Eric possessed for Lenny: he was black.

When Lenny would take off for a couple of days and broom down to L.A., he'd jump right back into the gang of crazies with whom he'd played those Marx Brothers scenes in the lab at UCLA. Fast Harry's cache of dope had long since been exhausted. Now the gang was into scoring through brilliant scams. Chic Eder recollects one such masterpiece:

Early in the morning, Lenny, a tall, skinny piano player and I were driving to the connection's in a car wanted by the finance company. We're all icky-sick and have scraped up barely enough bread to cop a three-way "wake-up" taste. The news comes over the car radio that Welk is suing Lenny for $100,000. Lenny tells me to head for my pad, drop him off at the pay phone on the corner, get my big Zenith Trans-Oceanic portable radio and pick him back up. When this is done and he gets back in the short, we learn that he's called the radio station and ascertained that they broadcast the news every half hour. Now we're moving on a tight schedule. Lenny tells us our timing has to get us to the connection's four or five minutes before the next news segment. Meanwhile, he dials the portable to the proper station. After the build-up and the hush-hush of listening to the news at the pad, Lenny convinces the bag-men that this publicity will skyrocket record sales to the tune of thousands in his pocket within a week's time. Needless to say, Lenny plays the dude like an instrument, and we leave there with half a piece [half an ounce] of stuff—on credit!

The legal hassle with Lawrence Welk did not put a lot of money in Lenny's pocket. Fantasy had to go through all the albums beeping out the bandleader's name with a funny sound—like cellos bowed staccato. What the record, the lawsuit, the reviews in the trade and local papers (combined with the steadily accumulating word-of-mouth publicity) *did* achieve was a Lenny Bruce boom loud enough to carry across the country. In Chicago, a team of nightclub owners named Shelley Kasten and Skip Krask was getting set to go out on a talent-buying trip. They had decided to redecorate their jazz club in the basement of the Hotel Maryland and reopen it with a new entertainment policy featuring comics and singers. The club, called The Cloister, was also a pet project of Hugh Hefner, a close friend of Shelley Kasten. When a jazz musician told Kasten about Lenny Bruce, the very next day Hugh Hefner also mentioned the name (Hef having gotten the word from West Coast friends). At that moment both partners decided to join Hefner on a business trip to San Francisco.

Shepherded over to Ann's by the ever-courteous Herb Caen, the talent buyers were delighted by Lenny's performance. A bright, hip, terribly funny comic whose potential hadn't been exhausted by over-exposure, he was just what they needed to attract the attention of the press and fill up their club with the sophisticated clientele they were courting in that day of clever young nightclub acts. The bargain they struck was a real coup for Lenny. He would open the club in September, right after Labor Day, play there the first week for $850, then, if he was held over, jump up the next week to $1,250. It was not only the best money he had ever made—it was a giant step professionally.

Chicago meant that Lenny was out of the joints, once and for all. Chicago meant that he was heading back East for the first time in five years, taking the road that was certain to lead to New York. Most of all, Chicago meant that Lenny Bruce was no longer a freak attraction enjoyed in little oddball places but a strongly bidding new talent, who might in time become just as successful as the biggest names in the business. Lenny's old dreams of starring in pictures or becoming a national celebrity—or just having the money to live comfortably and do what he pleased—these once flimsy dreams of a not very talented and hopelessly unprofessional kid were now about to materailize. In —of all places—"Chi-*ca*-go, Chi-*ca*-go!"

Chapter Eight

THE SICKEST OF
THE SICK

There was a line around the block on the first night of Lenny's appearance at the Cloister. Word had spread that this new young comic was sensational. Lenny's initial record accounted for some of the business; but the owners felt they were scoring off some strange underground word-of-mouth thing, a sort of jungle telegraph that had sounded the news of Lenny's advent clear across the country without benefit of conventional publicity. Keyed up for a killing, Lenny stepped out on the floor that night—lean, keen, and dapper in a dark, narrow Ivy League suit. "We have some celebrities with us in the audience this evening," he announced. "Sitting ringside are two boys in show business who got their start right here in the Windy City—the wonderful *Loeb and Leopold*!

"We're also privileged to welcome the star of the show that opens here two weeks from tonight. The management is sparing no expense in bringing him to you. Let's have a big hand for the lovable *Adolf Hitler*!"

Walk out there and BAM! An old show-biz trick, getting the drop on the audience. That first big laugh that starts the ball rolling. But Lenny wasn't shooting for anything as simple as a laugh. He was playing into the image of the *sick comic*—the tag that had been tied on him during his last months in San Francisco.

"Sick" was the magic word in American humor that season. Sick jokes and sick cartoons, sick comics and sick singers, sick, sick, sick —till it almost made you sick. One of those things like knock-knock

jokes and hula hoops that start with the kids, the subadolescents, and
then spread like the measles. "Can Billy come out and play?" "You
know he has no arms or legs." "That's all right, we just want to use
him for home plate." The archetypal sick joke was an incredibly in-
human response to physical deformity, disease, disaster—all the fe-
tishes of liberal piety and compassion. The humor surfaced first in the
playgrounds of the middle-class schools. Then it turned up in the pages
of *Mad*, the sick, cynical comic book of the new generation of sick,
cynical kids. From the junior high kids it jumped (as rock did later)
to the senior high kids and then to the college kids. At which point it
suddenly became the latest entertainment fad among sophisticated
young adults. Eventually "sick" embraced everything from the wistful
social desperation of Nichols and May, to the businesslike cruelty of
Don Adams ("Sitting over there I see Mr. Thompson. He lost his wife
and two children in the crash. Stand up and take a bow, Mr. Thompson.
Let's give him a nice hand . . . no tears now! Just take your bow and
sit down."), to the silly sadism of an ex-Harvard math instructor named
Tom Lehrer who always *sang* his sick jokes: "I ache for the touch of
your lips, dear / But much more for the touch of your whips, dear."
Along with the ghoulish cartoons of Charles Addams and the strips of
Jules Feiffer (those Village types with contorted, twitching bodies and
no less contorted minds, endlessly analyzing their neuroses), the sick
comics were the big pop-culture phenomenon of the fall of 1958.

Lenny scorned the label "sick comic," insisting the term was just
a lazy journalistic cipher for a very complicated and heterogeneous
clutch of comics. A good point. Yet the word "sick" was never out of
his mouth; and the way he used it made it equivalent to "funny,"
"bizarre," "fascinating," "imaginative"—all the values that characterized his own comedy. As soon as he spotted the new trend, he
tailored his act to strengthen his image as "the sickest of the sick
comics." He would open with a bit on John Graham, a kid who blew
up an airplane carrying forty passengers and his mother. Then he'd
segue into other items in the news: a recent mine disaster ("Get away
from there, kid—quit kicking dirt in the hole!") and the current trial
of an American soldier for killing a Japanese woman ("So sorry. Verdict has been changed from life in prison to two weeks at Waldorf
Astoria."). The mine-disaster bit was a favorite with Lenny. The biggest laughs occurred when a TV crew arrives on the scene and the
producer instantly sees the commercial possibilities of the miners' predicament. Yelling down the breathing tube, "Stop that whining!" he
orders his men to lower a Salem cigarette on a string. Calling down
to the miners, he says: "Listen, you men!—here's a chance to make

a few bucks. When you get the cue, I want you to say, 'Though we're trapped, Salem is trapping our tars!' "

After the first night in Chicago, Lenny's sick humor did so-so business. The critics didn't know what to make of him. There were the usual epithets—"shocking," "outrageous," "not in good taste." The word-of-mouth continued strong, however, and each week of the month that Lenny spent at the club showed a gradual improvement. By the end of the run, he had achieved two of his prime purposes: he had gotten an invitation to return the following year at a better price, and he had become a client of MCA, a major talent agency.

When Lenny got back to San Francisco, he passed up Ann's 440 to work a much slicker and better-paying club called Fack's No. 2. The joint's crazy name was explained by the fact that it was called *Jack's* No. 2 until the owners of the original Jack's, a restaurant on Kearney, complained that their rights to the name were being infringed. George Andros, the tough-talking proprietor of Jack's No. 2, said, "Fuck you, Jack! If the name is so goddamned precious, we'll change our billing and call ourselves not Jack's but Fack's—and fuck you, again!"

The first time Lenny met Andros, he flashed—Al Capone! The club looked like "a Filipino gym decorated for a high school prom"; yet he did some great shows there and invented some fresh routines. The big news story of the day was the Sherman Adams scandal. Adams—a former governor of New Hampshire and Ike's number one adviser in the White House—had accepted a whole series of gifts from a wealthy Boston businessman, Bernard Goldfine. Among the items that made the headlines were a vicuña coat, a deep freezer, and a very big hotel bill. Lenny applied his now-standard technique to the incidents in the newspapers and came out with a picture of dealings in the White House that was pretty close to his image of life behind the scenes of organized religion.

During Lenny's engagement at Fack's, Fantasy was again taping him, building up its stock of bits for a projected second LP. Recording was still seen as a rather costly and uptight operation, and every time the engineers came into the club, Lenny worried that something might happen that would spoil his performance. One night, Lenny had no sooner made his opening remarks and settled into the groove than a middle-aged man and two young women sitting at ringside began to make so much noise that he felt obliged to silence them. His first shpritz was a delicate needle shower designed to shock them into silence without employing any heavy weapons. Stopping suddenly, he turned to the table, scrutinized them closely and quipped: "We've got at ringside a very distinguished-looking gentleman and two ladies—a Mormon wedding!" Wanting to take the edge off his crack, he hastily added, "I'm a little hostile . . . I'll get rid of the poison in a minute."

Ten minutes later, right in the midst of a new bit, the noise from the table became so annoying that he suddenly spun around and barked in a strong, angry voice—"All right! Now shut up, you *hooker*!" Shifting gears quickly and adopting a slightly more humorous tone, he added: "And get out of here, Daddy Warbucks! Never mind the Diners' Club shtick! The convention isn't in town anymore. I had to get these two girls here from Sally Stanford's [a famous madam]. You don't understand [adopting tone of uptight parent admonishing child]: *You can't talk here!* [Then the fast hip shpritz] You'll get the towels and leave!"

One of the girls screams something back at him, and Lenny really lets her have it: "You'll end up in the trunk with Dr. Sheppard. [Screams of laughter] They'll get you . . . the gas in the face . . . you'll like it!" When the girl replies, "Do you think we're all together?" Lenny suddenly adopts his coolest, sexiest delivery. Casting moody eyes at the trio over the top of his hand-held mike, he murmurs, "I like what you're doing. I want to go home with the three of you. I'll sit on the bed. I won't touch anybody. [Howls from the audience] I'm one of those guys who like to watch and listen. A lot of guys promise . . ." Then giving up in despair, he sighs. "Oh, well, there goes the tape, money down the drain."

One more time, Lenny returns to the bits, having now done everything in his power to squelch the offenders. It's no use; much as he tries to concentrate and ignore the chattering trio, their voices are goading him into hysteria. Suddenly, he stops and demands: "How did you happen to come in here? Was it the Mystery Bus Tour? [Laughter] You got your slacks cleaned free . . . then the roller rink. You have eyes for me, I can tell. Later, 612 [Sotto voce], the key's under the rug. Take the elevator to the seventh floor and walk down one. Later. Oh, you're getting a different take on me? Lenny Bruce is hostile? Yeah, we might as well continue in that vein. I'd like to *put* something in your vein—an overload! You're another biological failure, a result of fallout. See the second generation of genetics we've suffered! We're getting paid back for Hiroshima . . ." On and on and on it went through "You love me!" "You hate me!" "I love you!" "I hate you!" *The Comedian's Nightmare* could have been the name of the tape. Frank Dell, Dean of Mimicry and Satire, fighting like a bitch to keep his slippery footing on the stage. Regrettably, Fantasy saw nothing of commercial value in the battle, and so another great document in the history of American humor hit the cutting-room floor.

During this second engagement in San Francisco, Lenny saw his first cabaret-theater revue—and was enchanted. It was a little home-made piece, starring two young girls of semiprofessional status; nothing very special, yet very typical of that day. For alongside the advent of sick comedy, another trend had surfaced in American humor: the coffeehouse stage. The origins of this experiment go back to the early years of the fifties at the University of Chicago, where Mike Nichols, a pre-med student from New York, and Elaine May, an "auditor" from the West Coast, met by doing shtick in an Illinois Central station near the campus (*Foreign accent*: "May I seeet down?" *Foreign-spy look*: "EEEf you vish"), and then went on to become the stars of a tiny off-campus cabaret, the Compass Theater, founded by Paul Sills and Sam Shepherd. Three years of endlessly improvising skits before solemn, beer-drinking U. of C. students produced enough material and enough chutzpah to send neurotic Mike and super-neurotic Elaine to the Blue Angel in New York, where Max Gordon and Max Jacoby played them for a week (frowning at the way Mike's cheap hairpiece kept sliding off his head) and then shunted them downtown to the Vanguard. Their subsequent success in clubs, on records, and in the theater made them famous overnight.

Lenny Bruce saw Nichols and May on TV. He loved them and even went so far as to offer to write them a couple of bits—but they turned him down flat. Actually, they were wise to do so: Lenny's genius certainly didn't lie in dramatizing the hang-ups of upper-middle-class intellectuals, neurotics, and analysands. His strength lay in mimicking the lumpen and the shinglemen and the hysterical little comics at Hanson's. Still, there was something about this new medium, the cabaret theater, that beguiled him. A tiny theater, you dig? Like a children's theater with booze. You had the tightness of a small club plus the respect you get in the theater. You weren't on the floor anymore—you were up on a little *stage*. The skits could be like in the Mountains, with blackouts. Or you could go with music and do a little revue. Something like *New Faces*. A whole new area of the business, and there just wasn't any saying where it could go. Lenny felt it was worth a shot. One shot, O.K.? A chance to write a show that could go to Broadway. He would script the book and write the tunes—he had a couple of ideas for melodies—and he would get some girls to work with him. He couldn't do all this in San Francisco because his gig at Fack's wound up at the end of October, and he had to get down to L.A. to work at the Crescendo. But when he got settled in L.A., he could look around for a groovy theater and build up the show by working on it, night after night.

By the time Lenny got home, he had the story of his "musical"

half plotted. Built out of autobiographical fantasy and observations of
the new world of the black-stockinged Beatniks in San Francisco, it
concerns a small-time comic who bombs in the clubs and decides to
get out of the business. Applying for a civil service job, his application
is mixed up with some other papers, and he is assigned by mistake to
J. Edgar Hoover's office in Washington. His job is to write all-purpose
speeches that can be used by public officials, like the President, every
time some emergency arises. The speeches are exercises in double-
talk: they sound like something left over from an old Sid Caesar script.

Apart from writing speeches, the comic sometimes works as an
undercover agent. His latest assignment is to infiltrate the coffeeshops
of San Francisco by posing as a comedian. Getting a job in an espresso
alley in North Beach, he immediately befriends two girls in black
stockings and long stringy hair. Their first conversation turns on the
topic of marriage. Explaining that his old lady has just left him, the
comic asks first one girl and then the other if they want "to do it."
Both turn him down flat; at that point he goes into his first number,
"All Alone." As the stage lights come down and the mood turns blue,
Lenny steps to the footlights and sings wistfully:

> All alone. All alone.
> Oh what a joy to be all alone.
> I'm happy alone, don't you see!
> I've convinced you, now how about me?
> All alone.

When the comic finishes his song, he asks the first girl, "Where
you from?" When she answers, "Lansing," he demands to know why
she would leave such a nice safe little town for "Phoneyville." The
girl replies with a typical Broadway revue number: "In Lansing girls
with glasses/Never got any passes made at them." The girls then exchange enthusiastic reports on their new activities: attending Neo-
Physical Free Love classes and Group Guilt Conscience Gang Bangs.
Then, abruptly, their sketch breaks off. The rest of the show is a series
of bits and blackout skits.

The funniest piece is about Forest Lawn Cemetery. Lenny, sitting
behind a desk, talks on the phone to the cemetery's customers:

"Yes, madam? Please, don't take up our time with a lot of extraneous details. We do a volume business here. What time did you
say your husband died? Three o'clock? Well, put him out on the
front porch, and we'll pick him up at five. Yes, honey, our ad is
absolutely correct. You read it right. The basic price of our funeral

is eight hundred dollars—to break ground. Well, we have a dirt-saving plan where we bury you in cement. Wouldn't you like to be part of that new freeway that's going out to Sawtelle?

Another skit, titled *The Defiant Ones*, presents Lenny and his new pal Eric Miller doing a parody of the film that focused on the image of a black and a white man shackled together, fleeing prison. The routine foreshadows Lenny's great bit *How to Relax Your Colored Friends at Parties* by scoring heavily off the clichés of the currently fashionable rhetoric of "integration."

For the *pièce de résistance*, Lenny hoped to recruit his other new friend from San Francisco, Lou Gottlieb. Lou had been a jazz musician in his day, and no Broadway revue could be considered complete without at least one travesty on that popular comic figure, the wild, whacked-out Be-Bopper, with his shades and drugs and crazy unintelligible music. So Lenny planned a beautiful jazz parody that would actually demand high musical skill. Herb Geller had figured out a way to make the exhaust of a vacuum cleaner power an alto sax. Lenny wanted Lou to come onstage dressed straight except for a pair of enormous nurses' shoes. (Lou wore size 15s; Lenny's idea was to have his father make up a special pair of hospital gunboats.) When he got on, Lou was supposed to plug his sax into the vacuum, throw the switch with his huge foot, and play—without ever putting the instrument to his lips—the Dizzy Gillespie–Charlie Parker classic, "Groovin' High." When he finished, he would take a cap of heroin out of the heel of his custom-built shoes, pop it, and walk off stoned. Lou broke up over the bit but declined the invitation. Lenny promptly put on his "Jewish sea-gull" voice and croaked like his Aunt Mema: "You're mekking a tellible mistake!"

Once the show had been roughed into shape, Lenny's next problem was finding a theater. Russell Bledsoe, Honey's lawyer (but a good friend of Lenny's), came up finally with a guy who owned a club called the Highland House. It was located on Highland Avenue between Hollywood Boulevard and the freeway. Lenny wasn't impressed by the joint, but when the owner took him upstairs and showed him the attic, he flipped. "This would make a beautiful little theater!" he gushed, and instantly the wheels of business began to spin. Conning Bennie Shapiro, a coffeehouse operator, into advancing the money for the fittings (in exchange for 30 percent of the profits) and persuading the two girls he had seen in San Francisco to come down and join him, Lenny was soon into rehearsal for his big little show. Casting about for a replacement for Lou Gottlieb, he hit on Frankie Ray, who was never very busy, being, in the words of Shecky Greene, "a man who has been out of work for thirty-three years." Frankie obviously couldn't do the jazz bit, but he could play in the main skit with Lenny and help with the decoration of the theater.

The week before they opened, he and Lenny launched their advertising campaign. The show was billed as *A Wonderful Sick Evening with Lenny Bruce*. The ad gimmick was a trio of giant posters, each about twelve feet high, that Lenny wanted to attach to the front of his newly dubbed "Attic Theater." The posters were pictures of Lenny Bruce, Charlie Chaplin, and Adolf Hitler. Lenny's picture bore the legend, LENNY BRUCE NOW APPEARING. The Chaplin poster was the familiar shot of Charlie from the rear, shaking his ass and peering back with an impudent grin. WELCOME LEGIONNAIRES, read the bold print below. The real stunner was the giant shot of *Der Führer* casting his eyes up into *der Himmel* with a maniacal stare while thrusting out his arm in the Nazi salute. COMING ATTRACTIONS, blared the poster, ADOLF HITLER.

By the time Lenny and Frankie got to hanging this last placard, the rush-hour traffic on the freeway was at its peak. Hundreds of cars were streaming along bumper to bumper, as tired workers poured home to their tract houses in the Valley. Suddenly, some of the drivers caught sight of the enormous picture of Hitler. *Clonk!* One distracted motorist rams into the tail of another. *Clonk!* Another follows suit. *Clonk! Bam! Crash!* Cars are smashing into each other on the freeway like Bump-mobiles in an amusement park. Frankie Ray is mortified. Lenny is elated. The shock effect on the motorists is a good augury for the success of *A Wonderful Sick Evening with Lenny Bruce*.

"All Alone," Lenny's wistful, Donald O'Connorish theme song, impressed most of the friends who saw him at the Attic Theater as a poignant expression of longing for his lost love, Honey. In truth, it was the opposite of nostalgia: the first sign of a thoroughgoing reconciliation. Not long after he wrote the tune, Lenny applied to the authorities at Terminal Island for permission to visit his former wife. She had already received many visits from Sally, who had fallen into the habit of bringing along Kitty. The three-year-old child expressed a confused curiosity about her mother's strange surroundings. Honey told her that she was working in a hospital on the island, and that she would be home very soon. So far as Kitty was concerned, there was nothing very terrifying about the prison. Honey wore a neat cotton dress instead of a uniform. The female prison guards were also dressed in street clothes. There was no wall around the prison, no bars or cells. Honey lived in the Honor Cottage overlooking spacious green lawns, well-kept flower beds, and a cozy picnic area. Kitty's visits with her mother were among the most pleasant experiences of her little life.

Honey's privileged position at the prison was based on her excellent record. She had labored as a seamstress ever since she arrived, converting government-surplus parachutes into silk underwear, bedspreads, drapes, and curtains. She had been a model prisoner. Everybody was pleased at the pleasant, soft-spoken, highly cooperative appearance she presented. Indeed, they were so satisfied that they recommended on several different occasions that portions of her sentence be discounted for good behavior. At the time, in late 1958, when Lenny was scheduled to visit her, Honey had accumulated no less than 144 days of shortened service. Then in one wild five-hour spree, she blew it all!

The story begins like a scene out of *Mister Roberts*. Directly adjacent to the prison at Terminal Island was a tiny Coast Guard base. The favorite goof-off game of the sailors was watching the female inmates of the prison through high-powered binoculars. One day two of the men decided to make a move. As Honey was walking to lunch that afternoon, she was startled by a tennis ball bouncing before her face. When she turned around, she saw two sailors standing behind the triple row of barbed wire that circled the prison, signaling to have their ball returned. As Honey tossed the ball over the fence, she flashed them a big grin. The sailors shouted, "Can we come and visit you?"

"Why, sure," she teased, "you can come over any time you like."

"When?" asked one of the men.

"Any time," she repeated. "Just make sure the lights are out before you come."

The lights were dimmed that night at 10 P.M. Fifteen minutes later, the two sailors set out for the Honor Cottage. They were dressed in dark-maroon sweat suits and dark socks. Keeping a wary eye on a guard stationed in a distant tower, they flung a mattress over the barbed wire and successfully scaled the three fences.

Inside the Honor Cottage, which had no locks on its doors, Honey had left her room to go to the toilet. Suddenly, in the dim blue lighting at the end of the hallway, she saw two men tiptoeing through the door, shoes in hand. They spotted Honey and waved two bottles of liquor in the air. Honey eagerly ushered one of the sailors into her room and introduced the other to her grateful friend, June McLaughlin.

Honey and her Coast Guardsman, who identified himself only as Tex, lay in bed for the next four hours, alternately drinking and screwing. Every hour, just before the guard conducting a bed check shone a flashlight into the room, Honey hustled Tex underneath the bed, draped a bedspread down to the floor to conceal him and hid the bottle of liquor under her pillow.

"I got paralyzed drunk and passed out long before Tex and his friend left," Honey recalls. "Later, they went around and visited a few of the other rooms."

Back at the Coast Guard base the next day, the two sailors could not restrain themselves from bragging about their incredible conquest. Word eventually leaked to the warden of the women's prison, who immediately called for a full-scale investigation.

No actual proof of the persistent rumors circulating around the nearby men's prison and Coast Guard base was ever uncovered. So the warden threatened to revoke the "good time" of every one of the forty-five Honor Cottage occupants unless the truth was revealed to him. Honey bravely stepped forward and offered a full confession. She was placed in solitary confinement for thirteen days and forbidden to receive any mail or visitors.

Lenny had planned to visit her for the first time the same weekend she was locked in solitary. A prison official contacted Lenny and informed him that Honey would be unable to have any visitors.

"Why?" Lenny asked.

"Well," the official evasively replied, "she's too busy."

Lenny phoned the prison the following weekend and was again informed that Honey was too busy to see him. Unable to understand this feeble explanation, he concluded that Honey was deliberately trying to make him suffer.

It was a month after her release from solitary that Honey finally got to see Lenny. He was still upset about the two earlier rebuffs, until Honey explained in detail exactly what had happened. Instead of being shocked, Lenny doubled up in laughter. When he finally came up for air, he congratulated her on her amazing ability to have sexual relations whenever she wanted—even inside a state prison!

On a subsequent trip to the prison, Lenny noticed the cornerstone for a brick wall being built around the cottages housing female prisoners. "I don't know why they're going to all that expense having that wall built around you," he jokingly told Honey. "You're only going to be here for another six or seven months.

Lenny's increasingly frequent visits gave him a chance to act out his profound ambivalence toward Honey. One time they'd be really close, picnicking on the lawn, sneaking kisses like young lovers. When it was time to leave, Lenny would break down. "Oh, baby, oh, darling, I'm so sorry for hurting you!" he would gasp, while crying and kissing her. "Just wait 'til you get out. Everything's going to be beautiful, and we're going to start all over again."

Sometimes, though, after staying awake all night on bennies, following a performance at the Crescendo, he would drive directly to the prison and cruelly announce: "I'm not coming to see you anymore."

To add to Honey's comforts, he arranged for Fantasy to send scores of albums and a stereo record player to the Honor Cottage. Honey had also begun to paint portraits with oils and brushes provided by Lenny. His attitude became even more optimistic as the scheduled date for her parole neared. He often signed his letters, "Your pen pal, Lenny." Then, he'd cross out that line and write, "No, you're in. I'm out. You're *my* pen pal."

While Lenny was dreaming of a new life with Honey and monkeying around at his Attic Theater, word of his talent was spreading all over the country. In New York, David Yarnell, the program director of Channel 5, called up an agent named Jack Sobel and said: "A comic named Louis Nye tells me that Lenny Bruce was dynamite in Chicago. How do I get him to audition for our network?" Sobel answered, "I've heard about him. I'll get him for you." And so was born the most profitable actor-agent relationship of Lenny's career.

Jack Nathan Sobel was a very sharp guy who had worked in the TV department of General Artists Corporation (after MCA, the biggest talent-management organization in the country) and made a lot of money for the company by selling the *Captain Kangaroo* series to CBS. Then he got into a hassle with the executives and decided to go out on his own with an independent management agency. A brilliant operator, much classier than the usual cigar-smoking vulgarians, Sobel began to make his mark immediately. Lenny used to say that if Jack ever got an act that was a thick-necked Hungarian, he would make a lot of money for him. Sobel was a thick-necked Hungarian.

The first proposition that Sobel laid on Lenny was to make a pilot for a "strip show" (nightly program) that would run on Metromedia opposite Jack Paar on CBS. The show would be aired locally with a feed to Washington, D.C. A novel feature would be the use of the recently perfected videotape machine which would enable the network to repeat the shows as often as it wished. Lenny was delighted to get on the tube, but he was worried about the shift from his usual raunchy material to the white-on-white stuff demanded by television. He decided that he needed a taster, an arbiter of gentility: an intelligent and reliable person who would curb his worst excesses and spark him to TV concepts. So he called up Kenny Hume, the drummer who had been his pal during Strip City days, and asked him if he would like to come out to Palm Springs for a week, while they struggled to get the pilot project into shape. Kenny was amenable.

The big script conference out in the desert turned into a straight dope orgy that lasted three days and left both men right where they started—without even the semblance of an idea for the strip show. Then, Lenny went off to play at the Cloister in Chicago. When Kenny joined him in February, Lenny was in the last stages of an exceptionally crazy period of dope experimentation. To understand how Lenny got so strung out at this time, you have to page back to his first engagement at the Cloister.

During that month, he had gotten friendly with a man we shall call Sol Holzer, a druggist who operated a pharmacy in the Rush Street nightclub district. Holzer was a "hip square," a guy who loved to hang around with jazz musicians and junked-out entertainers but managed to keep his own life in tidy bourgeois order. He was married, the father of two children and the proprietor of a large Gold Coast mansion known as "the shooting gallery" because so many shooting stars ran up there to turn on. Holzer's friends included many famous jazz musicians, singers, and entertainers, but the one he loved the most was Lenny Bruce.

Almost as soon as Holzer met Lenny, he learned that the comic was a runaway junkie with a habit that had soared to six hundred dollars a week. Lenny spent half his life out in the street trying to score; sometimes after a whole night of hustling he'd make a buy that turned out to be a handful of aspirin. It was a ridiculous and pitiful predicament for a young man of genius. The druggist decided to spare Lenny some of the worst scenes by becoming his supplier. No one will ever know how much stuff he provided—free of charge—but the quantity must have been enormous. Apart from the Dilaudid, Desoxyn, Methedrine, mescaline, and "Dollies" (Dolophine: a synthetic morphine invented by the Germans during World War II and named after that famous junkie, Adolf Hitler) that Lenny consumed while working Chicago, there were the "long brown envelopes" that followed him all over the country, wringing ecstatic cries from their recipient:

Dear Sol:
    Today the postman came to our house, and Gloryosky what goodies!! I stood in front of the bldg and mommy tricked the mailman. And I ran in the house with my package, locked the door—flung open the window and fucked donder and blitzen.

Holzer's value to Lenny was not confined merely to supplying drugs; he was related to an influential Chicago journalist and in a position to introduce Lenny to Chicago's trendiest people. Lenny was rather ambivalent about meeting people socially for the purpose of advancing his career (which was moving nicely without such extra pushing); on one occasion, he went upstairs when the company began to arrive at the Holzer mansion, took off all his clothes, stepped into the house elevator, descended to the ground floor, and sat there in the buff with a supremely unconcerned expression on his face as the notables arrived.

Apart from his involvement with Holzer, Lenny's most absorbing occupation in Chicago was his budding affair with the only woman—aside from Honey and one other lady in his last days—who ever inspired in him emotions serious enough to be called love. (Feeling a personal obligation to protect this woman's privacy, the author has altered her name and certain details of her life; no change has been made, however, that would distort the character of her relationship with Lenny Bruce.)

Francie, as we'll call her, was just becoming famous at this time after many years of ups and downs as a singer and actress. Born in Europe, she had been brought to this country by a relative and featured in Hollywood movies when she was just a child. Then she had struck out on the treacherous road of the jazz life with only enough talent to survive and never enough to succeed. Involving herself with a whole succession of often nasty drummers, she got hooked on drugs, dragged into bad scenes, and appeared destined for the tragic fate of a Billie Holiday, when she made a lucky strike by joining a highly original trio that became famous overnight by vocalizing instrumental jazz.

A very attractive woman, with good features, pale, translucent skin, and authentic red hair, Francie was quiet, cool, and undemonstrative. Yet she implied lots of heat. A sultry air of sexiness exuded from her deliciously low voice and her relaxed and sensuous manner. Though she didn't really look anything like Honey (being shorter, smaller, less voluptuous in face and figure) she did conform closely with Lenny's fantasy image of the sweet, hot shiksa punim crowning the yielding, enfolding body.

Lenny's engagement ring was a hypodermic needle. Francie was off drugs when Lenny met her. He turned her right back on again. That was one of his tricks with women. If he really liked them, he always hooked them. Francie was a pet of Sol Holzer; when he discovered what Lenny had done, he was enraged. "How could you do such a thing!" he shouted, like an angry Jewish uncle. Lenny mumbled, "That's the way it is, man."

As soon as the Chicago date was played out, Lenny and Kenny took off for New York. Setting up temporary headquarters in the Hotel America, they started working on the TV pilot. Nothing remains of the tape. Chances are that it wasn't anything special. The producer recalls one sight gag. Lenny is sitting behind a desk. As the camera backs up, slowly enlarging the scope of the picture, he stares earnestly at the viewer and demands: "What is wrong with this picture?" After a moment of apprehensive staring, you suddenly spot his left foot—it's naked.

When the pilot was finally completed, the people who made it couldn't decide what they were holding. "Show it to Pat," everyone said, meaning Pat Weaver, the great TV impresario who had dreamed up landmarks like *Your Show of Shows* and directed the fortunes of NBC all through the golden decade of the fifties. Pat had been bounced from the network and was now running Channel 5. When he saw Lenny's tape, he said: "He's brilliant but TV is not ready for him at this time." That trite little phrase was Lenny's television tombstone. It meant that the biggest and most lucrative market for his talent would be closed forever to him and that no matter how hard he worked in the dying nightclub business, the success he earned could never be translated into big money. How he felt about this limitation is not altogether clear. In his moments of braggadocio, he would say that all he wanted was two thousand people in each town who really dug him; that he wasn't interested in the mass audience. This snap-your-fingers attitude was totally contradicted, however, by the eagerness with which he accepted offers from the media and by the conviction he voiced in this period that his destiny was to become another Charlie Chaplin: writer, producer, and director of classic comic films.

Though the pilot was a miss, Lenny scored heavily with his next TV project, a guest shot on the *Steve Allen Show*. The idea of inviting Lenny was Steve's, always one of the greatest diggers of comics in show business and a thoroughly good and generous host who went to bat time after time for people who were on the TV blacklist. Steve had his hands full with the Lenny Bruce appearance. After he received the expected veto from the network officials, he got into a very heated debate over the merits of the case. The network people were terrified by Lenny's reputation for doing unexpected and outrageous bits. They knew all about his pranks on the stages of the Cobblestone and the Slate Brothers. They weren't going to allow him to go crazy on camera with maybe ten million people watching. They had a point. The show was live and if Lenny winged even a single dirty gag, the calls would start pouring in from all over the country. Steve pointed out that Lenny was strictly business these days, that he was represented by the widely respected Jack Sobel, and that he was willing to have his material checked out by Continuity. Just to make sure that the brass knew he was serious about getting Lenny on camera, Steve volunteered the information that if Lenny was turned down, there would be no more *Steve Allen Show*.

When the network officials and Steve's staff (which included Lenny's old buddies Marvin Worth and Arnie Sultan, now TV gag writers) assembled for the obligatory run-through, they found a very charming and cooperative Lenny Bruce. He had chosen several of his most innocuous routines and he aimed to please. So deep was the network's fear of offending, however, that even Lenny's most innocent jokes provoked crises of censorship. He had, for example, a little anecdote about the tattoo on his left arm. When he first showed the strange mark to his Aunt Mema, washing his hands with Rokeach soap in her kitchen in Jamaica, she had screamed, "You'll never be buried in a Jewish cemetery!" Offered the stupid-sounding reason—"You must go to your grave with your body just as God made it!"—Lenny had quipped: "O.K. So they cut this part off and bury it in a gentile cemetery!"

The gag always got a laugh. It was simple, honest, amusing. Just perfect, he thought, for TV. The TV people thought otherwise: they objected that the joke would be found offensive by Jewish people. Lenny insisted that it wouldn't; he knew what offended Jews—after all, he was Jewish! Still dissatisfied, the officials went into a huddle. When they came back, they had the punch line for yet another Lenny Bruce routine. "We've thought it over carefully," said the spokesman, "and we've decided the joke is also offensive to gentile people." "What!" exclaimed Lenny, staring at the man in astonishment. "How could it offend gentiles?" "Well, what you're really saying," continued the earnest official, "is that *gentiles don't care what they bury!*"

Having finally appeased the censors and dispatched to Continuity a script of the night's performance (Kenny sat down in the hotel and typed out from memory a couple of randomly selected routines), the two men went busily to work capitalizing on the Big Break. Lenny, with his hustler's instincts aroused, got on the phone to California and started bargaining with a plug broker. This was a guy who arranged plugs on TV shows for set prices. If you dropped one of his client's names into the script, you were entitled to fifty or a hundred dollars. If you were a regular panelist and always pulled a pack of a certain brand of cigarettes from your pocket, you might earn a couple thousand. It was a well-established racket, and Lenny had been planning to cut into it from the moment he left the Coast. Working back and forth across his lines, he discovered ways to throw in no fewer than seven plugs during his ten-minute guest shot. When he went into the tattoo bit, for example, he would roll up his sleeve, expose the anchor, and ad-lib: "I smoked Marlboros since I was six, and it just grew with me!" (In those days, the Marlboro Man always had a tattoo on one hand.)

When the great night, April 10th, arrived, Lenny was buzzing with excitement. Elizabeth Taylor had recently married Mike Todd. The air of New York was alive with jokes about intermarriage. In a typical gag, Marilyn Monroe (who had just married Arthur Miller) is talking to Elizabeth Taylor in the ladies' room, when Jayne Mansfield walks in. The two new Jewesses look at the outrageous shiksa and Monroe whispers to Taylor: "Be careful—*red* [speak] *Yiddish!*" Lenny, with his Jew-gentile obsession, could hardly let such a great event pass unnoticed. Mulling over the situation all afternoon, he had finally come up with a line. What if he were to walk up to the camera tonight, stare out from the screen, and ask: "Will Elizabeth Taylor become bar-mitzvahed?" What a great opening for his act! Just the sort of thing he would do in a club . . . but on TV . . . hummm. It bugged him until show time; then, as he was going down in the hotel elevator with Kenny, he said: "Lissen, man, what would happen if I went out on camera tonight and said, 'Will Elizabeth Taylor become bar-mitzvahed?' " Kenny chuckled, a sly grin on his face: "I don't see anything wrong with the line—do it!" Both relieved and disquieted by this sudden go-ahead, Lenny cast a worried look at his arbiter, observing, "So, I've reached you, too." Then, slowly shaking his head, he stepped out of the cab, walked through the lobby, and silently, thoughtfully, signaled for a taxi.

An hour later, every viewer watching the *Tonight* show saw one of the strangest walk-ons in the history of the medium. Trying to ward off trouble, Steve Allen prefaced Lenny's appearance with a long preamble:

> We get a great deal of mail from our viewers commenting on our sketches (heh, heh, heh!), indicating their likes and dislikes, and whether you realize it or not, there is just about no joke or sketch, particularly of a satirical sort, that will not offend somebody—a cowboy or a drunk—I don't want to equate those two; already I can see the cards coming in!
>
> Here is how we are going to face the problem—we have decided that once a month we will book a comedian who will offend *everybody*.

The audience laughs, but Allen is deadpan, looking straight into the camera.

> Then we'll get it all over with, see? A man who will disturb a great many social groups—I'm serious—his satirical comments refer to many things not ordinarily discussed on television; it serves you right. That way the NBC mail department will know in advance

that complaints are coming in, they hire a few extra girls, and they get the answers ready—"We're very sorry, we didn't mean a thing"—and the whole thing is handled with neatness and dispatch. So, ladies and gentlemen, here is the very shocking comedian, the most shocking comedian of our time, a young man who is sky-rocketing to fame, Lenny Bruce!

After this great build-up, the camera pans right, focusing on the curtain at the back of the stage, and out comes a small, neatly dressed young man with a most extraordinary expression on his face. Roguish, puck-ish, mischievous-looking, he resembles a little boy about to say a naughty word. Minutes seem to elapse before he finally gets front and center with this secret word practically pushing out of his mouth. Darting several nervous looks toward Steve, he confronts the camera, full face close-up, opens his tense lips, and—almost blowing the line from nervousness—blurts out, "Will Elizabeth Taylor become bar-mitzvahed?" As the audience roars with shocked delight, Lenny does a hipster crack-up—bending from the waist, his head shaking merrily like a little doll's, and pointing his finger at Steve with an "I gotcha" gesture.

The watching network officials are alarmed by this crack, but as the terrible seconds tick by, it soon becomes obvious that Lenny has discharged with his first gag his obligation to be shocking: the rest of the show is going to run along smooth professional lines. Settling down, he confides to the audience: "You might be interested in how I became offensive. I started in school with drinking. I was really a depressed kid, seven or eight years old, and I really got juiced. So the teacher would really get bugged with me singing and carrying on, and calling Columbus a fink, and boosting Aaron Burr, and smoking." While he is saying all this, he starts slowly rolling up his sleeve, having a little trouble with his jacket cuff: "Can you see that from here? I've got a tattoo—I smoked Marlboros when I was six and it grew up." "Marl-boros," of course, was bleeped out by the network censor, but everyone knew what Lenny meant.

Lenny's first sketch, *The Glue Sniffer*, is a fantasy about the first kid who discovers that you can get high on airplane glue. The bit builds to a very funny flash. Lenny comes into the neighborhood candy store, looking wonderfully childlike, with his eyes eating the candy out of the case, and gives his order: "Gimme a nickel's worth of pencils, and a Big Boy tablet, and some erasers and"—his voice changing to zonko madness—"*two thousand tubes of airplane glue!*"

Firing the last line dead into the camera with a great mug, he scores an explosive laugh and tracks right into a next bit, his satire on the typical "brotherhood" film. Playing Juan, a Pachuco kid, he combs his hair into a ponytail and a pompadour, while talking over the shoulder to his whiny, weepy, good-girl sister, who exclaims: "Juan, you're making a big mistake, hanging around with that gang. Mr. Mendoza, the shop teacher, says you're making wonderful earrings out of those espresso machines."

Running the bit through to its conclusion—Juan standing in the schoolyard making a we-all-got-to-stick-together speech that ends with the line "We all got to stay together—and beat up the Greeks!"— Lenny strolls over to Steve, who is sitting at the piano, and remarks: "I'm going to write a musical with Steve Allen, and it's a nice kind of thing, it's about a couple. If you've been married or are now, you know the kind of scene that happens. You've had a million beefs with your old lady, and you break up and go back together again. But this couple in the play are a little eccentric: they've broken up and gone back about fifty-five times in seven years, but they keep going back for the kid's sake. Finally, they go to a marriage counselor. It opens up and they're together, and they're happy, without one argument— but the kid's a complete nut! Because there was no adjusting to that scene. Breaking up and going back together, it's been too much. So they decide, for the kid's sake, to break up!" (Lenny at this point is standing in back of the piano, leaning on it with Steve to his left.)

"In the scene," he continues, "my friend and I are hanging out together, and he's got the first line."

Steve, playing it very straight, calls: "Hey, Lenny, where's your old lady?"

"We had a beef, man, we broke up."

"Don't worry, you'll get back together."

"No, that's it. We had a million fights, and finally we decided, that's the one—we've had it. I finally got the guts and got rid of her. I don't believe it, man, but I finally did it."

"How'd you do that?"

"She left me."

As the audience laughs at this remark, Lenny pensively strolls over to center-stage, the lights are dimmed a little, and Steve tinkles moodily across the keys.

"But it's better, you're better off alone. I'm really going to swing! I'm going to fix up my own pad . . ." He brightens. "That's it—I can really fix up that pad, you know? I'm going to get that shiny black furniture, and I'll get a bullfight poster, and I'll get a coffee table and make a door out of it. Then I'll really swing. I'll get everything nice: I'll get a satin smoking jacket, and a pearl-white phone, and I'll sit back and relax, and finally I'll be all alone. That's the best way to make it—all alone . . . all alone."

Crooning the refrain, he abruptly resumes his patter: "I don't know, I get so dramatic about it. I'm better off alone. I'm going to get a whole bunch of new suits—you know, I've been wearing the same dumb suit for ten years. You walk in her closet and you can't even breathe. I'll get a whole bunch of suits, and I'll get a chick that likes to hang out. I'll have vodka parties—that's smart, vodka parties, live it up and all of that. I'll get a chick who likes to drink."

Lenny's voice takes on a faraway, schmaltzy quality: "Boy, my wife sure used to look good standing up against the sink . . . I don't want some smart chick who can quote Kerouac and walk with poise. I just want to hear my old lady say, 'Get up and fix the sink—it's still making noise!' "

Lenny, looking very poignant, goes into the song again:

> All alone, all alone,
> like a near-sighted dog wears a bone . . .

The violins get louder.

"That's it, she's young and swinging now, and she can get a lot of guys now, but when she's old, I can see her about twenty years from now—how you doing, Francie?

"You look pretty good, baby. You still washing your hair with Dutch Cleanser, I see. Yeah, you look good. Gained a few pounds— what happened to your *neck*? I heard you got married a few times, eh? Me? No, I've always stayed single. I've been investing in property. I picked up a little place in Mexico. Maybe you've heard of it, called Acapulco. Where are you living? Furnished room? That's nice—you cook on the radiator, the paper drapes, sit in the lobby and watch television. That's cool, yeahsssss. Yeah, that's cool—you have the Diners' Club, you sign, you go first class in those joints."

Now Lenny is half singing: "Her future's spelled a murky gloom. I'll be rich and famous, and she'll be living in a furnished room, but it's going to be too late. I won't hear her moan. I'll be living in my Nob Hill mansion, and all alone."

Then, the lights are slowly turned down all the way and a pensive, sexy Lenny ends the song: "All alone, all alone, I'll be rich, but so all alone."

It was over. Lenny was off and the applause was rising in the studio mikes and Steve Allen, probably drenched with perspiration, was smiling that well-we-got-through-that! smile. And Lenny Bruce has been seen by millions!

Lenny had done such a good job on the first show that Steve wanted him back, but the network officials were wary. There were certain vibes that Lenny gave off, a certain uneasy feeling of anything-can-happen. The people in charge didn't want to take another chance. Still, they had to concede that Lenny had delivered a fairly straight, tight, professional show and was well received. So after long hassles with the higher echelons—and after Steve promised to work out a tightly structured bit with Lenny in which there would be very little chance to get crazy—Lenny was allowed back on.

On April 5th, Steve Allen's viewers were again exposed to Lenny Bruce: this time to a smoother, more confident young comic. Whipping through a take-off on Sabu in *The Thief of Baghdad* and the genie in the candy-store routine, Lenny wound up the show playing a hip-talking jazz musician being interviewed by a square DJ. Making a comical contrast with Steve, big and solid, dressed in his host's tuxedo, Lenny looked like a cute but crazy little speed freak. Holding his hands tightly pressed against his sides (to keep them from flying in the camera's face), he twitched and jerked and gave off so many fractured vibes that finally Steve, noting with disapproval his guest's head wagging from side to side, mumbled like a prim old lady: "Starch your collars!" Probably an ad lib, it was the funniest line of the show: a lot more clever than the tediously scripted interview, which concluded with the obligatory joke about dope:

DJ: "Where do you get most of your inspiration?"

Jazzman: "Wheat germ."

DJ: "You eat wheat germ?"

Jazzman: "No—I *smoke* it!

The audience laughs in amused approval and Lenny Bruce is safely off the air again—no misbehavior, no foul-ups, no schandah! But, though the network officials breathed a sigh of relief, they decided not to chance it again. Lenny was never asked back till years later, when the show had a whole new format and was no longer broadcast live.

Lenny's greatest adventure in TV land—his biggest shot at the medium in a whole lifetime—took place at this same time but on another show. This was a one-and-a-half-hour blast on Channel 13 (not an educational station at that time but an independent broadcasting company known as NTA); the program, called *One Night Stand*, featured bright new entertainment personalities. The engagement was the brain spawn of Jack Sobel, who worked hard not only to get the time but to raise the money that was needed to supplement the show's skimpy budget and surround Lenny with all the talent he wanted for his first "spectacular." Projected as a hipster's vision of New York, *The World of Lenny Bruce* was to be a map of Lenny's sensibility: his favorite neighborhoods and entertainments, his private discoveries and special kicks. Above all, it was to be a dazzling demonstration of Lenny's *sophistication*—of his absolute and effortless command of all those mysteries that were being touted to the general public as the preoccupations of the existential heavyweights, beginning with jazz and ending with Monet.

The fact that Lenny really didn't know much about jazz or Monet, the fact that he had no comprehension of the television medium (being himself a rival medium), the fact that his own material was vastly more entertaining than anything he could conceive of as a TV producer— none of these considerations appears to have caused Lenny or Kenny or any of the people at Channel 13 the slightest concern. The mood was Right On! Soon Lenny had the bit between his teeth.

His first task was obtaining film of his favorite areas of Manhattan. Ordinary stock footage wouldn't do, he insisted: he had to shoot just what he saw. The problem was how to make the film without spending a fortune. One night when he was hanging out in the kitchen of the club where he was working, he learned from the cook that his brother owned a big dump truck. Click! That gave Lenny an idea. What if they were to rent the truck, erect a blind in the back, and conceal inside it a movie camera? The thought was the deed. Within a week, a pedestrian in any of Manhattan's funkier neighborhoods might have been puzzled by the sight of a dirty old dump truck with a canvas tent on its back crawling slowly up the street while a frantically gesticulating man in the cab leaned out to shout directions into the vacant air.

The laboriously acquired footage makes its bow in the first moments of the program, as the screen fills with pushcarts, tenement fire escapes, and old Jews fishing pickles out of brine barrels. The voiceover is Lenny; adopting a fake-o March of Time voice, he intones this pompous spiel:

Strange locales hold an enigmatic fascination for the average viewer. As a general rule, and unfortunately so, war is usually the vehicle that provides men with the opportunity to travel. In traveling time, we are now two hours and forty minutes from a New York airport. Not two hours and forty minutes by jet, as you might have presumed, however—I walked it. This is New York.

Now Lenny materializes, perched on a high stool under moody down lights. Looking oddly angular and awkward in this unaccustomed pose of casualness, he launches into an ad-lib introduction of his first guest that is long on enthusiasm but short on clarity. Finally, you figure out that the guest is David Allyn, the hipsters' favorite male jazz singer. Lenny's gimmick is to have Allyn sing "Brother, Can You Spare a

Dime?" dressed in a windbreaker and standing in an alley lined with garbage cans. As the song proceeds, the camera begins to reel off pictures of bums standing in dirty doorways and picking rubbish out of bins.

When this mish-match is over, Lenny comes bopping up the alley, lifts the lid off the nearest can, and cracks—"Let's eat!" Next he starts pouring effusive praise on the befuddled-looking Allyn while buckling at the knees, popping his fingers, and carrying on as if he was in the midst of the wildest, most swinging party—instead of being out in the alley with a TV camera staring coldly at his antics. What he really wants to say about Allyn is that he won a poll once in a jazz magazine, but the great hipster gets so hung up trying to remember the name of the *other* magazine—"you know, not *Down Beat*, the one that's not so hip, [*Metronome*] you know, man," pop, pop—that he completely loses track of what he set out to say.

A ragged transition follows to some 42nd Street exteriors focusing finally on the sign for Hubert's Museum. Now the viewer is introduced to Professor Roy Heckler, who is sitting at a table with his flea apparatus. Perching himself on a stool like a saucer-eyed nine-year-old, Lenny practically hugs himself with glee as the old man starts to go through his act. "Now, Brutus . . . No! . . . That's Hector!" Then the feats of flea strength. Then the explanation of how it's all done—the flea is kept in a test tube where every time he jumps, he bangs his head, thus teaching him to hold to the straight and level. And finally the unconscious humor of the Professor's explanation of why he uses human fleas instead of dog fleas: "Dog fleas live only six weeks; if I were to use them I wouldn't get much work out of them."

After the flea circus, everything begins to go downhill. Lenny does his genie in the candy-store bit. Then he shows films of the outside of Birdland, one of the least imposing club fronts ever seen. Francie's group makes a brief appearance, looking and sounding much too strident for TV. More jazz follows with Buddy Rich and Cannonball Adderly, at that time a jive Charlie Parker. Lenny criticized jazz because it lacked visual appeal; so for his show, he came up with the weird idea of covering Cannonball's number with footage of a painting by Peter Blume, titled *The Eternal City*. As Cannonball's group plays low-keyed blues, twelve bars for each segment, Peter Blume's semi-abstract imagery oozes across the screen in the worst tradition of *Omnibus*.

Next, Lenny announces that he's going to sing "How Are Things in Glocca Morra?"—and goes right into the tune! A real song, unlike "All Alone," with big melodic jumps, sustained notes, and all the hard things that look easy when professional singers do them, "Glocca

Morra" proves too much for the pipes of that wee lad, Lenny Bruce. Just imagine someone with the merest wisp of a voice, no very certain sense of pitch, and a distinct frog in his throat negotiating the first strain, with its Celtic leap. Poor Lenny! Doomed from the first notes, he hadn't the wit to break off and turn the whole thing into a gag.

Ratings were actually sought for this program; Lenny was annoyed when they turned out to be the lowest measurable. Once again, he had had a shot at the media and missed. He never could seem to learn the obvious lesson that the kind of cool, calculating temperament that is suitable to films and TV is something you don't cultivate by being a hopped-up, off-the-top nightclub comic accustomed to doing everything with your mouth.

Lenny Bruce's proper medium was the small, dark, intimate nightclub, where he could take complete possession of the audience's mind, alternately seducing and antagonizing it, making it laugh and think, fascinating it with the rapid zigzag of his own mind, and imprinting upon it finally an indelible impression of himself as the most brilliant, funny, charming, handsome, and wise young man in the entertainment business. That was the impression he achieved effortlessly in dozens of club settings all through his career, and it was precisely the impression he was making now during his first engagement in New York, at the Den in the Duane. For all during the period of his TV appearances, he had been playing a regular nightclub gig, six nights a week, two shows a night on week nights, three on weekends.

He was shrewd as well as industrious. When he came to do the filming, Jack Sobel told him that it was time he worked a date in New York. "Where do you want to put me?" asked Lenny. The obvious answer was the Living Room, a club that specialized in comics of the second rank, people who were just coming up in the business. Lenny didn't dig the idea at all. The acts that played the Living Room were straight show-biz types; he was trying to establish a much different, more contemporary image. Soon he found the right spot, the Den. Not a well-known club, it was a new room specializing in bright new talents. Nichols and May had played there; now Milt Kamen (who had worked as Sid Caesar's understudy) was the resident funny man. Tiny, murky, cave-like, with a stage as high as a coffee table and barely big enough for a piano and bass, the club was cul-de-saced at the foot of a steep stairway leading down from the lobby of the Duane Hotel, an obscure hostelry situated on the corner of Madison Avenue and 37th Street. Lenny was so convinced that he would do business that he accepted an offer to work for scale, $125 a week, against the covers, which were $5. The room was an eighty-seater that could be stretched through police payoffs to a hundred and twenty.

Lenny's act in this period comprised virtually all the major pieces that were to appear on his records: *Religions, Inc.*, *The Prison Break*, *Lawrence Welk*, and *Bela Lugosi*. Soon, Lenny was packing the Den not just with customers, but with celebrities. All the heavyweights of show business, jazz, theater, television, and journalism were stacked up those stairs night after night, waiting to get into the magic room. Even to this day, most people in New York who remember Lenny Bruce recall him from when he worked "Down in the Depths."

The financial rewards of such success were extraordinary: at five dollars a shot, Lenny was making a thousand dollars a night! The management was stunned. They had been *taken*! Quickly they negotiated a new deal. *They* would take the covers, and Lenny could take a salary—for as long as he wished—of $3,000 a week, plus some very fancy extras: a lavish suite at the Tuscany, right around the corner on 39th and Park, unlimited phone bills, cleaning bills, cab bills—anything Lenny could justify as a business expense. Meanwhile, the club agreed to serve as a recording studio for Lenny's third album. (Unfortunately, the tapes made by Peter Ind were of such poor quality that they couldn't be used on records—a sad waste.)

Not only did Lenny receive the usual attention from the press, he became the subject of scrutiny for various serious magazines, commencing with the Sunday magazine of *The New York Times*, which ran a piece on May 3, 1959, with the very un-*Times*-ian title "Man, It's Like Satire." The writer, Gilbert Millstein, a specially chosen *Times* phrase-turner, described Lenny as "a four-button mongoose, imbued with a fidgety sense of moral indignation." He compared Lenny, rather cleverly, with Lou Holtz, "who was wont to prod chorus girls with his cane." He skimmed the punch lines off a few rich routines, then dug in for the obligatory interview. On this particular afternoon, Lenny was doing his bit about "We're all hustlers—we're all as honest as we can afford to be." He was also very frank about his business methods at the Den, citing numbers and percentages in a manner that was unprecedented in a show-biz interview. He offered the usual fantasies about his life, including the "facts" that he had lived for five years on a farm (in Wantagh) and had jumped ship in Naples to go to Turkey and, eventually, China. (Lenny was always on that China run when the reporters came around.) The one really funny line in the piece was a crack Lenny made about the girls in the burlesque clubs: "The strippers in those clubs had four words in their vocabulary—'I'll have the same.'"

Lenny worked the Den on and off for about three months. Though this was one of the peaks of his performing career, it was not, generally speaking, a great creative period. Lenny was most creative when he was most unhappy. During this happy time, he lacked the powerful motivation of tsuris, the etching acid that thrown on the soft shifty surface of his mind would burn away all the illusions and nonsense and reveal the stark outlines of his deepest emotions and convictions. Yet so compelling was the creative momentum that he had built up in the preceding two years that even at this moment of eccentric tinkering with TV and cabaret theater—and every-night dope-partying—he could still gather his wits together and fashion a masterpiece: the single most important composition of his entire career.

The Palladium was Lenny's favorite among all his bits. He regarded it as something apart from the general run of his work, and he treated it accordingly. After he had finished blowing it up, like a giant balloon inflated with countless puffs, night by night for several months, he tied it off by recording it at the hungry i in San Francisco in the fall of 1959. Then he virtually never performed it again. Unlike the other familiar pieces from his early years, which he would offer as crowd-pleasers in carelessly cut-down and half-heartedly performed versions, Lenny never did any tricks with *The Palladium*. He put it in a mental closet and rarely removed it. About the only motive that would make him perform it was the entreaty of some very good friend hitting on him at a particularly compliant moment. Otherwise, it was as if he had never heard of the piece. The one time I quizzed him about it, in the fall of 1964, he got a peculiar look on his face, started to say something about how it had begun in his mind—and then he abruptly changed the subject.

What makes *The Palladium* great is simply the fact that it is Lenny Bruce confronting his own essence. There was only one world that Lenny ever mastered and that was the smarmy little world of small-time show biz. Everything that Lenny achieved as a satirist depended on his ability to translate the great world into this little world. Having used the show-biz metaphor brilliantly to burlesque the high and mighty from the Vatican to the White House, Lenny finally turned the genius of his satire on his own metaphor, his own world, and his own self in this climactic bit.

Employing instinctively the technique of the movie scenario, Lenny opens the bit in Sherman Oaks, a newly hatched suburb in the San Fernando Valley, home of comic Frank Dell, whose cards reads: "Dean of Satire and Mimicry—Fun Acts." The milieu is neatly evoked with a deft one-liner: "The pool isn't in yet, but the patio is dry." Dell is having a business conference with his manager, Bullets. Shifting into the dialect of the comic (whose speech style is not consistent because he has to represent at various moments every sort of mediocre laff-grabber from some dumb Irish or Italian banana on up to the most

hysterical Jewish prima donna putzo), Lenny outlines the comic's dilemma: "I'm not movin', I'm not movin'!" the restless, worthless little
vuntz whines. Like all of his kind (and like Americans generally), he
thinks of his career as an arc of success that should ultimately explode
in the dazzling fireworks of stardom. His manager, Bullets, has the
job of joshing him out of these delusions of grandeur and getting him
back on the trolley that sends him one month to Montreal, the next
to some lounge in Vegas. Bullets represents the reality principle in a
world of fantasy-ridden egomaniacs. When the comic tells his agent
that what he needs is a "class date, a class room," Bullets good-
naturedly asks, "What do you have in mind?" The answer is sheer
madness. This dummy, this nothing, this twerp wants to work The
Palladium in London!

"That's a *vaudeville* house!" Bullets explodes incredulously.

"It's a vaudeville house? O.K., I'm gonna tell you somethin' about
vaudeville houses. Alan King played it! Joey Bishop played it! Frank
Marlow! Frank Fontaine! Look, I don't wan' no grief widya, man!
Either get me the Palladium—or get me a release from the office! I
can't keep goin' back to Montreal!"

Jumping ahead two weeks, the story resumes with the boozy, La
Primadora chuckle of the agent, who is reading the contract to the
comic: "Awright, ya creep, ya got it! You open up the nineteenth with
Georgia Gibbs, Bobby Breen, Helen Noga, and Bruno Hauptmann's
son, for some insurance. He's doing a double with Barbara Burns called
'Smoke the Bazooka.' For the weekend, they're getting in Leibowitz
and The Scottsboro Boys for Poetry and Jazz." (Bruno Hauptmann
was the kidnapper of the Lindbergh baby; Barbara Burns was the
daughter of Bob Burns, a rube comic whose trademark was a stovepipe
kazoo called the bazooka; and Judge Leibowitz was the heroic attorney
who defended the Scottsboro Boys, six black youths who were charged
with raping a white woman in Scottsboro, Alabama.)

When the agent finishes reading the contract, he warns the comic
again that he's going to bomb—"You're all right in the joints, man,
but here you'll end up booking the house!"

"Are you kiddin'?" the little banty rooster crows. "I'll *murder*
these people—*murder* 'em! I got my act tight now! I know every laugh!
I got twenty-four minutes o' *dynamite*! I can work to all kindsa people,
too. Work ta Jewish people—I learned to say *'toe-kiss.'* Ahright? For
Italians, I got the 'Mama mia!' bit. When I work to musicians, I got
a bit called 'Hep Smoke a Reefer.' For the eggheads, I do all that
Stevenson stuff. I even got a Jolson finish. You jes' haven't seen me
work in a year!"

Jubilant that he's finally going to join the ranks of those big-time comics who consider themselves "entertainers," the funnyman goes out and buys a new mohair suit, a ruffled shirt, and shoes with tassels. He gets a big going-away party from The Saints and Sinners, who present him with a pair of gold cuff links inscribed on one side, "Knock 'em Dead Sweetie!" and on the other, "From the Gang at Lindy's." Wearing these talismans, he takes off for London.

The next scene opens in the dark and empty theater, where a very bored and jaded orchestra conductor is putting the acts through a morning rehearsal. Lenny Bruce was always a very erratic actor, sometimes striking sparks of histrionic brilliance, sometimes sounding like a freshman dramat. Impersonating this English conductor and the house booker, who enters the story later, he achieved a perfection of tone and attitude that is unusual in his bits. What these characters represented in Lenny Bruce's scheme of things was the coldest, most sharply crystallized ice of contempt for show business, with its mediocre talents and idiotic stage tricks. The fact that they're English and therefore—in Lenny's eyes—innately snobbish and condescending makes the irony of the comic's aspiration to "class" even keener.

In the recorded version of the bit, Lenny manages to convey acoustically the lonely figure on the podium talking and singing in the eerily resonating auditorium. The essential musicality of Lenny's imagination is apparent in everything he does in this routine, from vocalizing the various tunes, fanfares, and run-ons to conveying the rhythms of the voices, the intonations of the speakers, and the gradually building madness of the conclusion, which he orchestrates to a tremendous vocal rave-up. (As might be expected, the least impressive thing in the bit is Lenny's English accent, which constantly slips out of place like a badly fitting Halloween mask.) The whole tone of the rehearsal is one of intense preoccupation, the conductor having his nose down in the score as he cues the orchestra from "letter H back to the coda."

After clapping his hands and shouting at the stage manager, Freddie, who is supposed to pass out the "books," the conductor announces that the first act will be the Dunhills—an unknown English act that winds up with a "Nick Lucas Tribute." Imitating them singing "Tip Toe Through the Tulips," Lenny has the conductor mumble to himself, "Tacit banjo and chorus. All right, into Maria Callas—*canceled?*"

The next act after the notoriously undependable diva is Bronko and His Dogs. Singing along in the mechanical rhythm of a bar counter and beat marker—"How *much* is that *dog-gy* in the *win*-dow"—the conductor reads aloud: "Next cue—drummer catch it with a rim shot when he says, 'What do we do when we see Hitler?' Dog lifts leg—*crash!*" Turning the page, he goes right into the next act: Bill and His Bells. "Awright, Bill, work it!" he calls, as Lenny sings in a quaky, shaky voice—imitating a Swiss bell ringer—"The bells of St. Mary's are ringing for me." Suddenly, the astonished Englishman looks up and exclaims: "An epileptic! They put him to work! That's smashing! The Americans are mahvelous at rehabilitating people!"

The next act on this fabulous bill is Wanda and Her Birds. "No use working the beasts, sweetheart!" the understanding conductor calls out; "we'll just take it for time." Then Lenny sings a big fanfare—"Yah-da-daaaah! Dah-yaht-da-da-daaaaaaaa!"—while the conductor mutters, "Sustaining the chord . . . Key bird come out . . . Takes the flag out of her mouth . . . Goes into 'Over there!' . . . 'It's a long way to Tipperrrary!' . . . 'My Buddy Cha Cha'—and off!"

This leader is really murder on dumb acts, yet he has no prejudice: When he calls out, "Get the comedian up here!" he evinces an attitude no different from that of a meat inspector calling for another load of carcasses. "Come up here, son!" he calls out in the affected-kindly tone of the old pro. Then he plays the comic's run-on music, a brassy, breathless Busby Berkeley–style tune called "Who?" ("Who's the one I've always wanted? No-body but *you*!") When he gets to the first cue, he balks: "Hold till comic reaches mike. Cue: 'That's why . . . (Oh, crap!) . . . that's why . . . Christine can never come home!' " (The allusion wrenched from the old song—"Christine Can Never"—is to Christine Jorgensen, a notorious transsexual of the time who had had a sex-change operation in Denmark and returned to the United States a woman.) The faggot theme continues in the next bit, whose cue word is "Liberace." The conductor is offended at all this cheap humor. When he finds, mumbling through the music, tunes like "Remember Pearl Harbor," he grunts cynically. "Oh, really?" and chuckles mirthlessly. By the time he gets to the end of the comic's act—"Let's go up to show-business heaven and Al Jolson"—he's really hacked. "Same *crap*, week after week, disgusting!" he mumbles—till the comic asks him what he's saying. Instantly altering his tone, he smiles and carols: "Oh, we were just talking about some boys that were here before! I'm sure you do the impressions different—you probably do them as children!"

That night everybody who walks onstage tears up the house. The comic is slated to follow Georgia Gibbs, who has been on for forty-five minutes and is really killing the people. As Lenny used to say at this point: "Ben Hur, daddy! She's got 'em like *this*!"—holding up his hands as if clutching a brace of chariot reins. Aggression, however, is really the subliminal theme of her performance; as she reaches the climax of her act, Lenny empathizes with the comic standing in the wings and registering every song as a boxer's blow smashed into the head and guts of the audience. "Now she goes into her heavyweight

numbers—'Eli, Eli!' Boom! Boom! 'The Tribute to Sir Harry Lauder!'
Boom! Boom! 'Vaccino Mare.' 'Sorrento.' *Killing* them! Off! Now
back! Standing ovation! Finally, gets off."

The poor little comic has been forced to witness his rival's triumph.
Finally, though, he gets his chance. The English announcer calls out:
"Mr. Frank Dell! Ahmericah's fastest rising young comedian!" The
band plays him on raucously, fading rapidly on the last notes of the
theme. And with a swagger and bluster and vulgar, gamey little smirk
of self-conscious cleverness, Frank Dell makes his entrance—with his
head shaking from side to side and his arms flapping like seal
flippers—saying in his strident, nasal, Bronx ball-park voice:

> Well, good evenin', ladies and gennelmen. It's certainly nice to be
> here at the most famous theater in the world, the wonnerful . . .
> *Palladium Theater*! Ha-ha-ha! [The dumb gag is that he almost
> forgets the name of the theater.] Well, I jes' got back from *Lost
> Wages*, Nevada! Funny thing 'bout working *Lost Wages*, folks
> . . . the way to make a lotta money there . . . when you get off
> the plane, walk right inta the propeller! I tellya, folks, this little
> pansy walked inta the bar . . .

And so he goes, Lenny would explain, through the motel jokes, the
Army jokes, the impressions—ten, twelve, fifteen minutes—and he's
bombing! "Nothing! But not laugh one! Now he goes into the dying
jokes: 'I wasn't born here but I'm sure dyin' here! A lotta different
ways to die . . .' " Finally, he starts putting the audience down:

> Well, Freddie, Freddie boy, I see it's little Squaresville, little
> Squaresville, for the first show. [Louis Armstrong voice] Buh-dah-
> bah-dah-dah! [Vaughn Monroe voice] Rac-ing with the
> mooooooooon! Let's go to show-business heaven! How 'bout it,
> maestro? How 'bout it, my-*ass*-tro? Ha-ha! Alec! Alec-*trician*!
> Let's hit it, boys! [Al Jolson voice] Rock-a-bye my baby . . .

"Walks off," Lenny would say, "gets a little courtesy applause—sounds
like *Citizen Kane*—plop! plop! The only two people who are laughing
are the usherettes—who ball everybody who plays the theater!"

When the comic gets back into his dressing room, he starts to
puke. In the midst of his retching, there's a brisk knock on the door
and in walks the house booker. Val Parnell (who was, in fact—like
Frank Dell—a real person, though just a name to Lenny Bruce). The
scene these two play is as close as Lenny ever came to writing straight
drama.

Vomiting sounds, then a knock at the door.

COMIC: Come in.

PARNELL: [British accent] Oh, you're getting it all over! Here's some Kleenex. Here, son . . . hahaha . . . and we just had the rugs done. Hahaha . . . Get it on the dog, at least . . . However, my name is Val Parnell, and I'm the house booker here. This is Hadden Swaffle, the critic from the London *Times*, and, ah, *goddam* they were grim, weren't they, son? I don't know what went on out there, we were in the box office, you know, when all of a sudden I heard that unnatural silence. And we walked out, and there you were, you poor bugger. You were on there for about three hours, weren't you? I really wonder what it was? You're quite good—that reefer bit was quite unique. My wife loved you —she's been to the Catskyull Mountains, she got all those esoteric references about Grasshangers and the Concoward, and all those places, but I, ah—what do you think, son? I mean, you're a clever chap, you've been around, ah, ah, I don't think it went over, did you? You're too damn *good* for them, that's what it is. Too clever. Fact, I got some ideas. I said, 'Hadden, this boy here's going over their heads, he's got all that hip stuff.' Ah, we got one idea, think you're going to get a kick out of it. Look, ah, ah, about leaving Thursday, now, I wonder if you'd mind signing this release here—

COMIC: *Hey!* Sign what? Sign your *chooch*! Whaddayou, kiddin'? Whaddayou, kiddin', sign a release? Look, you had a lotta kids out there, how you gonna make kids laugh, huh? I didn't do my fag-at-the-ballgame bit yet!

PARNELL: Thank God, son! Ah, ah, look, ah, I'm only the booker here, but it would seem to me that—son, this is no reflection on your talent, you're damn clever! Here, sign it, you're too good for them! You'll laugh at *them* years from now. Here, sign it, here.

COMIC: [Surly tone] Now look, I dunno if you're kiddin' me or what, but, ah, I gotta hot temper, you know what I mean? I wanna tell you somethin, now, c'mere, c'mere! Where you going? [*Very angry*] C'MERE! I wanna talk to ya now! Now look, I'm not horseshittin' you, now! Now, ah, I dunno if you think you're dealin' with some Johnny-come-lately here, I worked alotta good rooms, now, and I wanta tell you somethin'. You can't cancel me after one show! I got a union here, and, ah . . . [Collapses] Look, man, I'm sorry I got hot with ya, but ah, ah . . . look, man, you don't . . . you see . . . I donwanna hafta work in shithouses my whole life, man . . . My wife didn't want me to have this date, and my, ah, manager didn't want me to have it . . . I hate to cop it to ya

like this, man, but, ah, *ya can't let me go like this*, you unnerstan'
what I mean? . . . You *gotta* let me do the nighttime show. I gotta
lotta bits, I'll change around, but, ah, you know—they gave me
a party an' everything . . . I'll tell you how much this date means
to me—*I'll kill you!* Really would, man. You think I'm horseshittin'? I'll *kill* you! . . . You gonna let me do the nighttime show.
I don't give a shit about the money, man. Look. I tell you what
. . . I'll give you my guitar, man. I got two hundred dollars that
I brought over with me—you can have it, man. Just don't junk
me after the first show. Whaddaya want me to do, awright? Gimme
a break, or I'm gonna kill ya. I'm not horseshittin' ya, I'm telling
ya the truth.

PARNELL: You're obsessed! You'd really do me bodily harm?
Dear, dear! Well, if you think one show'll do it, well, ah . . . Son,
ah, isn't comedy, ah, it is a bit of a joke, isn't it rather, the totality?
I know it's rather an amorphous craft, son.

COMIC: Look, never mind widdat Commie horseshit! Lemme do
the show, awright? Don't break my chops. You said it's O.K.—
it's O.K.

After a traumatic scene like that, the comic should be shattered.
But no! This guy is a real animal—nothing gets through to him. He
takes off his makeup, cabs over to the one delicatessen in Soho, loads
up on hot pastrami and soda, and comes back ready to do it all over
again. This night, though, as he stands in the wings, his anger at
Georgia Gibbs comes out in a great display of "artistic temperament":

Whatthehell is she doin', that talk out there. Go ahead, *talk*, ya
fat-ass broad! *I'll* sing when I get out there. Hey Bobby, she supposed to do all that talk? Ahhh, sing some of *this*, awright? [Gives
her the finger] 'At cunt, what is she kiddin' with that horseshit?
Hey, tootsie! Hey, what's she gonna do, ten hours out there? . . .
I'll do my Peter Lorre . . . no, I'll do my Army bit first . . . [Sings]
'Racing with the moon' . . .

While the comic is fuming in the wings, Georgia Gibbs is getting even
more outrageous with the audience than she did during the previous
show. Lenny had a great line for this moment: he would say, "She's
now into her 'Tribute-to-Sophie-Tucker-Hello-God' number!" At the
same time, she's playing on British nostalgia for all it's worth. She's
got these offbeat Scotch numbers, like Will Fife's "My Heart Belongs
to Glasgow"—stuff that can't be capped in this theater. Cap it she
does, though, with one final genius-stroke of super schmaltz-'n'-shlock.

Coming out for her last bow, she suddenly adopts a serious, thoughtful "mien." Lowering her mouth into the mike, she gets a tone of solemn piety as she intones:

> Ladies and gentlemen, I know a vaudeville stage is not the place for sentiment . . . but I wonder if at this time, we could have a moment of silence . . . [Crooning tragically like Lady Macbeth] for the poor boys who went to Dunkirk—and never came back! Boys who will never agayne see the bright lights of Picadilly . . . boys who are gone. Why are the boys gone? [Whispering] The boys are *dead*!

Aspirating the last word like her own death gasp, Georgia Gibbs leaves the stage drowned in tears. In Lenny's words, "Those who aren't sobbing uncontrollably are clutching for digitalis!"

Now the comic is really screwed—he's been swamped in the singer's wake. Every time Lenny did this bit at the Den, he would try to imagine how you could follow such an act. You'd have to come up with something really incredible. "You couldn't follow that with Art Baker whacking it in Bert Parks's face! You couldn't follow that with a leper on the Art Baker show: 'You asked for it—an arm!' " And he'd make as if to wrench an arm off a leprous body! Poor Frank Dell has to go on with the show. The M.C. is sobbing—but he manages to squeeze out the words of introduction: "And now—boo-hoo—it's comedy time! C'mon, crybabies! We all lost a boy or two! Now, here's Frank Dell."

Any performer with an inch of give would do something at this moment to save his ass. But not our boy! He's one of those mechanical men who begin every night with the same line and end every night with the same line. Though the whole world has fallen down in front of him, he insists on breezing out on stage and blithering in his brassy voice:—"Jes' got back from a crazeee, crazeee little place called Lost *Wages!* Funny thing about working Lost *Wages* . . ." Ring-a-ding! He goes straight into the shithouse! Lenny used to describe the audience at this moment as "an oil painting," or, better, "Mount Rushmore— Washington, Jefferson, Lincoln!" Yet the comic is hip to what's happening to him, even though he can't change his act. As he rushes like a rat in a maze from his Army jokes to his motel jokes to his singing impressions, he begins to squirt a little poison into the audience: "Hey! C'mon, you limey assholes! Whaddya kiddin'? I was in the service too, guys! Nice way to treat a serviceman, folks! A few bucks o' mine made it over here!" Then he decides to try another tack, and he shmeers the audience: "I can tell ya getta kick outta me! Ya gotta dry sense of humor. Ha-ha! You're alright!"

Neither hostility nor flattery will turn the trick this night. So, just before he's driven off the stage by the movie, he decides to go completely nuts—and ad-lib a line. Inevitably, the first thing that comes to mind is something hostile and vulgar. Sticking up his middle finger in a "Fuck you!" gesture, he suddenly yells, "SCREW IRELAND!" Then he adds, "How 'bout that, eh? They really bum-rapped ya, the IRA. *Screw the Irish!*"

At that instant, a heckler in the balcony leans out, cups his hands around his mouth, and shouts: "That's the funniest thing you've said all night, Buster! SCREW IRELAND!"

Instantly, the comic realizes that he's gone too far. Things are getting out of hand. He tries to restrain the heckler. "Take it easy, mister, that's just a joke, ya know!"

"Not *here!*" shouts the man. "SCREW THE IRISH! SCREW IRELAND!"

Suddenly the somnolent theater erupts into riot. Screams of "Get the bobbies!" are mingled with shouts of "Blast the Irish!" "Rip the seats off!" and the endlessly repeated chant: "SCREW IRELAND! SCREW IRELAND! SCREW IRELAND!" The comic's one moment of freedom has triggered a full-scale theatrical riot.

Rushing back to his dressing room, he starts to throw up when an urgent beating is heard on the door. In comes Val Parnell.

Oh, *goddam*, son, you're a bloody Mau-mau! Oh, dear! Bar the door, Freddy! Oh, dear. Whew! I don't *believe* what's going on out there. You've destroyed the second balcony. Go ahead, you leper, get in there, do it up right! I've never seen anything like that! *Goddam*, son, do you know what's going on out there? You've changed the architecture of the oldest theater in London! Here. Sign it right here.

Now, just a minute.

What? Did I hear "Just a minute"? Just a minute for what? The return of the Crusades? Look, Bomb-o, you stunk it up out there, you know that, don't you? Why don't you get a nail and do it up right, you sadist! How old a man are you? Thirty-three, thirty-four, I would say. Maybe you should join the evangelists. You might be good at saving people. You don't use narcotics, do you? That's the only rationalization I could have . . . how you could be oblivious to the cacophony of sound that went on out there. Son, well, why . . . what are you *looking* at me for, you psychotic bastard, you? You're not funny, you sonofabitch! Get up! When

I came out this afternoon I thought that—you're not funny. Every-one in the whole world is funny and *you're not* funny. That's crude, you see. But, I mean, the world is filled with unfunny people, and you're one of them, you *leper!* Now, you sign this or I'll black your eye right now! And I'm not a violent man. You sign this right now.

Now, just a minute.

Just a minute for what?

I didn't do my spicy-blue-risqué number yer.

Get my digitalis—my face is becoming paralyzed! Your spicy-blue-risqué number? What did you call that, ah, what did you call that bit of classic mime you did? No, son. We'll get you out of the country some way. I believe years ago, Julian Eltinge left a wig in the closet!

Lenny Bruce never had a good closer for any of his great routines. *The Palladium* breaks off with a weak allusion to the most famous female impersonator of the thirties.

Where the routine really ends, though, is not with a punch line but with a prophecy. Having made his ultimate statement about show biz—having castigated its desperate whoring after status, its prepos-terous smugness, its crybaby sentimentality, and its secret contempt for the public it fawns upon—Lenny Bruce forecasts with the anarchic conclusion of this bit the future of his own art. Inspired by moral rage, alienated on every level from the business, scorning and deriding the very idea of the stand-up comic, he obviously had to make a move now that would dissociate him completely from the despised image of the laff-grabber. How he would do this, what steps would lead him off the stage and into the arena of violent gladiatorial contention with the lions of law and order—all this must have been remote from his con-scious mind when he created *The Palladium*. That it was not so remote from his imagination and his unconscious mind—much the same thing in his case—is proven by the bit. At the end, the message is perfectly clear. When the comic gets good and angry at the audience's failure to respond, he reaches for something heavier than a joke. He reaches for an emotional hand grenade and lobs it right into the house. Not surprisingly, it explodes—and the first person it kills is the comic! That was the prophecy implicit in the conclusion of Lenny Bruce's greatest routine. That he was talking about himself is clear from the booker's last speech, in which he mentions both Lenny's actual age at this time—thirty-four years old—and his addiction to narcotics: a stroke of characterization that would be utterly inappropriate to any Frank Dell type.

Lenny Bruce was talking about Lenny Bruce in *The Palladium*. He was castigating and casting out the ghost of his old self—the dumb putzy kid with his picture in the shoe-store window—and he was unconsciously predicting the course of his future career after the time when he had abandoned comedy for something far more desperate and earnest—*the reshaping of the theater*. For which you may read: American society, which more than any society since ancient Rome has taken show business as the model for its national values.

While New Yorkers tried to figure Lenny out, he went merrily on with his accustomed style of living. A man of regular habits, once he had established himself in a particular locale, Lenny lived as much according to schedule as any suburban businessman. He awoke promptly at two in the afternoon, dopey and depressed, fumbling for his ever-present bottle of bennies. Gobbling down enough uppers to give some men a heart attack, he would order coconut champagne from the papaya stand around the corner from the hotel or tea from the luncheonette at the Duane. After shaving meticulously, taking great care to circumnavigate the little mole on his left cheek, he would dress up in the new Ivy League clothes he had bought at Richman Brothers— suits, jackets, and topcoats both for himself and Kenny—and sally forth on his first mission, which was, invariably, scoring.

Unlike Chicago, where he could obtain an unlimited supply of drugs, New York made Lenny scuffle. Things were so tight in Times Square, you couldn't buy an eyedropper in a drugstore. New York narcs were the hippest, and they took particular delight in busting jazz musicians and show people. If they couldn't nail you, they would lift your cabaret card *on suspicion*, thus putting you out of business in any place that sold liquor. That was how they got Charlie Parker.

Considering the danger of arrest and the disastrous effect a bust would have had on his career, Lenny was amazingly careless about scoring, holding, and shooting up in his early years. His principal connection in New York was a jivey black singer on the order of Babs Gonzalez, who looked fifteen years younger than his real age and was always beautifully turned out in expensive Pierre Cardin suits. The connection was a coke head, perpetually tap-dancing with blow-powder jitters. Lenny would ring him up and put on his Jewish-businessman voice: "Listen, what's the matter with you people? I'm waiting and waiting and still you're not making delivery!" After carrying on this dopey ruse for five minutes, he'd suddenly cop out and say: "O.K., we'll be over to score tonight."

Scoring at the pusher's meant enjoying his hospitality, which included the curious pleasure of talking to his beautiful blond mistress

—who was a mute. Lenny would say to her, "Gee, it really gets me hot talking to a girl who can't talk back." Then maybe they would split uptown to Harlem to some heavy coke-blowing party in a protected tenement. The first time they made one of these scenes, Lenny couldn't believe his eyes. They walked into the building and up the twisting stairs toward the uproar of the party without observing any signs of precaution—no lookouts, no alarms, no protection whatsoever. Yet once inside the party, they found the whole place awash with dope. The host—a big ugly-looking black with a fearful scar on his face—said he wanted to offer them a toast. Going into one of the rooms of the apartment, they found a dining-room table on which had been laid a large plate-glass mirror. In one corner of the mirror was a huge pile of coke. The glittering white crystals looked like somebody had dumped a sugar bowl on the glass. Reaching into the snow mound with his big horny hand, the host spread some of the coke evenly across the mirror and then politely inquired Lenny's full name. When he heard "Leonard Alfred Schneider," he drew a big L and a big A and a big S in the white powder; then he handed Lenny a fat straw, urging him to start at the top of the first letter and snort up all three initials. When Lenny finished, the host made the same offer first to Kenny and then to the pusher, standing back and watching, bemusedly, as the men gagged and gasped in mingled shock and delight at the sinus-burning blast of the fiercely medicinal coke.

Not only was Lenny heedless of the risks of detection, he was supremely indifferent to the medical dangers of shooting up garbage scored in the street through a set of works that was rarely washed, much less sterilized. Instead of the elaborate pharmaceutical and surgical arrangements he later adopted, instead of a gold-plated syringe and carton of beautifully polished needles, he used an old Murine eyedropper wadded around with a dollar bill and attached with a rubber band to a No. 26 needle that had seen better days. When he had mainlined and Kenny had skin-popped off the same set of works, he would toss the battered instrument up on the shelf of the closet. His attitude toward detection was utterly fatalistic: "If they're gonna bust you, they're gonna bust you." And that was that! No grab-bagging or concealment. No taping goodies over doorjambs or above bureau drawers.

Nothing was to be feared, of course, from the maids at the Hotel America. They knew the scene and were not likely to cop out, especially on Lenny, who always lavished heavy tips on them. About the worst thing that could happen would be an occasional goof in which the brown bottle with the Dilaudid pills or the silver paper with the heroin would get buried in some newspapers or other trash in this hopelessly littered room—and thrown into the garbage. Once when this happened, Lenny rushed down to the incinerator room at 4 A.M. and began to rummage through the trash bins. After a long and disgusting search, he finally found a brown bottle and eagerly screwed off the lid. Astonishingly, there were forty pills inside—much more than he remembered having in his own bottle. "Is this ridiculous!" he flashed. "I've found *someone else's stash!*" The fantasy was dispelled a second later, when he put one of the pills in his mouth and discovered it was saccharin.

Kenny often used to wonder what the maids made of him and Lenny. For example, what did they think the afternoon they cleaned up the room and found the wastebasket filled with rock-solid plaster? That was the residue of one of Lenny's craziest whims—his attempt to cast a death mask. The instructions for making a plaster-of-Paris face mask were in a magazine he was reading. They seemed simple enough. You smeared the face with olive oil to keep the plaster from sticking, protected the eyes with little shields, and stuck two rolled-up dollar bills in the nostrils. Then you mixed up your plaster and molded it on the face. Kenny followed the instructions as best he could, but before he was half finished with the job, the damn plaster began to harden. Pausing to consider what he should do, he got a snap of Lenny's face—half buried under white muck with two green tubes protruding from his nose—and he started to laugh. Lenny caught the laughing bug from Kenny, and his first yack cracked the mold. In a couple of seconds, both men were screaming and yelling and rolling around on the floor as Lenny struggled to remove the wet plaster and Kenny abandoned his last effort at self-control. When the fit had passed, they filled the wastebasket with the heavy plaster. Then they waited for the maids to beef. No one ever said a word. After all, the maids at the Hotel America had seen a lot worse things in their lives than a bucketful of hard plaster.

During this same period Lenny was reunited with his old playmate Joe Ancis. Joe would come up to the hotel room and rave on about his latest adventures and enthusiasms. Lenny would try to capture him on tape, but the moment Joe saw a mike or heard the words "tape recorder," he clammed up like a hood taking the Fifth. Actually, he wasn't as funny as he had once been, because now he was entering his feinshmecker phase. He was becoming a great connoisseur of classical music, painting, and ballet. Oh, he could still paralyze you with some incredible story or line: like the time he was doing the bit about the guy getting sucked off and he screamed out, *"Grab my thrill hammer, baby!"* That was marvelous. Thrill hammer! Who could think of such a word? It was all the Tilly and Mack books in the world, all the Jiggs and Maggie jobs sold in trick shops and hawked down the center aisles of burlesque theaters rolled up into a single image. Yet Joe's shpritz these days was less about sex than it was about painting. He insisted on dragging Kenny and Lenny to the Metropolitan and the Museum of Modern Art, taking them on whirlwind tours of both collections with his rapidly wagging tongue doing service as a catalog, guidebook, and art-history course. "The fuckin' Monet, schlepped out, half dead, in his last period, you dig? Painting *water liles*—is that ridiculous! Water lilies, man, giant genius paintings, man, like the cat is ready to pack it in, but he has to blow one last out-chorus!"

Lenny would chuckle delightedly and that night at the Den the slightly bewildered audience would be treated to an impromptu lecture on Monet. "What a man!" they'd think. "The guy is so hip, so funny, so far out!—yet he has time to schlep in museums during the daytime and dig paintings!" Another Charlie Chaplin! A true artist and sensitivo!

The most exciting event of Lenny's private life, however, was the appearance in May of Francie, who arrived in New York with her group to play a date at the Apollo Theater. Though Lenny was living in a bed-sitting-room at the America, with just a little sliding-door alcove for Kenny, he insisted that Francie move in with him and share his big old bed. Lenny was really crazy about Francie. He treated her with tenderness and affection. He loved to make her laugh. He even revived the Jewish-mother role he often played when he was married to that other career girl, Honey. Every morning at eleven, Lenny would take the call from room service and rouse Francie for her twelve-fifteen show at the Apollo. Then he would go back to bed for a couple of hours. When he awakened in the afternoon, he missed her and felt sorry for her sitting up there in one of those dreary upstairs dressing rooms, filing her nails between shows and smelling the creosote they used to keep down the rats and bugs in that vile old workhouse of a theater.

One afternoon his thoughts spluttered into a great idea. Explaining to Kenny just how dismal it is to sit around between shows, he suddenly picked up the phone and asked to be connected with Western Union. He would send Francie a telegram, cheer her up with a nice sweet message. "Hello? Western Union? I have a message for Miss Francie Williams, Apollo Theater, 125th Street and Seventh Avenue, New York City. Here is the message: 'Dear Francie—stop—You have the most beautiful pussy in the world—stop—signed, Lenny Bruce.' "

The Irish Catholic girl on the other end of the line gasped with horror. "You can't send a message like that!" *"Why not?"* "Why, why . . . ." The girl pressed the panic button and summoned the supervisor.

"What was the message the gentleman wished to send?"—"Dear Francie . . . pussy . . . Lenny." More horrors, more schreck. "No, absolutely no, such messages are forbidden by federal laws." Now, Lenny was really getting hot, insisting that he held stock in the company, that the supervisor would be reported to the highest authorities, that she had exceeded her bounds in imposing censorship on a public communication. Finally, Lenny changed his tack, lowered his voice, and said reluctantly, "O.K. You win. I'll rephrase the message. Here we go: 'Dear Francie—stop—You have the sweetest pussy in the world—stop—Love—stop—Lenny.' " SLAM! Down went the receiver into its Bakelite cradle and up to the sniggering gods of sick comedy went the quenchless laughter of those immortals at the Hotel America.

When Francie, Lenny, and Kenny would finally get together, after the day's work, at two or three in the morning, life would take on a different character. Kenny would reach up—ole Modesto High boy reaching up for that rebound under the basket—onto the top shelf in the closet and haul down the works, that shaky rubber-ridden contraption. Kenny would pull his belt around Lenny's arm while he probed for a hit. Then he would settle back languidly in an armchair while Francie hit him. "Talk to me dirty, Francie!" he would quip as she slipped the spike into his shoulder. Then as Kenny worked the old whip around there, trying to get that little skin-pop moving toward his higher cerebral centers, Francie would take the clumsy geezer and shoot herself in the thigh with the sure, neat efficiency of a diabetic taking an insulin injection.

Those were happy moments, but they always had their edge of terror. One night Francie must have geezed up some shit with a lump in it. (The smack you scored in the street sometimes contained lumps of pure heroin that were enough to kill a man.) She sank the spike into her leg and squeezed the black dropper. Suddenly, she was dying! Turning a horrible shade of blue-white, she gasped and fell off the chair onto the floor. Lenny was just getting his head up after the flash. Kenny was in his end-of-the-day lethargy. Though they weren't *feeling* any panic, they recognized that their dear lady was dying. Galvanized into action, they seized the prostrate girl and turned her on her back. Lenny crouched over the body and began mouth-to-mouth resuscitation. Kenny massaged the area around her heart. Minute by minute they labored while Francie lay there, as stiff and torpid as Snow White in her glass casket. Finally, Lenny looked up and croaked, "We gotta get a doctor!" Just as Kenny was reaching for the phone, Francie groaned and moved. As soon as her eyes opened, they got her up on her feet. For the next hour, first Lenny, then Kenny, walked her back and forth, back and forth in that hotel room. Eventually she came around, but everybody realized, somewhere deep down inside his mind, that they had brushed wings with death.

The day after Francie O.D.'d, Lenny began to ponder his habit. He was consuming shit in Charlie Parkerian proportions. Sometimes it gave him a sort of grim satisfaction, a feeling of super-machismo, like a high-roller at Vegas pushing an enormous pile of chips across the green baize. One thing they'd always say about Lenny Bruce: he could really shoot shit! Still, it was stupid to destroy himself with this dumb habit. He wasn't one of those junkies who couldn't stop. Are you kidding? Lenny could stop on a dime. The problem was—should he *now*? In terms of reducing his load, the time had definitely come for a cutback. He was burning up an enormous amount of money just keeping straight. From the Den alone, forgetting about TV deals, he was drawing three grand a week. That was a lot of bread, Jim! He should have been banking half of it, maybe two-thirds. Instead, he sent Seymour (Seymour Grush, his accountant in L.A.) these little money orders, $500 here, $850 there. Meanwhile, Seymour kept receiving canceled checks to "Kenny Hume" for $1,000 and $1,200 that represented the cost of Lenny's weekly habit. Now, instead of pissing away all this money, wouldn't it be a smart move to just kick? Take Francie and split for Miami? Sit in the sun and suck in some health and let the fuckin' shit go by the board! He could do it, and he could make her follow his lead. It was the end of the season down there; they could still have some fun—and nobody'd know he was in town. No pushers or weirdos would come after him. He could get by on pep pills for a week or ten days, and his lousy habit would sink back into the depths.

So he told Francie: "Look, let's take a break. Go down to the Beach. I love it there. We'll have a really good time for a week or so. And we'll kick." Francie had been trying to get off drugs for a long time. She agreed without any argument. Then they had their honeymoon. It started with a funny incident. Arriving very late at the Fontainebleau, Lenny went to the desk and asked for his room. The clerk consulted his records and informed him that there was no reservation. Embarrassed in front of a chick, Lenny flew into a rage. As open-mouthed spectators gathered around the desk, he yelled: "What is it with this shithouse? I'm not gonna stay in this fuckin' dump! My manager called you blah, blah, blah!" Finally, the flustered and defensive clerk found him a room, and the pair, exhausted from their trip, fell into the sack.

Exhaustion and sleep were not interchangeable terms in Lenny's vocabulary: so he took the precaution of swallowing a whole handful of Tuinals before he buried his head in the pillow. Even so, he couldn't sink under the waves. Twitching and turning, feeling the pangs of frustrated drug hunger, he spent several wretched hours trying to sleep. Then he got up in the dark room, put on his clothes, and went downstairs at dawn to scrounge some breakfast at the next hotel up the avenue. Looking really ghastly in the morning light, he sat at the luncheonette counter and ordered coffee, toast, and jam. Every so often, he gave an uncontrollable twitch. The house detective, who was having coffee at a neighboring table, began to watch this odd performance with interest. When the waitress brought the toast and jam, Lenny laid a big glob of purple jelly on the bread, took a deep breath, as if to steady himself, and then thrust the morsel desperately toward his mouth. He missed—and his first big bite of breakfast went straight into his eye! The security officer got up at that point, and offered to escort Lenny back to his room. Quick to come up with an alibi, Lenny explained that he had been out all night drinking and now he was getting the d.t.'s The officer believed him. When Francie woke up, she was greeted with Lenny's latest bit.

That week in Florida was a sweet experience for both Lenny and Francie. They stretched their pale dissipated bodies under the hot moist sun at poolside. They took funny pictures—Lenny posing as a beach beauty, Francie submitting to his heavy gigolo embrace. They played practical jokes on the guests and employees of the hotel. Lenny would go over to the page girls and say: "There's a call here for Cary Grant; would you please page him?" Or he would nervously solicit an autograph from Dear Abby (Van Buren), who would sign the proffered menu without dreaming that this was the notorious Lenny Bruce putting her on. Best of all was the good time they had in bed. When Lenny was off drugs, Francie observed, he was very tender, the tenderest person she had ever known. He was constantly kissing and hugging her. Constantly making love to her. Holding her from behind as they dozed off to sleep. Eventually, Francie concluded that the personality the nightclub public knew—the hard, hostile, super-hip comic—was largely a product of heroin. Lenny was a junkie Jekyll and Hyde. When he turned on, he became the opposite of what he was naturally. Francie was grateful for the reversion to sweetness.

The love idyll couldn't last. Two careers demanded to be pursued. After a week or ten days, Francie went off to meet her singing partners; Lenny broomed back to New York. Before they split, they discussed very earnestly the possibility of marriage. Lenny wanted to get married again. He wanted a mother for his daughter. He wanted a wife in his kitchen. He painted the joys of domesticity like an article in a ladies' magazine. Francie was interested, but she decided to let Lenny make all the moves. She knew he still had a lot of feelings about Honey, and she knew that two careers don't make one marriage. He was at the peak of his success—or fast getting there; she was at the peak of hers: it would be very hard to work things out without somebody making a heavy sacrifice. So they decided to wait, to keep in touch by telephone, to work hard at coming together in the same towns at the same times—and see what happened. As it turned out, that week in Miami was the best moment they were to have together. Though they continued to see each other at erratic intervals all the way up to the moment when a radically changed Lenny visited briefly, absent-mindedly, with a radically changed Francie in London in 1962, the love affair was really over.

Honey is what ended it. No sooner did Lenny get back to New York than Honey called from the Coast with the stunning news that she was out of prison and free. Even in the midst of his high romance with Francie, Lenny had been making quiet but extensive preparations for Honey's return. Working through his trusted "Seymours," Seymour Grush and Seymour Lazar, his attorney, he had rented and renovated the second floor of a Spanish-style duplex on Spaulding Avenue in Hollywood, just off the Strip. A team of painters, carpenters, glass cutters, and mirror-installation men were paid double- and even triple-time wages as they worked around the clock readying the premises for its new occupants. For the plan was—incredible as it may seem—that Honey was to assume the responsibility for rearing Kitty, with the housekeeper, Lucille, remaining only for as many weeks as it required Honey to take matters into her own hands. Lenny had worked all that out in his head in recent months, and with characteristic indifference to reality—without even discussing the matter thoroughly with Honey—he was intently realizing the most minute features of his scheme, such as the sort of crystal chandeliers and expensive antiques that were to be installed in this new love nest. He had also deposited a sizable sum of money in Honey's bank account and rented a shiny new convertible for her use. Lenny's favorite self-image with those he loved was always Daddy Warbucks.

When the great day arrived and Honey was released, the phone lines between New York and Hollywood were practically melted down by the intensity of Lenny's passion. He insisted that Honey run out of the house, dash to the airport, and board the first plane for New York. He had to see her *at once*—he had to *have* her immediately! Pouring out his excitement to Kenny, he hastily made his arrangements. During Honey's visit, Kenny was to be quartered at the Hotel America. Lenny would remain in their suite at the Tuscany, which was instantly transformed from a littered pigsty into an immaculately ordered Park Avenue apartment. When Honey actually appeared, Lenny couldn't believe his eyes. She had an almost angelic appearance in her new short haircut, with her figure slimmed down through diet pills that Sally had smuggled to her in prison. Her manner was quiet and demure. She was a young girl just out of a nunnery.

Their first ball must have reached epic intensity. Yet, just three days later, Honey was on the plane heading back for L.A., and when Kenny moved back into the suite he found Lenny pensive and depressed. Kenny was too tactful to pry, but something had obviously gone wrong with the great reunion. Lenny was still determined to carry through his project of reconciliation, but he wasn't so sanguine as he had been when Honey was in prison.

When the tar began to soften in the New York streets, Lenny and Kenny finally pulled up stakes to head back to the West Coast and a three-week engagement at the hungry i. Their path led through Chicago, where Lenny worked at Mr. Kelly's and got into a tiff with columnist Herb Lyons. It was the first of a series of wrist-slapping hostilites between Lenny and pressmen who had originally liked him but who now began to carp and find fault with his increasingly caustic and bitter manner. For just a taste of success was enough to curdle the sweetness of Lenny Bruce. Though he was still charming when he wished to be and though his relations with his friends were still warm and generous, Lenny began in the summer of 1959 to adopt the biting, antagonistic tone that characterized his work all through his period of greatest satiric power.

When Lenny touched down in L.A. on the 25th of June 1959, his first thought was of Honey. With a heart filled with the excitement of a triumphant homecoming, yet troubled by a persistent intimation of disaster, he came roaring along the freeways to his love nest on Spaulding Avenue. Two seconds of looking at Honey, standing there in the doorway of the house, told him the whole story. His moody forebodings had been right: Honey was high!

He could see it in her eyes, painfully blinking in the light; he could hear it in her speech, slightly false and fumffering; it was obvious from her overrelaxed, super cool bearing, her reluctance to talk. The cunt! She was strung out like a dog! How could he have ever dreamed that she would stay straight once she was out of the can?

What made it all the worse was the fact that he was clean. Ever since his return from Miami, he had been off the heavy stuff. He had worked Chicago for two weeks, hanging out with Sol Holzer—"Soulman" he called him now—and had taken nothing wilder than a little drugstore cocaine, snorted off a hand mirror through a rolled-up dollar bill. Now after all his sacrifices and will power, he comes back home to his wife—in fact if not in law, you dig! the mother of his child, the lady he plans to lead his life with—and this goddamned cunt, this fucked-out, fucked-over hillbilly whore has got herself a goddamned habit! It was enough to make you kill! Yet, there was more to this than met the eye. He, Lenny Bruce, could have been a private detective, so shrewd was his sense of happenings behind the scenes. Honey had been off the turf for two and a half years. She couldn't have one old connection left. An ex-con, she was too hot to run around and make obvious buys. Somebody had hooked her! Now, who was the nigger in the woodpile?

Putting on his most charming, disarming manner, Lenny gave Honey the big hug and kiss routine. Soon he got into a relaxed rap about his adventures back East that segued easily into inquiries about what Honey had been doing since she got back from New York. Who had she been hanging out with, besides his mother? Oh, she told him unwarily, Joe Maini and Sandra had come over. Joe had been such fun, and Sandra was still so in love with him. "And was Joe holding when he came to visit?" "Yes, he offered me a little taste. I wasn't even interested. Then he and Sandra got down on the floor and gave me a little exhibition, a little freak show. They were still as crazy as ever!" "You never once fixed?" Lenny persisted, fixing her with his deepest eyes. "No! Are you crazy! Of course not! What are you trying to pin on me?" *"Just this, bitch!"* he shouted, as he practically tore the sleeve off her sweater, pulling it up above the elbow to reveal—wouldn't you know?—a long, fresh track of needle marks.

Tears, words, curses, apologies, all the old crap came pouring out—and Lenny and Honey were right back where they had started, three years before. This time, though, Lenny felt much stronger. His success had given him an I-can-do-everything determination to save Honey. From this time forth, he told her, she was going to be under his care. If she would do exactly what he told her, she would be able to kick the shit and stay off it forever. The most important thing was that they always be together. When she got the impulse to get high, she would tell him and he would help her fight it back. Together they would win. Separated, she was doomed.

So they drove up the coast that weekend in Lenny's old white Jag, with Kenny at the wheel: Lenny, Honey, and Kitty, heading for San Francisco and the hungry i. Times had changed since Lenny last played the bay city. No more would he have to work cheap little joints like Ann's or hood clubs like Fack's. Now he was a headliner, right up there with Shelley Berman and Mort Sahl. He could work the best room in any city he played—either the Fairmont or the i in Frisco—and the number would be a big one, like $3,500 a week. Enrico Banducci could count on him to do just as much business as his college-boy entertainer, Morty "The Sweater" Sahl. Lenny was twice as hip and ten times the showman.

"So this is where Jonathan flipped!" cracked Lenny as he surveyed the interior of the hungry i on his Thursday night opening. Instantly, the whole house was convulsed. Everybody had read in *Time* the story of Jonathan Winters's engagement the previous May. Leaving the club after a late night show, he had gotten into a taxi and ordered the driver to take him to Fisherman's Wharf. When he got out on the waterfront, he made a beeline for the *Balclutha*, an old sailing vessel that had been berthed there as a tourist attraction. Nobody was allowed on board the vessel at night, but Winters had barreled past the guard and climbed up the mainmast before the police could arrive and pull him down. Hauled to headquarters, he informed the startled magistrate: "I'm John Q from outer space!" The judge took one sorry look at the famous entertainer and ordered him conveyed to a mental hospital.

Lenny had a genuine affecton for Winters, whom he recognized as being in an entirely different category than most of the "new-wave" comics. A real character who talked compulsively and changed identity every other minute, Jonathan was a nut case after Lenny's own heart. Indeed, Johnny was in some ways closer to Lenny's ideal than was Lenny himself. Just as blue as Bruce when he was talking off the record, Winters was an astonishingly fluent improviser, whose off-the-cuff stuff was just as clear and crisp as any ordinary comic's scripted material. In the mid-fifties, he had been taping a cigarette commercial in a New York studio, when he got bored with the endless repetitions of the same cues and wording. Launching into a stream of dirty, funny improvised bits, he soon had the engineers in the control room laughing hysterically. One of those guys caught the whole crazy show on tape and that tape had quickly become one of the hottest bootleg records in New York. It contained choice items, like a Harlem disk jockey selling hair straightener for a Jewish sponsor: "You cats want to score for those fine ofay broads, don'tcha? Well, man, you gotta get *straight!*"

After his droll opening, Lenny went into his usual free-form vamp, leading up to the big set-pieces. On this particular night, his mind was full of Honey and their recent reunion. He spoke about all the problems they had experienced in the past and his hopes and fears for the future. As always, he was remarkably candid for a nightclub performer, and some in the audience were made uncomfortable by his remarks. One of these was the rather prim Herb Caen, who noted between strings of dots: "Confidential to comedian Lenny Bruce: We're all sorry you're having personal problems, but an endless airing of them does not constitute nightclub entertainment, sorry." It was just a slap on the wrist, and, on Wednesday, Caen softened the slap to a pat of reassurance: "After a most peculiar start, sickomic Lenny Bruce is getting back into his old insane stride at the hungry i; it must have been somthing he etcetera'd." Any other performer would have suffered such a mild rebuke from such a friendly critic in silence; not Lenny Bruce.

The night after Caen's first item ran, Lenny opened his act by remarking: "Herb Caen is not a transvestite, he is not a commie, he does not tint his hair." As Enrico Banducci looked on in horror from the back of the room, Lenny added: "It's true, I did look down in his Corvette and saw him with his garter belt showing." This was an act of *lèse-majesté* unprecedented in the recent history of San Francisco. To insult and abuse Herb Caen—a local monument on a par with the Golden Gate Bridge and the Coit Tower—was not only unthinkable, it was insane! Herb Caen *made* performers—he'd helped make Lenny Bruce. What was to stop him from unmaking his once-favorite comic? That night every San Francisco bureau was filing. The next day, though, they got even better copy. Lenny gave them a night letter to Caen which read as follows:

> Dear Herb,
>   A columnist of your genre should write a truthful and enter-
> taining column. No one questions your truthfulness. I'll stand up
> and fight anyone who questions your honesty. You write the swee-
> test, most honest, most *boring* column in the Baghdad by the Bay
> [the title of Caen's best-known book] area. This praise is com-
> pletely divorced from any personal feelings. One should be able
> to give an appraisal of any art form without involving personalities.
> The fact that your column is of the where-to-go-what-to-see qual-
> ity, chiefly concerned with senile reminiscences of fog horns, sea
> gulls and Louis Lurie [a local tycoon] does not make you a bad
> guy, just a bad writer. I'm still very fond of you as a person,
> although you are a disgrace to the newspaper industry.
>   —Love
>   Lenny

It was a clumsy put-down. The interesting question, though, was why Lenny had overreacted.

Partly, it was personal pique: Lenny could never accept criticism gracefully. Partly, it was his latent hostility toward Caen coming to the surface; his contempt for the pretentious little "square," who enjoyed such apparently undeserved prosperity and prestige. Partly "the Caen incident" was simply a deliberate effort to grab attention by being provocative and "controversial." "*Controversy makes money*"—that was one of the operative principles of Lenny's early career. Every time he had a chance to grab space in the newspapers, he grabbed it. That was why he had shpritzed Herb Lyons just a couple of weeks before, during his Chicago engagement. Lenny's story was that Lyons wanted him to make a free appearance on his local TV show. When Lenny refused, the columnist printed an item about how Lenny had been asked to cut the blue material out of his act. As Lyons and a friend walked into Mr. Kelly's a few nights later, Lenny grabbed for the first line that came to mind and quipped: "Here comes the Loeb and Leopold of show business." Again, not very funny, not very zingy—but good enough to make the morning edition.

Lenny's days of fighting for attention in the press were really almost over. Even as he shpritzed Caen from the stage of the i, the entertainment department of *Time*, under the direction of Henry Grunwald (later the magazine's boss) was preparing a feature story that would put Lenny Bruce right up there overnight with Mort Sahl, Shelley Berman, Nichols and May—put him above these performers, in fact, by naming him "the most successful of the newer sickniks." "The Sickniks" was the title of the piece that ran July 13th on *Time*'s show-business page. Looming in the upper left-hand corner of that glossy page was Lenny, looking cross and embattled, like a reform rabbi denouncing the treatment of the Jews in the Soviet Union. Beneath his name was inscribed one quintessential sick joke: "Bobby Franks was snotty." A half-inch down the page, in the left-hand column, began the tolling, alliterating *Vorspiel* of a typical *Time* "trend" piece:

THE SICKNIKS

They joked about father and Freud, about mother and masochism, about sister and sadism. They delightedly told of airline pilots throwing out a few passengers to lighten the load, of a graduate school for dope addicts, of parents so loving they always "got upset if anyone else made me cry." They attacked motherhood, childhood, sainthood. And in perhaps a dozen nightclubs across the country—from Manhattan's Den to Chicago's Mr. Kelly's to San Francisco's hungry i—audiences paid stiff prices to soak it up. For the "sick" comedians, life's complexion has never looked so green.

Great! That was worth a couple of million in advertising. Needless to say the article had nothing to say. After dropping a few names and salary figures, firing off a few sick jokes, and quoting a few big men in the industry, like "Comic Joey Bishop" ("Those guys tried their hardest to make it our way; when they couldn't, they switched") and

"Comic Joey Adams" ("They all act like big noncomformists, but they're all aiming to get on the Ed Sullivan or Steve Allen show"), "The Sickniks" ground to a typically inane and fence-straddling conclusion: "What is really funny and fresh about the sickniks may be around for a long time, and possibly reinvigorate U.S. humor; what is really sick is bound to evaporate." None of it really mattered, however, because not only had they spelled Lenny's name right, they had broadcast it across the country even farther than Steve Allen had done with his TV show.

The weeks at the hungry i were rich in every sort of career food. Lenny's first big album, *The Sick Humor of Lenny Bruce*, was about to be released—with a sickly green picture of Lenny lying on a picnic cloth decked with watermelon, grapes, green onions, cheese-bits, catsup, chili sauce, relish, chow-chow, and a single quart bottle of beer. Four paper cups are positioned across the cloth, but Lenny is all alone, staring at the camera with a most peculiar arch of brow and glaze of eyeball. Perhaps the explanation is to be sought in the background of the photo, which is an extremely well-kept cemetery with rows of polished marble tombstones reaching out beyond the spooky picnicker and his strange feast.

Eager to promote this product, Fantasy arranged a party at the hungry i and invited the press to meet its newest star. Lenny disappeared after the first ten minutes. When a reporter caught up with him the next day, he explained: "It wasn't only the sandwiches that made me sick. Seven people asked *me* who Lenny Bruce was. Finally, somebody asked me if *that* was Lenny Bruce and pointed over in a corner to a guy with long hair, dirty sweatshirt, blue jeans, Pernod, and Peter Orlovsky—it was Allen Ginsberg!"

Chapter Nine

"AMERICA'S NO. 1 VOMIC" (WINCHELL)

The hot August sun had already bleared into the Pacific, when Detectives Joel Lesnick and Carl Trout pulled off the Sunset Strip and into the parking lot of the Crescendo. They were on stake-out. Now they would sit and wait. Smoke a cigarette and shoot the breeze.

"This Lenny Bruce," says Trout, "have you ever heard of him before?"

"Yeah, I saw him a few years ago when he pulled a stunt on *Rocket to Stardom*. He came on as a trumpet player and passed the audition. He had a couple of professional musicians who were backing him. He wasn't too well known then, so nobody recognized him. Then, when he got on the camera, he yelled out, 'H. J. Caruso is innocent!' So they chased him out of the place screaming and yelling—the cameras were bouncing around! That's the first time I ever heard of the guy."

"And now he's a star. Right?"

"Not exactly. He's working here with Frances Faye; so he doesn't carry the whole show by himself. But they tell me he's good for twenty-five hundred dollars a week. So maybe you're right. He's a star by *our* standards!"

A cab pulled into the parking lot. Lesnick peered at it intently. The door swung open and out crawled a good-looking young guy dressed in an open-necked white shirt and dark trousers. He was carrying a freshly pressed suit on a hanger. To the trained eye of the undercover narco, Lenny Bruce was obviously stoned.

"Let's go," mutters Lesnick to his partner. The two detectives step out of their unmarked car and quickly overtake their man.

"Hey, Lenny!" calls Lesnick. "Can we have a word with you?"

As Lenny stares uncomprehendingly at these two square-looking guys with their neat haircuts, he suddenly realizes that this is a bust! Here he is standing in the parking lot of the club staring down into a shield! Either that or he's completely out of his nut because the guy is saying, "You don't mind if I just roll up your sleeve?" Before he can say "Yes!" or "No!"—or whatever the hell you're supposed to say—one cop is unbuttoning one cuff and the other cop is rolling up the other sleeve, and suddenly, he's totally exposed! Each arm has a ladder of white Band-Aids ascending from six inches below the elbow pit to three inches above it. Lesnick peels off the bottom Band-Aid. He lifts the arm and stares at the spot. He sees a small patch of black-and-blue centered on a tiny red dot. Smiling a slow, wise smile, Lesnick looks up into Lenny's face, still holding his arm, and says: "Lenny, I gotta take you in."

The next thing Lenny knows, he's been turned around and steered into the cops' car. Sandwiched in the front seat between these two guys, he's got his dark suit folded neatly in his lap. They're rolling along the Strip like they were out on a date. The whole thing is utterly unreal. Until it hits him! Then, fiercely, the flash rolls up from his gut! He starts to panic. He's staring out the windshield. He's seeing head-lines. SICK COMIC ARRESTED FOR NARCOTICS. A voice, a radio announcer's voice, is intoning in his ear: "Controversial comedian Lenny Bruce was arrested last night in the parking lot of the Crescendo nightclub in Hollywood and charged with using dangerous drugs. Bruce is free on bail, but if convicted . . ." He's starting to flash pictures. Sally screaming, crying, "Lenny, how could you!" Honey trying to flush the stuff down the toilet. Oh God! What will they do to Honey! A two-time loser caught with the shit in her hand! And his *career*! Imagine what *Variety* will make of this scene! Every schmucky little act in the business will be reading about this bust and saying: "Whadid I tell ya! I told ya he was out of his kug! I told ya he was on the stuff! Genius, shit! He's a lousy, dirty-mouthed, fucked-up junkie! This finishes him in the business. Good riddance!"

As the car makes for the West Hollywood sheriff's substation, Lenny finally pulls himself away from his fantasies. He has to talk to the cops. He's scared shitless. He's never been *had* before. Yet he's spent years listening to other cats tell their stories. How Joe got it here and chic caught it there and how they served time in Lexington and Fort Worth. Oh, God! This is bad! This could be the finish! He's got to talk to these guys!

So he starts coming on to the cops. "Geez! Wow! Whew!" He makes noises that mean: Hey! Fellas! Let's slow down! Let's cool it! "Look," he says, shaking his head in disbelief, "I'm terribly sorry, I don't even know your names."

"Joel Lesnick," says the heavy at the wheel. "Carl Trout," echoes the cat on his right.

"Well, listen. Uh . . . this is ridiculous. You don't have to take me in . . . I mean we're just people who could talk and work something out! Couldn't we? I mean . . . O.K. . . . You got something on me. But don't you realize what this will do to my *career!*" Now his voice is starting to climb. "I mean, man, I've worked for years just to get a break . . . you understand! I've broken my ass for ten years to get into that club where you grabbed me tonight! Please! Don't destroy me! Don't kill me! You don't have to kill me! I made a mistake. O.K. Lots of people in my business make that mistake. We work under terrible pressures. We need relief desperately. I know how it looks to you! But think what this is going to do to my mother and wife and all the people that I have to do business with! Don't you understand? You could kill me tonight! This is *it* for me! This is the *end of the line!*"

Beautiful! He got that high note off like Caruso. Now what? The two cops are strangely silent. They're calculating. The way this bust went down was that they grabbed some guy the night before and they made him sing. He said: "Well, yeah, a guy that's strung out real bad . . . it's Lenny Bruce, who's over at the Crescendo." That was how they got on to Lenny. Now at $2,500 a week, a real hype is going to be scoring from a lot of big dealers. What the hell does Joel Lesnick care about Lenny Bruce and his lousy little habit? The thing that would change his name from Detective Joel Lesnick to Sergeant Joe Lesnick would be busting some of the heaviest dealers in Los Angeles. And this scared-shitless little hype by his side knows *all their names and telephone numbers.* You dig?

So they played with Lenny. The way you'd play with a fish on the line. First, they give him the heavy goyishe conscience shit: "We can't make deals, blah, blah, blah." Then they threaten him: "Trying to corrupt a police officer is a serious matter, Lenny. More serious than drugs!" Then, finally, they let him exercise his *rights.* They tell him that he can go in that room there and make some calls and try to get whatever help he can obtain. Actually, since he didn't have any shit on him, the most they could charge him with was "under the influence"—a misdemeanor. But *he* didn't know that!

So Lenny goes over to the pay phone on the wall, where thousands of cats have begged and pleaded and poured out their hearts. He starts to make his calls. And *nothing* happens! One cat doesn't answer.

Another panics and hangs up! A third says, "Lenny! You *know* I can't get involved in a scene like that! Not with *my* record!" Finally, sweat is running down the crack on the front of his chest. He's trapped like a rat in a corner and he's fucked! What's he gonna do?

Lesnick and Trout have lots of do. They have to fill out Form 934567821. They have to type out a report. They have to call and run and hustle all over the station house. But it's all an act. A stall. They're watching. They're waiting. Using psychology. They dig that Lenny's scared. Scared hypes are cooperative hypes. Scared hypes snitch. They sing and jabber and talk their faces off to save their asses. Lenny Bruce figures to be *very* cooperative—if they just keep the heat on him.

Finally, Lenny is down to his last dime. He's got to save his life. He dials a man he despises—Gene Norman. "Hello? Gene? This is Lenny. Yeah, I know I'm late. Only I'm gonna be real late if you don't help. I've been busted. In the parking lot of the club. They've got me down here . . . it's for *drugs!*" Christ! Isn't there another word in the English language for that fuckin' shit! "Drugs!" "Narcotics!" Such a terrible word—"*narcotics!*" Hey—something is happening here! The cat is not hanging up. He's not giving me the brush. He wants to get involved!

"Gene, please! I know there've been bad scenes . . . but man . . . this is it! If you don't help now, I'm finished. Gene! Whatever I've said about you . . . I've made money for the club! Right! I mean, I'm a property, an investment! Please, Gene, come and talk to these cats. They'll listen to you. You're their kind of people. You're a big businessman. They're not gonna fuck you around the way they'll fuck me! Gene, in the name of God! Please Gene, for the baby, please, man, *help!*"

Now, Gene hates Lenny's guts. It isn't even personal. He despises *his* kind of people. Secretly, he's glad that Lenny's been busted. Glad the little shit's getting his ass kicked. Yet whatever his private feelings may be, they mustn't be allowed to fuck up his business. He's now the exclusive owner of the Crescendo. He's starting to face hard times. The nightclub business is bad and getting worse. Lenny draws. He's at his peak. Got all that publicity in *Time*. There are lines in front of the club on the weekends. Gene can't afford to lose Lenny Bruce. Besides, how would it look for one of his acts to get busted in the parking lot? That's the last thing he needs—that reputation for hiring dope fiends. Bad enough with the jazz musicians. Now with Lenny . . . He'll have to work out a deal. Go down to headquarters and talk to these guys. See what can be done. God! How did he ever get in this business?

So Gene rumbles and bumbles and rolls heavy sounds into the phone, but when he hangs up, he tells his maître d' to stall the acts, while he takes off for the sheriff's station, only five minutes away. As soon as he steps in the door, he is ushered into an office occupied by Lesnick and Trout. They're nice guys. They're very polite. They explain the situation, and they also explain that they are engaged in a war against narcotics on the Strip—and he can help them. Lenny's problem is a minor one. Yet it could make a lot of trouble. While they were waiting for Lenny to make his calls, they sent a couple of men over to his house on Spaulding and found drugs. Honey, Lenny's wife, is obviously strung out like a dog. If they want to press all possible charges, the whole family could end up behind bars. What they really want is simply cooperation. If they get that, Lenny can go back to the Crescendo in time to make the late show. How about it? Will he get this guy to talk?

Gene says he'll do his best. He hates drugs and hopes the officers succeed in stamping them out. When he is left alone with Lenny, he tells him about the offer. Lenny looks woebegone. He hates to be a fink. Yet what is there to do? The cards are on the table. So he says, "O.K. I'll talk." Then they go back in the office, and Lesnick lays his heaviest rap on Lenny. First, he asks, "Who you been buying from?" He hears old names and new names. He listens and takes notes. He asks a few questions. He seems very noncommittal. When he's gotten the names of the connections, he goes into his act. He tells Lenny: "Look, this is all fine as far as it goes. But it won't mean a thing in court. It's rumor, hearsay, your word against theirs. What we need is solid evidence. You've got to call these guys and arrange to make a buy. We've got to be there when they hand you the stuff. Otherwise all this is nothing."

Lenny looks horrified. Set guys up! Do whole big entrapment shticks? Christ! That's worse than finking. That's Judas! "Still, Lenny," bores in Lesnick, looking for the kill, "you can't expect us to play ball with you if you won't play ball with us. We're looking for convictions. Something that will stand up in court. If we can't receive your full and total cooperation in this matter, we'll just have to press our charges against you. I think you're crazy to sacrifice a career that's making you twenty-five hundred dollars a week to protect a bunch of scum who would cut your throat for ten cents—but that's *your* decision."

"O.K., O.K., O.K.," Lenny finally mumbles. He'll do the deed. And he did. That night about 3 A.M., he opened the door of his house to a dealer whom he had phoned from the club. Just as the goods were changing hands, in came Lesnick and Trout. About 5 A.M., the same scene was repeated with another dealer. By the time the night was over, Joel Lesnick had arrested some of the biggest pushers in Hollywood.

The essential details and lots of the language of Lenny's first drug bust come directly from the mouth of the arresting officer, who came to be interviewed with a scrapbook documenting Lenny's career and the detective's subsequent relations with his most famous "collar." What is extraordinary about the story is not that Lenny got busted (that was inevitable) nor that he finked (many junkies snitch) nor even that the police disclosed the name of a secret informant (Lenny had been dead for years when the interview was conducted). The most remarkable feature of the story of Lenny Bruce and Joel Lesnick is that it went on and on for years after this traumatic episode—went on, in fact, almost to the day of Lenny's death. Joel Lesnick became an important figure in Lenny's life, one of the people with whom he regularly checked in. Lesnick was a guest at Lenny's house. A recipient of numerous phone calls and private communications. For years he never knew when he picked up the phone at 4 A.M. whether the voice on the other end of the line might not be that of Lenny Bruce, smashed to the eyeballs. As a matter of fact, that was how the game began.

Very late one night, Lesnick was at the station making out his reports and cleaning up the evening's work. A call came in for him on the switchboard. Reflexively, he picked up the receiver. Suddenly, he froze! The call was from Lenny Bruce! The man he had busted just a few months before! Lenny was talking a mile a minute. His speech was so fast and garbled that Lesnick could hardly follow the darting movements of his mind. Jokes, shticks, hip words, and junkie phrases came pouring out of the instrument. Lenny was trying to make the officer laugh—and he succeeded. Then it got to be a regular thing. At odd intervals of six weeks or a couple of months, Lenny would call Lesnick and Trout with more shticks and bits. Or he would send them a letter. The letter is especially important because Lenny hated writing and would put pen to paper only under the most extreme need to communicate. Lenny had two distinctly different types of letters in his repertoire. One was the straight letter: sometimes scrawled, sometimes typed by a secretary, making some demand or making some complaint or sending funny greetings to a friend. The other kind of letter was the big paper-and-scissors, paste-up super Valentine—which he sent only to those he loved just when he felt the love most keenly (right after you had done him a favor). Now, strange to say, Lenny sat down on several occasions and cut up magazines and newspapers and fumbled with Scotch tape and marking pencils to concoct one of those super Valentines for the *police*!

One day about a year after the arrest, Lesnick and Trout received a six-page manual which Lenny had compiled "for the use of peace officers interrogating narcotics suspects." It was a thorough rundown on all the lies and bullshit that junkies use when they want to deceive the cops, every trick and cop-out that Lenny had learned during his many years on the scene. By sending such a letter to the police, he not only confirmed his character as a hype, but actually improved the efficiency of the heat's interrogations.

The last straw in this strange burden of placation came the night Lenny called up in a rather more coherent manner than usual and asked Lesnick whether he would like to have some names of guys who were dealing heavy stuff in the L.A. area. The police officer was all ears as Lenny explained that his dear friend Eric Miller had been burned badly by these cats and Lenny wanted to see them put away for keeps. Lenny gave the police such detailed information on this occasion that they made a whole series of arrests, virtually every one of which stood up in court. For that night's work alone, Lenny Bruce should have earned a special citation from the LAPD Narcotics Squad.

Lenny was always fascinated by the cops. He capered with them in Chicago and was destined to do so again in Miami. What's more, he had a philosophy about this hanky-panky, as about every other thing under the sun. He used to say that cops were just "players," like crooks—only they'd gotten a "license for their hustle." So Lenny played his little game of cat and mouse with Joel Lesnick and this little taste became the *forshpice* to the epic banquet of police persecution that Lenny was destined to prepare and consume in the latter years of his life.

It was bescheert!—fated—as the old Jews would say, that Lenny Bruce should get tight with the heat. That they should try to catch him and that he should try to worm out of their grasp. That he should provoke and they should react. That he should score his innings and they should have their victories. That, in a word, the most fundamental pattern of Lenny's soul—his love-hate, taunter-victim, provoking-placating relationship with Mickey, his father—should repeat itself on the big screen of later life. Lenny wanted to be busted. Needed to be busted. Deserved to be busted. If not in fact, then in his own mind! And eventually, he got his wish.

Now Lenny began to repeat the whole sickening cycle he had experienced years before with Honey. His efforts to keep her off drugs were completely unsuccessful. The harder he struggled to police her habit, the more she hated him and fought back against his mastery. The more he preached about the evil of drugs, the more she threw it back in his teeth that he was a confirmed junkie who had taken a bust. After a couple of months that never provided a moment of security, the pair split. Their relationship wound up just where it had been when they blew apart in Hawaii. The same old swinging door of love and hate.

As soon as Lenny broke up with Honey, he started to cast around for a new way of life. He decided to get himself a reliable companion and go out on the road again. After all, he had been happy with Kenny. They had worked together for almost six months without ever once having a quarrel. Lenny had been loose and creative. He'd even had his little fling with Francie. Everything was beautiful till that fuckin' Honey came along and loused up his life again! So, fuck her—the bitch! He'd go off and live. Only this time, he'd do it up right. He was in demand everywhere. He had his price way up there. He was the new sound, the new generation! Well, he'd live the part. He and Frankie Ray would take some wild pad and party every night. Live the way big men in this business always lived.

At that time Frankie had teamed up with former Dead End kid Huntz Hall to do a double at a newly opened strip joint on Santa Monica Boulevard called the Pink Pussycat. They were in the middle of their second week when Lenny walked in one night and buttonholed Frankie as he came offstage. "I want you out of this shithouse immediately," Lenny declared. "I'm gonna take you with me as my manager."

"Lenny, look. Don't bullshit me. I got a steady job now. Don't take me away from here. I *can't* leave."

"I'm making money and I want you to be my manager," Lenny insisted. "We're gonna leave right now. If you don't leave now—that's it! You'll *never* be my manager!"

Poor Frankie. That was all he had to hear. He turned around and walked out of the club without even telling Harry Schiller, the owner, he was splitting. Walked right out and left everything behind: top hat, cane, whistle, the works.

The two men moved into a luxurious apartment in the Regency Apartment Hotel in Hollywood, a pad that had once been occupied by Virginia Hill, mobster Bugsy Siegel's girlfriend. Partying every night, Lenny and Frankie had a marvelous time. Lenny was busy every day with an interesting little project that deserves a delightful chapter in the history of advertising.

He was taping *the first erotic commercials*. For a hip haberdashery on the Strip, Zeidler & Zeidler, right around the corner from Schwab's. The store was a hangout for actors and entertainers. Lenny would come in and do two, three hours. Break everybody up and finally buy a shirt. One day, Marvin Zeidler, the boss's son, says: "Hey, we're gonna do some radio spots for that jazz station, KBLA. We're trying for something fresh and original. Why don't you do one, Lenny?" "Hmmmm," he mused, head cocked like an alert puppy, "I never made a commercial but it's a wild idea. Yeah. It sorta grabs me. Suppose I do it! You could pay me in threads!"

The late-night jock on KBLA, Tommy Bee, had tied up in 1957 with another DJ named Jack Rose, and this pair had become the pioneer jazz-hip jocks in the L.A. area. Bee's model was Symphony Sid, and he affected the latter's cancer-throat growl as he announced: "And now Horace Silver with 'Señor Blues'—MAKE IT!" And that signature phrase would leap out of the radio like King Kong's paw.

With the attention of hippy-dippy late-night L.A. focused on the station, Lenny obviously owed it to his image to cut some commercials that really set a bench mark in pitchmanship. Two things came to mind instantly: the commercials should make fun of commercials—and they should insinuate into the mouth of advertising the hook of sex. The first blue commercials in history, they must sully the purity of the airwaves. Else, why MAKE IT?

Setting to work, in his most creative period, on an absolutely foolish and utterly unprofitable project—precisely the circumstances that always drew from him his greatest stuff—Lenny produced a series of ads so resourceful and so prophetic of everything to come that they still sound way-out and remain too kinky for network radio. Only on the whacked-out West Coast and only during the hours from midnight to six in the morning (on a station whose status with the FCC was always dubious) could such bizarrerie and grotesquerie and plain old-fashioned smut go winging out for minutes at a time, polluting the already filthy air of Freak Town.

Dig the first flash that lit up Lenny's mind! He decided to introduce the microphone into the intimacies of the bedroom. That was a setting he had mastered and it was perfect for radio. The ultimate studio. Hushed, intimate, curtained, and tight on the ear. "Oh! . . . Oh! . . . Oh! . . . Oh! . . . Oh! . . . Oh! . . ." moans the woman on his first commercial, her voice ascending the scale of orgasmic urgency. Slicing in with the classic radio announcer's voice, Lenny demands, "Oh? Oh, Oh *what*?" Then his tone switches from puzzlement to discontent, "Ooooh, *oh, oh,* Zeidler & Zeidler, 800 North Vermont," he distinctly enunciates, as the commercial detumesces.

"Ringa ding, ringadangdong," he lilts into the second commercial, jabbering away like a five-year-old girl playing hopscotch. Abruptly a mature girl's voice breaks in saying, "No! Not now!" Instantly, the mood of carefree innocence shifts to that of careworn experience. In a voice halfway between those of an old Jewish candy-store owner and Count Dracula, Lenny protests: "Vhy not now? I'm getting weak! It's almost daylight! Pleeze, pleeze, give it to me now!"

"No!" snaps the girl petulantly.

"Vhy not?"

" 'Cause they're the only *pair* I've got!"

Then Lenny drops into his normal voice and tells the chick off. "I can get the only pair—of Italian shoes—at Zeidler & Zeidler! And you can *keep* your pair!"

The sexual intimacies of Lenny's first two commercials are puns. In the third he starts off like a porno soap opera and winds up like an animated cartoon. "Can I touch it? Can I touch it?" he implores in this urgent bit. "No!" says the dreadful little shiksa, obviously lying in bed with him and offering some insane final resistance. "Please! Just once!" Then, like a child—and dig! this is literally the way he came on with chicks—he whispers, "I'll tell you a secret!" And he goes into the ad—how Zeidler & Zeidler has stores in three convenient locations, blah, blah, blah. Having discharged his responsibility to God and sponsor, he coaxes, "Can I touch it now?" In a quick warning voice, she gasps, "It'll explode!" Suddenly, there's a long, drawn-out bomb whistle followed by a shattering, mike-smashing explosion. When the pieces settle down, Lenny adds: "It was worth it, though!" The girl laughs irresponsibly.

In yet another, this one staged at a Hollywood premiere, Lenny, the reporter, says: "We have to be cool here—there are many people in the industry that actually aren't *in* the industry anymore. And now, the first voice from the past.

"Ah, sir, you're a movie star, aren't you?"

"Well, I don't like to put it that way, but, yes, I have hopes of making a comeback."

"It's people like you that made Hollywood what it is today. You get a lot of respect . . . fan mail."

"Yes, I'm loved."

"Of course, you know you're *nothing* in this town. Don't go by that fan mail—you're just a failure. You live at the Haney Hotel."

"But my agent . . ."

"Your agent's a *nut*! Listen—you want to get hip? You know anything about papers?"

"Papers like what?"

"Like picking up papers!"

"You'll hear from my lawyer," the man protests as people in the background laugh. Lenny tells him to beat it and then gets serious. "That man was helped by Zeidler & Zeidler at three locations. Don't forget—you're not only buying a suit—you're helping an old-time movie star."

The next ad that Lenny made is a classic of the art of kidding the commercial. It also anticipates the tell-it-as-it-is ad, which disarms the listener (or viewer) by offering a very simple, honest, soft-sell pitch through the mouth of a perfectly ordinary and rather likable character. The ad begins with one of those apocalyptic announcements shouted by an announcer with a voice like a cannon. "ZEIDLER & ZEIDLER! FOR BIGGER SAVINGS! FOR BIGGER AND BETTER BUYS! THE THRIFTY WAY TO SHOP!" Then you hear Lenny asking querulously, "How do you like that, Mr. Zeidler?" Then comes the switch, as Lenny dons his German accent and comes on like a slow, thoughtful, decent immigrant, a nice old German Jew who can't bear the vulgar schreidiche quality of America. "No . . . zat's not zee vun . . . zat's not zee feeling!" the old man adjures. "Well," spits the ad man, "maybe we otta grab 'em with the bargain angle?" Mr. Zeidler: "No, mein friend . . . it's not cheap clothes zheir . . . it's about zee same competitive price of zee other firms . . ." When the ad man says, "Well, how about this? Zeidler & Zeidler, it's real conveniently located!" Mr. Zeidler responds, "Yeah . . . but vhat's vith zhat? Sure, it's conveniently located . . . but everything's conveniently located . . . it's got a front door to it, my friend." Finally in desperation, the ad man cries, "Well, gee, Mr. Zeidler, I don't know what you want —don't you want a sincere pitch?"

As Lenny got deeper into the groove, his ka-ka, pee-pee toilet obsessions eventually came to the surface. Starting off a series keyed to "unusual occupations," Lenny taped a you-are-there interview with a shopper in the store. This cat has a one-of-a-kind occupation: "I am what's known as the Original Party Sound. They send for me and party favors." Asked what kind of sounds he does, the guy demonstrates one for people who are too poor to own a pool—but who want to hear the sound of someone diving in. You can hear water pouring, as though from a faucet—and Lenny getting uptight: "Oh . . . that's . . . you can't do that in front of children, can you?" As the man tries to explain, Lenny goes on, ignoring his expostulations: "You're lucky this is a *men*'s store! I didn't appreciate that! That was a little out of left field!"

The Sound assures Lenny that he can do other noises, such as smoking. Breathing in deeply, he sounds like he's toking a toke on a joint. "Oh!" is Lenny's unimpressed reaction. Then, reverting to the mysterious water music, Lenny continues his protest. "I didn't care

for that first one you did. That was *disgusting*!" The Sound shrugs:
"Oh, well, it's a little wet—but it's a big store! They'll never notice it
. . . this maroon rug. May I show you my other noise?"

The Sound tries next to be three people talking about Zeidler &
Zeidler, acting out each part—but making no sense at all. A glass
crashes in the background, Lenny asks suspiciously: "Have you ever
worked anywhere?"

"Huh? Oh yes . . . at Joe Zingo's Blue Room in Memphis . . ."

"I don't . . . Why are you sweating so much?" [A reference to a
common symptom of heroin.] Lenny is now very suspicious. "You've
never worked anywhere!"

"These are my props—this is my prop here for this gag, y'see. If
I don't sweat, I can't get the water, there's no water here . . ."

"Hey, listen, you're a wacko, you're a nut, right—are you a nut?"
asks Lenny in a confiding tone.

"Huh? No."

Lenny gets very sneaky, insinuating: "Tell the truth now—I'll
never cop—you're a *wacko*, right?"

The guy is very straight: "Well, I'll tell you why I come to Zeidler
& Zeidler—they've got pretty bags, you know, with the pictures of
old men on them, and I make paper slippers out of them."

Lenny is still playing along, humoring him. "Paper slippers?"

The guy muses, "Yeah . . . I like paper slippers."

Lenny begins to change his tone, whispering so that no one can
hear them, trying to make the other man paranoid: "You better get
out of here—quick! Split! Split!"

The Sound tries to suppress the giggle in his voice: "Why? Are
they coming?"

Lenny also is about to laugh: "You're a nut!"

"Just one more . . ." The guy whistles, and another glass shatters.
Lenny raises his voice and shouts: "Get outta here, you nut, and *stop
wetting on those coats!*"

Like the first guy who made a blue movie, Lenny was ranging
around freely in what was virgin territory. He loved scouting with the
tape recorder or sitting up on the couch of Jack Rose's house in Hollywood doing a bit with the neighborhood children. When the commercials started playing over the air, they received a lot of attention.
Everybody was talking about them. Lenny would come into the store
for his payoff threads (maybe a thousand dollars' worth of clothes, all
told), and he would do bits on his own bits, mimicking the effect of
hearing the commercial come on after some jazz tune while everybody
was kacked out at three in the morning. He hadn't had so much fun
since he appeared on *Rocket to Stardom*.

Not all the reaction was favorable, needless to say. The store got a very vigorous protest one day from a woman who identified herself as being the head of the local PTA. The commercial that bugged her was the one called *Your Dyke Alert Bulletin*. It was another twist on the radio interview, with a deep-voiced Paul Coates character interviewing two naked women who have been caught stealing men's clothes from Zeidler & Zeidler. When "Coates" gives the wrong address, he's corrected by one of the shoplifters, and between them they manage to give the store's three locations. Lenny interrupts the interview, saying he's a nightclub owner, and wants to know *why* the women were stealing men's clothes. Asking if they *like* to wear men's clothes, he suddenly breaks off and says in a police-radio voice: "Watch out for these two women. They're wearing men's clothes. These women may be found in neighborhood bars. This is another Zeidler & Zeidler public service—Your Dyke Alert Bulletin!"

Most of Lenny's commercials had nothing to do with his act, though he did use a couple of his standard voices. The best of the lot was, however, an extension of one little idea in the famous Lawrence Welk interview. One of the things that Lenny ridicules about Welk is the way he dresses. So in an elaborate three-man skit—Frankie Ray and comic Jackie Gayle playing salesmen and Lenny playing Welk—the whole theme of square and hip clothing is dramatized by making Welk walk into the store and order suits for his band.

"I vant to get suits for the boys. I like gabardine one-button rolls," announces Mr. Square.

Incredulous, the hip salesman laughs: "Wait a minute—Oh, man! You're too much, baby! Go to Robert Hall or something, you dig? I mean, you can't make it now, son, because we only take Joe Williams, the Basie band, Sonny Payne, Philly Joe—music of that ilk, ya dig?"

Like a spoiled child, Welk insists: "But I vant to buy a suit."

Jackie replies condescendingly, "Well look, baby, I don't think you're ready for suits yet."

"I got four dollars for the layaway . . ."

Jackie laughs again: "Wait a minute, daddy—you're not even ready for underwear!"

"I'm not your daddy—whassa matter?" Welk's voice becomes more and more babyish as the ad disintegrates: "Yes you are! . . ." "Wait a minute! . . ." "Now get outta this store, man! . . ."

A March of Time voice gets in the last word: "That was an example of the courteous service you receive at Zeidler & Zeidler."

One night, Lenny overheard a lengthy phone conversation between Frankie and his ex-wife, who had been living in Chicago since their separation seven years earlier. The sound of her voice had inspired Frankie to suggest a reconciliation. "We were very foolish," he said. "Maybe we should try to get together again." A look of utter despair flashed across his face as the woman rejected the proposal. Empathizing deeply with Frankie's pain, Lenny began to cry.

"When you were talking," he said, after Frankie had slammed down the receiver, "I heard so many words that I said to Honey. Like, all the things about getting back together again. All the same things that I've said to Honey."

A couple of nights later, while Frankie was packing his clothes for a long road trip with Lenny, Sally visited the suite. Smiling, joking, but worrying behind her mask of merriment, she watched the operation for a while; then suddenly she lowered her voice and said, "Maybe you shouldn't go." "What do you mean?" asked Frankie. "He's liable to change because he still has Honey on his mind," Sally warned. "Honey will call and you'll be out!" Frankie couldn't believe it.

The first stop on the tour was the Crystal Palace in St. Louis, where Lenny gave one of his rare press conferences. Playing up his image as the far-out sick comic, he received the reporter for the *Globe-Democrat* sprawled across a bed, draped with an oriental spread, eating jello with a beer-can opener. "Comedy is not an art form," Lenny informed the perplexed correspondent. "I don't . . . I honestly don't think I have a function as a comedian—except maybe to make money for the guy who books me. My normal show runs about forty-five minutes, and I guess about eight minutes is free-form. The rest comes from bits I've written here and there. I guess I replace about fifteen minutes or so every week. The only people who really see the changes are the waitresses."

Quizzed about his character as a "nonconformist," Lenny replied: "Sure, I say things that may offend people. But they don't have to pay to listen to me. I feel deeply about a lot of things, and I can say them. But when it's in a bit, it has to be well-mixed. After all, I'm supposed to be funny." Then he paused, furrowed his brow, snapped his fingers a few times, and looked up with a better explanation. "Look," he said, "it's a question of timing . . . like this!" Then he snapped his fingers, tapped his foot, and bobbed his head. "A serious comment," he explained, "then another, then a laugh." Asked the inevitable question about the Sick Comics, Lenny snorted derisively and snapped: "Sick? Ridiculous! It's strictly a commercial proposition. Mort is having two television spectaculars this season. Think they'd take chances? And Shelley has done a great job on the *Ed Sullivan Show*—the blandest, most soya-bean type of show in existence. It offends me . . . says nothing!"

Pausing for a moment, Lenny added with perfect comedy timing —"But the bread is *great!*" Pausing again, he anticipated the next question: "Sure, I'd like it!"

The interview concluded in the ornate saloon-baroque theater, gussied up to remind the customers of the Good Ole Days when St. Louis was "The Gateway to the West." Waving an arm around the room, Lenny quipped: "It looks like a church that went bad . . . started with a bingo party, then a dance, then . . ." His voice trailed off, as it always did when the inspiration flagged and it was time to change the topic. Wandering around the stage for a few minutes, he finally perched on a stool, tucked his legs underneath him, and raised his head to speculate. "Sometimes, I wonder how this town swings. First thing I do here, people are telling me about the tornado. But it happened eight month sago! Hasn't anything happened since?"

The dullness of the town had its advantages. With no scenes to distract him, Lenny worked hard developing new material. You could sit in the club night after night, show after show, and watch the stuff grow, like those paper pellets the Japanese drop in water to expand into full-blown flowers.

Between shows he and Frankie would go over to the Grand, the local burlesque house, where they would hang out with the baggy-pants comics and the strippers. Frankie had once owned (with Shecky Greene) an after-hours club in New Orleans called Wits End. It was the kind of place that opens at two in the morning and does its whole business with pimps, whores, gangsters, strippers, and actors. Frankie knew everybody in burlesque and so did Lenny. They felt a kind of loyalty to the old scene, even though they were glad to be out of it. It was sweet to go backstage and sit around in the dressing room for an hour reminiscing and doing bits. A nice feeling of coming home without having to stay. What especially pleased Frankie about these two weeks in St. Louis was Lenny's complete indifference to drugs. You didn't even see an aspirin lying around in his room. It was the best time Frankie ever had with his hero.

The next stop on the tour was Mr. Kelly's in Chicago. Lenny had no sooner arrived in town than somebody told him that Rocky had given up Duffy's and was back home in Chicago working in a pharmacy. "Let's go find Rocky!" Lenny yelled impulsively to Frankie. Without a second's hesitation, they ran out of the Delaware Towers and jumped into a cab. Minutes later they pulled up in front of a drugstore. Lenny dashed out of the taxi and entered the store; in a few moments he dashed back out of the store and into the taxi. Giving the driver a new address, he raced on to another drugstore, where the same scene was repeated. Every time he would hit a pharmacy, he would come back with the address of another pharmacy. In the first hour, they made a dozen futile stops. Finally, Frankie complained: "Lenny! Look at the meter! Let's rent a car." But Lenny had made up his mind that this was the way he was going to find Rocky. He was a bloodhound on the scent. By the end of the day, he had spent over seventy dollars in cab fares and still not found a trace of Rocky. Finally, he had to go to work. Next day, the idea had vanished from his mind.

During the first ten days in Chicago, Lenny and Frankie continued to live quietly and in perfect harmony. They went to the last ball game of the season. They sat through a couple of lessons at a local typewriting school. They made plans for further tours and junkets. Then, one day, during the last week in September, Lenny received an incoherent phone call from Honey. An hour or so later, Frankie was downstairs in the lobby, writing a letter. Lenny aproached him looking terribly tense and nervous.

"What are you doing in town?" asked Lenny.

"What!" exclaimed Frankie, thinking Lenny was kidding.

Two days later, Frankie found a note from Lenny in his mail slot.

"I don't have the heart to do this," it read, "but for the money that I pay you or spend on you, I could have Honey with me. I can't tell you this to your face because I like you so much. I think Honey's going to join me, and I just want to say goodbye to you." Enclosed in the envelope was a check for three weeks' salary, a generous payoff.

Honey was in a dreamy state when she arrived in Chicago with Kitty. Lenny had hoped that by bringing the three of them together he could help Honey to stay away from narcotics. During the day they visited places like Grand Park and the Lincoln Park Zoo. At night Lenny went to the club—which blew the whole deal. By the end of the week it was obvious to Lenny that Honey was scoring from someone in the hotel. Disheartened, he sent her and Kitty back to Los Angeles, telephoning his mother with instructions to pick up his family at the airport.

From this point on, he sought to preserve his relationship with Honey not by involving himself with her directly but by putting her into the hands of various doctors and psychiatrists, while at the same time he labored tirelessly to buy and renovate and furnish the most elaborate home that he could afford for himself, Kitty, and Honey. In many ways, it was an old-fashioned middle-class solution. He was no longer married to Honey, but he couldn't divorce her. Like thousands of conventional businessmen, he simply put his marriage on ice. Handed the wife over to the doctors and went on about his business. He wouldn't go near a psychiatrist himself; but he started auditioning doctors all over the country seeking the right man to cure his wife.

His first choice was a young man named Harvey Karman, a friend and a student of psychiatry. Karman was a medical school dropout who had turned to free-lance writing. Lenny had been impressed by some reviews Karman had written for *Variety* and by an article in which he analyzed the precocious daughter of the actress Pamela Mason. On this slender recommendation, he dispatched Karman to Honey's house to begin a series of listening sessions that were supposed to sort out all her problems. Karman visited his patient regularly three times a week. He listened to her free-association ramblings, if she felt like talking. If she seemed reticent, they would sit and watch television together. Resembling an adult baby-sitter, Karman kept an eye on Honey until Lenny could get back to L.A. and make better arrangements.

Meanwhile, he proceeded straight into fantasyland by commissioning his accountant, Seymour Grush, to seek out a suitable house and property for himself and his family. The house he bought was a conventional and unattractive glass-walled box lodged in a spectacular location at nearly the top of the Hollywood Hills. The approach to 8825 Hollywood Boulevard is dramatic. You make a sharp turn off Sunset Boulevard at Sunset Plaza Drive and start a steep airplane climb up Queens Road and then onto the winding, twisting, perpetually climbing hill trail of Hollywood Boulevard. After what seems like a quarter of an hour of wrestling with the steering wheel, you finally reach a level not far below the summit, where, in the middle of a serpentine curve, a steep little driveway jumps up, helicopter-style, to the parking lot of a house that has been cantilevered out over the hill. Originally, the house had only one floor, the lower part being used as a carport. There was no pool and the steeply sloping hill behind the house threatened mud slides. When Lenny brought his father up to see the house, the sensible senior Schneider, who knew something about houses, told his son that this precariously perched box was a bad deal. That advice may have clinched the deal. In any case, sometime in the spring or summer of 1960, Lenny purchased the property for $65,000 with a $500-a-month mortgage. Most of the money came from two generous sources: Fantasy Records, with whom Lenny had signed a five-year contract (designed to spread his earnings and reduce his tax load), gave him an advance of $25,000 expressly for the purpose of buying the house; another $25,000 came from Samuel Barnett, the owner of the El Patio nightclub in Miami, with whom Lenny became familiar during an engagement late in December. Lenny immediately began pouring money into his new house at such a rate that within two years he could claim (with perhaps a little exaggeration) that the place had cost him a couple of hundred thousand dollars.

After Chicago, Lenny went back to the Den for another long engagement. The little basement club had now become his base in New York. He felt so comfortable there that he got into the sort of stream-of-consciousness rapping that he had done at Ann's and before that at Duffy's. One night he was talking to the audience as if it were an intimate friend and the subject became his career. With his voice reaching lyrical intensity, he looked into the future and made a prophecy: "I know," he chanted, "that in six months, I'll be making five grand. I feel, I *smell* it! The sweet smell of success. I know it won't last. It's like bullfighting. You only feel that love when you're building him. Then you want to see him die! You resent him. Well, you just have to beat it by using a little junk!" The line got a big laugh. After all, it was a typical "sick" snapper.

Lenny was always looking to cop out in public about his habit: that was the secret meaning of bits like the kid with the airplane glue and the whacked-out pilots flying Non Skeddo Airlines and the jazz-movie parodies and, a little later, *Stamp Help Out!*, the comic picture and caption book that tells the history of a pot smoker's life, illustrating it with pictures of Lenny Bruce. Lenny often joked about dope and sometimes he preached about it, taking the line that everybody was hooked on something, whether it was sleeping pills, diet pills, mood elevators, tranquilizers, or just aspirin. It was the hypocrisy of the world that allowed people to denounce dope fiends while they themselves built up legitimate habits with the help of their prescription-writing doctors. No matter how wild Lenny got onstage, however, he could never really confront his addiction. It was a forbidden topic, a great big hole of omission in what was supposed to be a thoroughly examined and candidly revealed personality. As the years wore on and Lenny's comedy became more frankly autobiographical, the gap between the life he led and the pose he struck undermined completely his public credibility.

The job at the Den was Lenny's last regular gig for the year 1959. The year really ended on Saturday night, December 27, when for the first time in his life Lenny apeared "in concert." It was a great moment for him because it represented his graduation from the ranks of the ordinary café performer into the privileged class of the one-man-show stars. Concert appearances for comics were still a novelty at that time, and just the word "concert" was enough to fill most comedians with pride. "Concert": that was something an artist gave, like Heifetz or Toscanini. It meant that you had an "audience," not just a lot of drunks at ringside grabbing for your legs. At a concert you stood up on a stage, and hundreds, maybe thousands, of people paid strict attention. They didn't smoke or drink or talk among themselves. Heckling was unthinkable. If you wanted to stretch out, go over the usual forty-minute limit, there wasn't any location owner signaling you from the bar to get off. Nobody was worrying about turning over the house. It was a nice clean shot for an hour and a half or even two. You got out there and did exactly as you pleased—and even the money was good. In a big house, seating three or four thousand, you could reach as many people in one show as you played to in a nightclub in a whole week. Just in terms of dollars and cents, concert work was worth a lot more than the club business.

The guy who booked Lenny into Detroit was a young bespectacled Jewish boy, with a big nose and a little wife, named Bennett Sims. Ben had aspirations to be a writer but while he was getting up his nerve to hit the typewriter, he worked as a clerk in the largest record store in Detroit. It was on this job that he first encountered the humor of Lenny Bruce, listening to the first Fantasy album, then the second, each of them, in Ben's opinion, the funniest thing he had ever heard. It was just a step from cracking up over the records to saying to himself, "Hey! There's a fortune to be made in presenting this guy in concert!" Ben started negotiating with the local theater impresario to book Lenny into the huge old Riviera Theater, seating capacity, 3,400. Right away, problems cropped up. This guy Bruce was a weirdo: he demanded payment in cash and a jazz group had to work forty minutes before he took the stage. The jazz group was understandable; but the cash payment? The theater owner said that in thirty years of booking acts he had never encountered that demand.

Ben was not to be thwarted. He signed papers and wrote checks and picked up Lenny at the airport on the Friday night before the show. The next night Lenny showed up backstage with a little shaving bag to carry the cash and went on for an hour and forty minutes. It was a pretty strange scene because the huge house was virtually empty. He played to about four hundred people, of whom only eight were paid admissions. The mood was that of a séance; even the professional entertainment writer for the *Detroit News* walked out. Strange to say, none of this appeared to have any effect on Lenny. He was so delighted to be working a concert that he hung in there for almost two hours, giving a marvelous performance. After it was over, he appeared tired and wan. Ben insisted on schlepping him to a party at his mother-in-law's. After about twenty minutes, Lenny said, "Where's the bathroom?" He locked himself inside for half an hour with all sorts of people banging on the door. When he emerged, his mood had changed completely. He was happy and charming. He hung around for two more hours and then split.

After winding up his gig at the Den, Lenny took off for Miami.

It was another first for him: his first appearance on the Beach since his novice years back in '51. The thought of Honey really made him nostalgic for that time. She was going to join him at the hotel because this gig promised to run for a month or more. They would be making it again, like they always did, hot and heavy. Honey could always get him horny. She was the ultimate ball. The trouble was that he wouldn't be able to maintain his strict image with her now that he was back on the stuff himself. He wasn't really hooked. He could quit whenever he wanted. In fact, he'd been trying a new rhythm. On for a couple of days, then off. Then on and off. Funny! It reminded him of jerking off when he was a kid.

The other groovy feature of this gig would be Eric Miller. Lenny had really leaned on Jack Sobel, a couple of months before, to get Eric some work. The old Hungarian had come through with a booking in a very hip place, the lounge of the Sir John, the black hotel in Miami. Lenny was crazy about Eric, and he wanted to work things out so they could go on the road together in the spring. They had one bit, *The Defiant Ones;* now he would think up something better for them to do. Eric had told him about a party he once played, where some white businessman had come on to him real friendly, but everything he said was really a racial putdown. Like: "That Joe Louis was a helluva fighter!" Hmmmm. Lenny could structure that into a great six minutes. Do all the stereotypes: the food, the smell, the hair, the sex! "Hey, why do you guys want to do it to everybody's sister?" Yeah, it would be a heavy piece. Give everybody the bends. Hah!

The club where Lenny was going to work was called the El Patio. It was in the Waves Hotel, 11th and Ocean. A former fag joint owned by two brothers, it was now going into a show-and-music policy, with Lenny in the big room and Tito Puente in the lounge. Mambos and cha-cha-chas were pouring out of the joint the night Lenny arrived. The Jewish hase schoenahs were out on the floor shaking their asses. It was so funny to look at: the stiffo accountants and shinglemen down from New York trying to remember what they learned at Arthur Murray, while their zatskahed-up wives made with the Champagne Hour tooshie action. Jewish girls were the hottest—till you got them in bed. Then they always wanted to lecture you on "warmth."

Once he dropped into the Miami groove, Lenny had a ball. He loved this town for many reasons: because it was hot and tropical (he insisted that Jews had an innate longing for torrid climates), because in some neighborhoods you could still catch the flavor of old-country Yids, whom he always extolled in contrast to the self-infatuated and sentimental Jews that he met in the business, and above all, because the "Beach" was where he had fallen in love with Honey. He also dug the lifestyle. He would hang around the pool all day, until it was time to fix and shower and shave and fix and dress for the gig in a new denim jumpsuit. Then he would hop into a rented convertible and drive to the club, where he would do the first show and fix and the second show and fix. Then it was time to go out and play.

About 2:30 A.M., he would arrive at one of his favorite "pickle palaces," Wolfie's at 21st and Collins or Pumpernik's up in the 70s. After gobbling up six slices of French toast drowned in maple syrup at Wolfie's, he could go next door to the Five O'Clock Club and put on the strippers. Or he could drive out to the Black Magic Lounge on the 79th Street Causeway, one of the few late spots he enjoyed. Or he might cruise the hottest corner in town, 23rd and Park, where you could score for any drug and where there was a little tonk strip comprising the Night Owl, one of the country's skinniest bars (with a juke box containing only Frank Sinatra sides), the Grate, a bar-restaurant featuring live jazz, and the Pin-Up, a hooker spot that also had a jazz combo. The hip way to end the night was to go out on one of the ocean jetties and watch the sunrise.

When he told the boss, Sam Barnett, how much he wanted to come back the following year, the guy made him a fantastic offer. He told Lenny that he wanted him back—even though the crowds hadn't been as great as they both hoped—because he was sure that by then Lenny would have built a big following. In fact, he wanted Lenny to come back so much, he was willing to help him in his personal business. Lenny had said he wanted to buy a house back in L.A.: that he had gotten twenty-five grand from Fantasy and was looking for another twenty-five. Well, Sam Barnett would loan him the money. Give him twenty-five big ones for three years, on condition—"you hear, meshugana?"—that Lenny come back next Christmas and play the club till business slackened off. Lenny could pay him back in pieces, whenever he got the money; he would just have to sign a paper that made it all legal. Barnett didn't even want interest: he just wanted to guarantee Lenny for the future.

It seemed like a pretty crazy deal at the time—but Lenny never forgot it. A year later, when Barnett's brother had been bumped off by the Mafia for not giving them their share, Lenny got a frantic message from Sam. He needed Lenny desperately. He needed him to save his life. He couldn't pay Lenny's price, but he warned that if Lenny didn't save him, he would have to die, like his brother. Everybody tried to talk Lenny out of the move, telling him it was foolish to break his price for even one man. Lenny wouldn't hear of their objections. He remembered that loan for his house. He played El Patio the following Christmas and bailed Sam Barnett out of the worst jam of his life.

Winding up at El Patio, Lenny took off with Honey for a brief vacation in Havana. You could still breeze into Castro Cuba, and Lenny was dying to see what changes had been wrought in the most sinful city of the Western world. No sooner did they arrive in their Havana hotel room than Lenny was out on the balcony with Honey's black sleeveless cashmere sweater around his chin doing a take-off on Castro. Honey roared with laughter as Lenny spouted Cuban double-talk, making up nonsensical Spanish-sounding words in his phlegmy spic accent.

An hour later, Lenny rang down to room service for a meal. The food was long in coming, but when it arrived it was delicious. They wolfed down a load of roast pork with rice and beans. Thirty minutes later, they became desperately ill. Vomiting and shaking with chills and fever, they called frantically for the house doctor. Instead, they were confronted by the manager, who was enraged about something and demanded that they leave his hotel—instantly. Barely able to walk, constantly doubling over with terrible spasms of nausea, now become the dry heaves, they were conveyed swiftly to the airport and shoved aboard a plane for Miami. When they arrived, they rushed to a hospital. Describing their painful condition to the physician on duty, they received a cursory examination and a fast diagnosis. Cause of condition: *poisoning*. Making fun of Castro wasn't healthy in Cuba.

By March, Lenny was ready for the road again. He had written his new hit with Eric Miller, and he was dying to try it on the sophisticated customers in the northern cities. In 1960 civil rights agitation was at its peak. Everybody was talking about sit-ins and marches and demonstrations. When Lenny hit them with this new black bit, he knew he would make another sensation, just like the one he triggered off with *Religions, Inc.* Even down here in Miami, he could see that he was becoming the darling of the in-group. There was a bunch of very hip college kids at the club every night. They were young and rich and Jewish. They were from New York, Boston, Philly, but they went to the University of Miami. Every evening they'd sit outside the club in their cars and smoke a little tea. Then they'd come in and sit at a long table with fake I.D. cards. They really dug his head, his looks, his clothes—the whole image. They were the wave of the future, his next audience. Mort Sahl was across town at the Americana, but Lenny's crowd ignored him. Sahl was just too ridiculously uptight to be a hipster.

When Lenny breezed into New York that March—to play the

Blue Angel—he was at the pinnacle of success. His act had never been stronger nor his delivery more impressive. He had done fantastic business all over the country in the last couple of years, even in a town like St. Louis, which was not exactly the hub of the nightclub circuit. *How to Relax Your Colored Friends at Parties* was one of the greatest pieces he ever invented. Nothing funnier, truer, or more zestily iconoclastic had ever been presented on the American stage. Lenny expected a big hand in New York for coming home with just the sort of gamy bacon his hip, cynical, Big City audiences delighted to savor.

He roused himself from sleep the afternoon after opening night and started reading the newspaper reviews. As *Variety* summed up the press reaction: "For the first time within memory, N.Y. dailies really let the stops out on a [nightclub] act." "Obnoxious, arrogant," snarled Gene Knight in the *Journal-American*. "Diarrhea of the mouth," vomited *Cue*. "The man from Outer Taste," cutesied Bob Sylvester of the *Daily News*. "A vulgar, tasteless boor," huffed *Billboard*. The punch line was delivered, predictably, by Walter Winchell, who reached deep into his pun bag to dub Lenny "America's No. 1 Vomic!"

Shaken by the critics' cries of outrage, Lenny was disturbed even more by the news that one famous columnist had phoned police headquarters after the show and lodged a formal complaint. That night when he got to the club, he received word that police were present in the audience, armed with a tape recorder. For the first time in the big time, he was being confronted by the protectors of the society he had grown accustomed to scourging without complaint. Reacting instinctively to the threat of arrest, he presented a show that was completely free of obscenities. Just by repeating his recorded performances—all of them neatly shorn of nasty words and thoughts—he gave a performance that practically had the audience cheering and sent the cops back to the station house with nothing incriminating to report. Afterward, Lenny was moody and reflective. "It wasn't natural," he brooded. "I wanted to talk to the audience like I do to my family and friends. It wasn't honest. I don't care for myself, but the club could lose its license if I turned on the heat."

By the end of the week, Lenny was opening every show with an impressive demonstration of Christian charity. Walking onstage with a rolled-up copy of a newspaper in his hand, he rehashed all the charges against him in the press and then publicly forgave his critics. "I'm the only guy who got a bad review in 'Where to Go and What to See,' " he remarked wryly. Then he turned the other cheek: "I don't blame the critics for not liking me. It's not their fault they don't understand. Each generation is incoherent to the next. They can't help it—they're old! They're still hung with that Al Jolson–George Jessel garbage . . .

And I'm not knocking age. I'm relatively old myself. I can't relate to Fabian. Paul Anka probably says: 'Who's that old creep, Presley?' I'm really sorry for Abel Green [*Variety*'s chief editor]. There's nothing sadder than an old hipster."

The important issue, though, as Lenny knew, was not whether he could understand or forgive the critics but what exactly had provoked their anger. Lenny's latest hanger-on, a writer named Art Steuer, who free-lanced for Clay Felker at *Esquire*, figured that the problem was one of outraged moral sensibilities. Writing some months later in the newly sophisticated men's mag, he stressed Bruce's role as an iconoclast.

A contemporary Isaiah, Bruce execrates all that is unctuous and sanctimonious in our society: Mother ("We say we love our mothers, yet when any foul imagery is needed they are always intimately involved"); dogs ("The only dog with a function is a Doberman pinscher. You raise him—train him—and ten years later he kills you"); charity ("A lot of people don't know about the Ku Klux Klan. The B'nai B'rith is behind it"); Santa Claus ("Been under analysis for years. Loves to flagellate the reindeer"); liberals ("It's getting chic to be liberal. I figure I'll be the first hip bigot"); Eleanor Roosevelt ("She projects a good image of herself because she can afford to do things without getting paid for it"); child rearing ("This kid was abandoned in Yellowstone Park. His parents remembered to put out the fire, but forgot him. He was raised by a pack of wild dogs. Years later he was found walking on all fours, eating raw meat. In two years, he raced through grammar school, high school, entered Cal Tech, astrophysics. In a year he had his degree. The day after he graduated, he was killed chasing a car"); TV ("I'd like to kill myself on television. It would be a real 'first.' Of course the producer would be nervous ('You're not gonna say anything dirty, are you?' 'No, it's a very clean act. I just take four pills and die')"); mothers-in-law ("I think it's unfair to make jokes about them breaking up marriages. My mother-in-law *did* break up my marriage, though. My wife came home from work and found me in bed with her"); and even himself ("Of course I'm corrupt too. If I wasn't I'd pick up your tab").

Most of these little cracks were as nothing compared with the outrageous things he had said and done in his first years or would say in his last period. The year 1960 marked a time of high professionalism in Lenny's development. When he began to pick up flack, it wasn't so much because of what he said as because of the attitude with which he articulated these witticisms.

The hostility that had always lain at the back of Lenny's soul, the cruelty that sometimes emerged in his personal relations, the cold, radar-directed destructiveness that darted out in his deadly putdowns —these traits were now beginning to inform his nightclub act. Instead of superficially shocking the audience while subliminally wooing them, Lenny was now presenting an act that was authentically shocking because the nasty cracks appeared more and more to emerge from a nasty mind. Lenny was getting cold and bitter on the stage; his act was becoming an act of provocation. Always the self-conscious craftsman, he knew exactly what he was doing—or, if you want to get tricky about it, he had furnished himself with a convincing rationalization for what he was prompted to do from the bottom of his heart. Arguing back and forth with his closest friends, like Richey Shackleton, Lenny would insist that there was nothing wrong with becoming controversial because "Controversy makes money." Shack would counter, "Controversy catches up with you. It only lasts so long and then some people get a hard-on for you and want to do you in." The only way out of the dilemma, according to Shackleton, lay in structuring the material so cunningly that he couldn't take a bust. If he really went far enough into the existential-black-humor-Jean-Genet bag, he might grab the intellectuals, or at least the pseudo-intellectuals, and pass for an artist. Otherwise, he was setting himself up for martyrdom. Structure, though, was exactly what Lenny was trying to free himself of. He was utterly sick of the long, carefully plotted bits on which he had based his fame. Doing *Religions, Inc.* and *The Palladium* hundreds of times had not only turned him against these once favorite pieces—it had turned him against the very idea of the bit as a miniature drama. Lenny had always seen himself as a jazzman, a cat who just walks out there and blows. Now he had the confidence and the technique to be a real jazzman and work free-form every night. That was exactly what he intended to do.

Paradoxically, at the very moment Lenny Bruce the entertainer was horrifying his closest advisers by the recklessness of his attitude toward public performance, Lenny Bruce the would-be writer was similarly exasperating his literary adjutant by the timorousness of his attitude toward exposing himself in print. Like many oral personalities, Lenny was upborne by an exaggerated sense of self-confidence when he was shpritzing an audience and dashed by extreme self-doubt when he had to confront the cold steel of type. His terror of print came out in an abortive attempt to dictate an autobiography, titled *How to Talk*

Dirty and Influence People, with that same Art Steuer whom he had met at the Blue Angel.

A man of fitful brilliance, Steuer had the unfortunate knack of initiating ideas that other men brought to fruition, while he languished in angry obscurity. He had written pulp fiction in the early fifties and then turned to serious fiction, producing a story on life in a military school that ran in *Life* and clearly foreshadowed *End as a Man*. Then he had written a film script that anticipated *Mad, Mad World*. For a short time he worked on a series of articles about comics in *Esquire*, quitting to carry out yet another bright scheme: a collaborative biography of Lenny Bruce. His original proposal to Lenny was that they travel together and work on the book during spare moments. Lenny would shpritz and Steuer would write; together they would get the book together. Delighted by the suggestion, Lenny jumped in with his usual enthusiasm for any novelty and proposed very generous terms: a fifty-fifty deal.

All through April and May, the collaborators worked together, grinding their cigarettes out in paper coffee cups in the dingy hotels Lenny inhabited in Philadelphia, Washington, D.C., and finally, Chicago, where he worked in the recently opened Tradewinds for a record price of $4,500 a week. At the end of this marathon stint, Lenny pulled the stunt of dragging in a hooker off the street to test the readability of his book. Though eminently readable, what Steuer and Lenny produced together wasn't truth. Steuer had assumed that they would write a really tough, nitty-gritty account of a famous nightclub comic and how he got that way. He wanted Lenny to talk frankly about his traumatic childhood, his wrenching marriage with Honey, and his restless, tormented life on the road, always clamoring for attention and never satisfied with it, even when he got more of it than he could absorb. Steuer had a real fix on Lenny. He viewed him as the existential hero of our times. He wanted him to go all the way in the book and talk about his addiction to hard drugs. "Nothing is more important to you than drugs," he lectured. "Therefore nothing is more central to your autobiography."

Ultimately, Steuer was inspired by a vision of Bruce that was completely at odds with Lenny's vision of himself. Steuer saw his New Wave hero as essentially a *"criminal mentality."* When Lenny was given the choice of doing something straight or doing it crooked, he invariably chose the crooked way. He was always looking to beat something: a tab, a chick, a club owner, a doctor. He would cop out on any sort of excuse. Risk everything on the most ridiculous sort of scam. Waste hours and hours in the pettiest sort of cheating. Criminals were Lenny's heroes. He loved to talk about gangsters, imitate gangsters, and work in gangster-operated nightclubs. Lenny's favorite form of recreation was to sit late at night in some tacky hotel room or shabby bar lapping up the confessions of some hoodlum who would murder his own mother for a free trip to Miami.

The more Steuer brooded over his history of Lenny Bruce, the stronger grew his conviction that he held the key to this infinitely complex and baffling personality. He could see, for example, that Lenny had grown into a liar and a cheat by trying to elude the authority of his father and the amorous advances of his mother. Honesty was impossible for him. He was the King of Lies. Indeed, when you got right down to it, the source of Lenny's genius, of his incomparable humor, was precisely this criminal temperament. Unlike the ordinary Jewish comic who fuels his humor with displaced aggression or over-compensated depression, Lenny Bruce worked out of a weird antisocial impulse that reversed its negative thrust in laughter. Hitler was Lenny's ultimate hero. Lenny was a little Hitler who expressed his identification through comedy. A peculiarly inverted comedy in which the bad guys were the invention of the good guys, who turned out, therefore, to be much worse than the monsters they created. Lenny Bruce was just such a monster, attributing all his faults to the "manufacturer," and evading all moral responsibility through slippery ethics and even slipperier wit. Now, how could Art Steuer get him to confess to all these charges?

He couldn't. Lenny insisted that his biography be a charming, disarming, poignantly amusing sort of concoction, about eighty percent lies and the rest Chaplinesque fantasies in which he alternately played the Tramp and the Kid. Whenever Steuer would complain that Lenny was "bullshitting," Lenny would counter by telling Steuer that he didn't know anything about the public—which is why his books had bombed! Lenny said that if he told the truth, people would put him down. They would never understand what he suffered. They would think he was some kind of asshole. The trick—that was a big word with Lenny— was to give these dummies just what they wanted. Bullshit them blind. Make up silly little, cute little stories about his life on the farm and his seduction by a society lady and his first fuck, a hot Italian grocery girl—all of which had never happened—and titillate their tooshies off. Steuer would see that he was right when the book came out. Lenny knew his public. Above all, he sure wasn't gonna cop to any drug habit. "Are you crazy, Art? Do you know what they would do to me, man? You gotta be outta your kug, baby, touting me onto that shtick. Uh, uh!"

One day Lenny told Steuer he was rewriting their original contract. "Shit!" said Lenny. "When I made the deal with you I thought writing a book was a big job. Now I know I can write. So I don't need a collaborator. I just need a typist. If you want to take ten percent of the action—groovy! If not, forget it! I'm not giving you equal billing when I've done all the work!'' That was the signal to leave. Steuer walked—into a lawyer's office, where he sued Lenny. And won. Two years after the commencement of their collaboration, he received a check for $700, and the book lay just where he had left it. At a very critical juncture. At what even Art Steuer would have had to concede was a moment of truth. At the description of Honey Bruce, lying on the street in Pittsburgh, with the wheels of a Mack track cracking her bones like fortune cookies.

As the summer of '60 ripened into July and Lenny began working dumb time, like the Racquet Club in Dayton, he got a strange idea. He decided to take a break. A compulsive worker with no idea of leisure, he hardly ever took a vacation; but he was making a sincere effort to clean up, while Honey was pulling in the opposite direction. The only hope of saving Honey was to take her under his personal twenty-four-hour-a-day supervision. For this purpose, he had a perfect retreat. A Mr. Lansburgh—a man he met in Miami, who was the owner of the Flamingo Hotel in Las Vegas—had told Lenny: "Whenever you want to come to Vegas, you'll be my guest in the hotel." So Lenny decided to take him up on the invitation. It turned out to be one of the most self-destructive sorties of his career. The basic problem was that Lenny had come to Vegas not as a professional but in the embarrassing role of a tourist.

The vacation began happily enough with a bellman ushering Lenny and Honey into a sprawling suite usually reserved for high-rollers. The rooms were decorated with sprays of fresh flowers and the bar stocked with choice brands of whisky. That night, one of Lenny's friends arranged for a ringside table at the Folies Bergère, the girlie revue at the Tropicana. Compared with the sort of schmutzy burlesque that Lenny had worked in for many years, this European-style show was staid and decorous. To Lenny the tourist, however, the show was a shocking exhibition of sexual merchandising. When a patron at the next table began to talk to his girlfriend about "tits and ass"—those were the words he used and they were swiftly to become Lenny's verbal symbol for the whole Las Vegas operation—he grabbed Honey's hand and started hauling her up the main aisle of the showroom.

Frankie Ray happened to be sitting at the back of the room with the bosses of the club. His first impulse was to hail his friend; then he checked himself when he saw Lenny turn around at the main entrance, raise his fist in a fig gesture, and shout loud enough to be heard onstage: "Ahla fungoola!"

"Christ!" thought Frankie, "I better not introduce him to the bosses—he may want to work here someday!" At that moment, Lenny spotted Frankie. "Frandank! I want you to get me in the lounge to see Shecky."

"Of course," says Frankie, escorting Honey and Lenny through the lobby and noticing that they're both bombed. "It's his first time in Vegas," thinks Frankie; "maybe he's been drinking a little wine."

Still fuming about "tits and ass," Lenny settles himself at a table at the back of the lounge and immediately starts to heckle Shecky Greene. Mimicking the gross-out drunks that every comic dreads, he yells, "When is the show gonna start?" Shecky pins Lenny and shpritzes him right back. Instantly they're engaged in an insult contest that gets more and more obscene as they struggle to cap each other. Most of the audience love it. One man isn't so sure. He's Sol Jaffee, the owner of the building: the sort of preposterously proud proprietor who pats the furniture as he strolls through the lobby. Fidgeting nervously as the insults fly back and forth, he's trying to force a smile, when suddenly he finds himself the target for one of Lenny's gags.

"Look at that guy!" needles Lenny, pointing to Jaffee leaning against a post. "Look how cute he is! When he's not standing around here holding up fhat post, he's holding up the customers!"

Lenny chuckles at his own joke. The owner looks dour.

"You better watch that, Lenny," warns Shecky with mock sternness. "You may be working here next year."

"I wouldn't work in this *shithouse!*" Lenny shoots back.

"Shithouse!" Jaffee almost drops to the floor. "Shithouse?" His place, his palace, his prah-put-ty! Oi. The word hits him like a lump of shit. Quickly motioning to two security guards, he orders Lenny evicted.

Lenny is not in a mood to go quietly. When the guard says to him, "Could we see you outside for a minute," he starts yelling and making a scene. "Shecky! Frandank!" he calls. "They're trying to throw me out!" Finally, after a big hassle, they get Lenny out of the room and into a cab heading back to the Flamingo.

Lenny is in no shape to cool it now. He's hopping mad. That night, for the third time within six hours, he gets himself into a scrape. He and Honey are seated at a ringside table in the Flamingo Hotel's showroom, which has been reserved for them by the hotel's entertainment director. Joe Maini is playing in the band behind the room's headliner, Pearl Bailey. One of Pearl Bailey's gimmicks is an audience-

participation interlude in which customers are coaxed onto the stage
to sing along with her. This gives Joe an impish idea.

"That's Lenny Bruce," he whispers to Pearl, pointing to a front
table. "Get Lenny up here!"

"Ah don't know . . . there's somebody out there named Lehnny
or somethin'," drawls Bailey in her stone coon accent. "Get up here,
Lenny!"

Now the last thing in the world that Lenny wants, especially after
what had happened that day, is to be schlepped up on the stage and
made a fool of in some dumb entertainer's act. So he leans up toward
the stage, and murmurs, "Please don't get me onstage. That's not my
shtick."

"I don't know nuthin' 'bout no stick or nuthin' like that," deadpans
Pearl. "You jes' get on up heah!"

With the aid of a blinding spotlight, she finally compels Lenny to
take the stage. Then she realizes her mistake. As soon as she starts
into her bit, reciting the lyrics she wants him to sing, he reaches
over and grabs her big fat rump. The audience explodes with laughter.
Pearl makes one of her dumb chitlin circuit faces and struggles to save
the day.

"Whatchoo do that foh?" she cries in her best Aunt Jemima tone.

"I told you not to get me up here," grins back Lenny with an evil
glint in his eye.

Figuring that she better get out of this thing fast, Pearl calls a tune,
"What a Little Moonlight Can Do." Meanwhile, Lenny wanders off
the stage, deliberately distracting the audience by putting on a Stepin
Fetchit walk. Coming into the wings, he notices a fire extinguisher
hanging on the wall. His mind suddenly flashes back to his days on
the *Brooklyn*, when he and his shipmates used to relieve the tedium
by battling each other with these shpritzers. Before the stage manager
can stop him, Lenny's torn the big red bottle off the wall and is rushing
back on stage. Aiming the nozzle at the huge black singer, he zaps
her right in the face with white foam.

The effect is fantastically funny! The audience cracks up! The singer
is choking and gasping, her hair coming down, her white satin gown
ruined—and the audience loves it! Just at that moment, three stagehands come running out to grab Lenny, but before they can reach him
they start to slip and slide on the gooey foam until they lose their
balance and fall down.

The audience of eight hundred jumps from their Naugahyde banquettes cheering! They have no way of knowing that this Mack Sennett
comedy wasn't planned. Pearl Bailey is outraged. She won't get off.

She starts making a speech. She sees the whole prank as a racial slur: "I guess, folks, my generation will never see the freedom of blah, blah, blah."

Finally, drenched and feeling ugly, she hastens to her dressing room and discovers a hand-printed note on her table. It's a letter from Lenny Bruce. "Dear Pearl," it says, "I couldn't take your act. All the Uncle Tom bits you did like a lazy Negro." The last straw! Reading the note over and over again, she is stung to the quick. Summoning the manager of the hotel, she lays it down, hard and clear. Unless Lenny Bruce is thrown out of this hotel—"*You heah*?"—she won't set foot onstage again.

When the security men break into Lenny's room, they find him on the toilet. Grabbing him under the shoulders, they pull him off without even giving him time to hike up his pants. Dragged before the manager with his trousers dangling around his ankles, Lenny receives a white-faced lecture. "We have an angry performer here! Do you know what that means, Mr. Bruce? There could be no show tonight if you don't leave at once! Now, go!"

"Well, let me pack!" yells Lenny.

"No," says the chief guard, "we'll send the stuff wherever you want." And with that he starts to hustle Lenny toward the elevator.

"Well, at least let me get my pants up!" explodes Lenny as he scuffles out the door, down the hall, and into the waiting elevator.

Word of the Pearl Bailey incident soon filtered back to the Negro press, which castigated Lenny. That Lenny Bruce—who prided himself on his freedom from racial prejudice—should be singled out as an example of nasty Whitey was grotesquely ironic. The whole incident had been triggered precisely by Lenny's extreme sensitivity to what he regarded as a demeaning Negro self-image. But the black press had a point. Whatever Lenny thought about Pearl Bailey, he had no business humiliating her in public. He should have apologized.

Eventually, he received a reprimand from the American Guild of Variety Artists. The national administrative secretary, Jackie Bright, chastised Lenny in a letter that is a gem of show-biz huff and puff self-righteousness. First comes the fraternal salutation and self-absolving cop-out:

Dear Sir and Brother:
I regret exceedingly that circumstances force me to write the following type of a letter to you, but I would be remiss in my duties, both as the National Administrative Secretary of AGVA, and as one who knows you, were I to remain silent.

Then, after this profoundly "responsible" and "concerned" opening, he really schloogs into poor Lenny:

> Your conduct toward your fellow member and artist, Miss Pearl Bailey, at the Flamingo Hotel, was irresponsible, to say the least. Your conduct ill became you and cast a shadow upon all of us in the variety field . . . I have read your letter to Miss Bailey . . . I feel you should have apologized; instead you wrote a concoction of gibberish which not only did not make any sense, but further compounded the action taken by you in a most disgraceful manner. You further compounded this with your disgusting utterances at the Tropicana Hotel during Shecky Greene's performance . . . Should you continue to repeat such vulgar displays of bad taste, we will have no alternative but to take such action as we deem proper to safeguard the best interests of the sincere members of our organization.

When Lenny received the letter from AGVA, he just laughed. The entertainers' union meant nothing to him.

Fucking up in Vegas was something else again. As everybody knew, Las Vegas was the future entertainment capital of America. Already there were guys working the lounges there who made almost as much as Lenny in the nightclubs. Headliners made enormous, unheard-of salaries: $15,000, $20,000, $25,000 a week! Making a stink in Vegas was committing financial suicide. Shouldn't he be ashamed? Or should he?

The more he thought about it, the more he realized that Vegas could never be his market. His future lay in *controversy*. In Fun City, controversy was out of the question. "Tits 'n' ass"—that's what they sold there. "Tits 'n' ass" and a few feeble jokes. Now he was accustomed to the in-crowd: smart, sophisticated people who could dig his style. Why mess with fat, bald zhlubs in fuckin' casinos? The apes who stood there at the tables at 6 A.M. pissing away their mortgage money with a Bloody Mary in one fat hand? He was too good for those animals. He would have to go another way. That way was obvious. The time would soon come when he would be seen only in a few top rooms in a dozen top cities. He would become a cult figure, a hipster genius. People woud pay a lot to hear him say the unspeakable. Yes, that was the way. The Vegas thing was not simply a goof. It was a message. The message read: "Go right on, baby, and don't worry about the assholes!"

Meanwhile, he did have one big worry, the same one he always had —Honey. Though "Big Red," as he liked to call her in his more affectionate moments, was taking care of Kitty—after a fashion—and talking every week with her psychiatric baby-sitter, Harvey Karman, she was still getting loaded every time he turned his back. He heard the stories from mutual friends, and he knew what they meant. Some drastic cure would have to be found for Honey or she would go right down the drain like any other tapped-out junkie. The big problem was keeping her away from her suppliers. Availability—that was the most important factor in making and maintaining the junk habit. If Lenny could keep an eye on her all the time, there wouldn't be a problem. He could spot a head or a connection miles away. Nobody could bullshit him about drugs. The trouble was that he had to work, go out on the road and leave Honey behind where she could easily cop. Now, what was he going to do to keep her away from temptation?

He was sitting with Seymour Grush, his accountant, one day, talking about the procedure for setting up a Swiss bank account, when suddenly it hit him that the ideal person to send overseas to make the arrangements would be Honey. He could trust her, and she was shrewd enough to handle the business without goofs. More important, once he got her over there, he could keep her there until she was really cured. Sure, he could set her up in some nice pad with the kid—be great for the kid, she'd come back talking French!—and he'd get her a good doctor; they had all these drug doctors in Europe; and Honey would have to stay for a long time, maybe even a year, because he wouldn't send her the money to come home. He would send her just enough each week to live comfortably but never the heavy taste for the plane. At first she would squawk and kick. They'd run up a big transatlantic phone bill. Eventually, she'd get used to it and realize it was her salvation. The trick was to get her over on the other side, where she couldn't score because she didn't even know the language. Once she was there, things were bound to get better.

He called Max Weiss at Fantasy Records and told him about his plan to save his wife. Lenny knew that Max had been to Europe many times; couldn't he come up with a good idea about what to do for Honey? Back and forth they talked until Max agreed to rent a villa outside Rome as a business expense and install Honey and Kitty there for as long as necessary. Overriding Honey's nearly hysterical protests, Lenny arranged for the flight, packed up Kitty's clothes, drove them out to the airport, and practically shoved them aboard the plane.

Honey was not able to smuggle any drugs aboard, but Lenny had arranged for a fix at the airport in New York. When she arrived in Rome she was already sick. Holed up in a hotel room, she got more and more sick, sweating, vomiting, and fainting from weakness. Every time she hit bottom, she dragged herself to the phone and called Los Angeles. Lenny struggled with her on the phone, six thousand miles away, alternately commiserating with her suffering and lecturing her on her responsibility to Kitty. When she saw that she couldn't move him, she went out into the street to score. Searching for the seediest neighborhoods she could find, this striking red-haired American woman went from one disreputable-looking character to another, begging, "Dopa? Dopa?" Nobody knew what she meant. After three weeks of unrelieved horror, she got in touch with her close friend Barbara Lum; and she sent Honey the return fare to the States.

Feeling like an escaped prisoner, Honey headed straight for Detroit and her mother's house. Still feeling terribly ill, she noticed with alarm that she was puffing up like a balloon. She couldn't release her water, and the doctor had to give her injections of mercury to dehydrate her. Eventually, she realized that some of her symptoms were quite familiar. In fact, she had experienced them seven times before—and each time she had been pregnant! Immediately she went to a gynecologist. Blood and urine tests failed to show any signs of pregnancy. A rabbit test also proved negative. Weeks, then months elapsed: the symptoms became even more marked. No question about it now—she *was* pregnant. Pregnant without being married and pregnant while using drugs. She would certainly have a "narcotics baby." The only solution was an abortion.

Honey's mother made the arrangements with a Detroit abortionist to do the job for $900. The old butcher, who had performed thousands of such operations, didn't even bother to examine her. When she refused an anesthetic because she wanted to keep an eye on him, he slipped on his gloves, turned up his radio loud to drown the noise of screams, and started scraping out her womb. The pain was excruciating. Honey could barely restrain her sobs. It was nothing, however, to the shock of seeing the bloody mass that was extricated from her belly and held aloft before her horrified eyes. She had been six months pregnant and the fetus was well formed. You could even see the child's sex. It had been a boy.

The shock of this vision triggered Honey into hysterics. She realized now that she had murdered her own child. One month more, at twenty-eight weeks, the child could have been born prematurely with a good chance of survival. The abortion had been sheer insanity.

Calmed down by a powerful sedative, Honey was driven to her sister's home in a private ambulance. Complications began to appear. Her uterus was hemorrhaging. She was running a high fever. A hastily summoned doctor examined her and concluded that she was suffering from pneumonia and pleurisy. As she lay in bed, feverish and coughing up huge gobs of phlegm, she was tortured by recurring glimpses of the mangled fetus. She felt she was dying. She was wrong, however. Once again she pulled through.

While this horror story played out in Detroit, in L.A. Lenny Bruce was having the healthiest summer of his life. Off heavy drugs for the time being—though always taking uppers and other goodies—Lenny had gotten on a health kick. Like all heavy junkies, he realized dope was damaging his body. Unlike most, he made a serious effort to kick and stay off forever. He was helped considerably by the company he was keeping. Richey Shackleton was now a vigorous advocate of healthy living. Lenny would always say to people who were urging some new philosophy on him, "Don't tell me—show me!" Well, Richey could show him. Another good teacher was Richey's pal, Ted Markland.

A tall, skinny actor and comic, who fascinated Lenny because he was such a super-goy, Ted, like Richey, was always dressed in rough-out clothes and boots. The boys were always roaring up the Pacific Highway on motorcycles, always konking out in strange people's pads in sleeping bags—things that made Lenny marvel. He was still wearing tight dark suits and white shirts with cuff links. He had to have daily baths and clean sheets and maybe two or three changes of clothing just to get through a single day. Yet he found the outdoorsy life of these younger guys very appealing. He found himself hanging out with them more and more. Eventually, he allowed them to change a lot of things in his life—for the time being.

The third musketeer in this group was Jules Buccieri, who had been a talent manager and an agent and is today an antiques dealer in Hollywood. Jules was a yoga and health-food nut. He was always bugging Lenny to change his diet and take more exercise and practice the art of breathing. Lenny could dig anything as a kick; he picked up on Jules's recommendations. Lying out on the beach, he soon acquired a wonderful bronze tan. Working out with the boys, he firmed up his gelatinous muscles. Lenny had a good body; his proportions were right, his weight was still 155; even his back straightened up when he got off the heavy downers. Now with all these health measures going for him, he began to take on a lean, muscular, physical-fitness look—which he was eager to record in pictures.

Richey was the photographer. Whenever the gang took off for one of its weekend excursions—down to Mexico or out to the desert or up the beach to Malibu—Richey would capture Lenny in action. In Mexico, Lenny loved to shop for junk: corny whips and knives and sombreros, which the boys would flaunt when they got home, up and down the Strip. Sometimes they would poke around in old churches and graveyards, taking ghoul pictures or posing for a crucifixion, with Lenny pinned on the cross and the other cats hung up around him like the thieves with Jesus. The thief on the cross—that was an image that Richey implanted in Lenny's mind during one of their trips and it stuck for years. At one point, Lenny wanted to make a movie about Christ and the thief; he would have played the thief. Instead, he did a bit in which the thief is locked up in a cell with Christ, and when the holy one says spookily to him, "You'll go with me, brother!" the thief panics and screams, "Not me, schmuck! I'm in here for check-signing!"

All the young guys with whom Lenny was hanging out were desert rats. They loved to get high on peyote or mescaline and make the run out into the great open spaces. This was the time when peyote was just going out and mescaline was coming in. Peyote was an old trip that Lenny and Richey had first tried back in the middle fifties when nobody knew what the hell it was. In those days you could order the stuff from botanical supply houses for a penny a button. When Richey got his first batch, he didn't know how to take it. Still, he didn't do badly. He sliced it down, as you would potatoes for frying. Then he ground up the slivers in a blender until they were just powder. Then he loaded the powder into big double-O capsules. Finally, Richey announced: "I finally got it together, man. I really don't know what the fucking thing is, but it's supposed to be something like opium." On the way to Lenny's place on Las Palmas, they dropped the caps. When they went up to the Gaiety Delicatessen to get the beer, the peyote suddenly hit them and they became hysterical. They laughed so hard and behaved so outrageously at the deli that the manager had to ask them to leave. When Lenny got home, he called Richey to tell him about this big, beautiful, fantastic rose that he kept seeing wherever he looked. Then Lenny called back again to say that he had balled Honey and how that had been. Meanwhile, Richey was getting into a Doppelgänger scene, staring into the bathroom mirror. It seemed to him that the face in the mirror was another cat staring back at him. Bit by bit the figure in the mirror began to hypnotize him. It was the most insane trip!

Eventually, mescaline, the artificial derivative of peyote, started coming in and the cats began to drop the pure hallucinogenic ingredient of those nauseous little buttons. That moment corresponded with Lenny's summer of health and creativity. He was just crazy with energy that summer, getting into some new number every day. He decided that what he really wanted was to be the head of a street gang. He was living on Spaulding at the time, and he invited a whole bunch of young dudes to come and stay with him. He got Richey Shackleton, Ted Markland, Dick Sinatra, Tom Gilson, Dave Resnick, and another guy, who was going to law school and whom Lenny called "Gary the Barrister." He bought them all bull whips and switchblades. He called them his gang. He cavorted with them in front of Schwab's. One night Lenny flipped. He tore all the phones out of the house and kicked everybody out. He was finished with that fantasy.

The next kick was the dry orgy. One hot night in August, after he had dropped a lot of mescaline and bennies, he got crazy to do something. Rounding up Richey, Ted, and Joe Maini, at two in the morning, he went over to the Pink Pussycat and grabbed all the strippers. Throwing the girls into the back of a big car, he tore out to the desert. By the time they got near Joshua Tree, it was dawn. The spectacular pink dawn of the desert. All the guys were rushing. The chicks didn't know what was going down. Lenny was in his manic mood, jabbering away on the front seat like a little bird. Some cat had offered him a pad in the desert. The guy had laid directions on Lenny, who was now acting as navigator while Richey did the driving. They wandered around and around in a timeless daze until miraculously they found the pad. Everybody spilled out of the cars and into the house. Then the party got going—a righteous naked bacchanal, with the dropping of the grapes and the swilling of the wine. The only odd thing was that nobody wanted to ball! The strippers couldn't figure it. Here were all these usually horny cats carrying on like madmen—and nobody could raise a hard-on. Weird!

Mescaline enjoys the reputation of being a happy high—unlike shrecky acid. With the pure stuff obtainable at that time—uncut with speed or hyped up with psilocybin—you could get off for twelve hours at a stretch. Twelve hours of ravishingly beautiful desert colors, sensuous ecstasies achieved by simple bodily acts, like taking a shower, fantastic distentions of time, and the humorous, whimsical delight of catching yourself in some familiar act, like scratching your arm, and asking yourself: "Why am I doing this?" It shows a lot about Lenny Bruce that he never experienced mescaline in this normal way. As the bennies would wear off and the hallucinogen took hold, Lenny would get very quiet and withdrawn. He would begin to feel emotions that he usually repressed. The strongest of his choked-back feelings was anger. Behind mescaline, Lenny would get very hostile. He didn't rant or provoke quarrels or put people on. When Lenny got hostile, Lenny got quiet. As a kid, he had been a sulker. A pouter. A polluter of the emotional atmosphere. He wanted to be questioned, to be drawn out, to be relieved of these unwonted and unwanted feelings. With the gang, though, there was nobody to draw him out. They were all too stoned to care what trip he was on. Eventually, he would come out of the mood and go into a deep rap about religion or philosophy.

Lenny didn't know a thing about God or Sartre. But the thought of these mysterious subjects filled him with awe. Even the most rudimentary theological concepts, the stuff every freshman learns in Philosophy I, could blow his mind. He felt a great craving for basic truths. It had a lot to do with his act, which was rapidly changing from straight shtick comedy into a new mode of conceptual rapping. Shack—taking note of the angry tone of all the new bits—dubbed this new style "unstructured vitriolic humor." Lenny thought of it more in terms of simple honesty. Like every great performer, once he reaches the first plateau of acceptance and fame, he wanted to personalize his act. He wanted to make his act himself. This, after all, is the great difference between an actor and an entertainer. An actor spends his life getting into the lives of his characters; an entertainer spends his life focusing attention on himself. An actor fears that he will not be able to sustain the feigned life of the person he portrays. An entertainer fears that his true identity will become submerged in the image he has created with his most successful material.

Lenny knew very well that his private life was not a model for anyone. He would have been the first to reject it as a good way to live. His wisdom, though—the truths he had learned through so much crazy living—that was something else. Now he felt the time had come to get up on that stage and simply state his truths. Talk about God and sex and politics and the flag and communism and doctors and the clap and fags and dykes and Las Vegas and Honey and drugs and childhood and parents and life and death—talk about everything in a way that he had never talked before. He didn't feel he had to be so funny anymore—no, that wasn't it! He *did* have to be funny; as he told George Crater the next winter, "A comedian should get a laugh every twenty-five seconds for a period of not less than forty-five minutes and accomplish this feat with consistency eighteen out of twenty shows." Yes, that was professionalism and professionalism is giving people value, like laughter, for dollars. But the laughs needn't come out of highly structured routines that are pitched invariably to the ludicrous and acted out with comic-book faces and voices. The laughs can be thoughtful laughs and the bits can be just fast sketches in which you don't need so much acting and impersonation. Maybe two or three times in the whole show, you do a "bit" bit, a full-scale skit; the rest of the time you free-associate and touch on many vital themes and ideas.

His big new theme was *tolerance*. A new take on the ancient

Christian virtue of charity. Turning the other cheek, acknowledging that what people did they were compelled to do. You had to accept it *all*—that was the only alternative to fighting with everybody about everything. You had to recognize that this cat would rip you off and that cat would help you and the third would do some other bit. Everybody was doing his own thing. Everybody was just as good as he could afford to be. The question was: could you dig it? If you could just take the comic's attitude that everything is funny and stretch it to the Christian's attitude that everything is lovable or the Hindu's attitude that everything is sacred—imagine that, *sacred!*—you might open the door on a whole new universe of love and beauty and goodness. You would relate to people with love instead of hate and competition. Relating love to them, they would be moved to relate love back to you. Eventually, instead of all sorts of warring peoples, there would be just one great sacred family. Everybody sitting around the same table and having a ball. That was it. The end. You could see it so clearly out here in the desert.

Sometimes the trips on mescaline would take unexpected turns: especially if Lenny took the stuff while he was working and feeling the bad vibes in the nightclubs. One night in particular, he really got down in the depths on mescaline. It was an extraordinary moment because Lenny was not one to show really deep and unguarded emotion. He could laugh and cry and carry on with a lot of feeling, but his deepest and most painful emotions were always hidden behind an impenetrable veil. This night, though, the drug overcame his resistance and he split wide open and poured out the deepest gut emotions—his primal scream.

It began after the show. Lenny picked up Lou Gottlieb and drove him to the House on the Hill. There they found Richey projecting *Black Leather Jacket* on the wall by the pool. Ted Markland and a couple of other guys were sitting around digging the flick. Lou felt there was something decidedly homosexual about the whole scene, but he stayed on as Lenny began to explain to him the plan of his projected autobiography. Lenny was already very high by the time he stumbled across the page in the manuscript that described the terrible accident he had had in Pittsburgh. He insisted on reading the passage out loud. Richey Shackleton recollects what happened next:

He wanted to read Lou a funny incident from the book, but as he continued reading, he got into the description of where Honey got wasted in the automobile accident. As soon as he started reading that, he began to sob hysterically. Lou got very embarrassed for him. Lenny wouldn't stop. He made up his mind that he was going to read that whole passage—I guess for the experience. And he sat there and read the whole thing from beginning to end—but I mean *convulsions*. He couldn't stop and yet he would stop. He'd get himself in control and would start back again. Everybody got really bent out of shape. It took him three hours to do it. He made everybody sit and listen to it. Man, I've never seen anybody with such a need to get it out. That's the only time in his entire life that I ever saw him do that, and I'd known Lenny since he was twenty-seven.

At the end of the summer, Lenny settled down at the Crescendo for one of his longest runs on the West Coast. It was also the most creative stretch that he had experienced since the period in 1957 when he had been working at this same club. Getting the date had taken some doing because Gene Norman was terrified that there was going to be another bust like the one that had gone down the year before. He wanted Lenny badly because his business was dying—but he didn't want trouble. Lenny told Gene that he had nothing to fear because he was clean. Gene had his doubts. Finally, Gene got together with the L.A. Narcotics Squad, and they told him that if Lenny was really clean he should be able to take and pass a Nalline test. This was a chemical test that had received legal sanction in California in 1957 and was now widely used to determine whether a man was using narcotics. The test involved the injection of Nalline, an opiate antagonist. If the recipient of the drug was using opiates, he would be precipitated immediately into withdrawal symptoms.

Gene proposed the test to Lenny and he accepted willingly. He went down to the doctor's office with Richey Shackleton, and they found a very nervous physician. Evidently, the doctor had been told by the police that Lenny was a junkie. He feared that when he hit the mainline with the Nalline, Lenny would instantly go cold turkey. Lenny was so clean, however, that the drug had a paradoxical effect. Instead of exhibiting the symptoms of drug withdrawal, Lenny got whacked out of his nut! The doctor reported that none of the patient's behavior bore any resemblance whatsoever to being *deprived* of drugs. Very funny!

With the heat off his back and the steam coming steady up his pipes night after night, Lenny set to work in his old stronghold and created an entire new nightclub act. This may not sound like a great achievement to those who know little about the business and its terrible tendency to repeat itself. It may strike Lenny Bruce worshipers as just another example of Lenny's remarkable facility and creativity. But the truth is that the creation of forty-five minutes of absolutely fresh material is the entertainment world's equivalent of writing a major novel. It's something that even a talent like Lenny Bruce could do only a few times in a lifetime. During this hot August he poured out the material that was to carry him for the next two years—and beyond. Practically all the great second-wave Bruce routines date from this engagement: *Tits 'n' Ass*, Lenny's revenge on Vegas; *Christ and Moses*, the next turn of the satiric screw on organized religion; *To Is a Preposition, Come Is a Verb*, the symphony of sex sounds.

When Lenny got ready to go out on the road again in the fall of 1960 to open a season that would cap every other expedition he had mounted up to this time, he hated to part with all his wonderful California friends, his gang. Faced with the prospect of living for months in dreary hotels without any assured companionship, he offered Richey a generous salary to go along with him. Richey was willing to travel, but he wanted Lenny to take Ted also. He told him that Ted was going to be an important new comic because he presented a fresh image. Instead of the usual Jewish jazz, he was tall, blond, and gentile. The idea interested Lenny. He saw himself as a molder of talent. He knew there was a market for "a funny goy." Indeed, the first time he saw Bob Newhart at Mr. Kelly's, Lenny had told Art Steuer: "He'll make more money than me, Sahl, and Berman because Paar, Sullivan, and Moore need a goy comic so bad their teeth ache!" So Lenny made a deal with both men: he would go out and play his dates in Pittsburgh, Milwaukee, Dayton, and Philly; when he got to New York, where he was going to do three weeks at Basin Street East, the boys would join him and stay with him for the rest of the tour. Ted and Shack were delighted.

Most of the stops on Lenny's route were familiar; one, however, was a ringer: Milwaukee. The origin of this odd date was a direct invitation from the owner of the club. He had caught Lenny's act at the Crescendo and enjoyed it so much, he wanted to present it to his own people back in the land of championship bowling and free brewery tours.

The folly of the idea becomes apparent to Lenny the moment he arrives in town: the dinner show is at six-thirty and the men's room is full of kids playing hide-and-seek! When he looks at the people, they strike him as oddly familiar. Suddenly, it hits him: "These are the Gray Line tours—*before they leave!*" The first fifteen minutes of his show, he doesn't get one laugh. The people are staring at him in disbelief. Then the shock wears off and he starts to hear:

"You like him?"

"I wanna go to the toilet."

"Awright . . . I'll go with ya."

"I donwanna walk in front of him."

"Yeah, but everybody's walking out. And he's still up there—
'poots,' 'schmook,' 'dig', 'hip'—he's up there. Whaddishe, crazy?
. . . How come he hasn't got any music? No singing, nothing. Sure,
even the band left him. Ha ha ha! There's no band up here! Sure *they*
know he's crazy."

From those opening minutes the road leads steadily downward;
Lenny sees himself slipping toward disaster . . . "I'm stepping on my
dick, I dunno where I'm at, man. O.K. And finally I get off and the
owner goes, '*Lenny, Christ!* We had so many walkouts!' "

"I'm hip, man, they were stepping on my feet."

Lenny was bombed out of his nut by the time he got to New York.
Richey, Ted, and he had planned to go see *The Balcony* at The Living
Theater the night before he opened so they could do a bit on the show;
but Lenny was so boxed he could hardly see straight. Deciding to clean
up, he pressed his "kick" button and plunged into withdrawal symptoms. All night he flailed around at the Hotel America, sick, agitated,
tortured by the yearning to go out and score. Finally, he starts taking
Tuinals to knock himself out. Eventually, he takes so many of the little
triangular pills that he can't wake up. Next day the situation is desperate. The boys drag him out of bed and walk him around, but he
keeps collapsing like a rag doll. Finally, they find a doctor who agrees
to shoot him full of caffeine. The first show drags like a 78 record at
33⅓, but Lenny gets fairly good reviews. After that he hangs it up and
doesn't go back on the heavy stuff for a couple of months.

It was a good thing he did, too, because he was beginning to get
some heat at the club. The first night several plainclothesmen from
one of the special squads checked out the performance. They had a
chat afterward with Ralph Watkins, the owner of the room, and demanded to see the cabaret book. This is the record of every employee's
cabaret card. It turned out that Lenny's card had been revoked for
some reason or other, which meant that he had to go down to police
headquarters on Varick Street and obtain a new card. Phoebe Jacobs,
who was doing publicity for the club, recalled that Lenny was treated
to a humiliating interrogation that entailed, among other things, taking
him into an examination room and stripping him down for a thorough
search for needle marks. Lots of questions were asked, innuendos
made, and provocations offered. If Lenny had been less cool and in
control, he could have easily ended up in an argument that would have
cost him his card. As it was, he was a very gentle soul that day, and
the police had to license him. Even so, Ralph Watkins took the precaution of labeling the show: "An Evening of Adult Entertainment."

In a few days, life at the America settled into the familiar pattern. Go to bed about six in the morning. Sleep until three or four. Then Fran Lewis—one of the most shook-loose, head-down, yeah-that's-Bird-man hipsters—would arrive. Fran, whose maiden name was Pizminoff and who had grown up in Brighton Beach, was a lean, fragile, beautiful Jewish girl, with a tense curve in her back and a very quick head. She was the sort of helper that Lenny really dug. Every afternoon she would show up carrying coffee and rolls. Lenny would lie in bed, popping bennies and dictating portions of the book, while Fran sat at her table and typed up the rough draft. Shackleton would try to cue Lenny into stories he had heard him tell before. Lenny would balk and fret and finally break free to run down a particular episode. Around nine-thirty they would eat, and Shack would go over to Fran's apartment to work up the day's draft, while Lenny split for the club.

All during this period, Lenny was in constant telephone communication with Honey. Her illness in Detroit had spurred him on in the race to find a sure-fire therapy before she drugged herself to death. In New York he had heard of a "heavyweight" psychiatrist named Dr. O. A. Battista, who had published a book titled *Mental Drugs: Chemistry's Challenge to Psychotherapy*. Deciding that drugs were the best answer to drugs, Lenny worked for several afternoons on a long letter of "submittal," which was supposed to grab the doctor by presenting Honey to her as an absolutely unique and fascinating case with an enormous potential for social good—and a husband who was a very famous man.

Shack knew Honey from way back, being a native of Detroit himself. He harbored a secret desire to make her suffer for the way she had treated Lenny. He knew that Honey had nearly fingered Lenny in the early years of their marriage when she was having an affair with the boss of the Mob in Montreal. This hood had wanted to set Honey up as his number one girl, and he kept urging her to let him take care of Lenny. Honey came very close, insisted Shack, to giving him the go-ahead. Naturally, Lenny knew nothing about these backstairs maneuvers. But Shack knew, "and from that day on I did not break his bubble, but I saw to it that that fucking shit paid dues like you wouldn't believe!"

Entrusted now, for example, with the important mission of securing for Honey the best psychiatric attention available, Shack laid it down as preamble to the letter of submittal that "Harriet Bruce has been since puberty an out-and-out homosexual." Honey's lesbianism was the last thing Lenny could bear to confront. "No, man, no!" he moaned to Richey. "You can't put this shit in the letter to the doctor!"

He made Richey take it all out and use another line. Nothing in this world could pull down Lenny's head harder than thinking of Honey as his "die-girl dyke."

Sometimes, after the last show, the boys would go over to the apartment of Gloria Stavers, later the editor of *16*, then a high-fashion model. Gloria kept her fridge filled with all the baby foods the boys loved to eat: peanut butter and Yoohoos and bulk ice cream. They would turn out the lights, get the candles going, and lie around on the floor listening to Miles Davis in his spookiest mood. All night they'd be there noshing, listening, touching, grooving, with the blinds shut tight against the morning light and the night extending into day, as the cool sounds poured out of the pick and their eyes slowly grew weary of staring at the candle flames. It wasn't yet the era of psychedelics, but Lenny and his California friends were already deep into that bag. One night they got a couple of Gloria's nightgowns and black chiffon scarves (used by models to protect their makeup while they pulled dresses over their heads), and they camped up a sacred service: getting into a line and entering the room chanting solemn syllables and kneeling down before Lenny while he made the sign of the cross.

Other nights Lenny would come over alone and talk for hours. Lenny was obsessed with his addiction, and he often treated Gloria to long sarcastic lectures on the wiles of the dope fiend. He warned her that a junkie would do *anything* to score; that no relationship was too sacred, no bond too tight for a junkie to violate when his dope hunger grew to famine. He told her that junkies have a weird ESP affinity for other junkies: "I could land in a small town where there was only one junkie in the whole population, and I would hit on the cat within the first day." One night he explained in the most minute detail how to make a set of works out of a Murine dropper and a needle. The important thing was to seal the joint between the geezer and spike with a strip torn off a crisp green dollar bill. Another night, he leveled a deadly attack at the whole myth of "the poor devils" who went through "the tortures of the damned" when they had to kick "cold turkey." The agony of kicking, he assured her, was a myth promoted by junkies to excuse their habits and to gain pity from the straight world. Kicking was actually something anybody could do. It was no worse than a bad cold or a case of the flu. He had kicked many times. Once he went out to a shack on a remote island; after sweating for a whole day and a whole night, he suddenly had a terrific wet dream. The next morning he woke up feeling better. He stayed off drugs that time for four whole months—a record!

Another myth he ridiculed was the notion that dope killed the sex drive. She could see, he laughed, what bullshit that was. The first night they made it, he had come three times! How many men his age could do that? Sure, there were times when he couldn't get it up. Fatigue, nervousness, resentment, lots of things could make you lose your hard-on—but dope? Never! The only bad thing that dope did to your body was scar up your arms. Here, he rolled up his sleeve and let Gloria look at the ugly tracks marching up his right arm. Punching into the same vein hundreds of times, you eventually developed scar tissue and had to shoot in other places. Some of the ugliness you could erase with a product called—are you ready for this one?—Erase! That's right! There was a cream known to junkies that was sold in every drug store for "removing skin blemishes."

As far as his personal preference went, there was no drug like heroin. It was greater than any pleasure on earth—greater even than an orgasm. The flash made him feel like "a sunflower opening in my stomach! That sensation lasts only thirty seconds, but it is so powerful that it feels like three minutes. Imagine having an orgasm for three minutes! Sometimes, if it's dynamite shit, you vomit. Then you nod out and sleep for a quarter of an hour. When you wake, you feel cool and groovy. Afterwards you can go for hours in a state of controlled euphoria, working, balling, digging, getting your jollies. Eventually, it's true, you get numb behind heroin. You don't get the same flash, no matter how high you push the dose. You have to switch off to morphine or Dilaudid. Morphine is a drag. Instead of a glorious flash, you get a nasty kick. Dilaudid is better, but it doesn't hold half as long as horse!"

What Lenny didn't tell Gloria was how much he loved the spike and the sight of his own blood. Given the choice of taking a drug by mouth or by injection, he would always go for the needle. Then he would get into playing with his blood, not just jacking it back and booting it home, but sometimes using it like paint or as makeup. Chic Eder recollected a number of these macabre stunts:

> He once stood on the rim of the bathtub and wrote his name in blood on its bottom while holding the outfit like it was his prick. "Remember how we used to piss in the snow when we were kids?" he lugged. Once, in a cheap motel room registered in *my* name, he shpritzed it all over the wall; then played finger-painting games with it. By the time he was done, it looked like Richard Speck [the multiple murderer] had freaked off there with a few of the Manson tip. Another time he was in the bathroom alone when I heard a crash. I rushed in to see him trying to rise with blood streaming down his face. I flipped when I heard his groggy moans. Then it turned out that he'd taken a syringe full of blood and

squirted it into his hairline so it looked as though he'd cracked his skull open. He'd also put some in his mouth, mixed it with his spit, then let the bloody foam run down his chin and jowls.

These ghoulish games alternated with another pastime that is characteristic of junkies: studying the changes in their physical appearance produced by taking a shot.

The most obvious way to check your response to dope is to gaze in the mirror as you turn on, but you can't stare at the spike and the glass at the same time; so many junkies get a friend to take their picture at the same instant that they feel the jolt. Ideally, the picture should be taken with a movie camera, which can record the whole series of transformations. Lenny did the next best thing by getting someone to take a series of stills that he gave eventually to Terry Southern. At the critical moment, he looks like a puppet that is being violently jiggled on its wires, with its head awry and its features contorted and its expression almost idiotic.

At the end of the Basin Street run, Lenny and Richey said goodbye to Ted. Lenny was going back to play El Patio, living up to his word. Anticipating a couple of weeks of easy riding, he was taking along Fran Lewis; between the end of the three or four weeks' run at the club and the beginning of the spring concert tour, they would go off to one of the Caribbean islands. *Stamp Help Out* was virtually finished. The autobiography was coming along nicely. The holiday crowds at the club would enable him to push his price up week after week.

For once, everything worked out exactly as planned. Not only did the work go smoothly, Richey even persuaded Lenny to take a trip to the Everglades, where, high on mescaline, he had a marvelous time floating along the swamp waters, digging every bird and tree and hanging moss. When they got back to Miami, one last burst of energy polished off the brochure. Richey took off for the Coast late in January to see the copy through the lithographer and to bring back the completed booklets for the first concert, which was to be held in Philadelphia on February 3, 1961.

Just as Lenny was about to take off for Philadelphia on an Eastern Airlines flight, the news broke of the fantastic blizzard that was fast burying all the Middle Atlantic states. By the time the plane reached the vicinity of Philadelphia, the pilot was on the intercom explaining to the passengers that they would have to fly around the storm and land in Boston. In Boston! What the hell would Lenny do in Boston? His Philly date was shot. The next night he was due in New York for the second concert. Was that one going to cancel, too? As soon as he got off the plane, he began running around the airport trying to line up a flight back to New York. None of the commercial lines were flying? Solid! He'd charter a plane. Talking first to one pilot and then another, he found that no one would risk flying into the blizzard. He offered two hundred, five hundred, a thousand dollars! No one wanted the money. He started getting desperate. "Suppose you fly me over the city and let me bail out?" he urged one guy, who had said that landing was suicide.

"Did you ever use a parachute?"

"What's there to use? You just pull the thing and zippo-bang— you make it!"

Unfortunately, the Boston airport did not have any movie stunt flyers or fire divers. He ended up on a slow, drafty train that took eleven hours to reach New York. When he got out of Grand Central, the city was completely snowbound!

The Big Apple looked spectral. It could have been Nome or Fairbanks. Everything was blanketed with a thick carpet of sparkling white snow. The side streets were snow canals, innocent of even a single pair of car tracks. The atmosphere was thick with falling snowflakes and flurries blown up from the ground by cold, gusty winds. You couldn't see four blocks down the street. Once in a while you could hear a car grinding its wheels or a solitary shout. There were a few people clambering up 42nd Street, huddled, bent over, and walking in Indian file.

Unable to get a cab or a bus, Lenny slogged across town to Sixth Avenue and slogged uptown to 47th Street. He stamped into the lobby of the America looking like a snowman, coated from bare head to black boots in wind-stuck white powder. "What's happening?" he demanded. The whole story came tumbling out. How the snow had started yesterday afternoon and continued through the night and was sure to fall all that afternoon. Mayor Wagner had just been on television, proclaiming a state of emergency. No private cars were allowed on the streets and no motor traffic was permitted to enter the city. The whole Northeast was knocked out, but New York had caught the worst of the blizzard. It was amazing that any trains were still running. Maybe by tonight it would stop snowing and the Sicilian contractors could start digging the city out of the drifts. That would take days. Meanwhile, thank God, the power and the heat were working—and there was plenty of food. Lenny could forget about his concert.

Getting on the phone to Don Friedman, Lenny heard a different story. Don was determined to hold the event. He had raised a fortune from his backers by using Lenny's name. The Philly concert had been wiped out; if New York was also canceled, he might be ruined. The subways were running. Some buses were moving. The snow couldn't come down much longer—it was already twenty-four hours! So Lenny should be ready to make it at midnight.

Lenny didn't know what to believe. He holed up for the afternoon in his room, watching an old beat-up TV, into which you had to put a quarter for every half-hour. At 5 P.M. the snowfall stopped. Seventeen point four inches had fallen. Calls for volunteer shovel workers were going out. Big earth-moving equipment was being brought into the city.

On the eleven o'clock news, it was announced that the city would have to stay shut down for another day, but by Monday—or at the latest—Tuesday, the traffic would roll again. As for tonight, are you kidding? Nobody was going to schlep like an Eskimo lunatic across this wasted town to hear some little putzo make with the bits.

At eleven-thirty the brave little soldier, still bare-headed but wearing his white suit underneath his black raincoat, marched out into the street and up Seventh Avenue toward Carnegie Hall. He'd been geezing all afternoon and evening; so now the snowbound city appeared surrealistic. Those new WALK and DON'T WALK traffic signals really looked wild, blinking away in red and green to entirely empty avenues.

Then he reached the corner of 57th and Seventh—and flashed! The intersection was crawling with people. They were coming across the snow like ants. Coming up out of the subway and schlepping along by foot. A bus groaned to the corner and some more people got out! Hey! Is this a bit? The Underground People of New York Come Up from Beneath the Snow! Fan-fuckin'-tastique! There was a whole gang clomping up the steep old steps of Carnegie Hall! He'd made it! He'd pulled them in! The concert was a sellout!

Backstage, Lenny was aflame, cooking with the greatest ego charge of his entire career. So touched, so moved, so overwhelmed was he by what the people had done for him that he decided to give them his greatest performance. He could hardly stand still while that dumb, dopey, steppin'-on-your-dongo Don Friedman got off his crappy introduction. "It is not that Lenny Bruce *per se* (oi!) is a 'sick comedian' (oi!), but that Lenny Bruce comments, reflects, holds up the mirror, so to speak (come-on! . . . come-on!) to the 'sick' and corny (corny!) elements in our society that should be reflected upon and that should be spoken about!" (Applause.) That was it! The sound system sounded terrible . . . "eiii, uhhh, ahhh" . . . every vowel schlepped out like salt-water taffy. Frig it! Here goes!

Charging out on the enormous stage, Lenny looked up—and flipped! WOW! Hundreds, thousands of people stacked up in those old-fashioned, diamond-horseshoe balconies. Why, it was *The George Gershwin Story! The Jascha Heifetz Story! The Chaim Dreichel Story!*

Throwing up his beautiful hands before his glowing face, popping his fingers in ecstasy, he seized the mike and started off with a burst of energy that did not exhaust itself until well past 2 A.M. He ran through a dozen major routines, improvised material he didn't know was in his head, and lectured the audience intermittently on moral philosophy, patriotism, the flag, homosexuality, Jewishness, humor, Communism, Kennedy, Eisenhower, drugs, venereal disease, the Internal Revenue Service, and Shelley Berman. He wound up describing a recent operation which he had undergone to remove a bone splinter from his hip.

It was the greatest statement to date of his new unstructured humor. It may have been the finest all-round performance of his career. Brilliant, vivid, spontaneous, variegated, moody, honest, fantastic, and incredibly candid. Never since the days at Duffy's or at Ann's 440 had he succeeded so completely in removing the barriers that divide one mind from another. Never had he achieved more perfectly his ideal of coming on like an oral jazzman. He didn't want laughter anymore, he hated applause—"Please don't applaud!" he would beg, "It breaks my rhythm!"—he just wanted to get so far down into his own head that he felt that he was totally alone. He needed three thousand people so he could be alone!

What else is the whole jazz trip? You take your seat inside the cat's head, like you're stepping into one of those little cars in a funhouse. Then, pulled by some strong dark chain that you can't shut off, you plunge into the darkness, down the inclines, up the slopes, around the sharp bends, and into the dead ends; past bizarre, grotesque window displays and gooney, lurid frights and spectacles and whistles and sirens and scares—and even a long dark moody tunnel of love. It's all a trip—and the best of it is that you haven't the faintest idea where you're going! Lenny worshiped the gods of Spontaneity, Candor, and Free Association. His greatest fear was getting his act down pat. On this night, he rose to every chance stimulus, every interruption and noise and distraction, with a mad volleying of mental images that suggested the fantastic riches of Charlie Parker's horn.

The first flash was simply the spectacle of all these people piled up in America's most famous concert hall. He had two great associations with that picture. First, he imagined himself coming out onstage with a violin, bowing politely and then going into the heaviest shit you could play—Bach, Bartok, Stravinsky! Soon as he finishes, he turns around and splits! That's it! No bits, no lines. Just wails his ass off and splits! Wouldn't that leave them paralyzed! The other fantasy is that his concert is a sneak event. "This is a twelve o'clock scene . . . maybe the people who own this place don't even know we're here!" he confided to the delighted crowd. "Sure! You meet a guy who's a good, corrupt janitor . . . [Janitor's voice] 'All right, don't make no noise and clean up after you finish!' . . . Great!"

A few minutes later, during a bit on the Ku Klux Klan, a mike screech sets him off again, like a needle jiggling across a record. "I have done a cursed thing!" he intones in his sepulchral George McCready voice, the screech with its eerie reverberation reminding him of a dozen horror movies. "It's Andrew Stone in *Freekoscope!*" he shouts, aping the old radio ads, even to the pulsing, fading reverbs—"Wee! . . . Wee! Wee! We dare you . . . Bring a doctor . . . Twelve midnight show." The associations are coming in volleys now, all throw-away lines, blurring at the ends like phrases in a bebop solo. Meanwhile, Lenny's mind is racing, even as he forms the words, onto another track, another groove—Bela Lugosi! "Blub-blub-blub-blub!" he tumbles down a vocal scale, his abstraction of the famous Lugosi vocal delivery. Then into the familiar, lilting Transylvanian accent: "Pairmit mee to interoduce myself!" Boom! He throws up his arms in the classic vampire batwing pose and quips: "Those kinda guys, I dig, like to smell under their own arms!" By the time the laugh dies, Lenny's right back on track at the point where he bounced off, muttering thoughtfully, "Ku Klux Klan . . ."

Everything he did this night—and scores of other nights in this period—was summed up in those stunning mental leaps, those volleys of association and recollection, that dot-dash-dot of mental telegraphy. Lenny didn't move consistently in double-time—that would be too hard to do, too hard to take. Instead, he changed his rhythm and tempo repeatedly as he moved from one theme to another. Doing a couple of set pieces, back to back, on dykes and fags, he built up an enormous amount of show-biz excitement, getting the crowd to laugh on the beat, like Bob Hope. During a long introspective passage on America and the flag, he got down to a hushed adagio that had the whole hall hanging on each of his low-pitched, barely articulated words. Virtuosity springs out of the total confidence and freedom produced by splendid technique. On this night, Lenny was totally free. He could have flown up into the fourth balcony if he tried. Indeed, he even had the nerve to ask the balcony birds how much they had paid for their seats—"What's the taste, man?"—and reprove them for shouting "Louder!"

Lenny decided to leave the audience with a joke. That was always his problem: getting off the stage. But this night, he did it very neatly. He told a joke. Something he virtually never did. Yet, for once, he did it. A corny, dirty, sort of cute and faggy joke. A guy is seated in an airplane, zonked, sleeping—with his fly open. His cock is clearly visible. Next to him is another guy reading a newspaper. This guy looks over and pins the sleeping cat. Digs his joint and signals to the stewardess. "Stewardess!"

"Yes, sir! . . . Some gum?"

"No . . . uh . . . I'd like a pencil and paper, if you don't mind."

"Yessir."

Then the cat writes a note: "Dear sir, I am seated across the aisle from you. Your fly is open and you are completely exposed. I know this note will avoid any embarrassment. Yours truly, Frank Martin. P.S. *I love you!*"

A week after his triumph in New York, Lenny joined up with Richey again in Baltimore to play the next concert on the tour. Richey had done his work well. The first afternoon in the hotel he reached in his bag and pulled out a big square package, wrapped in brown paper and containing a couple hundred copies of *Stamp Help Out*. Blue, white, and shiny, they smelled of fresh ink and paper. Lenny turned the pages with unconcealed delight. Here it was. His book. Not *the* book, you dig. But a book. A beauty. The best, the funniest goddam concert brochure in the history of the business. That night, Richey was to stand outside the door to the auditorium and watch the book hawkers as they cried aloud: "Lenny Bruce souvenir booklet!" What a gas! Lenny was much more excited about the prospect of selling the brochures than he was by the concert.

Most of the copy in the 56-page booklet was taken from the unfinished *How to Talk Dirty:* the two longest sections were Lenny's reminiscences of vaudeville and the fictitious story of his first lay: an Italian chick who ran a grocery near the Brooklyn Navy Yard and made it in the back room among the cans of Progresso tomato purée and Medaglio D'Oro coffee. After these two swatches of recollection, the booklet settles down to its true theme: marijuana. The big idea is to recount with pictures and captions the history of a typical pothead, Russell Dreck (alias Lenny Bruce), from his first score on the school playground through his gradual addiction to "the stuff" to his final desperately strung-out condition as an addict. The pictures are a mixture of Lenny's scrapbook—his Navy I.D. card, his liberty pictures, and the delicatessen-window shots from the Hanson's days—with the pictures that Shack had been taking that summer and a handful of other weirdo stuff picked out of old photo files. Every page offers another gag. One of the most successful is the simple juxtaposition on two facing pages of Lenny as he looked in 1947 with his carefully groomed hair, smoothly rounded baby cheeks and hound's-tooth jacket and Lenny as he looked that summer of 1960, staring directly at the reader with his face slightly unshaven, his hair carelessly cut and his mature features, rendered free of baby fat, set off by an open-neck Levi jacket, with the twisted wire of a cyclone fence behind him. The funniest picture is one illustrating the word "zonked." Posed inside a thicket of leafless trunks and branches, Lenny nods forward from a sitting position, his eyes incredibly blank and stony, inhaling the aroma of a bizarrely ugly plant of sinister suggestion. The caption reads: "Marijuana that is not smoked. The user sits approximately 18 inches from the stalk and inhales the fumes."

The very next day after the Baltimore concert, Lenny and Richey flew to Philadelphia to make good on that concert. The next night, Lenny played the last of the series at Boston. Bam, bam, bam—four heavies in a row. Every concert, in the language of *Variety*, "Smash B.O." Now they were back in New York, getting set to negotiate the sale of the autobiography to *Esquire*. Lenny wants so many thousand in front for himself, plus another little piece to buy off Art Steuer. Just at that moment, he gets that emergency call from Sam Barnett at El Patio. Sam needs Lenny at the club and he needs him now! Lenny decides to go. Richey argues against the move. The argument soon spreads to other matters: the bum deal Lenny handed Richey on the booklets and the interference he's been guilty of in Richey's negotiations with the magazine. Back and forth they fight, until Richey says, "O.K. Give me my money and let me get out of here." Now, Lenny could never bear to be put in the position of the bad guy, the one who is morally inferior. So he decides to placate Richey. "I'll give you the money, man," he says, "but"—and here he put on all his charm— "come with me to my next date in Philly." When Richey remained adamant, Lenny got hacked. Adopting the childish tactics that he often used when he was angry, he went out and got ten 50-mm. ampules of Meth, knowing that nothing would make Richey feel guiltier than seeing him get good and whacked. Lenny was sure that he could both escape Richey's rage and punish him at the same time—all by simply getting high. Richey didn't give an inch; so Lenny left for Philadelphia alone.

The following week Richey got an urgent call from Lenny. He was running a fever, feeling weak, and geezing an enormous amount of Meth. Richey was troubled by the symptoms because they didn't correspond to anything he had ever heard of: neither dope reaction nor sickness nor infection of the blood. He consulted a doctor immediately. Lenny said that he was going to wait until he got down to Florida.

That was the beginning of his most terrible illness. Getting off the plane in Miami, he was reeling with fever. Standing on the stage of the El Patio that night, the whole room seemed to be spinning around. Finally, it got going too fast and he heard a loud thump! Later he realized that it was the sound of his own body hitting the floor. Rushed to Mount Sinai Hospital, he was put under the care of a Dr. Woodrich. The doctor took one look at his arms, and decided that he was dealing with either a case of hepatitis or a staphylococcus septicemia. Staph infections are common among junkies. The bacteria that lie on the skin and are harmless there become deadly killers when they're punched into the bloodstream. Lenny's fever was typical of blood infections; it went up and up until it reached an alarming peak of 107 degrees. At that point, the doctor despaired of Lenny's life. Ordering him packed in ice, he watched carefully as bottles of antibiotic were dripped into one arm while bottles of glucose and dextrose were dripped into the other. When Lenny's seriously damaged veins collapsed from lack of pressure, the doctor made surgical incisions in his arms to reach deeper-lying blood vessels and continue the flow of life-giving fluids. When Lenny's breathing became labored, the doctor ordered an oxygen tent and eventually an oxygen tube stuffed up one nostril and taped to his face.

Soon Sally arrived, bringing Kitty. They put up in a bungalow on the grounds of the Shoreham Hotel. While Kitty played all day at the pool, Sally kept an anxious vigil at Lenny's bedside. Things had reached a desperate pass when Honey suddenly appeared. She had been going through a terrible spell herself, out in Hollywood, trying to kick and get her life back together. When she heard the news of Lenny's illness over the radio, she flew to Miami. Coming into the hospital room that first day, she almost fainted. Lenny was lying in a coma, mumbling incoherently, as if he were mad. Though his eyes were open, he could not see. He seemed at the point of death. Finding nothing to do, Honey wandered forlornly back to Sally's hotel. Every time Lenny got sick, Honey would begin to feel as if she were losing her mind. That was exactly the way she felt that afternoon when she went into the Shoreham bar to steady her nerves with a couple of drinks. After the second vodka martini, she recognized a guy she had known in the old days: a friend of both hers and Lenny's. Then, her craziness took hold of her and made her behave shamefully. "I moved this guy I had no eyes for at all," she recalls. "I just flipped out for some reason, like I was madly in love with this guy, and just moved him right there."

When Sally arrived at the bungalow shortly after 4 A.M., she found Kitty asleep in a chair on the front porch. Cautiously opening the door to the cottage, she discovered Honey naked in bed, sleeping with the guy she had picked up in the bar. "I wasn't even concerned with her sleeping with a guy," remarks Sally. "When I saw the child, I saw the whole picture. I had never seen that picture before."

Greatly embarrassed, Honey bolted from the bed and hastily

pulled on a pair of Levis, a dirty T-shirt, and leather sandals. She ran toward the beach; after walking for an hour, she blacked out. Miami Beach police spotted her later weaving in and out of traffic on the Arthur Godfrey Causeway. They stopped her car in the middle of the street and made her get out. Seated on the curb, Honey began screaming incoherently at passing motorists. She was arrested and charged with driving while intoxicated and following too closely. As soon as she pleaded guilty on the latter charge and paid a $25 fine plus court costs, she headed back toward Lenny's room at the hospital. Walking into the room, she stared in horror at Lenny's supine body, crucified with needles and tubes. Impulsively, she decided to save his life. Rushing to his bedside, she began tearing out the tubes and pulling off the tapes and bandages. "Help!" screamed Lenny. "She's trying to kill me!" An instant later, the room was filled with nurses and orderlies, who seized Honey and led her into the corridor. A few minutes later, two police officers arrived and handcuffed her. She was driven to the psychiatric division of Jackson Memorial Hospital and locked in a padded cell. When she was released four days later, Sally would not permit her to see either Lenny or Kitty. "From then on," Sally declares, "she and I were at razor's edge!"

After twenty-eight days on the critical list, Lenny finally began to mend. He had had a close brush with death. His recuperation was slow. About two months from the time when he fell sick, the doctors pronounced him well enough to travel. Getting on a plane with Sally and Kitty, he flew to Los Angeles. Another spell of recuperation was spent in the healing climate of Palm Springs. Finally, in June, he felt strong enough to take a trip. Richey Shackleton and Ted Markland were planning to drive down the Baja peninsula to Guaymas and Mazatlán. They knew a guy down there named Tony, who had a great pad and was making a lot of money counterfeiting race-track tickets. They had visions of lovely country and crazy capers.

They rented a Hertz car and started south, but no sooner did they really get going than the whole trip began to deteriorate. By the time they reached the charming fishing village of Guaymas on the Gulf of California, they were veering toward madness. What happened after that is anybody's guess. The trip was aborted, and the next thing Shack recalls is driving into Tucson. He jumped a plane for home; Ted and Lenny came back by road.

It was mid-July when Lenny resumed his touring. His first date was the Dunes Motel in Neptune, New Jersey: a three-day weekend for $5,000—$1,500 after each of the first two shows and the balance after the third, all in cash. Lenny pulled in from New York, where he had persuaded Don Friedman and his wife to join him for the weekend.

Sizing up the place fast, he wasn't happy about what he saw. The crowd was heavy and integrated, which was good; but the owner and his "boys" were a bunch of dangerous-looking shtarkers. The first night's show was a bomb: Lenny played to thirty or forty people and a dozen walked out. The next night was not much better. The management was very unhappy. No stacks of clean green bills were forthcoming after the evening's work. One boss complained to Lenny about all the "filth" that was in his act. How could he use words like "kike" and "nigger"?

By the third night, the show was sold out, and the manager wanted to extend him one more day. Lenny smelled a rat. Going into the office to collect his money, he received not cash but a check. Normally, he would have refused to accept it, but with these guys glowering at him, he had to be polite and take the possibly worthless slip of paper. He refused to do another show and announced that he was leaving immediately. Going back up to the room, Lenny told Don to pack fast: they were going to have trouble if they remained another hour. Sure enough, as they're throwing things into bags, there is a heavy knock at the door. It's a hood from the office. He's been sent up to threaten Lenny. As the guy walks into the room, Don's big Doberman Pinscher spots a moth and leaps into the air, his savage teeth snapping at the insect. One look at the killer dog and the hood stops cold. Sensing a momentary advantage, Don puts on his most determined manner and tells the guy that they are leaving *right now!* A few minutes later they are in the car speeding back to New York.

When they got back to Don's apartment, it was midnight. Everybody's nerves were jangling. Lenny was desperately in need of a fix. Snatching the phone, he called a doctor. After a lot of hassling, threatening, and pleading, he finally got the guy to go for a prescription. At three o'clock in the morning, Don and his wife saw Lenny hightail it out the door, on his way to the doctor's apartment.

When Lenny reached Detroit for his next date, he was traveling alone, and feeling blue. What bugged him even more than the deadening sense of isolation was his frustration at not being able to write up a proposal that he had promised International Talent Associates, a big booking agency like MCA. Jack Sobel was not working for this outfit, but he had told Lenny that if he could get his ideas together on paper, there was a chance that the company would lay real money on him as an advance for a book or movie. Indeed, if he had a really great idea for a picture, there might be as much as a half million dollars in it for him as writer-producer-director. Maybe even more!

Lenny was sure that he could make a good pitch, but he needed someone to work with, getting the stuff down on paper. He needed

Richey or Kenny or even Fran Lewis. Someone! And he was bugged
that this golden opportunity was slipping through his fingers just because he couldn't get the simplest kind of help. Actually, Detroit
harbored at that time—unbeknownst to Lenny—the ideal helpmate.
The young Ben Sims—he of the record store and the historic first
concert—was at that very moment preparing himself for the rare pleasure of seeing his hero at close quarters. Ben still recalls, with bemused
delight, the sudden and startling swerve his life took when one day he
walked down a street in his hometown and looked up at the marquee
of the Club Alamo:

One day I passed by the biggest club in town with live entertainment. I saw "Coming Next Week, Lenny Bruce." I took two seats
at a table and got there very early. Before he came on, I wrote a
little note and gave it to the waiter: "Do you remember a tall,
thin, married guy with glasses and a big nose? Well, he's still tall,
thin, with glasses and a nose but no wife anymore. I wish you
well."

Lenny always had this big hesitancy about starting a show. I
always felt a great forlornness in his beginnings. That night he was
wandering around, complaining, fixing the microphone, when he
starts looking for me in the audience. "I have a note," he says,
"and I'm going to read it." I said, "No! Please don't do that!" So
he said, "O.K." and ate it. Swallowed it!

A waiter came over between sets and said, "Mr. Bruce would
like to see you backstage." We went back, and he was in the middle
of some complex hassle that always used to go on with club owners.
He said, "Stick around after the next show." Then, later, we went
downtown and had something to eat in the local show business
deli. Then we went back to his hotel and he said, "I have some
long distance calls to make, so you wait in the lobby and I'll meet
you there." Then, we went back to my apartment and rapped for
three or four hours and eventually drove back to the hotel. He
said, "I'll see you tomorrow."

The next night I showed up again and there was a table waiting.
It was the same routine as the previous night. To the deli, back
to the hotel. "Wait for me in the lobby 20 minutes"—which was
more like an hour. Then back to my apartment for four or five
hours. Again he said, "I've got to go back to the hotel." This time,
though, he said. "Listen, come on up." On the way up in the
elevator, which was self-service, he said, "Do you know anything
about drugs?" I said "No." "Have you ever smoked marijuana?"

"Three or four times." "Do you think there is anything terrible about it?" I said "No! What's wrong with drugs?"

He said, "O.K. Listen. I have to take some medicine." He walked down the hall and there was a bellboy in the corridor. Lenny was walking very cool and very slowly up to the door. The key goes in and the door opens. Then, faster than the human eye can follow, the sleeve is up, the spoon is out, he's cooking away, got a towel wrapped around his arm. Zap! It was a blur to me. It was so quick!

He said, "That's why I come back to the hotel. Does it disturb you?" I said "No." Because at that time, in a way, I had fallen in love. He was like the funniest, grooviest—and my head was in a lot of weird places at that time anyway.

One of the things Ben had his head into at this time was writing. When Lenny learned that this dedicated fan was a literary type, he instantly put him to work. Every afternoon Lenny would pace back and forth in his hotel room dictating to Ben, at the typewriter, the details of this smashing new proposal that might make millions.

Lenny prided himself on his ability as a P.R. man. Not only did he love to write funny put-on ads and promotions and commercials, but at an early point in his career, when he first got into nightclubs, he used to take space in the daily *Variety* and publish these big thank-you notes. You know those hats-off-to, I'll-never-forget bullshit acknowledgments that the show-biz assholes are always making to the third assistant janitor and toilet flusher? Well, Lenny would write this big thing saluting or hailing or throwing candy kisses to "All the People Who Have Helped Me in the Business." Then he'd print the names of his worst enemies—everybody who had fucked him or gypped him or ripped him off since he was two months old. An honor roll of pricks, with each shithead getting his ironic personalized tribute. "Boris Belt, who didn't hold me over at the Crescendo. Tony Cazatska, who blah, blah, blah." People in the business cracked up over those thank-you's.

Lenny had the same attitude going for him when it came to raising money for his career. He had the problem that many entertainers face. He was a success, a star, a name—but he wasn't into the big bucks. Sure, he made a nice taste in the clubs. If he wanted to stay out on the road all year and hustle every location like a whore and rip off the income tax like an accountancy Ph.D. and play the Portuguese sardine fleet on Bless the Boats Day at Gloucester, he could come home at the end of the year with $350,000. What's more, with the talent agencies he was always in this strange bind: on the one hand, he wanted to talk big money and really blow himself up like a billboard on Times Square;

on the other hand, he wanted to get cute with the copy and make the whole pitch a bit on making pitches. That's what he was into with his new collaborator in Detroit. He'd decided that they'd use some of the flicks from *Stamp Help Out*, showing him in different phases of his career, and get a special typewriter with an extra-long carriage and a script typeface. Working on extra large sheets of paper, they would do a big knock-'em-dead pitch. The basic proposition is spelled out on the first page: YOU OUGHT TO BE IN PICTURES, reads the heading in bold black type and underneath in script:

> I will sign an exclusive contract for a period of two years with no options with I.T.A.; to give I.T.A. ten per cent of all monies I earn in all medias of the entertainment industry—i.e.,
> * Film Producing and any
> profits I will derive from film . . .
> * Television . . .
> * Concerts . . .
> * Night Clubs . . .
> * Any Personal Appearances . . .
> * Phonograph Records . . .

If, you raise the sum of three hundred thousand dollars for Lenny Bruce Enterprises . . .

Then Lenny describes his potential "draw" and the financial advantages of making a deal with him instead of the usual movie package:

> Aside from the poetic market, I feel that individually there is the obvious, untapped, guaranteed market of the veneer followers . . .
> *Readers of "Mad Magazine," The Paper . . .
> ** Pot Smokers—Pill droppers . . .
> *** Subscribers to "Playboy:
> Rogue;
> Dude;
> Swank;
> Gent;
> Grove Press" . . .
> Nelson Algren;
> Norman Mailer;
> Hentoff and Camus;
> Thelonius;
> John Cage————

——who is so in—and the package becomes so damn in—that
they drop the n and only the i is left——
The I that is the one that I can understand
and can ENTERTAIN——
****Bartenders, Coctail Waitresses and "B" Girls and . . .
        . . . All Juniors and Seniors in colleges
        that can't see me on their campii because
        the Faculty considers me "unfit" so they have
        to sneak away and pay $4.75 to hear me at
        Carnige Hall . . .
*****The Village Voice, Emerson, The Realist . . . . . ************
Another unique facet is that I, the artist, have
started the investment by spending about $20,000 on
the first 15 minutes of the feature that is to run
65 minutes
      Explain This To The Investors:
   If a group of people got together $300,000—
which is a low figure for a "B" package . . . they
would need another $100,000 for publicity—
    They Would Never
             Have
the easily guaranteed five hundred thousand to
perhaps one million dollars worth of publicity that
this package will surely receive . . .
    This figure . . . . . .
           $500,000 to $1,000,000 . . . . .
can be corroborated by any publicity agency an investor
wish to employ as an inquisitor.
    The Press That Lenny Bruce receives. . . . . .
without ever having any publicity agent . . .
    Is Phonomenal.

As the proposal goes on for page after page straining to impress
the reader with Lenny's genius, the whole character of the pitch de-
teriorates into the ravings of a speed trip. Lenny boasts, jokes, ad-
libs, and throws in lines from his act. He indulges in all sorts of ty-
pographical gimmicks. He parodies old movie schmeers: SEE—
DANCEHALL RACKET—A TICKET TO DANCE IS A TICKET TO DOOM. He
offers quotes from favorable reviews; letters from magazine and book
publishers soliciting contributions; and even leaves one page blank
with the heading: SOME MAIL THIS MONTH. He even slips in some
random erotic fantasies:

*****The package will attract*****
         the kind of guys that would be uncomfortable
seeing two guys perform a homosexual act,
but would get horny if they walked into a
room in a millionaire's mansion and saw
         an auburn hair Miss America beauty
         tenderly caressing a fu-l-busted
         blue-eyed Irish airline hostess
         who was wearing a soft white pleated
           skirt;
the kind of aduience that wouldn't be gauch enough
to assume they could enter the erotics but would
remember it and have it to be a favorite fantasy when . . .

By the end of the rap, Lenny is talking to himself and asking:

       —Number what and why and number up—

    ? ?
      / / He doesn't believe that "religious"
        people believe in God. He is in conflict
        with a group that tells him that God made
        his body but only the parts that can be
        seen on Television. The other parts are
        alluded to by the "naughty" Charlie
        Weave / / / and / / /
He believes that whore houses should be legalized . . .
if he has trouble getting laid or is continually
rejected by his wife . . . or is in jail for running a whore
house.
    ? ?
      / / He's waiting for I-us . . . / /
what   I   am   going   to   do;
         WHAT I AM GOING TO DO. . . . .
    PRODUCE
     A
   FULL LENGTH
P A T H O F A R C E F A N S I C F I L M
andanotherandanotherandanotherandanother / / / / / / / /
Ready
   % $ # ¢ ") (*
 — $ " ' ( )* & ¢ *
    = * & ¢ % $ ( ) *

— % %) *
—
*

Needless to say, none of this raving made the slightest impression on the chain smokers at I.T.A. They probably passed it around like a comic book and shook their heads in amusement, concluding that any dealings with this nut would be commercially suicidal. Instead of putting the boys away, Lenny had driven another nail into the casket of his badly blocked career. Yet, such being the fantasies of omnipotence inspired by dope, he thought he had hatched a brilliant piece of work. Years later, he was still mailing copies of the prospectus to interested investors.

After a week of working together, Lenny and Ben were getting tight. They were just about to have a "shared experience" that neither of them would forget. It all began with Ben offering Lenny a bed at his pad. Lenny was pleased by the invitation.

He moved in with me. After three days watching him take drugs, I discovered Methedrine. It all came about through my friend, Ezra Gross, who had come to Detroit to visit me. Ezra was an anesthesiologist from Pittsburgh. He was the wildest human being I have ever known. An electrical genius who had gone into anesthesiology only because his family had put so much pressure on him to become a doctor. When you'd go into his apartment, you'd find the whole place littered with electrical parts and gadgets. To sit down, you'd have to scoop a whole handful of tubes or switches off the chair. Once Ezra demonstrated for me a little gadget that would dim out the lights of a whole neighborhood. He screwed it into a socket in the apartment and told me to go out in the street. When I yelled "Ready!" even the street lights dimmed! You could see TV pictures shriveling and imagine ice trays melting. It was magic!

In the army, he had been stationed in Europe, where he learned about Methedrine. He really believed in the drug. It began with Lenny weaseling a prescription for Dilaudid. That was the only drug that would get Lenny off. He couldn't get off on heroin, he couldn't get off on morphine sulphate, all he could get off on was Dilaudid. So Lenny goes to fill the prescription. When he comes back, he pulls the pills out of the bottle, stares at them, and says, "These are morphine sulphate!"

"How can you tell?" I said.

"The shape is different."

Well, you'd have to be Jimmy Valentine, the safecracker, to tell the difference. A micrometer is what you'd need. Yet when we actually compared it with Dilaudid, we found Lenny was right! The drugstore had palmed off morphine sulphate as Dilaudid. I got very interested.

Now, at that time Lenny was using Biphetamine, a black span-sule-like capsule, which he would take, an hour and a half before he went on, by mouth. Ezra said to him, "Have you ever taken Methedrine?"

"Yes, but it's not as punchy as Biphetamine because it's five milligrams in pills."

"Well, you can get it in intravenous solution, 20 milligram, 1 cc. ampules."

Lenny was willing to try anything. When he got the Methedrine in him, he said, "It's very groovy!" I said, "I'd like to try it."

The next day I was heavy into it with a prescription for 100 ampules. The next week I went to the medical library to read all about Methedrine and the opiates. From then on, one of my functions was to report back on all the latest advances in medical technology: little things, like don't use disposables or sterilize with alcohol. Use polished needles and sterilize them by immersion in jars of Phisohex, using them in cycles, one day's jar alternating with the next.

Dope-taking involves a lot of ritual and most of it has nothing to do with getting high. I said to Lenny once, "Why don't you take five Dilaudids and drop them in sterile water and shake it a couple of times a day for a week. Then, all you have to do is open the jar and take it out—you don't have to cook all the time." "Oh, no!" he said. "Cooking is part of the ritual. You want that."

I heard a shrink once use the term "present." Lenny's father was always present. I think more present than his mother, though that's the one he would talk about. He rarely spoke of his father, but when he did, it was always with a feeling of betrayal. You could always hear it in his voice. There would always be an edge to his voice. So all the hurt and all the ritual of the drugs was important to him as a way of paying his dues to his father. He had to pay dues for the fact that he got his pleasure that way and got away from the world. Ezra once said: "He sits there like a fucking toad: every once in a while his eyes open, he looks around and his eyes close again." This is when you're very high on opiates. You don't want to be bugged by a lot of stuff. You really just want to get away. That was Lenny. He had to remove himself from that feeling that the world was coming in on him. People came on very hard to him. They treated him like fucking property. He really hated that. So all the pain and ritual and scrambling for drugs was paying dues for the fact that the drugs were the one time he could get away from it all.

An example: there are two main arm veins. One doesn't hurt a bit and the other hurts like a bitch. The big one going up the inside of your arm is the easiest to see and the one where the doctor usually hits you. There's another one on the top side that doesn't hurt at all. In the one vein, if you miss, you get a terrible burn. In the other, even if you spill, there's hardly any burn at all. I used to say to him, "Hell, why don't you shoot up *that* vein?" The answer was: "I don't know. I always go here." What he really meant was: "I go here because it hurts more here than anywhere else." He shot there so much he got a great big embolism. Then he had to get down to shooting the back of his hand—which is really painful. To me, the same masochism was behind the fact that he was such an easy touch. He was always worried about money because when you're a junkie there's never enough money and never enough pills. Yet he'd throw money and pills away. Once he copped a huge bottle of over a thousand pills. That should have lasted him a long time. No, he gave most of them away—because he liked the feeling of panic, having to scramble. That's paying dues. Good Jewish dues.

Lenny and I traveled together for about six weeks. After we left Detroit, we went to Toledo. By that time I had seen Lenny do his act dozens of times. I had memorized most of his bits, and I was beginning to feel that I'd like to take a shot at being a comic myself. One thing worked in my favor. Lenny would always be preceded in the clubs by some sort of warm-up act. Because Lenny demanded so much money—at that time he was getting up to $5,000 a week—the club owners would try to get the cheapest act they could find. Generally, it was some chick singer with no talent and an accompanist who was her husband. Lenny had a real vendetta going with these chicks. Everywhere he worked, he tried to drive them out of the club. The way he would do it was really wild.

As soon as he came on, he would start to make jokes about the chick: the way she looked, her clothes, her hair, her voice, her music, her arrangements, her accompanist, her stage name— Lenny didn't miss a beat! And this wasn't just a few throw-away lines while he was adjusting the mike. This was five minutes of heavy needling. He even worked out one whole routine about these chicks. That's the routine where he says that he's bored with girl singers but he has a great idea for making them hot again. The

idea is to get a girl singer to let the *hair* grow under her arms.
When she does her act, she wears a low-cut gown. Every once in
a while she flashes! "In the still of the night" . . . bam! An arm
movement, a glimpse of bush—and the whole club is shook! "Did
you see that?" "What?" "That chick . . . I'd swear *she had hair
under her arms!*" "Aaaaah, you're nuts!" "Yeah, must be the
lighting in here. Weird!" Then at the end of her act, while she's
doing her big farewell-Sophie-Tucker-hello-God number, she
throws her arms up for a second and gives them a real blast of
bush! The house panics and her career really begins to move!

Well, two nights of this routine in Toledo, and the chick goes
into the manager and says, "I want to get out of here." Now that
was the time when I asked Lenny if he thought I could try doing
some of his material. We sat in the room one afternoon, and I ran
down fifteen minutes' worth of stuff—mostly his but with a few
things of my own thrown in. Lenny was nice at first. He said
anybody could be a comic if he was willing to work hard enough.
He agreed to put me on that night as an experiment. We went to
the manager and told him that I was a bright young talent and
would work in the girl's spot for nothing. The manager was delighted. So that night, for the first time in my life, I came out
onstage. It was beginner's luck because from the first line out of
my mouth the audience was completely with me. I did five minutes,
ten minutes, 15 minutes—and it seemed like 15 seconds. I could
have said anything and gotten a laugh. I even thought of doing
The Palladium! When I came off I was flying high. "Is it always
this easy?" I giggled to Lenny. He looked real glum and said,
"You'll see."

Next show that night I walked on a different man. Between the
success and the Meth, I came on like I was Mr. Confidence. And
did I bomb! I couldn't get one laugh. I couildn't do one thing right.
Later I was told that I did 12 minutes. It seemed like a hard day's
work. When I came off I said to Lenny, "How often is it like *this*?"
Lenny was smiling and breaking up. "Sometimes," was all he could
say. Then he had to go out and win the crowd. I'm sure the reason
he wanted me to try was so I could see what a treacherous monster
is an audience. Once I learned that, I vowed never to speak in
public for money again. I've kept that vow.

The day before Labor Day Lenny and Ben pulled into Philadelphia
to work at the Red Hill Inn. The Red Hill was one of the best and
most famous jazz clubs in the country. It was also a regular stop along
Lenny's East Coast show circuit. A big barn of a room in suburban

Pennsauken, just over the state line in New Jersey, the club was noted for its excellent acoustics and congenial atmosphere. The house booker was Sid Mark, a Philadelphia disk jockey, who ran a popular afternoon and early evening radio show called *Mark of Jazz*. Sid, a good friend of Lenny's, loves to tell the story of how he first made Lenny's acquaintance.

It was back in the late fifties, when Lenny was appearing in Philadelphia for the first time, at a square joint called the Celebrity Club. Mark had heard the first two albums, and, like every hipster in the country, he was gassed right down to his alligators. Trying to line up Lenny for an appearance on his program, however, proved an absolute impossibility. Lenny wasn't doing any freebies, and when pressed he got downright vicious, snapping over the phone: "All DJs are faggots!" Fortunately, Mark knew a lot of people in Philadelphia. One of them, a dentist to whom Lenny had gone for a quick repair job, called up Sid at WHAT-FM one afternoon while he was on the air and crowed into the phone: "Guess who I've got in the chair—Lenny Bruce!" Sid has a quick mind. "Tune me in on your office radio!" he barked. Then, after the next record, he pressed the button on his mike. *"Lenny! Lenny Bruce!"* he called over the air. "Get out of that chair! That guy's a *quack*!" Sitting up suddenly, with a comically alarmed expression on his face, Lenny turned to the dentist and said, "That's pretty funny. Who is this guy?"

That night they met, and the next afternoon Lenny was on the air rapping with Sid for two hours. They rammed right through the time segments, the commercials, all the stop signs, except the federally enforced station breaks. It was a great rap, combining comedy and personality and philosophy and shticks on the jazz scene that only a real hipster like Lenny Bruce could get off. Sid Mark was overwhelmed. He got so warm and friendly that he schlepped Lenny out to his home for dinner. That was a gig that Lenny *never* made. Dinner with a respectably married middle-class Jewish couple? Are you kidding? It was the same scene he ridiculed in one of his funniest bits, *Lima, Ohio!* But for Sidney . . . O.K. He'd be nice, he'd be a person. Yet he couldn't sit down to the table without complaining about the people who corner you at ringside and insist you come to dinner. What a drag! How can you say no? Then he looked down at his plate and pinned the fork. "Did you ever notice," he smiled, "that wherever you go there's always a *funny fork*? Yeah . . . one fork with a bent prong . . . that's the one I always get!"

Actually, it was hard for Lenny to sit through a meal. He was just like a little kid you bring to the table and prop up on the top of a telephone book. He plays with his food and talks out of line and gets restless and bored with the whole dumb ritual. Really, it's torture for him just to sit there that long. He's dying to get away from the table and run in the living room or out on the back porch where he can play. That was Lenny at meals. On this night, as soon as he could decently leave, he got up to go. Then his eye fell on a movie camera, lying on a chair in the living room. "Hey!" he yelled. "Let's make a movie!" Immediately, they were caught up in his fantasy.

It was going to be a really sick movie. *Dracula Meets the Jews*. How's that for a title? Lenny would be Dracula and Sid and his wife would be the Jews—type casting. The big scene is when they go to kill Dracula. The cross doesn't work—those dumb goyim! So they go for heavier weapons. The Jewish wife, right? The heaviest! Especially when she's pregnant—and Loretta is very pregnant. Who could stand up against one of those Jewish broads? Only it should be *really* heavy. She should come at him dressed up in a yarmulka, a mezuzah, and a tallith! That's like overwhelming . . . only it doesn't work! There has to be something even heavier . . . a fuckin' atom bomb that even Dracula can't stand! Lenny the writer-director-producer is really cooking now. Standing in the living room popping his fingers, sucking in his lips, looking wildly around. "Got it!" he shouts. "You're a DJ, right? A jazz DJ. O.K. You got some Charlie Parker sides? Something with Bird's picture on the cover? A Dial? A Mercury? Beautiful! That's it! Now we'll cook."

So as Mark points the whirring camera, Lenny poses in his long black cloak, his wolf-fang teeth, and begins to advance menacingly toward Loretta. Suddenly she holds up the album—with Bird grinning idiotically under the be-bop beret. Dracula stops dead in his tracks and clutches his throat. He reels back. Yet, he's not done for. Reaching under his cloak, he produces a mean-looking pair of garden shears and makes for Sid's pecker. A Jewish Dracula, he doesn't want to suck anybody on the neck—he wants to circumcise them! The power of the Bird album is too much for him, however. Toppling backward across the sofa, he raises his middle finger in one last fungoo of defiance and dies. The very next frame shows him toppling into a toilet bowl in the form of a Charlie Brown doll. Then the lid—emblazoned with the words THE END—slams down on the human excrement. Lenny even insisted that they shoot credits for the film with himself posing moodily, his head stuck through a hole in a huge sheet of white paper. Sid sent the film to Rochester to be developed, and it came back with the scissors episode blacked out!

Oh that Lenny! He was so young and beautiful at that time. He looked great and he came on clean. No junkie lunatic bits, like the time a couple years later—a thing that really shook Sid—when he tore off his shirt and blew his nose in it. That was the first time Sid realized that Lenny might be going crazy. Up to that point they had always had a ball. Like the time when Passover came out on the same day as Easter Sunday. Lenny was staying at the John Bartram and Sid called him up. Sid had just bought a new convertible and his wife was again pregnant. It was a holiday and he just felt like going out for a ride. So he goes over and picks up Lenny and they're heading out of Central City toward the club. As they pass through Independence Square, where a crowd has gathered to see the Liberty Bell, Lenny gets an inspiration. "Sid!" he drums on his shoulder from the back seat, "when you get to the red light, don't go when it changes green. We'll cause a traffic jam . . . we'll get some attention." Then he climbs up on the top of the back seat and cups his hands around his mouth and starts yelling at the people: "O.K. We're gonna shoot this scene one more time . . . that's it! If all the women could move to the left . . . and I want all the guys to move to the right . . . please cooperate with us!" Instinctively, everybody starts to move as Lenny waves them this way and that. Meanwhile, the motorists behind Sid's car are leaning on their horns, making a tremendous racket. "Should I go now, Lenny?" yells Sid over his shoulder. "No, I'll tell you when," shouts Lenny. Poor Sid, it's Passover, and he's sitting in this open car with a piece of matzos in one hand and a cup of coffee in the other. He doesn't know what's coming off. At that moment a patrol car pulls up, and the cop gets out of the car and walks over and says: "What do you think you're doing?" Lenny leans down to the cop and confides. "This is a diversionary tactic—we're blowing up a synagogue around the corner." As the cop squeezes his face into a frown of perplexity, Lenny snaps to Sid, "Go now!" Off they go across the bridge and right quickly into New Jersey.

Lenny was always doing the unexpected. Not just stunts and put-ons but really beautiful spontaneous things—like the time he bought all those clothes for the band at the Red Hill. They were a new jazz band from Wilmington, Delaware, a quintet led by a policeman named Lem Winchester. Lenny worked with them one Friday night and dug them so much that he went out the next day and bought everybody in the band new clothes and shoes. Except the conga player, a giant named Big Black. He must have weighed 350 pounds and there was no fitting him. Lenny didn't know what to do. As he was driving around with Sid, he suddenly got a flash. As they passed an A & P, he yelled "Stop, man!" Then, ducking into the store, he got two big shopping bags at the checkout counter and filled them up to the brim with every piece of candy in the store. A fortune in penny candy. That night at the club, he walks up to Big Black schlepping the candy bags and says,

"I really don't know what's good for you, but this is what I got!" The guy lost about ten pounds laughing.

As far as drugs went, Sid figured that Lenny was clean until he got that frantic call on the afternoon of Friday, September 29. He was on the air when the call came through. "Sid!" Lenny shouts through the phone, "I'm in jail! Get me a lawyer! Get me out of here!"

"What have they got you for?" gasps Sid.

"For taking stuff that I have prescriptions for," cries Lenny in exasperation. It was really a shocker. A crazy confused story that everybody tells a different way. Only when you've talked to a dozen different people and sorted out a dozen different versions do you finally realize exactly what happened.

It all begins with Lenny checking into Haverford State Hospital, a mental hospital, a few days before the bust. Lenny and Ben had broken up at that time because Ben was doing so much Methedrine that he was beginning to develop the initial symptoms of amphetamine psychosis. He was hysterically manic and increasingly out of touch with reality. Unlike Lenny, who had to get himself together every night to work the gig, Ben had nothing on his mind but drugs. At that point his consumption of Methedrine had reached 1,000 milligrams a day. He had discovered that you could buy crystalline methamphetamine in wholesale lots by representing yourself as engaged in pharmacological research. You could mix large batches of the crystal with water, throw in a little salt, and carry this liquid around with you in a plastic baby bottle. The crystal didn't have quite the magic of ampules, however; so on every possible occasion Ben would pop off to Pittsburgh, where his friend would dole out fifty or a hundred of the precious vials. In those days Methedrine was so new that very few laymen recognized the dangers of running up a speed habit.

What finally stopped Ben was the spectacle of Ezra constantly disassembling and reassembling his electrical gadgets without any discernible purpose. That crazy compulsion combined with a lot of crazy talk one weekend to persuade Ben that his brilliant buddy had blown it. Ben flashed, "I'm next." So when he got back to Philadelphia, he told Lenny that he was going off to write the Great American Novel.

That was the moment when Lenny shifted from working in blue jeans to working in black Nehrus. In the blue outfit he had looked passably well: sort of bloated and baggy-eyed but really O.K. The moment he donned the black high-collar jacket, his skin revealed a terrible yellowish pallor. Lenny didn't feel well, either. He was suffering from lethargy, even though he was doing up hundreds of mils of speed every day. Eventually, he began to suffer from fever and chills. Fearing that he was coming down with a recurrence of the illness that had laid him up the previous spring—a disease that had also begun in Philly—he decided to consult a doctor. He called up his regular man in Philadelphia and got a peculiar brush-off. The doctor, who had always been so helpful before, who had written so much script for him—the last prescriptions were from only six months before—suddenly balked. He told Lenny that he should consult another man. The new doctor put Lenny in the hospital and discharged him a couple of days later, with prescriptions for twenty-seven bottles of pills. It was quite a haul: Methedrine and disposable syringes; Dilaudid, Tuinal, and Dolophine. (Lenny always stockpiled drugs because you can't take script over state lines.) So he hightailed over to the Spruce Street Medical Pharmacy, where he was a regular customer, and then schlepped all the stuff back to Room 616 at the John Bartram. There he piled the bottles and boxes on his coffee table. At some point that night he fell into a deep sleep. He was still sleeping at noon the next day, Friday, September 29th, when he was awakened by an insistent knocking at his door.

Boom-boom-boom-boom-boom!

Hauling his dopey, woozy head off the pillow, Lenny mumbles, "Who's there?"

Boom-boom-boom-boom! "Open up the door, Mr. Bruce!"

Exasperated that his strict do not disturb order should have been ignored, Lenny levels his voice like a gun, barking: "Look, I'm gonna check out right now. You know my scene—that I sleep a certain time. I never want any calls. I told you, 'No emergency calls'!"

BAM-BAM-BAM-BAM-BAM! "PLEASE, MR. BRUCE— OPEN UP THE DOOR FOR YOUR OWN GOOD!"

Enraged, Lenny shouts: "WHO IS THAT?"

"It's the manager! Open up the door!"

Absolutely bewildered by such insane persistence, Lenny finally thinks to himself: "It must be some nut. After all, I'm a good guest, a heavy tipper. What is this shit? Reaching quickly across the bed for the phone, he barks: "Desk! There's a madman here who says he's the manager. Get me the police!"

CRAAAAAAAAAAAAACK!

The door bursts off its hinges—and there stand the *police.*

"Gee!" exclaims Lenny, "this *is* service!"

A bust is what it really is. The three gentlemen in plain suits standing inside the doorway are patrolmen Martin Miller, Albert Perry, and John Zawackis of Lieutenant Anthony Bonder's narcotics squad. They are armed with a search warrant. They know exactly what they are doing. They've caught Lenny with his pants down. But if Lenny is surprised by their sudden appearance, the plainclothesmen are no less surprised by what they discover in Lenny's bed. To their dismay, they soon realize that they have netted not only a dirty-talking dope fiend but the beautiful wife of one of Philadelphia's most prominent Main Line aristocrats. The instant the lady identifies herself, clutching a sheet to her naked bosom, the detectives fall into a stunned silence, broken only by Lenny's suppressed titter from the bed. (Who was she? Oh, some rich broad whose husband either didn't know or didn't care. She had come into the club one night, Ben Sims recalls, and taken a shine to Lenny. She sent a note backstage on the sort of stationery you don't ignore. Lenny had come out and stood at a vantage point to check her out. She was wearing a lot of jewelry and she looked like class. Lenny took it from there.) Now she is throwing on her clothes pell-mell, while the police huddle in the hall. When she emerges from the room, they suggest that she go home and say nothing about what has happened. They, for their part, will erase her name from their memories.

When they return to the room, the first thing they spot is the pharmacy on the cocktail table. Immediately, they swing into action. One cop grabs a big green box labeled "Burroughs-Welcome: Methedrine." Another holds up to the light a glass bottle of a clear liquid tagged with a prescription number prefaced by the letter *N,* for "narcotic." Another ponders the plastic bottles containing orange pills, white pills, and blue pills. "What's this? . . . And this? . . . And this?" they chorus. Now, Lenny knows that he has prescriptions for all his drugs—or nearly all. He knows he's got a cast-iron alibi with his hospitalization and his doctor. So he decides to play it cool and not submit to the shakedown. All the cops want is money—he knows that.

"I'm not feeling well," he mumbles in a feeble voice. "I just got out of the hospital."

"Come on, you dope fiend," growls one of the cops, his voice heavy with sarcasm and disbelief.

"What do you want to know?" says Lenny, the picture of injured innocence.

"What do we want to know?" sneers the detective. "You know damn well what we want to know! Wheredya get this stuff?"

At this moment, Lenny's anger catches him again and he decides to switch his tactics from sick to sullen.

"My name is Lenny Bruce. I live at 8825 Hollywood Boulevard, Los Angeles, California," he replies, as if he's reciting a formula.

The cops stare down at him, waiting for more.

"I'm gonna tell you again," says Lenny firmly. "My name is Lenny Bruce. I reside at 8825 Hollywood Boulevard, Los Angeles, California. That's it!"

"Hey," growls one cop, "what are you—a wise guy?"

Meanwhile another detective has been examining the library that Lenny always carts around on his tours.

"Hey, whaddya doin' with all these books here? Hee-hee!" he chuckles, as he starts to read the titles.

Getting more bugged by the minute, Lenny answers: "I smoke them at night. They're all dipped in secret shticklach." Then, he shpritzes the cops with an old bit: "I'll tell you something: if you're ever in a strange town, just clip the ad for the local jazz club out of the paper, roll it up, and smoke it—and you'll be right out of your kayach!"

"Come on—he's putting you on," one detective says to the other, jabbing him with his elbow. Then turning to Lenny, he barks: "All right, get out of bed!"

"I just got out of the hospital!" exclaims Lenny, his voice rising in disbelief.

"If you're so damn sick," says the cop, "we'll send for a doctor and have you examined."

"No you don't!" snaps Lenny. "I'm not going 'cause *your* doctor says so. I want *my* doctor."

"O.K., smartass," says the cop, "we'll getcha your doctor."

Dialing up information, getting Dr. Blatt's number, and calling his office are the work of a couple minutes. The instant the doctor gets on the phone, the policeman starts running down the situation: "making an arrest . . . claims he can't be moved . . . police surgeon . . . blah, blah, blah . . . thank you, Doctor." Down goes the receiver and the cop cracks a big grin. "*Your* doctor says you can go out and play!"

Lenny doesn't flinch. Cursing Dr. Blatt in the back of his mind, he repeats slowly and firmly through pursed lips: "I'm not leaving this bed!"

"All right, if you insist," sighs the officer, as he picks up the phone again, calls headquarters, and asks that a police ambulance and a stretcher crew be dispatched to the John Bartram, Room 616—"at once!" Minutes later, the whine of a siren in the street announces the arrival of the ambulance. Clomping into the room come two uniformed cops with the poles and canvas of a seven-foot litter. Following them at a more relaxed pace comes a civilian crisscrossed with leather straps and boxes. He introduces himself as Charles Myers, photographer for the *Daily News*.

The sight of the photographer and the uniformed bulls really enrages Lenny. Though he's holding himself in check, murder is stirring in his heart. Now he is absolutely determined not to cooperate. He'll resist like all the civil rights guys resist—he just won't move a muscle!

When the cops tell him to get his clothes on and lie down on the litter, he bursts out in exasperation: "What's the matter with you? You tell sick people to get out of bed and get in a stretcher? I'm in my shorts! I'm not even dressed."

So they start to dress him. They take his suit of Levis and pull on the pants, button up the jacket. Socks go on his feet and shoes—but the shoes are Thom McAn boots with high rises and no laces. Lenny has trouble putting them on himself. The cops find it impossible to get them on his feet. Finally, one cop suggests that they slash the leather.

At this point, he explodes: "You schlub! You'll do *what*?" Then, pointing at the cop's uniform and motioning with his head at the plain-clothesman on the other side of the bed, Lenny sneers: "See how this guy over here is being nice and subdued? And you're coming on so crude. You schlub—that's why you're still in uniform!"

With that, the uniformed bull gets very angry. A big red-faced old man, he picks Lenny up like a baby and throws him onto the stretcher. Then both patrolmen pick up the litter and start carrying him out of the room and down the hall.

The photographer has been recording the action with his camera. As soon as they get Lenny decently dressed, he yells, "Hey! How about a picture?" Lenny could kill this bum—but instead he obliges with a gracious open-armed bow from the waist, seated in bed. The expression on his face, though, tells the whole story. Such a sour punim, such a grapefruit grimace! Next morning that disheveled, grimacing head and torso with its theatrically extended hands will occupy page one of Philadelphia's hottest little tabloid. As if that isn't bad enough, one of the cops decides to punish Lenny for being a naughty boy by clamping a pair of handcuffs on his wrists. The photographer gets that one, too. Lenny Bruce, in profile, head lowered, like a felon, holding out his hands resignedly as the plainclothesman clamps on the cuffs. That shot will make even the boldest café owner wince with horror. Oh, it's going to be a beautiful stink!

Finally, four cops position themselves at the four corners of the litter, and they start schlepping Lenny through the corridors of the hotel, taking care to bump him good and hard—the little prick!—every time they turn a corner. When they reach the elevator, another problem presents itself. Elevators aren't built to accommodate seven-foot stretchers. No matter how they insert the thing, it simply won't fit. So one bright bull suggests they put the litter on a slant. Strap him in tight—like a papoose on a squaw board—and then angle him up against the wall. "Great!" growls the old uniformed cop, and he proceeds to raise the foot of the litter so that Lenny is resting against the elevator wall *upside down!* The other cops get a big kick out of that one, and as the doors of the car close, Lenny is followed down the shaft by a barrage of wisecracks and phlegmy laughs.

In this preposterous posture he makes the trip down, with the imperturbable elevator operator making his stops at every floor, opening and closing his doors and gates, taking forever to reach the ground floor. Meanwhile, Lenny is seeing the John Bartram from a novel perspective. For the first time he notices the beauty of ceilings.

Loading him into the ambulance, the cops start off for the hospital, when suddenly the farcical aspect of the bust gets another bizarre highlight as the ambulance sideswipes a car. *RUMP!* A fender tears and an irate motorist starts berating the driver. "You damn cops! Don't you know how to drive? I demand to see your operator's license, blah, blah, blah!"

Finally, they arrive at the headquarters and schlep Lenny up to the third floor. Lieutenant Bonder is waiting to greet him. Lenny gives him a little shpritz.

"Oh, is the Lieutenant a drug addict too?"

Slap! Bonder smacks Lenny across the face.

Oddly, the Lieutenant's brutality offends Lenny less than the plain-clothesman's sarcasm or the patrolman's crudity. Suddenly, sobering up, he makes a little speech. It's the first of many such speeches that he will make to the police over the next five years. It's his way of maintaining his dignity in this hideously degrading situation. Fixing the officer with his great dark eyes, ringed now with purplish circles, he says very reasonably: "Look, Lieutenant Bonder. You don't know me, but I'll tell you now that I'm not going to tell anyone that you hit me. I realize you guys are always meeting somebody that's psychotic and that wants to thwart authority and—whammo!—you lay one on him. Right? Well, I understand you have to. I mean, where would you guys be? So I'm not going to be bugged with you if you rap me around. But it's going to take a lot of rapping to get me to be affected. So I want you to know the story . . . that I'm hip and I want to save you all that work."

Sustaining Lenny through this whole ordeal is the thought that help is not far away. He knows he can count on Joe De Luca, owner of the Red Hill Inn, to bail him out. It's the weekend and Lenny is good for six thousand dollars Friday and Saturday night. So once the doctor has examined Lenny and determined that he is not dangerously ill, he is schlepped over to City Hall, Room 625, Central Magistrate's Court, where Magistrate E. David Keiser sits. Here he is met by an intense, young, sandy-haired lawyer named Malcolm Berkowitz, who has been summoned to the rescue by Sid Mark. Working briskly, efficiently, he gets the magistrate to sign a writ of habeas corpus and set bail: $1,500, which is instantly forthcoming from a bondsman. Once the papers are signed, Lenny is at liberty.

He is also beside himself with rage. Rushing to the nearest telephone, he begins calling everybody who can help, calling every friend and connection, calling all cars—HELP! Later he said that he hired fifteen lawyers in that one afternoon. The man in whom he reposes the greatest confidence, however, is not a seasoned attorney but a young apprentice lawyer named David Blasband.

The son of a prosperous and respected Philadelphia businessman (once an owner of the Yellow Cab Company), David Blasband had met Lenny Bruce as dozens of people met him over the years: in a nightclub where he had gone with his wife and sat at a front table and laughed appreciatively at Lenny's jokes and somehow caught his eye and aroused his interest sufficiently to make him say hello after the show and sit down with the young, good-looking couple and join them for a Coke. To talk to them was the same thing as putting them away. Instantly, they were friends, confidants, virtually intimates. Every time Lenny came to Philadelphia, he'd always call this young couple and they'd laugh and talk and even hang out together.

Now Lenny needs Blasband. Needs his advice, his connections, his legal savvy. Cabbing over to the young lawyer's prestigious firm on Walnut Street, he is ushered into Blasband's office, past towering shelves of leatherbound law journals and case books. Lenny smells dignity, knowledge, power. "A client could just hide out behind all those books," he quips. Blasband takes Lenny's arrest very seriously. He urges Lenny to hire an experienced criminal lawyer. "What do you mean?" exclaims Lenny. "The law says you can't have it without a prescription—well, I *have* a prescription."

Lenny is angry but he's also smart. He, too, smells danger. Blasband is right. He ought to have a good lawyer—but who? Blasband dials up Charles Rogovin, a former associate of the firm, who in turn calls Emmett Fitzpatrick, the second assistant district attorney of Philadelphia. Fitzpatrick says that Garfield Levy is the best man for a case of this nature. A call to Levy and a quick explanation of the problem secures an appointment for that night at the Red Hill Inn. Levy will come backstage between shows and go over the whole matter with Lenny. If Lenny wants Levy in court the next morning, he will be there.

Somewhat relieved but still frightened—and terribly angry— Lenny walks out on the stage of the Red Hill Inn that night and promptly launches into a narrative of his bust. The news had been flashed all over the area already by radio. Many people believed it was some kind of crazy publicity stunt. Lenny plays the arrest for laughs, capitalizing on the joke of calling for the cops when they are actually breaking down his door. Naturally, he says nothing about the society lady in his bed. When he gets to the examination by the police surgeon, he's so carried away by the indignity of the proceeding that he actually rolls up his right sleeve and exposes his scabby and discolored arm to the audience. Pointing to the pencil line which the police photographer had drawn around the puncture marks, he jokes: "The only thing missing is an arrow and the words: 'Insert here.' " The people who are sitting up front, where they can really see his arm, are shocked by its appearance.

When the first show is over, Lenny goes back to the dressing room, and prepares to meet Levy. He's uptight and nervous, asking himself over and over again, "How much is this gonna cost me?" Finally, Levy and the bondsman enter the room. After listening carefully to all the details, Levy picks up the phone and calls Dr. Blatt, to confirm Lenny's story. When he finishes talking with the doctor, he turns around in his seat and says: "Lenny, this will cost you ten thousand dollars."

"Whaaat," explodes Lenny. "That's a telephone number! Are you crazy?"

Unperturbed, the lawyer spells it out. He explains that the magistrate before whom Lenny is scheduled to appear the next morning is a notorious crook. On a salary of $18,000 a year, he has become a rich man, presiding over his business in bribes and gratuities from a palatially furnished office better suited to a big corporation head than it is to a local judge. Though Lenny's case is strong in one sense, it is weak in another. The judge could, if he wished, call the prescribing physician into court and threaten him with an investigation. The doctor then might testify that only a portion of the medicine had actually been prescribed by him. The pharmacist would back him up—and Lenny would be out on a limb. So far as actual evidence is concerned, it's in the hands of the same cops who tried to shake him down. Who knows what they might do with it—or add to it? As far as the police go, Lenny has to realize that the payoff would be split many ways. Magistrate Keiser has to get his and Levy has to have his fee, but there is also the police lieutenant to consider, and the doctors. Levy then hands Lenny a list of payoffs. "Everybody wants a taste," thinks Lenny, as he runs his eye down the list.

So he begins to bargain with Levy. The more he bargains, the lower the price sinks. Finally, just before the midnight show, he has him down to $3,500. Turning to go out the door, Lenny says, "Mr. Levy. I want you to represent me in court tomorrow—but I must sleep on this. Let me call you first thing in the morning." Levy nods his assent, and Lenny walks out onstage to tell his story for the tenth time that day.

When the show is over, at 1 A.M., Lenny drives off with Sid Mark toward the city in a friend's car. They go to this guy's house, and settle down in the kitchen over a cup of coffee. "Lenny," says the friend, "this is a serious business. Apart from the morality of offering a bribe to a judge, you have to realize that the minute you do this you become a mark for crooked cops all over the country. Every time you come into a new town, they'll be waiting for you with their hands out. Is that what you want?"

"Are you kidding?" says Lenny. "I've never paid for protection. Never made a deal with the police. And I'm not gonna start now!" So the decision is made to ditch Levy and hire another lawyer.

At this point, it's about two in the morning. Everybody is fading into the mood of the hour. If they are to show up with counsel at the hearing, they will have to act immediately. Sid Mark hasn't been able to contribute much to the discussion of legal matters, but now he makes a good suggestion. "How about Malcolm Berkowitz, the guy who bailed you out this afternoon?" says Mark. "Solid," says Lenny, reaching for the phone. When he gets Berkowitz on the wire, Lenny is his old charming self.

"Malcolm," he says, "I understand you're a groovy cat—Sid told me about you. I understand you'll represent me and won't charge me a whole lot of bread. Otto Kruger (already Lenny had a name for Garfield Levy) wants telephone numbers to get me off. How much do you want to represent me at the hearing?" Berkowitz's normal fee was $150, but with all the pressure and notoriety—and Lenny making $5,000 a week—he figured he could ask for a little more. He pegs the price at $500 and Lenny agrees.

The next morning, Berkowitz recalls:

I was in the office (room 306, 20 South 15th Street) about 9:45, when Lenny Bruce walked in wearing a black Nehru jacket, a pair of tight-fitting pants and zipper boots. He had his entourage with him: Count Fleet, a pasty-faced rock organist from South Philly, a young fellow and a big guy who looked like a bodyguard. They all walked in like Lenny was king of the hill. He sat down on the chair opposite me, and put his boots up on my desk. I said: "We got a hearing at ten. I gotta hear what happened, and I gotta get some money because I always count money." It was $470. I said, "What happened to the other thirty dollars?" "Well," he says, "I had to buy breakfast for the gang." He Jewed me out of thirty bucks, which he never gave me.

Lenny's story is a good one, and Berkowitz approaches the hearing with a great deal of confidence. He needs it because the hearing, conducted at the magistrate's office at 1301 South Broad Street, is stormy. Berkowitz's nominal antagonist is the fourth assistant district attorney, William Harris, a decent man, whose behavior at the hearing is a model of rectitude. His real opponent, however, is Magistrate Keiser, who never loses an opportunity to put words in the arresting officer's mouth, to assume the role of the D.A. and to stymie the efforts of the defense to have the case dismissed.

The first witness is the chief arresting officer, Patrolman Perry. He testifies about the difficulties he and his fellow officers had in making the arrest and then details the drugs they found:

20 plastic and 5 glass syringes

4 hypodermic needles

36 ampules of Methedrine

11 tablets in a plastic vial

A glass bottle containing a clear liquid with a prescription number indicating that it was a narcotic.

6 orange-colored capsules

13 white tablets, etc.

When Perry has completed his testimony, Berkowitz begins to cross-examine him. The attorney hammers away at the fact that the search warrant that prompted the arrest was unjustifiably broad and vague, containing a catch-all phrase—"any and all other tablets, powders, or liquids"—that could have produced an arrest for aspirin or talcum powder. Berkowitz also raises hell about the fact that no analysis has been performed by the police chemist on the unidentified liquids and capsules. Magistrate Keiser dismisses all of Berkowitz's objections and parries his demand for a chemical analysis by offering a later date for the hearing.

Finally, after a lot of acrimonious wrangling, the two prescribing physicians are called to the stand. One doctor testifies that he has been treating Lenny for "fever and migraine." The medication is Methedrine. The other doctor testifies that he has prescribed, on an earlier occasion, Dolophine. Neither doctor is able to idenify the unlabeled pills. That is the extent of the hearing.

The Commonwealth did not have a strong prima facie case for narcotics violations. Lenny had a lot of drugs in his possession, but he also had a lot of script. The doctors had come to court and backed him up. He had neither bought nor sold any drugs illegally, so far as the evidence showed. What is more, if the case were continued, it would obviously work a hardship on Bruce. He was scheduled to wind up his engagement at the Red Hill that night and fly out to San Francisco to begin work the following week at the Jazz Workshop. If Magistrate Keiser couldn't make up his mind that day, Lenny Bruce would have to fly across the country twice merely to complete a hearing that offered little likelihood of leading to a criminal prosecution. Another magistrate would have thrown the case out for insufficient evidence. E. David Keiser ruled that Lenny must return to continue the hearing on the 9th of October.

When Lenny and Malcolm left the courtroom both of them were boiling. As they walked down the Parkway, Berkowitz recalls:

Lenny took $500—he didn't count it, just a wad—and stuck it in my pocket. "Malcolm, when I'm gone, see if you can get somebody to get Dave Keiser to go for the five hundred dollars." He wanted Keiser to eat shit! I said, "Lenny, *I'm* not going to do it!" He talked to me like I was his child and he was my father: "Don't let it bother you . . . you're not really doing it . . . you're doing it for me, blah, blah, blah." I said, "Maybe I'll keep it!" He said, "Maybe you will."

After that, there was nothing left to say.

Chapter Ten

"ZUG ME, ZEYDAH!
ZUG ME!
TAKE IT,
YOU LITVAK LOLITA!"

Five days after the Philly bust, Lenny opened at the Jazz Work-shop in San Francisco. He had worked out a fast deal over the phone from Philadelphia with Art Auerbach, the club owner. Not only did he insist on his customary conditions, but he now made a new demand: that every show be professionally taped. Whether he was anticipating further trouble with the police or whether he was simply gathering material for a new album is not clear. When Lenny played back the tapes after opening night and found them indistinct, he flipped! He called up a radio engineer he knew, Gene DeAlessi at Station KSFO, and asked him to record the shows. Gene was on duty during the hours of Lenny's show, but he recommended another en-gineer who had just been fired from the station. Everett Hill was actually a good engineer, Gene explained, who had lost the union's support in a dispute with the station because he was too loose in his life-style. That was recommendation enough for Lenny; that night he and Lee Hill met for the first time, beginning what was to become a long and tight relationship. Lee was an Andy Gump type: quiet, loose-strung, with the spaced yet intense look of thousands of West Coast pre-hippies. Nervously fingering a piece of copper wire, he wordlessly concluded his deal with Lenny and took up his station in the basement of the club with a tape machine spooling before his eyes and this extraordinary show pouring into his earphones.

Lenny got off to a very slow start that night. He had kicked after the Philly bust and was feeling ill. When he got out onstage, wearing

his familiar Levis, he looked pale and bloated. He didn't seem eager
to work. For a long time he fussed with a light that was shining in
someone's eyes. Then he did a little free-form rap about that afternoon,
when he had put a quarter into the hotel TV and seen George Shearing
(the blind British jazz pianist) complaining about the idleness of the
blind beggars on American streets. It was so ironic, Lenny thought,
that Shearing—of all people!—should be getting heavy and moralistic
about blind people. The audience wasn't very amused. He changed
topics. Staring at the piano, prominently displayed on the stage, he
speculated: "What if I'm an eccentric millionaire, and the only way I
can go is on the piano—with Kenny Drew playing!" That got a few
laughs, as did his ironic rundown on the current entertainment scene
in Frisco: "Ferlinghetti is going into the Fairmount and the i has a
Gray Line Tour." The show was still dragging when Lenny looked
down at the piano player and abruptly slipped into a vein of pure
recollection.

Thinking out loud, he recalled: "The first gig I ever worked up
here was a place called Ann's 440, which was a place across the street.
And I got a call, and I was working a burlesque gig with Paul Moore
in the Valley (that's the cat on the piano here tonight). And the guy
says: 'There's a place in San Francisco but they changed the policy.'

"Well, what's the policy?

" 'Well, the['re] not there anymore, that's the main thing.'

"Well, what kindava show is it, man?

" 'You know!'

"Well, no, I *don't* know, man. It sounds like kindava weird show.

" 'It's not a show—it's a bunch of *cocksuckers*, that's all. Damn
fag show!'

"Oh, well, that is a pretty bizarre show, I don't know what I could
do in that kindava show.

" 'Well, no . . . it's . . . we want you to *change* all that.'

"Well—I don't—*that's a big gig!* I can just tell them to stop doin'
it." Now Lenny was finally in gear. His reminiscences brought cas-
cading peals of laughter.

Later, he walked to the stage apron, where he perched on a stool.
Barely whispering into the mike, he announced: "I want to help you
if you have a dirty-word problem. There are *none*, and I'll spell it out
logically to you.

"Here is a toilet. Specifically—that's all we're concerned with,
specifics—if I can tell you a dirty-toilet joke, we must have a dirty
toilet. That's what we're talking about, a toilet. If we take this toilet
and boil it and it's clean, I can never tell you specifically a dirty-toilet
joke about this toilet. I can tell you a dirty-toilet joke about the

toilet in the Milner Hotel, or something like that, but *this toilet* is a clean toilet. Now obscenity is a human manifestation. This toilet has no central nervous system, no level of consciousness. It is not aware; it is a dumb toilet; it cannot be obscene; it's impossible. If it could be obscene, it could be cranky, it could be a Communist toilet, a traitorous toilet. It can be none of these things. It's just a dopey toilet, Jim!

"So nobody can ever offend you by telling you a dirty-toilet story . . ."

The room was quiet. The people were no longer laughing. Lenny's lecture on semantics was respectfully received.

Then he drifted back into the private vein again, telling the crowd about his recent difficulties with those nightclub owners whom he imagined were stealing from him.

"I sent a letter to the Thomas Burns Detective Agency," he began. "They are bonded and you know what *that* means; anybody who is bonded could *never* steal from you. Very good . . . write the Burns Agency.

"Get a letter back, get an answer back. St. Louis, Missouri:

"Dear Mr. Bruce:
  Received your letter, blah, blah, blah, blah. We have ticket sellers, bonded. We charge two and a half dollars per ticket seller per hour. We would like to have some more details blah, blah, blah.
                                  Yours truly, C. E. Hoxie"

Reacting to the name, redolent of the red-dirt South, Lenny echoed:
"C. E. Hoxie? C. E. Hoxie! [Southern cracker voice] 'Hoxie, Buddy!' C. E. Hoxie, from the Criminal Correctional Florida Institution for the Criminally Insane, who beat up a spade-fag junkie before he was thrown off the police force, and then became a Pinkerton man and was later arrested for shtupping his stepdaughter. C. E. Hoxie, Hmmmm.

"All right. Now, because I have a sense of the ludicrous, I sent him back an answer, Mr. Hoxie. Dig, because I'm going to miss some of the real goodies I had in the letter, you know. He wants to know details.

"Dear Mr. Hoxie:
  It would be useless to go into the definitive, a breakdown of what the duties will be, unless I can be sure that the incidents that have happened in the past will not be reiterated, such as ticket takers I have hired who claimed they were harassed by customers

who wanted their money back, such as the *fop* in San Jose who is suing me for being stabbed. Claims he was stabbed by an irate customer, and it was a *lie*! It was just a manicuring scissors, and you couldn't see it because it was below the eyebrow, and when his eye was open, you couldn't see it anyway. So—and I have a lot of problems like that . . . my father . . . has been in three mental institutions, and detests the fact that I am in the industry, and really abhors the fact that I have been successful economically and has harassed some ticket sellers. Like in Sacramento, he stood in line posing as a customer and—lightning flash!—grabbed a handful of human feces and crammed it in the ticket taker's face!

And once in Detroit he posed as a customer and he leaned against the booth so the ticket seller could not see him, and he was exposing himself, and had a sign hanging from it, saying: 'When we hit $1500, the guy inside the booth is going to kiss it.' "

More laughs.

Perspiration beads Lenny's forehead. He walks toward the rear of the stage and hits the cymbal.

" 'To-ooooo,' " he croons—prolonging the note as if he were blowing a pitch pipe—"is a preposition.

"*Come* is a *verb*!" He breaks off the song and drops into speech, thumping the snare drum before the word "come," as he does throughout the routine. Reciting with increasing speed, he chants:

" 'To' is a preposition,
'Come' is a verb,
'To' is a preposition,
'Come' is a verb—
The verb intransitive."

Modulating to a softer voice: "To come . . . To come . . ."

Then, flatly, he confides: "I've heard these two words my whole adult life and as a kid, when they thought I was sleeping.

"To come." [Softly, reflectively] "To come."

He explains again: "It's been like a big drum solo."

"Didja come?" He hits the drum.

"Didja come good?" He hits the cymbal.

"Didja come *good*?" He hits both instruments as he repeats the line, occasionally changing the emphasis.

"Didja come *good*?

"Didja come *good*?"

As he races toward the climax, the lines come more urgently. Lenny chants like a kid in the street:

"Didja come good? Didja come good?

"Didja come good? Didja come good?"

"Recitative!" he shouts. Then he drawls in a he-man voice: "I come better with you, sweetheart, than anyone in the whole goddam world! I really came so good.

"I really came so good 'cause I love you."

He sings the next line: "I really came so good."

Then he speaks quietly and very slowly: "I come better with you, sweetheart . . . than *anyone in the whole world!*"

Singing again: "I really came so good, so good." (On this line Lenny starts high, using one note for "I really came," and ending low on "so good," setting up a new rhythm.)

"But don't come in me! Don't come in me!" (Here he sings a do-re-me-do scale, emphasizing the low-noted "me," and starts going faster and louder, building up to a crescendo, with drums rolling in the background.)

"Don't come in me, me, me, me, me! Don't come in me, me, me, mememe. Don't comeinme."

He slows down again: "Don't come in me. Don't come in me," lowering his voice from song to speech.

"Me me, don't come" [Sung again on a high note] "in me, me me."

There's a slight pause and Lenny hits the cymbals, creating a low dissonant clang as he says in a very frustrated, stopped-up, staccato tone: *"I can't come!"* Again he hits the cymbals, and adopts a complaining voice: " 'Cause you don't love me, that's why you can't come.

"I love ya, I just can't come," Lenny sighs. "That's my hang-up. I can't come when I'm loaded, awright?

" 'Cause you don't love me.

"Just what the hell is the matter with you? What has that got to do with loving you? I just can't come, that's all." Lenny slides the two voices together, so that you can't tell anymore who's saying what. He pauses, and peers through the hazy smoke shrouding the stage.

"Now," he says hoarsely, clutching the microphone, "if anyone in this room or the world finds those two words decadent, obscene, immoral, amoral, asexual . . . the words really make you feel uncomfortable . . . *If you think I'm rank for saying it to you, you, the beholder, think it's rank for listening to it,* you probably can't come! . . . And then you're of no use because that's the purpose of life, to re-create it."

It was a typical performance of that period, part free-form rap, part carefully rehearsed shtick, nothing very special, no unusual attitude—just the long haul up from the lassitude of the opening to the genuine engagement of the last portion of the show, when he finally got off. The audience was well satisfied, and Lenny received a big hand before the club began to empty for the next performance.

When Lenny comes out from the backstage, he spots Ralph Gleason sitting with a friend in a corner of the now-empty club and goes over to him. Lenny is sweating and shivering. He'd stopped using after the Philly bust; now he's going through withdrawal. As they sit and talk, Gleason has written, two policemen enter the club and stride purposefully toward the men's room at the back. Gleason suggests that they might be putting the make on the owner. Lenny laughs. He thinks they might want to make a pinch because he has noticed one of the cops at the show both nights. A few minutes later the cops come out and stride up the center aisle of the club and into the street. They are followed by Art Auerbach, the owner of the room.

"Lenny," he says urgently, leaning over to whisper, "he wants to make a bust."

"O.K.," says Lenny, as if it were a matter of no moment. Then he asks where he can find the sergeant.

"Outside," says Auerbach.

"O.K.," says Lenny, "let's go."

All the way to the door, Auerbach keeps up a nervous chattering. "I don't know why they want to do this . . . you weren't out of line tonight . . . blah, blah, blah."

Lenny, eyes forward, lips tight, keeps saying, "It's O.K., man!"

The patrolman is standing outside the club; when Lenny sees him, he says, "Cold night." "Yes," answers the cop, adding, "You understand the sergeant wants to have a word with you." The sergeant appears and begins marching the whole party along Broadway toward Kearny, where there is a police call box in front of Enrico's sidewalk café. Lenny gets into a probing discussion with the sergeant. "Was there a complaint?" he wants to know. The sergeant says something about "an anonymous phone call." Then he tells Lenny:

"I took exception . . . I took offense. We've tried to elevate this street. I'm offended because you broke the law. I mean it sincerely . . . I mean it! I can't see any right, any way you can break this word down . . . Our society is not geared to it."

"You break it down by talking about it," answers Lenny, adding, "How about a word like 'clap'?"

The sergeant barrels out his chest and says, "Well, 'clap' is a better word than 'cocksucker.' "

No sooner does he say that than Lenny snaps back: "Not if you get the clap from a cocksucker!" The crowd that has gathered around the police officers, including the novelist Herb Gold, gets a good laugh out of the gag. The sergeant isn't amused.

Shouting into the call box above the noise from the Finocchio's upstairs in the same building as Enrico's, he yells: "I'm not going to wait here till midnight!" Soon after, three patrol cars pull up, lights flashing, and after them comes the paddy wagon, which backs up to the curb. Meantime there is much haggling over whether the cops should take the license number of the Jazz Workshop now or later. The sergeant is fuming: "I don't want my wife to hear things like that!" Lenny asks, "Did you ever cheat on your wife?"

"Never in twenty years!"

"Not even for one minute?" persists Lenny.

"Not even for one minute!"

Lenny turns away saying, "I can't talk to you, man." The conversation ends for good when the sergeant wrenches open the door of the paddy wagon, makes a gesture toward Lenny, and says, "Mr. Bruce, if you will please step into the car." Lenny gets inside, waves at the crowd, and is driven away.

An hour later, Lenny is back onstage at the Workshop. Art Auerbach, who is a lawyer, has bailed him out for $357.60. Now he is stoked up to white heat. Standing before the crowd in his raincoat, he ad-libs an opening that he was to use many times again: "I better keep my coat on—I may have to go out again." Then, like a kid bursting with news: "Oh, you people don't know what happend to me. I've been busted! No, no! Not in Philly—that was *last* week! Right now! Right after the first show." Then he runs down the arrest for them, going through the conversation with the cops, the confrontation with the lieutenant in the Hall of Justice, and his answer to the question "Do you really think it's right to use a word like that?"—"Well, you use it right here, don't you?" At the end of the show, he is so wound up, he flies off the flat terrain of prose and begins doing poetic loop-the-loops, chanting: "Did the cop ever cop a joint? Did the cop ever get his joint copped?"—and so on ad nuttiness! Just before walking off, Lenny feels a qualm of conscience about not having entertained the audience. He apologizes in words that are prophetic of his whole future course. "I wasn't very funny tonight. Sometimes I'm not. *I'm not a comedian. I'm Lenny Bruce.*"

Whatever hour Lenny got to bed the next morning, he certainly didn't get much sleep. Awakened with loud knocking on his door, he was informed that the management of the hotel no longer desired his presence. For once he was staying in a very good old hotel, the Clift. As soon as they read the story of his arrest in the morning *Chronicle*, they decided that they had to get rid of Lenny Bruce. An intense argument took place, with the hotel manager complaining about the appearance of the room and Lenny threatening a lawsuit. Finally, he packed up and left. He was really starting to feel hounded at this point, but he continued at the club for a few more nights until it was time to fly back to Philadelphia.

On the morning of Monday, October 9, Lenny turned up again at Malcolm Berkowitz's office on 15th Street. He and Malcolm had chatted on the phone a couple of times, Frisco to Philly, but nothing had been said about the bribe. Lenny was dying to hear what had happened. He and Malcolm left the office and went to a little coffee shop. As they confronted each other over their restaurant crockery, Lenny said: "Malcolm, what happened to the five bills?" Malcolm was prepared for the question. Reaching inside the pocket of his tweed jacket, he pulled out a small white envelope. "Here's your money, Lenny," he said—and that was the end of the discussion.

Lenny was really miffed. He grew silent and withdrawn. When the reporters approached Lenny and Malcolm at the hearing, they could see that lawyer and client were not communicating. "What goes?" said one reporter.

"We're like husband and wife," wise-cracked Malcolm; "we have nothing left to say to each other." Berkowitz had plenty to say to the magistrate, however, and the press was extremely attentive because Lenny had made a radical decision. He had resolved to denounce publicly the whole judicial setup in Philadelphia, naming names and quoting prices and proving that in this town justice was for sale. He leaked just enough of this information to the media to have the whole press corps on hand that morning when the hearing began.

When Emmett Fitzpatrick got Lenny's doctor on the stand, he cut right to the heart of the issue. He demanded to know for what disease the doctor had been treating Lenny and whether he had actually told his patient to inject himself with twenty-eight bottles of medicine. The doctor replied that the disease was neuritis and the treatment a drug called Dolophine. The reason for allowing Lenny to inject the drugs was that "oral preparations were not effective."

That testimony should have ended the hearing; but there was a catch. Twenty-seven of the bottles seized by the police bore labels; one, however, a small plastic tube containing a few white tablets, did not. When confronted with this single unlabeled bottle and asked if it was something he had prescribed, the doctor shook his head and said no, *it was not*.

"You're lying!" burst out Malcolm Berkowitz, leaping to his feet to begin the cross-examination. "You're just saying that because you've probably been threatened with prosecution by the narcotics people or Captain Ferguson's Vice Squad. If you had the guts of a titmouse, you'd tell the truth and say this was one of the twenty-eight you prescribed!"

The doctor would make no such admission. So the hearing concluded that on the basis of this one unlabeled bottle, Lenny Bruce could be held for trial as a narcotics violator. Lenny had anticipated this conclusion and arranged his own courtroom in the street. A film made for TV news—whose sound track, alas, has been lost—shows Lenny out in front of the magistrate's office giving a very animated press conference. As the camera soaks in his face, handsome, dark, deeply shadowed around the eyes, with the lips moving fast and the hands speaking eloquently, the words come pouring out. What he had to say was summarized next morning by the *Philadelphia Bulletin*:

> Outside of court, the 35-year-old Bruce charged that an offer had been made to him to have the case forgotten for $10,000.
>
> When he refused, he charged, the price was dropped to $5,000 and then to $3,500.
>
> Bruce said Garfield Levy, Philadelphia criminal lawyer, made the offer.
>
> "He's a liar," Levy said last night when told of Bruce's charge. "He's a sick kid. The kid's crazy."
>
> Levy said he will sue Bruce for slander.
>
> As TV cameras ground and a crowd of about 100 gathered, Bruce stated that Levy made the offer at a backstage meeting at the Red Hill Inn on River Road in Delair, N.J., the night after Bruce's arrest on Sept. 29th.

The balance of the article details every feature of the proffered fix. David Keiser said: "This is the first time I've heard anything of this nature. I saw Bruce for the first time when he was brought before me on the original narcotics charges. What he says outside of court I can't say anything about. But it sounds ridiculous."

However ridiculous Lenny's charges may have sounded to Magistrate Keiser—who was eventually disbarred and committed suicide —the sound of the whistle being blown must have been heard far and wide among the officers of the courts, the district attorneys, and the policemen of the cities where Lenny worked. Police, in particular, must have taken a keen interest in what Lenny had to say. Big-name entertainers who had "problems" were accustomed to paying off to keep the heat from ruining their careers. Lenny knew this as well as any man. What he couldn't seem to get into his head—so schizzily divided by the double standard that allowed him to break the law but

insisted that lawmen be honest—was that calling attention to this arrangement could only bring more heat on his head. Considering the
vulnerability of his own position, his behavior in declaring war on the
cops, D.A.'s and magistrates was suicidal. Worse than paying off wherever he went was the prospect of being arrested everywhere. This
possibility apparently never dawned on him as he played the classic
role of the movie crime buster. The Philadelphia charges were eventually dropped, but henceforth it was open season on Lenny Bruce.

Actually, the people Lenny was denouncing were not ultimately
the people responsible for his predicament. The real question was:
Why was Lenny Bruce being busted for dope in the first place? The
police in many cities knew that Lenny was a junkie. They knew, as
Garfield Levy said, that he was a "legal junkie." Unless they caught
him in the act of scoring in the street, they had nothing to gain by
beating on his door. Why, then, did they come down on him in Philly?

Once you get down to Philadelphia and start talking to people
there—street people who knew Lenny, hung out with Lenny, scored
with Lenny, and formed his local gang—you hear a lot of strange
stories. You hear a lot more such stories from the eminently respectable
people who knew Lenny in the business or who met him socially and
were involved with him in other connections. What comes through
such a large and frequently conflicting body of testimony is the fact
that many people in Philadelphia didn't like the charming Lenny Bruce.
At the peak of his career, Lenny was riding roughshod over convention.
Not only was his act becoming a little too outrageous for many middle-
class patrons, *he* was becoming a little too outrageous for many of the
presumably sophisticated people with whom he associated. Lenny was
flirting outrageously with everybody's wife—and probably balling quite
a few of the ladies. He also couldn't resist putting on the guys: taunting
and teasing them. He seemed to get a kick out of rubbing salt in the
wounds he made in many people's sensibilities. He was becoming
intolerable.

Perhaps the story that sums up this whole scene most perfectly is
that told by Tab Murphy, a skinny, shadowy street cat, who was one
of Lenny's closest buddies in Philly. Old Tab (his Christian name is
Tobias) with his canny, cagey look and elegantly articulated street
slang, his midnight visits and rolled-up-in-newspaper sleeping bags, his
amazing street cat's memory and gossip and moral judgment, offers
the same shrewd measuring of men and motives found in old convicts.
He loved Lenny and recollects him now with mingled humor and pity.
Pity for the way people ripped him off, taking his money to cop and
then coming back an hour later to say, "Man, I was burned!" or worse!
Bringing back some shit that would bend him out of shape, all stiff

and sore up the arm from poison dope. Lenny would lay with these cats night after night. They would hang out at the Harvey House around the corner from the John Bartram. Or they would go out to late-hour joints. They would make the dives and play with the hookers. Some raunchy broad would say to him: "Let me take your joint out and hold it!" Lenny, spaced on shit, would say, "Go ahead! So now you got my joint—so what?" Or, he'd go up to some fat-assed broad and say, "Let me just put my hands on your ass and feel your girdle!" Some of these people were scum: petty thieves and winos, dirty errand boys, the lowest sort of leeches, waiting for Lenny to buy a sandwich so they could eat the half he left.

These cats may have been implicated in Lenny's bust as informers, but the real heat came from above: from those upper-middle-class types who were alternately fascinated and repulsed by Lenny Bruce. Lenny secretly (or not so secretly) loathed these hip businessmen and sub-urban swingers. One night one of them invited Lenny to his house in North Philadelphia. Lenny felt compelled to go because the cat was thinking of bankrolling Lenny's vaguely defined movie project. When Tab and Lenny got to the cat's house, they found a big party in progress. Lenny was the star attraction. He was supposed to get up and put on a show for the people. Something went wrong. Somebody said the wrong thing or showed the wrong attitude. Lenny took offense. When the assembled party gathered around him in their fashionable suits and cocktail dresses, he said, "O.K., people—here's my act!" With that, he whipped out his schlong and pissed on the carpet. Before anybody could catch him, he and Tab beat it out the door.

Someone in that crowd, some nice Florida-tanned businessman or martini-hoisting senior partner or aspiring political big-shot, blew the whistle on Lenny Bruce. He wanted Lenny driven out of town forever; and he knew that the scandal of a drug bust—whatever the outcome —would do the trick. He put pressure on the heat and the cops were sent in to make the kill. Everybody says so in Philly who claims to know the story, and as Lenny would say: "When you hear it from not one but *two* hookers [and a lot of very straight people], you better believe it!"

Lenny's final appearance in Philadelphia was made on the Monday night after the hearing at Count Fleet's pad in South Philly. Malcolm Berkowitz remembers the scene well:

> After the second hearing, he invited me down to Count Fleet's apartment. It was like a mob scene. Everybody was there. I walk in and Lenny comes up to me and grabs me in a bear hug. He kisses me on the cheek. He says: "You're beautiful! You're won-

derful! I've never seen an attorney fight so hard for anybody! Now, *David Blasband is going to draw up my next contract for my next engagement!"* That Lenny sure could snap a shiv—and shove it in!

When Lenny got back to L.A., his principal preoccupation was finding a lawyer to defend him in San Francisco. The lawyer that Lenny finally engaged was Seymour Fried. It was a natural decision because Fried had been Lenny's attorney on numerous previous occasions, representing him in his divorce action, arranging for his official change of name from Schneider to Bruce, and even setting up one of more of those goofy corporations, like Lenny Enterprises 9SV or the one that got the controller general uptight, the corporation so titled 4Q2.

When Lenny got in touch with Fried, the lawyer conceded that he had never tried an obscenity case before; but he concluded that this particular case would pose no difficulty and breezily accepted the assignment. "I had the feeling that I could get thrown it out without a trial," the young, bespectacled attorney recalled. "I told Lenny that I could do this by a motion. In a million ways, I felt that this was going to be a lark. I told that to Lenny. He wanted a trial. He felt the publicity of a trial would help his career tremendously. So we were going to have a trial. I told him I felt that we'd be silly to have a jury trial. He took my advice on that."

Lenny could envision headlines announcing his acquittal. There was no need to doubt such an outcome after the preliminary hearing in San Francisco before Judge George Axelrod. The judge agreed with Fried that a jury would not be necessary, and he also informed Fried that the case would be quickly resolved, leading the lawyer to believe that Lenny would be acquitted.

Fried prepared his brief based on the results of his meeting with Axelrod. It approached the issue of obscenity from a legal standpoint, noting all the constitutional issues involved, including the most recent Supreme Court definition of obscenity, promulgated in 1957 and eventually adopted by every state in the union:

> "Obscene" means that to the average person, applying contemporary standards, the predominant appeal of the matter, taken as a whole, is to prurient interest, i.e., a shameful or morbid interest in nudity, sex, or excretion, which goes substantially beyond customary limits of candor in description or representation of such matters and is matter which is utterly without redeeming social importance.

Clear as this carefully worded statement appears, it had already given rise to numerous legal arguments. Thus, it had been said that what constitutes "shameful" or "morbid" interest (except in the most extreme cases) is likely to be decided not as a matter of law but as the highly subjective reaction of the individual judge. "Prurience," the key term, had been defined by high legal authorities in two distinctly different formulas: as "inciting lustful thoughts" or as "filthy and disgusting." Lenny was pretty safe as far as the first formula was concerned; he was not so obviously blameless in terms of the latter.

The night before the trial, Fried had expected to confer at length with his client. "I'll be back in an hour," Lenny told him, suddenly bolting from Fried's room at the St. Francis Hotel. Lenny never returned. Alone in his room, Fried spent the night reviewing his planned defense. The California Legislature had recently passed legislation amending the two sections of the Municipal Code on which Lenny had been arraigned. He knew the sections would be "preempted," i.e., knocked out. This was merely a formality. His defense would be the Supreme Court decisions, which ruled that performances must be considered in their entirety, rather than in isolated excerpts. He felt the court could certainly find some redeeming social importance in Lenny's monologue if the show was taken as a whole. Lenny was practically a social philospher. What court would find him obscene!

On the morning of November 17th, *The People vs. Bruce* commenced with Judge Axelrod pounding his gavel. "Take the pictures now," he told the press corps assembled in the rear of the courtroom, "take the pictures now." The cameramen scampered down the aisles to make their shots. Spectators rose to get a better view of the action. Some of them stood on their chairs. The flashing strobe lights and loud chatter gave the courtroom a carnival-like atmosphere. Lenny was in costume. He wore his "Chinese rabbi" jacket, a Nehru suit that had been specially made for his court appearance.

While Lenny was still smiling for the photographers and exuding all the confidence in the world, the stern-faced Judge Axelrod put an end to the commotion. He again pounded his gavel and ordered the courtroom cleared.

When order had been restored, Lenny stood erect, like a young priest, and proceeded to plead, as Fried had advised him, not guilty.

District Attorney Schaefer solemnly rose to call the first witness for the prosecution, San Francisco Police Officer James Ryan. After he was seated on the stand, Ryan testified that he listened to Lenny's performance at the Jazz Workshop on the evening of October 4, 1961. Schaefer asked what Lenny had said during the performance which had prompted him to make the arrest.

"Well," said Ryan, "at one particular point in the show, he was talking about some past experiences he had in different clubs that he had worked, and one club in particular was a club that is across the street from the Jazz Workshop called Ann's 440 Club. And while discussing that particular club, he said that after he had seen the club for the first time, that he called his agent and advised him that he wouldn't be able to work in that club because it was overrun with cocksuckers."

Ryan was then asked whether Lenny said anything onstage which warrranted an arrest. Later in the same show, Ryan replied, Lenny discussed how he distrusted the ticket taker at the door. One day, he quoted Lenny as saying, a man would sneak by the ticket taker and situate himself at such a point that the ticket taker would not be able to see him, ". . . and then would expose himself and on the front of it, he would have a sign hanging, 'When we reach fifteen hundred dollars, the man in the front booth is going to kiss it.' " Ryan said that after hearing these remarks he went out into the street and discussed what he had heard with Sergeant James Solden. "We decided there was grounds enough to make an arrest," Ryan recalled.

Lenny sat quietly as Fried proceeded with the cross-examination. Ryan said that he was prompted to investigate the Jazz Workshop after receiving a complaint from his "direct superior that on the evening before, the show in the same place was of a lewd nature." Apparently, no complaint had been lodged by any of the nightclub patrons.

Ryan told the court that Lenny had been performing for about ten to fifteen minutes before using the words about which he had just testified. Fried asked him what the early portion of the act encompassed. "One reference was to a toilet, I believe," Ryan replied, "and the other something to do with butterflies. I don't recall too clearly now."

"Do you have any recollection, sir," said Fried, "of what was said by this defendant prior to the use of the term 'cocksucker' which you just told us he used . . . prior to the use of this particular phrase?"

Ryan cleared his throat. "Well," he said, "I can't give you the exact wording, but in effect what he was saying was that words are dirty only because what people . . . make out of them. And any word, without people's minds making them what they want to make them . . . itself isn't dirty."

"What reference was made by Mr. Bruce to the use of the word 'toilet'?" Fried queried.

"The fact that . . . the word 'toilet' was, to little children . . . a dirty word . . . because, I guess, of what their parents had told them about toilets," said Ryan. "And that if you took a toilet home and boiled it, it wouldn't be a dirty toilet. It would be a clean toilet."

"As a witness to the performance," Fried continued, building to a climax, "is it your feeling, sir, that the performance itself was, although done in a comic media, was intended to be a philosophical discussion of semantics?"

Schaefer quietly objected that this was irrelevant and immaterial.

"I think it calls for an opinion," Judge Axelrod agreed, "but irrespective of that, it wouldn't make any difference what his intentions were. The legislature has enacted a certain law that is worded very clearly. Section 311.6: 'The use of obscene song, ballad or other words in any public place'!"

"Well, of course, your Honor," Fried humbly replied. "that is true, and we have no argument with that. We have an argument, however, with the interpretation of the listener of whatever this defendant may have said and as to whether or not it is obscene as used by the defendant in context with this place at this time. For instance, if we had a situation where a group of very literate language professors had a discussion in semantics, clearly that could never come within the purview of this statute."

"You find it in the dictionary," Axelrod persisted, "then I'll go along with you. I'll sustain the objection."

"Now," said Fried, redirecting his attention to Officer Ryan, "was there any particular word used in the part of the ticket taker that you are referring to as being obscene?"

"Not a word, no," he replied.

"What then prompted you to feel that the statement was obscene?" asked Fried.

"Well, the inference," said Ryan. "I think everyone in the place understood what it meant. I know I didn't have any trouble."

Fried then asked whether there was anything else said by Lenny that led to his arrest.

"Well," Ryan answered, "he has a chant that he gave that particular night and I believe everyone in the place understood, including myself, that the dialogue that was used was meant to be the dialogue that would take place between a man and a woman during an act of sexual intercourse."

"Did Mr. Bruce say that?"

"No, I don't believe he said that."

"And, now, can you tell us a little more about . . . what you heard . . . in regard to the chant?"

"Well, he started off by tapping a drum and saying: 'I'm coming,

I'm coming.' And then later on, in a little higher or a little different pitched voice, he would say: 'Don't come in me. Don't come in me,' and so forth."

"Can you recall, sir, what did he say preceding this chant that you just related to us?"

"I believe again he said that words and actions are dirty because what people make them, not what they are, but what people make of them."

"Now, in the chant itself, it contained no other words than 'come,' is that your testimony?"

"That's correct."

"That you felt was obscene?"

"Yes."

Ryan then repeated that he had determined there were enough grounds to arrest Lenny after conferring with the sergeant outside the club. "Between the two of us, we have probably witnessed more than the average, I'd say, entertainment shows, and so forth, because a lot are in our particular areas, and between the two of us, we neither one had ever heard such an expression used before, so we felt that it warranted arrest."

"Did you have in mind then the language that was used in the Municipal Code Police Section 176, such as 'indecent, immoral, impure, bawdy'—those words?"

"Yes."

"It is your testimony, then, Officer, that because you never heard this before that you felt it was obscene?"

"I didn't say I'd never heard it before. I never heard it used in a show of any kind before."

"Is that the sole test that you applied?"

"The fact that I never had seen it used on television or movie theaters or in any place where people normally assemble for entertainment."

Fried then asked if the word "cocksucker" in any way aroused ". . . any particular feeling in your mind other than you felt it was a dirty word?"

This time Schaefer objected more vehemently.

"I don't think it matters what feelings arise," Axelrod ruled. "You already have a definition of what is obscene by . . . the Penal Code."

Fried argued in vain that the United States Supreme Court had handed down various decisions and that he was trying to elicit testimony from the officer applicable to the Supreme Court's definitions of obscenity.

"We don't need that," said Axelrod impatiently. "Penal Code

311.6 says: '. . . which goes substantially beyond customary limits of candor and description or representation of such matters and is a matter which is utterly without redeeming social importance.' I don't think I need the officer to tell me. I know whether it comes within that definition."

When Axelrod sustained Schaefer's objection, Fried realized that his chances had vanished of winning the case on legal grounds. Axelrod's about-face amazed him. He had prepared to try the case on constitutional issues. He was not properly prepared to try the case on facts. Now, Fried would have to play it by ear.

The second witness, Sergeant James Solden, took the stand and substantially supported Ryan's testimony.

As Schaefer slowly approached the witness stand, he asked Solden to relate the conversation he had had with Lenny just prior to the arrest.

Fried sprung to his feet and objected on the grounds that the people had not yet proved that a crime had been committed. Doggedly, in a last-gasp effort to restore his planned defense, he reminded the court that it was distinctly unconstitutional to select excerpts from a given piece of material and to rely upon such excerpts in determining whether or not the material was obscene.

"You have got to realize from the testimony that is being adduced here so far," Axelrod declared, raising his voice, "had it been a professor lecturing in a college who is discussing words and giving a lecture to students and using . . . these . . . vulgar words, that would be one sense . . . the sense in which he used them and the reference to which he made . . . In the manner in which the words were used by the defendant, they *were* obscene. I'm not picking out a part. I'm picking it out the way the officer testified he said he heard it. It makes a difference."

Ironically, Axelrod was now using the same argument previously used by Fried—the analogy of the professor using vulgar words before his class. When Fried used this analogy in arguing that the sense in which the dirty words are used is important, the court answered that intentions were irrelevant in the face of the law. Without realizing it, Axelrod was supporting Fried's earlier contention while answering his latest objection.

Seasoned courtroom reporters, who had patiently waited to hear Bruce, were amazed by the court's statement. They perceived that Axelrod had failed to discern the difference between the constitutional issues of this case and the petty issues of everyday misdemeanor work normally brought before this court. Axelrod stated that he felt the words, in the manner used by Lenny, were obscene: this was the whole issue in the case. Quite prematurely, he was drawing a legal and factual conclusion, thereby prejudging the case before hearing all the evidence.

Sgt. Solden recalled his conversation with Lenny prior to the arrest. He stated that he asked Lenny "if he felt his choice of words were proper for a nightclub, for the public, and Mr. Bruce's reply was: '. . . there are a lot of cocksuckers around so why shouldn't I speak about them?' "

Schaefer rested the state's case.

Lenny was still confident and waited patiently to take the stand.

Fried began his defense by rising from the counsel table and renewing his objection that no corpus delicti or proof of the elements of the crime were presented by the prosecution, that ". . . . the dominant theme of the material taken as a whole must appeal to the prurient interests."

"Whether a word is obscene is the real question," he concluded, "and whether it is obscene depends on whether it appeals to prurient interests!"

"I don't need any points and authorities to tell me that this language which was used and which was quoted by the officer and the context in which it was used is obscene," Axelrod replied with great anger. "Now, if the Supreme Court takes a different view, that is up to them! But to me, it is obscene and I certainly wouldn't let my grandchildren sit in and listen to a show like this. Now that is my viewpoint."

His statement echoed through the silent courtroom. Fried was stunned. *"Gornisht helfen* here [Nothing will help here]," he muttered to Lenny, thoroughly demoralized. Lenny's face reddened. He leaned across the table, and for the first time addressed Fried in rapid-fire words. He pointed out that Axelrod's grandchildren certainly would not have had access to his performance at the Jazz Workshop, even if they were accompanied by the judge. Even more apparent, Lenny declared, was Axelrod's legal error. What he would allow his grandchildren to witness was obviously not the standard used to determine obscenity.

Even Schaefer was shocked by Axelrod's statement. Later he admitted that at this point he became infuriated at the shabby treatment Lenny and Fried were receiving.

Lenny now became passionately involved in the proceedings. He waited nervously to take the stand, while Axelrod continued his premature evaluation of the testimony.

"And the other feature I think is obscene is the drum act, as described," the judge declared. "The manner in which they were spoken, I think the whole context, in my opinion, is obscene, so that is my ruling."

That was as much as Fried could take. "My stomach hit the ground, and I knew I was in for it," he later recalled, "and I had to get out of this thing!"

"If the court please," he interjected, "I won't belabor the point any further with oral argument."

He then submitted his memorandum of points and authorities for the court to consider and quickly played the tape recording of Lenny's October 4th performance.

Axelrod ordered the barely audible tape stopped midway through its playback. "I think I have heard enough," he sighed, after hearing the word "cocksucker." "If the Supreme Court doesn't think that is obscene, then I don't know."

"Your Honor," Fried desperately pleaded, "if the court please, that is one word in an hour tape. That is the only word that could possibly be considered obscene."

"That is enough in my book," Axelrod snapped. Then, he apparently had second thoughts about quashing the evidence. "I mean," he stammered, "if you want to play the rest, all right . . . If it is anything like the other, I don't want to hear any more, but go ahead. That is your privilege. I can't stop you. It is a matter of testimony."

"It obviously wasn't a case where you're picking up a guy on Market Street because he turned around and called some guy a cocksucker," Schaefer said privately, after listening to that portion of the tape. "You could see immediately that Lenny had a message to convey and was sincere and honest about it."

Fried again turned on the tape recorder but the tape had jammed. Frantically, he tried to respool the tape. His efforts were fruitless. He pivoted toward Lenny and muttered, "The damn tape recorder won't work!"

Lenny glanced at the press gallery and threw up his hands. His impatience could no longer be restrained. He ordered Fried to put him on the stand. Fried then called Lenny as the defense's only witness and hastily laid the proper foundation for the introduction of the tape into evidence. Here was the chance Fried had promised Lenny to convey his message to the world.

By the time Lenny strode to the witness stand and took the oath, he was seething with anger. He had pinned Axelrod as a loathsome stereotype: a sour-breath Bronx mockie brought up during the Depression, with all the bitterness of that period; a mean-spirited moralist: in a word, an ugly human being. Now here was this Jewish sourpuss sitting up there behind the bench handing out sixty days to this poor guy and ninety days to that poor guy, without a semblance of sympathy or compassion or even fairness. The judge was obviously prejudiced; he made a mockery of justice. So Lenny felt he ought to give him a taste of his own priggishness. He determined to take every opportunity presented by his questioning to lay moralisms right in the judge's moralistic punim.

When Fried asked him the first question, whether the tape just heard was in fact a recording of the show in question, Lenny answered: "The show was made for the purpose of keeping the standards of this community at a certain level," and then looking directly at the judge, "and having the children's interests at heart."

"I'm glad my children are not raised under the same standards as yours," Axelrod bristled.

Fried repeated his question concerning the identity of the tape.

"I must to . . . if this is the tape that I made . . . to question a father's concept of God made the child's body," sputtered Lenny, wildly searching for the words of a routine he often did, "but qualified the creativity by stopping it above the kneecaps and resuming it above the Adam's apple, thereby giving lewd connotation to the mother's breast that fed us and the father's groin that bred us, then this is the tape, yes."

Fried offered the tape into evidence and again asked to play it.

"The only testimony I'm concerned about is what the officer testified," Axelrod declared with exasperation. "I don't want to hear the whole show. The officer didn't testify that the whole show was objectionable. It was three portions. The one that you just played there was one of them. The other one was the drum act and the third was the reference to the ticket-taker. Now, *Those* were the three. If you want to play that portion of it and you think there is any redeeming features [sic] to that portion of the show, you can play it. But . . . we are not objecting to the whole show."

Fried was still arguing that the tape had to be heard in context as he turned on the recorder. This time it operated properly. But the tape recorder was so weak, it still could barely be heard.

Suddenly, Lenny pushed back his chair on the witness stand and jumped to his feet. "I agree with the court," he shouted, interrupting Fried. "Those who have ears will hear us, and so I waive the right to play this."

"Why don't you let your attorney try your case?" Axelrod archly advised Lenny. "You're a better actor than a lawyer." Lenny slumped in his chair, seething.

"I have had enough experience sitting in this court in this particular department to know what is obscene or not obscene," said Axelrod, replying to Fried. "This is what is known as the Women's Court, and I think I am pretty much of an expert of what is obscene and not—at least according to San Francisco standards. In my opinion, this is obscene language, no matter how it was used. *The decision of the court is that he's guilty based upon the evidence. I'm finding him guilty.*"

"Lenny was visibly shaken and shattered," Fried recalls. "He was demoralized and disturbed by what he considered to be the indignities of the attitudes. He adopted this particular judge's attitude as being the attitude of the law."

Fried then made a motion for a continuance in order to procure more points and the authorities, as well as a typed transcript of the tape recording in its entirety.

Axelrod granted a thirty-day continuance, stating that the defendant should have every opportunity to present his case properly, especially the chance to play the tape recording under better circumstances.

"My feeling at this point after what I've heard, I'm ready to make a decision," Axelrod said. But he could not resist this one remaining occasion to chide the defendant. "It is my understanding he's got a show Sunday, a concert at the Curran Theater in San Francisco," he declared. "If there is any repetition of this conduct at that show, I'll deal with him accordingly. The next time he comes to court, he better bring his toothbrush with him."

Every antagonistic impulse in Lenny's being flared up! Two nights later, he walked out onstage at the Curran Theater ready to kill both Axelrod and Keiser in a full-scale public execution. Unfortunately, he picked one of the worst nights in the history of the Bay Area to make his appearance. The rain came down in such torrents that most people were afraid to drive. In a hall that seats 1,768, Lenny got about 300 people. It hardly mattered, however; Lenny laughed off the size of the crowd in his opening fantasy, and then settled down to the business at hand: his recent busts in Philadelphia and San Francisco. In each case, he was determined first to explain exactly what had happened in court and how manifestly prejudiced both magistrates had been. He went over the obvious points in a style of tense, struggling, pent-up anger and frustration, the pushes and pulls in his guts being almost audible as he emoted into the mike. After he had gotten through a tense but not very detailed picture of his hearing before Judge Axelrod, he took a breather and explained to the audience that since the judge made such a mockery of justice, Lenny felt he was entitled to do the same. In fact, he had given a lot of thought to just what he would do the next time he had to appear in court. His plan for bugging the judge and sabotaging the legal process was hilariously funny. It sounded like something out of *The Magic Christian*.

Lenny would get himself a screaming faggot for an attorney, some "fop" who was too fruity to practice but who had been educated in law by his doting parents and hidden away in an accounting firm. This queen would get himself all fapitzed in a chic Continental suit and then begin camping it up in court. Putting on his high, shrill Kiki voice, Lenny vocalized some of the exchanges. "Now, offithah, when Mr. Bruce said—Whoops! Oh, is it all right to say it? He-he-he! Well! Now, blah, blah, blah." Finally, when the fruit has driven the judge up the wall, he screams one last time and falls to the floor in a dead faint!

Then Lenny's next lawyer takes over. This one is the former mayor of a small town in the Deep South. He's fifty-seven years old with silver-gray hair and an obvious respect for God, country, and mother. The only problem is that he tahahoks so-ho slooooooooooooooooooow that he drives everyone crazy. He has a couple of other problems, too. Right in the middle of his leisurely rhetorical perambulations—"Now, Yah Honor, Ah'd like to cite a case: the case of *Wahton vs. Wahdell*. 'Scuse me. Snnnnirf!" Wow! He takes a great big snort of snuff, then offers some to the bench! When the judge implores him to make haste, he comes on with all that Southern butterball bullshit, commending the judge on his war record and praising his mother and bowing politely to "mah wuthy opponent." As if all this isn't bad enough, Lenny has planted a couple of people in the courtroom, a juror and a spectator, who occasionally burst into applause for the judge or yell out, "That's right, Judge! He was way out of line!" Finally, the poor magistrate can't stand it anymore. He gets up from the bench and walks out of the courtroom.

The final plan was to take vengeance on Judge Axelrod and make him pay according to the strictest poetic justice. What had bugged Lenny most about the judge was his constant flaunting of his grandchildren, as if the fact that his kids had kids made him some sort of morally unassailbale human being. So Lenny had hatched this plot to entrap the judge and expose his human fallibility. The whole plot hinged on Lenny's intimate knowledge of this type of Jewish man: his prejudices and weaknesses. For example, you could never tempt a mockie like this with straight-out sexual allurement. He would never go for it. You had to disguise the sex with innocence—innocence and *illness:* because Jews always identify with disease. So here was the plan, he whispered conspiratorially to the audience: he would set things up with Honey, his old lady—"who looked like a cross between a kindergarten teacher and a $500-a-night hooker"—to meet the judge in an elevator.

Now, I tell her, "Sweetie, look, do me a favor. I want to entrap the judge. You gotta be very cool, you can't come on with him. He'll freeze right away. Be very cool. Meet in the elevator of the courthouse. Have a heart attack, a slight one."

And she goes into the elevator: "OH!" *Thunk.*

He runs over: "What's the matter with you?" Rubs her wrist, gives her the dopey Jewish-doctor speech: "Look, you're a young girl, your body is like an automobile. If you give it too much gas, and the clutch—" That crappy dumb parallel. All right.

But to get him to a pad is very tricky. Drive drive drive drive. If she said she had to change clothes, he would freeze. 'Cause he'd wait in the car. To change a bandage—that's legit. He can watch her take off a bandage, nothing dirty about a bandage. But a bandage may make it less than sensual.

Supp-Hose! Perfect. A little varicosity. "*Oi*, got Supp-Hose?" And he's digging her. How do we get her over to the sack? Another heart attack.

"OH!" *Boom.*

He runs over.

"What's the matter, *another* heart attack?"

"Oh, Judge, I'm just so embarrassed, I'm just in from Oklahoma . . ."

It's horny enough to be white, but *Oklahoma*—it's such an *ofay,* the Jews'll go blind if they look at her.

"I'm in from Oklahoma. I was doin' a benefit for crippled Catholic Jewish war children from the Ronald Reagan post in memory of Ward Bond. And you've been so good to me . . ." And she kisses his hand, very dry, very respectable, except a little wet at the end.

Now one deft move—a pop-off bra, toreador pants. *Pow!*

Now we have to record all this, see? How to record it? Six months previous, a genius operation, a tape recorder set inside the throat: no wires, one small goiter scar.

Now the damnation.

CHICK: Judge?

JUDGE: Uh.

CHICK: I wanna tell you something, but I'm afraid that, oh, that you're gonna think that I'm, oh, perverse.

JUDGE: Look, who's to say vuts normal? It's what?

CHICK: Well, I—do you know why I was attracted to you?

JUDGE: Why?

CHICK: You remind me of my grandfather.

JUDGE: That makes you hais [hot] meshugana, you like that, right?

CHICK: Yeah, and I would, it would sorta knock me out if you would sort of enjoy the fantasy with me, and imagine I was your granddaughter.

JUDGE: All right, meshugana, you like that? What'll I say?

CHICK: Just, "*Zug* me, Zeydah."

JUDGE: Vuss?

CHICK: Tell me I'm only six years old.

JUDGE: All right. You're six years old.

CHICK: Do you like giving it to your granddaughter?

JUDGE: Do I? *Take it! Give it to me, tochter! That's it, take it! Sock it to me! Give it to me! you Litvak Lolita! I'm gonna give it to you—and your pony too!*

That's all. Play that back in court:

TAPE RECORDING: *Give it to me Zeydah! Rip me Zeydah! Sock it to me Zeydah! Give it to me, you Litvak Lolita!*

That's the end of the lower court. That just blows it right there!

Lenny was so carried away by his fantasies and his emotions and all the new ideas that had come swarming into his head since his busts that he couldn't get off the stage that night. He raved on for over *three hours,* and he didn't lose a single listener until the last twenty minutes.

If he had only retained the attitude he evinced during the Curran concert, he would never have succumbed to the madness of his later years. He possessed a magic weapon in his humor that could defend him and revenge him and vindicate him against any amount of judicial prejudice. The pity is that he never recognized his own strength and always insisted on playing the game in the terms established by his enemies. Once he started taking the courts and the lawyers seriously, he was doomed.

In the aftermath of the municipal court fiasco, Fried made plans to move for a jury trial and ask for a mistrial on the basis that Lenny had never been properly arraigned on the amended complaint. But Lenny had no desire to win the case on such a technicality. He felt that his right to say what he wished must be proven. Consequently, he dismissed Fried and began looking for another attorney.

Several weeks later, Lenny visited the City Lights Book Store and got into a conversation with Lawrence Ferlinghetti. Eager to help, Ferlinghetti suggested that Lenny contact Albert Bendich, a former staff counsel for the American Civil Liberites Union in northern California and now a University of California (Boalt Hall) professor. Bendich was one of a team of three lawyers who, in 1957, had successfully defended the City Lights Book Store and its right to sell Allen Ginsberg's poem *Howl*. The case ranked as the most significant obscenity proceeding until that time in the Bay Area.

Bendich had never seen Lenny work, nor had he heard any of his four record albums. He invited Lenny to his home in Berkeley, where Lenny played the entire tape of the performance for which he had been arrested. Bendich listened intently and readily agreed to take the case.

The lawyer studied the transcript of the trial during the Christmas holidays, and made a court appearance before Axelrod. On January 22nd, he made a motion for a new trial. He wanted to present the case in a different manner from hitherto, and he wanted a jury trial because the obscenity law was based upon community standards and he deemed it essential to have as broad a cross-section of the community as possible. Twelve persons seated on a jury would give him a better chance than one person seated on the bench.

Lenny received Bendich's letter outlining the prospective courses of action in Chicago, where he was appearing at the Gate of Horn and staying at the Hotel Maryland. While he enthusiastically approved Bendich's thinking, he began to have second thoughts about going to trial with an attorney who was not well known outside of the San Francisco area. His confidence had been shaken by the first trial. He was still disillusioned and he had even thought of handling the case himself. One night, after his last show, he returned to his tiny hotel room and paced the floor. He kept telling himself, as he watched the traffic flowing twelve stories below on Rush Street, that the publicity accompanying the second trial would be a distinct aid to his career. His advisers had also agreed that a more prominent attorney would add to the publicity.

Finally, Lenny took a pencil and paper and wrote to Jack Sobel in New York. The letter was hurried, his scrawled handwriting moving in and out of the margins.

Dear Jack:

If I go to trial and lost I have to appeal the trial fly back and forth another time makes spend $750 although it is only a misdemeanor. I guess you know I don't want to lose, I'd like you to get me the best lawyer possible. I don't have that at present. Marvin Beli or Bel eye is how it sounds, phonetically.

I want to take over get me the best representative you can. Al

Bendich is the attorney on the case now he wants $200 to get character witnesses why don't you introduce yourself mail wise.

Only twelve hours later, Sobel received a wire reaffirming Lenny's desire to hire Melvin Belli, the flamboyant San Francisco attorney.

PLEASE MAKE SURE YOU PROTECT ME IN SAN FRANCISCO MARVIN BELLI HE IS THE MAGIC MAN LOVE LENNY BRUCE

Belli was unavailable but volunteered to help in the future. Lenny received the news from Sobel in Miami Beach, where he had begun a $2,500-a-week engagement at the Bel Aire Hotel. He still insisted that he wanted a prominent attorney. Then, one night, as he sat in his room at the Brazil Hotel watching the *Sam Benedict* show on television, he found another Magic Man. The program was a fictionalized version of the career of Jake Ehrlich, a dapper San Francisco lawyer who had defended Harry Bridges and other famous figures. Unknown to Lenny, Ehrlich had donated his services as the principal attorney on the *Howl* case, the same action in which Bendich had functioned as counsel on behalf of the American Civil Liberties Union.

On Wednesday, February 28, five days before the trial, Lenny phoned Ehrlich, who seemed interested. Then he called Bendich, suggesting that he associate with Ehrlich in Lenny's defense. Bendich refused; later that day, he received a terse wire from Miami Beach.

Dear Al,
Our deal was you handle my case for about $1,500 plus $250 for rounding up character witnesses. Seymour Fried bowed out gracefully and you bowed in at my specific request consistent with university law you teach at California. I assume if client wants other counsel, first counsel should be paid even if you don't do work for trial, etc. So this wire is notice from me, Lenny Bruce, that I will pay you $350 for your services and discharge you officially as my counsel and it is my intent to use Jake Ehrlich as my attorney and would be grateful if you would turn over all material to him and tell him of my financial stress. I will have a thousand dollars in cash for him before he goes to court and $350 for you March 5th. Cordially. Love.

Within twenty-four hours, Bendich met with Municipal Court Judge Clayton Horn, who had been assigned to the case in place of Axelrod. He informed the judge in his chambers of the difficulties he had been experiencing with Lenny and considered making a motion to be allowed to withdraw as his counsel.

Part of the trouble between Lenny and Bendich concerned the manner in which the case would be controlled. Bendich recalls: "I insisted that if I were going to be the attorney in the case that I would have to have control of it, that it would be presented in the way that I thought was my legal responsibility to present it."

Bendich never turned over the material to Ehrlich because the latter advised Lenny to retain his original counsel after learning that Bendich had been intimately involved in the case for months. The night before they went to court, Lenny agreed to Bendich's conditions. The jury selection, list of witnesses, and general strategy would all be decided by Bendich.

The second trial began on the morning of March 5, 1962, before Judge Horn. No special significance could be attached to Horn replacing Axelrod, the practice in the Hall of Justice at that time being that one set of judges tried non-jury cases and a second set handled jury trials.

Five years earlier, Horn had freed several teenagers in a misdemeanor trial on the condition that they attend *The Ten Commandments*. Horn had been attacked by the *San Francisco Chronicle*, which observed that it was not within his province to mix law with religion. *The Ten Commandments* affair did, however, indicate that Horn harbored a more liberal attitude than his predecessor, Judge Axelrod.

Albert Wollenberg, Jr., became the new prosecuting attorney, replacing Arthur Schaefer, because the case had been shifted to a different department at the Hall of Justice.

Wollenberg and Bendich were busily engaged in the process of selecting a jury for *The People vs. Bruce*, when a bailiff marched up to the bench and interrupted the proceedings. He handed Judge Horn a special delivery letter that had been mailed from Los Angeles.

Horn temporarily halted the jury selection, adjusted his eyeglasses, and carefully read the letter. It appeared to startle him. Immediately, he called a recess and requested that Bendich and Lenny accompany him to his chambers. Bendich listened in amazement as Horn read the typewritten letter aloud:

Dear Judge Horn:
   The monstrous rumor Judge Horn feels the defendant takes the matter lightly motivates this letter. Odious is the matter, my arrest for obscenity has enfilmed my career with a leperous stigma that St. Francis could not kiss away at ethereal peak. Objectivity is

impossible for me. I have searched the matter out morally—"Let yea cast the first stone"—is the answer I keep hearing.

Lest this letter be misinterpreted, its intent, not to placate, but to clarify a preconceived concept of my attitude.

This inference you would pre-judge is the fear of the courts as a result of Axelrod Palace. His statement "I don't understand a thing on this tape but, as far as I'm concerned, he's guilty"— without hearing one witness.

Sincerely,
Lenny Bruce

The letter lacked a signature. Horn asked Lenny if he had written it. Lenny admitted its authorship but tried to explain that he had not written it to the court but rather to the judge as a personal note. He said that a friend had typed and mailed it from Los Angeles. Bendich, who was openly distressed, said that he could only hope that Judge Horn would view this embarrassing letter in the context of the special problems with Lenny of which he had spoken to the judge on the preceding Friday. Lenny could not appreciate the gravity of the matter. He declared passionately that he was not at fault, remarking lamely that the post office had disturbed the court and that it should be held in contempt.

Judge Horn thereupon found Lenny—not the post office—in contempt of court. Bendich attempted to explain that Lenny had not meant to be sarcastic or contemptuous. His letter was the product of his naiveté in legal matters and his fear of losing after an unfair trial. Judge Horn insisted that the charge must stand, but deferred sentencing until the end of the proceeding.

After leaving the judge's chambers, Lenny walked back solemnly to the counsel table. He was costumed in his black frock coat, buttoned to the chin in the manner of an ecclesiastical vestment. (The rationale for wearing such bizarre garb in court was that he didn't want to adopt the customary tie and jacket.) As soon as the examination of jurors resumed, Lenny's mood brightened. The observations he whispered in Bendich's ear had a determining effect on the selection of the four men and eight women who comprised the panel.

Following Wollenberg's short introductory statement, Patrolman James Ryan was called to the stand. He testified much as he had at the first trial. When Wollenberg began to question the witness about Lenny Bruce's testimony at this trial, Bendich objected, as had Fried, that the prosecution had failed to establish that a crime had been committed, remarking that no corpus delicti had been produced and that therefore it was objectionable to bring in an admission made by the defendant in a previous action.

Unlike Judge Axelrod, who had insisted that the defendant's use of the word "cocksucker" was innately obscene, Horn postponed his ruling on Bendich's objection and suggested that Wollenberg defer this question until the rebuttal.

Wollenberg asked Officer Ryan next to repeat his conversation with Lenny following the Jazz Workshop performance. Bendich objected that the conversation was irrelevent until the corpus delicti had been established. When the objection was sustained, it began to appear that this trial was destined to take a different course from its predecessor.

Bendich began his cross-examination of Ryan by asking him to name other nightclubs on his beat. Wollenberg objected that this was irrelevant.

"We're talking about community standards," Bendich argued, revealing the heart of his defense.

The objection was overruled. Bendich had won another major point.

Ryan named five neighboring nightclubs—the Gay Nineties, Casa Madrid, Moulin Rouge, Finocchio's, and La Casadoro. He was then asked what his standards were for judging whether or not a show was objectionable.

"Well," said Ryan, "any part of the show that would violate any police or penal code sections that we have."

Bendich resumed his cross-examination of Ryan on Tuesday morning, seeking first to elicit from him the fact that other clubs along Broadway—like the notorious Finocchio's—presented shows that were just as unconventional as Lenny's. He also quizzed the patrolman about the word "cocksucker," which the officer admitted he had heard before, even in his precinct station. Having underscored the fact that the police had made the arrest without receiving any complaint from the patrons of the club, Bendich concluded his questioning.

Surprisingly, at this moment the People rested its case. No special efforts were made to convict Lenny; the matter was being treated as if it were a routine misdemeanor. Bendich was taking no chances; he had lined up an impressive array of expert witnesses to attest to the social and artistic value of Lenny's performance. His first witness was Ralph J. Gleason, who was eminently qualified as an expert, having written about Lenny's work and attended the performance in question.

"Mr. Bruce's performances are improvisatory and spontaneous, creative comedy in nature," he explained. "Therefore, the performances will vary from night to night and even from show to show, in quality as well as content. And some of the performances will be very good and some of them will not be so good. And this performance was of the same general nature as the continuing satirical social comment that he engages in." The theme of the show on the night in question, he noted, "was a social criticism of stereotypes and of the hypocrisy of contemporary society." Asked to recall the themes Lenny developed during the course of that evening's performance, Gleason noted: "He attempted to demonstrate to the audience a proposition that's familiar to students of semantics, which is that words have been given in our society almost a magic meaning that has no relation to the facts, and I think that he tried in the course of this show that evening to demonstrate that there is no harm inherent in words themselves."

Gleason testified next to the context in which the word "cocksucker" was used during the show. Gleason felt that the use of this particular word had artistic relevance, since it was common in show-business language to use the word "cocksucker" to describe homosexuals, just as other people use the words "faggot" or "fairy." Ironically, it had taken one trial and a sizable portion of a second before the meaning and usage of the word had been properly explained.

Bendich then asked whether Lenny's performance, in the judgment of the witness, had social importance.

"All of Mr. Bruce's performances do," replied Gleason. The social importance of the use of "cocksucker," he explained, was "the way in which one aspect of our society functions and some of the hypocrisy inherent in the fact that you can discuss these things in one sense and in another you aren't supposed to."

Gleason went on to explain that a Lenny Bruce performance had to be taken in its entirety in order to be properly understood. He then read an article, which had been introduced into evidence by Bendich, written by Nat Hentoff in *Commonweal*, a Catholic intellectual weekly. Like Gleason, Hentoff was a jazz and social critic of liberal persuasion. Hentoff's article attested to Lenny's social significance.

Wollenberg began questioning Gleason about the contents of a *New York Times* article about Lenny, written by Arthur Gelb. The prosecutor was interrupted by Judge Horn.

"Mr. Wollenberg," said the balding magistrate, "at the sake of being facetious—I'd like to carry on the trial without further levity. But at the sake of being facetious—your shirttail is out."

Lenny folded his arms akimbo and, like everyone else in the courtroom, howled over Wollenberg's unintentional breach of etiquette.

"I don't think it's terribly relevant to the issue here, Your Honor," the lawyer stammered, his face reddening. He tucked in his shirttail.

Gleason read Gelb's article into the record with great flair, along with a *Reporter* magazine piece written by Hentoff that dealt with the work of Bruce in a critical and analytical fashion. Gleason concluded his testimony by affirming that his prurient interests had never been aroused by one of Lenny's performances.

Lou Gottlieb took the stand next, as the second expert witness. He testified that he had published articles dealing with the work of jazz performers and had reviewed the work of comedians. "Like many other professional comedians," he said, "I make every attempt to see Lenny Bruce."

Bendich asked the nature of the themes presented by Lenny in his performances.

"May I say that Mr. Bruce's attempt is to evoke laughter, which he does supremely well," replied Gottlieb. "In so doing he caricatures society, emphasizes certain elements which strike him as grotesque . . . he creates sympathy, again as a by-product, within his audience for socially produced problems, such as racial and religious bigotry, perhaps even narcotics addiction, the problems of inverts and other people whose problems, I think, must be regarded sympathetically before they shall ever be ameliorated."

"You say the main theme of Mr. Bruce is to get laughter," Wollenberg asked, beginning his cross-examination.

"That's the professional comedian's duty," Gottlieb replied.

"I see. And do you see anything funny in the word 'cocksucker'?"

"To answer that question with 'yes' or 'no' is impossible, Your Honor," said Gottlieb, addressing Judge Horn.

"You may answer it 'yes' or 'no' and then explain your answer," the court ruled.

"I found it extremely unfunny as presented by Mr. Wollenberg, I must say," Gottlieb responded, timing his barb perfectly. Lenny and Bendich both joined the spectators in uninhibited laughter.

"All right, wait a minute, wait a minute!" shouted Horn, rapping his gavel for the first time.

Gottlieb was again asked whether he found anything funny in the word "cocksucker."

"I do not," he said, "but as Mr. Bruce presents his performances he creates a world in which normal dimensions . . . become . . . how shall I say? Well, they are transmuted into a grotesque panorama of contemporary society, into which he places slices of life, *phonographically* accurate statements that come out of the show-business world . . . and sometimes the juxtaposition of the generally fantastic frame of reference that he is able to create and the startling intrusion of slices of life in terms of language that is used in these kinds of areas, has an extremely comic effect."

Bendich called next a professor of speech at Berkeley, Dr. Don Geiger, who read a John Berryman poem containing the word "fuck"; a high school teacher and his wife, Mr. and Mrs. Kenneth Brown, who had been members of the audience and had volunteered to testify; a writer named Nathan Asch; a former deputy D.A. of San Mateo County, Clarence Knight; and an assistant professor of English at Berkeley, Robert Tracy, who pointed out the analogies between Lenny's routines and the satires of Aristophanes, Rabelais, Chaucer, and Joyce by reading sexually explicit passages from the latter two authors.

The parade of witnesses made Lenny restless. He cupped his hands and whispered in Bendich's ear, asking to be allowed to take the stand. Bendich shrugged him off. Several minutes later, during the testimony of Grover Sales, another witness to the October 4th show, Lenny again distracted Bendich. He wanted him to play the tape. Bendich told him to have patience.

Sales testified to the style and themes employed by Lenny at the Jazz Workshop and compared his style to Joyce's stream of consciousness. The theme of religious hyprocrisy he connected with similar attitudes in G. B. Shaw and Dostoevsky.

Wollenberg, sated by this time with the pyramiding literary references, finally asked Sales whether he enjoyed Lenny's performance. Like the other defense witnesses, most of whom gave qualified assents to this question, Grover Sales answered hesitantly: "I would say that it was profoundly moving and emotionally disturbing in an unforgettable way."

Wollenberg then attempted to lead Grover into admitting that the word "cocksucker" was not essential to the show.

"It's very difficult for me to answer that question without saying that anything that Mr. Bruce sees fit to put in his show is necessary to that show," he replied evasively.

"In other words," Wollenberg suggested, "you'd give Mr. Bruce a license to say anything he wants, because he's in show business?"

"It is not my place to give Bruce a license," the witness replied. "I paid two-and-a-half to get in the Jazz Workshop, and the only way I could register my protest, if he offends my sensibilities, is to walk out of the Jazz Workshop without hearing him through. And I assume that anyone else that paid two-fifty has a similar right." Many spectators applauded this statement, which again made the point that nobody had objected to Lenny's show except the police.

The reporters, who had been amused repeatedly by the messages

Lenny would pin on his back, now became aware of the disturbance at the counsel table. Lenny and Bendich were arguing vehemently in whispers, their heads no more than an inch apart. Apparently, they were fighting over whether Lenny should be allowed to take the stand. Bendich felt his case was going well; he was dubious about whether Lenny could control himself on the stand. Lenny stabbed his chest with an imaginary dagger, suggesting that Bendich was being treacherous. "You want to fire me?" Bendich said hoarsely. Lenny insisted that he must testify. Finally, he won.

The clerk of the court called him. He walked toward the witness stand clad in tight white pants, a faded zippered jacket, and a pair of slightly torn white boots—his third striking costume in three days. His eyes rolled toward the ceiling as he took the oath. Two chairs stood side by side on the stand. Lenny sat in the wrong one. With great embarrassment, he moved to the chair equipped with an overhead microphone.

He shook his head, took a deep breath, and clasped his hands behind his head as Bendich began the interrogation. Lenny, his voice sharp as a guillotine, acknowledged that he had used the word "cocksucker" during the Jazz Workshop performance. He testified that he could not remember every word of his act, insisting that without a verbatim recital the meaning of what he said might be lost.

Bendich noted that Wollenberg had previously stated that Lenny used the phrase "Eat it." He asked Lenny if he had used that phrase on the night in question. Crossing and uncrossing his legs, Lenny replied that he did not use the phrase "Eat it." Instead he had said, "Kiss it."

He was then asked if there was a significant difference between the two phrases. "Kissing it and eating it?" he responded, blinking his eyes. "Yes, sir! Kissing my mother goodbye and eating my mother goodbye—there is a quantity of difference!"

The spectators howled. Lenny went on to deny that he had said anything vulgar about butterflies or that he had any intention to inflame the Jazz Workshop audience sexually. He also denied having said, "I'm coming, I'm coming," during his routine. He explained that his only theme was semantics, the interpretation of words.

Lenny's emotional fifteen minutes on the stand, characterized by much squirming and gulping, ended when Judge Horn adjourned the court for the day.

"He was under the influence of a drug when I saw him in court," Wollenberg later declared. "Across the inner aspect at the wrist of his hand he had four fresh puncture marks. I debated at some juncture whether or not the guy was competent. He appeared higher than a kite. This was quite apparent to me, having had experience in the narcotics court previously."

Before the trial resumed on the morning of March 8th, Lenny looked balefully at the witness chair in which he had sprawled the previous day. "That's the most humiliating place in the courtroom," he told reporters.

The long-awaited playing of the tape recording of the Jazz Workshop performance began shortly after Lenny calmly slid into the chair. As the performance unfolded, the jury heard the word "cocksucker" tumble from Lenny's mouth. By now, they had heard the word so many times that it came as no shock at all. "If sometimes I take poetic license with you," they heard Lenny say, "and you are offended, now, this is just with semantics, dirty words . . . If I can tell you a dirty-toilet joke, we must have a dirty toilet . . . obscenity is a human manifestation. This toilet has no central nervous system, no level of consciousness . . . it is a dumb toilet; it cannot be obscene . . . impossible." Though the jurors were visibly shocked during several portions of the half-hour-long tape playback, they were now able to understand the meaning of the entire show. Soon thereafter both sides rested their cases.

Wollenberg's closing argument noted that the question before the court was not what college professors considered to be literature or comedy. It was a question of what the community felt, the people on the street, not "the self-appointed high and mighty."

After the closing arguments, Judge Horn explained carefully to the jury the law of obscenity. They retired to the jury room, bearing the stack of complimentary reviews that Bendich had introduced into evidence. The prosecution, which had chosen to call no additional witnesses besides the arresting officers, had failed to provide any other type of negative criticism of Lenny, which was readily available.

The first ballot was ten to two for Lenny's *conviction*. The jurors returned to the court asking for additional instructions. Judge Horn patiently complied with their request and again repeated the "clear and present danger" instruction, which had not been requested by the jurors.

The jurors interrupted their deliberations for dinner shortly before 6 P.M. When they returned, they took two more polls. After deliberating for a total of five hours and twenty-five minutes, they filed back into the courtroom.

"We find the defendant, Lenny Bruce, not guilty," announced jury foreman George H. Casey III, his voice resounding through the silence. Lenny clasped his hands over his head like a champ. As the spectators rejoiced, defendant and attorney leaped from their chairs and embraced each other. Unabashedly, before reporters and photographers, Lenny kissed his counsel.

"Based on that instruction," Wollenberg explained later to the press, "the jury had basically no other alternative." The ruling, as Lenny interpreted it, affirmed that his material possessed redeeming social value. "You couldn't get Horn to convict two people of obscenity if they were caught having intercourse on a street corner," a disgruntled city attorney said afterward. "Under the letter of the law," jury foreman Casey explained, "we had no choice." Another juror stated, "We hate this verdict."

One additional matter remained unresolved following Lenny's acquittal—the citation for contempt of court dating back to the first day of the trial. Bendich explained that mailing the letter could not constitute contempt, because it had not interfered with the due process of justice. He reiterated Lenny's ignorance of legal procedure. Lenny was then put on the stand and questioned. "I am not rebellious by spirit, nor do I want to thwart authority," he said passionately. "Judge Horn and I had never met . . . somebody said I took the case too lightly and I wanted him to know in all seriousness . . . I did not . . . it had placed a leprous stain on my career, cut my income in half. I have a six-year-old daughter in Los Angeles that will be a real hardship in this case. It's really blacked out my career, knocked out all the college dates I had and, you know, I don't want to hang you up with my problems but it's really been a bug to me. Since my arrest in San Francisco for obscenity, all the jobs—'too dirty, too dirty, got arrested,' and that's it. I was afraid to come into a court where, perhaps, he, the judge, felt I'm a snotty kid and I'm just here to tell the people what I've got to tell them. No. The letter was just meant to entreat with you, not to placate, not to be sycophant. I just wanted to let him know that I was not one to thwart authority. And that is all, just wanted a fair hearing."

Horn wanted to know what Lenny meant by the phrase "Axelrod's Palace," to which the court had strenuously objected. "Hostility," said Lenny. "He violated every concept of what I thought was law, what a judge did; he told people to shut up, and he said: 'I have to hurry to go to Phoenix, my grandchildren, and I can't— Well, how long does it take?' It was disappointing to me, my concept of a judge was one who would listen and weigh and it was just adverse to anything I had ever seen, and he was just completely in control; nobody could talk —would listen to no one . . . And that's what I said. He was a 'palace.' There was a king in his dominion. All the people were subservient. Humility is the worst form of ego," Lenny added, speaking with a soft voice, "and I would not do that to Your Honor."

Judge Horn then revealed that he had originally intended to send Lenny to jail for five days. His humble statements, however, had made him change his mind. Lenny was fined $100 and the court adjourned.

The San Francisco newspapers devoted front-page eight-column banner headlines to the outcome of the trial. RELUCTANT JURY— LENNY BRUCE CLEARED, trumpeted the *Chronicle* in an early edition. Although he had still not had the opportunity to tell his full story to the world, as Fried had promised, he was already reaping the publicity dividends he had originally anticipated.

That night, as Lenny flew to New York for a one-night concert appearance at Carnegie Hall, he reflected on how the publicity would undoubtedly stimulate sales of his record albums and of *Stamp Help Out*, which he had recently delivered on consignment to the City Lights Book Shop. He still owed $394 of Bendich's $2,100 fee for the conduct of the case. Before leaving San Francisco he had assigned four hundred copies of *Stamp Help Out* to his attorney to cover the outstanding obligation. It would be ironic, he thought, if the publicity would produce enough sales to cancel his debt.

Before drifting off into a fitful sleep, Lenny took a piece of airline stationery and scrawled a note to his accountant, Lowell Demurs:

Dear Lowell:
   If there's any chance that any attorney's fees may be disallowed, refer it all as theatrical advice for recording contracts and the fact that I knew I was going to get arrested in San Francisco. 9SV [a Lenny Bruce company] set up the arrest for the publicity. If that was the only press job they did for me, it would be worth $50,000.

Chapter Eleven

PERSECUTION

L enny in London! Sounds bizarre, doesn't it? Like James Brown at the Bolshoi. Or Little Richard at La Scala. Yet, it happened. In the spring of 1962, Jack Sobel and Nicholas Luard, of The Establishment Club in London, negotiated a satirical exchange program that sent Lenny Bruce to England and dispatched to the USA Peter Cook, Jonathan Miller, Alan Bennett, and Dudley Moore in *Beyond the Fringe*. These four lads, who, along with Luard, the businessman, had met at Cambridge in their undergraduate days, had improvised a satirical review that had played at the Edinburgh Festival; and on the strength of their success there, they had come down to London and launched a two-pronged drive against the proprieties of British society. One prong was their relentlessly sarcastic show, which speared Macmillan, the Queen, commercialized religion, African nationalism, Beaverbrook journalism, semantic philosophy, and Old Vic Shakespeare. The other, more deeply gouging tine, was thrust out from the second floor of a private club in Soho called The Establishment.

London's first and last cabaret theater, The Establishment was designed to elude the censoring scissors of the Lord Chamberlain's office (which since the sixteenth century had been maiming English stage plays) by invoking the privilege of private, membership-only entertainment. Financed partly by private capital and partly by member subscriptions—five thousand people contributed two guineas apiece to provide an initial capital of 10,000 pounds—the club was located at

18 Greek Street in a renovated strip joint called the Tropicana. The basement of the building was a dance hall, the ground floor was furnished with a bar (where a modern jazz ensemble performed), and the dining facilities were upstairs in a simple, purely functional room, vaguely Scandinavian in style, which contained three rows of tables ranged around a bare platform and backed by a long bar that offered an unobstructed view of the stage. Cramped and crowded to bursting since its riotous opening night, October 5, 1961, the club offered its members two seatings for dining, at eight-thirty and eleven, followed by a show. Operating under the direction of Peter Cook and Nicholas Luard, the regular company consisted of John Bird, Jeremy Geidt, John Fortune, Eleanor Bron, and Carol Simpson. At midnight, when the second performance was scheduled, Cook, Miller, Moore, and Bennett would race into the club from the theater where they were appearing in *Beyond the Fringe* and lend their improvisational talents to the supper show.

So beguiling was the appeal of such a privileged entertainment and so clever were the young university men at concocting daring and original skits that the club became an overnight sensation. At virtually the same time that the Lord Chamberlain was ruling that it was permissible to say "Christ" on the stage but not "Jesus" ("Christ" being merely the Greek word for "messiah" not "the Lord's name"), The Establishment was preparing a skit that depicted Christ Jesus as an upper-class gent hung on the cross between two cockney-talking thieves, who complain in their petty, rancorous way, " 'E's gettin' all the vinegar sponges!"

None of these young Cantabrigians had ever seen Lenny Bruce, their only contact with the master being through his apostle, Kenneth Tynan, who, during his brilliant stint as drama critic for *The New Yorker*, had witnessed Bruce's shows at the Den at the Duane. Tynan had been profoundly impressed and had praised the fascinating American effusively. He wrote that Lenny Bruce was the "sharpest denter of taboos at present active . . . a true iconoclast . . . who breaks through the barrier of laughter to the horizon beyond where the truth has its sanctuary." That was heady stuff—and so were Lenny's albums, which The Establishment played over and over again, struggling to understand their compelling but often enigmatic language. Eventually a deal was worked out, not a very good deal because it piled financial insult atop cultural incongruity. Lenny was offered $350 a week plus expenses. Sobel advised him to work for short line because England would open the door to the Continent and eventually a world-wide market for his talent. The obscenity trial in Frisco had knocked out some markets and made others cautious. O.K. They'd travel off limits and make the foreign buck. One thing would balance out the other. Lenny would stretch his wings. Nineteen sixty-two would be the year of his First Great World Tour.

Lenny's notions of England—compounded from old Hollywood flicks and Alec Guinness imports—were queer, to say the least. As Jonathan Miller summed them up, Lenny saw Great Britain "as a country set in the heart of India bossed by a Queen who wore a ball dress. The population had bad teeth, wore drab clothes and went in for furtive and bizarre murders."

The first time Miller laid eyes on Lenny, he was taken aback. Walking into the office of The Establishment, he found the famous comedian wearing "a black Nehru jacket, unbuttoned at the neck to display a bright orange T-shirt, and wearing what looked like white high-heeled cricket boots." Perched atop a secretary's desk, Lenny was trying—and apparently had been trying for some time with complete absorption—to fix a tape recorder with a bread knife. The two men were introduced by this nervous, flustered woman. Staring at Miller's crash helmet, Lenny excitedly inquired: "Hey, man! Whaddya ride?" Expecting for answer some classic British bike, such as he'd heard about from his West Coast motorcycle pals, Lenny was appalled when Miller sheepishly confessed to riding a motor scooter. That admission queered their relationship for a long time.

A nation of newspaper readers, the British got their first intimation of Bruce's character from a thoroughly muddled daily press. Two weeks prior to Lenny's arrival, on April 1st, the *Observer* warned its readers against the "farthest-out of all the American sick comedians." "Among his more favorable reviews," the paper continued, "have been the following sobriquets: The Man from Outer Taste, A Vulgar Tasteless Boor and Diarrhea of the Mouth." When Lenny finally reached London, in the middle of April, the *Observer* heralded his arrival with a few pertinent facts: "This is Bruce's first visit to England; it is said that he's had such a rough time from American audiences that he is seeking fresh fields. He is 36, small, stubbly, with a drawling voice. His mother was a burlesque actress (an extraordinary woman from whom he gets some of his jokes)—and his training was in the old Burlesque School." (Whose school tie, we may presume, is a G-string.)

On the day after Lenny's arrival, assembling for a press conference at the club, the more cynical reporters anticipated a meeting with an incoherent, obscenity-spewing, mad-dog narcotics addict. They were astonished to discover a piquant Lenny, whose insatiable curiosity turned the tables and made the press corps the highly flattered subjects of relentless nonstop front-page interviews by the star himself.

Opening night was a triumph for Lenny and the hand-picked audience of connoisseurs who gathered in the upstairs room to hear him, after a fine dinner crowned with snifters of fuming brandy. As always when the chips were down, Lenny soared. The dinner show ran over an hour; the supper show went on for eighty minutes, ending finally at 2 A.M. Jonathan Miller was struck dumb by the performance. He agreed with Tynan that "If *Beyond the Fringe* was a pinprick, Mr. Bruce was a bloodbath." Later, in educated afterthought, he and his fellow enthusiasts would reach the outermost limits of literary analogy in describing Lenny's style and character. Lenny was a "nightclub Cassandra," a "Yiddish Ariel," "the prophet of the new morality." Watching him perform was like reading *Finnegans Wake*. To prepare for the experience, Kenneth Tynan suggested that the listener read a long list of books, including the words of Marx and Freud.

The second night, the real public appeared. This audience was comprised largely of what Peter Cook called "SW 1" types, referring to the most prosperous portions of London. Solidly middle-class, drably conservative, piously dedicated to proprieties that Lenny had never heard of, much less concerned himself to observe, this audience was far from enchanted by the "Yiddish Ariel." Cries of "Shame!" punctured Lenny's monologues and interfered with his flow of thoughts. Hostile glares met his prying eyes, and when people decided to walk out, instead of silently rising and departing (with, at most, an angry glance), these Britishers made demonstrations. A well-dresed attorney had come with his wife and son. He sat sniggering and chortling through the first part of the performance; then Lenny swung into a bit about cancer. Paling at this startling medical reference, the man bellowed, "CANCER!" and leaped to his feet. "Cancer! That's it! Helen, Nicholas . . . he said 'Cancer' . . . we're going!" And he trundled his family out of this obscene club and into the clean, wholesome air of Soho—where on every block you are accosted by pimps who politely inquire, "What are you seeking, sir?"

Walking out—even in this dramatic fashion—was as nothing, however, compared with the vehemence of what happened when the show reached its final intensities. People actually began to throw things! First, it was a penny, tinkling on the stage. Then a water goblet smashed into the wall behind Lenny. "Who did that?" he challenged. Silence, save for another flying glass! Jonathan Miller recalls the scene as "like a séance; and Bruce himself seemed dazed . . . in a trance, creating effects, cries and levitations, beyond his and the audience's control . . . the whole occasion was weirdly supernatural as if his disturbing routine and the dreamy mesmeric delivery had galvanized some deep communal energy of the darkened audience. It was this necromantic style, as much as the scandalous *things* he had to say, which accounted for most of his hectic effect."

The readiness of the English audience—which Lenny had imagined as a crowd of "stiffos"—to express its disapproval through physical violence was rather less startling to Englishmen than it was to Lenny Bruce. A couple of years after this engagement, when the English critic Brian Glanville observed Lenny's performance in New York, he wrote that though the comedian's images were "deeply shocking . . . on each occasion, the words themselves were perhaps less significant than the fact that they brought absolutely no protest. Nobody shouted, nobody walked out, let alone threw things." As Jeremy Geidt, who toured with The Establishment company in the United States, remarked: "American audiences are more polite than those in England. You get the feeling they have finished their jobs for the day and have come to watch you do yours."

From the second night on, the fistfights and walkouts were many and celebrated. Yevgeny Yevtushenko, John Osborne, and Penelope Gilliat walked. Siobhan McKenna, the well-known stage and screen actress, went further. She appeared one evening with a party of eight, including her escort, a nineteen-year-old photographer. The party was loud and hecklish, until they decided to walk out in the middle because of "extreme boredom." Peter Cook took the trouble to thank them for finally leaving, causing Miss McKenna's escort to grab Cook by his tie and punch his face. Holding his bloodied head, Cook accused Miss McKenna of scratching him. The belligerent actress actress strode around the downstairs bar, proclaiming in Gaelic bellows: "These hands are clean. They are Irish hands and they are clean." Cook retorted, "This is a British face and it is bleeding!"

Lenny countered the hostility of the British public with an ingenious strategy. Still taping all his shows as a matter of course, he rigged a speaker on the stage of the club and played to one audience the recording of the previous audience's rudeness and violence. He rebuked the British through their own mouths. Nor was he loath to castigate them more directly. "You people, having dutifully read the newspapers, are calling me a sick comedian," he declared one night; "yet in this country and my own, children can see in the cinema as many beatings as they can stomach. But to show anything that approaches the act of love would bring forth the anger of the righteous. Who is really sick? You or me? Your very obscenities betray your sickness!"

Critical response in the British press was, as might be expected, sharply divided. Kenneth Tynan still loved Lenny thoroughly and unabashedly. Of Lenny's opening-night performance, he wrote: "By the end of the evening he had crashed through frontiers of language and feeling that I had hitherto thought impregnable." On the other hand, there were critics who scorned Lenny and sought to sink him by one-upping him at his own game of transvaluing values. More than one reviewer sneered at Lenny for playing the naïf, taking every moral injunction literally and "being on the side of the angels." Probably the best-balanced of all these expressions of British taste appeared a couple of years later in *The Spectator*. Having studied Lenny Bruce and the other "sicks" on both sides of the Atlantic, Brian Glanville wrote:

> Bruce has taken humour farther, and deeper, than any of the new wave of American comedians . . . Indeed, the very essence of the new wave is that one hears an individual voice talking, giving vent to its own perception and, in Bruce's case, its own obsessions. An act such as his requires a good deal more than exhibitionism; it also needs courage and passion. Essentially, it is not "sick" humour at all. The word is a tiresome irrelevance—but super-ego humour: a brave voice calling from the nursery.

Lenny's offstage life during the five weeks he lived in London is illuminated only by flashes of anecdote. Nicholas Luard, who was, among the members of The Establishment, the man who had the closest contact with Lenny, has never been willing to divulge what he knows about Lenny's life in this period, though he has been quizzed by many journalists. Actually, it isn't difficult to imagine Lenny in London, strange as that setting was for a man who was so absolutely the urban American primitive.

Lenny's first problem would have been scoring. Tempted by the British legalization of narcotics for confirmed addicts, he wanted to test his chances of finding in England a fall-back position should he ever get into serious trouble in America. Undoubtedly, his route to the "right" doctor would have begun with men like Luard, whom he could trust. Victor Lownes, who knew Lenny pretty well immediately after this period, reports that Lenny told him that "at the time he was in England he had been off drugs and had been receiving some sort of drug substitute therapy." One thing is clear: Lenny didn't stop sticking himself with needles. He was expelled from a hotel when an irate plumber discovered that the commode had been plugged up with discarded spikes. (Another hotel manager took action when, at the urging of sleepless guests, he walked into Lenny's room at 4 A.M. to find him conducting a trio of blondes singing in shrill three-part harmony an original composition with the refrain "Please love me,

Lenny!") Certainly, Lenny did not leave London in good odor. His drastic and humiliating experiences there the following year owed a lot to the fact that the British government suspected him of desiring to use England as a base of supply for his then well-publicized addiction.

Search as you will through the mountain of tapes that he accumulated from this time on, you never uncover any bits based on the English scene—save for one pungent little item. In his study of the British narcotics program, Lenny had encountered again that irresistibly comic narcotic, the morphine suppository. Like a fantastic metaphor or a Joycean pun, it fused in a single object the two most profound features of Lenny's psyche: his addiction and his anality. "Shit" is the oldest name for dope, and this shit was shit you shoved into your own shit—an epiphany!

Inevitably, Lenny worked this image into his act. Apropos of nothing he might suddenly exclaim: "When I was in England all these faggots were strung out on sleeping pill suppositories. *Emmis*. So I says to this cat, I says, 'Do they really make you sleep, man?'

"He says, 'Are you kidding? Before you get your *finger* outta your *athth* you're *athleep*, Mary.'

"That's a beautiful ad: BEFORE YOU GET YOUR FINGER OUT OF YOUR ASS—YOU'RE ASLEEP!"

That shitty little bit was all that Lenny treasured of London.

Returning to the U.S., Lenny settled down to serious work on *How to Talk Dirty and Influence People*. He had a good customer for the book in Hugh Hefner, who wanted to serialize the chapters in *Playboy* and take an option on the hardcover rights. Art Steuer, who had done most of the actual writing, had been aced out of the game the previous February for $700. The additional parts that Lenny had worked up with Richey Shackelton were lying around in various states of preparedness. All that was really needed was one last burst of energy and the project would be complete. Lenny figured there was a good taste in it for him: say $50,000 in advance. What's more, he had a new literary collaborator: Paul Krassner.

Krassner and Lenny had been getting tight since 1960, when Lenny gave a concert at Town Hall. Lenny had wanted to advertise the event in *The Realist*, Paul's magazine. He told Don Friedman to buy some space. When Friedman reported back that *The Realist* accepted no advertising, Lenny was intrigued. Actually, *The Realist* did print ads —for itself. Krassner decided to use the Lenny Bruce concert to publicize his magazine. He stuck a copy into every seat for the Saturday night concert. Sunday morning the hall began to fill with members of a religious organization. Many of these pious people picked up what they assumed was a work of devotional literature, only to discover the dirtiest little magazine in America. Lenny Bruce never again worked Town Hall.

Meanwhile, Krassner wooed Lenny in the pages of his rag, printing long, slightly sycophantic interviews, at first by other writers, like George Crater of *Downbeat*, later by the Realist himself. Krassner was actually the perfect Lenny Bruce groupie. A runty, ugly guy with a fantastic ego and the chutzpah to match, he was an ambition in search of a career. What Krassner wanted out of Lenny Bruce was precisely what everybody wanted out of Lenny Bruce: the vicarious thrill of being a bad boy. With Krassner, though, the intensity of the craving was a great deal stronger than with most of Lenny's pals. *The Realist* was willing to sit for hours in the Playboy mansion, with no bunnies, no revels, no fun—just to enjoy the spectacle of Lenny Bruce pacing endlessly back and forth, racking his brain for the words, the ideas, the bits that should go in the last part of the book.

Lenny's real problem was not creative or literary—it was political. He saw his life as a chance to sell himself to the public. To achieve his purpose, he had to watch his words. So he worried and calculated and second-guessed himself, which is why it was so devilishly hard to bring the book to completion. Krassner was a competent editor; even Lenny had to admit that. The question was simply one of truth versus fiction. How much should they make the book an autobiogrpahy, how much an autofantasy? The revisions and deletions continued to the eve of publication.

While the brain-racking proceeded in the mansion, the money-wrangling proceeded by wire, letter, and phone between Lenny's man, Jack Sobel, and Hugh Hefner's man, Victor Lownes. Sobel wanted Lenny to concentrate on writing the book while he took care of business. Lenny could never keep his nose out of any pot that was boiling. Even though Hefner sent him $1,000 on April 25th, before any agreement had been reached, and $3,500 on June 4th—on the strength of a verbal agreement to print five pieces in *Playboy* at $1,500 a shot—Lenny was very upset by the negotiations. He barraged Sobel with calls and letters, insisting that Hefner was "dangling" him and screwing him and getting away with murder. By July the pressures all around had built up so high that Krassner was writing a letter of resignation and Sobel was ready to follow suit. Finally, on July 23rd, Hefner sent the contract, which confirmed the serialization offer and stipulated that the balance of the $7,500 for the five installments would be paid when Lenny signed the agreement. Hef requested a ninety-day option and assured Lenny that he almost certainly would exercise the option, in which case he would pay another $2,500 as an advance on the hardcover book. The royalty arrangement for the hardcover would be 8 percent on 5,000 copies, 10½ percent on anything from 5,000 to 15,000, and 13 percent for sales of more than 15,000 books. The paperback deal was 3 percent up to 200,000 and 5 percent over that figure. Krassner was also to receive a sizable advance, plus royalties on the book.

After a month of recriminations, during which Lenny repeatedly called Hefner a liar (because Lenny believed he had been promised $7,500 for three, not five pieces), after further pleas from Sobel that Lenny steer clear of business and after a lot of haggling between Sobel and Hefner, the final contract was typed up on September 4th. In this version the option period is reduced from ninety to thirty days; the book advance is increased from $2,500 to $5,000; and the royalties— which were a little low—are justified by a commitment to pay Paul Krassner the additional portions of the customary author's percentages, 2 percent on the hardcover and 1 percent on the paperback. A total advance of $16,000 ($11,000 to Lenny and $5,000 to Krassner) is promised on completion and acceptance of the manuscript. To this revised agreement, Hefner appended a statement of his personal motives:

> I hope that Lenny also realizes that there is a good deal that is personal in my own motivations on this project, too. As a pure business deal, the risk is really not worth the potential return, but if it is possible to put together a really good book—one that will renew interest in Lenny's talent, help build his career, and get him out of his financial difficulties—then it will certainly all have been worth it, and the special consideration that we have all brought to this project will have been very worthwhile. I just hope that Lenny fully understands and appreciates how much a number of us who care about him, both as a talent and as a person, are willing to gamble on him, even at relatively high stakes.

Hefner also pointed out that Lenny was receiving a considerably higher royalty than was generally the case with ghost-written material.

Lenny was not able to respond to this final offer until the middle of October; then he wrote Hefner: "Paul Krassner is not a ghost writer. All he has done is transcribe tapes." He also complained that payment of his share of the royalty was tied to delivery of the manuscript, a process controlled by Krassner. Eventually, after a series of other messages, some of them couched in a tone of grateful-for-past-favors-but-don't-you-think-you've-changed?, Lenny agreed to sign the contract providing he obtained "etymological rights," i.e., the right to emend and delete from the galleys. On December 17th, after nine

months of negotiation, Lenny, Krassner, and Hefner signed the contract for *How to Talk Dirty and Influence People*. Lenny acknowledged
receipt of an additional advance of $3,000, briging his total front money
up to $9,000. The target date for delivery of manuscript was set at
March 15, 1963.

While the hassling over the book contract reached its climax, Lenny
was busy making trouble for all his other business associates. He had
long desired to break his contract with Fantasy because he wanted a
more prestigious label and the nice lump of sugar that would be stuffed
in his mouth when he changed houses. Phil Leshin, who worked for
Jack Sobel, recalls that record-company officials were always calling
up and saying: "Get Lenny away from Fantasy, and we'll lay twenty-
five thousand dollars on him and five thousand dollars on you!" The
only problem was that Fantasy's contract—which Lenny usually referred to as a "toilet-paper contract"—was perfectly valid. It stipulated
that Lenny receive 5 percent as a performer and 5 percent as a writer
of all material which was copyrighted by Fantasy in his name (approximately 43 cents an album). Lenny claimed the company was cheating him on royalties and censoring his material. "He always thought
we had a secret pressing plant somewhere in the desert," laughs Saul
Zaentz, the current president of the company.

The charge of censorship, however, is one that cannot be denied.
Lenny Bruce's material was not presented to the record-buying public
in the same form that it was delivered to his nightclub audiences. The
question is: would any other record company, especially a big outfit
like Atlantic (where Lenny was eager to move), have taken a more
liberal attitude? Judging from the subsequent history of the record
business and its long history of scandals over trivial things, like the
Rolling Stones singing "Let's Spend the Night Together," Fantasy's
caution about printing sides sprinkled with expletives like "cocksucker"
and "motherfucker" was perfectly legitimate. The one charge against
Fantasy that Lenny could make legitimately was that the company had
refused to issue his greatest single performance: the Carnegie Hall
concert of February 1961. Objecting to the length, the language (which
was unusually clean), and various other features of the tape, which
had been made by the producer, Don Friedman, Fantasy refused to
cut the album. (It was released in 1972 by United Artists without the
slightest degree of censorship.) Putting all the claims and charges together, it does not appear that Fantasy took advantage of Lenny Bruce;
but he felt he was being screwed, and he brought a suit against the
company that was thrown out of court.

Consulting Earle Warren Zaidins, an attorney who had been recommended by Don Friedman, Lenny received some interesting advice.

He was told that the only way to pry Fantasy loose was to conduct an audit of its books and establish that they were cheating him. Lenny agreed enthusiastically to this proposal and in a letter of May 21, 1962, he formally requested Zaidins to take action in the case. The lawyer was given a retainer and provided with a first-class plane ticket to San Francisco, where he received the full cooperation of the company. The resulting audit—a long and detailed document—claimed that Fantasy owed Lenny $19,000 in unpaid royalties. The company claimed that Zaidins had simply tabulated all the merchandise shipped by them without allowing for returns and back orders that were booked but never shipped because of subsequent cancellations. It is a little late at this point to be deciding the fine points of the case; but one indication that Fantasy was right and Zaidins was wrong is the fact that the highly principled and sincerely devoted Al Bendich refused to take the case.

Money had become a great issue with Lenny because his trials and troubles had reduced his income and threatened him with further losses. It was imperative that in addition to making money he also think of cutting his costs. The easiest cost to cut was the 20 percent bite which Jack Sobel took as Lenny's personal manager. (Managers normally receive 25 percent, but Lenny had worked a deal that allowed him to pay the extra 5 percent to a lawyer-accountant named Wallace Magaziner.)

Sobel had been an extremely loyal, skillful, and hard-working manager-agent. He handled Lenny's affairs with a great tact and resourcefulness, negotiating and renegotiating endlessly with club owners who were unhappy with many features of Lenny's act as well as his unprofessional behavior. Sobel was not only very patient about waiting for his fees; he often advanced his own money to pay urgent bills. Lenny respected Sobel and knew how to value his services: which made the decision to ditch him that much harder—and guilt-inducing. Characteristically, he deided to solve the problem through a stratagem, outlined in a note to Zaidins:

> I want to go out this year with Jack. I know he is very emotional temperament . . . . . Let's see what his reaction is to the loss of power of attorney. (Don't tell him you knew.) What I want from you to protect me from any emotional rash that may occur here on in.

Having hatched this little Sicilian plot—designed to make Sobel resign by stripping him of one of his prerogatives—Lenny wrote to Sobel as follows:

I don't want anyone to have power of attorney. I don't want anyone to have the power to sign my name on any documents. I don't want Jack Sobel to have power of attorney. I don't want Jack Sobel to sign my name on any document. This is effective as from this date, May 21st 1962.

It's obvious that you have my welfare and interest uppermost in your mind. Your honesty is unchallengeable; you let me owe you money, get ahead of you on commission, and with my rating security-wise this isn't the surest gamble. You have made excellent moves for me showbusiness-wise. However some of the business moves in other areas are not satisfactory. This letter voids any power of attorney I may have given you, and I instruct you not to sign any document relating to me or my business.

I want you to do everything as before and don't change a hair, except send me that documented piece of paper that will say you have informed Magaziner that the only one who can sign my name is me, Lenny Bruce. I still want you to be my agent and do everything as before, except leave the last 'yes' or 'no' to me.

Love,

On September 3rd, after a meeting in Los Angeles, Jack Sobel resigned.

One of Sobel's last acts before he packed it in was to book the balance of Lenny's 1962 world tour. The next stop was Vancouver, British Columbia, the largest city in western Canada. Jack must have been harboring unconscious feelings of hostility when he arranged this date because the world capital of logging, salmon fishing, and paper mulching was simply no place for Lenny Bruce. Not that he did badly with the audiences—it was the press and city administration that broke his balls.

To take it from the top: the gig was a joint with a comical name —Isy's Supper Club. Isy Walters was a shrewd operator. He dug in front that Lenny could bring a lot of heat on his club; so he stipulated in his contract that Lenny would be paid on a pro-rata basis if his performances were canceled or prohibited by the authorities for obscenity. He deposited a cash bond to that effect with the American Guild of Variety Artists' Portland office, then he sat back to await developments after Lenny opened on Monday night, July 30th. Unfortunately, the unusual protective measures came to the attention of a local columnist, Jack Wasserman. Writing in the *Vancouver Sun* a good ten days before the show, Wasserman advertised the fact that Isy Walters was bringing an act into Vancouver in which he had so little confidence that he was paying it only by the night. This publicity set the stage for the strange sequence of events that followed.

Lenny's two shows on opening night were typical of the performances he was doing in this period; they won considerable applause from packed houses. No one who was present as a spectator made any complaint; but the next afternoon, Jack Wasserman reviewed the shows scathingly, with the critical barbs falling equally on Lenny as a performer, as a person, and as the author of a totally objectionable act. Oddly, Wasserman copped out at the end of his column with the pious wish that regardless of his own viewpoint the authorities would permit the comedian to complete his engagement. The authorities, after reading the column, were instantly interested in Mr. Lenny Bruce. On Tuesday night Chief License Inspector Milton Harrell and Assistant License Inspector Ernest Akerly, accompanied by two Morality Squad detectives, appeared at the club. Immediately after the show, Harrell summoned Bruce and Walters to the club office. He informed them that Bruce was finished in Vancouver. Taking the line that the show "might be all right for some U.S. cities but is indecent and improper for Vancouver," Harrell cited as his warrant a city-licensing bylaw that empowered him to "prohibit or prevent any lewd or immoral performance or exhibition." If Walters did not cancel Bruce, warned Harrell, the club's operating license would be suspended forthwith.

Walters exercised his escape option immediately and canceled the balance of the engagement, inducing Lenny to sign a release that protected the club against future litigation. As no charges had been preferred, no contracts breached, and Lenny had been paid for his work, the comedy appeared to be over—when suddenly a new actor appeared on the scene. This was Howard Bateman, operator of the Inquisition Coffee House. He got in touch with Lenny that same night and offered to pick up the remainder of his engagement. Lenny agreed to reopen the following night, but he insisted on certain special provisions: neither Jack Wasserman nor any other *Vancouver Sun* reporter was to be admitted, and the shows were to be taped and sealed as evidence, in the event that any court action followed.

Harrell, when informed of this development, said he would be present and would suspend the Inquisition's license if Bruce performed. Then Lenny made an unexpected move: declining a direct challenge to the inspector, he went to Harrell and signed a voluntary pledge that he would never again perform in Vancouver. Appearing Wednesday night on TV stations CBC and CHAN, he reiterated his pledge and added that he had nothing against Harrell, remarking: "He's a nice guy, simply doing his job as he sees it." Actually, Lenny had tried to make a deal with Harrell, offering to clean up his act for the rest of the week. When Harrell assured him that no such changes would be acceptable, Lenny decided to put a good face on the matter by signing his pointless pledge and publicly absolving the inspector of blame.

The next week the whole story was minutely detailed in *Variety*. Nightclub operators everywhere were put on notice, in effect, that if they hired Lenny Bruce, they stood in danger of having their licenses revoked. Revocation was a much graver threat than an obscenity indictment. Obscenity is a misdemeanor, carrying a light penalty and subject to appeal to higher courts, where lower-court convictions are usually reversed. Suspension of an operator's license means instant death to his business, with no clear line of appeal or assurance of restoration. The *Variety* article ended by questioning the propriety of placing in a single, admittedly ill-qualified individual's hands the right to act as an arbiter of public morality. That same week an editorial in the *Sun* provided unwittingly a prophetic answer to such queries. Slugged "Who Should Remove Manure?" the editorial read: "Some may complain that a city license inspector has no qualifications to judge the quality of night club acts and no right to close those which he finds offensive . . . But it is hard to blame Mr. Harrell. To him, his duty seemed clear. If you piled manure on the street, someone would demand that a city sanitary inspector order it removed. Mr. Harrell, knowing manure when he sees it, ordered it removed from a night club."

After the freeze-out in Vancouver, Lenny was grateful for the hot moist breeze of Atlantic City, his base for the month of August. As usual, it was Le Bistro and the boardwalk in the wee hours of the morning and scoring dope and shooting up in hotel rooms. He amused himself with the old Jewish pensioners on the Steel Pier and goofed on the ancient shooting galleries, fortune tellers, knish stands, and vendors of salt-water taffy. Atlantic City was low camp: its tone was the moody decadence of a Coney Island. For Lenny Bruce it was a pleasure dome.

All through the dog days he lingered, putting through his calls to New York and Jack Sobel, his now-on, now-off manager and agent. The author of his great world tour was planning at this moment another precedent-making overseas engagement for the most famous of the sick comics. The target was another British dominion, one that was much farther away than England and even more morally conservative than Vancouver: "*Australia!*" Lenny barked. "What am I gonna do with those kangaroo heads down there?"

Sobel reasoned that Lenny might make a score in Australia because the country seemed starved for American acts. Every name comic of the old school—Bob Hope, Red Skelton, Danny Kaye—had gone down under and come back up with a pile of money. People like Frank Sinatra had made fortunes in Australia. There was an American agent in Sydney named Lee Gordon—a real hustler who used to book strip acts and now had graduated to the big time—who was a genius at booking Americans. He had read about Lenny; now he wanted him to fly out there and play at a place called Aaron's Hotel. It was $2,000 for a week's work plus expenses; but if Lenny did well, there were a million spin-offs. He could go around the country doing concerts, maybe work the universities.He might take a shot at TV, and Sydney had at least one very sophisticated nightclub, named Andre's. So why not go? If he bombed, he was so far away from home, nobody would know or care.

Lenny's gig in Atlantic City wound up on Labor Day; he was due to depart for Australia on September 4th. The timing was tight. When he got back to L.A. on the evening of the 2nd, he was gunning his motors for a quick takeoff. Two days of frantic lafeing brought him around to the afternoon of the 4th so quickly that there were still all sorts of chores to be performed before he could embark on the flight. Chic Eder recalls exactly how the game was played:

A few hours before Lenny's departure for Australia—and the entourage is gathered playing "get the insane star off to the plane." Lenny is giving orders (which he's subject to contravene within minutes) to his accountant and lawyer and their secretaries. Lenny gets a bankbook and a withdrawal slip from the accountant, signs it, and gives me those super-explicit instructions which were such a fantastic manifestation of his insecurity: "Dig chic! You take this to the Gibraltar Savings and Loan on Wilshire . . . you know where that's at?"

"Yes, Lenny, the address is right here on the form."

"O.K.! Now they've been using my bread since '59 so I want you to make sure they give me all the interest I've got coming. You've got a good kup for figures, so make sure they don't burn us, right?"

"Right, Lenny."

"O.K., as soon as you're sure you've got the right number, you take care of the business we discussed earlier, and get back here as quick as you can." (The "business" is scoring.)

I get to the bank, give the teller the paperwork, and tell her I want to see the figures on the updating of interest and close out the account. She goes to a file to make a signature comparison, over to a bank officer's desk where she raps for a moment, then comes back to invite me to talk to this vice-president. I explain to

the dude that I'm acting as Lenny's agent in this transaction, and
he tells me that the signature on the withdrawal slip isn't even a
reasonable facsimile of the one recorded at the time the account
was opened. It turns out that he knows Seymour Grush, so I explain
that Lenny'd signed the slip while laying in bed, and he lets me
use the phone to call the house. Needless to say, the line is busy
and, after maybe ten attempts to get through, I'm starting to get
a bit nervous. I'm strung-out, down to my running weight of 120
pounds, have more tracks than the Sante Fe, and can afford no
contact with the heat; so I dial the operator and have her break
into the circuit via the old "emergency-call" shtick. Lenny is steaming when he gets on the line—I've interrupted a call to Chicago.
When I hip him to what's happening, and the fact that I'm about
to get rousted for trying to pilfer his account, he cracks up. We
put Seymour on the phone to the bank official, and he tells Seymour
that he needs a properly signed form before he can give me the
bread. Lenny gets back on, and we make arrangements for someone to meet me halfway between the house and bank. The bank
dude is a winner guy, and by the time I get back he's got everything
ready for me.

I get to the connection's, make the deal, but don't like the weight
he's given me. He tells me that he's just scored the stuff from his
main-man, that it's "killer brown"—and that it's the same strength
as when it came across from Mexico. I tell him that if I ain't happy
with it I'm coming back, and split for the hill.

Back in the bathroom, Lenny also comments on the size of the
bag. I tell him that the connection claims it's dynamite shit that's
never been stepped on. Lenny counters with: "They all say that.
Did you ever know one to tell you he was selling you Harlem
garbage?" He calmed down when I reminded him that he, as a
headlining star, might be subject to getting burned; it was doubtful
that the cat would cross me. Despite this, Lenny puts a glob into
the spoon that was out of line even for the mediocre shit we'd
been geezing. While he's talking to the Seymours through the
practically open door, and explaining what he wants me to do
about the trouble he's having with his building additions while he's
gone ("Do't let those building inspectors on the property . . . Stand
them off with a shotgun if you have to; like that old broad they
wanted to move to put the freeway through. Don't forget to water
the tree every day . . ." etc.), he's filling these super-legitimate
drugstore vials with the smack from the bag. I surreptitiously knock
half the shift out of the spoon, put in an amp of Meth, cook it up,
and suck it up into a Discardit disposable syringe. He gets a register

on the first try (unusual for him at this stage of the game, since most of his veins have long since collapsed), sending it home after jacking it back once. Then the shit hits him. It drives him to his knees, and when he finally gets his head out of the toilet—where he pukes up his breakfast—I show him how much I've taken out of his spoon prior to cooking up his taste. There's no doubt in my mind that he'd have offed himself had he fixed as much as he originally planned. Meanwhile, it's obvious that Lenny's going to be late getting to the airport, so we've called Qantas Airlines, and they've agreed to hold up the plane's departure. The cab is parked in the driveway—facing downhill—and Lenny hits the steps carrying his oversized attaché case. (Actually, that tschechel is a portable pharmacy—and taped to the inside lid is a glowing testimonial of Lenny's almost unbelievable ability to move croakers to write scripts for him: it's a letter from Dr. Norman Rotenberg that's virtually a license for Lenny's tracks!) Anyhow, Lenny spots Sally at the bottom of the stairs holding Kitty by the hand. Without even breaking his stride, he lugs, "Will you stop it with those Stella Dallas goodbyes?!!" and bops into the cab.

Lenny was so bombed on the flight to Sydney that he never really got himself together until he reached Fiji. Here, at a tiny, moist, hibiscus-dotted airport called Nandy, he spent an hour poking around the duty-free shop. Everything in the store appeared to be made of beads or grass. The help were giant Fijians, who reminded him of all those *National Geographics* he had perused as a child: "and the ancestor of the modern stroke book, *The National Geographic* . . . 'Hey, Manny, look at the tits on these natives!' " Picking his way through a rack of postcards that looked like sets for old Dorothy Lamour movies, he selects a beauty and laboriously addresses it to Seymour Lazar. On one side is a vista of tropical beach and palm tree; on the other side a simple message: "Still throwing up!"

Landing in Sydney around noon on Thursday, Lenny cabbed out to a little hotel in Kings Cross, the seedy, run-down Greenwich Village of the city. Soon he was in a huddle with Lee Gordon. The promotor told him that he was booked to play the next night at Aaron's Hotel, where he would do two shows a night to about three hundred a sitting. Gordon—a Hebe about forty with a bad nose job, married to a stripper named Sharon—was proud of the way he had handled the advance publicity. He had addressed his ad: "To the free thinkers of our community." His spiel? "After having brought 471 American entertainers to this country, most of whom were virtually devoid of talent, I now

deviate with Lenny Bruce, who prefers to be called a philosopher."
How's that for a smart pitch? That should blow some of the stink off
him! Lenny, changing from his Levi suit to his black Chinese rabbi
outfit, wasn't so sure; but he was willing to give it a try.

Next night he walked out on a stage that had been erected in the
dingy dining room of the hotel. Screwing the cheap mike off its stand
and confronting an audience of beat-looking cats, who were his only
Australian fans, he started bitching about the lighting and the sound
system. For five, ten, nearly fifteen minutes, he complained, until the
crowd began to feel restless and guilty. Finally, he settled down and
began doing his material. The show was full of dynamite: he slammed
into one highly charged topic after another—"niggers," divorce, Adolf
Eichmann, religion, sex, the whole bag. In a sophisticated nightclub
in New York or San Francisco, it would have been a heavy dose; in
Australia it was pure insanity. The audience gasped and tittered with
nervousness. The laughter was of that strangled variety that denotes
anything but merriment. Four women got up at various points and
walked out. By the time the show ended, Lenny had kicked an enormous hole in the local proprieties.

Backstage during intermission, he got into a fight with Gordon,
who begged him to tone down his performance. "You don't know
these people!" the promoter kept repeating. Lenny would hear nothing
of retrenchment. In fact, Gordon's entreaties only fired him with an
even stronger desire to needle this audience of unappreciative squares.
Jumping up on a chair at the beginning of the second show, he told
the audience: "I'm going to do something that's never been done before
in a nightclub—I'm going to *piss* on you!"

Piss on you! The phrase rang out with the stunning impact of a
pistol shot. The audience cowered, its only response being a few masochistic giggles. Some people thought Lenny was mad, some that he
needed a fix, still others that he was being deliberately outrageous
because he wanted the engagement canceled. Actually, the line was
"material," something he'd said before and would say again. This
possibility never registered with the Australians. They sat there listening to the second show like people at a wake. The less they responded, the more bizarrely obscene Lenny's performance became.
At one point he ran through a whole series of descriptions of sex acts;
then, having exhausted the subject, he turned to religion, avowing:
"We Jews killed Christ, and if he comes back, we'll kill him again!"
One member of the audience refused to be shocked: she was Barbara
Wyndon, a young Joyce Grenfell, with a big beak of a nose, one of
the best-known comic actresses in Australia. Getting up toward the

end of the show, she called out, "Tell us something we haven't heard before!" The hostility of the heckle triggered an automatic reaction: spinning around and fixing the woman with a black stare, Lenny snapped, "Fuck you, lady!"

Next morning, the Sydney papers went after Lenny like a pack of baying hounds. "DISGUSTED BY SICK JOKES—FOUR WOMEN WALK OUT," blared the headline in the *Sun*, with an elongated picture of Lenny, getting off the plane in his Levis and white boots, clutching his pharmaceutical briefcase and looking completely bombed. "SICK JOKES MADE AUDIENCE ILL," quipped the *Daily Mirror*, with an onstage picture of Lenny in his black Nehru, thrusting his arm out in what appears to be a Nazi salute. The horrified *Mirror* writer noted that Lenny gave a blasphemous account of the crucifixion and used a "steady stream of dirty words." It also reported that the vice squad would attend the next show. The *Sun* intoned, "Sydney has never seen a public performance of such blasphemy and obscenity." Both papers made much of the fact that Lenny had used repeatedly "the Lady Chatterley word," and concluded that "it will be astonishing if the Chief Secretary's Department allows the shows to continue." The shows were not to continue, in fact, because the manager of Aaron's, Nicholas Devery—announcing himself "shocked and disgusted"—had hastily informed Gordon that the engagement was canceled.

As the storm of controversy began to build around his ears, Lenny retreated to his hotel room and refused to answer the phone. Consoling himself with a rich diet of ice cream and heroin, he remained incommunicado until the next day, Saturday, when a newspaper reporter finally made his way into the room. He found Lenny "red-eyed, unshaven and lying in bed . . . He hardly slept Friday night and had just recovered from an asthmatic attack . . . At first he was nervous, hesitant, suspicious . . . I told him after two performances in Sydney (one of them mostly inaudible to 50 percent of the audience) he had been judged and condemned . . . *'Don't I know?'* he said, with his face in the pillow." In the ensuing interview headed, "The Four-Letter Word Man Talks," Lenny appeared to speak spontaneously; actually, everything quotable came out of his act. He did lines like, "If the Messiah returned and said, 'All is pure,' I'd be standing in the bread line—right back of J. Edgar Hoover, Jonas Salk and Jesus Christ." He did his "obscenity is in the ear of the beholder" bit, and rounded off by insisting—as would any comedian—that he had done better than was reported in the press. "It is not true to say that my show was met by 'stunned silence.' You were there. You heard the laughter, the applause—and it wasn't only because I was using four-letter words!"

Three days later, the Lenny Bruce controversy got another shot in the ass when the directors of the Australian Broadcasting Company banned an interview that had been scheduled on a popular Tuesday-night show called *People*. The program's host, Bob Sanders, protested vigorously, offering the network the choice of viewing a pre-show airing or filling in the time themselves. When the network officials remained adamant, Sanders threw up his hands. Lenny had wanted to carry his case to the people via television. He had agreed not only to pre-tape the show but to submit it to censorship. When he got a point-blank refusal with no explanation, he immediately booked a flight back home on Qantas. Meantime, Lee Gordon had been hard at work arranging other bookings; finally he persuaded Lenny to remain. Dates had been set up with two universities, Sydney and New South Wales, and a concert arrangement had been worked out with the management of the Winter Garden in Rose Bay, a posh eastern suburb near the most beautiful beaches and the seaplane basin.

On September 14th, just a week after his fiasco at Aaron's, Lenny stepped out on the stage of the Winter Garden—a huge old movie palace with draped goddesses on either side of the stage—nearly an hour late, to play a concert before about two hundred devotees, curled up in the first few rows of the cavernous old house. Joking about the emptiness of the theater and the possibility that it was haunted, he went off into a subdued but brilliant show that included some of his finest pieces, such as *Lima, Ohio* and *How to Relax Your Colored Friends*. The tiny in-group audience loved Lenny and would have killed themselves laughing if only they had been able to penetrate his fast Brooklyn accent. Again, as in England, the purity of his dialect defeated those who were unfamiliar with the language; yet Lenny was adored by these new fans. This warm reception led, in turn, to yet another offer; this one from Jim Callaghan, to work at Andre's. Lenny accepted and on the second Sunday of his stay below the line, he was spotlighted in yet another newspaper interview (a medium he always shunned in America), pacing his hotel room like "a jaguar with a toothache."

"I'm not a comedian," he said. "And I'm not sick. The world is sick and I'm the doctor. I'm a surgeon with a scalpel for false values. I don't have an act. I just talk. I'm just Lenny Bruce . . ." Then, after pointing out some examples of condoned obscenity from the Sydney papers, Lenny wound up by explaining what had spoiled his opening-night performance: "I can't stand rejection. I can't give a good performance if the people in the audience reject me."

Two days later, he scribbled a note to Callaghan saying that he had received an urgent call from home. Leaving instructions that the message not be delivered until his plane had cleared the airport, he took off, leaving behind him a thoroughly puzzled and irate Sydney.

Lenny's return from Australia landed him in a morass of serious problems. He found that the federal government was auditing his past income tax returns. Fantasy Records had refused to come through with any additional royalties since the Zaidins audit. GAC would not cough up the agency fees that Lenny claimed had been unjustly deducted from his paychecks. Most annoying of all, his house on the hill had become the source of a major controversy with the City of Los Angeles. At issue was the $20,000 guest cottage, adjacent to the main house, which had been built while he was working out of town. Lenny had supplied minutely detailed instructions for its construction and interior layout. But he had refused to make arrangements, despite repeated warnings, for the most basic requirement—a city building permit. "I don't give a goddamn fuck about the city," he told the building contractor when he was informed that the city would never O.K. his ideas. The upshot was that the Department of Building and Safety had condemned the structure the previous August. A safety inspector had already served three notices to "demolish and remove the illegal building" and to "restore to its original state the dwelling and garage." He had also threatened to turn off the electricity.

Belatedly Lenny agreed to compromise. William Spivak, Jr., an attorney associated with Seymour Lazar, won a last-ditch stay of demolition by offering to hire an architect to design alterations that would be acceptable to Building and Safety. This decision prompted another detailed advisory from Lenny, while he was working at the Establishment. He proposed the construction of two retaining walls, one inside the guest cottage and the other outside. He also ordered the installation of a new carport, new plumbing, a stairway connecting both floors of the main house, and that a portion of the upper story be fitted as an astronomical observatory "maintained for the purpose of mounting telescope to scan the horizon and sky for enemy and friendly aircrafts, saucers."

With all these problems bugging him—plus a recurrence of his old staph infection, which laid him up in the hospital for three days—Lenny began to run up his habit. He needed fresh supplies and new connections. It was for this purpose that Tony Viscarra picked him up on the afternoon of October 5th—a date neither of them would soon forget.

It was about one in the afternoon when Tony steered his green classic MG down the driveway onto the roller-coaster curves of Hollywood

Boulevard. Lenny basked in the balmy autumn sun, regaling Tony with the story of how he had registered at the hospital under an assumed name and then ducked out without paying the bill. High on Meth, Lenny even had words for the beauty of the day and the serpentine road littered with leaves fallen from live oak trees. He had stuffed several extra Methedrine vials into his pocket, knowing the first injection would soon wear off.

It was Tony who suggested they go to the Grand Prix Hobby Shop, just a couple of miles away in North Hollywood. The owner of the shop, Robert Coogan, Jr., brother of Jackie Coogan, was one of Tony's good friends. They had met at Normandy Village, a dilapidated apartment complex that had become a cheap housing hangout for hookers and would-be actors and singers. Tony had frequently cut Coogan's hair at his beauty salon, located two blocks from the Village. The two men were now contemplating a round-the-world pleasure cruise. Only one thing was lacking—the money.

Tony parked in the lot behind the Hobby Shop; they entered through the back door. Lenny had never seen slot-car racing, which had replaced trampolining as the latest Southern California fad. Like a child absorbed in a new Christmas toy, he spent the better part of two hours pressing the remote control devices which sent the scale-model Ferraris, Lotuses, and Jaguars careening over a simulated Grand Prix course. He and Tony took time out only to drive to a hot dog stand three blocks away and browse in the nearby veterans' salvage store. It was the same sort of aimless afternoon they had spent together on many previous occasions.

This day, however, unknown to either of them, the Hobby Shop had been placed under surveillance at 2 P.M. by four Los Angeles County narcotics officers, under the command of Sergeant Joel Lesnick. Tipsters had informed the police that Coogan was using and selling large amounts of narcotics, utilizing the store as a front. Customers were required to buy model cars for each hundred dollars' worth of heroin they purchased. Often the heroin was packed inside the cars.

Dressed in plainclothes, Lesnick sat with another man in an unmarked 1961 Dodge Lancer parked forty yards from the Hobby Shop's back entrance. Plainclothesmen Benjamin Lopez and Bobby Hill were staked out in civilian automobiles on either side of North Lankershim Boulevard. From his observation post, Lesnick watched Tony and Lenny park the MG on Magnolia Street and reenter the Hobby Shop through the back door. "There's something going on here," Lesnick thought to himself; "Lenny Bruce isn't too interested in little cars." Waiting patiently behind the wheel, chain-smoking Camels, Lesnick talked on and off with the new man on his squad, Sergeant John Lee White.

Suddenly, the back door of the Hobby Shop swung open and Lenny, Tony, and Coogan emerged. Lesnick tensed up at the wheel. Coogan retreated inside the building. Tony and Lenny continued up the alley. Tony walked toward his MG. Lenny lingered behind, peering in the window of an ATV appliance store. Lesnick glanced at his watch. It was a few minutes past four. He'd seen enough. Switching on the engine, he released the brake and pulled up to the curb behind Lenny. When Lenny spotted Lesnick, he panicked. He slipped his hand into his pocket and dropped something on the pavement. Then he strode up the block two doors and ducked into a bicycle shop. White was out of the car in a flash. Scooping up the object Lenny had dropped—a matchbook—he rushed into the bicycle shop. When he returned with Lenny in tow, he saw Tony Viscarra frozen in his tracks confronting Lesnick. The sergeant tossed both suspects into the back of his car and gunned away from the curb. Lesnick was worried lest Coogan stick his head out the door and pin the bust.

Driving over to a nearby parking lot, Lesnick stopped to question his prisoners. White had been examining the matchbook. On the outside, it read UNITED CALIFORNIA. Inside, tucked between the matches and the cover was a square of neatly folded notepaper. Opening the blue-lined paper, White discovered that it was filled with a familiar-looking white powder. A quick search of Lenny's person turned up a packet of Methedrine vials and a lot of marks on his arms. There were old patches of scar tissue on his right forearm, which also showed eleven fresh punctures. The elbow hollow of the same arm was bruised and perforated with ten more fresh punctures. Lenny's left wrist was badly bruised and scarred, and it, too, showed signs of recent injections. Lesnick counted fifteen fresh wounds. During the search and examination, Lenny struggled to explain that his tracks were legitimate. He was taking Methedrine for lethargy on prescription from Dr. Rotenberg. He even had a note from his doctor. "Lenny kinda laughed when he showed it to me," recalled Lesnick.

When the suspects had been questioned, Lesnick drove back to the Hobby Shop to bust Coogan. When he walked into the store, he could hardly believe his eyes. Coogan had dropped about a hundred pounds. There were abscesses all over his arms. He had two more packets of heroin in papers identical with the one Lenny had concealed. He also had a pile of United California Bank matchbooks. Lesnick hung around for a while, and sure enough, a couple more cats came to score. By the end of the day, the sergeant had made a half-dozen pinches and sent several packets of white powder to the police chemist.

On the drive from the Hobby Shop to the West Hollywood sheriff's station, Lenny remained silent, his face concealed in his corduroy jacket. Occasionally, he glanced over at Lesnick, thinking of how at the Crescendo he was able to wiggle out of the collar and make a deal. This time there was no way out.

An audience of photographers, stenographers, clerks, and police awaited Lenny as he entered the station house. "I'm not the only one in jail," he proclaimed, after being booked on suspicion of possessing narcotics. "I'm proud to be in the company of Ross Barnett [segregationist governor of Mississippi] and other eminent Americans who have been arrested this week." As usual, Lenny had something quotable to say.

A city news-service reporter asked whether he was worried about the charges. "I'd say we're living in the time of the end," he replied; "probably Cuba will bait us into attacking her and that'll be it."

The laughter generated by these remarks had barely subsided when Lenny suddenly whirled on Tony and Coogan, snarling: *"You all turned yellow."* Burying his head in his hands, he muttered, "I want a priest." A deputy told him he could phone for a lawyer. "I got one," he said, quickly changing his mood; "I talked to Gerald L. K. Smith [the once notorious leader of the Silver Shirts of America, a fascist organization]."

A late-arriving reporter asked Lenny where he was arrested.

"Lawrence Welk's pad."

"What are narcotics like?" asked a stenographer, joining the impromptu press conference.

"Baby," said Lenny, employing a hipster's voice, "it's a weird, dizzy, crazy scene!" To punctuate his statement, he twitched convulsively.

Before being jailed, he placed a phone call to Burton Marks, a lawyer who had visited his house on the preceding night. (Oddly enough, he made no effort to phone Seymour Lazar, his manager and attorney of record. Apparently Lenny was reluctant to involve someone of Lazar's stature in a matter that shamed him.) Marks had known Lenny since 1954, when he was attending law school during the day and moonlighting as an assistant manager at Strip City. In the interim he had handled various minor affairs for Lenny, including booking contracts for local nightclubs. Marks was a fat boy, a good laugher, talented but on the make—and titillated out of his toosh by his intimacy with Lenny Bruce. He was the sort of cat Lenny would describe as a "fan."

"They got me busted for narcotics," Lenny yelled at Marks over the phone, "and it's a bad scene." He mentioned that Tony had also been arrested. "Don't bother about Viscarra," said Lenny, after Marks offered to bail him out as well: "They're going to let him go."

Lenny never cracked a smile as he joined Coogan in the stark detention cell. He slumped on a cot and reflected on the ignominy of the situation—being arrested on narcotics charges just after playing with toy cars. "Who could have done it?" Lenny repeatedly asked Coogan, implying that he was framed. "Who could have done it? Bobby, you know I didn't buy it!"

Within two hours Marks arrived with his wife and a bail bondsman. Lenny was freed on a writ of habeas corpus an hour later. Tony, who had been booked for investigation, had been released earlier when the inquiry at the station proved fruitless. "They couldn't find any marks of any kind and my eyes weren't dilated," Tony explained. "I wasn't high. They had to turn me loose."

Outside the station house, Lenny tried to convince his hulking 240-pound attorney that the police were lying. He insisted that he had not discarded any narcotics. "I've got to get to that car," Lenny declared. "Drive me over there!"

When they got to the Hobby Shop parking lot, they found the car gone. Lenny called Tony and was informed that the car was back in Hollywood, just off Santa Monica Boulevard. Marks, his wife, and Lenny drove over the hill again to the MG. Jumping out of Marks's car, Lenny darted over to the MG. He opened the right-hand door and reached into the glove compartment. When he returned, he was holding a capsule of white powder in his hand. "You see!" cried Lenny, displaying the capsule. "I told you they were lying. They never found the stuff. Here it is. It was in the car where I stashed it!"

Who knows what was in that cap! Heroin was virtually never sold on the West Coast in those days in that manner. According to chic Eder:

Bobby Coogan was dealing papers of stuff, i.e., the heroin is placed in the center of a piece of paper approximately two inches square. The paper is then folded in such a manner as to allow it to be tucked into itself, thereby making a small, easily concealable packet to envelope "God's medicine" without danger of spillage. The quantity contained in each paper denotes its price as well as its name. In making a purchase, you would request "a nickel paper," "a dime paper," etc. Caps entail considerably more time and trouble to package, but are not uncommon back East. In L.A., however, I can count the number of connections who've dealt caps on the fingers of one hand.

Marks knew nothing about drugs. He swallowed Lenny's story without batting an eye.

The lawyer was unhappy about defending Lenny, however, in such a serious case. Lenny wasn't eager to have him either. Lenny viewed Marks as an unimaginative, plodding attorney who was always available. He called him because he could be counted on to move fast in obtaining bail and filing a standard habeas corpus brief. Lenny didn't want Marks defending him on a rap that could put him away for years. He wanted a "top daddy," like Melvin Belli.

Two days following his own arrest, Lenny learned of the unrelated narcotics arrest in Los Angeles of Eric Miller. Without hesitation, Lenny championed Eric's cause. Seymour Lazar received a frantic, barely legible note from Lenny offering a 7½ percent interest in the Alberts, an English musical comedy act Lenny was managing, in exchange for handling Miller's defense.

> Your office takes Eric to the highest court to beat his case. Handle my beef. I *don't* want Eric's case to be lost just trial. The police, they found one joint in Eric's blue jacket he was wearing . . . Eric did porter work at hotel where the jacket belongs to a rock and roll group label sewn in and they left the jacket . . . but sincerely, I'd appeal to Supreme Court because he has no record and I don't want him to have ever.

Lazar understood the message but he declined the deal. Eventually, Eric entered a "negotiated plea" and did six to nine months in the county jail.

When Lenny turned up on the morning of October 10th for his arraignment at Van Nuys Municipal Court, he found a swarm of cameramen outside the small courtroom. Whereas he had been anxious to attract publicity after his San Francisco obscenity arrest, the stigma of the narcotics charge now made publicity something that he sought to shun at any cost. Sighting the waiting photographers, he suddenly became camera-shy. Sprinting toward the front of the oak-paneled courtroom, he wrapped himself inside the bear flag of the State of California, remaining in this enswathed state until a bailiff escorted him to a seat in the spectators' section.

Photographers' strobe lights flashed as Lenny cowered now behind the railing, hanging his head between his legs, while trying to hide his face. Finally, he employed a strategy that he had long meditated for such a contingency. He printed two words on a sheet of paper, which he held in front of his face. The message read: "Fuck you."

More strobe lights blinked as an apprehensive deputy sheriff hustled Lenny into a vacant women's rest room, where the accused waited until the session was ready to begin. When he emerged from the room, he had his five-button, mandarin-collared black jacket buttoned over his head. As the spectators laughed and applauded, the cameras clicked and hummed.

Gaunt and unsmiling, Lenny was arraigned finally before Judge Howard Schmidt. Marks stood beside him, having agreed to represent Lenny until he could obtain other counsel. Lenny was formally charged with possession of narcotics and released on $2,500 bail.

The surrealistic side show resumed when Lenny bolted out of the back door of the courtroom into a narrow alley with the photographers in hot pursuit. He was able to elude all but one of them, Ed Clark, a stocky television cameraman employed by local station KTLA. Clark shouted after Lenny, demanding that he halt his flight. Lenny obliged by stopping short and allegedly throwing a roundhouse left. Clark fell to the ground amidst the clatter of film gear. He quickly arose, though, and continued the chase.

Lenny dashed around the building, finally outdistancing Clark, who circled the block and ducked back into the courthouse looking for Marks. While Lenny was catching his breath, he graciously took time out to give his autograph to a fan. Again the amused photographers spotted him and resumed their chase. The Keystone comedy concluded with Lenny weaving his way through the heavy traffic and vanishing among the passers-by on the opposite side of the busy intersection. Marks, who had been patiently waiting in the getaway car, watched in astonishment as Lenny left him behind.

The bizarre event in Van Nuys received almost as much attention the next day in the *Los Angeles Herald-Examiner* as the first meeting since 1869 of the Ecumenical Council, which Pope John had convoked in Vatican City. That night Lenny watched his escapades unfold on several television news broadcasts, one of which used Mack Sennett background music. He compared these reports with the pictures and accounts in the *Herald-Examiner*. Television, he concluded, told a far more realistic story.

On the weekend following the bust, Lenny decided to cool out by the pool with Eric Miller and chic Eder. As inevitably happened when Lenny Bruce decided to lower the volume of his life, circumstances conspired to turn it back up again to blasting intensity. Years later, writing from an "adjustment center" cell in Folsom State Prison, chic was able to recall sixteen hours of that wild weekend in astonishing detail:

On Friday or Saturday night, about a week or two after his junk-bust in the Valley, Lenny, Eric, and I spent a quiet, relaxed afternoon—swimming, noshing on tidbits we'd scored from Gold-blatt's deli, and just enjoying one another's company. It wasn't the kind of rapport that we'd ever talked about—that would have killed it immediately; its duration was always uncertain; and it certainly couldn't be "planned."

Then, over a period of a half-hour, about a half a dozen people show up. All of a sudden Lenny's "on" in his usual frenetically manic way, and the mood is shattered. Eric's the first to react—he slips out and swings with Lenny's rented car. (Eric was notorious for disappearing for days at a time with the wheels.) About an hour later, I'm ready to get in the wind; not a simple move under the circumstances. The front door has this huge wooden bar across it that's difficult to remove without making so much noise as to be heard in the bedroom where everyone's congregated. The simplest exit for me is out the sliding glass doors in the living room which lead to the balcony from which I can drop down next to the pool, then go around the house to the driveway and my car. Lenny, though, is so fuckin' hip that when I get my jacket and start out of the bedroom he picks up immediately and calls me into the bathroom (the only place for good conspiratorial Howard Hughes–type conferences.) "You're gonna pull a fade, too, right? Where ya going?" "I figured I'd go down to my pad, get showered and changed, go for something to eat, then make the party that I hear the freaks of the Vito set are having. [Vito "The Sculptor" Paulakis was the Socrates—half philosopher, half satyr—of the early L.A. freakscene. A fifty-year-old artist and ex-dancer with a studio near Kanter's Deli, he was the leader of a pack of body-painted, mini-skirted girls who would descend on rock clubs, where they would dance with abandon.] Lenny allows as how the party might be a winner, and suggests that as quick as I change I come back up the hill and get him. He mentions that Eric might be back by then, and we crack up at the absurdity of that possibility.

(Lenny had a tremendous amount of personal feedback, and I believe he was aware of the exact point of transition in his tempo—from largo to vivace—and felt uncomfortable about hav-ing relinquished the rare, special thing we'd had for that short span of time. There was something whimsical in his plotting in that bathroom—as though the act of going to the party might recapture the continuity of the mood we'd had in the afternoon. He was like a kid who'd broken a toy that belonged to all three of us; knew it, and wanted to fix it.)

Anyhow, when I get back up the hill Lenny's still rappin' and hasn't even hit the shower. He's explained to everyone that we have some super-important business to take care of. By the time he gets showered and decked-out in a wild outfit, and we both geeze and get out of the house, it's ten o'clock. Only after he tells me, "When we hit Sunset, cop a right," do I realize there's been a change in plans. While I'd been down the hill, he'd gotten a call inviting him to a different party. I argue that there's a particular fox going to be at the Vito shindig with whom I'm anxious to get down; that I'm hungry; and that I've no eyes to make any of those phoney "Hollywood" scenes. He counters with the information that he's got to meet a guy there who can swing some juice regarding his recent bust; that this kind of affair's always catered better than a Temple Emanuel bar-mitzvah; that it's a party being given by and for very high society types—not new-rich mockies; that nothing ever gets to shakin' at Vito's till after midnight; and that we'll split the scene should either one give the other the "office" [the warning signal in pickpocket slang]. Of course, he has no intention of honoring this last commitment; but he sells me, as usual, and when we get to Sunset I head west.

All things considered, the address is easy to find. It's one of those "estates"—like you find in Connecticut, Westchester County, eastern L.I. or, as in this case, the Westwood/Pacific Palisades section of L.A. My piece-of-shit-short really looks incongruous in amongst those foreign and domestic chariots, limousines, and sport-cars. Lenny points out how you can immediately spot the difference between a shvar pimp's Caddy and one belonging to the truly rich.

Lenny finds the alleged juice man who'd invited him to the party, and I make a not-too-subtle zig-zag for the scoff—a buffet that wouldn't quit! I grease to a bust-out!—sturgeon, pâté de foie gras, all kinds of rich meats carved by smilin' "yassa-massa" Toms (who give me the feeling that they know I don't "belong" even before I fress up plates full of their epicurean delicacies). It isn't as much a party as a "social event." There are about 300 people there, a six-piece band, a slew of servants who take your order and are back within seconds with your drink. I've never been present at anything like it before, or since. We're in this huge ballroom, the glass doors of which lead out onto a sort of combination patio/garden—which in turn slopes down to a damned-near Olympic-size pool, with cabanas on the back side of it.

The band goes into a four-bar fanfare, and the cat who's fronting the group introduces a young dude who's just returned from

France, where he's been studying with Marcel Marceau. The guy does about five minutes of pantomime that's dynamite—and it's obvious from the response that he's working to a sophisticated, appreciative audience. Lenny hips me to how people on this strata invite fresh, chic talent to add spice to their affairs (some get paid, but most work for the exposure and social contacts). We move down to the wall by the raised bandstand while the next act is being introduced—two chicks who do risque parodies of show tunes, accompanying themselves on piano and guitar. Not bad, if you dig that goyishe shtiklach. Then the cat introduces "the controversial Lenny Bruce," and even more people move inside from the patio. Remember, Lenny'd recently had a shit-pot full of publicity behind his bust, and not too many of those in this audience would ordinarily catch his act.

Lenny comes on, extends his usual quieting, suspense-building pause, and starts shpritzing from the jump. "None of this is real —it's life imitating art! For those of you who haven't met your host, he's the Great Gatsby." Then he does a thing about how John O'Hara is really down with scenes like this: "The society chick horny for the sexy-looking Italian in the band . . . who's actually a Puerto Rican closet-queen."

Some asshole in the audience hollers up a Yiddish phrase, and Lenny slams him with: "Dig him! . . . He's passin'!" A lug like that, which you'd assume would be "in" only on double-hip sets, just killed them. He goes back to capping—addressing the band, he points to the audience: "They all went to college . . . never learned how to get laid." Then: "The servants were hired through Central Casting . . . work days playing the same parts on antebellum plantation sets at MGM." He's doing standards and one-liners, and he's laying them out. This is righteously *his* room, and he's gassed by the reception he's getting from these people, who it turns out are not at all unlike his regular audiences.

Lenny hates to get off when he's hitting that good, and there just aren't any acts who can follow him—both of which only heighten the unreality of what follows. He explains how he's got this expert teaching him about prison—"just in case they manage to railroad me." (I'd hipped him to the prison pecking order, general milieu, cultural aspects, etc., and explained how Oscar Wilde wasn't unique in having written poetry while doing time.) Lenny runs this down briefly to the audience, then goes into his Catskill/burlesque M.C. bit: "Direct from an extended engagement in the United States Penitentiary at Atlanta . . ."

Feeling like a lone Mousketeer about to follow the Mormon

Tabernacle Choir, I hit the stage and went into a classic prison
"toast," *Junkie's Lament:*

High-Rollin' chic, a rogue known to be slick,
Stood watching a game of pool.
His vines were fine, he was dressed to the nines,
He knew he was lookin' real cool.
He was choked up tight in a white-on-white,
Had on a charcoal continental that was dap.
A Countess Mara tie hung down to his fly.
On his head was a sportin' cap.
It was the 15th frame of a straight-pool game,
And chic stood watchin' the play.
With an idle shrug he suddenly dug
A strange cat moving his way.
He was a slender-built cat in a funny-lookin' hat,
Looked about ten years old.
Wore a fucked-up vine, needed a shine,
And he shivered as if he were cold,
As he moved in close wipin' his nose,
And the water ran from his eyes.
Chic pinned him, as the cat moved in,
And measured him up for size.
To all them other hicks but High-Rollin' chic,
He looked like an ordinary flunky.
But from well-trained eyes and many past highs,
Chic dug the cat for a junkie.
Chic had to grin as the cat came in,
And asked if he knew Joe Moore.
'Cause Joe wasn't around, his habit was down.
He'd gone to his man to score.
The cat looked drugged, as if he would bug,
When chic told him Joe had gone.
He said, "Where is he at," and "He can't do that,"
He was sick and he wanted to get on.
"I can see you're sick and in need of a fix."
[Chic and the guy turn on; the guy turns out to be an FBI agent.
Chic gets busted and convicted. His last words in court are:]
Now I ain't cryin' 'cause the agent was lyin',
And left youse all with a notion
That I'm a big-wheel in the narcotics field,
Hell, I hope the cop gets a promotion!
But I dug from the jump they were holdin' all the trump

When you wouldn't let my lawyer object.
A fact is a fact and a stack is a stack,
And I never got to shuffle the deck.
But it's all the same, it's in the game,
And I dug it when I stay in to play.
To give all the odds and take all the low cards
Is the price a junkie must pay.
I just want you all to note, and you reporters can quote,
Ol' chic he lost with a grin,
And there's those who know, and they'll tell you it's so,
It's the same grin I wear when I win!

By the end of the sixth stanza—where the plot opens up—I know I've got 'em. My timing, diction, and characterizations are *down*! I'm moving all over that little stage, playing to the whole audience, and acting my ass off! This kind of material, which is indigenous to slums and prisons—and even barracks—is original and mind-blowing to these squares, and really reaches them. When I close, the applause, laughter, and yelling are astounding—it's so heavy for me that I'm close to *coming*.

Anyhow, the band starts playing again, and Lenny and I get to mingling with different groups. I wind up in a corner talking trash to two Bennington-brat-broads who'd cut into me—and who just exude authentic "class" (the kind who never show any ostentation—wearing "simple" dresses that you *know* had to cost big bread). One of them's got that Barbie Doll punim—for which there must be a mold somewhere—which invariably turns Lenny on. He sidles up and tells me: "Why don't I wait here while you get that out of the car." I bop out to the short—graciously accepting kudos along the way—and get our outfits and stuff from the super-cool stash in the kickboard.

When I get back, Lenny runs this story on the chicks about how you get sweaty, onstage, and do they think we could maybe score the use of a nice quiet bathroom for a few minutes. They know their way around the layout, and the four of us wind up in a second-floor guest room. Lenny and I strip down to the waist, and hit this far-out bathroom—so wild we wonder what the one in the master bedroom must look like. We wash up; get the works, skag, and Meth lined up. I'm wired like General Electric, and am telling Lenny how my wasting this audience only proves that I can build an act around my prison background. At that moment he successfully ended my show-biz aspirations—although I didn't realize

it until I'd had a few days to think about his right-on statement:
"Forget it! You were just a freak to them! That shit's great for
living rooms, but there's no way you're going to build a professional
act around it. Why don't you just face the fact that you're an
amateur, and quit wasting your time. Besides, you gotta keep your
nights open to burgle!"

What with all the rapping, we're in there quite a while. Just
after I get everything cooked up, there's a knock on the bathroom
door, and a chick's voice: "What the hell are you *doing* in there?"
Lenny's just been through that bust, so you'd think he's at least
developed enough protective paranoia to be cool, right? Without
hesitating a lick, he opens the door and says: "We're about to
administer a large quantity of heroin and methamphetamine hydrochloride into our bodies via intravenous injection." Before I
can get over my astonishment at his audacity, he's got these two
foxes in the bathroom, goes into a description of the various ingredients and instruments, and has them fascinated. I get the two
syringes loaded, sit down on the toilet, tie off, get a hit, and geez,
all in about a half a minute. (Lenny sure envied me my "ropes"
—claiming I could get a hit from across the room.) All during the
"operation" Lenny's giving a running commentary on my actions.
I yank the spike, look up at these two chicks with down-dropping
jaws, and lug: "I can't speak for this dope-fiend, but I'm merely
a poor, unfortunate diabetic." They crack up, and Lenny switches
positions with me. Even his tracks have tracks, and he has to hit
four or five times before he gets a register. By now I'm smacked
down, my mind's wailing behind the crank [speed] and I'm digging
the chicks digging Lenny. They're both enthralled, but mine looks
like she's about to be sick (I say "mine" because the pairing off
is implicit); so I get her out of the bathroom before Lenny starts
jacking it back.

Right away she starts sounding me about how did I get started,
why do I use, what are the sensations—all the standard square
shit. I pull her up with: "Send me a sociological questionnaire,
and I'll fill it out sometime when I'm kicking." In no time we're
into some lightweight huggin' and muggin', and I figure I'm moving
pretty swift, 'til Lenny and that pretty-girl come out of the bathroom beautifully bare. I never wear underwear, so I'm balls-ass
naked in under 10 seconds. Then I stand out from between the
two king-size beds, so he can push them together to enlarge the
playing field, and I go to lock the door. It's already locked—which
could have been done by the chicks after Lenny and I'd gotten

into the bathroom—so we get off some good zingers about how far ahead of us they are. My fox tells us: "We needn't be concerned about appearances—the host and hostess are exceptionally broad-minded."

We get into sucking and fucking and freaking real good. The chick I'm making it with is one of them short-rolls moaner-groaners. Crank affects me as an orgasm retardant, and just as it's starting to get righteous good to me, Lenny's head pops up and he asks my chick: "What are ya doing—auditioning for the Ray Charles Singers?" That line is so applicable to the wild, chantin' rhythm she's grunting, that I fall out—literally! Lenny's screaming with laughter, I jump up, start pummeling him, the beds slide apart, and he gets caught between them. The scene's hilarious, and turns into an insane pillow fight.

We finally get back to balling—and switching chicks—and then into rapping. The Barbie Doll is blithering in triplets—some mean-ingless shit about her older sister who falls in love with every cat she makes it with—when I suddenly snap that she's cranked out of her gourd! (During that five to ten minutes they were in the bathroom together, Lenny not only got her out of her threads but turned her on to some Meth!) With the three of us working on her—and explaining that it's nothing but liquid Benzedrine—the other chick, who's starting to fall by the wayside at this late hour, and after that much activity, drinks down an amp. Then Lenny decides it's time for us to get off again. We do and, as we're cleaning the outfits, start a water-fight—using the syringes for pistols. We go out and shpritz the chicks, and Lenny gets Barbie to let him give her a douche—sans spike. By this time the four of us are so wired that we're rapping and tummuling simultaneously.

One of the chicks suggests a foray to the kitchen, and we four naked savages make a good simulated commando raid. The kitchen has a walk-in refrigerator—like you find in restaurants—and a large, heavy-duty blending machine. We throw in all kinds of fruit, and a few vegetables, and make a smooth, delicious concoction.

When we get back upstairs, you can see light on the edge of the world. Lenny and I get dressed, pack our drugstore, take our leave "nicely," and drive off into the sunrise.

Coda: The cat who'd invited Lenny to the party knows his way around the political set but, because of all the publicity the case has received, can't do him any solids. (I don't recall if he said it then, or at some other time, but Lenny contended that "what I really need is a lawyer with enough juice to get Ray Charles a driver's license!")

> A couple of days later we discover we've both got crabs . . .
> Lenny kind of liked the idea of having scored "high-society lice."

While Lenny and chic laughed at the aftermath of their riotous weekend, a notice was posted on the varnished front door of the Troubadour, a West Hollywood nightclub on Santa Monica Boulevard, where Lenny was scheduled to open a twelve-day run on the night of October 17th:

> *The Troubadour neither condones nor condemns*
> *Mr. Bruce's statements since it is our policy*
> *not to interfere or limit in any way an*
> *artist's performance on our stage.*

Attorneys had advised owner Doug Weston—who had previously presented many protest folk singers and controversial comedians without incident—to post the disclaimer for his own protection.

On Wednesday, October 17th, the folding chairs at the Troubadour were filled to capacity for Lenny's opening-night performance. Among the two hundred hardcore fans and curiosity-seekers were two vice squad officers, Sergeant Sherman Block and Deputy George H. Koga. They were joined by two other policemen far off their customary beat, Sergeant Joel Lesnick and Officer John L. White.

The presence of all four plainclothesmen was reminiscent of Lenny's past experiences at the Jazz Workshop in San Francisco. No complaint had been lodged by a private cititzen; yet the West Hollywood police felt it necessary to keep him under surveillance. Obviously, Lenny's public pronouncements were not helping his relations with the police. Lesnick and White were on hand presumably to determine whether or not Lenny would be performing "under the influence of drugs."

"I'm so bored with what you're interested in hearing about," he told the audience at the outset, referring to his recent legal hassles. "It's O.K. to get busted once, but I've been busted so many times this year." After the audience failed to react to this remark, he promised not to discuss his current problems any further. Instead, he recapped the highlights of his bust in Philadelphia. Lenny's tale of the Philadelphia elevator ride got him into a freewheeling dissertation that ranged from narcotics to marriage ("Makes you wonder why married men have to jack off more than anybody else") to midgets ("When you're a midget, you have a very limited point of view—the whole world's a crotch"). In one breath, he told a story about a man who liked to expose himself in public and in the next moment delivered a mordant commentary on church hypocrisy. "Religious leaders have missed the boat," he bellowed, the hand microphone close to his lips. " 'Thou Shalt Not Kill,' they say, and then one of them walks comfortingly to the death chamber with Caryl Chessman."

Seated at a rear table, Sergeant Block scribbled busily the notes that ultimately found their way into an official police report. One of Block's special qualifications was fluency in Yiddish. "During the course of suspect's narration," the dapper police officer reported, "he uttered obscene and offensive words including a reference to his ex-wife as being the type that became upset when he entered the bathroom while she was 'fressing' the maid. The term 'fressing' is Yiddish and means 'eating.' To 'eat' a person is a reference to committing an act of oral copulation upon that person. Throughout his narration suspect interjected the terms 'shmuck' and 'putz,' which are Yiddish, and mean 'penis.' Suspect also used the word 'shtup,' a Yiddish word meaning sexual intercourse when used in the context that suspect used it. Also uttered during narration by suspect were the terms 'asshole,' 'jackoff,' 'tits,' and 'ass.' "

Two days after his debut at the Troubadour, Lenny ran again a gauntlet of photographers in the corridor of the Van Nuys Municipal Court. He managed to temporarily sidestep the cameramen by rushing directly into the court of Judge Charles N. Hughes, which was already in session.

Burton Marks had bowed out by this time as Lenny's attorney; now he was represented without fee by the celebrated Melvin Belli. A partner of Seymour Lazar, Belli had never been averse to reaping a little publicity for himself. Even a momentary association with Lenny Bruce was certain to put the flamboyant lawyer's name in the papers.

To the charge of punching cameraman Ed Clark, Lenny pleaded not guilty. After Judge Hughes set November 19th as the date for a jury trial, Lenny dashed from the courtroom into a nearby rest room, locking himself inside a toilet cubicle, remaining there until the time arrived for his preliminary hearing before Judge Francis A. Cochran on the narcotics possession charge.

Silhouetted in a blizzard of strobe lights, Lenny entered Cochran's courtroom and found a seat in the front row as the persistent photographers continued to shoot pictures. Hunching his head inside his Chinese rabbi jacket, he got down so far that only his oily, wavy hair was visible. After gasping in this position for several minutes, he leaped up on his seat, whirled on the cameramen, and screamed: *"This is too much!"* Covering his face with a paper towel on which he had lettered the word "SHIT," he disappeared into a jury room from which photographers were barred. When the court day ended, Lenny had still not appeared before the judge. The preliminary hearing had to be continued to October 26th.

Six days following his opening at the Troubadour, on October 23rd, three other members of the sheriff's vice detail—Sergeant James L. Cline and Deputies Thomas P. Frawley and Gerald Schayer—turned up to catch Lenny's 10 P.M. show. The words they heard seemed more obscene than those first noted by Block:

> Suspect's act primarily centered around sexual activities of various sorts. In one anecdote the suspect described an individual as a "cocksucker" (a term used as slang to indicate an act of oral copulation). Various descriptive words such as "bastard," "asshole," "goddam" were interjected at various times through his performance.

As soon as the show was over, the three cops arrested Lenny and drove him to the West Hollywood precinct station four blocks away, the same station where he had been booked in the narcotics possession charge. This time he was charged with a misdemeanor: violation of Penal Code section 311.6. The ever-ready Marks was called; he arranged promptly to bail Lenny out.

The next night, Sergeants Block and Cline paid a return visit to the club, accompanied by Deputy District Attorney Richard Hecht, the city's expert on obscenity. Block reported:

> On this date October 24th, suspect Bruce's act was similar in content to those performances previously mentioned . . . At one period suspect started complaining to the person controlling the stage lights that they were too bright. After a brief period during which time the lights were not dimmed, suspect looked up to the control booth and hollered, "Where is that dwarf mother-fucker?" He subsequently bent over to the first table in the audience and stated, "The prick thinks I'm kidding!" In one of his anecdotes relating to New York policemen dressing as women to apprehend mashers, he stated, "This would never stop a real rape artist because some of these cops have pretty nice asses and the rapist might even want seconds."

The porno expert from the D.A.'s office advised the two vice-squaders that sufficient evidence existed to issue a complaint.

At 11:40 P.M. Lenny was arrested again, in his dressing room, and charged with the same misdemeanor, violation of the penal code and speaking obscene words in a public place. The squad car traveled the familiar route to the West Hollywood station house, where Lenny was booked and fingerprinted for the third time in less than three weeks. Cops and D.A.'s dig seeing their names in print as much as the next guy, so they made sure some reporters had been alerted to this latest bust. Lenny made no statement until he was released on $525 bail, which he paid himself, pending an appearance in Beverly Hills Municipal Court the following Tuesday. "I'm broke and I'm also having money problems," he plaintively told the press. "I don't know when or where I'll get an attorney."

In fact, he was already formulating plans to market the minutes from his San Francisco trials, as well as the eighteen-minute tape recording of his Jazz Workshop routine that had been played in court. In a phone conversation with Melvin Belli, he predicted that such a recording would sell at least half a million copies, although none of the four Bruce LPs previously released by Fantasy had sold more than fifty thousand copies.

Belli headed an imposing three-man brain trust at the narcotics preliminary hearing before Judge Cochran in Van Nuys, which had been postponed from October 26th to November 9th. Two of Belli's partners, Seymour Lazar and Samuel Brody, happened to be handling other cases in Van Nuys Municipal Court that day. The fact that they had taken time out to sit in on the hearing made Lenny feel even more confident.

Deputy Sheriff John Lee White took the witness stand first and described the events that led him to arrest Lenny. He indicated that Lenny had dropped from his left hand the matchbook containing heroin. He recalled that he had apprehended Lenny in Gunn's bicycle shop by ordering him to "hold it right there and raise your hands," and that he had then informed the defendant: "You are under arrest for violation of the State Narcotics Act." White stated further that he did not examine the contents of the packet found inside the matchbook until after he took Lenny into custody. His testimony indicated that he had arrested Lenny before ascertaining that a crime had been committed, a fact that would later have considerable significance. He told the court that Lenny had denied ever having seen the matchbook.

Brody cross-examined Sergeant Lesnick, who was called as the second witness. Lesnick corroborated White's previous testimony. After hearing the sheriff's forensic chemist, Harry McKeehan, testify that the powder found in the matchbook was heroin, Judge Cochran ruled that there was sufficient cause to believe that Lenny was guilty of a felony. He ordered Lenny to appear in Superior Court for arraignment on December 10th.

Amidst all these difficulties, Lenny was forced again to seek new counsel. He had signed a $3,000-a-week contract with the Gate of Horn, a Chicago nightclub, to begin a four-week run on November 27th, which would have him in Chicago during the period of the Beverly Hills obscenity trial. Meantime, he needed someone to replace Lazar—who had thrown up his hands and resigned—for the next court appearance and to arrange a postponement. Burton Marks seemed to be the man for the job.

Marks had recently received widespread publicity defending Carol Lane, a Los Angeles hooker. The case clarified the state's right to preempt the city's statute in a case of prostitution, establishing a major precedent. Impressed by the victory, Lenny asked Marks to represent him, explaining that with Lazar gone, he was the only expert to whom he could turn. At first, Marks was reluctant; but sensing apparently the opportunity to obtain more publicity for himself, as well as to help out his hero, Marks eventually capitulated. He agreed to handle the Beverly Hills obscenity and Van Nuys battery cases, but only after Lenny promised that he would allow Marks a free hand, an agreement confirmed in a letter dated November 30, 1962. Enclosed with the letter was a check for $500 and a tape recording specifying how Marks should obtain and interview expert witnesses, but in the very next sentence, after he agreed to allow Marks complete freedom of operation, Lenny made it clear that he would not be taking a back seat:

> The three trials will be all jury and I'll be allowed to pick the jury in a manner that will be unpretentious (I will not upstage you nor behave badly while we are in court).

Lenny also made mention of a six-page letter he had sent to Lesnick, typewritten on both sides, on how rookie police officers should interview narcotics users: "I should like to remind you about the letter I wrote to the boys that was rather incriminating and everybody felt, including Belli, will be my downfall. Well they didn't use it and I still think they are my friends."

Late in November, Lenny took off for his eagerly anticipated job in Chicago. It had been nearly a year since he had played the chilly city, and those who hadn't seen him for that period, or longer, were shocked at the change in his appearance. The once handsome, animated, brilliant performer and commentator was now a fat, bent, shabby-looking street cat, a horribly dissipated, baggy-eyed, numb-fleshed junkie, with a tragic darkness in his eyes. Walking slowly through the room and up on the stage, he gave off a creepy, repellent air, like some deranged old bum who had wandered in from skid row. Instead of the carefully bleached Levi suit or the somber black Nehru, he now wore a cheap blue car coat, hanging loose around his body to hide his growing obesity. There was something ominous about this new Lenny Bruce, something that began with the title of his show—*Let the Buyer Beware*—and extended through his beat, sinister appearance to emerge full-blown when he opened his mouth and began his hour-long jeremiad. Talking in bursts and slamming from one grimly phrased bit to another with the air of a man restlessly groping for some combination of words that will adequately express his rage, pain, and vindictive antagonism toward the world at large, Lenny Bruce loomed before his audience in Chicago as the opposite of a comedian.

What he had to say wasn't so much the issue anymore as the way he chose to say it. There were old bits like the Shelley Berman number and the Negro at the party; there were recent pieces like *We Killed Christ*, or the election of Norman Thomas; there were things that came out of that week's newspaper or out of his recent arrests in Los Angeles; but what characterized all this material and held it together—in a unity that Lenny's act had never before possessed—was the mordant, biting tone with which every subject was seized and slashed and slapped in the audience's face. By pressing and compressing every bit until it achieved a harsh, strident musical line, by volleying these bits one after another into the audience's mind with no softening of tone or relenting of vigor, Lenny created a phantasmagoric nightscape, a wretched, suffering, and embittered world. Like another Juvenal excoriating another Rome, he lashed out at the hypocrisy, the cant, the self-deluding moralism of the police, the politicians, the liberals, and the journalists. He also lashed himself in the guise of the Good Man, the man who says: "When I cheat, I always tell my wife." That was a new bit and its sour-mouthed irony encapsulated the mood of the whole show. "When I cheat on my wife, I always tell her. Because I'm an honest guy, and I come from a good culture, a decent culture, and I can't lie. Whenever I cheat on her, I gotta tell her—'cause I like to hurt her. I like to make her throw up!" That was the tone of all the new material: the bit on *Custody*, a mixture of memories from Lenny's childhood and his marriage, all turning on the idea that the "good man," the "good father," who obtains custody of his children from his "tramp" of a wife—who "shtups in front of the kids"—is really just a vengeance-seeking prick, out to inflict pain on his old lady. Yet the wife is just as bad in her own way, feigning fatigue and headache while her poor dumb schmuck of a husband stands there in his shorts begging her to "touch it once!" Men and women, husbands and wives, they make each other wretched and they drive their kids crazy, schlepping them back and forth in endless family quarrels.

So much for the family, that happy American home a whole generation of Americans had spent their lives celebrating. Now, up the next step of the ladder of social organization to the body politic: our country, right or wrong. How right is our country, Lenny began to ask, when it stations its armies over half the earth, lets its troops rape Italian mothers for candy bars, and burns up its enemies at long range with atom bombs? Where is the right and wrong of war? "If the Japs had won, Jim, they would have strung up Truman by his balls!"

What about patriotism? "I was a gunner's mate second class on the U.S.S. *Brooklyn* for six years," Lenny would tell his audience, establishing his own standing (with a little exaggeration); "I made five invasions at Anzio, Salerno—the whole scene!" Then he'd ask the audience whether that made him a hero and Gary Powers—who had just confessed to the Russians after being shot down in a U-2 spy plane—a traitor to his country? The question would suddenly transform itself into dialogue: the anonymous man-in-the-street dialogue that was spinning through Lenny's brain in these dark days:

"Goddamit, *I'd* never sell my country out!"

"You ever been tested?"

"I'm not the kind of guy that would. I know it. I'd *never* sell my country out. Powers is a fink. That's why I'm gonna cast the first stone: he's no good. A wrong guy, bad apple. If *I* get on the jury, *I'll burn his ass*. And he's going away for a long time. That's it, no bullshit. I've got secrets right here. *I'm* a loyal American. No, *I'd* never sell my country out.

"They got the other guy? They got his *pants* down? But I don't give a goddamn *what* they do to him, I'd never sell—What're they putting a funnel in his ass for? Can't put a funnel in his ass! Geneva Conference! Tell 'em to take the funnel out—they can't do that. . . . What're they heating up that lead for?

"You're not getting these secrets from me! Forget that with those tricks!

"They wouldn't put hot lead into that funnel that's in that guy's ass, now, would they? For a few dumb secrets! Would they? Would they? . . . They *are*? . . . Well, that's *ridiculous*!

"Oh, the secrets? *Surprise!* Here they are buddy! I, ah, I mean I got *more* secrets, too, you wouldn't even believe! These are bullshit secrets, I'll *make up* shit. I'll give you the President and the White House!

"I just don't want to get hot lead in my ass, that's all . . ."

That was the new Lenny Bruce. Not brilliant, imaginative, or "inside." Not hilariously funny. You sure couldn't sing it in the back of the cab on the way home from the show. But it was true and it was *right*. Right in every sense of the word. Right for that audience that was reading articles at that very moment about how the CIA had equipped Powers with a little poison needle that he was supposed to use in case he got captured. Right for Lenny Bruce because the bit was directly inspired by the guilt he must have felt after he had finked on all those dope dealers. Now that Lesnick had caught him again, the whole psychodrama had come zooming up to the surface of Lenny's mind. The bit was right, too, in terms of the vision that Lenny had suddenly gained in the wake of his current troubles. Like many a man before him, like that archetypal character—the old mad king out on the blasted heath—Lenny Bruce had been humanized through suffering. That was the meaning of it all—the obesity, the shabby clothes, the harsh tone, the *ad hominem* appeals to "Jim." Lenny Bruce, the Golden Boy of American comedy—the cute, the clever, the sick little, mean little, bright little master of the Funny-Funny-Funny pinball machine—had become a man! It had taken years. It would cost him his life. But he had finally found his fate and his theme.

Some nights he would end his act with a bit that had no precedent in the history of American nightclub humor. It was inspired by a poem of Thomas Merton that Lenny had read and treasured for a couple of years. Gloria Stavers had told him when he read it to her: "Some day you're gonna read that thing onstage!" It was much too strong for a nightclub audience. Lenny had been holding back with it, waiting till the time was right. Now was the time. Every night he would enact that chilling poem. He would call for a single pin spot. Then he would put on a very straight German accent. Staring sternly at the audience, he was Adolf Eichmann standing in the dock:

> *My name is Adolf Eichmann.*
> *The Jews came every day*
> *to vat they thought vould be*
> *fun in the showers.*
> *The mothers were quite ingenious.*

They vould take the children
and hide them in
bundles of clothing.
Vee found the children,
scrubbed them,
put them in the chambers,
and sealed them in.
I vatched through the portholes
as they would dahven and chant
        "Hey mein Liebe, heyyyy."
Ve took off their clean Jewish love-rings,
removed their teeth and hair—
for strategic defense.
I made soap out of them,
I made soap out of all of them;
and they hung me,
in full view of the prison yard.
People say,
        "Adolf Eichmann should have been hung!"
Nein.
Nein, *if you recognize the whoredom*
in all of you,
that you would have done the same,
if you dared know yourselves.
My defense?
I vas a soldier.
People laugh
        "Ha ha! This is no defense,
        that you are a soldier."
This is trite.
I vas a soldier,
a good soldier.
I saw the end of a conscientious day's effort.
I saw all the work that I did.
I, Adolf Eichmann,
vatched through the portholes.
I saw every Jew burned
und *turned into soap.*
Do you people think yourselves better
because you burned your enemies
at long distances
with missiles?

> *Without ever seeing what you'd done to them?*
> *Hiroshima . . .* Auf Wiedersehen!

At the conclusion of this cold, flat, reasonable recitation, Lenny would suddenly hurl his voice up into a cantorial wail that made your skin crawl. He would cry out in anguish, in a strange tongue, and then disappear into the darkness.

Though Lenny's act ran this same grim course night after night, he was still perfectly capable of throwing the script away and winging a wildly original free-form show whenever he was in the mood. On the night of November 28th, a Wednesday, he did the supper show in his usual pattern, then came back at eleven o'clock to repeat the same performance, with minor changes.

Between the middle and late shows, the members of The Establishment Company come into the club to see Lenny work. They were appearing in *Beyond the Fringe* at a Chicago theater, and were keen on digging Lenny, their hero. When the time came for the last show, Lenny was flying. Walking onstage and seizing the mike, he cries out "Sophie Tucker! You're a *cunt!*" Then he starts telling *The Lawrence Welk Story:* how Welk was born in Strasburg, North Dakota, "the only son of poor Polish immigrant parents, his father a famous Dixieland drummer, Ben Pollack." Already the lines of reality are flexing into the shapes of fantasy: Welk isn't Polish and his father is certainly not the old Jewish bandleader with the comical name. Welk's mother, Lenny continues, said in a recent interview: "Dankyou veddy moch, ledies and chentelemen. I vud like to say bud vahn ting: dot——is a fink! She balled da proputty man to get da paht." The voice and the bit belong not to *The Lawrence Welk Story* but to Lenny's impression of Maria Ouspenskaya on his first album.

Operating under the laws of Free Association, Lenny caroms next into *Count Dracula,* another classic bit; he soon swerves back onto the track of *The Lawrence Welk Story* and does his famous interview between the bandleader and the junkie spade trumpet player.

The next bit he announces is also from the early period, the *Airplane Glue Sniffer;* but before he can even get off the first line, he suddenly gets a better idea and goes into a rarely heard recollection of his days in the Mediterranean Fleet when he would make liberty in the North African ports and the Arab pimps would dog him through the strets offering all sorts of bizarre temptations.

> "Hey Yank! Wanna see a resbian show?"
> [Embarrassed voice] *"No, thanks!"*
> *"How about a resbian show, two girls, a dog . . ."*

"No, thanks a lot."
"How about two girls, a dog, a cat and a bear?"
"No. That's O.K. I jes' gotta get back to the base."
"How about two girls, a dog, a boy, and a camel?"

Then, when he's strung the Arab's offer out to ludicrous lengths, he swings back to the airplane-glue bit, goes up to the line, "I'm out of my skull for a dime!" and starts to head out on one of his favorite closers. Opening a closet door at the back of the stage, he tells the audience that he's going to take them backstage and show them the "secrets of show business." Then he starts to inventory the contents of the closet: "Some old shoes with dog shit on them that belonged to Ed Wynn. Ed was queer; used to pay girls to smear him with shit. Jerked off before every show to steady his nerves. Wanna Kleenex, Ed?" That bit cues him into his insult humor. Standing and shpritzing into the mike, as an invisible rhythm section plays stop time in his head, he fantasizes about the following celebrities (with increasing attention to the British citizens in the audience):

1. Sophie Tucker and Alan Ribback, the owner of the club, "who gets all the nooky he wants."
2. The British royal family: all suffering from syphilis and feeble-mindedness.
3. The British critics, especially one who had championed Lenny: "A flaming fag!"
4. Dinah Shore: "who never gets laid. She's the kind who laughs guys out of it. 'Oh come now . . . ha, ha! . . .' Her one sex pleasure is pushing Connie Boswell off a chair." [Connie Boswell was a crippled singer who worked sitting down.]
5. Eddie Cantor: "who takes it in the keister from Bobby Breen, which makes his eyes bulge!"
6. Chiang Kai-shek: "who never takes the puttees off. He'd fall over if he did."

After his lightning-fast shpritz, with the audience going bananas around him, Lenny suddenly puts on an Irish accent and recites a long poem about a hermit caught bathing nude by some girls who make his pecker stand up like a hat rack. The phallic image triggers one last association: a corny joke about a couple of lovers balling during the Blitz in a London underground station. When the girl asks the guy why he keeps nodding Yes! while they screw, he replies that his muffler is caught in his fly.

Years later, Jonathan Miller wrote a piece in the *Partisan Review* in which he compared Lenny to a mad projectionist cutting up and pasting together scraps of film in his booth atop the theater. It is the perfect image for this sort of madly inspired collage performance, which Lenny gave so rarely in his later years. Here it was offered as a tribute to his English fans: an *anthologie sonore* plucked off the shelves of a thousand nights, cut up like a jackpot, and paid out on the spur of the moment with improvisational genius.

Lenny had been working at the Gate of Horn for a little better than a week when he was busted again. The arrest took place at 1:10 in the morning of the 6th of December toward the end of a show that began at 12:30. The show was preserved in its entirety because *Playboy* was recording Lenny for an article they were preparing concerning his recent legal problems. As the shows were running that week, it was a rather good-natured performance. Lenny had walked out onstage complaining about the laundry service in the Hotel Maryland. He was wearing, he explained, a pajama top and rumpled denim trousers, with no underwear and socks that didn't match. The raincoat covered most of his body, but he really looked a mess. He did some of his punchy new bits, but seeing lots of people walking out of the club, he switched in the middle of the show to sure-fire material like the Negro at the party, the bit about his appearance in Milwaukee, and the closely related story of Lima, Ohio. He had just gotten into a bit about marijuana, when suddenly he noticed a couple of men rise up up in the audience and stride purposefully toward the stage. Sensing instantly that he was about to be busted, he used his last few seconds to shpritz the oncoming heat: laughing maniacally, he cried: *"Bolt the door! . . . Oh, shit! . . . Wake up! . . . Quick! . . . Out the back way! . . . The bricks move! . . . Anything! . . . It's SUPERJEW!!!"*

"We're police officers," declares the next voice on the tape.

"Oooooh, I knew that," teased Lenny as the cop vaulted onto the stage apron. "I knew that. Yeah!"

Many people were now standing to get a better view.

"Let's go, Lenny," orders the second cop, taking his arm.

"All right, man," he snaps.

"The show is over, ladies and gentlemen," the first cop tells the customers. "We're police officers. Everybody have a seat."

"Everybody have a seat, please," echoes the second cop. "We're vice officers." He turns to Lenny and says, "Let's go."

"After you," Lenny replies with mock formality.

"We'll check your I.D. cards as you're leaving," Cop One shouts to the audience, many of whom he suspected were not yet twenty-one, the legal drinking age. "We'll go downstairs. Your identification will be checked on the way out. If you do not happen to have a license, a description . . ."

"I don't have any," Lenny interrupts. "I don't even . . ."

Cop Two grasps his arm more firmly.

"Ladies and gentlemen," the Gate of Horn manager announces as Lenny is being led down the stairs, "we now have a new star of the show."

It took a long time to check three hundred I.D.s. The cops got irritable doing this dumb job. When the last guy in line said he "didn't believe in identification," one of the blues grabbed him by the back of the neck and the seat of the pants and hustled him down the stairs and into the patrol car where Lenny was sitting with Alan Ribback, the Gate's bartender and a writer who was doing a piece on Lenny for *Swank*. "Whatta hell are *you* doin' here?" cried Lenny when the door of the car opened and comedian George Carlin was pushed inside. "I got stupid with a cop," explained Carlin. Then the whole party was carried to headquarters, where they spent the better part of the night being shunted around from cell to cell until finally they were all bailed out.

The prime mover behind Lenny's Chicago bust was the Roman Catholic Church. The first unmistakable evidence of the church's involvement appeared during the following week, when the captain of the vice squad walked into the Gate of Horn and the following dialogue ensued:

. . . I'm Captain McDermott. I want to tell you that if this man ever uses a four-letter word in this club again, I'm going to pinch you and everyone in here. If he ever speaks against religion, I'm going to pinch you and everyone in here. Do you understand?

Ribback: I don't have anything against religion.

McDermott: Maybe I'm not talking to the right person. Are you the man who hired Lenny Bruce?

Ribback: Yes, I am. I'm Alan Ribback.

McDermott: Well, I don't know why you ever hired him. You've had some good people here. But he mocks the Pope—and I'm speaking as a Catholic. I'm here to tell you your license is in danger. We're going to have someone here watching every show. Do you understand?

Ribback: Yes.

Lenny worked that very same night, and the next morning Ribback was informed that his license had been suspended. The charge was "presenting a lewd show."

Variety—which had never taken a favorable view of Lenny's work and had warned at the very outset of his career, back in 1959, that "by satirizing such a wide range of subjects he is certain to offend someone eventually"—saw the Chicago arrest as more a case of blasphemy than of obscenity: "The prosecutor is at least equally concerned with Bruce's indictments of organized religion as he is with the more obvious sexual content of the comic's act. It's possible that Bruce's comments on the Catholic Church have hit sensitive nerves in Chicago's Catholic-oriented administration and police department." How much importance the feelings of Catholics might have in such a matter could be inferred from the simple fact that out of a total population of three and a half million, Roman Catholics numbered two million, two hundred thousand. The proportion of Catholics in the police and legal administration was even higher. Most important, the number of Catholic jurors impaneled for the Bruce trial was forty-seven out of fifty. Eventually, the trial assumed the form of an inquisition, with a Catholic judge, a Catholic prosecutor, and an all-Catholic jury, every one of whom showed up on Ash Wednesday with a black smudge in the middle of his forehead. (The judge had to order the jurors to remove the mark.) As Brendan Behan exclaimed: "That scares *me*—and I'm Catholic!"

On the very day that Lenny was arrested in Chicago, Marks made a perfunctory appearance for his client in Beverly Hills Municipal Court, where he was allowed to substitute for Lazar. Two days later, on December 7th, he returned to the same court and agreed with the district attorney's office to postpone Lenny's obscenity trial until December 28th. He discussed with the court the possibility of proceeding with the jury trial on that date in Lenny's absence.

Marks summarized the status of Lenny's crowded legal calendar in a letter dated December 10th, the same day his client failed to appear for arraignment in the Los Angeles narcotics case:

> It will be necessary to order a reporter and also to have from you some names and addresses, if possible, of persons who were in the audience (preferably female) who might testify favorably regarding the emotional impact of your act upon them; i.e., funny, not revolting, not appealing to prurient interest, etc. The battery charge is scheduled for Feb. 4th, 1963. A brief interview with interested parties indicates that the possibility of a satisfactory compromise in accordance with the spirit and letter of the law may be reached

prior to the trial date. (I do not recommend, nor contemplate, a civil action against the news agency Station KTLA.)

Marks also suggested that Lenny appear in court on December 18th to offer a not-guilty plea in his narcotics case and be re-released on bail until the trial.

Even as Marks was trying to impress upon Lenny the seriousness of his case, and at the same time exercise proper restaints upon his client, Lenny was thinking up new schemes to save himself. He phoned Belli in San Francisco, pleading that he associate with Marks in his defense. Flushed with his success in the Lane case, Marks insisted that he try the case alone.

Adding to the endless distractions in Lenny's life were the latest developments at the House on the Hill. The city had ordered the guest house torn down. While he was performing in Chicago, a salvage company had carted away the bricks and lumber, leaving an exposed foundation, a maze of pipes, and several pathetic-looking toilets.

The obscenity trial got under way in Beverly Hills Municipal Court on December 28, 1962, with motions by Marks to dismiss the case because of the prior obscenity acquittal in San Francisco. Lenny had given his consent for the trial to proceed in his absence, while he fulfilled a nightclub commitment. Judge Dulin denied the motion to dismiss before excusing the jury until Wednesday morning, January 2nd.

New Year's Eve found Lenny opening at the club Le B, in south Miami Beach. The owner had hired Lenny hoping to capitalize on his recent notoriety. Lenny took the offer because he was strapped for money. His legal bills for 1962 had reached $12,188, over 15 percent of his gross earnings.

The new year held little joy for Lenny Bruce. His thoughts were focused on the twisted, confusing logistics of his life. It was a time of head-banging, as he obsessed over the mess in which he found himself. Back and forth he paced in his Miami motel room, thinking through the biggest decision of his career. By New Year's Day, Lenny had made a resolution that he was bound to keep. In order to survive, he needed to thoroughly familiarize himself with the law. Instead of entrusting such matters to attorneys, who frequently failed to comprehend what he was attempting to convey to the public, he would have to control and guide his own defense.

Lenny purchased a copy of the United States Constitution at a Miami Beach bookstore, as well as a $14 copy of *Black's Law Dictionary*. Instantly he became fascinated with the legal terminology and the recitation of past cases and precedents. At the outset, however, his lack of education held him back; simple matters of grammar and even the use of punctuation confused him. For two nights he stayed awake, while devouring *Black's*, taking shots of Methedrine every three hours to sustain himself. Inspired by the material he had just read, he scribbled a letter to Marks on both sides of a manila envelope, the only paper he could find to write on. The Meth did not allow him to sustain a line of thought; his brain skipped from one idea to another like a jerky teletype.

Dear Bert

Tell absolutely no one the following. The . . . obscenity trial will be taped and I will be allowed to put it out as an album. And nobody else will be allowed to because you will get releases signed and give them to me four days before the trial . . . Al Bendich, the S.F. att. had so many witnes that the issue got confused. I know how a show should be run. Most of the wittnes in the S. F. trial were under 40. A 50 year old Irish security guard is worth more than 6 30 yr. old Jewish physicists. Put yourself in the jury box, who's going to be sweeter to his daughter and less likely to rape her and kill her, the Irish father or the Jewish father? I asume that you will allow me (with no ones knolage natcherly) to handle this case and I will be able to give $1500 for it (and $1000 for the narcotic trial) I pick the jury, wittnesses . . .

. . . Take lie detector test . . . to prove to newspaper that photographer heap full of shit. Other news photographers told me today thats his gimmick falling down and sueing . . .

Help me. Their trying to pin a phoney rap on me.

Lenny worked at the Village Vanguard from January 3rd to February 10th. The terrible mental pressure of his fears and anger continued to distort his act, until finally something broke in his brain and he emerged as a startling new stage character—the shaman, exorciser of demons.

"In every primitive tribe," writes the Hungarian psychoanalyst Geza Roheim, "we find the shaman in the center of society, and it is easy to show that he is either a neurotic or psychotic: or at least that his art is based on the same mechanism as a neurosis or psychosis. The shaman makes both visible and public the systems of symbolic fantasy that are present in the psyche of every adult member of society. They are the leaders in an infantile game and the lightning conductors of common anxiety. They fight the demons so that others can hunt the prey and in general fight reality."

The shaman is not a priest, nor is he a medicine man. The closest thing to him in the Western world (shamanism is primarily a phenomenon of oriental civilizations, especially of the peoples who live along the line that descends from Siberia through Tibet to Indonesia) is the exorcist. The shaman, however, is also an artist—an artist who employs his art for the well-being of the tribe. What he offers the tribe is a performance, an act of intense make-believe. Gathering the people together in a lodge, he first puts himself into a trance. Then, through the use of drugs, drums, chants, and other devices, he reaches a state of ecstasy. Eventually, he launches out on a spirit voyage, traveling in an imaginary boat or climbing an invisible tree. His destination is the other world. Along his path he encounters demons and gives battle. Every encounter and blow he describes vividly to his audience, which sits around in fearful concentration. If the shaman reaches his goal in the spirit world and obtains the information or the powers which he is seeking on behalf of his people, his voyage is celebrated as a triumph for the whole tribe. If the shaman fails to reach the goal or loses control of the spirits, he must be killed.

Lenny's act—the drugs, the lights, the chants and drumbeats—was pure shamanism, as was his spooky appearance, and his symbolic acts, like climbing on chairs or throwing open doors, or threatening violence. You could picture him perfectly in the darkened, cavelike club, charged with tension, where the audience sits hunched over, tense, breathless, its eyes fastened on the weird figure in the center of the magic circle. While the tribe looks on in fearful absorption, the shaman prepares himself with drugs in anticipation of his terrible struggle with the tribal demons. Then when the "unspeakable" has been shouted forth, there is mingled with the urgent applause a sigh of release. Purged of their demons, the tribe has been freed for the moment, to "hunt the prey and . . . fight reality."

A wondrous achievement! But it entails a danger: losing control of the spirits. Some people want to be aroused and put through profound and shocking experiences. Others not only resist and resent such treatment but want to make it impossible for anyone else to undergo such a séance. As you pondered Bruce's amazing record of recent arrests, you could see that one of his troubles was simply the fact that he was turning everybody on. He had polarized the public; while one group was worshiping him, another was seeking to lock him up. If you followed the parallel of the shaman to its logical conclusion, it was clear that Lenny Bruce *was* letting the spirits get out of control. He was arousing more demons than he was defeating. If things got bad enough, Lenny might suffer the fate of the failed shaman. The tribe might turn around and kill him.

Chapter Twelve

TRIALS AND ERRORS

On Monday morning, February 11th, Lenny's obscenity trial began at Beverly Hills Municipal Court. The first day was spent in quizzing prospective jurors. The next day was Lincoln's Birthday, a holiday for the court—but not for the sheriff's department. Two officers caught Lenny's show that night at the Unicorn and arrested him, charging again that he had delivered a lewd and obscene performance. When the proceedings resumed on February 13th, all three obscenity arrests—the two at the Troubadour and this latest at the Unicorn—were consolidated and ordered tried together. The following morning the trial finally got under way.

Sergeant Sherman Block, whom Lenny called "the Yiddish Undercover Agent," testified, as did Deputy Sheriff Gerald Schayer. As in the trial in San Francisco, the officers pulled words and phrases out of context and reduced the meaning of Lenny's act to the level of grafitti on a men's room wall. Marks was able to introduce as evidence excerpts from Bruce performances similar to those he had given at the Troubadour and the Unicorn. There was frequent laughter from the jury, and Lenny was encouraged by this response to think that this panel was more sophisticated than the jury he had encountered in San Francisco.

The laughter—and the sympathy it betokened—died when Lenny was called to the stand. He looked bizarre in his faded blue chambray shirt and Levi jacket. He had ignored Marks's demands that he have his shaggy hair and long sideburns shorn. His only concession to the decorum of the court had been a fast makeup job in the lawyer's car: dabs of Max Factor applied to the bags around his eyes. What provoked the bench was his refusal to take the customary oath. He promised to tell the truth, but he refused to raise his hand and swear.

Cross-examined by Deputy District Attorney Ross, Lenny proved to be a slippery and elusive witness. Instead of replying directly to the questions, he used every response as an opportunity to state his views on society and the world. Asked what effect he wanted to produce on his audiences, he replied: "I want them to stop punishing each other, and I want them to open up the jails and have rachmunis [compassion]." The incongruity between such lofty moral purposes and the dirty words with which the jury had been bombarded was so extreme (and the mechanisms of Lenny's comedy so completely unexplained) that some of the jury must have thought he was bullshitting. No expert witnesses were called to make up for this deficiency in the defense. In fact, the only witness Marks called was his wife, Jenny, who had been at one of the shows for which Lenny was busted. Nervous, fidgety, and discomposed on the stand, Mrs. Marks blundered and fumffered. Compared to the elaborate defense marshaled by Bendich in San Francisco, this L.A. strategy was utterly inadequate.

At 4:40 on Friday afternoon, February 15th, the jury entered a private room to begin its deliberations. Two hours later, it was still out. Judge Drager called Marks and Ross into his chambers. He said that he doubted the case was important enough to be held over the weekend. He wanted their permission to bring back the jury and expedite its verdict. Both attorneys agreed to this unusual procedure.

A poll of the jury, which returned at 7:00, revealed six favoring acquittal and six opposed. They were sent back to their room for further deliberations.

At 7:30, Drager recalled the jury to the courtroom. They were still hung up, deadlocked at six and six. The judge declared a mistrial. He set February 25th as the date to hear a motion for a new trial. But the question of whether he had the right to hustle the jury hung like a cloud over the completed proceedings.

Lenny was very unhappy about the trial. To him the hung jury was tantamount to a conviction. To Marks it was a victory.

Following the disappointing Beverly Hills verdict, Lenny caught the first plane to Chicago, where his third obscenity case would begin the following Monday. Samuel Friefeld, an attorney for the Gate of Horn, and Donald Page Moore, the lawyer who won a 1962 reprieve from the electric chair for convicted murderer Paul Crump, had made several preliminary appearances in Lenny's behalf while his Beverly Hills trial was still in progress. A conflict of interest caused Friefeld to drop out. Moore stepped aside when Lenny made it clear that he intended to direct the case himself. Still smarting over the inconclusive Beverly Hills decision, he could no longer resist the temptation to play attorney and thereby achieve total control over his fate.

Several weeks earlier, Lenny had asked Earle Zaidins to coach him from the sidelines. Zaidins was a member of the New York and Wisconsin bars, but he was not conversant with Illinois law. He didn't want to get mixed up in the case, but—as always—he melted in the face of Lenny's pleadings. Lenny assumed that because he had witnessed several obscenity trials, he was capable of conducting his own defense. Legal history doesn't record many instances of men with so much to lose taking such grave and unnecessary risks.

The trial opened on Monday morning, February 18th. The judge was Michael J. Ryan. There was no doubt that Lenny was running the show, as he conducted lengthy interrogations of the prospective jurors. Lenny asked each one of them if they would be shocked by such words as "fuck," "piss," "tits," "jack-off," "balls," "schmuck," "friggit," "condoms," and the phrase "stepping on my dick." The words rolled off his tongue as he moved across the room with catlike strides, firing questions at the jurors with surprising skill.

Lenny had some quirky notions on how to choose a jury. He felt that one of the crucial factors in his San Francisco victory had been the presence on the jury of an old lady who couldn't sit through the lengthy deliberations of the panel because she needed a drink. He wanted to embarrass the Chicago jury with such another old boozer. Finally he found the woman he was seeking: her name was Bridey Finnerty. When Lenny started questioning her, he said: "Do you know who I am?" When she said, "No," Lenny was furious because he was certain she was lying. He decided to disqualify her by proving that she lied about other matters. He asked her, "Do you ever masturbate?" Judge Ryan summoned Lenny to the bench and told him that he would not permit such questions in his courtroom. Lenny explained that if the woman had said no to this question, it would prove she was a liar because scientific statistics had established the fact that everybody jerks off. The judge was a sly old dog. He invited Lenny to his chambers and offered him a glass of brandy—to test whether he was an addict. Lenny accepted the drink and choked it down. He then went back to the courtroom and eliminated the old lady on a direct challenge.

The opening remarks by the prosecution, Assistant District Attorney Samuel V. Banks, had barely begun when Judge Ryan interrupted. "Ladies and gentlemen," the judge declared, noting several youthful faces scattered among the spectators, "all of the children will please be escorted from the courtroom during this part of the jury trial. Will the parents please take all the children out?" Lenny and Zaidins watched the ensuing exit impassively.

"There are certain terms and words used [at the Gate of Horn performance] which are not the acceptable standard of our community," said Banks, "but I will be forced to use them in the opening statement to you so that you will all be apprised of exactly what is the issue here." Now it became obvious that Lenny was not the only actor in court, as Banks played the white knight preparing to slay the foul-mouthed dragon. "I don't like to use these terms," he continued apologetically, "but I have to. Mr. Bruce, throughout his performance, used the word 'fuck' constantly . . ."

Like a veteran performer, Banks paused to allow the impact of that word to register on the minds of the jurors. "Truthfully," he said, "I am not permitted to say what I feel. I am sure that you have noticed the perspiration on my nose and my upper lip." The jurors strained to get a better view. Sensing that he had them set up, Banks swung hard now with his knockout punch. "You will hear the mockery of the Church," he warned, his voice quavering, "not just any church, not just the Catholic Church, not just the Lutheran Church, but the Church *per se*. You will hear mockery that is vulgar and obscene."

"Objection!" shouted Zaidins. He said that his co-counsel was not on trial for mocking the Church, but merely for using allegedly obscene language. Ryan informed the jury to disregard the previous impassioned comments delivered by Banks. But a telling point had been made.

"Ladies and gentlemen of the jury, I am Lenny Bruce," the attorney of record began nervously, speaking in short, choppy sentences.

I am a comedian. I am going to prove that my intention is not to degradate the community, to lower the standards. I will support this theory of my intentions with letters from specific Catholic priests who heard this performance, and an Episcopalian priest who also heard this show. I will prove that the State must have heard a different show. Certainly there is no relation to any of those words that he, Banks, said.

I will prove that the police officer who arrested me unfortunately did not have sufficient academic exposure to understand the meaning of the stories which preceded the words, and I feel that I will prove also that although the eating of pork would be disgusting, it would not be obscene.

I will prove that the wearing of most vulgar clothing like platform shoes or ankle straps, although it is most vulgate, would not be obscene. I will prove that although it may be blasphemy, religious ridicule is not profanity. I will prove that there has been damage to my career, irreparable damage. I will prove that through a tape recording of that show. Every word was taped. Thank you.

The second act of Lenny's courtroom performance—following his dramatic selection of the jury—was very nearly a flop. His hesitant delivery made a poor contrast to the emotional philippics of Banks. What's more, the meaning of his remarks was largely incomprehensible because as often happened when he essayed "correct" English, he put his foot in his mouth. The embarrassed Zaidins wished he were anywhere else. Lenny soon sensed that he was fucking up. As he returned to the counsel table, he slumped into his chair.

Arresting Officer Arthur Tyrrell took the stand as the first witness for the prosecution. His testimony indicated that he had merely heard the dirty words Lenny was using, without understanding their context. Following instructions from Lenny, Zaidins preceded his cross-examination of Tyrrell by making a motion to play a tape recording of the disputed performance. Lenny felt that the early introduction of the tape would effectively demolish the testimony of Tyrrell and Banks. He had also taken care to doctor the tape so that some of the most offensive passages were cut out. Ryan decided, however, to recess the court and listen to the forty-minute tape in his chambers. Eventually, he ruled that the tape could be heard by the jury.

The cross-examination of Tyrrell by Zaidins resumed the following morning. Testing Tyrrell's knowledge of the Chicago obscenity statute, Zaidins, acting on orders from Lenny, asked the officer if the expression "strung up by the balls" related to a morbid interest in excretion.

"Give me a definition, please," Tyrrell replied evasively.

Zaidins asked if he knew what "excretion" was.

"Somewhat, yes, sir," Tyrrell said, hesitating.

Zaidins wondered aloud how Tyrrell could be certain that Lenny's reference to Truman's genitals did not represent a morbid interest in excretion.

Tyrrell replied that he knew what was obscene.

Before Officer Michael Noro took the stand as the second prosecution witness of February 21st, Ryan requested that thirty students from a Catholic girls' college—who had just entered the room on a tour of the courts—be asked to leave the premises.

Noro gave substantially the same testimony as Tyrrell. He told the court that he felt the performance in question was obscene. Again, Lenny declined to conduct the cross-examination, preferring to count on the playing of the tape recording and the appearance he would make in his own defense. In cross-examination, Zaidins introduced evidence of Noro's previous testimony at a hearing before the Illinois State Liquor Licensing Commission, at which time the Gate of Horn was fined and lost its license for presenting an obscene show. At the hearing, Noro had admitted that none of the things that Lenny had said appealed to his prurient interest.

"No further questions," said Zaidins, abruptly discharging the witness.

The prosecution rested its case.

All during the first week of the trial, matters were going from bad to worse in Lenny's private life. Boxed up with Zaidins in adjoining rooms at the Hotel Maryland, Lenny was constantly plotting defense strategies that just as constantly collapsed. He had promised, for example, to present a Catholic priest as a defense witness. The cleric he had in mind was Father Norman O'Connor, "the Jazz Priest," a man who had associated himself closely and publicly with jazz musicians and cabaret entertainers. Father O'Connor promised Lenny that he would testify on his behalf; then he reneged on his promise, sending a wire saying that he would have to "cop out." Lenny was instantly on the phone, calling the Paulist Father in New York. After a heated argument, he yelled: "If you come, what can they do to you? Bust you to nun?"

Catholic solidarity was demonstrated time and again that week. One night Zaidins persuaded Lenny to go out with him to a restaurant and have a good solid meal. They went to a steak house and noticed a drunken priest at the bar. When the priest heard that there was a famous comedian in the room who had appeared on the *Steve Allen Show*, he insisted upon meeting him. He came over to the table and was graciously greeted by Lenny, who invited him to share the meal and order another drink. Suddenly, the besotted priest awoke to the fact that he was talking to the notorious Lenny Bruce. Without saying a word, he jumped up and practically ran out of the restaurant. Lenny was terribly hurt. "What did I do to that man?" he exclaimed. "They're really out to get me! Look how they've poisoned people's minds against me!"

Even worse than the feeling that he was being persecuted by Roman Catholics was the agony Lenny was experiencing this week with his drug habit. The notoriety of the trial had closed off his normal sources of supply. Just at the moment when his craving for drugs was most intense, he was reduced to running around all night trying to score from the lowest sort of street pusher. On one night alone, he spent $350 for heroin; even so, he couldn't score enough dope to still his hunger. He got so desperate that he began taking pathetic long shots. He had a friend call up jazz drummer Art Blakey; when the musician answered, Lenny grabbed the phone, introduced himself, and in practically the same breath asked him whether he had any "smack." Blakey hung up fast. Finally, on Friday, when Ryan adjourned the trial for the weekend, Lenny decided to make a flying trip to L.A., where he could obtain both money and drugs. He made one call from the airport—to Honey—and boarded the plane.

Early Saturday morning, February 23rd, he landed at Los Angeles International Airport and ducked into a Yellow Cab. At the intersection of Sunset Boulevard and La Brea Avenue, the cab was intercepted and forced to the curb by an unmarked car. The police had noticed that one of the cab's headlights was out. (Every Los Angeles Yellow Cab had a switch on the dashboard that could extinguish the right headlight, thus indicating that the driver was being robbed.) Ironically, the darkened light in Lenny's cab was the *left* one. It's wires were defective. The cops never noticed the difference.

Lenny was ordered out of the cab. One of the policemen made a move to search his pockets, but Lenny pushed him away. He was subdued with a hammerlock, placed in handcuffs, and thrown into the car. A search of the cab turned up a gram of heroin inside a knotted balloon; several syringes and bottles of Methedrine were also found in Lenny's attaché case. The police also noted the heavy tracks on Lenny's arms. They took him to a local station house and booked him on suspicion of narcotics possession. He was not released until Tuesday. Even then, the terms of his $2,625 bail were such that he could not leave Los Angeles before a preliminary hearing scheduled for March 7th.

John Marshall, a noted L.A. attorney who had taken over Lenny's first narcotics possession case, appeared at the hearing in Los Angeles Municipal Court. He argued that Lenny had been illegally searched and seized and that the heroin had been found in a public conveyance; there was no evidence linking its possession to Lenny. He also noted that the police had no reason to stop a cab with a defective headlight. Judge Tante disagreed with Marshall's contentions; he felt that sufficient cause had been established for a belief that Lenny was guilty and ordered him remanded to trial. (Four weeks later in Los Angeles Superior Court, Judge Alfred O. Peracca dismissed the case. He ruled that Lenny's constitutional guarantees against illegal search and seizure had been violated.)

Back in Chicago, on the morning of the bust, Earle Zaidins began to feel uneasy when Lenny failed to call him, as he had promised to do. When he read about Lenny's bust in the afternoon edition of the

Sun-Times, his uneasiness escalated to keen anxiety. Unable to reach Lenny at the House on the Hill, Zaidins began frantically telephoning attorneys in the Chicago area. He was uncertain of the consequences if Lenny was unable to appear in court on Monday morning. Nor had he any clear idea of how to proceed with the case. Bit by bit, that afternoon, the seriousness of the situation became clear. Ignorant of Illinois law, Zaidins had allowed Lenny to leave the city without obtaining the necessary permission from Judge Ryan. Technically, Lenny Bruce was now a fugitive from justice!

Standing alone before the court on Monday morning (after a hasty telephone conference with Harry Kalven, a law professor at the University of Chicago), Zaidins informed Judge Ryan of the developments of the weekend. He explained that Lenny had been freed on bail in Los Angeles, but was unable at the moment to return to Chicago. Zaidins seemed as uncertain about California law as he did about the customs of the Chicago courts. Nor could he say when Lenny would be allowed to leave Los Angeles. He requested a delay in the proceedings until he had an opportunity to speak with Lenny and some knowledgeable attorneys. Judge Ryan granted a two-day continuance.

Zaidins finally reached Lenny on Tuesday night, confirming his suspicion that it would be impossible for him to return to Chicago without forfeiting bail. Throughout the course of the chaotic two-hour phone conversation, Lenny attempted to instruct Zaidins on how the case should be handled in his absence. He also brought Zaidins up to date on his latest and continuing legal problems, going so far as to suggest that Zaidins fly to California to handle the narcotics case. Lenny had become so desperate that he was unable to keep his mind on one problem at a time. Zaidins was left so thoroughly confused that he called Kalven the next day for further advice.

Zaidins presented a pathetic figure when the trial resumed on Wednesday, February 27th. First, he asked for another continuance. Somewhat perfunctorily, Ryan replied that he had granted enough time and continuances, reminding Zaidins that he had been unaware of Lenny's decision to leave the court's jurisdiction during the trial. He ruled that Zaidins must return that afternoon with a defense. Following the luncheon recess, Zaidins entered a motion for a directed verdict of not guilty, asserting that the jury had heard only the allegedly obscene words out of the context of Lenny's performance. He cited case law precedents showing that previous decisions had hinged on the significance of those words within the context of the entire work or show.

Judge Ryan overruled the motion.

Desperately, without laying the proper basis, Zaidins then moved for a change of venue, arguing that Lenny was not receiving a fair trial in Ryan's court.

Judge Ryan again overruled the motion. He was becoming increasingly irritated.

Zaidins, who had been backed into a corner and had run out of arguments, despairingly replied that Lenny was counsel and that he was merely co-counsel. "I may state," the disgusted Ryan interjected, "it was represented to this court that Mr. Zaidins was a duly licensed lawyer and attorney in the State of New York and also Wisconsin, but from the statements made it appears there should be some question as to whether he is a duly licensed attorney."

Zaidins's face reddened: "I would like until tomorrow so I could stipulate for the prosecution as to credentials," he replied, in a final, pathetic attempt to win a delay.

Judge Ryan rapped his gavel emphatically and ordered Zaidins to proceed with the defense. Zaidins was unprepared for this turn of events. The defense had no available witnesses. None of the people Lenny planned to call upon—Ralph J. Gleason, Nat Hentoff, Steve Allen—had actually been summoned. The whole battle plan had fallen to pieces.

Zaidins's only move was to play the doctored tape recording of Lenny's performance at the Gate of Horn. The jurors listened intently and court was adjourned at the conclusion of the playback.

The next day, Zaidins failed to offer any explanation of what Lenny was attempting to say on the tape. Likewise, he neglected to introduce any reviews of his act or any of the numerous magazine analyses which were not only flattering to Lenny but which intelligently interpreted his routines.

Ryan soon adjourned the court and immediately thereafter forfeited Lenny's $500 bail and issued a bench warrant for his arrest. The judge was outraged over the course of the proceedings.

In a phone conversation with Lenny that night, Zaidins described his pitiable plight. Rather than offering any concrete suggestions for continuing his defense, Lenny came up with another desperate angle.

Before resuming his woeful performance the next morning, Zaidins insisted that he wanted to examine a Captain McDermott concerning some allegedly prejudicial comments that he had made; but, he complained, he was unable to bring the witness into court. As instructed by Lenny, he asked for a further delay until McDermott could be called.

Ryan angrily retorted that Zaidins had already had sufficient time to subpoena McDermott. The judge declared that he would not continue the trial for so flimsy a reason.

"Since I am under instruction from the defendant, himself, as to how he wants this done today," Zaidins resignedly answered, "and since this decision throws off the interrogation in regards to how he wishes to have it related, I have no further orders from him on this, and consequently the defense must rest."

After the lawyers' summations, the jury withdrew, and returned after one hour with the inevitable verdict. It found Lenny Bruce "guilty as charged."

The Chicago conviction galvanized Lenny. For the first time in his life he was a wanted man. There was no end in sight to the pressures of the police. No way out of the legal morass. His only hope of survival lay in acquiring the legal knowledge that would enable him to win in court. Every day, he endeavored to visit new libraries and scan past cases. A discovery in one case invariably led him to another case. If the new case was unavailable in one law library, he would race to another library in search of it. He accumulated reams of paper, spending hundreds of dollars copying pages from trial decisions. Ultimately, to reduce spiraling costs, he had a Verifax machine installed in the bedroom of the House on the Hill. So engrossing was his research that he hated to waste time sleeping. To keep himself awake he stepped up his dosage of Methedrine.

Barricaded in his Spartan bedroom on the upper floor of the house, Lenny worked night after night trying to concoct schemes for his salvation. Many of the voices contained in the secret recording he had made during the Beverly Hills trial were barely audible. In his anxiety to transfer the wire recordings to tape—and thereby improve their poor quality—he jammed the capstans of his Uher tape recorders. Trying to repair them, he ended by tearing them apart.

Much of his time was now spent talking to Harry Kalven, the gray-haired University of Chicago law professor whom Earl Zaidins had consulted. Lenny sent Kalven a copy of the tape-recorded Gate of Horn performance. Kalven listened to the tape at the home of Robert Ming, a Negro attorney, who for years had handled much litigation for the NAACP and who was an expert on court procedure. They both thought the performance was funny, but terribly strong.

Kalven forwarded the tape to Maurice Rosenfeld, the skillful attorney for Hugh Hefner and *Playboy* magazine, who had conducted the negotiations on behalf of Hefner for Lenny's autobiography. Rosenfeld heard the tape the first time alone; he was startled by its content.

By March 14th, the day Lenny was to be sentenced by Judge Ryan, the three attorneys were still undecided about taking his appeal. Kalven prevailed upon another attorney to substitute for Lenny and Zaidins that day in Chicago Municipal Court. The lawyer was not prepared for what would transpire before Ryan passed sentence. The judge's face began reddening as he announced that he had recently received two telegrams signed by Lenny that he wished to read into the record. The first wire had arrived at his home after the jury returned its guilty verdict.

Dear Judge Ryan:
Here's what's happening to me. The reason I am contacting you is, that you seem very fair and you're extremely gracious to me and the objections you sustained and the ones you overruled showed a most impartial attitude, and with the pressure on you this is quite admirable.

To praise you more, I cannot, lest I am scurrilous sycophant.

If the purpose of the law is to cause coarcations and contre-tempts, the uneducated, then I would rather put my head upon the block to intercept the progress wheel.

I am not contemptuous of the court.

I respect, in fact, I fear the court and plead a judgment from the court that will begin when the last testimony has been given.

I am not guilty of the charge technically, spiritually, morally, legally, and yet the arrest was reported by Sunday Times has put me in league with the Cohens, the Dillingers, the Lucianos and the Curleys.

I dread the message that opens with "I."

So to alleviate this trauma I introduce as exhibit A to the court for evidence, wires sent to me.

"Lenny Bruce, 8825 Hollywood Boulevard, Los Angeles, California. Sir: It has come to our attention through news media that you are to be in court in Chicago today. May I suggest to you that you are not to violate the conditions of your bail. You are not to leave the jurisdiction of Los Angeles County. Considering all the other court appearances you are to make here in Los Angeles /s/ Salas Bail Bond, 139 North Broadway, Los Angeles County."

Please have mercy. I do not like, in fact I am quite unhappy when my view is barred.

/s/ Respectfully, Counselor Lenny Bruce

Judge Ryan received a second telegram from Lenny on March 9th and a duplicate copy on March 12th. This one reflected his true feelings and was not intended to placate Ryan.

Dear Judge Ryan:
    I was the defendant and my own counsel in an obscenity case that you were the judge. District Attorney Banks, Officers Tyrell and Noro were State's witnesses. Earle W. Zaidins was my co-counsel. When you adjourned, I left for Los Angeles, with your knowledge. Actually intending to return to Chicago and bring the case to a stunning close with a capper summation. I was arrested not long after I landed in Los Angeles. I have been arrested five times in Los Angeles this past year, and Salas, the bondsman I sent you stated, refused to grant me permission to leave the state or he would cause my arrest for pulling my bond.

    I beg the court to indulge me. I say this because I understand the trial of this criminal was continued minus two important factors. One the defendant, and two, the defender. What did you base your instructions to the jury on? It is my belief that this was illegal, unconstitutional and most fascistic in behavior. I never gave anyone permission to represent me solely. Zaidins was merely a co-counsel and did nothing without my approval and he received no instructions from me to make any summation. He told me that he did so under threat. He said that he tried everything, but they forced him onward. Regardless of any religious beliefs, I will go through a life of hard labor rather than succumb to those pagans who would reject every Christian philosophy that Christ proclaimed and think themselves quite just.

    I am reduced to cliche. Physician, heal thyself.

Lenny Bruce.

After reading the telegrams in court, Ryan immediately quashed the lawyer's motion for a new trial. He then found Lenny guilty *in absentia* and meted out an extraordinarily severe sentence—one year in the House of Correction plus a fine of $1,000. It was the maximum penalty provided by the Chicago obscenity statute. "If capital punishment were available to this crime," remarked one legal expert, "Ryan would have given it."

A cash bond of $2,500 was set on the warrant for Lenny's arrest. He received word of the sentencing in San Francisco. "Kafka!" he shouted to reporters.

When he got back to the House on the Hill, Lenny resumed his frantic telephoning and letter-dictating. He had not paid his overworked secretary in weeks. Finally, he suggested that she take some time off. For months she had valiantly tried to make some sense out of the increasing chaos of Lenny's affairs. She had typed letters from his hieroglyphic notes, handled his laundry and shoe repairs, and, most important, she had run his filing system in an efficient, businesslike manner. Now, Lenny's files were churned into hopeless disorder as he struggled to do everything himself. His secretary complained that it was becoming impossible to cope with his erratic actions and his inability to communicate rationally. Mounds of Verifaxed papers and carbon copies piled up in the corners of the rooms. Any visiting acquaintance who could operate a typewriter was immediately pressed into service. Jo-Jo D'Amore, a close friend of Sally's, could not type; so he wrote letters in longhand for Lenny, sitting on the bathroom floor, while Lenny dictated from the toilet.

Harry Kalven now agreed to handle Lenny's appeal without fee. Kalven was attracted to the case because it raised a basic issue that had never before been confronted: namely, whether obscenity could be justly defined in terms of *disgust* as well as prurient appeal. Lenny wasn't erotically stimulating, but he certainly was vulgar and sometimes disgusting. Was this a legitimate basis for prosecuting him, convicting him, depriving him of his living, and perhaps imprisoning him? This was the question the professor wanted to address.

Kalven's decision to handle the appeal gave Lenny the most prestigious representation he had ever received. Rosenfeld and Ming also agreed to assist Kalven in Lenny's defense. "We don't care what he said," Kalven and his associates agreed: "We'll defend him because it's a question of principle."

On March 19th, the triumvirate of Kalven, Rosenfeld, and Ming visited Judge Ryan in chambers in an effort to get Lenny's appeal bond approved—normally a routine procedure. They planned to show Ryan that Bruce was not taking the case lightly, that he was concerned and wanted to appeal. Ming did not want the fact that Lenny was a fugitive to obstruct the appeal. Ryan agreeably poured them cups of coffee. But when he heard what they wanted, he became as bitter and uncompromising as he had been on the day he passed sentence. He fumed over Lenny's failure to appear, doubting that he had been detained by the California bail bondsman. Finally, Ryan refused to issue the appeal bond. If Lenny had been a burglar, a murderer, or a rapist, the lawyers would probably have obtained the bond without any trouble, merely as a matter of professional accommodation.

Kalven next contacted the office of Illinois Governor Otto Kerner, requesting the issuance of an appeal bond. It was too late. Ryan had already taken legal action to return Lenny to Chicago. An Illinois fugitive warrant had been mailed on March 19th, requesting his extradition from California.

Lenny had still managed to evade the warrant when he appeared before Los Angeles Superior Court Judge LeRoy Dawson a few days later, on March 22nd, requesting that his March 25th trial on charges of narcotics possession be postponed. He was represented in court by John Marshall, who had now agreed to take all of Lenny's West Coast cases. Marshall explained that his embattled client had to appear in a Chicago court on the same day, March 25th, to post an appeal of his obscenity conviction. Judge Dawson again postponed the narcotics trial, this time until May 13th.

Lenny neglected to tell Marshall that he had become so frustrated by the inability of Kalven, Rosenfeld, and Ming to perfect the appeal bond with Judge Ryan that he had decided he would have to make an appearance on his own. Lenny felt confident that he would persuade Ryan—just as he had convinced Judge Horn at his San Francisco contempt hearing—if only he could plead his case personally. Falsely he informed Kalven by telephone that the Los Angeles Superior Court had granted him permission to visit Chicago on March 25th in order to file the appeal. The jubilant Kalven suggested that they meet for lunch. But Lenny failed to reveal his entire scheme: in particular, that he intended to risk jumping bond in an attempt to file an appeal of his conviction before Judge Ryan in propria persona. Afterward, he planned to meet with the attorney at the luncheon and gloat over his success.

Excited at the prospect of meeting the famous Lenny Bruce, Kalven invited Rosenfeld and Ming to join him at the University of Chicago Faculty Club. The three of them nervously began checking their watches twenty minutes after Lenny had been scheduled to arrive. But their client never appeared. The three disappointed attorneys left the club an hour later, in bewilderment.

What they didn't know was that soon after landing in Chicago and driving to the courthouse, Lenny had learned that Judge Ryan was out of town, vacationing in Florida. His wild plan had backfired. Now, he was in imminent danger of being prosecuted as a bond jumper as well as a fugitive. Rather than join Kalven and risk arrest, Lenny decided to double back to the airport. He sneaked out of the court building, making certain he was not observed by the police, hailed a cab, and raced off to O'Hare, where he boarded the first jet home.

When he arrived in Los Angeles, he discovered that Sergeant Lesnick had visited the house on the night of March 25th to serve the Illinois fugitive warrant. He found, instead of Lenny, two hookers living in the upstairs apartment, whom he arrested for possession of marijuana. The next day, March 26th, Marshall surrendered Lenny on the fugitive warrant and recounted his client's abortive journey to Chicago. Municipal Judge Maurice T. Leader set April 25th for a hearing on the fugitive complaint and ordered bail set at $2,500. "I would rather get the gas chamber in California than go to jail in Illinois," Lenny told reporters, feeling much like a man caught in a revolving door. "I really like it here in California . . . but the people don't seem to like me."

After their failure to perfect the appeal bond with Judge Ryan and the Illinois governor's office, the three Chicago attorneys were forced to devise some new strategy. Kalven decided to file an extraordinary motion before Illinois Supreme Court Justice Schaeffer, asking that Lenny be placed on appeal bond so that he would be free to travel as he pleased. Schaeffer suggested a meeting in chambers. But before traveling to the downtown courthouse, Kalven called Lenny in Los Angeles. He told him to stand by at some fixed place in case the three attorneys would have to reach him.

On April 2nd, they gathered in Judge Schaeffer's chambers to argue the matter of the appeal bond. Kalven informed the judge that Lenny was not a fugitive, that he intended to pursue his appeal.

"He's serious about the appeal," said Kalven. "If you want him brought back, we'll bring him back. If that will effect things so he can have the appeal, we'll do that."

"We don't know where he is," commented Schaeffer.

"We can bring him back right now," said Kalven, making the first move in his grandstand play. "We could call him right now and he'll come back."

"Well, go ahead and call him," Schaeffer suggested. "Use my phone."

Kalven experienced some momentary anxiety. He would lost the gamble if Lenny was not waiting by a telephone as he had promised.

"Well," said Kalven, "if that's the only point, what sense is it having him make this trip?"

"Harry, please," Schaeffer replied. "You've got to realize that the State needs a little concession to its prestige."

Kalven picked up the phone and asked for long distance. Deep down, he felt he could rely upon Lenny.

"We had more confidence in his word than anybody I think we ever met," Kalven said later. "If he agreed to do it, he would do it."

His fear vanished as he heard Lenny's voice. "Take the first plane," Kalven told him. "Come to Chicago and don't go any place tonight. Come in and go straight to Hefner's and don't get hooked up on the side someplace and get arrested."

It took guts to return to Chicago that night. There was no guarantee that local authorities would not arrest Lenny at the airport on the fugitive warrant. He could very well wind up in jail for a day or more—which would have been a terrible shock to him—as well as getting some more unwanted bad publicity. He managed, however, to reach Hefner's mansion without incident.

Next morning, Lenny arrived outside of Schaeffer's chambers. He still felt that he had entered some kind of a trap. Sheepishly he hunched himself up inside his jacket as he stood before Judge Schaeffer with his three attorneys. The formal procedure lasted no more than five minutes. His appearance alone prompted the judge to grant the appeal bond.

Kalven's strategy had worked like a charm. Lenny had rarely seen the law act so decently. He was suddenly liberated. Instead of being a fugitive from justice, he was entitled to go wherever he wished. "I can't believe what's happened," Lenny cried as he strutted down La Salle Street. He began doing a little dance step. Almost defiantly, he looked passing policemen in the face.

After briefly returning to Rosenfeld's law offices, the four of them stood in a corridor waiting for the elevator. "I want to give you something," said Lenny, dashing back inside for a moment. He returned with a broad grin on his face, offering them a matchbook. Each of the matches was twisted and bent. A handwritten label on the inside of the matchbook read: "Made by the handicapped."

Lenny reflected on the most recent events of Chicago as he boarded a plane for London on April 7th. He was still enjoying the flush of victory. It was the first time he had beaten the system since Albert Bendich successfully defended him in San Francisco. Again it was a law professor who had come through for him.

On the afternoon of April 8, 1963, as he stepped from a jet at Heathrow Airport, Immigration officials handed Lenny a slip of paper refusing him entry. He was detained for two hours in an airport waiting room before being forced to board an Air India 707 back to the United States. The British Home Office subsequently issued a statement explaining this apparently arbitrary action. "He was not permitted to land because in the view of the Home Secretary, Henry Brooke, it would not be in the public interest for him to be allowed in the United Kingdom." Actually, he was barred on a technicality—failure to obtain a work permit. Nicholas Luard had applied for a work permit a month prior to Lenny's arrival and inquired about his application each day. Normally, permits are granted within three days.

With the disheartened Lenny on his way back to New York, Luard posted a sarcastic notice outside The Establishment. It read: "Lenny Bruce's appearance has been postponed due to the courtesy of the Right Honourable Henry Brooke." Luard told reporters: "This is absolutely wicked. Lenny has admittedly been in trouble with American authorities many times, mainly on obscenity charges. But in this country, he has a completely clear bill. He is highly unusual and highly provocative and he has something important to say."

Haggard and bedraggled, Lenny returned to Idlewild Airport at 1:30 P.M on April 9th. He had been awake all night. American customs officials were more hostile than those who ejected him from England. Rummaging through his luggage, they ordered him to empty his pockets and strip naked. The cuffs and seams of his clothing were groped for contraband, and his shoes were closely examined. Apparently annoyed at discovering nothing illegal, they decided to give him a "finger wave." One customs man approached Lenny, pulling on a rubber glove and carrying a tube of K-Y jelly. With a determined look on his face he ordered, "Bend over and spread your cheeks!" Then he plopped a dab of K-Y on his index finger and jammed it up Lenny's ass, feeling around the entire rectal cavity for a stash. Lenny was outraged by this gross violation of his person, but being naked somehow made him feel totally defenseless. Events were happening faster than he could cope with them. For seventy-five minutes they worked him over until, finding nothing, they grudgingly let him go.

"Customs told me I had nice legs," he told reporters gamely after being released, struggling to repress his tears. "They also assumed I had a long series of convictions. They seized me and wanted to know why I didn't register as a narcotics addict. I don't use narcotics, and I've never been convicted of using narcotics." He was no longer smiling. "It's pure Kafka. It's trial without jury." The reporters asked Lenny to comment on charges that his nightclub act was obscene. "There is a point of view that I have offended illiterate Catholics," he replied, still referring to Chicago. "I have an act that would offend Al Capone, but that the Pope would like."

He recuperated from his latest ordeal at the Greenwich Village apartment of the English comedian Peter Cook, who was performing in New York. It was there, apparently, that the two of them hatched a new plan to smuggle Lenny into England. Five days later, on April 12th, Lenny flew to Dublin, where he was admitted as a tourist. Waiting at the airport was Peter Bellwood, a writer and performer at The Establishment. Early on the morning of April 13th, they drove a rented car across the border to Belfast, Northern Ireland, legally entering through what was known as the Irish Back Door route. Northern Ireland, in those days, exercised no control over traffic from Eire.

Lenny sent a cable to Home Secretary Brooke from Belfast, stating that he had traveled to Great Britain as a tourist in order to present documents that he hoped would validate his future application for a British work permit. He flew to London that same morning on a domestic flight, thereby avoiding a repetition of his prior confrontation with British Immigration authorities. The scheme seemed to be working.

But Lenny's face dropped as he arrived at The Establishment. Two plainclothesmen were waiting outside the door. They escorted him to the London airport, claiming he was wanted for consultation with a Home Office official. At the airport he was swiftly taken into custody by Immigration officials and, for the second time in five days, ordered deported by Brooke. The Home Secretary cited a section of the British Alien Act.

Lenny spent a fitful Saturday night waiting in a police station. On Sunday morning, he was hustled onto a plane heading for the United States. He walked down the ramp at Idlewild weeping. Tears still streamed down his anguished face as he moved through the Public Health and Immigration inspections. "This is all too embarrassing," he sobbed to reporters. "I feel sick. I'd like to talk . . . but I can't."

Meanwhile there had been a frantic scurrying about by Lenny's closest friends in New York. Faye Dunaway, whom Lenny had been seeing in New York (where she was a member of the Repertory Company), heard first that he had been expelled again from England. She phoned Earle Zaidins. Earle, just as worried as Faye, had told his wife that he had to go down to the office, even though it was Sunday. Once he slipped into his desk chair, he began dialing all the airlines, checking out every flight to discover on which plane Lenny was coming home. Faye soon joined him in the Schwab Building, and they maintained their vigil all through a dreary New York Sunday afternoon. Then Earle's wife called from the apartment: Lenny had just arrived from the airport. The moment he saw her, he had burst into tears. He was dead broke. She had had to pay for his cab. He hadn't slept in a week. So she had taken out the kids, and Lenny was snoring now on the living-room sofa. Earle said, "I'll be home in a minute." And he beat it out the door with the lovely Faye, descending in the empty elevator to 57th Street and hailing a cab for the fast ride through the empty streets uptown. When they stepped in the door of the apartment, Lenny was already awake. The instant he spotted Faye, he reached down to the floor and picked up a sack of laundry: "Would you do me a real favor?" he implored her. "This is all my shirts and underwear. Would you take it out for me to the Chinese laundry and bring it back when it's finished?" Startled and hurt, the actress took the proffered bundle and allowed herself to be hustled out of the apartment. A couple of days later, when she brought it back, Lenny turned her away at the door.

Lenny was hysterical at that moment. The last thing in the world he desired was some woman to whom he would have to relate like a man. He wanted to scream, to cry, to throw a fit on the floor. He was so hurt and humiliated that he could hardly breathe. And he was dying for a fix! He needed a taste *immediately*. He had the stuff and the needle but he lacked a syringe. He had to go out and buy a bottle of Murine for the eyedropper. Then he had to file and sand the slender glass tube to a point. When he blew the last dust off his homemade spike, he rushed into the bathroom. A half-hour later he emerged: he was still unhappy, angry, bitter, disillusioned—but he was once again Lenny Bruce. Whew! Those Limeys! They were somethin' else, man! Wow! When would he learn that there are no "good" people?

By the time Lenny recovered from his double deportation, he needed work badly. He had counted on his $1,960-a-week salary at The Establishment to pay off his soaring bills. Providentially, he was offered a job at this moment by Marvin Dubin, the owner of Le B in North Bay Village (a couple of little islands on a causeway between Miami and Miami Beach) who had booked him the previous December, following his arrest in Chicago. Dubin hoped to capitalize on the British publicity. Lenny's triumphal return was ballyhooed in newspaper advertisements showing him flashing a V for Victory sign.

Opening night at Le B, Lenny looked ghastly. A picture of him at the time shows him with his face ruined by suffering and dissipation, his tongue lolling out of his mouth like a crazy court jester and his once-beautiful eyes looking like black marbles coated with suet. His hair, long one of his vanities, was shaggy and greasy. His weight had increased still further and even under the car coat—so bizarre a costume for Miami in April—he looked fat and gross. The presence of the police and their recording equipment made every word he said sound like a death sentence. He was working while looking down a pistol barrel. Next day, the Miami entertainment columnists pulled the trigger on that pistol. They reviled him, one and all, treating him as if he were some dirty little freak. Miami had become Death Valley.

As if this weren't bad enough, while driving to the club the following night in a rented Chevy, Lenny was stopped by two cops on the North Beach Causeway at 11:15. First, they charged him with speeding and operating a vehicle with a defective taillight. Then a search of the car uncovered a hypodermic needle and syringe. Lenny protested that he used the needle for the administration of Methedrine to counteract a nervous disorder: his latest, and ironically apt, excuse for addiction. He showed the cops his folder of prescriptions and the letter from Dr. Rotenberg. He urged them to verify the medication with Dr. Jules Trop, his long-time local physician, whose offices were only a few blocks away. His pleading got him nowhere. He was schlepped to the precinct station and arrested for illegal possession of a needle and syringe. Then he was sprung for $50 bail.

Lenny worked at Le B for a couple of weeks. During that time he struck up an acquaintance with a girl who was destined to become one of his most sentimentally devoted followers; to this day, she speaks of Lenny either as if he were still alive (and she were intensely in love with him) or as if he had just died and she were in mourning. A tanned, black-haired, melancholically erotic girl with a whining intonation that makes the word "Lennnnnn-nnnnyyy" emerge from her pouting mouth as a long glissando, Sue Horowitz was probably typical of the young Jewish girls of that day in Miami Beach. Her father was a clothing merchant, specializing in cabana sets. She and her brothers had gone to Miami High. Tiring of college after her second year, she had gotten a job with Harold Gardner, the public relations man for the Club Le B.

Near the end of Lenny's previous engagement at the Le B, Sue's boss had given her a suitcase full of old *Playboy* magazines and told her to return them to Lenny Bruce—with the boss's apologies. (Gardner had been instructed by Lenny to have these back issues bound up in two stout leather volumes with their spines emblazoned in gold letters: STROKE BOOKS. Gardner had goofed on the assignment and now the magazines had to be returned.) Lenny's airplane ticket had also to be delivered. Sue not only spoke with Lenny and watched him work but accompanied him back to his hotel room between shows, where he lectured her on Australia, maintaining that "Australians are the ugliest people on earth. It all comes from the fact that the English sent their criminals out there." When Lenny put Sue in the cab that night, he saw she was shivering. Taking off his gray English lamb's wool cardigan, he draped it over her shoulders and said, "Now this is yours."

"What do you mean?" she protested. "What am I going to do with it? I'll never wear it!"

"I just want you to have it!" he said. (Sue still has it—a precious relic.)

Lenny had been lying in wait for her because, as he subsequently told chic Eder, he had spotted her as a useful tool. "She was lurking, man, driving around the hotel waiting for me to come out. What's more rank than a love-struck cunt? There's no fun, no mystery. Then I thought, 'Secretary! Right!' and decided to put her away." First, though, she had to pass a couple of tests.

Next day at noon, Sue returned to the hotel. Feigning casualness, Lenny said, "Would you do me a favor and just take this letter?" Sue wasn't a secretary but she obliged in longhand on a stationery tablet that Lenny had readied on the table. It was the first of hundreds of letters, transcripts, briefs, and legal documents that Lenny was to dictate to her over the next three years. Without knowing it, she had bitten the apple of sexually inspired servitude.

The next step was testing Sue's tolerance toward drugs. A few nights later, she came over to the hotel to drive Lenny to the club. Just before he left the room, he reached in his bureau drawer, took out an amp of Methedrine, and prepared to inject himself. Sue had a phobia about poking needles into veins; instantly she was nauseated. Lenny was seated on the edge of the bed; when he caught the disturbed and quizzical look on Sue's face, he reached down and picked up the instruction sheet that comes wrapped around the Methedrine vial. Wordlessly handing her the tightly printed slip of paper, he continued probing for a hit. Sue stared at the little instruction sheet, made out the names of many unfamiliar diseases, and kept her mouth shut. She had passed the test.

During this same period, Sue introduced Lenny to a local lawyer named Charles R. Ashman, who handled her boss's legal work. Ashman was a headline maker in his own right. He had just won a major decision in the courts against the sovereign state of Cuba. The six-foot red-haired lawyer had sued Castro for not paying a local public relations firm and received a judgment in favor of his client. He then attached a whole trainload of lard intended for shipment to Cuba. Lenny was impressed. In a flash, he saw Ashman as a new Magic Man. After his usual put-away pitch, alternating emotionally between complaints of persecution and heavy digs at his lawyers, Lenny popped the question: Could Ashman help? Yes. Yes. He would like to help. Lenny could count on him. "Great!" barked Lenny. "You're hired!"

On May 13, 1963, at Van Nuys Municipal Court, Lenny Bruce stood trial for possession of narcotics. This dope rap was far and away the most serious of all his many busts. The danger would not have been so great if California had been a less "enlightened" state. Normally, the offense with which Lenny was charged bore a penalty of one or two years' imprisonment. In California, however, liberal-minded legislators had created a special legal apparatus for keeping narcotics offenders segregated from the regular criminal population. Through Department 95 of the criminal courts system, they weighed each case to determine whether the offender was an addict or in danger of becoming an addict. In either case, if there was a positive finding the convicted man could be sent to a so-called rehabilitation center for up to *ten years*. This was the nightmare that Lenny was facing.

In contrast to his much less serious convictions for obscenity, Lenny's defense against this grave charge was hopelessly weak. Instead of batteries of expert witnesses and reels of tape and complicated legal arguments entailing precedents and decisions and points of law, all Lenny's lawyer, John Marshall, could do was point out trifling inconsistencies in the testimony of the arresting officers and pit the word of his client against that of the police. As usual, Lenny came to court looking beat and derelict. He shook up the jury by refusing to take the oath and disrupted the order of the court by his antics at the counsel table.

The trial went off like clockwork, and when the jury went out to deliberate, Lenny locked himself in a men's room stall and prepared for the worst. After deliberating for two hours, the jury came back to court to have Lenny's testimony read to them. Once again they heard his story: that he had been picked up on a public street for no apparent reason, forced into a police car, and driven to a parking lot where he was suddenly presented with a matchbook which was said to contain heroin. After hearing the story a second time, the jury required only eighteen minutes to arrive at a verdict. Standing up in the box, the black foreman said in a bland monotone: "We find the defendant guilty of illegal possession of narcotics."

Lenny was released on $1,500 bail, the day of June 4th being appointed for his probation hearing and sentencing. That night he started to make rough maps and sketches of the Hobby Shop and its environs. He wrote instructions for the ordering of transcripts from all his previous trials, forgetting that some had already been ordered. Somehow he would have to plot the total picture of where he stood and what he could possibly do to save himself.

With each new injection of Methedrine, his mind sprang wildly ahead. He brooded about his lack of success in battling the police, the courts, and the establishment. He had become their scapegoat. Now he needed some scapegoats of his own, someone *he* could go after. He thought about the little people—the jurors and court reporters who had sat in on his trials. If he could find that they had made errors, the burden of persecution could be shifted from his shoulders. Lenny's pursuit of the little people eventually became a major obsession. Again, he was off on a tangent and distracted from the big picture, which was still out of focus.

That same week, he reevaluated John Marshall. A skillful attorney of sterling character, he had lost the crucial case. Lenny decided to fire him. He rationalized that Marshall was too old. He wasn't hip.

Next he made several frantic phone calls to Miami Beach and finally located Charles Ashman. He pleaded with Ashman to help him by handling the narcotics possession appeal. He held out the hope that the publicity accompanying the appeal would hype Ashman's legal career.

Lenny was too busy with his books and the telephone to appear in Van Nuys Municipal Court to answer the almost-forgotten battery complaint lodged by KTLA cameraman Ed Clark. Marshall appeared on behalf of Lenny and succeeded in having the case continued.

Judge Landis had reserved sentencing until June 4th, wishing to be guided by the results of a probation report, a standard procedure in California. Lenny had been directed to meet with Leland C. Carter, a probation officer assigned to the Central Adult Investigations Division of the Superior Court.

Instead of taking his interview with Carter seriously, as would most men confronted with the prospect of a lengthy jail sentence, Lenny regarded it almost defiantly. Disillusioned by the workings of the courts which had found him guilty, he was in no mood to cooperate with another instrument of the law. He went into wild flights of fancy in describing his past life to Carter. At the conclusion of the interview, Lenny promised to furnish a written statement and other material that would substantiate that he was not a narcotics addict. He also promised to submit several letters of reference.

By May 27th, when Carter dictated his report, Lenny had failed to furnish any of these documents. Apparently, he did not realize the harm he was inflicting upon himself. When John Marshall heard of this stupid blunder, he became infuriated. Lenny resented the tongue-lashing he received from his attorney. Again he resolved to fire Marshall, and again he called Charles Ashman in Miami Beach, begging him to catch the first plane to Los Angeles.

Before convening the court on the morning of June 4th, Judge
Landis read Lenny's probation report in chambers.

There are significant indications that this 37-year-old defendant
has been a user of narcotics despite his denials . . . The defendant
is considered by many to possess unusual talent and a keen mind.
On the surface he appears forceful and confident and it is difficult
to set any hypothesis as to why he would find it necessary to
reinforce himself through illegal use of narcotics. He rationalizes
his present involvement and steadfastly maintains his innocence.
In this vein, he has not offered any information that is not already
a matter of public record. . . . It is the opinion of the probation
officer that a referral to Department 95 is indicated in order to
obtain an authoritative medical and psychiatric evaluation of the
defendant's use of narcotics.

John Marshall, now a lame-duck, understood exactly the newest
difficulties that awaited Lenny. He was finally able to impress upon
his client the urgency of the situation. Despite his abrupt dismissal,
Marshall felt concerned enough to make one last effort. He engaged
two Beverly Hills physicians—Dr. David Neimetz and Dr. Lawrence
Cahagan—to examine Lenny and administer a Nalline test. If the test
proved negative, it would help at Lenny's Department 95 hearing.

Lenny arrived with Jo-Jo D'Amore at the second floor of the
Beverly Hills Medical Building on the morning of June 6th, exuding
confidence. Lenny knew he was clean. He could not possibly flunk the
test. Dr. Neimetz conducted a short interview and asked Lenny to roll
up his right sleeve. A nurse applied an alcohol swab to his scarred
forearm. The doctor then injected two cc.'s of Nalline into a vein. Half
an hour later, Lenny was ushered into a darkened room and seated
within three feet of a gooseneck lamp equipped with a 100-watt bulb.
Dr. Neimetz flipped on the switch and carefully observed the pupils
in Lenny's eyes, as well as his general behavior.

If Lenny were addicted to narcotics or had used them recently,
the injection of Nalline would precipitate withdrawal-like signs and
other symptoms. Furthermore, if his pupils dilated as much as 0.5
millimeters, the test would be considered positive. If his pupils con-
stricted as little as 0.5 millimeters, the results would be negative. At
20-, 30-, 40-minute intervals Drs. Neimetz and Cahagan determined
the size of Lenny's pupils by matching them against a small card containing two vertical columns of circular black dots.

"Mr. Bruce was carefully observed before, during and after the injection," read their report, copies of which were forwarded to Judge Landis and District Attorney William McKennson. "From this test, we conclude that Mr. Bruce is not now under the influence of morphine and its derivatives Demerol and Dolophine, which are narcotics."

There was a big grin on Lenny's face when he heard the results of the report. He thought he had beaten the rap because he had been clean. But the overriding issue—whether he was in *imminent danger of becoming an addict*—would still have to be decided in Department 95, where such tell-tale signs as needle marks, scars, abscesses, and his past medical history would have to be taken under consideration.

Once Lenny settled down in the tape room of his house to audit the tapes of his narcotics trial, he began to slip over into the paranoid psychosis that dictated the whole future course of his life. Psychosis is the natural response of the mind to many destructive stimuli. Severe and prolonged emotional crisis, addiction to Methedrine, lack of sleep coupled with inadequate diet, a disposition inherently hysterical and neurotic—any and all of these factors can trigger off a psychotic episode. Is it any wonder, then, that Lenny Bruce—who was afflicted by *all* these conditions—should have experienced psychotic episodes? The wonder is that he remained as sane as he generally was.

He was acting pretty nutsy the day he called up private investigator Seymour Wayne. Wayne drove up to the house and climbed the steep stairs to the second-floor apartment. Sally scrutinized him through a crack in the front door before cautiously unlatching the chain. Still looking at him suspiciously, she disappeared down a darkened hallway to carry word of his arrival. Feeling like the visiting stranger in a horror movie, Wayne shifted uneasily, feeling the spooky vibrations in the house.

"O.K., follow me," ordered prison matron Marr, on her return. She led the way to Lenny's bedroom headquarters. When they reached the master bedroom, Wayne was astonished by what he saw:

There was Lenny sitting on the bed, talking very excited on the telephone, all upset. He hands me a kooky letter that's written by some teenaged girl, a stranger. It tells him how wonderful he is and that she wants to meet him so she can give him some marijuana.

He gets off the phone and starts talking to me. He thinks rapid-fire, faster than he can talk. He's way ahead of what he's saying, and he gets fouled up. I don't know what the hell is going on here. He just keeps jumping around from one topic to another. He starts telling me about the letter from the girl. He says it's a trap, the police are trying to trap him. He wants me to check the girl.

It had only been two days since Lenny was ordered to undergo a psychiatric hearing as part of the Department 95 proceedings. That challenge, coupled with the round-the-clock Meth watches he had been keeping on his legal affairs, had triggered him into madness. A two-day growth of beard covered his dirty, haggard face. He wore a sweat-stained T-shirt and a rumpled pair of Levis. His disheveled hair and bulging eyes made him look like what he was—a deranged speed freak.

Seymour Wayne was, by contrast, a solid, plodding investigator, a burly shtarker who looked like a plainclothes detective. He had been recommended to Lenny by Joe Speck, the latest sympathetic attorney to rally to his cause. Amid Lenny's confused ramblings, Wayne tried to pick out his client's desperate plan to exonerate himself.

Lenny had deduced from his legal research that he must find errors in questions of law rather than questions of fact in order to win a reversal of his narcotics-possession charge in the Appellate Court. Constant listening to the trial tape recording had convinced him that the judge had committed numerous mistakes. He was certain that members of the jury were familiar with his notoriety before they were selected, although all but one had vigorously denied such knowledge. Lenny felt that evidence of prejudice among the jurors could result in a reversal of his conviction.

Acting on his own behalf, while deliberately ignoring Marshall, Lenny was planning to file his narcotics-possession appeal by his own hand. For some unknown reason, he planned to have a brief written before the Department 95 hearing began the next week.

Suddenly, while pacing the room and unburdening himself, Lenny decided that Wayne could be his salvation—the latest Magic Man. As his voice filled with emotion, he pleaded with Wayne to start inter-viewing jurors immediately, at that very moment.

"He's nuts," Wayne thought to himself. "I don't want any part of this guy. I gotta get out of here." His head throbbing from Lenny's verbal bombardment, Wayne felt as if he had been listening to a record playing at twice its speed. Most of all, he was confused by Lenny's peculiar way of conducting business. Never had he been asked to produce the barest credentials or to comment on the efficacy of his client's plans.

"You know, Lenny," Wayne said with a sigh, "I don't think I can handle your case."

"What do you mean!" Lenny exclaimed hysterically. "Man, you gotta handle my case! You gotta!"

The desperation of Lenny's appeal caught Wayne. "I'll need a hundred dollars as a retainer," he tentatively announced, making one last effort to call Lenny's bluff. Lenny reached into the pocket of his

Levis and pulled out a hundred dollars. He pressed the money into Wayne's hand.

"Don't give me your phone number," Lenny warned him. "I'll drive you crazy."

"I know I'll go nuts with this guy," the detective muttered to himself as he drove home. Several hours later, a typewritten letter was delivered by messenger to Wayne's home.

Dear Seymour Wayne:
#265741 [the number of his narcotics case] is the number that will long live in my memory. Until the memorial day when I shall have my day in court and vindicate myself I must start at the basic start off place clerking . . . First to do . . . call the D.A.'s office tell them of my intent ask them if this would be in ann e manner violate the rights of the jurors If we get their sanction. Did the jurors ever HEAR OF LENNY BRUCE Except for one chick who saw me on Hefner's show . . . Then I've written out some ass of a boston blackie type questions. By the way . . . Tell all of them that you work for Lenny Bruce. TELL THEM IN FRONT SO THAT NO JIVE MOTHERF will say you entrapped them and oh yes tape them Tape them Tape every interview. Blackie questions to find out if they find me guilty possession of heroin . . .

By the next morning, Wayne had committed the questions to memory. When he returned home after purchasing some tape-recording equipment, there was a message from Lenny waiting on his answering service. Lenny told Wayne he was confronted with a rigid deadline for filing his appeal and then proceeded to supply him with an entirely *different* set of questions. Grudgingly Wayne proceeded to make arrangements for his first interview.

"I hope to hell it's a real bust so I can show the guy I'm not qualified," he thought to himself. "I'll give him at least half of his hundred bucks back. This way I can keep my conscience good and know that at least I tried."

As luck would have it, the first juror approached by Wayne—a Beverly Hills housewife—refused to talk. She would not allow him to enter her apartment, declaring that she had already had enough of Lenny Bruce. "I'm going to burn my turkey because of you," she complained, as Wayne stood on her doorstep. "I want you out of here. I'm not going to talk to you."

The woman's attitude irked Wayne. Now there was even more at stake than Lenny's cause. Wayne's own ego, his proven ability as a reliable investigator, had been put on the line. Rising to the occasion, he finagled his way into the kitchen and engaged the lady in a 45-minute conversation, all of which was preserved on the tape recorder he had concealed under his jacket.

She admitted that Lenny's appearance in court—the Levis, the T-shirt, the car coat—had helped convince her of his guilt. She resented his unshaven face. She was also offended by Lenny's refusal to take the oath and his statement: "Oh, this is the final mockery!" "What does he think he is," she exclaimed. "Some kind of a communist?"

An hour before Lenny was scheduled to be examined by state-appointed doctors as part of his hearing in Department 95, Wayne revisited Bruce's messy bedroom to personally deliver the tape recording. When Lenny heard the contents of the tape, he was ecstatic. First, he rolled around on the bedcovers, clutching his sides and shouting jubilant war whoops. Then he leaped to his feet, snapping his fingers, like a driving rhythm section. "Beautiful, man! Beautiful! You're great! You're fantastic! We got 'em!"

This overwhelming praise flattered Wayne and wiped out the last lingering doubts that hung at the back of his mind. But Lenny's exaltation changed abruptly to suspicion as he played one section of the tape over and over again, fascinated by a strange noise he heard.

"Dig!" he shouted. "Get that! Seymour, dig!"

"That's a screech," Wayne patiently explained.

"Screech? Balls!" Lenny snarled. "It's the fucking cops standing behind that woman's door. They know you're out on this goddam thing and they've probably got you bugged. Notice when the screech comes in? Every time you ask a key question. There's a fucking cop standing behind the goddam door and he's blowing a whistle to fuck up the recording."

"Lenny," Wayne assured him, "I'm certain there were no cops around there. Maybe it was a bird in the tree!"

Later they learned that the squeak had been caused by a malfunction in the mechanism of the cheap Japanese tape recorder.

Lenny was particularly impressed by an interview with juror Trevor Faux that appeared to show prejudice:

WAYNE: Had you ever heard of him?

FAUX: I had heard of him—I'd never followed his background or seen him or heard him on television. I just had scanned some of the numerous newspaper articles. Just a quick headline look and that was all. I really don't know anything about him.

WAYNE: What about when Bruce got up to be sworn in? What was your feeling about what happened there?

FAUX: Well, it certainly was confusing . . .

WAYNE: How did you feel about it?

FAUX: Well . . . I don't think it did him any good, frankly . . . I don't know what his . . . reasoning would be, but they certainly expect people to come up and raise their hand and swear to tell the truth.

WAYNE: Did some of the other jurors make comments about the incident?

FAUX: Yes, they certainly did.

The premature appeal of Lenny's narcotics-possession conviction in propria persona was only one of Lenny's current problems. Totally absorbed in these preparations, he had left the arrangements for Department 95 almost entirely in the hands of Charles Ashman, who had flown in from Florida to handle the case and had moved in with Lenny.

Even though John Marshall had been replaced by Ashman, he still felt obligated to help locate defense witnesses. Two days before Lenny was scheduled to appear for the hearing, Marshall arranged for him to be interviewed by Dr. Keith S. Ditman, a research psychiatrist known for his work among alcoholics, users of hallucinogenics, and narcotics addicts. Marshall asked Ditman to conduct a psychiatric evaluation of Lenny's current condition.

Lenny regarded all psychiatrists with suspicion. He entered Ditman's first-floor office at the UCLA Neuropsychiatric Institute accompanied by Harvey Karman, now a UCLA graduate student majoring in educational psychology. Karman had been invited to provide moral support and vouch for Lenny's honesty.

Lenny carried a portable tape recorder and a battered suitcase filled with documents and newspaper clippings concerning his arrests and trials. Without any prompting, he embarked upon a disjointed recital, describing his various jousts with the law. Waving newspaper clippings in the air as he padded about the room, he delivered a sputtering, fragmented monologue, continually wandering off the subject without ever concluding his reasoning.

He insisted that he had been victimized by the narcotics officers who arrested him outside of the Van Nuys hobby shop. To support his contention that the police had planted drugs on him, he switched on the tape recorder and began playing segments of the trial that had been secretly taped in court. Frequently, he turned the tape recorder off in the middle of a sentence and launched into a verbal description of what had happened almost a year before—impersonating the voices of each of the principals. Gesticulating wildly, he enacted the arrest as if he were doing a bit.

"He is kind of manic and hard to contact because he may be high on some drug," Dr. Ditman wrote in his notebook. "I get a distinct impression of a person who is very kind, not a mean person in a sense of being mean to people or being physically brutal to people. A gentle person. He is appealing in the sense that you get a feeling that he is very vulnerable. He appeals to people that might want to protect him."

What throbbed through Lenny's exhausting diatribe was the paranoid's fear that he was being persecuted by the police and prosecuted by the courts for no conceivable reason. A notable example was his arrest in the Los Angeles taxicab four months earlier. Although he had been upheld by the law, Lenny was unable to forget this humiliating experience.

He was just as paranoid about his relationship with Honey. Responding to Dr. Ditman's questions about his personal and family life, he poured out his grievances. "She was mean to me and never did her share of work around the house," he complained. "We had no sex life."

As Lenny got into his personal life, his agitation mounted even higher. "I thought he was in a borderline psychotic state," recalled the psychiatrist. Lenny rolled back his sleeves and showed Ditman the scars on both his arms. He gave the doctor a history of his experiences with drugs, admitting that from 1959 to 1963 he was addicted to Dilaudid.

"I had a habit going for four years," Lenny declared, adding that he had discontinued the use of Dilaudid only five months earlier. He also confessed that he had smoked marijuana and tried LSD but *denied ever taking heroin*. In the past five months, since he had denounced drugs, he had relied upon such substitutes as Doriden, a sedative, and Methedrine. He told Ditman that he had used Meth for ten years, the last four by hypodermic injection, claiming that various doctors— notably Dr. Norman P. Rotenberg—had prescribed the drug for him along with needles and disposable syringes.

Ditman was amazed that any doctor would freely prescribe needles and Methedrine for a patient to use on his own. Prodded by Ditman, Lenny claimed that he took the drug to counteract his underlying depression. He felt that Methedrine was of great benefit to him in his work. He failed to detect any hazards in its continual use.

In a phone conversation with John Marshall the following morning, Ditman said that Lenny was "very disturbed," that he needed treatment, and that he undoubtedly was addicted to Methedrine and probably other drugs, sedatives, stimulants, and possibly narcotics. "My opinion was that Mr. Bruce was an addict and that he needed treatment, which means confinement, although it probably would not be curative," Ditman later explained. "It was quite possible that Mr.

Bruce had frank psychotic episodes precipitated or aggravated by amphetamines." Since the doctor's testimony would undoubtedly harm Lenny's case, it was agreed that he would not appear.

Defense witnesses were becoming difficult to obtain. Lenny had gone so far as to write Harry Kalven, begging for suggestions. Lenny's trial attorney, Charles Ashman, eventually was forced to contact Ditman and ask if he would testify simply on the question of how drug addiction could be proven. The key point he wanted to make at the Department 95 hearing was whether one could tell what was injected into a vein merely by examining the scars.

Ashman was taking a big chance. If the prosecution questioned Ditman under oath about Lenny's past drug history, he would have to reveal what Lenny had already told him—that he was once addicted. Ditman—a law buff who had functioned as an expert witness in many previous narcotics trials—eventually agreed to appear for Lenny. He called Dr. Rotenberg to corroborate that he had written prescriptions for the use of Methedrine in intravenous syringes. Rotenberg told Ditman that he knew of no narcotics addiction but agreed that Lenny was ill and needed help.

Rotenberg had risked his professional reputation in writing out at Lenny's dictation that note of excuse. "You couldn't say no to Lenny," Rotenberg remarked, adding: "It's difficult to look at him from a professional point of view. I came from a small town and it was a thrill just to be out here. Everything I saw was just a thrill, and the idea of meeting someone who was well known at that time was one of the finer things to me." Before long, Dr. Rotenberg had written prescriptions for Demerol and any other drug requested by Lenny. He also supplied prescriptions for the purpose of disposable hypodermic needles to be used for the injection of Methedrine and instructed Lenny in their proper use. He demonstrated how to keep the needles sterile and showed him the location of the most palpable veins. "I was his friend now and not his doctor," conceded Rotenberg. "He was going to get dirty needles anyway. So I might as well prescribe for him a method that at least he would have clean needles so he wouldn't get hepatitis or some other bacteria in his blood. It wasn't a matter of treating him. It was more a matter of protecting him. So I gave him a prescription for clean needles and Methedrine."

Rotenberg had agreed already to testify on Lenny's behalf before he heard from Ditman. "There is no doubt in my mind that he was addicted to some drugs and had been addicted to narcotics for some time," Rotenberg admitted. "I felt I might be perjuring myself, but I said, 'What the hell, I'll be a nice Joe rather than some charlatan should get a hold of him and charge him all kinds of money.' I said,

'Hell, I'll help Lenny,' maybe against my own better judgment. I really had no business being his doctor. I was more his friend. By and large, all I'd do is pick up the phone and call Schwab's and order him a prescription, whatever he wanted."

Lenny called Dr. Joel Fort, a specialist in public health and criminology and a member of the Advisory Committee of the California Rehabilitation Center at Berkeley. He had been impressed by several papers written by Fort. Dr. Fort was, in turn, familiar with Lenny's performances.

In an examination of Lenny prior to the Department 95 proceedings, Dr. Fort took a history of Lenny's drug use and analyzed the findings of a series of Nalline tests, all of which were negative. "He was unhappy, restless, often depressed," noted Fort, before agreeing to testify as an expert witness. "He at times would describe himself as a megalomaniac. All of this goes along with being sensitive to the ills and wrongs of one's society and one's culture. It would be difficult for somebody to see the world as it really is without being, to some extent, unhappy, restless, and dissatisfied. He was a very unhappy human being."

When Judge William A. Munnell convened Department 95 of the Psychiatric Court at County General Hospital on June 12, 1963, he discovered that it was by no means easy to determine whether a man who was not still taking narcotics was "an addict or in imminent danger of becoming addicted." Five days before the hearing two court-appointed doctors, A. R. Tweed and J. R. Peters, had examined Lenny and come to opposite conclusions. Noting his jumpy, restless manner and the deep needle tracks on his arms, they had agreed that he was under the influence of Methedrine (Lenny told them, in fact, that he took two amps a day), but they could not agree whether the marks on his arms indicated that he had also injected heroin. Confronted with contradictory views, Judge Munnell decided to appoint two more doctors to examine Lenny. On June 17th, Drs. Harry Berliner and Thomas L. Gore examined the defendant. Both doctors concluded that the tracks were those of an old narcotics user and submitted their opinions to the court.

At the final hearing, no less than eight separate medical opinions were entered into the record. Some doctors argued that the condition of Lenny's veins could be explained simply on the basis of needle trauma; others insisted that the peculiar stippled appearance of the scars indicated narcotics. Some insisted that the Nalline test was conclusive evidence; others that the test was meaningless unless it was conducted regularly over a long period of time. By the end of the hearing, three of the four court-appointed doctors stated that Lenny was definitely a drug addict. That was basis enough for a decision. A few days later, Judge Munnell ruled that Lenny Bruce was an addict and should be confined for treatment to the State Rehabilitation Center at Chino, California.

With the pronouncing of sentence, Lenny's career as a working entertainer virtually ended. Worse than the loss of money or prestige was the feeling of having been branded a criminal. From this time forth, his primary energies would have to be devoted to saving himself from the clutches of the courts. Instead of standing back and castigating the society that committed injustices, he would offer himself as the victim of injustice. Instead of pleading his case in a nightclub or concert hall, he would have to focus his attentions on the courtroom as the only stage where his performance could be crowned with real success. Unconsciously, he was committing himself to a conflict that could only end in his destruction as an artist. No matter what verdicts he won or what justification he obtained in the courts, the distortion of his mind entailed in remaking himself from an intuitive, imaginative being to a legalistic logic-chopper would be artistically suicidal. Yet, in his masochistic and rebellious way, Lenny welcomed this ultimate confrontation with authority.

One night I went back to see Lenny between shows at the Vanguard. He was talking to two heavy schlubs, who looked out of place. When he finished, he said to me, "Come on, man. Let's take a piss!" As we went into the men's room, I started rapping about the show. Lenny didn't respond. Suddenly he asked, "See those cats in the kitchen there?"

"Yeah."

"They're *heat!*" he said, turning in the stall, with his prick in his hand, giving me a sad, wise smile.

I got a flash of that smile that I'll never forget because it felt like he was saying that they had come to arrest him and *he sort of dug it!* He seemed to be deriving some grim satisfaction from the fact that the heat was about to bust him again.

I was dismayed. That word, "heat," stopped me in my tracks. What could I say? How could I help? Lenny smiled his strange, ambivalent smile one more time and said, "Later, man!" That was all he said. But—that was everything.

Before the court handed Lenny over to the custody of the sheriff for transportation to Chino, Ashman asked to be heard on the question of bail. As a last resort, he requested Judge Munnell to consider further the testimony of Dr. Fort.

"This man is considered by this court to be an ill person," declared

Judge Munnell. "The court has great respect for the opinion of Dr. Fort. He is certainly a well-recognized authority on this subject, but the court cannot overlook testimony of court-appointed psychiatrists, who are also well versed in the field of narcotic examination and diagnosis."

Upon the request of Ashman, Judge Munnell postponed the commitment order for one week to enable Lenny to organize his personal and financial affairs. On June 26th, the same day Lenny was scheduled to be incarcerated as a narcotics addict, Ashman and a battery of three additional attorneys—James G. Cooney, Don Edgar Burris, and Vincent Cavanagh—moved for a stay of commitment pending an appeal of the order. The triumvirate were experts in California law whom Ashman had consulted in a last-ditch effort to keep Lenny out of prison. Amazing to say, the legal maneuver worked. Proceedings in Psychiatric Court were automatically suspended. Lenny was free to pursue his appeal. Coincidentally, the almost-forgotten Beverly Hills obscentiy case, which had begun eight months before, was finally dismissed on July 1st on a motion by the People. In the interest of justice, the prosecution had decided it would not be worth the effort or expense to retry a case that had ended with a hung jury.

As soon as Ashman flew back to Miami, Lenny took off after him to work on his appeal. He moved into Ashman's twentieth-floor apartment on the Miami side of the bay. He also took up again with Sue Horowitz. All day he would work with Ashman and his junior partner, Tony Aiello; at night he would dictate to Sue, sometimes working through to dawn and coming out with only two usable pages. He was always going off on wild tangents and getting himself involved in crazy experiments. One night he demolished Ashman's phone trying to figure out how phone taps work. Another night he completely stuffed up the toilet. He wasn't depressed, though; he was flying on a strange updraft of enthusiasm. Sue recalls him standing out on the balcony of the apartment at dawn after an all-night session, holding in his hand a toy-store megaphone and yelling nonsense down at the cars speeding by on the causeway. Then, one night, the party ended.

Lenny and Sue were working alone in Ashman's apartment when Lenny went into the lawyer's files. He began to read through Ashman's whole file on "Lenny Bruce." He seemed shocked at what he found. All of a sudden he decided to fire Ashman.

When Lenny got back to L.A., he was once again in search of an attorney. Deep into the law himself, he had come across the name of Sidney Irmas, a Los Angeles attorney who had recently argued and won two important narcotics cases before the California Supreme

Court. Both cases challenged the constitutionality of Department 95.

Irmas, a member of the Board of Governors of the University of Southern California Law School, considered tilting with the establishment as one of the obligations of his profession. Once, for example, he had been threatened with contempt of court for pointing out to a Santa Monica judge that the legal system was wrong on a certain point. Rather than defer to the jurist, he pulled out his wallet and offered to pay the fine for contempt right on the spot. Instead of pressing charges, the judge retreated to his chambers—a tacit admission that Irmas was right.

Ashman had already obtained a stay of commitment pending appeal of the Department 95 order, when Lenny got an impulse to call Irmas at home. After introducing himself and outlining his difficulties, he begged the attorney to represent him in his appeal from the Department 95 commitment order as well as his appeal from the criminal narcotics-possession conviction that he had filed himself. As luck would have it, Irmas had a guest, Harold Solomon, a New York City law professor. Not only did Lenny's proposal intrigue Irmas, it suggested a way to entertain his out-of-state visitor. Much to Lenny's surprise, Irmas said that he would come right over.

He and Solomon found Lenny in his office-bedroom, knee-deep in papers. Irmas was impressed with Lenny's gentlemanly manner, as well as his rational discussion of the charges. At the same time, Lenny sensed that Irmas could be another Magic Man. Aware that Irmas was a seasoned fighter where Ashman had been, by comparison, merely a street brawler, Lenny persuaded himself that he would be willing to take a secondary role if Irmas embraced his cause. The attorney took home copies of both transcripts and promised to call him back.

A week later, after carefully studying the transcripts, Irmas informed Lenny that there seemed to be several reversible errors in the Department 95 proceedings, and that he would be glad to handle this appeal. The only error he could detect in the narcotics-possession trial, however, was of such a technical nature that he could not imagine the conviction being reversed. He analyzed the narcotics case as being simply a matter of Lenny's word against that of the police officers, with the jury ultimately believing the police.

While Irmas was busy putting together his opening brief for appeal of the Department 95 commitment order, a tremendous stroke of good luck improved immeasurably Lenny's once quixotic but now promising efforts to save himself. In the midst of his search for prejudicial remarks made by the jurors in Van Nuys Municipal Court, he had asked his friend and temporary housekeeper, Lili Romney, to search back issues of suburban newspapers published after the verdict was rendered.

On the front page of the July 13th edition of the South Bay *Daily Breeze*, which had appeared just three weeks following the conclusion of the Department 95 hearing, she found an incredible story. Sergeant John L. White, one of the police officers who arrested Lenny outside of the Grand Prix Hobby Shop, had been arrested in Redondo Beach and charged with *suspicion of possessing and selling narcotics*.

Following several months of surveillance, prompted by a complaint filed by the mother of a woman White was dating, fellow officers had uncovered a quarter ounce of heroin concealed beneath the front seat of his car. Arrested along with White was his girlfriend, Mrs. Julie Mae Smith, a thirty-year-old convicted narcotics addict. White had met Mrs. Smith while investigating a narcotics ring he helped to break up.

A member of the police force since 1955 and father of two children, White had allegedly supplied Mrs. Smith with a quantity of heroin he had purchased from a Tijuana cabdriver. He was suspended at midnight July 12th, by Los Angeles County Sheriff Peter J. Pitchess and booked on two narcotics counts only a few minutes later.

"I got 'em! I got 'em!" Lenny shouted.

Proclaiming a day of rejoicing, he called all his friends gleefully to relay the good news. He spoke to Sally, Jo-Jo, all the people he had not seen in some time. Overnight, Lenny had broken out of his shell.

The only person he didn't inform was Irmas. Instead, after confirming for himself that Sergeant White had indeed been arrested, he decided to withhold the information until the outcome of White's trial.

Only thirteen days after White had been arraigned, he was arrested a second time at the border station separating San Diego and Tijuana. Federal customs officials discovered a half-ounce of heroin and a hundred Percodan tablets—a narcotic—concealed in his car. The smuggling charges against White stated that he was not only a user but an addict, and that he had failed to register his condition as required by law. He was locked up in San Diego County Jail, in lieu of $10,000 bail.

On October 16th, White pleaded guilty in U.S. District Court and was convicted of illegally importing a half-ounce of heroin and a hundred Percodan tablets into the United States. He was sentenced to five years' imprisonment, with the recommendation that he be committed to the U.S. Public Health Service Hospital at Lexington, Kentucky, for treatment of narcotics addiction.

Upon receiving a report of the verdict, Lenny immediately called Sidney Irmas. "You told me you wouldn't handle the narcotics-possession case," Lenny crowed into the receiver, hardly able to restrain his enthusiasm. "Would you change your mind if I told you that the officer who claimed that I dropped the heroin on the street was later arrested and convicted of being a narcotics addict? Would *that* change your mind?"

"You're goddam right it would," Irmas replied. "I don't know where or when I'm going to get you the relief or how I'm going to do it. Just off the top of my head, I can't tell you how it can be done. It rubs me the wrong way, and we're going to find a judge somewhere that it rubs the wrong way, too. Somewhere, some place, in some court, I'm going to have that judgment set aside."

On November 30, 1963, just eight days after the assassination of President Kennedy, Lenny Bruce walked out on the stage of the Village Theater in New York, half expecting that he himself would be assassinated. His fears were attributable partly to the plague of paranoia raging in the country; partly, though, they were well grounded in sinister premonitory warnings delivered in the language of violence. The theater where Lenny was scheduled to appear, the theater where his name had stood for two weeks in bold black letters against a white background, had been visited by arsonists just a couple of nights before his opening and nearly burned to the ground. The story was hushed up at the time because the promoter was afraid that people would stay away from the show. Briefly, it went like this:

The Village Theater, on Second Avenue at Sixth Street, was a former movie palace called the Loew's Commodore. Located in a dingy old edifice closed during the movie recession of the late fifties, it had recently been fitted out for live stage offerings and renamed. (Three years later it was sold to Bill Graham, who made it the mecca of East Coast rock—the Fillmore East.) Lenny had been hired to open the new house. That explained why his name glared so long from that marquee. Naturally, any crank walking around in that freak scene on the Lower East Side would build up an association between the theater and its notorious first attraction. The theory of Lenny and the other heavy diggers was that some gang of homicidal Catholic maniacs had attacked the theater because they really wanted to attack Lenny Bruce, whom they associated—dig it!—with the murder of President Kennedy. "Lenny Bruce—and other degenerates like him—killed our sacred martyred President." That was the thinking that Lenny attributed to the less enlightened elements of the community.

Actually, you couldn't blame him for being paranoid when you heard the chilling story of how these arsonists had gone about their work. They had broken in the stage door and lined up metal cans stuffed with gasoline-soaked rags along the curtain line. Then they had ignited the wastes. The flames licked up like quiet cobras, stinging the

fire alarms and sprinkler heads into instant action. The New York City
fire code demands that an auditorium be sealed off from its stage by
an asbestos curtain. Once the heat got high enough, the fire curtain
descended and confined the flames to the stage area. At the same time,
jets of water poured down on the blaze. That was the scene playing
in Lenny's head the night of the concert.

Lenny was in pretty bad shape, even apart from paranoia. Earlier
in the month, he had begun to complain of severe pains in his back
and chest. Reporting to Dr. John David Romm in Hollywood, he was
diagnosed as suffering from an inflammation of the pleura. Questioning
Lenny carefully, Romm discovered that a week or so before, Lenny
had been shooting up in his usual clumsy manner. He was having a
lot of trouble getting a register and the blood kept drying on the needle.
Lenny's blood coagulated with unusual rapidity, and if he were shooting Meth or some easily procured drug, he would simply throw one
disposable away and reach for another when the first became clogged.
This day, though, he was shooting expensive, hard-to-get heroin. When
a blob of congealed blood formed on the end of the spike, he kept
jabbing until he finally got a register. Then he jacked everything into
the vein—including the congealed blood. As Romm later reconstructed
the case, the blood clot circulated up Lenny's arm and around through
his chest until it became lodged in a small vein in the chest cavity.
There it formed a local blockage that gradually swelled into a full-scale
pulmonary embolism. Once the clot began to fester and abscess, Lenny
was in serious trouble. With every breath he took, he forced his lung
to rub against the inflamed pleural sac causing acute pain and worsening
further the inflammation. Romm bound up Lenny's chest to reduce
the friction and counseled bed rest. Lenny was not the type who could
lie around the house; what's more, he had this very important gig in
New York.

Don Friedman had come up with a deal to do two concerts on a
single night just after Thanksgiving. Another pair of concerts was
projected for Easter. The money was good—$5,000 for a night's
work—and Lenny was desperate for dollars. What's more, everything
pointed to a personal triumph. People were starting to pick up on
Lenny as the latest thing. The fame he could never earn with his talent
he had gained through the notoriety of his arrests and deportations.
No longer an underground cult figure, Lenny Bruce was in *Playboy*.
The previous month, October 1963, saw the first of six installments of
How to Talk Dirty and Influence People stuffed into several million
mailboxes across the country as it was sold off the newsstands of every
urban, suburban, and rural magazine dealer in America. No comedian
in modern times had ever received such a massive hype. You'd have

to go back to Charlie Chaplin's paternity trials or his persecution at the hands of the American Legion to find even a remote parallel.

The first installment of the autobiography was prefaced by a full-page reproduction of an oil portrait that had been done a couple of years before. The picture looked like something out of a faggot's fantasy: an exquisitely featured full face, with lips like a lipstick ad, eyes with the spooky stare and the hanging lids of a highly provocative queen, crowned with cosmetically arched eyebrows and a short, tousled thatch-cut coif that hadn't the faintest resemblance to Lenny's curly, greasy hair. Drawn in that style that resembles charcoal running down a wall, with heavy shadow mysteriously dissolving the left side of the face, the picture projected only one truth—that its subject was absolutely self-infatuated. Turning the page, you encountered an introduction running down the center fold, flanked by a zigzag layout of family album pictures: Lenny with his dolled-up eighth-grade classmates; Lenny shorn of his hair and staring with adenoidally parted mouth into the camera of a Navy I.D. photographer (against a wall scale that measured him off precisely at 5 feet 6 inches); Lenny in his summer whites, his salty sailor's hat cocked on the back of his head, posing with a slobbering pony; Lenny in his classic delicatessen portrait, looking like a chicken schmaltz version of Warner Baxter or Roland Young. The introduction was a big editorial hype.

"Once upon a time," *Playboy* winked at its readers, "when everybody was afraid to speak out about a certain infallible emperor as he paraded grandly through the streets, there was one little boy who insisted that the emperor was naked. That little boy grew up to be Lenny Bruce, the most controversial—and the most busted—comic of our generation." Then having gotten things off on a note of fairy-tale parable, *Playboy* settled down to tell the grim but irrefragable facts of the Bruce case. "Bruce says emphatically that he takes only certain legally prescribed drugs for physical trouble related to a couple of bouts with hepatitis years ago and carries with him letters by three physicians to that effect." Having disposed neatly of the drug problem, *Playboy* then dispatched the obscenity arrests, insisting that Lenny was simply "honest"—though cautioning at the same time that "total honesty, of course, is not necessarily total wisdom or even total goodness." Yet there was certainly nothing "sick" about Lenny's humor, *Playboy* argued, because this often misunderstood humor was, in fact, a "potent antibiotic capable of attacking—and perhaps curing—our *real* social ills." In any case, Bruce's problem was essentially no different from that of the scholarly, 670-page *Dictionary of American Slang*, "many copies of which were destroyed by the militant folk of Butte County,

California" because it contained some words they considered obscene. Indeed, Bruce was cleaner than the *Dictionary*, for, as columnist Ralph J. Gleason had written in the *San Francisco Examiner:* "Lenny Bruce . . . [uses] words that you and I may think are dirty, and in the process cleanses these words, [which] seems to me to have considerable reputable precedent, not the least of which is Lawrence and Joyce." And now having established the *honesty* and the *humor* and the *wholesomeness* of this unfairly maligned man, the truth of Lenny's life was to be offered up for the delectation of the *Playboy* bachelor lobbed out in his *Playboy* pad surrounded by his *Playboy* toys (hi-fi, Miles Davis records, color photos of classic sports cars, imported old-oak brass-hooped ice bucket, Chivas Regal, clean-picked marijuana, and last naked flicks of Marilyn Monroe) while he waited for his latest and hottest little bunny to come hop, hop, hopping out of that cab he'd generously offered to pay for to enjoy the supreme pleasure of having the mounted come to Mohammed.

With this kind of front-running ballyhoo, Lenny Bruce was not going to miss in New York City. The night of the concerts, you could stand in the sloping lobby of the theater and see a broad cross section of New York file into the auditorium. Most conspicuous were the celebrities who turned up in unprecedented numbers. Leonard Bernstein and Felicia Montealegre, Betty Comden and Adolph Green, Peter Cook and Jonathan Miller, Orson Bean—and Bob Dylan. Lots of heavyweight intellectuals turned out, too, their curiosity whetted by articles that had appeared in prestigious journals, like *Commentary*, *The New Leader*, and *The Partisan Review*, which had published Jonathan Miller's piece on Bruce, "The Sick White Negro."

Walking toward the theater after the first show, through a mob of departing spectators overseen by a whole detail of police, were Jack Kroll, the brilliant art editor of *Newsweek*, and Harold Rosenberg, the principal dialectician of modern American painting. Rosenberg was asking: "Who is this 'masked man' he keeps talking about?" Kroll's melancholy expression conveyed his impression of Lenny's show. Lenny had said he was "sick," but Kroll felt it was something more than physical illness. Lenny had also joked about this being his "last performance."

Pressing into the house with the audience for the second show were an astonishing number of kids. Lenny had always worked in nightclubs where young people couldn't gain entrance or were simply too poor to pay the tab. Now the kids had gotten a chance to dig their latest hero in the same setting later provided for the rock stars. A button hawker had set up his table in the foyer and was selling tin disks on which were printed the words "Lay Off Lenny Bruce." The kids, for their part, were pouring into the house chanting: "We love Lenny! We're Lenny's people!"

Don Friedman looked like he was at his wits' end. The arsonists hadn't destroyed the theater, but they had knocked hell out of the sound system. Cables, cords, insulation, socket boxes had been destroyed. Electricians had been working since the damage was discovered to ready the theater, but they still hadn't cleared up all the problems when the audience took its seats and Mongo Santamaria's Afro-Cuban conga-bongo band took the stage. Santamaria's hotbox singer had belted the whole first show into a dead mike, while first one and then another goofy, self-conscious electrician had crept out on the apron and screwed new mikes on the stands. Finally, the band had bowed off and a dazzling, blinding sequin-spangled curtain had closed across the stage. Poor Don had come out through the center gather to say a half dozen "good evenings" into the still-dead mikes. At the last moment, the system came to life and Don lugubriously intoned the story of his troubles in booking Lenny into the city, complaining about turndowns from both Carnegie Hall and Town Hall.

When Lenny got out onstage, the more sensitive people among the crowd were feeling a cramp in their guts. They were very worried about how he would treat the subject of the assassination. He couldn't avoid the world's biggest topic, and yet it was terrifying to think what might happen if he said something crude or "sick." What these people didn't realize was that Lenny shared every American's feelings about Kennedy. Ever since the President's election, Lenny had stressed in his act the importance of having a young man in the office. "I'm going to see a baby born in the White House" was his way of putting it. Eisenhower had been the butt of Lenny's humor because he was this old hydrocephalic grandpa: "The only thing a man of that age can say to me is 'Have you had enough to eat?'" Rubbing in the age and youth thing, he would add that the job of President was just too tough for a man of Ike's years. The spectacle of Kennedy's inauguration had provided fresh laughs, with Lenny doing a bit on Jackie and Jack in the inaugural limousine. Jackie had been caught in one picture staring with an odd expression at her silk-hatted husband. "Know what she's saying to him at that moment?" Lenny would quip: " 'That hat makes you look like a schmuck!'" Then there were all the jokes about what would happen when, the first Catholic having been elected, the American people decided to make a Jew President. It couldn't be allowed, Lenny would insist, because it would be so embarrassing to have some old Jewish lady—the President's mother—on television screaming, "Is that a toosh! Mmmmm! Let me kiss that toosh!" Now the hero was dead, the only President to whom Lenny could "relate." He was as sad as anyone in that audience that night. He would never say anything shocking about his dead President.

What he did, in fact, was a deft job of sidestepping the whole issue. When he walked out onstage, he appeared to be deep in reflection. Standing before the mike visibly thinking, he made the sounds of a man marveling at some strange, sad, ironic occurrence. With the audience fixed on him in utmost attention, he stretched the moment to its uttermost and finally spoke. Whistling softly to himself, he shook his head and said, "Wow! Boy! Sssssss! Poor *Vaughn Meader*!" Meader was just about to release Volume Two of his phenomenally successful impersonation of Kennedy and now he was deader than the President. Bang! That did it! The house erupted in laughter—and then applause. The topic had been both confronted and evaded.

From the death of one comic, Lenny made a direct segue to the sickness of another—himself! Opening his shirt, he showed the audience his chest swathed in bandages. "Tonight," he said, "it was a tossup between jail, the hospital or this date!" Nobody knew how to react to that statement. Some snickered, taking it for a gag; others frowned with concern. It was the keynote to the whole evening, which was dampened by a pall of gloom. A bootleg tape of the show survives; it records a sadly diminished Lenny Bruce trying to perform in his usual manner, moving along from bit to bit, comment to comment, in the free-form rap mosaic that he had perfected in recent years—but nothing works. The rap technique is based on a genuine flow of thoughts and images, one idea dissolving into another like the patterns of a kaleidoscope, fluency and ease of delivery being essential to create the effect of interior monologue. This night Lenny was sledging on sandpaper. His voice was small and tight. There was no thrust to his delivery. Each little bit was hard to launch, and once it ended, it did not immediately suggest another. An air of lassitude hung over the whole show like stale smoke.

The second performance was a little better. Lenny had to face an irate audience, which had been infuriated almost to the point of violence by Mongo Santamaria's refusal to end his part of the show after the normal warm-up period. The loud, vulgar Latin leader—who probably thought he was going over *beeeg*!—was finally forced off by a barrage of catcalls, shouts, and insults. Don Friedman delayed the proceedings further by insisting that each of the celebrities get up and take a bow. As each of the famous names was called out—"Leonard Bernstein! . . . Comden and Green! . . . Orson Bean!"—the audience booed and hissed. The people wanted Lenny Bruce and *only* Lenny Bruce.

Finally, Lenny appeared to tumultuous applause. Glancing down at the stage floor, he spotted a red slipper. The Mongo Santamaria band had beat such a hasty retreat that the singer had lost a shoe. Lenny picked up the garish-colored pump and stared at it with amusement. Just at that moment a burst of staccato Spanish emerged from behind the scenes. Lenny raised one finger to his lips, signaling the audience to remain silent. Mischievously, he eavesdropped on the conversation. After a moment, he turned around and explained to the crowd that the Spanish girl was complaining that she couldn't leave the theater without her shoe. Then, with an impatient wave of his hand, like some grumpy old Jewish doorkeeper, Lenny gave the band the "good-riddance" wrist-wag and said, "Go! *Geh!* . . . to your *Hector's Cafeteria!*"

That was about the funniest thing he said all night, the reference to the schlocky 42nd-Street-style cafeteria breaking up the New York audience. From that point on, it was mostly downhill. Lenny again confronted and eluded the assassination, this time by playing with Oswald's name. "Oswald is the name of a rabbit!" Lenny proclaimed, and "Ruby looks like Ruby!" It was true, of course—the befuddled, smiling, white face of the killer in manacles, and the gross, hysterical punim of the small-time Jewish club owner, who had suddenly busted out of characer and acted like a Western badman—Lenny had them pinned. His next association, between the pictures of Lyndon and Lady Bird Johnson and a trailer camp, wasn't bad either. Those were the kind of deep intuitive flashes on which Lenny had built great bits in the old days; but tonight he wandered right off the subject, remarking only that "Nobody ever gets kissed in a trailer. They're built to go nowhere!"

Fumbling for a lead, struggling to locate himself on this disorienting night, Lenny alluded briefly to the shocking fact that arsonists had tried to burn down the theater. Again, he hit the nerve, but he hadn't the heart to tell the story. Standing there after a week of paranoid hysteria, he probably feared that any reference to the event would bring a bullet smashing into his skull. Next he stumbled into his great obsession of recent weeks, the discrepancies he had discovered between his secret recordings of his trials and the official transcripts of the court reporter. Yet even the most compelling themes of his life coudn't rouse him this night. He stood there onstage, head cocked, mumbling "Uh-huh!" and "Hmm-hmm!" as if he were listening to a tape recording of his act playing through his brain.

When Lenny got back to L.A. in December, he scored an unexpected windfall by discovering a club that had nothing to lose by hiring him.

This was the Trolley-Ho, a 250-seater on the east side of La Cienega Boulevard, a few blocks south of Sunset. The club was in such serious financial straits that even the most extreme risks were justified. Lenny could easily bring down a bust, but he could also pack the house. The owners and he worked out a fast deal. They agreed to give Lenny all the proceeds from the gate plus some money for advertising (with the understanding that part of this bread would be deducted from Lenny's salary). Their piece was in the drinks.

Lenny opened on New Year's Eve, playing two shows to a packed house. Uptight as always about the door arrangement, he gave the job of checking the receipts to chic Eder, cracking: "You're just schmuck enough to give me a square count." Chic, with his powerful inverted moralism—all good to his brothers! Death to the *fremden!*—hovered over the till for two weeks, until Lenny's coffers began to fill with long-forgotten gold.

Good old chic, he was really a great henchman—when he was out of the can. He had been in Vegas earlier that winter, plying his wicked trades. Finally he had pulled up stakes and come back to L.A. The day after Christmas he blew in from the desert and made a beeline for Lenny's house. As always, his appearance signaled the beginning of a great romp.

When I show from Vegas I pull my VW Kombi up in the driveway and leave the keys in it because I'm parked behind another short. In the carport are Lenny and a black dude who's doing some interior construction work. The long trip has me dusty and sweaty, so I cop a leisurely shower, shave, and invite Lenny in to geeze some coke I'd scored in Vegas. We get out of the bathroom, and I notice my suitcases and clothes-bags have been brought into the pad. Since Lenny's actions are generally the antithesis of consideration, I look askance at my personal belongings being so neatly removed from the van for me. Lenny notices, and mentions: "The cat needed your truck to pick up some big stuff from the building supply joint." I commence to blow it, and Lenny wants to know: "Since when did you start worrying about 'tinnif' like wheels?" "I don't give a fuck about the short, Lenny; where's the other stuff that was *in* it?" "Oh, we took it out to make room for the load he's getting." I bop around to the driveway and he follows. The seats have been removed and are sitting against the fence at the top of the driveway—along with the cardboard cartons that had filled the van. I ask where the metal footlocker is, and he says they left it in the van since it didn't take up all that much room. I explain to Lenny that each of the small cartons contains two of the new model Polaroid cameras; then open one of the two huge cartons—which are filled with boxes of disposable syringes that I plan to trade for smack, since they're so hard to come by in L.A. I lay a couple of boxes of them on Lenny, and ask how long he thinks it'll be before the cat shows back. My concern is so obvious that he wants to know what's in the footlocker. I'm shining him on, and stacking cartons, when the van noses into the driveway.

Then the three of us get the van unloaded. I get a broom and tell the dude that I can get the stuff back in myself, since I want it loaded in a certain way. Lenny's sitting on the footlocker, studying its large, hinged, snap-lock, while I get the van swept out. He just sits there, with that shit-eating, Cheshire-cat grin of his and points down at the locker: "What's in it, chickie?" Knowing the futility of trying to strap a shuck on him—and wanting to wig him out anyway—I give him the key. A couple of friends and I have made a deal with a cat in Mexico City to cop some almost pure smack from him on the barter side. In the locker is the "merchandise" for our end of the exchange: 48 brand new tiny Sony portable radios; eight handguns of various makes and age; and two beautifully lethal looking Sten submachine guns—all smoking hot! Despite the fact that I tell him that those Stens carry five years each under federal law, he's got to schlep all that armament into the pad so he can play with it!

Knowing he's not about to give them up until he's exhausted his war/gangster fantasy trips, I split down to the "hideout" (a $10-a-week rooming house just south of Sunset) to stash the rest of that intense heat with which I'm driving around.

That type of Polaroid camera has just hit the market, and the Christmas season has wiped out every camera store's supply of the film for them, so all I've got is one magazine-pack. We get a couple of foxes up there the next day and use up the eight color prints on a fantastic series. Lenny and I are each carrying a Sten and have four handguns apiece on various parts of our bodies (he rigged a nylon stocking as a shoulder holster). He goes into his "director" bag and explains how we're going to do a sequence of armed-forcible-rape flicks. These two freaks are fully cooperative, but Lenny's shpritzing one of them because she's not emoting in the "proper terrorized" manner. He's expounding on Actors' Studio "Method" to her and she tells him: "But, Lenny! The thought of being raped at gunpoint gets me terribly horny! I just want to get these dumb pictures over with so we can fuck!"

The best flick of me is where I've ripped this chick's peasant blouse down the front so her tits are hanging out; she's quivering with fear, and my face radiates a leer of rapacious psychopathy. The last flick we take is the capper: the other fox is giving Lenny head. It's a profile shot, with both of their faces turned toward the camera just slightly. Her teeth are tightly clamped on Lenny's cock and he's screaming!

Chapter Thirteen

PRIVATE PARTS

By the winter of 1964, Lenny Bruce had become the victim of a nationwide lockout. He could still play San Francisco, where his one and only legal victory secured him from prosecution; but even in this sanctuary the heat was getting heavy: the locations that Lenny worked were under constant surveillance; the hotels where he shacked up were subject to narcotics raids; even the connections were shy of doing business with him.

Elsewhere, Lenny was as good as dead. Miami was very dangerous. *"Earle! Whattha hell am I gonna do?"* he had screamed through the long-distance wire to New York one night the preceding spring. Zaidins yelled back, *"Gettha hell outathere!"* That tore it in Miami. In his adopted city, the LAPD, the Los Angeles County Sheriff, and the state undercover narcos had established an all-time record by busting him seven times in two years, the most recent collar being at the Trolley-Ho in February. That put the dream on the train in L.A.

The smaller Midwestern towns—unthinkable! Chicago—out of the question! The heavy Maf strongholds in Atlantic City and Vegas—over the hill! All things considered, the Mob had proven a very tolerant employer. It had backed Lenny to the end. Now the heat was too high for even the greediest Tony, Dom, or Vito. In the gazetteer of cities, the only real question mark was New York.

Lenny had been rousted a couple to times the previous spring at the Vanguard, but nothing serious had happened. He had lost his cabaret card in the wake of his narcotics conviction, but he was still free to play concerts, theaters, and places that didn't serve booze. The tremendous turnout at his Thanksgiving concerts proved he was still a draw in Big Town. What was to prevent him from yo-yoing back and forth from New York to Frisco till he finally put out the fires in his own backyard? Absolutely nothing—save for the fact that no operator in the city would hire him.

One day in March, Lenny was sitting in his house, when the phone rang. It's a man voice. A guy named Howard Solomon in New York. He mentions Jack Yanov, who owns Basin Street West in San Francisco. He explains that he's got this new club called Cafe Au Go Go. He is down on Bleecker Street in the Village and he has just opened. Professor Irwin Corey was his first act, but he didn't do business. The man has put all his savings into the club—about $80,000—and he desperately needs a winner. If he doesn't find someone who'll do good for him, he'll have to close up. Solomon and Lenny talk back and forth, until they rough out an agreement.

Lenny is in no mood for giving discounts. What he wants is a theater concert and a minimum of one week's work in a club for a combined total of $10,000. Don Friedman can pick up the concert part of the deal, booking the Village Theater, as he did at Thanksgiving, and paying Lenny $5,500 for two shows in one night: $500 in front, the balance to be held in escrow by Jack Sobel. The other $4,500— "all right, if you're so broke, I'll make it $3,500"—will come from Solomon, who must not advertise Lenny's appearance until the second concert begins on Saturday night. Then he can start his pitch, and next day—Easter Sunday—Lenny will open at his room in the Village: a matinée and an evening show that very Sunday. After the first week, if things go well, they'll renegoiate. How's that? And . . . Oh yeah! . . . There is one other provision. Every show at the theater or the club must be tape-recorded by a competent professional engineer. "Someday those tapes will save your ass!" Lenny chuckles.

When Lenny hits the stage of the Village Theater for the Easter concerts—which have suddenly multiplied from two to four in the wake of sensational pre-show business—he is spoiling to shpritz. He knows how badly he stunk it up the previous Thanksgiving; now he wants to make amends. Good Friday, he doesn't quite get it together. Saturday night, he gets off the last great blast of his career.

The show was Carnegie Hall three years later, with all the enormous soul changes those terrible years had produced. Lenny was now a man who had nothing to lose, a performer without a hope, a show-biz kamikaze. When he got onstage, he became the Jewish equivalent of James Brown, stripping down his mind to the bare bone just the way the rhythm-and-blues cats tear off their clothes and scream out their guts and finally regress to tribal totems drenched in sweat. Soul, not jazz, was Lenny's final aesthetic. You can really hear his soul on this last great tape.

Everything was whirling through his mind in those latter days. One minute he'd be explaining how Lesnick and White planted dope on him because they were convinced he was a junkie and they were willing to "lie for the truth." The next minute, he'd be off on some religious fantasy, describing that great day when the elders of the tribe gave something up for God. St. Paul capped them all by scribbling on his pledge, "Fuck no more, Paul." God, religion, Jews, gentiles—Lenny was down to his final statements on these topics. He had a great little bit, for example, in which he explained that the superiority of the Christian God to the Jewish God lay in the fact that former had a face, a family, an image—"The Christian God has been in three pictures!"

Spliced right in there with the intellectual material was all kinds of highly personal stuff, as well as deep, primitive psychological fantasies. He did a whole thing that night on Sally, dramatizing their relationship back in the old days on Livingston Street. Sally is hotting it up around the apartment, humming lasciviously in the kitchen as she prepares drinks, and Lenny is protesting—"Ma, I'm not gonna be able to bring guys around here anymore, Ma, if you're gonna act this way—you old *kurvah*!" "Haven't I got nice legs?" Sally inquires flirtatiously. "Yeah, Ma, you got nice legs, nice arms—but that *means* something when you say that!"

The psychological-fantastical repercussions of such scenes emerge a little later in the show when he does an oddly affecting piece of material about Eleanor Roosevelt. In this way-out what if, Lenny goes into the bedroom and finds Mrs. Roosevelt "changing." "Haven't I got beautiful tits?" she asks him. "You sure have!" is his comeback. Then he asks her, "Do you work out or anything?" What it all comes down to is the idea of Mrs. Roosevelt, as the Mother of Us All, sporting a bee-u-tee-ful pair!

Probably the greatest piece of this last period was Lenny's fantasy on "pissing-in-the-sink." (The common yet forbidden act was one thing in his mind, so it was always titled with a staccato word burst that fused four words into one term.) On this particular night, he said that he was thinking of getting up at a giant Jehovah's Witness rally in Yankee Stadium and crying out to the assembled thousands: *"Is there one other sinner out there who has ever pissed-in-the-sink?"*

Then the bit begins with two guys asleep in a hotel room. One guy has to take a leak. He gets up and starts to piss in the sink, when the other wakes up and challenges him. "Whaddya doin' there?"

"Oh, my foot is cut—I wuz just washin' my foot!"

"Oh, that's better. I wuz afraid you were pissin'-in-the-sink. If you'd done that, I'd a *killed* ya! I gotta wash my *face* in that sink!"

The guy who has to take the leak is now frantic. So he slips out on the ledge and gets ready to piss into the street. Just at that moment, a Pat O'Brien priest appears and calls out: "Don't jump, son!"

"Oh, Father, I was jus' tryin' to take a piss! I wasn't gonna kill myself!"

Suddenly, the priest becomes Shaughnessy from Homicide shouting commands at him. Next, the fire department arrives with screaming sirens and the fire chief is bellowing order to the crowd through a bullhorn— the whole scene has turned into a nightmare. Finally, the guy's mother appears; he cries out deperately, "Ma! I was jus' tryin' to take a piss!" She cries, "Run the water! Run the hoses!" desperate to aid her hung-up son. The fear of arrest and exposure had mingled in Lenny's mind with excretory fantasies and the irrational guilt of the old-style Jewish toilet training, with its terrifying threats: "He made kaka? All right, we'll get a policeman!"

The most astounding—and frightening—thing that happened this night was the sudden appearance of a weird-looking guy with a beard and a crew cut. This big schlub jumps onstage and thrusts his hand out like an assassin with a Saturday-night Special! Our hero figures that he's had it! This is the lunatic attempt he has always feared. The ultimate act of protest. Yet what the cat is holding in that menacing paw turns out not to be a gun, but a five-dollar bill! Tearing the mike out of Lenny's hand, he screams "FUCK TEXAS!" and scrambles off the stage.

None of Lenny's comic bits—not even the shock of seeing him confronted by a possible assassin—produced such deep vibes as his now-standard routine about Jackie Kennedy "hauling ass to save her ass." This bit had been triggered by that astonishing strip of pictures printed across the top of two pages in the December 6, 1963, issue of *Time*. The photographs, cut out of the 20-second movie film made by Abraham Zapruder, were captioned: "The third shot, all too literally, exploded in Kennedy's head. In less than an instant, Jackie was up, climbing back over the trunk of the car, seeking help. She reached out her right hand, caught the hand of a Secret Service man who was running to catch up, and in one desperate tug pulled him aboard. Then, in less time than it takes to tell it, she was back cradling her husband's head in her lap." Lenny Bruce saw the sequence differently:

The conclusion that I've formed was denied by *Time* magazine, which said that she was going to get help. Now, I challenge them. To which checkpoint would she go? Where's her experience? "Oh, yes, when he got shot I knew and I went right off the car to get help, so I could bring back the help.'' No, I think that's *bullshit*!

Now, why did the guy get the medal? Certainly not the last caption, that he's being helped aboard. That's bullshit!

Why this is a dirty picture to me, and offensive, is because it sets up a lie: that she was going to get help, and that she was helping him aboard. Because when your daughters, if their husbands get shot, and they haul ass to save their asses, they'll feel shitty, and low, because they're not like that good Mrs. Kennedy who stayed there. And *fuck it, she didn't* stay there! That's a *lie* they keep telling people, to keep living up to bullshit that never did exist. Because the people who believe that bullshit are foremen of the juries that put you away.

As best as anyone can tell, the single most damning bit of evidence in the subsequent prosecution of Lenny was what his critics felt was his cruel and angry indictment of Mrs. Kennedy. One of Lenny's lawyers later recalled that even before his client's trouble began in New York, Richard H. Kuh, the assistant D.A. in charge of obscenity prosecutions leaned across a dinner table and snapped: "This Bruce ridiculed Mrs. Kennedy. He said, 'She hauled ass to save her ass!' Those who live by the sword, die by the sword!"

When Lenny went into the Cafe Au Go Go the afternoon of Easter Sunday, the place was filling up for the first time since it opened. The bill was a fantastic entertainment offering, one of those rare and unforgettable combinations of talent that forever haunt the imagination. Can you imagine who was appearing as the warm-up act? None other than *Tiny Tim*! At that time Tiny was the favorite entertainer of the lesbians at Page Three—a freaky street person who played for dimes and quarters at Bohemian parties and at Hubert's Flea Circus.

The link between the two performers was Ronnie Lyons, a small-time promoter who was managing Tiny Tim and also acting as Lenny's go-fer in New York. Ronnie had sent some tapes of Tiny Tim to Lenny in California and Lenny had loved them. Always a sentimentalist about old things and camp things and things fragrant with the musty odors of nostalgia, Lenny's heart leaped up the first time he heard Tiny Tim sing. When he got to New York for the Easter concert, the first thing he wanted was the author of those tapes. Tiny Tim recalls:

I was working at the Page Three, where the girls liked each other. They were all dear friends of mine, 'cuz it's the heart that counts, not the facial appearances. I was making $40 a week. Then Mr. Bruce came to New York and said he wanted to meet me. I felt very funny—I'll never forget. It was a Sunday and my nose started to bleed before I went out to meet him. I had to keep my nose up, put water on it, and go down to meet him. I felt funny because Mr. Lyons asked me to sing for him. I never like to use any star for success. I don't want no help from these people who have made it already. To this day, I'm sorry that I went down there. But I did go down and sang for Mr. Bruce.

He was at Mr. Lyons's place in the Village. I went up there to a little flat. I was waiting for Mr. Bruce, and he came out of the bathroom. He had a favorite song of mine: "When Will the Sun Shine for Me?" It was done by Irving Kaufman in 1924, the Bing Crosby of his day. I left feeling bad after realizing that I had auditioned for somebody who it would seem like I wanted something from. Mr. Lyons came to the Page Three a day later and said, "Mr. Bruce *loved* you! He wants you to sing on the bill with him."

The night we opened I really tore the place down. I did "Tiptoe" and several songs in my high voice and a duet with myself. After that I went into heavier ballads, which I never did except at parties. I sang one of Russ Colombo's songs, Jolson's "Avalon," "Sonny Boy," and "Walk Like a Man" in high voice. After that, tragedy came.

On Tuesday, March 31st, the third night of the run, at about 10:30, a small dapper man in a dark suit entered the club, bought a ticket for $4.70 at the curtained-off admission desk, and proceeded to a table just short of the stage. When the 11:00 show got under way, he drew a small notebook from an inside pocket and began to enter his observations. When Lenny got out onstage, the little man consulted his watch: it was precisely 12:01. As Lenny spoke, the man took notes: a word here, a phrase there, perhaps six little pages neatly written on both sides. At the conclusion of the show, he slipped the notebook back into his pocket and quietly left the room. No one had so much as noticed his presence. The next morning he got up early and went to his office, where he took a sheet of stationery headed "New York City Department of Licenses" and copied off his notes. His next stop was the office of Assistant District Attorney Richard H. Kuh. When Kuh read through the report of License Inspector Herbert S. Ruhe, formerly of the CIA, he quickly rose and went to see the boss—District Attorney Frank S. Hogan.

Hogan was a small, graying leprechaun, fifty-eight years old, nearing the end of his fourth consecutive four-year term as Manhattan District Attorney. His power was second only to the mayor's. Like any administrator, he had certain notable prejudices: one of them was against anything that could be constructed as pornographic. Way back in the thirties, he had indicted Edmund Wilson's *Memoirs of Hecate County* and had the book banned in Wilson's native state. What he had done to the dean of American letters, he could be expected to do even more punitively to a café performer with an unparalleled reputation for obscenity. As an eminent Catholic layman, Hogan must have resented profoundly Lenny Bruce's blasphemy of New York's leading priests: Cardinal Spellman and Bishop Sheen. He might very well have taken offense at Lenny's remarks about Jackie Kennedy "hauling ass." Indeed, there was very little in Lenny's act, language, or public attitude that would not have offended a puritanical man like Frank Hogan.

From the very start, all the investigative officers and attorneys were coordinated by a master plan. No crude bust ordered by a local captain and executed clumsily by the cops on the beat, the arrest of Lenny Bruce in New York was designed to ensure conviction. After Inspector Ruhe made his report, the D.A.'s office ordered the police to monitor Lenny's act that same night, April 1st, using special recording equipment. The Supreme Court had decreed that the work must be examined as a whole; it was necessary, therefore, to obtain a complete record of the performance.

So on Wednesday, April 1st, at eight-thirty in the evening, two gentlemen with neat haircuts and inexpensive but well-pressed suits purchased middle-priced tickets for $3.75 apiece and sat down at a table about fifteen feet from the stage. One was Patrolman William O'Neal, the other Patrolman Robert Lane, both members of the First Division's Public Morals Squad.

Patrolman Lane had been fitted out just a couple of hours before with a Minofon Recorder, a small wire recording machine that could be strapped to the body. As he sat at the coffeehouse table sipping a confectioner's drink, he could feel under his left armpit the bulk of the six-by-eight-inch power pack. When he pressed his chin down on his chest, he could see the tiny silver microphone gleaming from his cravat like a tiepin. During the first act—a folk singer—Patrolman Lane did nothing. The next act was an English comedy team. Again he did nothing. When Lenny Bruce walked out onstage at about ten, Lane reached discreetly inside his jacket and pressed the "record" button on the Minofon.

Lenny worked for fifty or sixty minutes amidst noises of laughter, applause, furniture scraping, people chattering—the usual uproar of a public place. The tiny mike was flooded frequently with noise that blotted out the words of the performer on stage. Even when the room was relatively quiet, it wasn't easy to follow Lenny's rapid patter and erratic delivery. The patrolman watched the show attentively, but he wasn't sure that he was getting everything. One comfort he had: looking around the room, he spotted two fellow plainclothesmen at another table further to the rear. They were Patrolman MacCambridge and Lieutenant Russo, also of the First Division. With four men covering the show, it wasn't likely that anything important would escape the police.

As soon as the show was over, Patrolman Lane got up from the table, walked out of the club and up the stairs to Bleecker Street, where he pressed another button on his machine and stopped the recorder. Later that night he recorded the second show. Next morning he played the recording at Assistant District Attorney Kuh's office and received orders to rerecord it onto tape—so the original wire would not be damaged—and then transcribe the whole performance on paper. Holing up in an office with O'Neil and MacCambridge, Lane spent the next six hours playing and replaying the tape dubbing, trying to "translate"—to use his word—the performance into writing. Many passages had been rendered inaudible by the noise in the club; other things were hard to understand. Nevertheless, by late afternoon he had eight pages of typed script, representing about half the show. Taking this up to a grand jury room in the Supreme Court building, Patrolman Lane was introduced to a panel of middle-aged jurors and quizzed about what he had heard the previous night. When he had completed his testimony, he saw the copies of his transcript being distributed to the jury. As he left, he heard the first words of the tape being played to the reading jurors.

Some time the following day, after further police testimony, further playing of tapes and reading of testimony, Kuh instructed the jury in the nature of the law. It was an archaic statute, numbered 1140-A in the City Code, whose anxiously overlapping adjectives—"indecent, immoral, impure"—had never been clarified through litigation. Vague, inexplicit, clearly out of harmony with current state and national laws, this creaky old ordinance was quite possibly unconstitutional. No conviction obtained under its catch-all provisions stood a chance of holding up under the scrutiny of the appellate courts; consequently, the only purpose that could be served by invoking it would be the harrassment of the defendent, who would have to spend thousands of dollars to free himself of its inhibiting grip. District Attorney Frank S. Hogan, however, was so firmly convinced that Lenny Bruce was obscene that he was willing to challenge even the appellate courts in order to bar Bruce from New York.

What was basically at issue in the Bruce trial was much more than a specific performance by a particular comedian. The issue was—as the chief prosecutor of trial, Richard M. Kuh, was to make abundantly clear in the book he wrote after its termination (a very able study of obscenity titled *Foolish Fig Leaves?*)—the tide of moral license flooding the contemporary arts, especially, the public arts of theater and film. Kuh wrote in 1967:

> The [Jonas] Mekas and Bruce prosecutions were not, as some had charged, politically or sectarian-inspired retaliation for political or religious irreverence. They were simply an inevitable reflex at what seemed to be a sudden effort to push too far too fast. Although, along with our sexual mores, standards of obscenity were obviously changing and changing rapidly, existing unrepealed and uninvited statutes still banned certain public "entertainments". . . if these [entertainments] chose as their channel of expression sexual imagery that stripped all privacy from sex and distorted it and made it ugly, whether this was done by film (Mekas), or in words and gestures (Bruce), such [entertainments] could not be blithely ignored by those charged with enforcing existing law. It was for law enforcement to start the process that would determine whether or not they accorded with our "contemporary community standards," and whether or not they were redeemed by any—or by adequate—"social importance."

The men who conceived and executed the New York prosecution of Lenny Bruce were not foolish bigots: they were not Judge Axelrod fretting about his grandchildren or Magistrate Keiser looking for his schmeer or Judge Ryan worrying about an election year and a Catholic constituency. Hogan and Kuh were moral conservatives who could see the future clearly—probably a lot more clearly than Lenny Bruce and his befuddled liberal allies—and were determined to offer it all the opposition they could muster. Theirs was a perfectly understandable and respectable aversion to change: the irony of it was that the man they selected for their test case was far from being the bellwether of the avant-garde.

Lenny Bruce was, in his own terms, just as moralistic, conservative, and "uptight" as Judge Murtagh and Assistant D.A. Kuh. From the very beginning of the trial, he felt a secret affinity with these men and a secret aversion to his long-hair hippie and short-hair libbie supporters. Lenny was an exacerbated conservative, a typical satirist seeking revenge for outraged moral idealism through techniques of shock and obscenity as old as Aristophanes and Juvenal. All satirists are conservatives. It's an axiom of literary criticism, a lesson for sophomore-survey students. Turn Swift or Juvenal or Aristophanes inside out:

insist upon the positive content of their beliefs—and what do you find? Something like the Houyhnhnms: a cold, abstract, unreal universe of "reason" and "common sense" and "sanity" that is simply the pale moral reflex of profound moral prejudices.

Satirists are the last men in the world with whom the liberals and the avant-garde should make common cause. They are radical only in their choice of words. What they have to express is not a passion for change and improvement or a millennial vision of the earthly paradise but an endless reiteration of the follies and sins of humankind. Satrists are moralists, and the moralists of this world are precisely those people who are in the rear—not the vanguard of society.

Lenny Bruce was a man with an almost infantile attachment to everything that was sacred to the American lower-middle class. He believed in romantic love and lifelong marriage and sexual fidelity and absolute honesty and incorruptibility—all the preposterous absolutes of the unqualified moral conscience. He stood at the opposite extreme from the psychoanalyst or the social worker or the lower-court judge who, day in and day out, is compelled to examine humanity precisely as it is and come to terms with human imperfection. Lenny doted on human imperfection: sought it out and gloated over it—but only so he could use it as a *memento mori* for his ruthless moral conscience. So that he could sentimentalize and rhapsodize and carry on as if Eve had never bitten the apple. That was the essence of his moral being: that noting and emoting over human sin. A world where things were not conceived in the first instance in moral terms was unthinkable to him—as unthinkable as a world where sin did not instantly bring punishment down upon it. It's true, of course, that when Lenny got very defensive, he would grab sometimes for the clichés of the liberals and radicals: he would say that there was nothing dirty about the body or that "fuck" denoted "warmth" and "love" and that "the mores" were more important than "the morals." That was Lenny "the philosopher" talking, generally for publication in a local newspaper. The man, the artist, the entertainer operated on different principles: he knew very well what dirty words were, how they struck a middle-class audience and what they denoted in terms of anger and ugliness. After all, in his day he had been "the sickest of the sick comics." The attempt to make Lenny superior to morality, to make him a hippie saint or a morally transcendental *artiste*, was tantamount to missing the whole point of his sermons, which were ferociously ethical in their thrust and firmly in touch with all the conventional values.

On Friday night, April 3rd, just before the 10:00 show, the sound of sirens filled the street outside the Cafe Au Go Go. Officers in uniform

and in mufti entered the club and arrested Lenny Bruce and Howard
Solomon in the former's dressing room. As soon as they left, an announcement was made that Lenny had been apprehended and that no
show could be expected that night. Two hundred patrons were about
to receive refunds, when Professor Irwin Corey jumped up and offered
to go on in Lenny's place. Some customers left, others remained,
curious to hear what Corey would say. He rambled on for an hour and
a half, making snide remarks about the police and their role as cultural
arbiters but never really daring to broach the serious issues that the
arrest presented.

When Lenny and Solomon were taken down to the Charles Street Station,
where they were booked; then they were taken to the Tombs, where
they were kept for a couple of hours in the yard while they waited to
be released on bail. Lenny was in high spirits during the whole procedure. Arrests always excited him and sent his spirits soaring. It was
his paradoxical reaction to disaster. He kept telling Solomon, "I told
you so," pointing out to him how wise he had been in stipulating that
the tapes be made. Eventually, both men were released.

When they returned to the café, they found about a half-dozen
lawyers gathered, involved in a grand confabulation on what should
be done next. Lenny, the leading authority on the subject of obscenity,
jumped into the discussion; as the feeble dawn gradually brightened
the narrow dirty streets of the Village, he led the lawyers to the conclusion that the show should go on the next night as a sign that the
defendants did not consider the performance illegal. Around eight in
the morning, a large breakfast was cooked and served to everybody
who had watched through the night: sausages and eggs, toast and coffee
crowned the counsel table as the mood rapidly elevated to that of a
cabinet which has resolved a national crisis. Lenny was especially ex-
hilarated: he saw all his trials as test cases, but this New York arrest
struck him as being an especially good opportunity to show that his
work was really blameless before the law. New York wasn't Los Angeles; it certainly wasn't Catholic Chicago; he would win here and then
he would go to the courts that had convicted him and demand "equal
protection under the law." That was the key phrase—"equal protection." If his act was innocent in San Francisco and New York, how
could it be criminal in Los Angeles and Chicago?

The next night the show went on and the crowds were huge. It
seemed that thousands of people were standing in the street clamoring
to get into the little club. People were waving twenty-dollar bills and
shouting for attention. More devious types were claiming that they
were press representatives or magazine writers or well-known café
performers. Every scam familiar to New York's highly skilled party

crashers and gate sliders was being practiced in the mad stampede to
see the notorious Lenny Bruce.

The newspapers were not playing up the arrest; their notices were
small and objectively worded. Only one paper made much of the bust,
The Village Voice. As soon as the arrest occurred, the *Voice* assigned
Stephanie Gervis Harrington to cover the story. Her reporting was
highly sympathetic, but inadvertently she destroyed Lenny's chances
of having the charges against him quashed. One of the biggest hopes
of stopping the trial before it began lay in the fact that the prosecution
had not succeeded in obtaining the kind of evidence it desired. Instead
of getting complete recordings of the shows in question, it had only
obtained fragmentary and inaudible tapes. The Cafe Au Go Go, however, had very good professional-quality tapes, which the prosecution
knew nothing about—until Stephanie Harrington's first piece appeared
in the *Voice*. In that article the reader was given a description of Lenny
Bruce sitting in the fancy Fifth Avenue apartment of a "prominent
civil libertarian for whom they played the tapes of the shows for which
Bruce was arrested." When the public prosecutor read that there were
clearly audible tapes of the show, he immediately demanded that they
be handed over to the court. A legal wrangle resulted: the defense
claiming that the tapes were the property of Bruce or Solomon and
their surrender would amount to forcing the defendant to testify against
himself. The prosecutor soon proved that the tapes were the property
of the Cafe Au Go Go Corporation, which had hired Bruce and executed the terms of his contract, including the taping of the shows.
Corporations are not included in the rule against self-incrimination;
hence their records are subject to confiscation; therefore, the tapes
were subject to the court's subpoena. Ironically, the very instruments
to which Lenny looked for his legal vindication became devices for
trying and convicting him.

On April 7th, at the conclusion of the first show, Lenny and Solomon were arrested again, and this time the owner's wife, Ella, the
club's cashier, was also apprehended. Now one show was over and the
next was about to begin.

The first lawyer to become deeply involved in the Bruce case was Allen
Schwartz, a young man who had once worked in the district attorney's
office in New York. Schwartz knew David Blasband, and it was a call
from the Philadelphia lawyer that brought him into the case. The three
men got together with Solomon one afternoon at the Cafe Au Go Go.
Lenny was fuming because he had just been to see Morris Ernst (Stephanie Harrington's "prominent civil libertarian"), who had agreed to
take the case for nothing but had told him that his material was "the

stuff you see on bathroom walls." Lenny was looking for a more congenial lawyer, but Schwartz could see right away that the comic would
be a difficult client. At this point, Lenny had been through three
complete obscenity trials, and he thought he knew the law inside and
out. He was much too confident about being acquitted in a New York
court, completely wrong in his presumption that he would receive a
jury trial, and clearly the type of personality who would interfere at
every point in the proceedings. Schwartz got into a long knee-to-knee,
nose-to-nose rap with Lenny; when he finished, he had won Lenny's
respect.

> Lenny said, "Come back inside. I gotta talk to you." So we go
> inside and he says to me—we're in the back where the pipes are,
> next to the boiler—"Listen, I like you very much. You know what
> you're talking about. But I warn you. I feel I need a big name. I
> think I want a big name. I'm going to be very badly treated! I
> know it! I've been in trials in California and Chicago. They shit
> on you if you don't have somebody who stands up—who's big—
> who's recognized in court. I gotta have a big name! But I want
> you to be my lawyer. I will pay you a thousand dollars for the
> trial. Oh, I'm sorry!—What's your fee for the trial?" I said, "My
> fee for the trial, if it lasts a week or less, is a thousand dollars.
> That includes the preparation for the trial and all preliminary ap-
> pellate procedures, not including filing the brief or preparing the
> record." So Lenny said, "That's very good, very fair. Tell you
> what I'll do. I'm a little light on bread, so I'll give you two hundred
> now and eight hundred later, if you catch me—which you never
> will."

Schwartz explained that the money was as important to him as it was
to Lenny and declined the cheap deal. Still he wanted to participate
in the case; so when Solomon offered to engage him, he pitched in on
that side.

The first point he raised as a line of defense was the doctrine of
"scienter": the concept that, in this case, the producer of a show cannot
be held responsible for what a performer does when the performer
works entirely extempore. When Lenny heard this argument, he went
through the ceiling: it was as much as saying that he was obscene but
that Solomon had no responsibility for his dirty act. That chilled it
between Lenny and Schwartz. Meanwhile, the long series of preliminary hearings had commenced, and Schwartz was involved in another
issue that concerned Lenny vitally: the surrender of the tapes to the
D.A. The same morning that the court ordered Solomon to produce

the tapes, Lenny had sent an investigator named John Dolan to the club to pick up the tapes for Lenny's use. When Schwartz asked Lenny to return the evidence, he flatly refused. The tapes were his, he claimed: his words, his act, his soul. Lenny's refusal to come across put everybody into a sweat; if Solomon didn't surrender the material, he could be cited for contempt. Finally, tapes of two of the shows were located; the third remained in Lenny's possession and was never entered as evidence in the trial. What took its place was the imperfectly recollected testimony of license inspector Ruhe—which undoubtedly did Lenny more harm than would have the tape recording.

Eventually, after a lot of fast auditioning, Lenny hired Ephraim London. He was the logical man for the job, being the doyen of censorship and obscenity lawyers, with an amazing record of two hundred and fifty cases, including victories on behalf of *Lady Chatterley's Lover*, *Tropic of Cancer*, and the films *The Miracle* and *The Lovers*. London commanded respect as a distinguished attorney who had frequently pleaded before the U.S. Supreme Court. He was also good at lining up expert witnesses with famous names and making magisterial statements to the press. He told the newspaper reporters at his first press conference that "he knew of no previous case in this state where a performer had been charged with obscenity on the basis of his words alone." Clearly the case of Lenny Bruce was not going to be merely a show trial—it was going to make history. Meanwhile, London was doing everything in his power to ensure that there was no trial at all. During the hearings, he came up with every conceivable reason for throwing the case out of court. When he had exhausted all his purely legal objections, he drew himself up to his full and imposing stature as the elder statesman of obscenity and declared with great dignity:

I must say that I speak with possibly greater experience than any other attorney in the United States on the question I have been discussing. I can say that, I think, without the slightest hesitation. I think this is generally recognized. . . . There is not the slightest doubt in my mind that any conviction, or a conviction of this defendant . . . for violating a law relating to indecency or obscenity, could possibly stand. I would stake my reputation on that!

Nothing London could do or say, though, could dissuade the magistrate, Judge Frederick Strong, from recommending the case for trial. The court took the position—fully in accord with London's statement to the press—that this *was* a unique case: that as a spoken performance it differed decisively from a book or movie or even from a stage play because the actor and the author were one and the same person. As there was no precedent for such a case, the court held that the matter would have to be determined by either a jury trial or by the appellate court. At yet another hearing it was decided that the matter did not justify a trial by jury. The crime was a misdemeanor and the decision of a judge was adequate. Eventually it was determined that the case should be tried by three magistrates sitting in concert with one presiding. The board was selected and the members announced: Judge James R. Creel, Judge Kenneth M. Phipps, and Judge John M. Murtagh, presiding.

During the hearings, Lenny suddenly became ill again with the lung ailment that had plagued him in the fall and early winter. Every time he took a breath, he got a searing pain in his chest or back. Consulting a doctor, he learned his lung was full of fluid and in danger of collapse. If an operation wasn't performed immediately, the lung would soon infect and he might die.

At this critical moment Lenny was appalled to discover that there wasn't a doctor in the city who would treat him. He was a notorious character, and the doctors didn't want to share the spotlight with him. Going from one office to another, he got about four or five turndowns. Finally, he decided to trick his way onto the operating table. Checking into Flower and Fifth Avenue Hospital under an assumed name, he inveigled Dr. Irving Sarod into performing the necessary surgery. The doctor explained to Lenny that the operation would be a very long, difficult, and exhausting procedure. He would be laid on his side on the operating table and a fourteen-inch incision would be made in an arc extending from his spine to his breastbone. Raising this huge gill, the surgeon would use a scissorslike instrument to cut away two ribs. Then he would spread open the rib cage with the surgical equivalent of a car jack and expose the lung. Once the pleural caul had been stripped away, the lung could expand to its normal size without grating against the inflamed membrane. The price for this operation would be $1,700 plus hospital costs. The patient would need at least two weeks of nursing before he could be released.

The surgery was performed on April 23rd; the operation consumed five full hours. When Lenny was finally wheeled up to his room, he was a very sick man facing a long and dangerous recovery period. Yet, when Kenny Hume came to see him just two days later, Lenny was leaning out a window from his bed, panning an 8-mm movie camera alternately on a junkie and an intern washing his car. Lenny was in amazingly good spirits, and his hospital room recalled the famous Marx Brothers stateroom scene. Not long after Kenny arrived, Paul Krassner turned up, followed next by Tiny Tim, who promptly unpacked his ukulele from a paper shopping bag; unfolding the old cardigan with which he protected the instrument, he began singing "On the Good Ship Lollipop" and "Tiptoe Through the Tulips." As Tiny Tim shrilled through his songs, Lenny recorded him on a portable Uher, carefully monitoring the ups and downs of the voice with his hand on the level control, his face fixed in a shy, bemused smile. When the recital was over, Lenny introduced Kenny to Tiny, saying "Here's a producer from Hollywood." (Lenny was always amused by Tiny Tim's longing for commercial success.) Just at that moment a sixteen-year-old boy breezed into the sick man's room and said, "Here are those pills you wanted. Lenny."

"Thanks, kid," ragged Lenny. "Meet Sergeant Jessup of Narcotics Control."

Life in Lenny's hospital room got so uproarious that the nurses complained to the doctor. The doctor scolded Lenny and warned him that he still wasn't out of danger; but nothing availed and the partylike atmosphere lasted to the end.

One day, after complaining that the hospital didn't provide the sort of service that he desired, Lenny picked up the phone and called Sally in L.A. He told her that he had decided to come home immediately and ordered her to make the necessary arrangements. He would have himself conveyed from the hospital to the plane in a private ambulance; she must have another ambulance waiting to carry him up to the house. His regular doctor should be standing by when he got home to give him an immediate examination and prescribe whatever drugs might be necessary. Then riding over the nearly hysterical protests of the hospital staff, who saw him rushing toward his death, he had himself dressed, propped up in a wheelchair, trundled through corridors, into elevators, down ramps, and out into a waiting ambulance, which whisked him out to Kennedy Airport, where he boarded a flight for L.A. When he finally reached the House on the Hill, he was half dead from the exertion; but his recovery recommenced the next day. Soon he was ready to return to New York to begin his longest, costliest, and most maddening trial.

While Lenny was flat on his back, the forces of the New York cultural community began to rally around him. The instigator of this movement was Allen Ginsberg, who was deeply concerned at this time with what he viewed as a citywide crackdown on the arts, especially the raunchy arts of the New York avant-garde. Ginsberg was the unofficial mayor of the new Beat community quartered on the Lower East Side. He was constantly receiving complaints from his ragged constituency that the New York City Department of Licenses, the New York State Division of Motion Pictures, the Vice Squad, the Fire Department, and Building Department authorities were engaged in a concerted campaign to drive the Beats to the wall. These agencies had padlocked theaters, closed down coffeehouses where poetry readings were held, served summonses, and made arrests. Just a month before the Bruce trial, they had tried and convicted Jonas Mekas, founder of the Film-Makers Cooperative, for publicly screening Jack Smith's *Flaming Creatures*, which offered fleeting glimpses of limp sex organs, and Jean Genet's *Un Chant d'Amour*, a sentimental vision of homosexual love in prison, containing one startlingly frank sequence in which the camera pried into a series of cells, all of them occupied by men who were masturbating. (Mekas's conviction was subsequently reversed.) To Ginsberg and his cronies, the arrest of Lenny Bruce was the capstone on a hastily built wall of repression.

Sitting in the lotus position in the living room of a squalid little pad down on 5th Street and Avenue A, sorting out the newspaper clippings that told the mounting story of arrests and threats of arrest, Ginsberg pictured a three-headed monster menacing his flock of Beat saints. One head was Robert Moses, who was suspected of wanting to clean up the city for the World's Fair, scheduled to open that summer; another head was Cardinal Spellman, who was at that time leading an antipornography crusade; the third head was the real estate interests, which wished to clear the Village of Beats so they could sell the houses to successful commercial artists and trendy fashion photographers at inflated prices. Possessing a rare gift for public relations, as well as considerable organizing ability, Ginsberg decided to make the Bruce case the focus of his campaign to stop "the harassment of the arts." Already, he had achieved some success in liberating the coffeehouses; now he would take on a case that did not lie exactly in his province but had the merit of commanding widespread public attention.

His first step was obvious: a committee must be formed and a petition drawn up and circulated. Ginsberg named the new organization: The Committee on Poetry; but his efforts to frame the petition, round up the appropriate signatories, and launch the whole campaign in the media were not very successful until he enlisted the help of two young women. Helen Elliott had worked for the MCA; she not only knew how to contact celebrities but how to walk right up to them and put the collar around their necks: that was the way she had approached Lenny a couple of years before. Now she put this talent at his service. Helen Weaver was a free-lance translator, who was useful on the literary side of the project. She had never met Lenny, but she felt strongly about his persecution. She was the person who framed the petition and wrote up the press release.

The whole campaign was timed to break in the Sunday papers just before the trial commenced. The court had set the date as June 16th; three days earlier every media office in New York received a boldly printed memorandum headed: ARTS, EDUCATIONAL LEADERS PROTEST USE OF NEW YORK OBSCENITY LAW IN HARASSMENT OF CONTROVERSIAL SOCIAL SATIRIST LENNY BRUCE. The document read:

We the undersigned are agreed that the recent arrests of nightclub entertainer Lenny Bruce by the New York police department on charges of indecent performance constitute a violation of civil liberties as guaranteed by the first and fourteenth amendments to the United States Constitution.

Lenny Bruce is a popular and controversial performer in the field of social satire in the tradition of Swift, Rabelais and Twain. Although Bruce makes use of the vernacular in his nightclub performances, he does so within the context of his satirical intent and not to arouse the prurient interests of his listeners. It is up to the audience to determine what is offensive to them; it is not a function for the police department of New York or any other city to decide what adult private citizens may or may not hear.

Whether we regard Bruce as a moral spokesman or simply as an entertainer we believe he should be allowed to perform free from censorship or harassment.

Signed: Woody Allen, Entertainer; David Amram, Composer; James Baldwin, Novelist; Arnold Beichman, Chairman, Board of Directors, American Committee for Cultural Freedom; Eric Bentley, Critic, Translator, Drama Dept. Head, Columbia Univ.; Theodore Bikel, Entertainer; Louise Bogan, Poetess; Bob Booker, Producer; Robert Brustein, Drama Critic, *New Republic*, Assoc. Prof. English, Columbia Univ.; Godfrey Cambridge, Actor; Fred Coe, Producer-Director; Gregory Corso, Poet; Malcolm Cowley, Poet, Critic, Editor; Merce Cunningham, Dancer; Severn Darden, Actor, The Second City; F. W. Dupee, Professor of English, Columbia Univ.; Bob Dylan, Folk Singer; Jason Epstein, Vice Pres., Random House Publishers; Jules Feiffer, Cartoonist; Lawrence Ferlinghetti, Poet, Publisher, City Lights Books; Robert Frank, Photographer, Moviemaker; Jack Gelber, Playwright; Richard Gilman, Drama Editor, *Newsweek;* Allen Ginsberg, Poet; Ira Gitler, Editor, *Downbeat* Magazine; Harry Golden, Social Commentator, Newspaperman; Albert Goldman, Asst. Prof. English,

Columbia Univ., Music Critic, *New Leader*, TV Critic, *New Republic;* Robert Gottlieb, Managing Editor, Simon and Schuster; Dick Gregory, Comedian; Elizabeth Hardwick, Novelist; Michael Harrington, Social Critic, Author; Joseph Heller, Novelist; Lillian Hellman, Playwright; Cecil Hemley, Poet; Nat Hentoff, Jazz Critic; Granville Hicks, Literary Critic; John Hollander, Poet, Asst. Prof. English, Yale Univ.; Richard Howard, Poet, Translator; Irving Howe, Editor, *Dissent;* Peter Israel, Managing Editor, Putnam; James Jones, Novelist; LeRoi Jones, Poet, Playwright, Editor; Alfred Kazin, Literary Critic; Walt Kelly, Cartoonist; Alexander King, Memoirist; Kenneth Koch, Poet, Asst. Prof. English, Columbia Univ.; Paul Krassner, Editor, *Realist;* Irving Kristol, Editor, Basic Books; Tommy Leonetti, Entertainer; Max Lerner, Author, Columnist, *N.Y. Post;* Alfred Leslie, Painter; Robert Lowell, Poet; Dwight MacDonald, Film Critic, *Esquire*, Staff Writer, *The New Yorker;* Marion Magid, Asst. Editor, *Commentary*; Norman Mailer, Novelist; Steven Marcus, Asst. Editor, *Partisan Review*, Assoc. Prof., Columbia Univ.; Jonas Mekas, Director, Film-Makers Cooperative; Henry Miller, Novelist; Jonathan Miller, Essayist; Reinhold Niebuhr, Theologian; Paul Newman, Actor; Frank O'Hara, Poet; Peter Orlovsky, Poet; Theodore Wilentz, 8th St. Bookstore, Publisher, Corinth Books; Arthur Penn, Stage, Cinema, TV Director; William Phillips, Editor, *Partisan Review;* George Plimpton, Editor, *Paris Review;* Norman Podhoretz, Editor, *Commentary;* Robert Rauschenberg, Painter; John Rechy, Novelist; Theodor Reik, Psychoanalyst; Jack Richardson, Playwright; Barney Rossett, Publisher, Grove Press; Meyer Schapiro, Professor, Fine Arts, Columbia Univ.; Robert Silvers, Co-Editor, *N.Y. Review of Books;* Susan Sontag, Author, Critic; Terry Southern, Novelist, Screenwriter; William Styron, Novelist; Harvey Swados, Author, Literary Critic; Jerry Tallmer, Drama Critic, *N.Y. Post;* Rip Torn, Actor. Lionel Trilling, Novelist, Prof. of English, Columbia Univ.; Louis Untermeyer, Anthologist, Poet; John Updike, Novelist; Rudy Vallee, Singer; Gore Vidal, Novelist; Dan Wakefield, Social Critic; Arnold Weinstein, Playwright; John Wilcock, Columnist, *Village Voice.*

Ginsberg's petition had the desired effect. The Sunday papers were full of the Bruce case. In a lengthy two-column article, *The New York Times* presented both the substance of the protest and the results of its own follow-up reporting. The most striking feature of the petition was the appearance of those famous names, Niebuhr and Trilling; the *Times* called both men. Their comments were revealing. Niebuhr, an old man, in delicate health, living removed from current affairs, was reached at his summer home in Stockbridge, Massachusetts. "I have never seen Mr. Bruce or read anything about him," the renowned theologian confessed, going on to say that he had signed the statement after hearing about the case from close friends. Professor Trilling was somewhat better informed: he had never attended a Bruce performance or heard a record but he had read the transcipts of the shows; he found Mr. Bruce "a very remarkable and pointed satirist."

When the public prosecutor, Richard H. Kuh, read these statements in the *Times*, he went into action immediately. Fearing that such prestigious names would point the spear of antagonistic public opinion, he fired off a letter to Dr. Niebuhr, explaining the seriousness of his endorsement of Bruce and containing, it has been said, a veiled threat to subpoena the sick old man and drag him back to New York at the height of the deadly summer. Niebuhr's reply must have been very gratifying to the relentless and resourceful Kuh. It read:

> Dear Mr. Kuh:
> I should like to communicate with you in regard to the petition I signed in behalf of Lenny Bruce. I want to confess that my signature was *ill advised*. It was prompted by conversations with friends who knew Bruce and who had competence to judge the merits of social satire.
> But I should not have signed the petition at all because I had *no first hand knowledge* of Bruce's performances; and therefore my witness about the charge of obscenity was useless; and it may have led other signers of the petition astray. Incidentally, I violated the habit of a lifetime in signing a petition which had to do with some issue about which I had no personal knowledge. I will make no charge against Bruce; but also I will not say anything in his defense.
> I am writing you this note in order to correct an error of judgment, of which I was guilty.
>
> Sincerely yours,
Reinhold Niebuhr

The district attorney himself called Professor Trilling. Hogan—a lifetime trustee of Columbia University and a long-time resident of Morningside Heights, the university's neighborhood—knew Trilling personally. When he questioned the propriety of the professor's endorsement of Lenny Bruce, and then mailed the eminent critic a copy of the satires which he had characterized as "remarkable and pointed," Professor Trilling replied that the monologues in question were "filthy" and "shocking," adding that the shock of the language had doubtless added a great deal to the impact of the performance. Invited to appear in court, Trilling explained that his interest in protecting freedom of speech would prevent his giving his critical opinion.

Critical opinion was precisely what the Bruce defense was least keen on having. The defense was organized along strict Lib-Lab lines of moral cop-out, with much talk about "artists," "social comment," and "satire," and particularly all those preposterous and irresponsible comparisons that Ginsberg had initiated with "Swift, Rabelais, and Twain." Lenny Bruce was never happy with this line of defense or with the legal grandee who authored it and vainly attempted to impose it on the court. Lenny was a pragmatist even before he was an idealist. His humor was based on a thoroughly disabused vision of *what is.* "Not what should be but what is"—that was his true philosophy. Now, with Ginsberg and his Beatnik pals, or the nice young ladies from the publishing firms and PR companies, with the professors from the universities, the students from the colleges, and especially with those damned rabbinical liberal lawyers, like Ephraim London, he felt that the whole concept of reality was slipping away.

London had never seen Lenny work, Trilling had never seen Lenny work, Reinhold Niebuhr had never seen Lenny work. What is more, there was something slightly condescending in the support of these people—like Park Avenue aristocrats patronizing some People's Poet in the commie thirties. When you really got down to it, did they or didn't they dig? Lenny was never convinced they did. Never! He hired London because his instinct for self-preservation told him: "Grab a top daddy!" So he bought the best. When he got him, though, he couldn't stand him. London was a stiffo, a ponderoso, a pretentious goy-Jew who was "passing" at the Princeton Club. Big deal!—he'd learned to juice with the other shickerniks and come on like a heavy. And he was always lecturing Lenny. One day, when they were arguing about whether or not Lenny would get a shot at the court, London told him that he didn't dare put him on the stand because he was "inarticulate." A man whom Kenneth Tynan had described as breaching "frontiers of language and feeling . . . hitherto thought impregnable." *Inarticulate! Oi!*

On the 16th of June, in hot, muggy weather, the onset of the worst summer in many years, the most remarkable legal contest to hit Foley Square since the days of Joe McCarthy and the Communist Conspiracy to Destroy America began unfolding in the Criminal Courts Building on the north side of the city's legal and administrative acropolis. One hundred Centre Street is a steep, tripartite skyscraper of smoke-stained granite, looming up like the ghost of the Depression; a somber, sawed-off skyscraper, it suggested not so much the majesty of the law as its stony weight and labyrinthine gloom. Here in Room 535, one of the largest courtrooms available, the little misdemeanor action that should have occupied a few days of the court's time swelled during the next six weeks into the longest, costliest, most bitterly contested and widely publicized obscenity trial in the history of American jurisprudence.

On the first day of the trial, the courtroom was jammed with spectators. They were like the guests at a wedding: the pro-Bruce forces sitting on the left-hand side of the room and the anti-Bruce forces sitting at the right. Many of those who had come were simply sightseers: Beat types in long hair and scuffle clothes, courthouse loungers, people who had come in from other sections of the court to while away an hour before or after their own business was conducted. Many of the spectators, however, were on assignment from the news media: *Newsweek*, *Time*, *The New York Times*, the *Daily News*, the *New York Post*, and *Herald Tribune*—all the papers were represented as well as the international news-gathering agencies. The intellectual journals had also sent some representatives to cover the trial, choosing their writers almost tongue in cheek. Philip Roth had an open assignment from the *New York Review of Books;* Jules Feiffer had come as an observer but was also looking for material to use in his strip in the *Village Voice;* I was covering the trial for the *New Republic.* There were also artists sketching the action for these same magazines, as well as poets like Allen Ginsberg and Peter Orlovsky. The defense of art was, when you thought about it, a pretty good subject for art.

The setting for this strange judicial show was a long, lofty courtroom, lined with heavy oak benches and illuminated by indirect ceiling lights. When the black-clad judges entered in a row from the robing room and assumed their positions on a lofty dais, flanked by a half-dozen uniformed officers, the spectacle suddenly assumed a theatrical image. Half the writers in the room started scribbling about the "court as theater," the trial as a "summer arts festival" or the "theater of the absurd." It was all working beautifully, just as they had foretold days before on the phone with an editor or whooping it up at a Sunday-evening dinner party. Then the flipper-armed Irish bailiff called out the case—"People of the State of New York versus Lenny *Brice*"—and everybody snickered appreciatively. The law was really a gas!

Every other second, the reporters cast curious looks at the defense table, where the object of this hullabaloo was seated. They saw a small neatly bearded man dressed in well-scrubbed Levis with high white boots and a creepy, obsequious manner. Lenny had come with a complete kit of legal tools: yellow-lined pads, Magic Markers, and clench-back notebooks filled with clippings and documents neatly protected by cellophane. He struck you as a kid at his first day in grade school with a new pencil case and a plaid book bag. Actually, his gear was rather less innocent than it looked. He had carried into court a hand grenade, which he kept on his lap under the counsel table. Every time the bench made an adverse ruling, he made as if to lob the grenade right in Judge Murtagh's lap. His leather attaché case, which looked so professional when he carried it down the aisle, actually contained a built-in tape recorder whose microphone was one of the locks. The cops had bugged Lenny's show with their dinky little Minifons? Well, Lenny was going to bug their bugs with his expensive little machine, which had been manufactured by the well-known recording engineer, Bones Howe. Sometimes after the lunch recess, Lenny would ask one of his friends among the press corps to carry the case into court for him; when the friend would make a face at the leaden weight of the case, Lenny would whisper the dread secret in his ear and then hiss, "Zug nisht!"

The other principals in the cast were all clearly defined characters. Judge Murtagh was the very model of judicial appearance and decorum: a stiff, prim figure, with powdered cheeks and expressionless face, he ruled the court with inviolable dignity. On that first morning he appeared open, sympathetic, cool but good-humored: everything that his reputation as a liberal-minded jurist would lead one to expect. As one reporter remarked that day at lunch: "If Bruce has a case, Murtagh is the man to hear it." Judge Phipps, who sat to Murtagh's left, was a faceless middle-class black, whose only appealing feature was a tendency to chuckle at everybody's jokes, until Murtagh shushed him. Judge Creel, on the other side of the bench, was a handsome middle-aged man of kindly demeanor, who was obviously puzzled by the defendant's language. He was capable of asking: "Is 'goy' a dirty word?"

The advocates who jousted back and forth before the bench for six long weeks were an oddly contrasted pair. Ephraim London was a tall, stooped college professor, removing his glasses to opine before his learned colleagues and putting them on again to read forth from documents and case books and from the thick wads of his client's transcribed monologues. Richard Kuh was a brisk, athletic YMCA prosecutor, always advancing and retreating, ducking in and out, grandstanding with feigned indignation, then sitting down with a smile to the spectators, like a fielder who has just made a shoestring catch. A typical product of the Kennedy years, Kuh even affected Kennedy's slight lisp in his loud but strangled voice. But he was on the wrong side so far as the liberal-intellectual audience was concerned. They kept trying to pin him with an image: Burt Lancaster, Dick Tracy, Spencer Tracy. Finally, Jules Feiffer got the picture: Dick Kuh was

Clark Kent, Superman. Lenny Bruce was Leonard Schneider, Super-jew! An immortal contest!

That first morning in court told a lot about the trial to come. London had planned to snow the judges with the expert witnesses he had been courting in countless luncheon appointments and private hearings of the much-hassled tapes at his Greenwich Village apartment. It had taken heroic efforts to persuade some of these people to come into court and testify, and they had specified that they were available only within certain narrowly prescribed times. Richard Gilman, the drama critic of *Newsweek*, was about to leave the city on assignment. He was a valuable witness in London's eyes because 1) he had seen Lenny work (though not at the performances in question); 2) he had never written about him before; 3) he had ben associated for years with *Commonweal*, a Catholic publication; 4) he had maintained a high literary and moral tone in all his writing. Bringing him on early seemed like no problem; but as soon as the pugnacious Kuh got wind of the plan, he threw up so many objections that London had the greatest difficulty in even getting his man on the stand. When it developed that Gilman had not seen the shows for which Bruce had been arrested, the barrage of objections assumed an even greater intensity; and when, to weather the objections, London had to answer that Gilman *had* heard the shows by means of tape recordings played at London's apartment, the whole procedure foundered over the court's concern over whether these tapes were in fact *the* tapes, blah, blah, blah. "The court finds confusion in the presentation of Gilman *now* before a proper foundation has been laid." Off with Gilman and on with the officers who observed, recorded, and transcribed the show for the trial.

That was how the first morning was spent, and by the time the hotshot writers and intellectuals went out to lunch, they were bursting with impatience. Wedged around a little table in a restaurant down in that uninhabitable region near Foley Square—oblivious of the delights of Chinatown just a few blocks away—Philip Roth and Jules Feiffer struggled to outdo Lenny Bruce in humor and verbal brilliance. Philip had never been sold on Bruce. He found him obvious and not that funny. When the records were played for him at social gatherings, he felt an acute sense of embarrassment. Lenny didn't know how to use words: that much was obvious. Like all semiliterates, he got a piece of the word—"like getting a piece of the ball, Al!"—and he didn't quite get it all. Couldn't send it neatly over the near-left field fence, as any really practiced, really schooled, really talented writer could do. What's more, like all these self-important show-biz types, he abused the language with dreadful phrases like "behavior patterns" or plumed himself with words he had no title to, like "neologize." Now how's that for chutzpah? Lenny Bruce talking about "neologizing"? —does the damn word really have a participial form? Oh, it was silly to go on and on about this latest pet of the cranky New York intelligentisia—Roth wasn't keen on what was coming out of Mr. Lenny Bruce. "Admit it, Al, I'm funnier many times!" As the IRT train roared up the East Side, I admitted it.

As part of the foundation for the prosecution, Inspector Ruhe was called to the stand the second morning, where he gave a remarkable performance, in every sense of the word. The state had no recording of Lenny's first indictable presentation, the one at 12:01 on the morning of April 1st. The only evidence was Inspector Ruhe's notebook, and the memories it revived. After a prolonged legal wrangle, the court ruled that Ruhe could use the notebook to recollect the performance, even though the recollection would be imperfect because the notebook contained only isolated words and phrases, selected, according to Ruhe, in accordance with "a system of memory recall . . . which would subsequently assist me in typing up a more complete report." Considering the number of words that poured out of Lenny Bruce in a single performance and bearing in mind the odd character of his language and the crazy-quilt texture of the show as a whole, it was not surprising that Ruhe should have failed here and there to recollect what was said or exactly how it was phrased. What was astonishing was the extent and accuracy of the recollection sparked by this little handful of notes. Not only the sequence of the bits and the substance of the bits but whole long passages sounding almost as if they came directly from Lenny's mouth were conveyed by the witness into the court record. As Ruhe warmed to his work, the reservation he had originally betrayed toward saying the dirty words melted away and soon he was *doing* Lenny Bruce—getting off Lenny's bits like an understudy mimicking the star. His success could be measured by the same standard that rules all comedy: he began to get a lot of laughs, till Murtagh hushed the court.

Lenny was outraged by Ruhe's performance. As he saw it, the little fart was stealing his act. "Listen to him!" he hissed into the ear of Martin Garbus, London's junior partner. "All he wants is to be an actor. This trial is his chance. Listening to him is like listening to Ezra Pound reading the Bible. He loves doing my act. He's looking to see if there are any talent scouts in the courtroom. And he'll look at tomorrow's papers for his reviews."

Ruhe not only stole Lenny's act; he offered the most fearsome piece of evidence presented during the whole trial. Before leaving the stand, he said that he had seen Bruce slide his hands up and down the

microphone as part of a "masturbatory gesture." He also said that
Bruce touched his crotch. Lenny blanched at the word "crotch."
"That's it! That's the trick!" he panted to Garbus. "That's how they're
going to get me, Martin! I would never do anything like that—I know
better. It's one thing to talk about tits and ass. But to show how to
jerk off—they'd put me away for life."

The next witness, Patrolman Lane, the officer who had made the
Minifon recording, also testified that Bruce had made gestures that
originated in the area of the crotch. When the D.A. asked him to
demonstrate, the big embarrassed-looking officer got up from his chair,
held out his arms as if he was holding a flagpole and slid his hands
back and forth along the imaginary pole. From that time on, the defense labored to prove that Lenny had not made such gestures. It was
far easier to convict Lenny on the basis of what he had *done* than it
was on the basis of what he had *said;* therefore, every one of a dozen
defense witnesses who were present at the shows was asked "Did Mr.
Bruce make any gestures toward his crotch?" One and all, they denied
it. Eventually, London raised the biggest laugh of the trial by asking
one witness: "Did you see Mr. Crotch makes any gestures toward his
Bruce?"

During Ruhe's testimony on that second day of the trial, Lenny
got up at one point and walked out of the courtroom. He complained
of feeling ill. Next day he did not appear in court and London announced that he had had a recurrence of pleurisy and was in the
hospital. The trial was adjourned for ten days. A couple of days later
Martin Garbus went to visit Lenny.

His room was dark, with just a small light in one corner. Flowers
sent by admirers overflowed into the hall. He was unshaven and
looked terrible, but scattered over the bed and floor were at least
two dozen law books. He had read our preliminary brief and said,
in an apologetic but still faintly accusing voice, "There was an
amendment to Section 1140 back in 1930 and it changes the meaning of the Section. The amendment excluded actors. I just came
across the case of a rabbi who was arrested for not having a license
to run a butcher shop, and that case, because of the amendment,
is the same as mine. He was acquitted because he was not the
principal. You didn't cite the case in your brief."

I tried to explain to him that the case of the rabbi had no bearing
on his own case, but it was impossible to get through to him. I
could not tell him what he really wanted to hear—that his research
was brilliant. Most of the law books he had poured over were

deadly dull, but he had read them thoroughly and with obvious enjoyment. "I read four of these from cover to cover," he said.

When the trial resumed on June 30th, 1964, the defense made a motion that the complaint be dismissed on the grounds that the People had not made out a prima facie case for obscenity. Standing before the bench in his drooping professorial posture, London argued—borrowing a page from Kalven—that vulgar language is not in itself obscene. When London finished his lesson, he received powerful seconding from Judge Creel, who said that though he deplored the performances and regarded them as the products of a sick mind, he believed that recent rulings of the Supreme Court had deprived local communities of the right to protect themselves against such scatological assaults and that there was nothing left for this court to do but concede that Bruce was not obscene under the law. The only remedy for this admittedly dreadful situation, he added, was to convene a constitutional convention and draw up new rules governing the principle of free speech. (A rather quaint suggestion in view of the fact that the last constitutional convention had been held in 1791!)

Confronted with the threat of having his case shot out from under him, Kuh summoned up all his powers and delivered what was probably the most damaging legal argument ever directed at Lenny Bruce. Eschewing for the most part the finger-pointing rhetoric that characterized the rather stupid prosecutions in other cities, Kuh hammered home point after point of solid legal argument. He insisted that Bruce's performances were obscene in *substance*, not just in language; that they were prurient even if they were not erotic because "prurience" as a legal term embraced not only the erotically stimulating but the "filthy and disgusting"; and he capped his case with the most crippling argument of all: that Lenny's work need not be taken as a whole because it was *not* a whole in any meaningful sense, being in fact a collection of "bits" that "meander, wander, and deal with a hundred things." "An anthology of filth" was, he said, a better description of the typical Bruce monologue; and under the law, the presence in such an anthology of some items that were not filthy was no defense against the condemnation of other bits that were obscene. Kuh's arguments were just what the court needed to continue the trial, and eventually they found their way into the judicial majority's opinion.

The defense now began to build its case by calling back to the stand Richard Gilman of *Newsweek*. The decision to put Gilman on as the first expert witness was forced on London by the exigencies of scheduling: the man had to get out of town. Psychologically, it was a

blunder. Gilman was a bad lead-off batter. Thin, pinched, bespectacled, with the dry condescending manner of a monastic academic stiff-
ened by the intellectual hauteur of the middlebrow-baiting sixties,
Gilman immediately betrayed his contempt for the bench and the
district attorney. Not only did he bristle with moral indignation, he
answered London's questions about the artistic value of Bruce's work
with such a huffing-puffing tone of critical self-righteousness that he
instantly drew fire from the judge. Actually, he was probably terribly
nervous, and he was suffering from the bluntness and broadness of the
questions. Literary critics—who spend their lives making narrow esthetic assessments—are the last people in the world to be asked: "Have
you formed any opinion with respect to the artistic value and importance of the performance of April 1st?" The question is simply too
vague. To answer in the form to which he is accustomed, a critic would
have to write an essay, deciding carefully where to begin, what examples to cite, how to make his transitions, where to point his argument, and how to round the whole matter up in some rhetorically
emphatic final paragraph. Asked point-blank, "Is this thing art?" he
is bound to fumble and stall, like a delicate diamond-toothed saw laid
across a piece of pot metal.

Gilman's answer to the question "Whether it has . . ." was so
vague as to be almost unintelligible: "I believe that the basis of the
artist's value is . . . the basis to have any art, which is that on the other
hand gives a form to an otherwise chaotic experience that reveals
beneath the person . . . that tells us what we are unable to know any
other way."

Immediately, Murtagh was directly involved with the witness,
questioning him, challenging him, taking over the examination the way
judges almost invariably do when they're truly perplexed. "You mean
you have to resort to this language to convey that thought?" said
Murtagh, cutting through the hot air of the witness's answer and pointing him directly at what was troubling the court.

"I don't know what language we resort to," replied Gilman, falling
back on the academic's classic posture of "define your terms."

"He asked for a definition," snapped Murtagh, underscoring the
fact that expert witnesses were supposed to come up in court with the
answers and not with expressions of doubt, confusion, or the inability
to put the matter into words.

"I have never heard a definition or explanation of artistic value
that does not deal with," expostulated Gilman, going completely on
the defensive when he should have been responding to the Judge's
questions.

"What is artistic value?" insisted Murtagh, forcing the line of questioning to its deepest and most impossible—and yet most vital and
promising—level. "What is artistic value?"

Answer: "That value which constitutes a work of art." Sensing
the folly of his reply, Gilman hastened to try again: "I would say it is
a form of revelation which takes experiences and allows us to see in
a way we are unable to see it without the artist's shaping and form
upon the material."

"Where is there art in any of these transcripts?" persisted Murtagh,
dragging the witness back to the issues before the court.

"I think it consists really of what we feel, actually feel or actually
say. What we actually do as distinguished from the way we follow
ourselves. The very use of a certain kind of language seems to me is
artistic, insofar as it makes a revelation about our life today, life in
society, life in relation to each other, sexual lives, imaginative lives,
lives as citizens . . . the value that rises from that is the value of the
liberation that we feel in seeing the truth."

Murtagh pressed on, asking for specific examples of the values
Gilman discovered in the monologues, and Gilman struggled stubbornly to come up with instances of esthetic merit. In fairness to Gilman, it must be conceded that he was facing some pretty rough shows.
The deterioration that had been evident in Lenny's work ever since
the preceding fall had now reached the point of virtual incoherence.
The effect of listening to him had come to be that of hearing a half-
intelligible internal monologue interspersed with obscenities.

Every afternoon, when the court adjourned, Lenny would go out
to the elevator bank surrounded by a cluster of reporters, friends, and
onlookers. Holding forth like a *chef de clinique* who has just finished
walking the wards, he would crowd into a car with this mob and descend
to the first floor, where he would invite his Pal of the Day to jump in
a cab with him and go up to his Greenwich Village hotel. Richard
Kuh, in one of his forensic flights, once described Lenny's hotel as
"the Marlton on elegant Fifth Avenue." The Marlton was, indeed,
just a few doors west of Fifth Avenue, but it belonged exclusively to
the honky-tonk world of Eighth Street, which it fronted with a façade
so narrow-shouldered and a lobby so inconspicuous that you could
walk up and down the street for years and never notice this tiny fleabag.
I used to sit in Lenny's "suite" on the second floor—perched on a
corner of the bed because there was only a single chair—wondering
when the wrecking ball would come crashing through the sick green
walls. The carpet looked as if it would crack if you tried to bend it.
The bedspreads were exhausted chenilles with fuzzy ridges meandering
across them. Everything was festooned with unstrung, twisted magnetic

tape. Adjoining the bedroom was a large kitchen whose chipped por-
celain table was generally crowned with an old electric typewriter and
a stack of legal documents.

This was the period when Lenny began to grow obese. He never
slept and he never ate regular meals: so he was always noshing at hot-
dog stands, sending out for Chinese food at 3 A.M., or guzzling down
bottle after bottle of Diet Rite soda. The empty soda cases at one end
of the kitchen reached almost to the ceiling. The staples that were
stocked in the pantry were dozens of bags of unshelled peanuts, great
quantities of fruit, and, in the refrigerator, numerous quarts of heavy
butterfat ice cream. Lenny doused everything he ate—warm or cold,
fruit or ice cream—with great gobbets of Red Devil hot sauce.

As he got virtually no exercise, it isn't any wonder that he puffed
up by the end of the trial to two hundred pounds. A bad sign, it showed
the degree of his suffering. Also the degree of his obsession and preoccupation. He was letting himself go. The supreme narcissist, the man
who once had his Levis tailored to his trim frame, didn't give a damn
how he looked.

Lenny had also changed his brand of speed, shifting from Methedrine to Desoxyn. After things got really heavy in court, he began
to use a lot of heroin. Inevitably, his first act when he hit the room
was to run into the bathroom and geeze. A good hour would pass
during this silent ritual, in the course of which his guest would invariably call out, "Are you all right, Lenny?" A mumbled reassurance
was about the most you could expect by way of reply. Then, as the
sky was darkening around dinner time, Lenny would emerge from his
lair and open up his attaché case to start auditing the day's sneak
recording. He could never get enough of these tapes, and by the time
his disciples began to gather after dinner, he was always deeply im-
mersed in the study not only of every word that had been uttered that
day but of every incidental noise, squeak, or murmur.

The crowd usually included Solomon's wife, Ella, who lived
nearby, Allen Schwartz, Earle Zaidins, Martin Garbus, Ronnie Lyons,
Tiny Tim, and a number of young women, whose names no one seems
to recall. As Lenny got deeper into his review of the day's proceedings,
he would gradually shift from listening to lecturing, bringing up points
of law, developing analogies with his other trials, suggesting all sorts
of new strategies and legal gimmicks, and finally ending up on his feet
doing the sort of performance that he should have been doing that
evening in a club for money. When the hour got really late, most of
the visitors would leave, and Lenny would get the urge to go out and
wander up and down the streets. He would take his 8-mm movie camera
and cab up to Times Square, where he'd prowl around his old haunts

and maybe wind up in Bickford's Cafeteria, stacking his tray with all kinds of soupy food while he aimed his camera at each old wrinkled counterman. Other nights he would go to the long lobby of the Flanders Hotel next door to the America and sit around holding court among the pimps, whores, connections, and other night people. He still loved to draw out weirdos and get off listening to their hard-luck stories or their fantastic boasts of former prosperity.

Another pattern he fell into was dialing up Allen Schwartz at his girlfriend's house at 10th Street and Seventh Avenue. The conversation would always commence with aimless chatter about the day's proceedings. Then, after listening uncomfortably to ten or fifteen minutes of mishigaas, Allen would say, "O.K., Lenny . . . I gotta go now." That would be Lenny's cue to start pleading: "Can't we get together later, man? I'll come up to your place or you come down here. Let's hang out tonight!" Though Allen's girl took a dim view of these seductions, Allen felt that he couldn't say no. Late in the evening, he would walk through the narrow, hall-like lobby of the hotel and take the cramped winding stairs to the second-floor front. Lenny would be on the phone or talking to one of his girls or listening in deepest absorption to a tape. He might take a letter off the desk and hand it to Allen wordlessly. Allen would glance down at a child's scrawl, with lines like "Daddy, don't let them send you to jail," the bottom x'ed across with mute kisses. Or the phone might ring, and it would be Sally begging Lenny to "Get off the hook! . . . Cop a plea! . . . Skip out of town!"—all the counsels of a born survivor. Lenny wouldn't listen to a word of maternal advice. Pumping himself up to his best Jimmy Cagney delivery, he would pace and fume and punch into the phone: "I don't give a shit! . . . I'll never give in! . . . They can hang me by the balls! . . . Fuck off with that bullshit! . . . blah, blah, blah, blah!" With his poor grieving mother he'd do the whole self-destructive hoodlum bit.

Finally, he and Allen would hit the street at one in the morning, the hot, moody New York night pavement: pacing up 8th Street toward Washington Park or going west into the old Village, Lenny would pass a Hoagy stand and stop for a frankfurter and a Coke. When he had wolfed down the food, they would continue their stroll, sitting down eventually on a bench in the park. As the night wore on, Lenny would get deep and confessional. Running his mind back over the years, he'd talk about when he was in the Navy and having his first homosexual experiences; when he was a child and could hear the sounds of sex in the next room—"Didja come . . . didja come . . . didja come good?" Just as he did with Martin Garbus, Lenny insisted to Allen Schwartz that he never took the "hard stuff." He was just a sick man taking his medicine according to the prescriptions he received from doctors.

When the procedural wrangles that had held up the trial in its first days were finally resolved, the defense called Richard Gilman back to complete his testimony. Then a remarkable thing occurred: Kuh objected that Gilman had no expertise in the area under investigation. At first, that seemed like a shocking and utterly unfair judgment. Richard Gilman, the drama critic, the observer of contemporary culture, the full-fledged New York literary intellectual, lacking in expertise? Yet Kuh had a point: the so-called expert had never made a study of nightclub comedy, had never even spent much time in nightclubs. He had not been present at the performances in question, nor had he written even a single article on the man upon whom he was supposed to be an "expert." The more Kuh objected to the characterization of Gilman as an "expert," the more obvious it became that he was no expert at all.

The truth was that none of the dozen expert witnesses called by the defense had much expertise in the comedy of Lenny Bruce. Though these articulate people were able to discuss Lenny's humor in the abstract, there was practically nothing they could say to which the judges could not take exception. They were not bearing witness to the performances for which Bruce had been indicted; they were not in close touch with the texture of the act in the transcriptions; they did not explain to the judges the way the humor worked or why it bore such a filthy aspect.

Actually, there were many good reasons why Lenny's language was black and blue. The obscenities established a no-bullshit tone of off-the-record honesty. They served to spark Lenny's imaginative processes and to wake up and stimulate his listeners. They evoked the hipster underworld that Lenny inhabited, as well as defining many other social groups and subcultures. They were satiric barbs, aggressive missiles, deflationary pins stuck into hollow values. They had the exhilarating effect of carnival and the hilarious effect of fun. Some grave, gray-haired professor should have told the judges, as a matter of expertise, that humor flourishes best in filth and that satire is essentially desecration. Instead, there was much talk of Aristophanes, Rabelais, and Twain.

As the trial turned into its third week and the stifling blast of midsummer blighted the city, the courtroom began to empty. Nobody was interested in the trial anymore, and those who commented in the press did so in a tone of irony or mockery. One of the very few people who seemed to care deeply was Frank Hogan. He came down from his office on the eighth floor several times to observe the proceedings. One day when he walked into court, a professor from his own university, Columbia, was in the stand comparing Bruce with Rabelais and Swift. Daniel Dodson, associate professor of English and comparative literature, was cool, crisp, and clearheaded in his appraisal. He concentrated on the sense of moral outrage in Lenny's work— precisely the point that rebutted most strongly the accusation that Bruce was a vulgar, cheap, laff-grabber. Hogan was visibly upset by the caliber of the witness and the character of the testimony. Looking around from his seat on a front bench, he saw that the rows behind him were full of young men from his own office. Here were his prize recruits from Harvard and Yale, sitting at the feet of this renegade professor and taking it all in as if they had nothing better to do. Tossing them a peremptory signal, Hogan stalked out of the courtroom. In the corridor he rounded on the young men. "What are you doing here?" he demanded, his fair complexion turning livid. "Is there anyone here who doesn't have work to do? If so, tell me and I'll find things to do. I don't want to see you here again!" Later that week Marty Garbus learned that Hogan had discovered that one of his young men was having lunch with Garbus and had denounced the lawyer—who had no connection with the trial—for "fraternizing with the enemy." He told him to stop it. "The performance is filthy," he fumed. "Anyone who doesn't agree with the prosecution can hand in his resignation!"

While the trial was proceeding, no less than four important decisions or legal actions in regard to obscenity were registered in the press. The most important was the Supreme Court's decision in the case of *Tropic of Cancer*. The book had been banned in Florida on the basis of its "vulgar and indecent" language. The court ruled that "dirty" language was not in and of itself sufficient grounds for finding a work of literature obscene. On the same day, the Court ruled in the case of Jacobellis, a film distributor who had been convicted of obscenity for presenting *The Lovers*.

Five different opinions were published on this case because the judges disagreed on almost every issue, but the majority verdict followed basically the line articulated by Justice William Brennan. He argued three cardinal points:

1. That the court had a right to review a case tried by jury because the right to free speech justifies such review by a higher court.
2. That the phrase "contemporary community standards" should not be interpreted in a narrow parochial sense, but should be taken as implying a *national standard* because "it is, after all, a national constitution that we are expounding."

3. That the balancing test—weighing social value against prurient appeal—was inappropriate. Henceforth, he said, "A work cannot be proscribed unless it is 'utterly' without social value."

Fifteen days later, on July 7, 1964, the Supreme Court of Illinois ordered Lenny Bruce's Cook County case reargued: which suggested that this court, which had previously rejected Kalven's appeal, would now reverse itself to preserve its alignment with the Supreme Court's views as embodied in the Jacobellis decision. The following week, the New York Court of Appeals, also reacting to Jacobellis, held that *Fanny Hill* could not be judged obscene.

At this moment the defense offered its star witness: the late Dorothy Kilgallen. London had gone to extraordinary lengths to get her to testify, and when finally she agreed to appear, everyone regarded it as a great coup. Cool, prim, and absolutely unflappable, Miss Kilgallen seemed to embody precisely those values of conventional morality that the district attorney was trying to protect by banning Bruce. If she approved of Lenny, if she found nothing objectionable or dirty or crazy in his act, what was the trial all about? Dorothy Kilgallen had been well coached, like all the defense witnesses, and she knew pretty well what she had to say to help Lenny. Under Martin Garbus's low-keyed, highly respectful interrogation, she made little speeches of endorsement. At one point she summed up her views very neatly by saying, "I think that he is a very brilliant man and that he has great social awareness: that basically, he's an extremely moral man and is trying to improve the world and trying to make his audiences think, which I think is a very good thing and very moral and to be applauded." Asked later about the esthetic value of the language Lenny Bruce employed, she remarked, "He employs these words the way James Baldwin or Tennessee Williams or playwrights employ them on the Broadway stage: for emphasis or because that is the way that people in a given situation would talk."

When Kuh got his chance to examine the witness, he appeared to be walking on eggs: he was terribly anxious not to give the impression that he was lacking in gallantry to a lady. Nevertheless, he pressed home his points in his usual relentless style. At first his probing produced nothing but answers that helped the defense. On the question of the unity of Lenny's act, Dorothy Kilgallen offered a better answer than any of the literary or dramatic critics. She spoke the simple truth: "He goes from one subject to another, but there is always the thread of the world around us and what is happening today and what might happen tomorrow, whether he's talking about war or peace or religion or Russia or New York—there is always a thread and a unity." That was excellent, and equally good were her interpretations of a bit on chicken-fucking—"He's making fun of the law as against sodomy"— and the "tits and ass" bit, which she said required the frequent repetition of that phrase to show how monotonous was the entertainment of Las Vegas. As the questioning proceeded, however, Kilgallen began to destroy the value of her own testimony by stumbling into glaring inconsistencies. When Kuh asked her about recent books that employed the same language as Bruce, she mentioned James Jones, Norman Mailer, and Arthur Miller; then she added, "There's another book called *Naked Lunch*, which I couldn't even finish reading; but it's published, and I think the author should be in jail!" "Unfortunately," interrupted Kuh, "we can't do everything at once, Miss Kilgallen," which got a laugh from the spectators.

Unquestionably, Dorothy Kilgallen thought she was helping Lenny's cause by indicating that she was not devoid of moral standards in art, but the effect of her testimony was to suggest that a line should be drawn between what is allowable and what is not—which was precisely the practice that the defense objected to as being an arbitrary exercise of judicial authority. The whole thrust of the defense was that no matter what language a man used, he was innocent of obscenity— providing his speech was not pruriently appealing. As if to make matters worse, Kilgallen answered, when asked why she found the book revolting: "It seemed to use the words for shock value, not for any valid reason and I object to that." This implied, of course, that if the judges found that Lenny Bruce used words for shock value and that his ideas could be expressed in polite language, then he, too, should go to jail. The last blow to the crumbling structure of Miss Kilgallen's testimony was struck by the lady herself when she was asked again about Lenny's tits-and-ass bit, especially about the repetition of that phrase. "It's just a word," she said calmly, "if you meant a donkey, you could say it and you wouldn't blush." At this point, it became pretty obvious that apart from a favorable reaction to Lenny Bruce, Dorothy Kilgallen hadn't much to tell the court on the subject of obscenity: her testimony was a tissue of unresolvable contradictions.

On July 9th the trial was adjourned for eighteen days so that Judge Murtagh could take his summer vacation. Though the interruption was unwelcome because it left Lenny hanging in air, it offered him a valuable opportunity to make some money. Flying out to San Francisco the same day, he planned to open the next night, a Friday, at the Off Broadway, a girlie club a few doors down the hill from Broadway on Kearney Street. The Thursday night Lenny arrived in town, he ran into chic Eder. The two friends hadn't seen each other for a long time;

they spent the entire night together talking, as chic drove up and down the hills. One of the first topics that came up was the recent and macabre death of Joe Maini.

During the first week of May, Joe had been gigging his buddy Ray Graziano. The men had just come home to Graziano's house. Joe had been drinking wine all night. Now he spotted a .25-caliber pistol on the cocktail table, a mail-order gun that Graziano had ordered after his woman had been frightened one night by a prowler. Joe picked up the piece and pointed it at his head, making one of his goofy faces. "Man!" Graziano burst out. "It's loaded for my old lady—be *careful!*"

Joe acted as if he hadn't heard. "Anybody for Russian roulette?" he quipped and squeezed the trigger. BANG! He got a bullet in the brain. After lingering for a couple of days in General Hospital, he died on May 7th without ever regaining consciousness.

Lenny took his usual tough-guy attitude toward Joe's death. When chic insisted that he was really hiding his feelings, Lenny turned and said: "Look, man, don't try to psych me out! The truth is that when a friend dies, the first thing you think is, 'Thank God it wasn't me!' That's the *emmis*. The rest is bullshit. If I were to die tomorrow, you'd miss me for a few days, maybe a week. Then you'd go right on with your life as if I had never been here. So why should I feel any different about you or about Joe? I don't live for *what should be*. I live for *what is!*"

The rest of the night was spent discussing Lenny's trials. He said he was much more worried about the dope rap than he was about the obscenity beef. The dope rap involved a lot of dirty pool. Not only had he stashed so that the fuzz could never have found the shit, but he had been victimized at the Department 95 hearing by some evil cats who were pretending they were doctors.

When the New York trial resumed on July 27th, the prosecution pulled a big surprise. For the first time in the history of Lenny's legal battles over the issue of obscenity a whole series of expert witnesses turned up in court to testify in support of the prosecution!

Normally, in an obscenity trial all the really heavy work of proof or demonstration is shouldered by the defense, with the prosecution resting on its factual presentation, its legal arguments, and its cross-examinations of the defense witnesses. Dick Kuh was not the sort of man who would leave a stone unturned. He went out with Frank Hogan and actively sought prosecution witnesses in exactly the same manner that London used to line up eminent people for the defense. Kuh and Hogan, however, were much less successful than their adversary because they were asking people to fink on a man who was by now a notorious martyr. Even though lots of prominent people in the press, the universities, and the ministry thought Lenny Bruce was smutty and sick and should be banned from public performance, they were averse to standing up in court and casting their stones at such a pathetic offender. Consider the case, for example, of Bosley Crowther, the lifelong movie critic of *The New York Times*. The Sunday after Lenny's trial had started, Crowther had written an all-out attack on a movie that he felt was morally objectionable and therefore a menace to the community. Upborn by the pulpit fervor that seems to infect so many writers for the Sunday *Times*, the usually mild and milquetoasty Crowther had written: "The critic must speak out boldly and let his anxieties fall where they may." The next morning Frank Hogan was on the telephone to Crowther: would he read the transcripts of Bruce's shows and consider testifying at the trial? The transcripts were sent off. A few days later Hogan received a note on the bold black Gothic letterhead of *The New York Times*. Crowther replied:

> Although I find the material distasteful and disgusting in the extreme, I feel it would be inconsistent with my concepts of free speech to participate . . . I deplore the fact that there are people who will listen to such stuff, but I don't feel it would help matters—or be consistent with our democratic principles—to lock up Mr. Bruce.

Despite the reluctance that most people felt toward voicing their opinions of Bruce in a courtroom, Kuh and Hogan did manage to obtain five witnesses, chosen deliberately to offset the types that had borne witness to Lenny Bruce. The Reverend Daniel Potter, Executive Director of the Protestant Council of America, was a set-off to the Reverend Sydney Lanier and to the Reverend Forrest Johnson. John Fischer, editor-in-chief of *Harper's* magazine, was the answer to Richard Gilman and Nat Hentoff. Robert Sylvester of the *Daily News* spoke for the popular press, as had Alan Morrison, editor of *Ebony*. Marya Mannes, a lower-middle-brow journalist, was the counterpart to Dorothy Kilgallen. Ernest Van den Haag, adjunct professor of social philosophy at New York University, was the defense's answer to academics like Daniel Dodson and Herbert Gans.

The prosecution, unlike the defense, was content merely to have these people get up on the witness stand and express a negative opinion of the defendant. Kuh, mindful of the judges' growing impatience with this interminable trial, simply wanted to show that he could muster as many and as distinguished witnesses for his side as London could for his client. Practically all the prosecution witnesses appeared on the last day of the trial, July 28th, and spoke their pieces with little in the way of direct questioning or cross-examination.

The Reverend Potter made the first big end run of the prosecution's offense. Taking up the ball with the customary question about whether the monologues transgressed contemporary community limits, he ran it way down the field with one of the most remarkable statements of the entire trial:

> In trying to imagine out of the various community involvements that it has been my privilege to have during the years, I was trying to picture some group to which this would not be offensive or would not be almost insulting . . .
>
> There is only one community I can think of where this would be acceptable, and that would be in the back wards of the Rochester State Hospital, in the mental hospital, where persons for the most part do get up on stumps and speak in this kind of random, irrational way and primarily employ filthy and vulgar words and play on them for the sake of playing on them.

The Reverend Potter's identification of Bruce with the mental patients he had served in Rochester State was stricken from the record by Judge Murtagh, but it expressed with admirable bluntness the opinion more or less openly held by a great many people at the trial (including many of Lenny's supporters) that the man who had once made such good sense as a comedian was beginning to lose his mind.

John Fischer, the next witness, testified that he found no social or cultural value in Lenny's work; comparing Bruce's use of obscene language with that of James Joyce, he argued that Lenny displayed none of the purpose or coherence that characterized the writer's work. Couching all his evidence in a tone of modesty and one man's opinion, Fischer neither made much ground for the prosecution nor lost any to the defense. He was at best a make-weight in the balance of justice. The witness who succeeded him, Marya Mannes, had originally been approached by the defense—so closely did the ambivalences of opinion lie in the matter of Lenny Bruce. She had refused initially on the grounds that she had never witnessed a Bruce performance.

Ten days before the end of the trial, however, she had seen Lenny in San Francisco and was surprised at the extent to which he had cleaned up his act. This fact apparently convinced her that she should testify *against* him in New York. What she had to say was not much more than an echo of Fischer's testimony to the effect that Lenny's monologue had no social or artistic importance. The fact that she was a woman, however, probably made some impression on the court,

which was destined to prosecute the male defendants to the limit of
the law and let off the female, Ella Solomon, with a generous extension
of judicial clemency. If Kilgallen had made any real impression in
Lenny's favor, Mannes helped to neutralize that influence by her presence on the witness stand.

The last witness at the trial was in some ways the most interesting.
This was the sociologist, psychoanalyst, and popular culture authority
Ernest Van den Haag. A European who had spent most of his adult
life in the United States and who was in close contact with the swinging
scene in Greenwich Village, Van den Haag approached the subject of
Bruce with considerably more sophistication than did many of the
witnesses pro and con. He took the view, reminiscent of the hostile
British critics, that Lenny's comments were without social value because they were obvious or platitudinous. He also pointed out that the
secret of Lenny's power lay in his violation of public decorum through
the use of language that is normally forbidden in such circumstances.
Oddly for an analyst, instead of seeing this violation of verbal taboos
as a cathartic or "liberating" experience, Van den Haag saw it as a
threat to the whole social order. All societies seek to protect certain
minimal social standards, he argued, and if one violation of these
standards is tolerated, others are certain to follow, until the whole
social order dissolves in anarchy. Nothing that was said at the trial
fitted in so neatly with the conservative philosophy of the district attorney's office—and this testimony came from a psychoanalyst and a
professor of pop culture at the New School.

When the last witness had completed his testimony and the trial
seemed destined to a quick conclusion, there was a sudden disturbance
on the defense side of the bar. Lenny Bruce stood up and addressed
the bench: "I would like the court to allow me to speak. I do have
counsel that ably represents me, but I have a problem communicating
with them and there is evidence that has been withheld from the court
and I would . . ." Murtagh cut in at this point and said that the court
would strongly advise Bruce to be guided by the wisdom of his counsel.
A quick recess was called, and London and Garbus huddled with Lenny
in the corridor. They told him that he was jeopardizing his whole record
by speaking out of line; that he had pulled this stunt in Chicago and
been convicted for his pains. If he would just play along with the
defense strategy here, he might win; and even if he lost, he would have
an immaculate record upon which to appeal. Lenny was unhappy about
going to the finish line without so much as speaking a single word on
his own behalf; after all, he had testified at all his other trials. Im-
portuned by London and Garbus, he finally consented; when the trio

returned to court, London informed the bench that Lenny had agreed
to be guided by his counsel's advice and the defense rested.

Murtagh asked that motions be made without oral argument and
that written briefs be submitted instead of the usual rhetorical summations. The lawyers left the court for their various vacation retreats
completely drained by the effort of the trial. Lenny took off again for
San Francisco, where he was booked for three more weeks at the Off
Broadway.

Lenny's favorite roost in Frisco was the Swiss American, a clean,
cheap, European-style establishment, with its little lobby at the top of
a long narrow flight of stairs on the second floor of a building located
in the heart of the Broadway tonk strip. Lenny occupied a different
room every time he lived at the hotel; there was, however, one constant
feature of all his occupancies—his San Francisco sidekick, Lee Hill.
No sooner would Lenny turn up than Hill would appear. He wasn't
registered at the hotel, but he would find some corner to sack out.
The important thing was simply that he be at Lenny's side every instant
of the day and night. Lee was Lenny's shadow. He was also a useful
guy to have around the house, a former radio engineer who was hip
to electric gadgets. For example, he could wire up a phone in Lenny's
room so that all calls would be billed to somebody else's number. By
this time, Lenny's legal business and his phone mania made his call
bills five or six hundred dollars a month. Getting off free with the
phone company was enough to endear Lee to Lenny forever.

The two men had other common interests: for one thing, they were
both speed freaks. Lenny had offered to turn Lee on to heroin, inviting
him to his house and telling him: "I'm going to give you something
you've never had before—all the dope you can use!" Lee used heroin
for two weeks and gave it up. It wasn't his bag. Long flights on Meth,
lasting days at a time—that was his real mania. Lenny was still purchasing the drug by prescription. He would go off to the doctor and
return with a large bag—like a laundry bag—full of disposables and
boxes of the Magic Vitamin. Then the boys would turn on, and clumsy
Lenny would go through four or five syringes trying to get a single hit.
Each time the blood clotted on the point of the spike, he would throw
the disposable across the room and crack open another package.

Once the pair got high, they would work and play for hours on
end. The work was the usual legal hassling; the play was more interesting. Lenny and Lee would make up Bob and Ray routines and
record them on Lenny's Uher. Lee was usually so shy and withdrawn
that nobody ever remembers him saying a word. Lenny knew how to
bring him out. He would make him shpritz into the mike and crack

up at all the funny things he said. "You're the funniest person in the world!" he'd yell at Lee—offering him the greatest compliment in the world. "Don't your friends think you're funny?"

One day they got completely obsessed with a strange and goofy-looking piece of furniture in the hotel room. It was one of those dumb combination pieces, part table, pole lamp, desk, and phone stand. Lenny said it was a monster and they should make a movie of it attacking them! Instantly, Lee was lying on the floor, doing horror takes, and Lenny was feverishly working to get the monster looking really scary in the finder of his movie camera. Finally, he shot the whole scene on split-frame film. When he got the stuff back from the developer, he couldn't wait for the proper projector. He insisted on dividing the long strip of film with a razor blade. The result was a total loss.

One thing that bothered Lee about Lenny was his growing obsession with suicide. Lenny was preparing for the day when he would kill himself. If you get yourself thoroughly accustomed to the thought of self-destruction, he argued, you could throw yourself out a window without hesitation. Halfway down, of course, you might be overwhelmed with horror. But then it wouldn't matter. The Hollywood way of checking out was to swallow a bottle of sleeping pills. Popping off on uppers appealed much more to Lenny. He would do whole bits for Lee on the theme of "Sick Comic Dies from Dexie-itis." Lee would laugh at the bits, but he was worried by the obsession. He knew—as the world did not—that Lenny's pride had been deeply wounded by his arrests and notoriety. The bravado of his behavior when he was busted or fought back in court was just a cover-up for the terrible pain of humiliation. Sooner or later, Lee feared, Lenny would hurt so much that life to him would become worthless. He would have to kill himself to save his pride.

Scoring was a constant problem in San Francisco because he was not so well connected in the city as he was in L.A. or New York. Sometimes, when things got really desperate, he would tell the club owner: "If you don't get ahold of a doctor and straighten me tonight—I'm not gonna work another show." Sometimes that threat would get him his medicine. Other nights, nothing would help. Suffering terribly, Lenny would collapse like a victim of leukemia. That was the state in which he was found by a man we'll call Don Goodwin, a hip-talking DJ with whom Lenny had partied years before.

Don came into the Off Broadway one night before the club had opened. Peering around the empty, gloomy room, so ugly in the work lights, he spotted Lenny slumped over a table like a drunk.

Instantly concerned, Don walked over and asked, "What's wrong with you?"

Raising his head off the table, Lenny stared at Don and groaned, "I'm in very bad shape!" Then fixing an imploring expression on his face, he said, "Do you know a doctor?"

"Yes, of course!" Don replied.

"Well, I need something only a doctor can give you. I can't sign for it. So *you'll* have to sign. O.K.?"

"O.K., man. What is it?"

"Morphine suppositories," mumbled Lenny, scrawling the words on a piece of paper.

When Don gets to the doctor that evening, the guy takes one look at the note and snaps: "Are you crazy? If I gave you a prescription for this drug, the druggist who filled it would make out a form in triplicate. One copy would go to the federal narcotics people, one copy to the state, and one would be attached to your driver's license!"

Don begged so skillfully that finally the doctor gave him the address of a druggist way out in the country, where he could have the prescription filled without any questions being asked. Then Don dashed back to the club and told Lenny that he would go after the stuff but that it would be hours before he got back; Lenny would just have to hold out through his evening shows. Don found the pharmacy in the sticks, made the buy, and drove back late at night to Broadway. About three in the morning, he walked into the bar and found Lenny sitting at a table awkwardly writing something on a little piece of pasteboard. Lenny looked up, reached out one hand for the package, and with the other offered the writing. Then, he split with a muttered "Later!"

Don examined the paper. It was one of those little cards that are placed on nightclub tables to announce the minimum. Lenny had half-written, half-printed on the back a desperate prayer:

> Dear Don, Oh God you call yourself a god O Don Dad o Mafia Mafia Don My-u ness Don I will sit upon your knee as you flee to bring Lenny the cure from the bad sickness that rings my balls & my chest taught some sweet Don sweet bird of youth Don wh wouldn drive upon si drunk to strike at phantoms

As Don sat there in the bar, bushed from his long ride, staring at this cramped, frantic writing, he suddenly recalled what the doctor told him when he left on his mission: "The guy who's taking this stuff will be dead in a year."

Around the first of September, Lenny wound up his gig in San

Francisco and returned to L.A. Immediately he plunged into his legal
work. Having spent months comparing the tape recordings of his shows
at the Go Go with the dog-eared police transcriptions used in his trial,
he had become furious at the way his words had been twisted and
mangled by the cops. He was even more furious at his lawyers for
accepting such garbled and damning nonsense as a fair representation
of his act. Poring over the tapes and transcripts, he claimed to have
found in thirty-four pages of transcription, "1,273 words omitted and
857 words inserted, clearly a total of 2,130 errors in wording alone."
What especially enraged him was the clearly discernible tendency in
the transcript to substitute dirty words for decent words that weren't
clearly audible. Drawing up a memorandum of law for submission to
the court, Lenny offered a whole page of astounding mishearings:

PAGE	PEOPLE'S TRANSCRIPT	CORRECT WORDING
11, line 12	"With a shit three sizes too big."	"With a *suit* three sizes too big."
23, line 3	"The lowest tit can the sight of blood of a (indistinguish-able) big ass"	"The Loew's Pitkin, haha, five vaudeville, *five big acts*."

The tendency of all these mishearings was the same: they made Lenny
Bruce out to be a dirty-mouthed lunatic who belonged, in the Reverend
Potter's phrase, in "the back wards of a mental hospital."

At the same time that he was making this natural and sensible
protest against the mistranscription of his work in the trial record,
Lenny was writing letters to his friends in the New York press corps
outlining a sinister plot to deny him his constitutional rights. "Someone," he insisted, was going through the record of the trial expunging
everything that offered a basis of appeal. Writing to Dorothy Kilgallen
on August 4th, he spilled out this paranoid fantasy:

Dear Dorothy,
I've got a secret. When a witness like yourself testifies on the behalf
of the defendant, the judge challenges the witness and tries to get
from the witness answers that will justify the judge's decision—
that the defendant is guilty as charged. That part of the trial is
over, someone (a mysterious force perhaps) takes "the record,"
reads it over, and upon the second reading is embarrassed and
takes out the part that challenges the wisdom and removes some
of the statements made by the judge and insures correctness of
the guilty verdict. (Vaudeville?) . . .

I was in awe as I listened to your resolving each theme under constant jabbing of the picadors, the social redeeming factor test. I guess women really are brighter.

> Love,
> Lenny

Lenny was by now very unhappy with Ephraim London. He felt that he was being shunted aside in the preparation of his own case, while his lawyer went out to lunch every day with all the fancy professors, critics, doctors, and actresses who contributed so little to the defense. The tension between client and attorney had heightened dangerously during the trial, when Lenny had sat next to London day by day, trying to communicate with him by notes, whispered words, and facial expressions that his lawyer had treated as the products of an unbalanced mind. "Insane" was a word that London had used more than once for Lenny. When London wasn't treating Lenny as a nut, he was treating him as a child. Once at the trial London smacked Lenny's hand right in front of everybody. Lenny had reached over to take a paper away, and he got punished like a bad little boy. Lenny was very funny at that moment. He turned to Allen Schwartz anbd gently smacked him in the face, saying, "It's Manny, Moe, and Jack. Pass it on!"

Now that they were in the final stretch, he was beginning to feel that London was really the enemy. Look at it like this: London had told him from the outset that he would never win on the local level. Now, what did that mean? It meant, basically, that instead of working to get through to Judge Murtagh and the New York court, London was simply compiling a record for the appellate court. What was wrong with that? Lots of things. For one thing, it cost a fortune to go the appeal route. For another, it took a long, long time. For yet another, once you won the appeal, what had you won? You had been vindicated on one or two shows performed years before, but you had no license to continue doing your act in the city where you were busted. The next night they could come in the club and grab you again. Now, suppose they had made a real effort to get through to Judge Murtagh. Granted, he was a stiffo, a real Judge Stone out of an Andy Hardy movie. Well, that was good: that was the way judges were supposed to be. Lenny wouldn't change Judge Murtagh for a million dollars. In fact he had this fantasy about the judge: that someday Lenny would come into court and do his act and make his comments about American society and when the show was over Judge Murtagh would say: "Are you kidding? Arrest this man for obscenity? Why, he's a true American! A moralist! An intellect! Case dismissed!" Then Murtagh would come down off the bench, put his arm around Lenny, and say: "Come along, son. I've got a rod and line in my chambers. Let's go fishing!" Now, what was London doing to make that fantasy come true? He was alienating the judge and bombarding him with a lot of so-called expert witnesses who couldn't relate to the court. So Lenny felt that the time had come for him to assert himself and demand that his lawyer act in accordance with *his* views on what must be done to save *his* ass. After an exchange of namby-pamby letters, he got off a really heavy letter on September 2nd. Pacing back and forth before his secretary, Jan Mathews, he dictated:

Dear Ephraim,

If the court had appointed you as a public defender, I would have less rights as far as instructing you. I promised to pay you $2000 and I have not fulfilled my promise. I have given you $1000, and the hi-fi equipment and camera I sent you were worth about $200, used. So I am instructing you with the power of a $1,200 client and an $800 debtor, and should you choose to ignore the following instructions for whatever reason you might have, then I ask you to accept this letter as notice that I don't intend paying you the money I originally promised to pay you. You accepted that money on the condition that you would conduct yourself in a manner that would be effective in the trial court and respect that trial court and not assume that the trial court is merely a recording studio waiting to be administered and overturned by the appellate court. . . .

You are an appellantophile, you are possessed with a "shameful and morbid interest" in finding statutes unconstitutional on their face. Your first duty, however, is to your client. Your second duty is to other clients who follow. Finding 1140-A unconstitutional on appeal will do nothing for me and you do a disservice to the community of New York by not working on the trial level. The disservice you do is the propagation of villain image that it places upon the courts that are already in a precarious position with the civil rights issues. The liberal gets another crack at the establishment. It would be okay if the argument was confined to liberals and conservatives. The liberals and the people who have seen my show have been given the opportunity that the trial court has been denied. And your statement, "I agree that your transcript of the performance at the Cafe Au Go Go is better than the one offered in evidence. There is nothing to prevent us from using your transcript . . . on appeal," is insanity. What the fuck is the matter with you Ephraim? Don't you know who will reap the hostility? The

poor policeman, the foot soldier. The newspaper article, "Lenny
Bruce found Guilty," brings forth the statement from the liberals,
"Gestapo police, how 'bout that, the God damn police." It's not
the God damn police, but it's "God damn you," for denying the
trial court something they can judge. Did it ever occur to you that
the expert witnesses couldn't relate to the court? The words they
used were too esoteric . . .

I wish to be put in propria persona and substitute Allen G.
Schwartz if you do not choose to submit these transcripts, tapes
. . . AND GET THEM INTO THE RECORD.

A week later, London, dictating into a machine in his office on
East 44th Street, slapped Lenny on the wrist again. Expressing resentment at Lenny's accusations, London retorted with a flat rejection
of his client's arguments and a demand that he pay the agreed price,
which, as London reminded him, was less than the amount Lenny
received for his own work. Appended to this letter was a bill for services
rendered that ran to two single-spaced pages and mounted up through
numerous "conversations and conferences," library research to "secure
favorable criticisms of Lenny Bruce performances," drafting motions
for jury trial, drawing memorandum of law, holding conferences with
the district attorney, drafting papers to be submitted in the event of
conviction and appeal, telephoning, duplicating, conferring, talking,
corresponding, appearing, blah, blah, blah . . . $15,541.00. Lenny had
paid roughtly a thousand dollars; so the bill stood at $14,000 and
change.

The day after London's letter was written, Lenny wrote to the
Honorable John M. Murtagh, substituting himself as counsel for
Ephraim London and offering in evidence the tape of the April 1st
12:01 show, plus a transcript of the same. Not resting content with this
"fresh evidence," Lenny offered the judge a philological analysis of
the "dirty words" which the court had deemed actionable, demonstrating from *Webster's New International Dictionary* that in almost
every case his language was listed in the dictionary as "slang." The
two leading exceptions were "motherfucker" and "cunt," which were
employed in dramatic contexts that exonerated the defendant from
guilt. Winding up his letter with correct transcriptions of the bits that
the court deemed particularly offensive, Lenny tried to argue the judge
into a more sympathetic view of his comedy.

After a further exchange of letters, telegrams, and phone calls,
Lenny flew back to New York for a hearing on the 5th of October.
Appearing before Judge Murtagh and two other judges—not the same
men who had heard his case—he insisted on being recognized as his

own counsel, to which the court agreed, stipulating only that the decision on the case be postponed a month to November 4th.

The day after the hearing, Lenny was back in L.A. Frantically busy, he still found time to draw up plans for another total renovation of his house and property. To reconstruct all the projects hatched by Lenny Bruce as he brooded over his "$100,000 view" would baffle an archeologist fresh from excavating the ruins of some polis in Asia Minor where fourteen layers of civilization have been piled one on top of another. His house was exactly like his nightclub act. Just as the one was like a manuscript, endlessly typed and retyped, two or three times a night, six or seven nights a week, month in, month out, so the house offered a record—in brick, stucco, wood, glass, and paint—of the endless flux of Lenny's fantasy life, becoming eventually a two-story allegory of his soul.

The basic thrust of Lenny's home and garden mania was revealed in his first year of ownership. Getting back from a road tour, he discovered he had about $35,000 in the bank. The house was finished, but Lenny couldn't stand the fact that nothing was happening. So he decided that the entire property must be transformed immediately into the Garden of Eden. This brown mudslide hillside must be made to bloom like a kibbutz in Israel! Calling up some big Japanese gardening company, Lenny ordered up the kind of job that Daddy Warbucks used to lay on Little Orphan Annie. Remember how the trucks would roll through the night at Daddy's bidding, hauling a whole orchard to Annie's house while she slept and blowing her mind the next morning when she looked out the window at a magic forest? Well, that's the kind of kick that Lenny got on that week with his Japanese gardeners. Eighteen of them spent two days cutting, grading, and planting the bare cliffs in back of the house and along the driveway with two hundred flats of Korean grass and rose bushes, a hurry-up banzai job that cost Lenny $3,000.

By October of 1964 Lenny was again determined to make the place bloom. This time, he decided to have three hundred and fifty irrigated trees planted and dozens of prize rose slips divoted into the ground along the driveway. Trees and flowers were the least of what he wanted, you realize, as you read over the specifications he drew up for the house at that time. In the past, he had been variously motivated in recasting the house, moving sometimes in the direction of enlarging, sometimes in the direction of subdividing, sometimes adding out-buildings, sometimes acceding to demolitions and cover-up jobs. The rationale for these latest modifications was greater comfort for himself in a future during which he would obviously be compelled to hole up in the house and devote himself to desk work and private amusements. He was fitting the house up as you would a love nest when your principal love object is yourself. It was largely a matter of relining everything with expensive fabrics and woods, like a guy who takes his favorite old tweed jacket to Rhodes and gets the cheap Greek tailors there to replace the faded and torn rayon with fine oriental silk. The skillful yet inexpensive tailor in this case was a man who figures very largely in the history of Lenny's last years, being none other than the noble John Judnich, Lenny's last roadie, go-fer, henchman, and man of skilled work.

Judnich was a shook-loose, spaced-out, inarticulate, Levi-clad version of St. John the Hospitaler: the saint who used to stand at the ford in the river and carry the weary traveler across upon his strong, serviceable back. Workmanlike in appearance, with those sinewy forearms on which you can see the vein cords passing and knotting, John Judnich appeared to have been designed by nature as the anti-type to Lenny Bruce. In fact, it was the total and absolute incongruity of their respective characters that brought them together and sealed them in indissoluble friendship. John was the kind of man that Lenny could never be but whom he intensely admired; Lenny was the sort of dazzling genius who was nearly beyond John's comprehension but whom he idolized. Lenny admired any kind of competence—especially if it took the form of physical skill. He was always thrilled by guys with "good hands." John was a *Popular Mechanics* Daedalus. Any task that demanded the shrewd and patient coordination of mind, eye, and hand he could perform flawlessly. His accomplishments ranged across the whole spectrum of craftsmanship. When Lenny met him, he was the foreman of a shop that manufactured stainless-steel sanitary food equipment. Before that he had worked in a boat-building yard. At one time in his life, he had invented one of the first artificial heart machines. Later he became a professional sound engineer and designed the colossal sound system that accompanied the Rolling Stones on their 1972 tour of the United States.

In February 1964, when John and Lenny linked up, the House on the Hill was a mess. The floors were scuffed and dirty. The glass walls were scaly with dust and streaked by rain. The rooms looked as though they'd been hit by a paper blizzard—piles of yellow legal papers were strewn all over the place. Most of the furniture had been rented to some Indians in the music business. They had ruined the pad and burnt Lenny for about four months' rent. The worst wreck in the place was its owner. Instead of being the neat, compulsive, high-velocity personality that John remembered, Lenny had become a stone speed

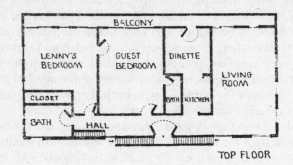

TOP FLOOR

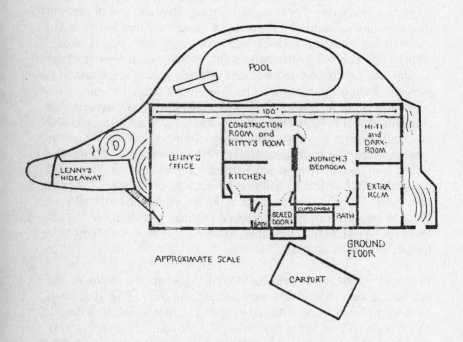

APPROXIMATE SCALE

GROUND FLOOR

freak, using 25 or 30 cc.'s of Meth a day and walking around in a kind of stupefied euphoria, like a drifter on skid row with a bellyful of canned heat. Finding no furniture in the house, John's first act was to take out his tools and begin building a whole new set of sofas, beds, chairs, and benches to make good the damages wrought by the former tenants.

Once Lenny had signed the contract with John Judnich to remodel his house, he was back on the plane heading for New York and the climax of the greatest obscenity trial in history. During the few days between his arrival and the hearing which had been set for November 4th, he enlisted another valuable new soldier in his private legal army. Selma Rovinsky, who worked in the office of the *New York Law Journal*, was a tomato-faced girl from Bensonhurst and the brightest lady who ever touched Lenny. She flickered for the next couple of months on the periphery of his consciousness as a bright, useful helper and iron-ically clucking mother hen, whom he ultimately despised and dis-missed. What she had to offer in the first instance was a lot of practical help. She had access to the Xerox machines and legal paraphernalia that were essential to Lenny's new home law practice. She also knew her way around the New York law circuit and could suggest lawyers to call, offices to visit, and procedures to adopt when the labyrinth of red tape seemed impenetrable.

On November 4th at 10 A.M., the fifth-floor courtroom at 100 Centre Street began to fill with many of the same people who had appeared on the first day of the trial, six months before. The press, the district attorneys, the sightseers, and the defense counsel were all in place waiting to begin, when somebody noticed that the defendant was not present. As the minutes ticked by and the judges waited in the robing room, the thought began to force its way into Martin Gar-bus's head that Lenny might not show. "I became apprehensive," he recalled later. "I had spoken to Bruce a few days before and didn't know if he was going to show up. He feared the decision: he knew he was going to lose and was terrified of jail and the stigma of being branded a 'dirty' comic. He also felt that a conviction would ruin him financially. He was becoming more and more confused." Shortly after eleven, Lenny came in, clean-shaven and, for the first time since the trial began, wearing a suit and tie.

As soon as the judges had taken their positions on the bench, Lenny stepped forward and said he would like to "testify." Murtagh informed him that the trial was over and that it could not be reopened. The judge was also disturbed by Lenny's insistence that he appear without counsel. Lenny was determined to speak: he had held himself in check for six long months, and if there was a way of getting his words into the record, he was going to find it. Seizing on the judge's concern over his solo appearance, Lenny asked for permission to explain why he was appearing without counsel, promising meekly, "I won't waste any of the court's time." Murtagh said, "All right," and Lenny launched into his plea. As the onlookers stared in astonishment, Lenny poured out the thoughts that had been whirling around and around in his head for months. He started by rehashing his argument with Ephraim London:

MR. BRUCE: Ephraim London told me that the trial court at its best could not understand me. He guaranteed me that the appellate court . . . they have the wisdom, they will understand. I discharged him. It cost me $14,000 to talk to Your Honors. That's what he is suing me for. I want to tell you what the performance is, what I do. I am not obscene . . . that there were 2,130 word-errors in the prosecution transcript, such as the word "shit, three sizes too big." "Lowest tit" was actually "lowest pit." If Your Honor will allow me to represent some of the gestures.

JUDGE MURTAGH: Mr. Bruce, counsel has been relieved. We are asking Mr. Garbus to stand in. Now, this case has been concluded. It's here today for decision. The court is prepared now to rule on the motions that were made.

MR. BRUCE: I haven't testified, Your Honor. The merits of the case, the obscenity, the moral play. The only thing presented is a screenplay, not the gestures. You haven't seen the visual. That's why the prosecution case is—I made gestures and there was the play. You have read a written play, but you haven't seen any gestures. May I give you the gestures? Would you judge a film listening to the soundtrack?

JUDGE MURTAGH: You were duly represented by counsel throughout the case, and the case was concluded.

MR. BRUCE: The last day of the trial I begged Your Honor, please, I don't have the ability to relate to my counsel, can I talk to the court; can I give the evidence. You said, no, you have very competent counsel. I don't think I did.

JUDGE MURTAGH: You elected to take his advice, and the case is closed.

MR. BRUCE: You won't let me testify?

JUDGE MURTAGH: We will not grant your application at this time to reopen the case.

MR. BRUCE: Will you hear it off the record then, Your Honor?

JUDGE MURTAGH: No, everything is on the record.

MR. BRUCE: There is nothing on the record, because the district attorney very carefully had the court reporter waived, so there is actually nothing on the record at all. It is barren; only a dirty show presented by the district attorney. Proof of that is Marya Mannes, a people's witness. She said she saw me in San Francisco. She said, "He certainly cleaned his act up." She had read about the dirty Lenny Bruce. Then she saw me in person. She said, "He certainly cleaned his act up." Your Honor, the gestures, masturbations, were gestures of benediction. I did a bit on Catholicism. How perverse Ephraim London would be to defend me for gestures of masturbation. They were meant to be gestures of benediction. I have the right to say "fuck you." I didn't say it. Please, Your Honor, I so desperately want your respect. I want the court to know. My profit has gone down from $350,000 a year before to $6,000.

JUDGE MURTAGH: The court has all of your arguments to that effect before it.

MR. BRUCE: The court hasn't heard the show. They haven't heard me testify. I can give you the show verbatim. When you see— please let me testify. Let me tell you what the show is about.

JUDGE MURTAGH: The court urges you to be represented by counsel.

MR. BRUCE: Counsel doesn't understand my show . . . They are defending me by throwing me in with a band of pornographers. My thinking is, I believe in censorship. I believe, as I said, in prior restraint. I don't believe a building has to burn down for the building inspector to look at the wires. I know what obscene means. I know more than the district attorney. . . . Let me do the show. Let me do the gestures. Let me show you what I did. This is not the gestures of masturbation . . . The name Jacqueline Kennedy does not appear anywhere in these transcripts. "Jackie Kennedy hauls ass": where is "Jackie Kennedy"? The name is not in there, no "Jackie Kennedy." I never did a "Jackie Kennedy" haul ass bit. . . . Naturally, I taped everything. That's my way of recording. *I tape every day of my life.* I can show you figures. I spent about $63,000 the last two years on tape recordings. I tape-recorded every day of this trial; tape recording of the tape recording, so I have an exact show. I have the tape here to play for Your Honors as it was played in court. There are 2,130 errors . . . Let me testify, please, Your Honor. Don't finish me off in show business. Don't lock up these 6,000 words. That's what you are doing, taking three counts, taking away my words, locking them up. These plays can never be said again. You are finishing me up in show business. I have no job. I got out of the hospital to come here, Your Honor. . . . I collapsed during the trial. I was in the hospital again. I came here. Won't you, after twice coming 3,000 miles, won't you please let me show what the form was? You asked for the form. Ephraim London said the judge knew what the form was; why he kept asking for the form. He wanted to do away with any prurient test, because he didn't, couldn't even say there is no form; ask to have the complete test. It's just hard-core pornography. The judge is interested in form. I can give him the form.

Finally, Murtagh could bear no more. With barely concealed disgust, he ordered Lenny to be seated. He then pronounced sentence:

> Having considered all of the evidence, after the deliberation, all of these motions are denied as to each count with respect to the defendants, Lenny Bruce and Howard Solomon. The court, Judge Creek dissenting, finds the defendants Lenny Bruce and Howard Solomon guilty as charged. The court by unanimous vote finds the defendant Ella Solomon not guilty.

The court then promised to file its opinion, spelling out the reasons for the conviction, and set the date for sentencing as December 16th. Lenny resisted to the end, asking the judge if he could be sentenced at once and spared the cost of remaining for a month in New York. No, said Murtagh, he could not be sentenced because first the court wanted him to undergo a psychiatric examination.

Martin Garbus had been watching Lenny's performance with a heart full of emotion. He realized now that curbing Lenny through the trial had not produced any better result than would have letting him have his head. He also was deeply moved by Lenny's naked effort at self-salvation, the desperateness of his plea, and his vulnerability before the implacable Murtagh. The whole scene was an oedipal nightmare—Lenny back again in his childhood, pleading, cajoling, placating, trying desperately to avert the punishment meted out by that stern disciplinarian, his father. No wonder Murtagh acted with aversion as he surveyed this whining, manipulating, unmanly defendant. The two of them were locked into roles that made each an affliction to the other. Garbus, full of sympathy, could only shake his head in silence. He recollects that "Lenny was left at the bench inside the court bar, rolling eyes toward the ceiling and muttering, 'If I could just show them my act!' "

The moment the newspapers got word of Lenny's conviction, they started besieging his little two-roomer at the Hotel Marlton. Most of the reporters had no knowledge of the case, no awareness of Lenny's history apart from his notorious reputation. When it came to asking him questions, about the best they could do was: "How do you think all this will end for you, Lenny?"

"What, the trial?" asked Lenny, "the appeal?"

"No, the whole thing, all the trials, the arrests, do you think they'll stop?" . . .

"O.K., here's how it ends. One day I'm going to get an order to appear in court. 'Shit, what is it this time?' But when I get there the courtroom will be all decorated, dig, with balloons and streamers and confetti, and when I walk in they'll all jump up and yell 'Surprise!' And there'll be all the cops that busted me, and the judges and D.A.s who tried me, and they say: 'Lenny, this is a surprise party for you, we're giving you a party because even after everything that happened you never lost respect for the law.' "

When Lenny walked out of the Criminal Courts Building that November morning in 1964, he was not exactly a changed man, but he was one consumed by a cause. Extravagant as his behavior had been on previous occasions, when, for example, he had hired a private eye to check out his jurors or when he played counselor at law in a Chicago courtroom or when he tied bits of metal around his neck to thwart the police "bugs" or imputed ventriloquistic powers to Dick Kuh—wild as all these actions had been, they were soon to pale into nothingness before the insanity of his final phase. Now he was taking that last fatal plunge into legal paranoia, into litigant's dementia, that had threatened on previous occasions to overwhelm his sanity but had never quite reached the level of insanity. Madness was now the port toward which he was steering, madness that often made sense when you examined his behavior piecemeal and listened to him lecture and considered the really terrible persecution to which he had been subjected.

Yet in one sense Lenny's tragedy had been his triumph. Through the law he had reached the "bigger life" he had always been seeking, the life of serious men and serious issues. From this time forth this bigger life was to take control of his thoughts and actions. The basic feature of his new career was simply the fact that he was now his own master in matters of legal maneuver. He had bombed in show business when he first set out, and now he had bombed as a debutant in the law business; but he would improve in the law as he had in the clubs

and end up a headliner working the big room, the Supreme Court.
That was how he saw it: as simply a question of time and procedure.
He had to find the levers and knobs that would jump him over the
tedious business of the appeal courts and send him zooming into the
big court on top of the pile. While lambasting Ephraim London for
not giving the lower courts enough respect, Lenny was intent on not
only circumventing these courts but leaping over the appellate courts
as well. That was the purpose of his first campaign that winter, beginning with the injunction that he got against Judge Murtagh.

"Declaration of Lenny Bruce in Support of Temporary Restraining
Order and Preliminary Injunction" was the heading of the document
that was delivered to Judge Murtagh's chambers on November 24,
1964. It was accompanied by a summons form indicating that the judge
had been named in a civil action (File No. 3574) to which he had to
respond within twenty days or suffer "judgment by default." The papers were delivered by a process server, who reported to Lenny that
"Murtagh was furious." The same documents were served that day on
Judge Creel, Judge Phipps, District Attorney Hogan, District Attorney
Cahn (of Nassau County)—everybody, in short, who had sat in judgment or prosecuted Lenny in the New York court. The declaration,
which was addressed to the United States District Court for the Eastern
District of New York, was a carefully drawn statement in proper legal
form:

I, LENNY BRUCE, hereby certify and declare as follows:
1. That I am the plaintiff in the above-described action.
2. As is set forth in the complaint on file herein, I am an author,
lecturer and social satirist. I appear before live audiences, through
the medium of phonograph records and tape recordings, and my
articles and expressions of my opinion have been published in
periodical publications circulated nationally. My expressions and
views (largely critical) are presented in a humorous manner and
are for the most part directed at contemporary persons, institutions
and social problems . . .
3. What success I have had (and perhaps my ability to influence
people at all) depends upon the expression I give to certain unorthodox ideas—controversial ideas—even ideas hateful to the prevailing climate of opinion. These deal mostly with politics, religion,
economics, sex and other socially topical matters.
4. Unlike the author who seeks vindication for the printed word
he has created, or the movie operator with film in hand, I can
attach nothing to this Declaration in support of the assertions and

charges made herein and in my complaint, because of the nature of my performance itself, which consists not of a simple speech, a transcript of which might be conveniently attached hereto; nor of a film, unchanging and rigid, which might be deposited with the court. This is because my performances before live audiences consist largely of dialogues between characters identifiable only by the tone of their voices and the subtlety of the attitudes they express. Thrown together on the printed page, as a single monologue, the presentation becomes pure gibberish. Moreover, there are gestures and sounds used in the presentation which are incapable of transcription on the printed page.

5. Based upon the foregoing, it is my intention to appear before this honorable court, at a hearing in support of the temporary restraining order, and preliminary injunction, or at other times and places convenient to this court for the purpose of delivering my performance to the court. It is only in this way that the court can be apprised of the performance, its meaning, its social importance, and can further determine whether or not it and I are entitled to constitutional protection as prayed for in the complaint.

6. As I have stated in my complaint, I not only present my views for profit, but I attempt (and I believe the attempts are successful) to influence and mold public opinion and direct the course of human conduct in the areas of religion, politics and social action.

7. The action of the defendants named herein has not only deprived me of my livelihood in this State, and of an outlet for the free expression of my ideas, but it has also deprived that part of the public which comprises my "audience" of the constitutional right to hear me and be influenced by me.

8. In this day, events move rapidly. There is a war in Viet Nam, Barry Goldwater suggests that control of the Republican Party will not be seized from the conservative without a struggle—Premier Kruschev will be put to trial—and Great Britain will nationalize certain basic industries. On each of these subjects I have ideas, some unorthodox—some controversial—some even hateful to the prevailing climate of opinion—but each of these ideas are expressed by me for the purpose of bringing about political and social changes.

9. As is more fully set forth in the Points & Authorities accompanying this Declaration, the need for intervention by this Court stems from complete suppression by the State of New York, and the named defendants, of those ideas which I offer. It is not as if a particular playlet or particular book had been declared obscene

and the author was free to perform other playlets or write other books. The ideas I have are now imprisoned within me, and unless this Court acts, will not be permitted expression.

10. While the Supreme Court of the United States has forbidden the abridgement of free speech except in the case of hard-core pornography, lower courts are loathe to apply this doctrine. The practical result of the defendant having to stand trial and to receive vindication, if at all, only from an appellate court, is to effectively silence him. Furthermore, were it not for my conviction in the State of New York, it would be almost laughable to suggest that sex in my performance is treated in a manner appealing to prurient interests, i.e., "having a tendency to excite lustful thoughts." Quite to the contrary, to follow my performance takes almost complete concentration of the listener, and only the most alert in the audience are able to appreciate and comprehend the complicated interplay between characters and ideas taking place.

11. I believe that the defendants, and each of them, are planning to arrest me each and every time I offer my performance. My information and belief is based upon (a) a conversation with a deputy district attorney Levy and an Inspector Vicviolo, on or about 5/64 at the Cork and Bib, in Westbury, Long Island (County of Nassau) New York. The conversation referred to was (unbeknownst to those gentlemen) recorded on magnetic tape by declarant and a transcript thereof made, which transcript is attached hereto, marked Exhibit "1", and incorporated by this reference. A tape recording of said conversation will be offered at the time of application for preliminary injunction or temporary restraining order; and (b) remarks made at the time of my trial in New York by the Deputy District Attorney prosecuting the case, indicative of a drive by New York County and Nassau County authorities to restrain me from appearing in either of said counties and from expressing my views therein, during the period of time the New York World's Fair is active. . . .

I declare under penalty of perjury that the foregoing is true and correct.

At the same time that Lenny was seeking to enjoin the court that had tried him and the district attorneys whom he maintained had conspired against him, he was pursuing another much more radical strategy designed to show that he was exempt from prosecution under the provisions of Statute 1140-A—*as amended*. How Lenny learned the history of this particular law is unclear, but sometime during that hectic November he was hipped to the fact that the original law, enacted in 1909, had read differently from the law that had been amended after a great deal of debate in the early thirties, when Franklin Delano Roosevelt was governor of New York. The Theater Padlock Law, as it was then called, had become an issue at that time because it contained no provision exempting actors and stagehands from arrest. Actors Equity had initiated a campaign for legislative reform of the law which resulted in the Post-Buckley Bill (named after the representatives in the State Assembly and Senate who stood sponsor to the legislation), which specifically ruled out the arrest of "any person participating in such performance merely as an actor, musician, stagehand or spectator." On the surface this provision did not appear to apply to Lenny Bruce, whom the district attorney characterized as a performer "who neither reads nor recites from his script nor memorizes lines penned by another" and who "functions as one who presents a loose and partially extemporaneous improvisation." Yet when Lenny looked into the matter in the course of his obsessive scrutiny of every possible escape hatch from his present predicament, he discovered that the phrase "merely an actor" could bear an interpretation that put him outside the law.

The way it worked was very interesting. First, you had to get hold of the bill jackets that accompanied the original legislation. These were files of correspondence by interested parties who had written Governor Roosevelt at the time the bill was before him for endorsement, either arguing for or against the proposed legislation. These bill jackets were available only in one place in the State of New York: the Legislative Library in Albany. At this time there had been a fire in Albany, and everybody was claiming that anything they couldn't lay their hands on had disappeared after the fire. Lenny kept insisting that the bill jackets existed, and he laid his heaviest commandment on Selma Rovinsky to go forth and find these vital documents. Miss Brash from Bensonhurst got on the phone and rang up everybody up to and including Attorney General Louis Lefkowitz—without scoring for the bills. Then she had a huddle with Lenny, during which he told her how to "deal with people." The trick was not, as everybody said, to "go to the top"— oh no, that was dumb as hell! The answer was to *"go to the bottom,"* the anonymous, irresponsible clerk or secretary who had the same power as the big shots but who didn't give a shit. *"Get the pusher!"* —that was Lenny's advice. And it worked. As Selma recalls:

> He called me one day, whining, saying that he had spoken to somebody in Albany. He never got anybody that he could get back to. So I put him on a conference call with the head librarian at the state archives. He heard me questioning the librarian, who

insisted that [the jackets] do not exist. Lenny claimed, on the contrary, that from an index of telephone numbers of libraries in Albany, he had spoken to somebody who said "not only do they exist but they could be xeroxed and sent off to any citizen, any layman." But *he didn't know who he talked to!* Typical Lenny fashion. Finally, he found the number, and I called and there was a lady sitting there who does nothing but xerox bill jackets. It was typical of every encounter I ever had with Lenny. He was always so wrong and so right simultaneously.

What the jackets told Lenny was that back in 1931, parties like the deputy police commissioner, the New York Society for the Suppression of Vice, the district attorney, the New York County Lawyers Association, the Society for the Prevention of Crime, and the Citizens' Committee for a Clean Stage had been attacking the proposed amendment excepting actors, using precisely the same arguments employed by Richard M. Kuh. These early conservatives had insisted that the amendment would "seriously weaken prosecution against obscenity on the stage," that it would involve "undue interference with police power," and that it would provide immunity for "filthy stag shows" and burlesque shows in which "dialogue is spontaneous and is not known in advance to the producer." This last was precisely Lenny's own case, and as he read the letter describing a burlesque show called *Ballyhoo* that had been taken over by its actors when the producer abandoned it, he recognized a perfect prefiguration of his own act. In a fascinating letter from the New York Society for the Suppression of Vice, dated April 13, 1931, the writer spelled out exactly the case of Lenny Bruce: he complained that in burlesque shows "the actors were of a peculiar type, hard to keep down and they became callous to situations which an outsider might regard as obscene." "It is quite apparent," continued the correspondent, "that the actor in this class of shows is a very important element in determining what is or is not displayed." That was Lenny. Now, what had F.D.R. done with all these warnings and pleas? He had discounted them. Signed the bill into law knowing full well that there would be shows where burlesque actors would be winging all sorts of wild lines—that now *would be protected by the amendment to the law*! Lenny Bruce was just such an actor, and he was outside the jurisdiction of the law. The only thing wilder than finding this correspondence would be discovering that 1140-A didn't exist at all—Lenny had that fantasy too.

While this far-ranging legal work was going forward at the offices of Bruce, Bruce & Bruce, 5 West 8th Street, a couple of other comedies were playing in other rings of the legal circus. One concerned the majority opinion, which had been written by Judge Murtagh and Judge Phipps and cleared for publication in the *Law Journal*. The *Journal* is an arid, nineteenth-century-looking, eight-column newspaper, with pen-and-ink illustrations of old jurists in wigs and ribbons signing documents with quill pens and perorating down the page in endless periods that made the run-on sentence of the freshman English textbook look curt and short-winded. Nobody but an attorney even knew the *Journal* existed, and you would have to be James Joyce's twisted idiot brother to ever think of looking in those dreary columns for anything pruriently appealing; yet, when Murtagh and Phipps delivered their opinions in the Bruce case and listed the dirty words and gestures which they felt merited punishment, the prim old editors of the *Journal* threw up their hands and refused to print this smutty screed. Ironically, they were willing to make space for Justice Creel to unreel his dissenting opinion (cut down from sixteen pages to about eight or nine), but they wouldn't allow the little column that would have sufficed to print the majority opinion in this case that had attracted so much notice. Finally, forced to give an accounting by lawyers like Charles Rembar, who were vitally interested in obscenity decisions, the *Journal* declared that it could not delete the offensive language from the opinion without destroying its meaning and it could not publish the opinion's original language without transgressing its own standards of editorial propriety; hence the case had been passed over despite the universal demand for its details. When Lenny heard the story from Selma, he demanded, "Why don't they bust Murtagh?"

Unbelievable as it sounds, in the midst of all this legal commotion, with complicated maneuvers to plot and numerous people to consult and the day-by-day study of the law to absorb his time, Lenny was planning at this very moment to take the Village Theater for three nights and stage another series of concerts. He was going to appear in concert with Tiny Tim. The title of the event? *Lenny Bruce Speaks for Profit—Tiny Tim Sings for Love*. That was the line that ran in the newspaper ads, which must have cost a pretty penny, and which announced the great event for November 25th and on, with a benefit price scale that went all the way up to a hundred dollars a seat for the first two rows. Most of the arrangements were made by Ronnie Lyons.

On opening night, I went down to the theater and was astonished to see a dark marquee. Lenny's name was up there, all right, but it was not in lights, nor were there any lights on in the theater. Huddled under the dark marquee were maybe thirty or forty people, one of the smallest crowds ever to assemble for a Lenny Bruce performance. Right in the middle of this little herd was Lenny himself, engaged in heated debate with a man later identified as Ben Bonus, the old Yiddish theater operator who owned the Village Theater. Bonus told Lenny that he was not going to allow him to perform because the show would cost the theater its license. Lenny was arguing that Bonus had taken a deposit and was legally obliged to open his doors. As the hassle spread from the inner to the outer edges of the crowd, I could see Lenny turn angrily on Ronnie Lyons, yelling: "You shoulda gotten him on paper, man! You shoulda gotten him on paper!" Then Lenny darted into Ratner's, the Jewish dairy restaurant next door to the theater, to continue the argument: soon it was apparent that the show would not go on. Just as I was about to leave, I noticed Nat Hentoff standing off to the side with a reporter's notebook in his hand. Feeling disappointed and rather annoyed by the fiasco, I said to Hentoff: "Lenny is acting like a madman. Next thing you know, they're gonna try to put him away." Hentoff gave me one of his sorrowful, soulful looks and quietly said, "I know."

Bad as things were in his professional life at this time, Lenny was about to receive some desperately needed encouragement and support from a wonderful new friend, a woman who was in every sense of the word a lady. Judy Peabody was her name, her husband being Sam Peabody, brother to Governor Peabody of Massachusetts and to Marietta Tree, the intimate of Adlai Stevenson and mother of the model Penelope Tree.

Judy heard about Lenny through an article written by Lenny's favorite New York journalist, Dick Schaap. The piece had appeared in the *Herald Tribune* late in November; it recorded in the quiet yet cutting irony of the New Journalism the decline of Lenny Bruce from cause célèbre to pain in the ass. "It used to be fashionable to be for Lenny Bruce," the article began; then it traced out the decline of Lenny's popularity as it became obvious that he was less concerned with lofty matters of principle than he was with the technicalities of law that might save his skin. Lenny was depicted as a man deserted by his good-time liberal allies, sitting in a room littered with legal documents, a hideous scar cutting across his back, and a secretary typing in the next room not because she thought he was a civil rights hero but just because she liked him. Sitting in her luxurious duplex across the street from the Metropolitan Museum on Fifth Avenue, Judy Peabody read this piece and felt the full force of its irony. She was one of those elegant, beautiful young society matrons beloved of *Vogue*, tall, willowy, blond, and dressed in the latest fashions. She believed strongly that the best test of friendship was when a person was "poor, miserable and unsuccessful." She was convinced that Lenny had no real friends. She wrote him a letter and said that she wanted him to know that he had one friend; and she enclosed a check—"a very small check."

Lenny, sitting in the squalor of his shit-green room at the Marlton, took one look at that heavy notepaper framed in turquoise, headed with that magical address, 990 Fifth Avenue, and endorsed with that bold, clear hand, "Judith Peabody," and he reached for the phone. Naturally, he discovered that the lady had an unlisted number; but he soon discovered that the building had a number—as do all first-rate buildings in New York—and by dialing that number and leaving a message, he soon got through to the magic lady. With the first words from her mouth, pronounced in a voice as mellow and low as a cello, he knew that he had struck pay dirt. They achieved "instant rapport"; immediately she felt that he was very "warm." Why don't you come up?" caroled the enchanting voice. Why not? Hours passed. He never appeared. Finally he rang again: "Why don't you come down?" he wheedled. She turned to her husband, he nodded, and they cabbed down to the Marlton. The hotel appalled her: "Tile floors and filthy carpets. Lenny's room was terrible: a toilet that never stopped flushing; a sink that never stopped dripping; windows that wouldn't shut tight; and a defective lock on the front door." Despite his surroundings, Lenny was undismayed; he marshaled all his charm and put on a great little show for the Peabodys. They were fascinated.

Soon Judy Peabody was going down to that wretched room every day. She rebelled against the self-destructive way in which Lenny lived. She would say: "Eat! Walk! Take care of yourself!" She would drag him out into the streets, compel him to walk a few blocks, until he would say: "Don't you want to go in here and have a cup of tea?" They would enter some greasy spoon and Lenny would instantly go into a number with the counterman, getting him to spill his story for her entertainment. Lenny was always very gallant, very kind and protective of Lady Judith. "He touched me very deeply," she recalled with obvious emotion. "He was a beautiful man. Very kind, very thoughtful, gallant, gentlemanly, funny, loving, appreciative. He was a tragic picture. Poor, overweight, tattered lovable creature!" As she got to know Lenny she could see that he had been deceived all his life. He didn't trust anyone. Every errand or favor was asked of half a dozen people. He didn't want to answer the phone or the door. He would ask her to do it. Weird people were always turning up. "The human defective would come knocking; Lenny would say: 'Get him out of here!' " Nobody was really doing anything for Lenny. His tape recorder needed fixing. He had asked so many to do it. She did it. He needed legal help. She got in touch with lawyers she knew, who really tried to help Lenny. Most of all, she went on missions. He would tell her to go to court and get certain documents. She would say, "Lenny, they're not going to give them to me. I'm not a relative or a lawyer." "They will!" he countered—and she would get the stuff. March off with her purse full of quarters for the copying machines and get a dozen copies of each document. Sometimes they would find pages missing. "Somebody got there before us!" Lenny would shout, shuddering in a fit of paranoia. "I knew I was being subjected to many tests," she says; but she rose to meet them all with the confidence of a mature woman of the upper classes. Judy Peabody was "class."

Supported on the one side by his elegant lady and on the other by his bright, witty Bensonhurst baby, who had more native intelligence in her little finger than most of the male "brains" Lenny had known, our hero began to make rapid progress through the mazes of the law. As his legal maneuvers advanced, he soon envisioned the day when he would walk into the federal appeals court and lay his case before some of the most famous magistrates in the city. On December 14th, his action against the judges and D.A.s was denied; on December 15th, he went to court at nine in the morning to appeal the district court's denial. Selma was beginning to get very worried that Lenny would make some terrible blunder by proceeding without a lawyer. Writing back to John Judnich on the West Coast, she confided:

I'm afraid for him to let it [getting a lawyer] go to the last minute. There is no way for me to get his attention. And the rare times I have and start to talk about a lawyer, he goes into a diatribe on how they're all thieves, liars, etc. Finally, on the eve of his big day before the federal appeals court, Lenny began to get nervous. He finally started talking about wanting one a few days ago. Then he wanted a law professor (which is his awful snobbery) and an authority, etc. etc.—well, you know it all. Nobody knows enough; and, of course, compared to him, it's certainly true. By last night he *really* wanted one and then when I came up with one or two they were just inadequate. I think he will just pick somebody up in court today, which is easy to do. His mental attitude is more than a little nervous. I thought he felt a little better about the possibility of being committed (everybody says it just won't happen) but last night he indicated again that he is genuinely frightened about it.

Lenny did not appear before the court without counsel: he took along Marty Garbus for moral support. Garbus is still haunted by the

strange scene that was precipitated by Lenny's appearance in one of
the most august courtrooms in the State of New York:

> The Court of Appeals is on the 17th floor of the federal courthouse
> in lower Manhattan. It is an elegant, large, high-ceilinged court-
> room. Because it is in New York, it hears a great number of
> commercial cases, anti-trust cases, violations of the Securities Ex-
> change Act, and the like. By and large, it is the more successful
> Wall Street lawyers who try these cases. The dozens of such lawyers
> getting together on a morning in the Court of Appeals to argue
> their cases make the room resemble a bankers' meeting. It was an
> incongruous scene when Bruce, in his white Nehru jacket, arrived
> to argue his appeal of the denial of an injunction. His fellow ad-
> vocates were stunned. He walked in carrying a suitcase filled with
> paper and legal books. When his case was called, he went to the
> podium and stacked his law books, place-marks protruding from
> many of the pages, all over the counsel's table. The bench he faced
> consisted of Judge Henry Friendly, a scholarly, conservative judge;
> Judge Paul Hays, formerly head of the National Labor Relations
> Board; and Judge Thurgood Marshall, who was later to become
> the first black judge appointed to the Supreme Court.
>
> Bruce rose and explained to the court, "I want them to stop
> prosecuting me in the future. I want you to enjoin them from any
> arrests for my act, and to stop them from putting me in jail. I'll
> show you some of it so you'll see there's nothing wrong with it.
> Under the law, before a judge can stop a performance and arrest
> the performer, he has to be shown the performance is obscene.
> What I'm doing is the other way around. But I'll have to show
> you some of what I'm doing."
>
> The judges listened with interest. Lenny first talked about Amer-
> ica's misuse of Christ symbols. He then went into a sketch com-
> menting on the kinds of justice all white men can expect from black
> juries, pointing out that black men would treat whites as badly as
> they themselves had been treated. He concluded with his imitation
> of the outraged liberal saying, "They gave me twenty years for
> raising my voice—those niggers!" Marshall's head jerked up and
> he nearly dropped a pen from his hand. Bruce saw Marshall's face,
> stumbled, tried bravely to explain the joke, but could not. Then
> he knew he had lost the case and sat down.

At the request of the Court of Appeals, sentencing in the Bruce
case was postponed from December 16th to December 21st, when
finally the great trial came to its long postponed conclusion. On that

day the faithful Martin Garbus turned up at the Criminal Court to
watch Lenny play out the climactic scene in the long legal drama.
Every time Lenny walked into the court, he seemed like a new man.
Today was no exception. Instead of the neatly dressed defendant of
the preceding appearance or the bearded concentration-camp rabbi of
the early summer or the white-frocked Nehru-suited scholar, Lenny
came to court for sentencing in his street-bum costume: "a dirty blue
trenchcoat over torn, faded blue dungarees and a blue-striped T-shirt."
"His shoulders were hunched," recollects Garbus, "his hands in his
pockets. He looked at the room as if he were trying to memorize it.
The night before, Bruce said, 'I know he's a good man. I can talk to
him. He's just insulated. He'll hear me. It's my last chance to get
through to him.' " Lenny wasn't simply interested in getting through
to the judge, however; he had already done that on the day when the
decision was rendered. What he intended today was something entirely
different from anything he had ever attempted before in court. Taking
precisely the opposite tack from the disorganized, scatter-shot approach he had employed on November 4th, he now intended to turn
himself into a legal machine and grind the bench into submission by
reciting into the record no less than forty pages of carefully organized
testimony bearing on the amendment of 1140-A and the various passages in the monologues which the court had singled out as instances
of obscenity.

   After the usual hassle over the fact that he was appearing without
counsel, Lenny started off dramatically by announcing: "It's twenty-
five to four and I speak for the record." Then he requested that Judge
Murtagh appoint a referee or "master" to receive the evidence he had
to impart because he feared prejudice on the part of the bench against
which he had recently brought suit in the amount of a half million
dollars, claiming that the judges had violated his civil rights by finding
him guilty. This mad motion summarily brushed aside by Murtagh,
Lenny dug in and began the reading of his treasured bill jackets. On
and on he droned through the correspondence of the various lobbyists,
reading the letters down to the signatures, the titles beneath the signature, the postscripts beneath the titles—everything but the water-
mark on the paper.

   After about twenty minutes of the bill jackets. Lenny suddenly
switched gears and started to argue point by point every item of the
majority opinion. Buttressed by his months of legal readings and re-
searches, he tore along from one item to another. The ears of the
judges were flooded by an endless succession of cases, precedents,
arguments, inferences, analogies, and reflections. Gradually, the monotonous Hasidic drone of the reader—Lenny was citing his opinions

directly from law books—turned into a surrealistic patter in which the
listener was idly struck by the most incongruous words and images:
"St Paul . . . fucking . . . Murtagh . . . celibacy . . . Ruhe . . . adultery
. . . *The Miracle* . . . *Burstyn vs. Wilson*, 343 U.S. . . . Mr. Justice
Roberts . . . *Cantwell vs. Connecticut*, 310 U.S. . . . my note . . .
gravamen . . . lust-inciting . . . *Tropic of Cancer* . . . St. John Stevas,
one of the soundest and sanest of today's writers on the law of obscenity
. . . Manual Enterprises . . . *People vs. Fritch*, 13 New York 2nd, 119,
127 . . . *Enterprises vs. Day* . . . homosexual magazine . . . the indecent,
the disgusting, the revolting . . . nudity or excretion . . . ellipsis symbol
. . . *Webster's New International Dictionary* . . ." *Und so weiter* until
one solid hour had elapsed.

When Lenny finally ran out of steam, Richard Kuh got his turn.
He rose and demanded punishment in the form of immediate imprisonment for Bruce and the maximum fine for Solomon. Winding up his
statement with what he probably regarded as the most inflammatory
thing he could say, Kuh inveighed against what he called "a notable
lack of remorse" on the part of both defendants, who had gone on
after their first arrest producing the same show and even daring to
raise the prices. The word "remorse" triggered a nerve of anger in
Lenny, and he instantly fell into the rhetoric that lay most closely to
his heart at this catastrophic moment: the rhetoric of Jew vs. Gentile.
"I am a Jew before this court," he cried. "I would like to set the record
straight that the Jew is not remorseful. I come before the court not
for mercy but for justice—and profit is everyone's motivation in this
country!" Strong—if stagy—words. Quite enough, you would think,
to relieve his feelings. No. Nothing could ever be enough for Lenny:
certainly, no mere form of words. Soon he had digressed from the
issue of remorse to the recent scandal caused by Jackie Mason allegedly
making a fuck-you! gesture at Ed Sullivan on TV. Lenny had to drag
in this extraneous issue to further annoy the judges, making the forbidden gesture right in the judges' faces, and probably erasing, in the
process, the last shade of doubt concerning the gestures that he was
alleged to have made during his act.

When the storm had passed, Murtagh calmly sentenced Lenny to
four months in the workhouse.

Chapter Fourteen

SHIT

Spit in my face!"

"I don't wanna spit in your face."

"No, I want you to spit in my face."

"I don't wanna . . . I don't wanna spit in your face."

"Spit in my face!" insists Lenny.

"O.K.!" shrugs Eric. "Tpwh!"

Lenny rubs the spittle all over his face. Then he starts taking off his clothes. Up there in the Swiss-American Hotel. Overlooking Broadway. At 3 A.M.

"Jesus! Put your clothes on, Len! The shades are all up and the people out there in the street are going to see you!"

"No, no, no! They have to know! They have to know where it is. It's *out there*! I have to tell them . . . it's *out there*!"

Lenny jumps up on the bed. Then he jumps onto the window sill. Standing there stark naked, outlined by the lights from the room, he starts shaking the big, old-fashioned French window. Once, he shakes it. Twice. Suddenly, the goddamned thing breaks open! Lenny topples out the window, head over heels!

Eric is up like a shot, lunging for Lenny's leg. He clutches his ankle for a second—but the weight is too much. His grip breaks. Lenny plunges into the darkness. Peering over the sill, Eric sees him hit the pavement, twenty-five feet below. Duhd! His body makes a sickening sound. Eric stares for an instant, aghast. Then he tears a blanket off the bed and darts out of the room. Down the steep narrow staircase he hurtles to the street. Out the door he bursts in time to see Lenny reeling to his feet. Christ! He looks pathetic under the street lamps. A fat, fucked-out figure of a man, struggling to stand upright. Eric rushes to Lenny's side and bundles him into the blanket.

"O.K., baby," he soothes, "everything's gonna be cool!"

"I love you, Eric!" Lenny sighs. "Jesus! I love you, man!" And he kisses Eric on the mouth.

Someone across the street has witnessed the whole scene. Already the cops have been called. When they speed up in their cruiser, they think they're nailing a couple of crazy fags.

"You motherfuckers!" Lenny screams at the cops. "You're all after me . . . but it's all right. You don't know where it is!" With that he makes a lunge for one cop's pecker. The officer grabs his hands and starts putting on the cuffs. Eric, meanwhile, is trying to explain what happened. He's frightened by the way Lenny's ankles are inflating like balloons.

"Motherfuckers!" Lenny screams. Then, suddenly, he bends over and whispers to Eric: "They're just trying to get me! They just want to take me and lock me up!"

"Oh, no! No!" says one cop, wise now to the fact that Lenny is in shock. "We just wanna take you to the hospital!"

"I don't wanna go!" says Lenny. "I don't *have* to go!"

"Yes, but you're hurt!" the cop insists, as the sound of a siren comes up the street. The ambulance attendants hop out and grab Lenny, who swings at them like a punchy boxer. They strap him down on the litter. They load him aboard and speed off into the night.

Their destination is the emergency room of San Francisco General Hospital. When they arrive at the entrance, the cops pull up behind them and start to help with the stretcher. Again, Lenny shpritzes them with all the heaviest words in the street vocabulary. "Cocksucker! . . . Muff diver! . . . *Skeevuse con gangaruse!*" He's getting off words that even the cops have never heard.

Then, inside the emergency room, Lenny pins a sister: *"I wanna suck a big fat nun's cunt!"* he screams. A muscular-looking doctor slaps a piece of adhesive tape across Lenny's mouth. Asked about this unusual medical procedure, the doctor explained: "We wanted to protect the sisters and the nurses. We took it off a half hour later. When we told Bruce what had happened, he seemed very amused."

Lenny was probably less amused by the doctor's diagnosis. The chart spelled out the damages in formidable words:

Complete transference fracture of the medial malleolus with some displacement of the right ankle. Bimiliar fracture with fracture

fragments in satisfactory alignment of the left ankle. Undisplaced
fracture of the left innominate bone, extending through the ace-
tabulum. Contusions, lacerations, etc., of the back, shoulders and
head.

Translated into layman's terms, Lenny had done a flip-flop in midair
and landed on his feet. He had smashed both ankles and driven his
legs up into his hips, where the bones had cracked. He had not struck
his head directly on the pavement. That is what saved his life.

What had driven Lenny out the window? As usual, it was his legal
mania; that, plus round-the-clock activity and massive doses of Meth.
Lenny had actually kicked his legal craziness for a couple of months
when he suddenly pulled up stakes at the Marlton in February and
flew back to the West Coast. Once clear of New York, he had drawn
a deep breath of life. He'd gone back to work, for a change, and played
Basin Street West and a community center up in Marin County. He'd
also made plans to work the Tender Trap in Sacramento and the
Shadows in Washington, D.C. When he got back to the House on the
Hill in early March, he seemed to be returning to normal. He saw his
old friends, made his old jokes, and behaved like himself. Then the
insidious virus of the law had started boiling again in his veins.

The disease began with a fresh legal connection: Ed DeGrazia, a
lawyer who had come to Lenny's aid at Judy Peabody's behest. He
wasn't absolutely sure what he could do; in fact, he suggested that
Lenny hire another man, a friend of his, who was just leaving Bobby
Kennedy's office and who had more "juice" than Bobby Baker. Lenny
wouldn't hear of it. He knew what he wanted: *he wanted to play the
Supreme Court.* He dug that he needed a better legal strategy than
"win on appeal." What he needed was preventive medicine; a lifelong
vaccination against cops. Now, how could he get it?

DeGrazia thought and thought. Then a couple of days before
Lenny went out the window, he came up with the answer. It wasn't
the definitive answer: just the first rough sketch. Lenny should claim
that his *civil rights* were being infringed. Obscenity was a schmutzy,
ugly issue the Court detested. The judges didn't want to become experts
in the dirty joke, the double entendre, and the stag movie. What they
dug, under Mr. Justice Warren, were heavy pronunciamentos on civil
rights. Now, suggested DeGrazia, why shouldn't Lenny argue that his
right to free speech was being continually and *unconstitutionally*
"searched and seized and silenced"? That was the groovy language he
used in a letter that Lenny got the day he fell, March 29th. DeGrazia
wrote:

"Our approach to the Supreme Court in your case would probably be that your expression was, and continues to be, unconstitutionally searched and seized and silenced. That the charge under which this unconstitutional activity gets exerted is 'obscenity' rather than 'blasphemy' or 'nihilism' makes little difference. I believe the U.S. Supreme Court is aware of this better than most.''

Imagine being up there with the civil rights martyrs! With Martin Luther King and Dick Gregory! Yeah, Gregory had actually asked him to join some march. Lenny answered: "No, man, I'd just bring a lotta heat on you! Besides, the marchers are sloppy: Al Hibbler [a blind singer] walks right into people." He had even repeated that conversation on the floor. But Gregory was right: Lenny Bruce *was* a civil rights case. He wasn't really being busted for obscenity; he was being busted for the truth!

Lenny Bruce—American. That was the title of his last album— the best he ever cut. Lenny Bruce was a fuckin' American hero, man. Fighting for the same shit that heroes always fought for in this country. If he was a martyr, it was only because the people of prejudice and limited education didn't understand what he was trying to do. Wouldn't the cats on the Supreme Court be different? Wouldn't they see in a flash what the other assholes could never dig? Damn well bet they would, Jim! If Lenny ever got up before the Nine Old Men—or whatever the hell they were called—he'd cook his ass off and from the highest bench in the land they would shout bravo!

On the day before he went out the window, a new fan came into the room. Lenny was already up on top of the bed, demonstrating how he would address the Supreme Court. He was already so high that he was ready to fly out a window. "I thought I could reach"—that's what he told Honey, echoing ruefully the old junkie joke weeks later when he was recovering—"I thought I could reach the bottom." He was so damn high when he went out that window that he probably did figure that he could do a Daddy longlegs and be down in the street in one stride.

Lenny, though, wouldn't have made the try if he hadn't been bucked up with some dynamite shit. It was rocket fuel that blew Lenny out that window. DMT, that nasty little agent of chemical warfare, cooked up in the research centers of the Pentagon, had made its way into Lenny's veins.

A friend had laid on Lenny some grass soaked in the new ingredient with a note reading: "Smoke this, till *the jewels roll out of your eyes!*" Mighty powerful words. Enough to make Lenny conquer his aversion to hallucinogens and blow a little of the brown "mint leaves." Who knows what such a stone freak felt? Lee Hill felt: "I was a tree and I was breathing through every pore."

Heavier still is what happened the next day. Lenny had been bitching about a toothache. Dissolving some Percodans, his current substitute for heroin, in a cooker, he had tried to inject the shit intravenously. Clumsy as ever, he hadn't been able to get a hit. Finally, in a paroxysm of frustration, he had taken the syringe in his left hand and jammed it into the back of his right bicep. "No! No! Lenny!" Lee had shouted across the room. "That shit abscesses in the muscle, man!" Lenny's impatient, impetuous nature had set him up for another ghastly affliction.

Then Lenny and Eric smoked some more of the tinctured grass. "You get anything offa this?" Lenny questioned. "No, man, I feel the same." Then, they went downstairs and across the street to make the gig. Lenny worked his show and came back to his room and dismissed his guests. When all the trouble began, Eric remembers, it was a couple of hours past midnight. He left Lenny's room and went up the hall with a chick who was also staying at the hotel. They lobbed out for an hour in her room. Then the chick asked Eric if she could try on his jacket. Next she went up to Lenny's room, knocked on the door, and showed him the jacket. "Lenny doesn't like this jacket on me," she reported when she came back. Eric was nodding out on the bed. It must have been three or three-thirty when he was roused by a terrible racket at the end of the hall. "That sounds like Lenny," he mumbled, hauling himself dutifully out of bed. "I better go see what he's into." Walking down the corridor and knocking on the door, Eric got no answer at first. He knocked again, and a voice inside challenged, "Who's there?"

"It's me, Eric!"

"Oh, come on in!"

"You gotta be a little quiet," Eric admonishes as he enters the room. Then he pauses to dig the scene.

Something weird is going on. Lenny is on his knees, caressing a girl seated in a chair. "Geez! I love this chick. Doesn't she have lovely red hair?" As he's saying this, tears are coming to his eyes. Eric is hip to Lenny's moods. He's seen him fall apart before. He sits down on the bed and starts to talk in a very calming manner. What Eric doesn't know is that Lenny has taken the liquid DMT and loaded it in a spike and shot it into his arm. Lenny is wildly hallucinating. At that moment he's clinically insane.

"Yeah. You're right, Lenny," Eric purrs, trying to be soothing. "Lissen! Why don't you quiet down a little bit?"

"No! Spit in my face!"

"I don't wanna spit in your face!"

When the cat who had laid the DMT on Lenny turned up at the hospital to apologize, Lenny took him off the hook immediately. "Man," he said, "I wouldn't have missed it for anything!" The San Francisco papers wouldn't have missed it for anything, either. Inspired by that sympathy and compassion that is such an essential feature of our free press, the headline writers struggled all day for the *mot juste*. "LENNY'S PAINFUL FLOP. COMIC GETS CARRIED AWAY. BRUCE BRUISED AND MUZZLED."

Meanwhile, the news was broken to John Judnich by a 10 A.M. phone call from Eric Miller. "Lenny fell out the window . . . He broke his right ankle . . . He's unconscious." John, reacting with instant paranoia, cries, "Were the heat on it?" "No, man," answers Eric and hangs up. John still doesn't know what's happened, but he gets on the phone and calls Sally. As always, Sally is great in an emergency. That afternoon, she's on the plane to Frisco. Walking into the ward where Lenny has been stuck, she flashes: "A Fellini movie!" Weird old men in white bathrobes are wandering around talking to themselves. Lenny is half whacked on sedatives. The whole scene is a nightmare. Immediately, Sally makes arrangements for a Schaefer ambulance plane to fly Lenny down to L.A.

The next day, they roll out to the airport in a big hearselike car, and a couple of attendants load the body on the plane. Lenny is stoned for the trip, but Sally is frantically awake. No sooner does the little plane take off than they're hit by a terrific storm. Bouncing around up there over the mountains, with the lightning flashing and the thunder rumbling in her ears, Sally figures, "This is it! We'll never make it!" When they finally touch down at the airport in L.A., Sally is almost as sick as Lenny.

By this time the House on the Hill has become the target of a frantic telephone barrage, fired off from all over the country. Under Phone Calls, John Judnich notes in his diary for March 30th: "Elly Solomon; Selma Rovinsky; Al Sexton; Ed DeGrazia; Kiberley; Janie; Barbara Lum; Paula Maguire; Judy Peabody—momentarily hysterical . . . back from Nassau; Sue from the Free Press; Frankie Ray."

For the next few days, Lenny lies in extreme discomfort in Cedars of Lebanon Hospital suffering from a high fever and being fed intravenously by a tube in his left hand. Then he slips into delirium with his fever hanging at 105. He raves incoherently, tears off his bedclothes and pajamas, and once writes John a check for $5,000! Dr. Romm, who has taken charge of the case, assumes that Lenny is suffering from a recurrence of his chronic staphylococcus infection. Yet blood tests, performed every two hours, fail to show the staph bacteria. Meanwhile Lenny's right arm begins to swell to gargantuan proportions.

On the fifth night, Sally and Sue Horowitz walk into Lenny's room and find him frantically searching his bed. "It smells like there's shit in my bed!" he exclaims with a worried expression. "Maybe I did something I don't know. Look in my bed. The smell is driving me nuts!" A disgusting, fecal odor fills the room, but the bedclothes are perfectly clean.

A little later the same evening, Fat Jack E. Leonard comes schlumping into Lenny's room wearing a hospital robe and slippers. He's a patient, too. When he heard that Lenny was in the hospital, he immediately offered to go in and cheer him up. When he takes a good look at Lenny, he turns white with anxiety. For the first time in his life, he loses the power of speech! What he expects to find is a sick man. What he finds is one who is nearly dead. Waxy-pale, black-bearded, his eyes bleared above purple-black pouches, Lenny looks ghastly. What really grosses Leonard out, though, is Lenny's feeble attempt at a joke. Picking up his hideously swollen arm—bulging above the elbow like one of Popeye's biceps—Lenny mournfully cracks, "Hey, Jack, look at my arm!" Fat Jack mumbles a hasty excuse and beats it out of the room.

The shitty smell that was driving Lenny nuts was actually the stink of gangrene. The Percodan shot he had given himself for his toothache a week before had festered under the skin and initiated a complex infection that had turned gangrenous. The fantastic swelling of his upper arm was caused by gas generated by clostridia bacteria, which proliferate in dead and rotting flesh. Next morning his arm exploded. Two quarts of pus and ooze came pouring out of the gigantic wound. The nurses and doctors were so overcome with loathing that they couldn't bear to enter the room. Finally, Dr. Romm steeled himself to make an examination. He found some bits of glass in the arm and a lot of dead tissue. Grimly he realized that unless Lenny was very lucky, they would have to amputate the arm at the shoulder.

The next few days were touch and go. Lenny was wheeled into an isolation room to protect the gaping wound from further infection. All visitors were barred. Delirious most of the time, Lenny slept fitfully. When he awoke, he complained bitterly about the pain he was suffering and demanded more drugs. In addition to all his other suffering, Lenny was actually going through withdrawal. Dr. Romm finally realized what was wrong and took appropriate measures, but the huge wound— which the doctor recalled as a "big, gaping, ugly, foul-smelling abscess!

Horrible-looking thing!"—stubbornly refused to heal. "There was obviously no way of closing it," Romm recollected. "It just looked like it was never going to close—like his whole arm was going to disappear." Calling in other doctors and experimenting with various antibiotics, Romm fought the intractable infection day by day. Once, the wound did begin to close; but it soon reinfected and opened wide a second time.

Romm was now deeply concerned. The septicemia he had been looking for since the time of the accident had begun to show up in the blood tests. Also, the longer the huge abscess lay open, the greater the risk of a fatal infection. Every day the doctor noted in his records, "continues to draw very foul-smelling, purulent material."

Finally, after about two weeks of medical battling, Lenny began to come around. His fever dropped, his septicemia was allayed, and the festering hole in his arm began to show signs of healing. As soon as Lenny could receive visitors, he ordered John to smuggle in some Percodan tablets. For about a week, he was high on pills; then a nurse busted him. "You bastards!" he screamed at the doctors, demanding the return of his pills. Nothing he could say would persuade Romm to allow him unlimited quantities of narcotics. He had to get along on what was prescribed. Eventually other people passed him the stuff he needed, and Romm never realized that the fine recovery Lenny made during his last week in the hospital owed a great deal to medicine the doctor never ordered.

On Wednesday, April 28th, a month exactly from his nearly fatal fall, Lenny came home. He was in a wheelchair with casts up to his hips. His pale, ravaged face was framed in a heavy black beard. He was absolutely helpless, requiring the attentions of a full-time nurse, who fed him, bathed him, helped him void, and, most important, washed out his ugly wound every four hours with antibiotic solution, covering over the hole each time with a neatly folded pad of gauze. John Judnich, a saint of a man, soon assumed this wretched chore. Six times a day—even in the middle of the night—he removed the gauze and stared down into the red raw wound, filling with pus and fluid. Into the hole he inserted a huge bulb syringe, like you'd use for basting a turkey. Sue Horowitz was just as brave and devoted. The first night Lenny got home, she put him to sleep in a hospital bed with high sides. Then, she made a bed up for herself on the floor and slept there all night wrapped in a blanket. Next morning Lenny told her: "You made me cry last night. I woke up—and there you were on the floor, sleeping like a little puppy."

Faithful Sue and Faithful John and Faithful Sally. Lenny was fortunate to have so many people dedicated selflessly to his survival, but what he really needed was money to pay the doctors, the nurses, the druggists and ambulance owners. Money for the first mortgage on his house and the second. Money for all his secret drugs and his long-distance phone calls. Money to put food in his mouth and Methedrine in his arm. O.K., he had some health and disability insurance to cool out the hospital. But he still owed $1,500 to Dr. Sarot in New York for the operation on his lung. Another grand was owing to the faithful Dr. Romm. His phone bill was $1,600. And the lawyers? Thirty thousand dollars would be the lowest number for all the cats that had gone to bat for him in the courts. On his latest album, *Lenny Bruce Is Out Again,* he had listed them all: Seymour Fried, Russell Bledsoe, John Marshall, Sydney Irmas, Jr., Stuart Kagen, Albert M. Bendich, Ephraim London, Marshall Blumenfeld, John J. Brogan, Jr., Robert Ming, Harry Kalven, Jr., Maurice Rosenfeld, Melvin Belli, David Blasband, Malcolm Berkowitz, Charles R. Ashman, Larry Steinberg, Richard Essen, Alex Hoffman, Earle Warren Zaidins, Joseph Steck. An honor roll.

Even when he was half out of his nut in Cedars of Lebanon, Lenny had been thinking about the gig he had been offered in Chicago. Le Bistro was a chic nightclub on Chicago's Near North Side. It was the answer to his prayers—a cool two grand a week for three weeks— $6,000 to quash all the liens on his life. At the same time, there was a point of honor. He could now return to Chicago a *free man*!

So the old Plastercaster gave his marching orders. Fanned down the hysterical objections from all the women in the family. Instructed John what to instruct the cats at the Bistro. They should build a ramp up to the stage—dig? He didn't want a hundred people in the back screaming that they couldn't see him. So they would build this ramp and get him up high and he would be wheeled out there night after night and given a hand mike and then he would cook from the wheelchair in a rare display of the old show-biz get-off, dig it?

So, at the midnight hour on May 18th, Lenny and John lifted off from L.A. airport and broomed back to Chi, where they landed at six in the morning. They were met at the airport by Jackie Gayle, Sally's former partner, who brought along the club owner. Lenny told them straight off that he was only working two, not three, weeks. His plan was to go on to New York, where he was going to present his appeal at the end of May. No sooner did he get into the limousine than he learned that absolutely nothing had been done at the club. Here he was, lobbed out in a wheelchair, and these jerks hadn't constructed the ramp to the stage. Lenny said that he could only promise one show a night—maybe two on the weekend. It was going to be a terrific hassle to work this club without the special preparations that he had ordered. What a drag!

When they got to the hotel, it was just like the old days. The phone never stopped ringing all day long and even into the late night hours. Finally, Lenny, who was exhausted, called down to the switchboard and told them to shut off the calls. Christ! What the hell did they think he was made of? Next day, Phyllis Mahoney, a really nice lady who trained Playboy bunnies, came over and washed out Lenny's arm. The gauze was heavily stained with pus; the wound didn't look good. Lenny was bombed out in his wheelchair. Late in the afternoon, he told John, "Man, we gotta split for home!" That was it. The cat couldn't make the gig. The owners flipped, but they cooled out when Lenny told them that he would come back June 17th. They had booked more reservations than at any time in the club's history. It would have been sensational business. The only trouble was that poor Lenny was dying in his chair. As John booked the flight for that night, Lenny started popping Percodans like they were candy. When they got out to O'Hare, Lenny flipped because their plane didn't have an in-flight movie. So John had to book another flight, rewrite the tickets, the whole shmeer.

Finally, they took off. Lenny got rowdy in his seat. "Hey!" he exulted, adjusting the headphones, "this is the first time I ever heard a stereo!" Really blew his mind. You could hear his voice above the roar of the engines. The stewardess was only too happy to lay a couple drinks on him. What with the pills and the booze, he was sound asleep by the time they passed over the Mississippi River.

During the last year of Lenny's life, the mood in the House on the Hill changed mysteriously. It wasn't easy to put your finger on the difference, but everyone who went up there came back down with the same impression. Lenny was slowly going crazy. He didn't look like Lenny or sound like Lenny or have any of the interests of the old Lenny. He was surrounded by a bunch of weirdos, who acted like his slaves. All he did from one end of the day to the other was sit inside his office and read law books. You couldn't talk to him about anything except law, and you could never lure him to come out and play. He didn't gig and he didn't earn. God knows how he paid the mortgage and put food on the table. The whole thing was unspeakably sad, and once you had seen it, you never wanted to go back and see it again.

Imagine someone arriving who had known Lenny for years and remembered both him and his house from a different era. The guy might not have seen Lenny for a couple of years because he was serving time or working in another part of the country or he had had some little tiff that took time to forget. One day, he gets the yen to see Len. He picks up the phone, dials the familiar unlisted number, 652-8961, and gets the old fake-out greeting he remembers so well. "Hhmmyeah?" "Hey, Lenny—it's me!" Billy, Bobby, Jimmy, Tony, Ernie, Eddie—whatever. "Heeeey—man!" exclaims the suddenly reviving personality at the other end of the line. "Wheryabeen?" Blah, blah, blah, the conversation sketches in a few fast details, and then the familiar nasal voice urges, "C'monup!"

Ducking into his short, the cat starts to cut across L.A., aiming for the Strip and Sunset Plaza Drive, the launching pad to Lenny's house high atop the mountain. Grabbing a hard right at Queens Road, he watches the hood of his car tilting up, like a jet taking off for Honolulu. Up, up he goes past neat white villas and sword-leafed tropical plants. Around blind curves, pointing steadily upward, toward the milk-glass sky. Whoosh! A descending car whizzes past his window as he cuts into the curve even harder, shifting down to second and soaring above the treeline. The road serpentines past houses on stilts and brown burnt-out hillsides, scored with erosion. The numbers on the houses are reaching astronomical altitudes—8825, 8847—when suddenly he spots Len's house hanging above his head, and he goes into his landing maneuver. Shifting down and wrenching the wheel to the right, he *va-rooooms!* up a thirty-degree driveway and lands *va-voom!* in the parking lot.

Now, he notices something odd. The parking lot is totally empty. Or maybe there's just one little Volks. In the old days, the lot was always jammed. Sometimes you'd have to park in the driveway with its ridiculously steep angle—the cause of numberless accidents, with cars coasting backward to land, tail in air, hung up on the retaining wall. Now, the carport looms out at a crooked angle from the house, like an abandoned railway station. Pushing open the big metal gate on the right-hand side of the house, the guy goes in back to the patio and pool. Here he gets another flash. The joint is deserted! In the old days you'd come back here and there was always a party. Guys and girls were lobbed out on towels or splashing around in the water. Music would be blaring from the hi-fi. Maybe Eric Miller would be seated on a chair, head down, knee cocked up, playing guitar for the gang, while everybody lay back, smoked tea, and grooved.

Now a telescope is perched on long skinny legs, peering down into the valley across the shoulder-high glass fence and the water in the pool looks turbid and green, as if it hadn't been cleaned out in a long time. Bramble weeds and tall grass creep raggedly up the sides of the stucco walls. Even Lenny's prize roses and garden lanai are weed-choked and dying. The only sound you hear is the distant *peck, peck,*

peck of a hunt-and-hit typist. Walking past the glass panes and cor-rugated panels of the first floor, the guy searches for the sound. It's coming from the other end of the house, the end where Lenny had his goofy little guest cottage. Pulling back an aluminum-framed glass panel, the visitor steps into the interior and pauses to catch the sound of the typewriter ringing through a door directly in front of him. Rap-ping discreetly on the door, he hears again the familiar voice. "C'min!" He opens the door and gets the shock of his life!

The bearded lady from the circus is rising to greet him! It's Lenny, but he's so freaky-looking that the visitor is almost afraid to take his hand. This giant fat person dressed in a denim muumuu with a head on him—a *pinhead*! Bearded like a Trappist monk, his head is so much smaller than the rest of his body that he comes to a point on top! When he walks around in this denim gown, you can hear his medicine bottles clanking around inside his big patch pockets.

The minute you walk in his room, he starts shpritzing you with the law. He's telling you about this shit that he's just been reading, some dumb cases.

While you're listening to him rave on, you look around the pad. He's working inside a nutshell. His "office" he calls it. It's a walnut-paneled rumpus room with everything built in. The desk he types on is a shelf that's growing out from the wall. The copying machine is grooved into another wall. He's got a library of law books stuck up on the shelves. Balled-up paper wherever you walk, yellow-lined pads slung all over the place and a giant spaghetti of unstrung tape spools floating on top of the floor. The real tip on the whole scene is the pillar that's holding up the ceiling. It's probably an I-beam. Lenny has encased it in walnut. Sticking out from one side of it, like the bima in the synagogue, is this giant dictionary, a great big khaki job laid open in front of him like a Bible. You haven't been in the office five minutes before he has schlepped you over to this volume—and you're looking up words!

He's got all these legal strategies. One is Declaratory Relief. Pub-lishers use it when they've got a hot book. They take the manuscript to a judge and say: "Look, I'm afraid there might be trouble if I publish this writing; could you read it and give me the benefit of your opinion?" The judge examines it and says, "O.K., go ahead." Now what good is *that* if you're Lenny Bruce and never do the same show twice?

His other mishigaas is a kind of civil rights action that enables him to sue the governors of all the states where he's been busted. He plans to sue Nelson Rockefeller in New York; Edmund Brown in California; Otto Kerner, Jr., in Illinois; Farris Bryant in Florida; David Lawrence in Pennsylvania; and maybe throw in the District of Columbia for good

measure. The beef? *Nonfeasance!* The governors, he will claim, failed
in their duty to protect his civil rights. He's pissed because a cop on
a beat can come in and bust him for giving an obscene performance
when the cop probably doesn't even know the legal definition of obscenity. The most the cop is really empowered to do is to take Lenny
to a magistrate. If the magistrate says he thinks the show is obscene,
then, O.K., the cop can bust him. But peace officers are simply chauf-
feurs between crooks and courts. What's more, the governors of the
states are at fault because Lenny's act was ruled legally clean in his
first trial in San Francisco. Whether those jurors realized it or not,
they cleared Lenny forever. Obscenity is part of the law laid down by
the Supreme Court. That law is uniform across America. Lenny's got
a punch line, his final genius stroke. With some of the biggest attorneys
in the country working for him—on contingency—and the whole press
corps alerted to his plan, he's going to initiate the suit *in a Southern
court*! He's gonna go down to Selma or Atlanta or Birmingham and
he's gonna sue there "to highlight the civil rights aspect of the case"!
Because this isn't any petty dirty book and movie case—this is the
daddy, the *biggie*, the heavyweight case that will blow the whistle on
the whole law-and-order scene in this country. This one will go all the
way. Lenny Bruce will play the Supreme Court, and he'll knock those
fusty old farts right off their swivel chairs. What a gas! What a show!
Who the fuck wants to work the Fillmore when you can play the
greatest court in the land and help save our country? To every schmuck
who calls him about work Lenny says, *"I'm not a comedian—I'm Lenny
Bruce!"*

Terry Southern was the only guy he couldn't use for a legal sounding
board. So on those rare occasions when old Terry came up, Lenny
would get charged up with a few Dexies and spend the whole afternoon
playing. What a team! Bruce & Southern.

Terry is sitting there in the tape room, slumped heavily, flaccidly
on a bed, his face covered by a thick scruff of beard, his eyes shielded
by dark glasses, hair tousled, blue shirt hanging out of dirty gray-white
pants: a beat Charles Laughton, laughing that sly laugh of his and
talking in that shy, British-accented voice. Drinking a lot of lush over
the course of a long day's jollys, he finally starts to thrash about and
get into his fantasies. Finally, he rears back and opens his mouth and
launches into this whole long red-dirt Texas shit-kicker speech—talkin'
jis the way people talk down in his hometown.

Lenny's bent from the waist, flinging his arms this way and that
as he registers every doubt, hesitation, or confusion of his speed-
smashed brain. One minute he's jumbling frantically through a pile of

mashed and broken and mislabeled tape boxes looking for this fantastic song by Tiny Tim; the next moment, he's gotten hung up on something entirely different—an excerpt from his trials or some hillbilly record off the radio or a party record by some dirty little no-talent comic doing straight whoopee-cushion humor.

If they have Terry's buddy Bill Claxton, the photographer, they'll spend a couple hours making funny pictures. That's what they did that afternoon when Terry and Bill came up the hill and found Lenny in his wheelchair. He was such a sight with his face ringed in a big black beard and one leg rammed out in front of him on a breadboard. Instantly, Claxton whipped out his camera and the boys went into their act. Lenny put on his fiercest, most glaring mountain-lion face and seized the rubber tires of his wheelchair in a knuckle-whitening grip. Fixing his eyes implacably upon Terry—who had drawn himself to the ramrod posture of a reporting sergeant slapping a French Foreign Legion salute against his forehead—Lenny had himself photographed as the grand old marshal, desperately wounded but grimly determined, ordering a final desperate onslaught against the foe. *"Oui, mon capitaine!"* the picture screams. (The real punch line came years after Lenny's death, when a dumb picture editor at *The New York Times* cropped away Terry's comic salute and printed the baleful picture of Lenny glaring in his wheelchair with the caption: ". . . the year before his death.")

When *The Magic Christian* was published in paperback, it bore a laudatory blurb by Lenny Bruce: "Hosanna! In only one printing Southern has achieved Second Coming. Funniest book I ever read." Years later, in the summer of '64, when Lenny was wrapped up in his New York trial, Terry tried to pay back the favor by offering Lenny a part in *The Loved One.* Adopting the classic put-on tone that he always used in his epistles to the Great Bruce, Terry wrote as follows:

31 July 1964

Len Big Bopper

Enclosed please find cine script by yrs truly and a crafty old fruit [Evelyn Waugh]. It is our very real hope that you will consider the role of the GURU BRAHMIN—which can be altered and grooved up infinitely, natch, to your own outlandish specifications. You will be rubbing shoulders, Len, (if not, in fact, pelvic regions) with such star and feature players as: Sir John ("Jack") Gielgud (Francis), Jonathan Winters (Harry and the Dreamer), Rod Steiger (Joyboy), Liberace (Starker), Dana Andrews (Gen Schmuck), Keenan Wynn (Immigration Officer), and a host of other show-stoppers of equally curious persuasions. Director is tip-top Tony R. [Richardson], the Oscar-copping madcap, and as I say, chief scripter is yrs tly. Perhaps you are wondering about so-called material recompense. Well, Len, we have two schemes going here—under one, you can take your pay in straight top-drawer starlet sugar-scoop; under the other it is one bill (*big* bill, Len) per day. The GURU's lines appear on pages as per follows: 75, 76, 93, 119, 120, 141, 142, and 143. Please note that Scene #131 gives you an excellent shot at the fantastic winner-quim of our beautiful young girl star, whose name I will not reveal to you at this moment due to its effect of instant shoot-off.

We'll want to move fast on this one, Len—for reasons I shall explain later. Please let me hear from you by return of post.

—Yrs. as per,
T.

Lenny declined the invitation. He was always loath to enlist himself behind anyone else's banner, especially in a matter like a Hollywood movie. He told Terry that he wanted his own film, not a bit part in another man's rave-up.

The correspondence continued, however, and after returning from the West Coast, where he had visited Lenny's pad, Terry wrote again:

Saturday

Len Big Bopper!

Hope this finds you in top form and fettle, Len. I've just returned from the film-capital where I saw, let me tell you, the fabulous DOOR that JOHN built for your shicksa-puss room! Believe you me, Len, I've seen doors aplenty, but *nothing* to compare with this. Approaching the door, with its suggestive slivers of soft light beckoning through its quality panels, one is so subtly overcome by the prospect of possible mystery, intrigue, and giant spurting member within! Horowitz, Lil, Nance, and the others were terribly excited by it, and I'm very much afraid that your so-called "Boss Joint" will be required to do yeoman-service after this period of absence. The fact is that these girls are actually *half-sick* from the abrupt withdrawal of your gross animal-dong—so much so that John and I had to render almost CONSTANT HEAD to keep their sugar-scoops from wasting away entirely. However, more of this later. Now then, Len—buzz along the rialto has it that you found *Candy* to be a darn fun-book. If this is, in actual fact, the case, why for gosh sakes let's have another of those dang Hosanna quotes (by return of post, if poss.)

Hope to see you soon—will bring copy of Tiny Tim disc! Take care.

> Your boy,
> Terry

RFD/East Canaan, Conn.

The door to which Terry refers was the item on which Lenny set greatest store in his newly decorated bedroom. It was the sort of door that you always see in Bela Lugosi movies: an old, cracked, weather-beaten door that makes a long, spooky squeak as it turns reluctantly on its hinges. Terry had been witness to the first inspection of the door some weeks before, when Lenny had registered deep disappointment over the effect. Standing before the forbidding-looking planks, he had bent his head this way and that and clucked his tongue in audible frustration. Phrasing his objection carefully—so as not to injure Judnich's feelings—he said: "Man . . . it just doesn't *make* it . . . it's not *quite* what I wanted. Can't you get it like they always have it in the movies? You know . . . so that when you approach, there's just a little light glimmering through? Can't you sorta *chink it*, man?"

The greatest prank Lenny ever played with Terry occurred during the last year of his life. Terry had called and said he was coming up to the house. There was a flurry of preparations. When the curtain goes up, Terry Southern is entering Lenny's office, where he finds the famous comedian obsessed as always with legal business, pacing back and forth, dictating a letter full of Latin terms to a seated secretary—who is stark naked! Nodding abruptly, peremptorily, to Terry, while signing him to have a seat, Lenny continues in full stride, pausing only to note, in his preoccupied manner: "Oh, yes . . . if Mr. Southern wants his cock sucked, you'll take care of that, too, won't you?"

Temperamentally, Lenny and Terry were ideally suited to one another. Lenny, the oral shpritzer; Terry, the quiet, introverted writer. Lenny a great practical joker; Terry with the same mania but playing all his pranks in print. The only sour note ever struck in their relationship was that *Loved One* letter. Lenny told John Judnich, "He's just trying to exploit me."

The only movie that Lenny could make would be a movie of Lenny by Lenny and for Lenny—which is precisely the movie he did make when it was much too late to make much of anything out of the once-talented Lenny Bruce. The project was the brainstorm of a San Francisco educational filmmaker, John Magnuson. Though his company was titled "Imagination, Inc.," Magnuson was not especially imaginative, nor was he a name in pictures. He concentrated in later years on producing filmed episodes for *Sesame Street* and doing little documentaries. What he did have in abundance and what especially endeared him to Lenny was character and absolute disinterestedness: so much of both that when Lenny made his will, he named Magnuson as his executor. When Lenny first met Magnuson at the bar of the Off Broadway in 1964, he pinned him for a priest. That's how Magnuson's short hair, earnest pale face, nervous, fidgety temperament, and obvious sincerity, etched into plain, unsmiling features, struck Lenny's imagination. Magnuson looked like the kind of guy who would walk the last mile with a condemned prisoner—precisely what he did with Lenny Bruce.

The mile began with three laps around the block that first night, as the two men fell into a very deep discussion of film. Lenny said that he was deeply interested in film making and that he had a great idea for a picture. He wanted to get a house somewhere out in the country and invite a group of interesting people for a weekend. The place would be wired up like a film studio, and everything that happened could be captured by the cameras. He was certain that once the people felt they were completely marooned, completely on their own, they would get into so many strange and fascinating psychodramas that the movie would prove a masterpiece. It was the same sort of idea that Norman Mailer acted on years later when he filmed *Maidstone* in a weekend on a Long Island estate. Magnuson, deeply impressed by Lenny, replied that he had the house they needed. It was out in the Napa Valley, a big old house that belonged to his little film company.

Many discussions followed that first evening; eventually Lenny and Magnuson settled on a much simpler scheme. In February 1965, they made a deal—two-thirds to the Bruce Estate, one-third to Imagination, Inc.—to film one of Lenny's nightclub shows in San Francisco. No effort would be made to gussy up the picture with editing, cutting, or special effects. The only condition was that Lenny would strive to give an outstanding performance. As he had grown very erratic over the years, Magnuson hit on the idea of recording many hours of Lenny's shows and then playing them back so that he could pick out the best things and combine them spontaneously. Over the next couple of months, thirty hours of performance were taped. Lenny listened to fifteen hours and said he was ready to go. Then he fell out the window of the Swiss-American, and the project had to be shelved.

The picture was finally shot in the spring at Basin Street West. After two half-hour run-throughs to check out lighting, sound equipment, and cameras, the last show of the evening was filmed. Though nothing more complicated was attempted than a head-on picture made by two alternating cameras—with an occasional slow zoom—several problems cropped up in the run-throughs. Lenny's eyes were too weak to bear normal studio lighting; so Magnuson decided to reduce the light and use a very fast film stock, which would project with a rather grainy texture. There was also the old problem of getting Lenny's voice clearly recorded. After a lifetime of performing with a hand mike, he still hadn't learned how to manipulate the instrument so that his mumbles and asides came through clearly.

The film has a strange dungeonlike setting, a wall of heavy stones, mortared together like a cell in *The Prisoner of Zenda*. This sinister backdrop was simply the fake cobblestone wall at the back of the stage, a stupid effort to lend the club "atmosphere." Like everything else in this picture, it seems like an unconscious metaphor for death.

Lenny's entrance is typical: he screws the mike off the stand and waves it over the first few rows. Then he explains that he can identify his audience this way: Catholics are offended at the parody of a priestly gesture—Jews think he's trying to hit them. Immediately he goes into his trials, slowed down and encumbered by a massive legal transcript through which he pages, seeking for examples of various absurdities and injustices. (Magnuson, afflicted by a mania for literal accuracy, had insisted that Lenny read the actual words from the transcripts— which produced a lot of cumbersome, time-wasting page-turning in what was supposed to be a brilliant and spontaneous show.) The basic thrust of the performance is an attempt to prove that Lenny never actually said the things for which he was tried in New York. He reads the often inaccurate or garbled phrases of the police transcript; then he tells the audience what he really said. One exception is a passage in which he describes how the police come in a club, make a few notes, and then impersonate him on the witness stand. When the cop is asked what Lenny said, he gives a dumb, glum glance down at his notebook and reads: "Catholics . . . Jews . . . shit!" Not a bad abstraction of Lenny's last act.

At the end of the film, Lenny drifts into some of his famous routines. How little he cares about this material is apparent in the way he throws it around, omitting huge chunks, going off on long digressions—which are funnier than the bits because they're fresher —and even going up on once-automatic lines and gags. Drifting from the *Prison Break* to *To Is a Preposition,* he touches the cymbals and drums, then wanders off to one side of the stage playing with the phrase "Don't come i'me!" until he finally shapes it into a Broadway show tune. At the very end, he's opening a door so that he can look outside and see the hookers taking the johns into the little scratch hotels above the tonks of Broadway.

After the 65-minute film—titled *Lenny Bruce*—was edited, Lenny screened it five or six times. He was enchanted by it and pronounced it "Maybe the best performance I ever gave."

Encouraged by Lenny's praise, John Magnuson went on to a more interesting and entertaining project: the animation of Lenny's last great routine, *Mask Man*. The fantasy on the Lone Ranger, which Lenny had been developing since 1962, lent itself nicely to the technique of the sophisticated animated cartoon. Actually, any of Lenny's fantasy pieces would have served just as well because there is an element of cartooning in the way these skits are drawn up and presented. Animated cartoons were a staple of Lenny's childhood, and they—along with newspaper funnies, radio serials, and even Tilly and Mack books—all fed his developing fancy. What you have in a piece like *Mask Man,* therefore, is an art form feeding off an imagination that once was fed by this very same art form—an esthetic circularity that will probably become more and more common as the age of media advances.

Apart from his filmmaking and a couple of concerts on the West Coast, Lenny's last professional commitments were all bankrolled by his principal patron, the famous rock 'n' roll record producer Phil Spector. Estimates vary as to how much money Spector laid on Lenny or how seriously Lenny worked at exploiting Phil. What is really important about this relationship is neither the money nor the few little bits of tape or nights of live entertainment it yielded; the crucial thing is that Phil Spector was the first and only embodiment of the new youth culture with whom Lenny Bruce allowed himself to become involved.

Lenny conceived himself as belonging to one brief moment: the Jazz Age of the late fifties and early sixties. As he saw it, when jazz went down, he went down with it. He never made this point more emphatically or with a more obvious relish of bitterness than he did during his brief run at the Cafe Au Go Go in the spring of 1964. Reflecting grimly on the current status of nightclubs, comics, jazzmen, and damn near everybody of his generation, he exclaimed:

[Tough, bitter tone] I know that I've *had it* as an art form! Oh yeah, definitely . . . You've been with me so long that my tits are sagging now. And that as much as I try *gnavitch* things with makeup—we've been married too long! And the reason you resist that and deny it is that if that happens with me, then it's the truth with you, too! "That the new is not the most desired"— but it is! *New is good!* [Girl-watcher whistle] And ah . . . [Long thoughtful pause] . . . the only salvation, the only comfort is that we all went *together*! We all *had* it together! The other generation couldn't measure the artistic viewpoint because they went forty miles an hour. But this had it from '56 to '61—that-was-the-end-of-it! That ended jazz—[Aside] it's in the shithouse—I-don't-know-if-you've-evaluated-that-yet! ANNIE ROSS! SHELLEY BERMAN! BAH-DE-DAH!!! DING-A-DING-DING-RIP-IT-UP-DA-DA-DAAAAAA! BAM! It's gone!

Now what happens is—there's enough people left over that made a business out of that, so that the business is *supporting* the business. . . . So now you'll fuck me if I see you once a year, Saturday, a quick shtup! You know, I'll still look *hot* to ya! But if it's an every-week scene, it's a complete *pass!* If I can split from you a couple of years, I'll still look heyss. I'll dress in a girdle, I'll get sharp, ya know, and I'll dazzle you with those soft lights, but . . . ah . . . No! . . . No! That's why it's a big mistake for older types to marry young chicks. They've *seen* Carmen Cavallaro.

Bitter. The truth is that the hippest members of the Rock Generation were very impressed by Lenny Bruce. Didn't the Beatles put him on the cover of *Sgt. Pepper?* Any time he showed up at the Whisky Au Go Go or the Troubadour or any of the new joints along the Strip, the musicians in groups like the Byrds, the Electric Flag (or in San Francisco, the Jefferson Airplane and The Mothers) made it perfectly clear to Lenny that even if they didn't understand exactly what he was doing, they regarded him as a hero. Lenny could never accept their adulation. He would just continue to stare, like a kid blinking at a Christmas tree, at the clothes and the hair and the manners and the morals of a generation that struck him as being absolutely futuristic. The only exception was Phil Spector: no small exception, when you consider the extent to which Spector was the author of the rock culture and one of its freakiest products.

At the time Lenny met Phil, back in 1965, Spector was twenty-four years old and the Magic Man of the music business. He was also the youngest millionaire in the United States—The First Tycoon of Teen, as Tom Wolfe dubbed him in a brilliantly caricatured profile. A little hippie from the Bronx, five foot seven, 130 pounds, Phil strutted through his trendy kingdom with the first head of really long hair that had ever been seen in New York. This pageboy hung down to his shoulders; on nights when he turned up at Arthur's, he looked like a little page, with his jerkin jacket, suede pants, and winkle-picker shoes. Talking in the bored, jaded, had-it-up-to-there! voice of a young misanthrope, Phil sent killing vibes thrilling yards and yards around his presence. For locked up inside that tiny, puny body was an ego as big as the Ritz: one of those Jewish princeling egos that are always sneering down at the ratty action of this schmucky world, where the gross, stupid animals are always fucking up the truly great, really "creative" people. "Animals!"—that was his word for the Brill Building types, the coin machine operators, the rack jobbers, the A & R men, the song pluggers, the guys who spent their lives reading *Cashbox* and *Billboard* and screaming: "Christ! The fuckin' tune jumped on the charts at No. 37—with a *bullet*!"

Phil was himself a bullet. A tiny, steel-jacketed bullet smashing with lethal force right through the ranks of the dummies and rummies of the music business and out into the world where his wildest shots brought down the big game of the hit hunters. Phil had fired off his first hits before he was twenty years old—and they were monsters! "Rose in Spanish Harlem"—a record Lenny loved so much that he used to play it from the stage on a portable pick—was co-authored and solo-produced, recorded, and mixed down by the eighteen-year-old Phil Spector. After that he became chief A & R man for Atlantic Records, at the age of nineteen. In his early twenties, he became an independent record producer, working with people like Elvis Presley, Ray Peterson, and Connie Francis. The capper came at twenty-one, when he started marketing his stuff on his own label, Phillies Records. His first twenty-one singles sold thirteen million copies, including nine gold disks, each representing a million dollars in sales.

The hits kept coming for four long years, until the Beatles knocked Phil out of the box. Suddenly, he retired from the competitive arena to cool out on the West Coast. There he pushed his image into even stranger forms. Remember the scene in *Easy Rider* where the freaky little millionaire with the wild limousine and the driver/bodyguard comes out to the airport to score for shit from Peter Fonda? That is Phil Spector playing his fantasy of Phil Spector. The fancy cars and the bodyguard were always Spector trademarks.

By the time Phil met Lenny, he was spoiling for a big fight with "the Establishment." He believed that everything he did was aimed at demolishing the old, uptight, fullashit society. Wasn't he the first hippie of America? The pioneer of long hair, wild clothes, and rock music? Every one of those things was anti-Establishment, ya dig. They were all little banderillas sticking out of the hump of that fuckin' American buffalo! Now it was time to go in for the kill. Get into something that would blow the minds of the animals. Something far out and absolutely outrageous—like Lenny Bruce.

Lenny, for his part, knew a mark when he saw one. He met Phil just at the moment when he was about to go under for lack of cash. Immediately, he flashed—bread! The two heavy-duty egos made an unspoken pact that allowed Lenny to mooch off Spector's millions, while it allowed Spector to bask in the reflected glory of being tight with the notorious Lenny Bruce, Public Enemy No. 1.

The mooching soon reached record proportions. Lenny was always in need, and he wasn't shy about asking. One day, it was money for Kitty's birthday: the kid had to have her big load of fancy toys. Another day, it was money for a transcript, being copied off the court tape at a dollar per page in New York or Chicago or L.A. Sometimes the sums were tiny: enough for a pack of cigarettes and a cab from Phil's office on the Strip back up the hill to Lenny's house. Sometimes the number ran up into the thousands: as happened when Lenny decided that what he really needed was one last shot fired from the stage of a legitimate theater, not a nightclub. Spector couldn't say no. So the crazy caper was cut.

An old legitimate house, the Music Box on Hollywood Boulevard, was discovered by Lili Romney. The building was a wreck, with holes in the ceiling and mud on the stage. It was scheduled for demolition. No matter. Lenny conned Phil into pouring enough thousands into this ruin to turn the lights back on and ballyhoo an audience into the dump for opening night. Danny Davis, Spector's right-hand man, was ordered to phone every celeb in Hollywood to assure Lenny a trendy opening night audience. The word was passed as it would have been for the latest super-freaky rock group opening at the Whisky.

The show was a bomb. Everybody was fed up with Lenny Bruce. Only a scattering of people appeared. Lenny got onstage and went right into his legal craziness. Phil's heart sank as he looked at the ruin he had backed. Next day he tried to squeeze out. After all, the ads said, "Phil Spector Presents Lenny Bruce!" He didn't need his name linked with a total loser. But he hadn't reckoned on Lenny's burrlike obstinacy. Ten days had been appointed as the length of the run; ten days were destined to pass before Lenny would get off that stage and allow the electricians to black out that doomed old house and forget the whole crazy business as a bomb laid—not by him but by Phil Spector, who had "failed to advertise the show," according to Crazy Lenny.

Lenny's occasional stabs at the stage in his last year should be seen for what they were: mere foraging expeditions by a mountain outlaw feeling the pinch of hunger. By the end of his life, Lenny hated to work at his profession; he regarded doing comedy as a sheer waste of time that could be devoted to his legal business. And his paranoia. To protect his privacy and secure himself from surprise police raids, he had fortified the house. The electric gates that were supposed to protect the property had been long since abandoned as irreparable. In their stead, Lenny had constructed defenses much closer to his command post. Behind the double doors that were the main entrance to the house, John Judnich had constructed a heavy wooden plank door fitted with massive steel hinges and secured by an oaken crossbar seven feet long. This medieval beam was so heavy that none of the women in the house could lift it. If there had ever been a fire, they would have had to either jump off the balcony or perish in the flames. To further secure himself within the house, Lenny attached numberless locks, chains, bolts, and fasteners of every description to each and every door, window, and closet. He had enough security hardware for a score of houses. To facilitate communication within the bunker, Judnich rigged a PA system that allowed the garrison to talk back and forth between all the principal rooms and areas of the house and grounds. John also rigged a tape recorder so that in case of a police raid, every word and sound made by the peace officers would be captured by hidden microphones. The telescopes and periscopes that everybody noticed when they visited the house were actually the instruments of John's hobby, astronomy. Lenny, however, would often train them not on the stars but on the West Hollywood police station and the approach roads to his barricaded castle.

Immured within his citadel, Lenny gave free rein to his fantasies. Though he spent most of his time pecking out words on his typewriter, pawing through his law books, or talking on the phone to attorneys, judges, private investigators, and legal archivists, he still found time to indulge himself in a couple of his favorite amusements. So long as there was the slightest bit of money, he continued to commission new work on the house. When Judnich brought to completion the massive rebuilding program detailed in the "specs" of November 1964, Lenny came up with new plans, new schemes for household improvements. The building up and tearing down of the house—always an irrational process—now became totally crazy.

Lenny's bedroom, for example, had been painted a beautiful shade of his favorite Dufy blue. Everyone admired the job and complimented Lenny on his taste and John on his skill. Lenny was not happy. "Paint it white," he ordered one day. John refused. He was beginning to realize that Lenny was nuts. So Lenny hired a painter and had the beautiful blue covered with many coats of dull white. As if this were not screwy enough, Lenny got into the habit of going into the bedroom every night after the painter had left and making all sorts of marks and lines all over the walls—completely defacing the man's work! Next morning, when the guy would return, Lenny would be lurking around the corner, giggling like a naughty boy, waiting for the anticipated outburst from the outraged artisan. Lenny would say that it wasn't his fault: the damn kid did it, or they had had a party. Eventually the painter failed to show up. He stayed away for a week. When he came back to collect his tools, he told Lenny that doing the same job over

and over again had gotten him emotionally upset. His doctor had told
him to quit.

Another time, a couple of bricklayers were summoned to the house
to construct a wall separating the parking lot from the left-hand entranceway. If you walked past the left side of the house, you could go
either around the house to the pool or you could walk out along the
narrow isthmus that led to the end of the property. Here John had
constructed a retreat for Lenny. Behind a high wooden fence, with a
swinging panel, he had installed a big bed and a table equipped with
phone jacks, light plugs, a periscope, telescope, and the inevitable tape
recorder. Lenny could lob out here for hours and bullshit on the phone
with his friends all over the world. Or he could dictate into the machine
or spy on all the houses up and down the hill. It was his tree house
and he loved it.

What bugged him was the fear that while he was in seclusion,
people could gain access to his property. A simple wire fence and gate
would have made the house secure, but no—Lenny had to have bricklayers and a big expensive job. So the men came with their load of
bricks and their trowels and mortar-mixing basins. Every morning
Lenny would get up and go outside and jaw with them. He loved
hearing about how they had learned their trade and the different jobs
they had worked on. It was real man's talk. When it was time for the
workmen to pack up and go away, Lenny was devastated. Desperate
to keep them, he ordered them to build a brick staircase leading up
the side of the house to a spot where there was no door! The men
couldn't believe he was serious. He lied and told them that an entrance
would be cut into the side of the building after they left; it was just
more efficient to have the staircase built first. So the bricklayers worked
on crazily for another couple of weeks building a staircase to heaven.

Another, vastly more important feature of Lenny's final withdrawal was the act of surrounding himself with women. During his last
years, he lived inside a harem. Like an oriental pasha sitting cross-
legged before his hookah, he sat all day before his electric typewriter,
sometimes high, sometimes low, while all around him the house re-
sounded with female voices, female steps, female odors of cooking,
washing, and cleaning—and the bright cheery jokes of female minds
intent on getting him away from that typewriter for a few minutes so
they could feed him, soothe him, and maybe satisfy him by kneeling
before his fat white body and sucking his distracted dick for the twenty
or thirty minutes it required to make him come.

Lenny wasn't a ladies' man at the end. He was a bearded baby,
passive, helpless, and totally self-absorbed, sustained—apart from his

one male companion, John—by this astonishing network of women whom he had carefully assembled for the purpose of protecting his life and facilitating his work. So many! It almost seems as though he deliberately set out to realize every possible relationship that can be achieved between man and woman—all at the same time.

First, there was Sally, running in and out, playing the heavy Momma, urging Lenny to *eat*, to look at the *child*, to see the *doctor*, to go to the *beach* and *relax*! Only he shouldn't hit on her for money when things were so tight and chancy at her end of the line! Lenny would get on the phone and bawl, "Hey, Ma! You got thirty-five bucks? The bank's closed. It's Friday night. I forgot to go to the bank and we need some bread." Sally would bring up the money and say, "Here! Let me put it in your pocket." When she pulled her hand out of his Levis, she still had the bills in her palm. A couple hours later, Lenny would go looking for the dollars; you could hear him shouting, "What did I do with those pants I had on?"

After the Momma came the Child. Kitty was then nearly nine years old, a little beauty, with a big heart-shaped face like Honey's and large womanly eyes and that little pursed-up mouth—an erotic-looking little plum! And they would pose for pictures: Lenny, with his big black beard and those tragic Jewish eyes, and Kitty, the little minx, lying on her father's chest, peering boldly into the camera. "Beauty and the Beast" was Lenny's caption.

The child's mother, Honey, was part of the cast right until the end: the Ex-Wife, the Ex-Favorite, the lady who went over the hill. The younger women, like Sue, could never understand what the big fuss was about Honey. I mean she was this ordinary-looking lady, youthful for her age, not bad-looking and not heavy or too beat-up— but what was the big deal? No great beauty in either that face or that figure. No tragic ruin either! What the hell was everybody talking about when they said that Honey had been this knockout who now looked like death. Beauty? Death? Bullshit!

Sally, Kitty, and Honey were the Immediate Family. But the extended family included many more ladies. Sue Horowitz, for one. She fancied herself Lenny's soulmate. She prided herself on her ability to mind Lenny's business and take Lenny's shit and never feel the slightest twinge of jealousy or anger or despair. Sue had been on and off the hill for years. She had nursed Lenny and loved Lenny and typed for Lenny and spent hundreds of hours discussing the deepest life themes with her beloved Lenny. All Sue cared about in this world was Lenny. He once joked with her about what a drag it would be if she ever got married and came up the hill with a fifteen-year-old son. "Don't worry," she had replied, without smiling: "I'll never marry." And she never has to this day. Sue was born to be Lenny's widow. His black-haired, dark-skinned, black-suited widow. "Black Sue" is what Lenny used to call her, joking cruelly about her swarthy Semitic complexion and the tiny black mustache on her upper lip. Black Sue is what she was, in truth: a dark, melancholic lady who mourned the dying prince even before he began dying. Sue was tightest with Lenny when he was sick or dead.

Getting deeper into the Bruce Family, you come upon an exotic like Lili Romney, ex-old-lady of the comic Hugh Romney (later known as Wavy Gravy, head of the Hog Farm commune), a very sexy-looking number who moved into Lenny's house in the final year with her child and occupied the upstairs apartment. Lili functioned as Lenny's business manager, cook, and helper. She was a female friend—one of the very, very few in Lenny's long female-crowded life. A great old lady, she was perfect to hang out with and get on with and bullshit with and never get into the sack with. Lenny had so many chicks he could ball that it figures there had to be one who was the Madonna.

The Balling Chicks came pouring onto the premises day by day without solicitation. Brenda Bernstein, as we'll call her, was a chunky Jewish girl from the East Coast, who had flipped out to the West Coast and was eager to make a mark as an actress.

Brenda was about eighteen when she met Lenny. She had grown up in Brooklyn, gotten in trouble, and cut out. While working at the *L.A. Free Press*, she asked for an interview feature and suggested as her first subject Lenny Bruce. "I've been in love with you since I was fifteen," she wrote to Lenny. He responded by telephone and told her to bring along someone who could type. Brenda drove up the hill for the first time with a short-haired, middle-aged lady who was a professional typist. Lenny greeted them with a burst of paranoid fantasy. Taking Brenda into the next room, he whispered that the lady looked like an agent for the CIA. He insisted she leave—at once! Next he retreated to the bathroom and began to interview Brenda through the slot under the door. Eventually, he got into his rap about the courts and the law, all of which Brenda got down on a tape recorder and printed in the *Free Press*. When Lenny finally got straight again, he emerged from the can and eyed Brenda strangely. Suddenly he asked her, "Can I touch your breast?" When she nodded, he extended his hand and muttered—as if he were standing off observing his own actions—"And then he touched her breast."

Brenda stayed for three days on that first interview. She went to bed with Lenny the first night and decided he was a fantastic fuck. The next day she began to get the hang of the house. She watched while Lenny threw cherry pits at Kitty, played hide-and-seek with Lili, and complained about how cheap his mother was. The next time they were in bed, Sally drove up the driveway and started yelling for Lenny. "It's my mother!" he gasped, seizing Brenda, as if he'd been caught in the act. "We've got to be very quiet," he warned. "If she catches us—look out!" Lenny liked to fantasize while he balled.

Soon Brenda was a regular around the house. She got a line on everybody. Honey was "an aging woman with a fantastic figure, dyed red hair and an unwrinkled face—ironing the same pair of curtains for two years." Lili "would walk around in a blue sarong secured by a safety pin." Hugh Romney would come up with "his latest magic object. A butterfly or a model of the universe made of styrofoam balls." Shel Silverstein, the cartoonist, would play with Lenny. Nick, a plumber, hung around. There was also a carpet mechanic. "Any competent act impressed Lenny." Then when he got the impulse to work, "Lenny would put on a babushka and sunglasses and send everybody home."

Another regular at the end was the Usherette. She was nineteen, tall, white-skinned, dark-haired, blue-eyed, with soft dimpled knees. She met Lenny while working at the Cine on Sunset Boulevard. Immediately she assumed a protective and helpmate role, laboring at Lenny's cases, filling Lenny's larder, and driving Lenny to his monthly meetings with the probation officer. Sometimes when she would go off to perform an urgent errand for her lover-boss, she would find at the office, library, or store another of Lenny's girls who had been sent out an hour before to perform the very same errand! As the two girls giggled over Lenny's insecurity, they would be even more amused by the appearance of still another girl charging into the building intent on checking out the previous two and seeing that the vital mission was performed exactly as ordered.

Lenny showed rare genius in getting all his girls to cooperate without visible friction. They all shared an understanding that Lenny was common property, that nobody could possess him completely. If there were wars between them—and there were—they were never shooting wars. Cold wars, wars of bitchiness, were the only struggles that would be tolerated in the House on the Hill. Even the slightest sign of encroachment would be met by Lenny with antagonism. The Usherette, he accused of trying to move in on him. "Every time she comes up here," he would complain, "she leaves something else in the closet. Dresses, shoes, shampoo—she's starting to crowd me!"

Sometimes a couple of girls would show up the same night with the same intention of laying claim to Lenny's body. This required fancy footwork. Lili Romney would have to lend a hand by telling one girl that Lenny was on the phone or sound asleep, while, actually, he was making it with another chick upstairs. Girls would duck out side doors and drive down the driveway lickety-split, while other girls raised eyebrows and asked, "Who is that running out of the house so fast?" Oh, it was touch and go some days up on the hill! Lenny outfoxed them all, though; and he kept them just where he wanted them. Probably the funniest instance of his fought-over status was the night he was sleeping with Sue Horowitz and a girl arrived at the house. Not willing to take no for an answer, the chick went into Lenny's bedroom and roused him from sleep. Hauling him out of bed and carrying him off like a giant teddy bear, she forced him to satisfy her keen desires.

You'd think with all these chicks, Lenny would have enough of women. Balls! He could never get enough nookey. Sometimes he'd wind up in the office at four in the morning. Stretching his body, he'd feel that horny itch. He'd go upstairs and waken Lili Romney: "Don't you know some girl you could call?" Poor Lili would get on the phone and talk to some chick and the moment the girl heard the magic words "Lenny Bruce," her voice would brighten and she'd say she was just getting up. "Hold it—I'll *be* there!"

Lenny had a regular seduction route planned for these newcomers. First, he'd take them to the telescope on the patio—or better still, he'd be discovered there, the lonely romantic stargazer seeking the future among the wheeling constellations. When it turned out this telescope, into which presumably he had been earnestly gazing all night, was not in working order, they would retreat to his hideaway out at the end of the property. Here they would get even tighter. Finally, when the time was ripe, Lenny would bring the girl back to the house, and they would enter the tape room. Here he had a number of harmless little toys that gave him a great deal of pleasure. He could discreetly record the sound of the girl's erotic moans—if she had an interesting vocal quality. Or, if the seduction was made while people were sitting out on the patio, he had a one-way window installed at the head of the bed that enabled him to spy on the visitors at the pool while he enjoyed the sensations of intercourse.

Casual seductions were often the basis for more enduring relationships. Once the young woman had experienced the thrill of that first night—like the knight in the fairy tale charging up the glass cliff toward his sweetheart—and talked the strange enchanted talk that Lenny offered at such moments; once she found him an eager, sensitive, and skillful lover and an affectionate and amusing playmate, she might wake to find the fairy castle blown away. His mind back on business, Lenny would ask the girl the next morning if she could type or file or take dictation. He would try to recruit her for his household staff. He was a very tolerant master, to be sure. He offered his new ladies as many plans as a Swiss hotel keeper. The girl could hang around for a few days and then split. She could go home that day and come back a few days later. She could, if she was really good, have the use of a room in the house when she wanted it, though there was no guarantee that Lenny would share it with her. She might even, if she was a very special favorite, be installed as a regular guest and entrusted with regular duties and allowed to bring up boys—whom Lenny would scrutinize like a jealous paterfamilias!

Back in January 1966, Maury Hayden was a comedienne, a bright, pretty, blond-haired, blue-eyed Jewish lass from Philadelphia, only twenty-one years old. She had gigged around the coffeehouse circuit in the Village; now she was working on the West Coast

doing a singing, dancing, and comedy act with Jimmy Gavin, the original coffeehouse folk singer. Lenny loved Jimmy. We were working at the Troubadour and John Judnich came by. He thought I should listen to some of Lenny's tapes. I was going with Tim Hardin at the time, but I wanted to make an impression on Lenny. [Tim Hardin and Lenny Bruce had met in Greenwich Village in the early sixties at the commencement of Hardin's career. Though he made his name as a star of the folk-rock scene, Hardin regarded himself as basically a jazzman, and that was how Lenny viewed him. Hardin wrote his early albums at Lenny's house, using a piano that Lenny had bought for him out of the proceeds of the Berkeley Concert. The strongest link between the men was their common addiction to heroin, which would have far outweighed any rivalry over a mere chick.] So that day I got dressed in a yellow dotted-Swiss dress (this is important because of what happened later), and my hair was just very Monroe-y and I wore perfume. (I'm a powder-perfume kind of person.)

I was just sitting in his office, listening to the tapes; and all of a sudden, he walked in, in a blue dungaree outfit. I had just been listening to a routine about "Where are all the girls with perfume, powder, and cleavage?" when he walked in and gave me such a look! He told me much later that he went out and said to John, "Is this your girlfriend?" Isn't that ridiculous? Then he came back in and sat down on the bench next to me and said "Listen, the dentist is very broke. He's liable to pull out a couple of teeth that don't have to come out." He just couldn't get over the way I looked because the sun was hitting the blue in my eyes, my blond hair, and my freckles. He kept talking about the way I looked. I was telling him a story, and he was running around so little-boyish. Oh! And Honey was there! She really looked like—at tops!—a stunt woman on a bandstand. He called her "Honey," and I thought it was just an endearing term for a woman. I thought . . . well, you know, she had on a plastic jacket and *whoopie socks*! He came over to me and said, "That's my ex-old-lady, and I don't even know who she is anymore!" There was no reason for him to tell me that.

Then his mother came in. She recognized me as Jimmy's partner, and she was just thrilled. She kept calling me Edie Adams. I was starting to enjoy myself, but all the time it was hanging over my head that I had to go to work. Finally, Kitty came in and everything was just perfect. When they all got out of the office, he said, "May I ever see you again?" I thought, Well, of course! Then I realized that it was important to him because he hadn't had a female who could relate to him on that romantic level. Also, more than that, I knew that it was time for me to talk to him.

So, we were sitting there, and he said, "May I see you or call you or anything?" And I went with the romance because he wanted it so much. He wrote down my number, and we talked and laughed at a lot of things. I had to leave. For some reason—it wasn't conscious calculation—I left my notebook at his house.

I left and I knew he was just overwhelmed with me. I really cared greatly for Tim Hardin. I didn't want to bust that up at all. I loved Tim, and I didn't want to louse up my thing with him. Lenny, though, was an exception. He made me break a basic rule: never invest your affection in more than one thing at a time. Anyway, I had to go back to Lenny's house between shows to pick up my notebook. When I walked into the center room, I ran into John Judnich. "He loves you!"—that's exactly what he said. I flipped. "Oh, that's groovy!" and walked into the office. He had a visitor, but he jumped up and said, "Oh, wow, am I glad to see you!" He wouldn't let go of my hand. It was almost as if I had come to feed him the life force.

He took me for a ride—we drove two miles per hour up around the mountains. He literally begged me to come back that night. I knew that if I came back I would have violated my whole relationship with Timmy. We went all the way up in the mountains. He was driving my car—a VW. He didn't have a license at the time, but he was desperate to be alone with me . . . He said, "Please, please, come back!" I said, "O.K., O.K." So I went and did my set.

When I got back to Lenny's that night, I was upset and uptight. I had had a fight with my manager, Roy. He's one of those types whose finger is always pointing to his cock. For two years he had been trying to tell me how to perform and what to say onstage. Now one thing I have is total integrity in terms of who I am. For me to repeat the same steps for the same people was more than I could ever do. I didn't care if I didn't get a laugh so long as people dug me for what I am. Roy, though, was always threatening me. So I started pouring out my troubles to Lenny. I was doing the tragic heroine thing, and Lenny said, "Boy, I'll bet you're the greatest actress in the world!" I wanted to relate to him in a more natural way but I was so upset after that quarrel. After an hour or so, I finally calmed down. Everything became incredibly beautiful. He just held my hands and said that I was the loveliest girl. I know he was extremely complimentary to everyone. That was what was so beautiful about him. I just loved to watch him relate to people because he had the capacity to make everyone feel like they were the most important person in the world. That whole night was truly beautiful and lovely. I slept with him. For me, it was the first time in my life. (I'd only made love with two men before.) He said to me, "Either you've only been with one man or you've had thirty men a week."

The next morning we had a lot of fun up at the house. Everything was funny and I made him laugh. The thing is that I was the first girl in his life—and the only girl—who gave him more energy than he gave her. His whole life, he did all the giving. When I met him, he was tired. He was really lonely. I was able to feed him. I kept his head going. The Methedrine only brought him to the point where he could receive my energy. He needed the Meth to start even. It was truly a chemical, physical, thing that he had to have. Lots of times when he dropped pills, it was just like eating. He wasn't looking to get any flashes or buzzes from it. He just wanted to be up to his brain. He just wanted his body to be able to keep up with what he knew he had to accomplish. He had to become Lenny to become a receptacle for me.

When I got home that day, I found a note from Tim. At first I promised never to see Lenny again. Then I broke the promise. It was a difficult situation. I had no illusions about Lenny. There were always going to be other chicks. There was this other girl. He said I was the only girl he had ever loved not for what I could do for him but just for what I was. Sue Horowitz, for example, was a good typist . . . The truth is that at the end, he didn't want those other girls—he wanted me.

Why was he so crazy about me? First of all, I don't think he had ever met a Jewish girl who looked so blond and white as me. He liked the shiksa look but he respected Jewish women. He told me, "I would never marry anybody but a Jewish person." Of course, he didn't mean someone like Sue Horowitz. What is Jewish about Sue Horowitz and many other Jewish women is that they are crisis-makers. They cause crises from day to day because they only operate on high-frequency levels. If nothing is left to discover about them, they cause a crisis so they can run away. Everything has to be on a very high emotional level, or it appears to the woman as being boredom. But I am not that way. Starting in March I was with him every day. He could see how different I was. He couldn't believe it. He kept teasing me, insisting I was really a goy. When I brought back New England clam chowder instead of New York clam chowder, he was sure that I wasn't Jewish. Yet I lived for a year in Israel and he loved that. I had the same Jewishness that he had. Lenny really thought that I was he in a girl's body. He thought that we had both transcended the stereotypes.

The proof of how much he loved me is that he asked me to marry him. It happened on July 9th, a Sunday [actually, a Saturday]. At that time I was extremely tanned. I was like black, and he got me these two little slips, which were very Italian—a pink one and a black one. I was very thin, very slight and I was wearing the pink one while I made him breakfast. I had a lot of hair and that day I had rubies in it. He turned around and he said to me . . . but first I have to explain that the night before, he was jealous of Tim Hardin. There were many reasons. It wasn't just that Timmy was young [twenty-five], vital and had a future . . . majorly it was because he knew that I had really dug Timmy for a long time. Now the night before, I had gone to a party with my manager, and when I came back, I was sitting around kind of restless. I had the attitude (I never usually got that way) of, like, Julie Christie in *Darling*. I called my friend Cathy, who had just gotten back from England, and she told me that she had met the Beatles and I ought to come over there because the Beatles and Peter Fonda were still there. I came back about two hours later, and Lenny said, "I was so afraid you wouldn't come back, so afraid!" He just held on to me.

Timmy was in the other room. He was always milling about. I must tell you that Lenny did not like Timmy. Lenny said something teasing, like, "You still love Timmy. If I ever catch you in a bar with him, I'll kill you!" Then he threw all his paperwork away, and we went upstairs and just held each other. "I really love you so much," he said. I was afraid to say anything because Lenny said "I love you" to so many people. But it did remind me of how he had taken me to meet his father just a couple of weeks prior to this, and how he told me that I was the first girl his father had liked. His father told me that day that if I married Lenny, he would die peacefully. It was simply because I was Jewish, clean-looking, and healthy. Lenny's father told me that Lenny said he really loved me but he didn't know what to do because I was only twenty-three. I had never really thought about marriage with Lenny. That day I was busy digging the connection between Lenny and his father.

His father was more of Lenny's conscience than anything else. His father was the duality in Lenny—the conflict. He was the place where Lenny started out from to get his comedy. The father was an overly opinionated man, overly-educated, living in Pasadena in a white picket-fence house with curios on each shelf. His father practically has a British accent. He was British-born, but it's an affectation all the same. He called me Marlene, my real name. Later, I spent the weekend at his father's house. He told me that once when they were keeping Kitty, Honey came to pick up the child with a black, black Negro. "You get away from here, you slut! Take that bum with you!" That was how he talked to her. Lenny couldn't bear to think there was any difference between black people and white. I told him, "Lenny, to deny the fact that they look and smell differently is denying their equality." He got so uptight about it. Two weeks later, he said to me, "You're absolutely right. I'm the one who's hung up about it. You're not." He said that the thing that really killed him was the time he saw Honey with a Negro. So, he wasn't so terribly different from his father.

. . . Just before he proposed marriage I had told him: "Don't say that you love me only, nobody can vouch for themselves." He said, "I just have to keep saying it, I just have to tell you, I have to tell you I love you. I cannot not tell you now." Then he started that business about how he didn't love me for what I could do for him. I told him, "There's lots I can do for you." He said, "No, I just love you, and I never thought I could love again. I never even loved Honey." I said, "Don't say that! People always have to destroy one thing to make another thing." He said, "It's just what I made of her. I didn't even know before I went to Europe. It was my fantasy." I said, "But it was her that lent herself to your fantasy—it's always that."

The next day he said, "I love you so deeply but I'm afraid to tell you that because I'm so promiscuous." Then he said—these are the exact words—"I don't want to fuck anyone else." That really bothered me. I said, "Please, honey, don't say that because if you do, then you're going to put up a promise. And promises are only an extraction of tomorrow. If you're going to make a promise, you're going to violate it. You'll feel so guilty, you aren't going to love me for it." The next morning, he woke up and in front of his mother he actually said, "I'm not going to fuck anyone else. I don't want anyone else."

Now, getting back to that Sunday morning, when I was walking around in my little slip: he said if he'd been the delivery boy and he came to the house, he would go in the bathroom and jerk off. He asked me to marry him right after he told me about the delivery boy. We were reading the stock-market page. I knew more about it than he did because my father taught me a little. I said, "You don't know what we're reading. You think these are tiny sentences." He thought that was the best joke he'd ever heard. He kept laughing, and then he said—"Will you marry me?" I said, "Oh, yes." It was right.

Timmy Hardin was there that day, and he came upstairs twenty minutes later. Lenny told him. "Oh!" he said and walked out. John Judnich said, "Congratulations." Sue Horowitz came over that night because he told her she looked lovely on Friday. She had a tan and her hair was—she had a fall on—and she looked as clean as she ever looked. He always thought she looked dirty. So she thought she'd come back that Sunday night. I was in the office with them. He said, "Maury and I are getting married." She said, "Congratulations" too fast and left very quickly.

After Sue left, he started to cry, saying, "You're getting such a lousy deal. I'm getting the most beautiful girl in the world. I can't imagine why everyone in the world wouldn't be in love with you. And all you're getting is a jailbird. The newspaper headlines will be: "DAUGHTER OF WOODEN KIMONO WEDS JAILBIRD." (He always called me Daughter of Wooden Kimono because my mother was a singer and her theme song was a thing called "Wooden Kimono.")

The day after he asked me to marry him, he told me a story. He said, "When you're sleeping, I steal your dresses and I take them to a seamstress and she makes them into full-length gowns of white kidskin." (You could feel the material the way he described it.) "And you're always being bathed by fifteen handmaidens." A couple days later, I bought the groceries. He called the store and made them come and take everything back. I was his princess, and he wouldn't take anything from me.

Sometimes he would say, "Honey's coming over," and I would split. What I had with Lenny, I knew nobody else in the world could threaten it. One day I came back, and Honey had been there earlier. He said, "You're gorgeous. You really make me hate Honey. She's such an apple dumb girl, I'm so embarrassed to talk to her. I can't believe it that I was ever with her." When he first met me, he was really embarrassed about Honey. Embarrassed that she was there. She kept saying dumb things. She was very stupid, I thought, or very weird. Honey's not bright—she's shrewd. There's a difference.

Originally, the thing he loved about me the most was my talent. He thought I was the only funny girl he ever knew. I played some of the tunes I'd written for him. I read my poetry. I was playing the guitar and singing some Hebrew tunes for Kitty, and he came out of the shower in Kitty's room and said, "Wow! You're the only talent left!" He looked up the word in the thesaurus for the "world's greatest entertainer."

The grooviest thing he ever said to me was: "You're the smartest girl I ever met." I actually fell off the chair. "Oh," I said, "don't say that if you don't mean it, please!" I just couldn't recover.

The Monday morning after the Sunday when he asked me to marry him, he said, "I can't wait—let's get married Wednesday." I got very uptight. I wanted a baby. He said, "I don't need my mother anymore." Actually, Sally and Kitty had moved into the house just two days before me. Yet I was very insecure. I worried because I didn't know how to cook. He was on a rice diet. His mother used to say to me, "When Lenny meets somebody he really loves, he'll lose weight." So one day, he went on an organic rice diet—right around the time he asked me to marry him. When everyone left, I cooked kasha for him, and I put too much salt in. He took one bite and said, "This must be what it's like when people are drowning."

Even love, true love, couldn't deflect Lenny from his legal obsessions. But he was coming to the end of that road. FINAL PERFORMANCE IN AMERICA!—that's what the court docket should have read on April 18, 1966, at Los Angeles Municipal Court where Lenny was to be finally sentenced for his narcotics violation.

Nearly three years had elapsed since he had been convicted of throwing a matchbook full of heroin into the gutter in front of a TV store in West Hollywood. All through those years, he had insisted that he was framed. Even to the cats he knew best, he insisted there was no way the fuzz could have found the shit he ditched. That was not an issue. The point was—*he had never been caught with the stuff!* Dig it! The cops knew he was a junkie; hence they had no moral reluctance about planting the stuff on him. That was Lenny's Big Lie. The fantasy to which he clung through all those years of litigation.

Facing sentencing by Judge Benjamin Landis (whom he had been barraging through this whole period with letters bitterly protesting his conviction), Lenny knew that acquittal was unlikely. Before they got into court that day, Sydney Irmas warned that there was a distinct possibility Lenny would be sent to the state penitentiary or at least receive a term in the county jail. At the same time, he assured Lenny—for whatever the hell it was worth—that the conviction was an "illegal" judgment that would ultimately be set aside by an appeals court reviewing the very same evidence offered to the sentencing tribunal.

Irmas was a man to believe. Just ten weeks before, on January 31st, he had succeeded finally in having Lenny's Department 95 commitment order rescinded. Appealing Lenny's case to the State Supreme Court, he had gotten a unanimous reversal of the earlier Los Angeles Superior Court decision. This action by the State Supreme Court would certainly affect the sentence that Landis would now deliver by disposing the judge to leniency. The important thing, Irmas whispered to Lenny, was to remain calm and leave the pleading to him.

If Irmas had known Lenny a little better, he would have realized that his client was like a bomb set to explode. But the Lenny that Irmas knew was an impostor, who showed up regularly at the attorney's upper-middle-class Jewish home, where he behaved like the misunderstood little Jewish genius. Normally, Lenny would sooner starve than sit down to a family dinner table; yet he sat down as often as twice a week with the Irmases because he considered it absolutely vital to put this daddy away. Though he always called himself the world's worst father and lived up to his reputation by ignoring for long periods his beautiful and charming daughter, he made damn well sure when he went to Sydney Irmas's house that he paid a lot of attention to the kids, especially the little one, who at nine was exactly the age of Kitty. Eventually he persuaded Irmas that he was "a person who, in my opinion, was diametrically opposed to the reputation that he had garnered, at least among the public officials that he took on regularly. . . . He was very quiet and a person who loved kids. He would come over and spend as much time with them as with me."

Under the pressure of his imminent sentencing, Lenny had gone back to heroin. That morning when he walked into court, he was probably stoned on Methedrine and skag. For weeks he had been working around the clock preparing for this appearance, living virtually incommunicado. Just three days before, his closest friends had tried to use John Judnich's thirty-second birthday as a device to lure Lenny out of his office. They had prepared a meal and were lighting the candles on the birthday cake when they came to the door of the office and begged him to join them for an hour. Lenny refused. Disgustedly, Sue Horowitz threw some food on a plate, as you would for a dog, and brought it down to the office. "You're just like an animal," she fumed when Lenny admitted her. "Soon, nobody's even going to come in and hand it to you. There's going to be a little gate on the bottom of the door, and they're going to slip the food through underneath!" Lenny laughed and turned back to his briefs.

With a rap of the gavel, Judge Landis walked into Hearing Room 201, took a seat on the bench, and arranged the legal documents before him. He had already read a supplemental probation report issued on April 12th that stated that Lenny was considered to possess "unusual talents" and that he gave every impression of being an "extremely intelligent person." The report noted also that he realized the seriousness of the charges against him and appeared to be sincere. The investigator suggested a probationary program for Lenny, advising the court at the same time to strongly admonish him, "so as to add to the shock value of these proceedings and bring home to him that conduct of this nature will not be tolerated from him." He also proposed that Lenny be required to pay a substantial fine.

Seated next to Irmas at the witness table, Lenny studied a typewritten statement he had prepared, as well as the transcripts of the most recent developments in his case. On March 25th, Irmas had filed a Declaration and Notice for a new trial in which he observed that because Officer White was involved with a narcotics addict, his testimony could not be believed. The declaration alleged that White had perjured himself on the stand; therefore, the document noted, Lenny should be allowed a new trial on the basis that facts that were not and could not have been reasonably discovered by the defendant either before or during the trial had since emerged.

Irmas amplified this argument as he stood before Judge Landis. "I think that the only fair thing to do in this case is to grant a new trial, let the People put on their case with the facts as they exist, let Sergeant White take the stand," he urged the court. "[If] my eight-year-old son [tried] the case, this man would be acquitted."

Landis denied the motion for a new trial. Irmas next moved for a continuance. Again, he was denied.

Following the course of the hearing closely, Lenny could already foresee a bad outcome. He envisioned himself again being muzzled.

"I just want to speak," he shouted, interrupting the proceedings as he jumped to his feet. Whether the judge liked it or not, he was going to have his day in court. Lenny refused to go down without

fighting. Permission was granted for him to speak to his attorney privately.

When he returned to the courtroom, Irmas announced that Lenny felt his civil liberties would be best protected if he were allowed to make a statement of several minutes' duration to the court. Judge Landis agreed to this unusual procedure.

Standing in front of the bench, clutching a sheaf of typewritten pages, Lenny looked like a pariah. The sixty pounds he had gained in the past six months had ballooned his once-slender torso to an incredible 225 pounds. His obesity was compounded by a terrible shortness of breath and crookedness of posture. His bearded face was set off by ugly black circles framing his exhausted, bloodshot eyes. He was in his latest combination: suede desert boots, white jeans, and a black car coat. He could have been on the stage of Basin Street West as he paced the courtroom, pleading for a stay of judgment in order to obtain federal injunctive relief. He claimed that he had been deprived of his just rights as the result of unconstitutional applications of state statutes. His lengthy speech cited obscure laws, cases, and acts of Congress, which he read excitedly from the papers laid out before him.

At various intervals, Landis attempted to interrupt Lenny, who would not be stopped. He continued to read from his prepared statement as well as speak extemporaneously. He threatened to file a complaint in the federal court for an injunction against the operation, execution, and enforcement of Section 11500, California Health and Safety Code (the narcotics-violation section) on the grounds of unconstitutionality.

Landis tried to explain to him that such a motion, whatever its merits, should be made in a federal district court, not in the jurisdiction under which he currently found himself. But Lenny continued to babble on, ignoring the judge's remarks.

"Mr. Bruce," Landis finally said, "the court does not wish to be disrespectful, but the court insists that all this material you have just enunciated is absolutely immaterial and this isn't a proper place to make this motion."

Lenny still insisted on being allowed to finish his statement, merely to have it read into the record so that a future appellate court would have the opportunity of reading it. Landis reminded him that if he filed a written copy of what he was reading it would appear in the final transcript as a matter of course.

"It is not [protected] if I haven't got it in the record," Lenny snapped, revealing his ignorance of the law in this basic procedural matter.

The petty wrangling continued as Landis again reminded him that he could put it in the record merely by filing a written copy.

"I could already have been finished reading it by now," Lenny complained.

"Mr. Bruce," Landis coldly replied, "you are not running this courtroom. I want to be respectful, and you have certain rights and I certainly don't want your rights violated. But I say to you: *you are utterly unreasonable!*"

"But I've got only three more paragraphs left," Lenny insisted, waving the typewritten pages in the air. Landis examined the paragraphs, ruled they were too long, and indicated he would not permit Lenny to read any further.

"May I read one paragraph?" he persisted, trying to bargain.

"You may not," Landis said with finality. "You have read enough. Now, you will stand up and be sentenced and the court admonishes you to keep quiet while court makes his observations."

Grudgingly, Lenny shambled forward from the witness table and stood before the black-robed judge whom he had unsuccessfully attempted to manipulate.

"Throughout the course of this trial," Landis began, taking the opportunity to castigate the witness, "you have taken great pains to manifest your contempt for the administration of justice in general, and for this court in particular. You have conducted yourself with obvious disrespect for the law. In your arrogance, you hold yourself superior to the society which has exposed you to this unfortunate experience." Irmas fidgeted in his seat. Landis continued, measuring his words:

But you are not charged with being in contempt of this court, or being disrespectful of the law, or of being supercilious. If I considered your personal attitudes in pronouncing sentence, I would be demeaning both myself and the law. My high regard for the law precludes me from taking such irrelevant factors into consideration in imposing sentence. I believe the law is the most stabilizing influence to a well-ordered society. Without it, we would have anarchy running rampant.

Your contempt for the law really reflects your contempt for yourself. Your bravado and your manifestation of heroics are nothing more than an ill-concealed attempt to exalt your own ego.

I have carefully reviewed the record in this case. I find that your conviction is due, in part, to the testimony of narcotics agents who themselves have been convicted of narcotics violations. I find also that this is your first offense. . . . These are mitigating elements. The record, in my opinion, does not warrant imprisonment.

It may be that your conflict is not with society, but with yourself. I believe you have a spark of talent in the field of your endeavor. If you resolve these conflicts, if you are given the opportunity, you may yet ignite this spark of talent into the flame of genius. I fervently hope so.

Then, to virtually everyone's surprise, Landis did little more than slap Lenny's wrist. He sentenced him to a one-year suspended jail term, fined him $260, and placed him on probation for a period of two years. The terms of his probation called for him to avoid the use or possession of any narcotics or narcotics paraphernalia, to stay away from places where addicts congregate, and to refrain from associating with known narcotics users or sellers. Furthermore, Lenny was required to remain in Los Angeles County, unless permitted by the court or by a probation officer to journey elsewhere.

In effect, Lenny had beaten the most dangerous rap still outstanding against him. Irmas later described the lenient sentencing as "an act of Christian charity." But the outcome of his most threatening trial did not satisfy Lenny Bruce. Speaking to reporters afterward, he still maintained his innocence and insisted that he had been victimized by "illegal search and seizure."

"I'm going to pursue this federal action and try to establish my civil rights," he promised. "Violations of civil rights are questions of equity. It has nothing to do with 'mercy' or with 'charity.' There are those who compare me with Kafka. But the difference is—he was in Russia and there's no constitution there."

Despite Irmas's immediate assurance that a conviction would ultimately be reversed by a higher court and that he would have no difficulty in having a new trial ordered, nothing he could say made Lenny feel other than a loser. He was after something far greater than victory in court. Getting off "light," with the judge treating him like a gifted neurotic, was not at all the sort of treatment he desired to promote his new image as a national civil rights hero.

Actually, the greatest problem that Lenny Bruce faced at the end of his life was the fairness of the American judicial system. The more he fought and protested and raised hell in the courts, the more the courts backed down and said, "O.K. You got a point. We want to be fair. Go ahead and try it again!" By the summer of 1966, Lenny was virtually in the clear so far as legal claims against him were concerned. He had beaten all his obscenity raps, except for the one in New York, which he refused to appeal in the proper form. (Howard Solomon, his co-defendant, *did* appeal, and eventually was exonerated—as Lenny would have been if he had simply taken the advice of his lawyer.) The whole drift of the Supreme Court in this period was so favorable to material like Lenny Bruce's that there is no question that if he had wanted to go back on the stage, he could soon have found ample opportunities to do so without the threats and harassments of the past. He would have had to use judgment and caution because, even today, the performer whose medium is himself is still the least protected artist in America. The land of free speech doesn't like people who are too free with their speech. Yet with the highest court constantly liberalizing the law, with public opinion setting in strongly against persecutions such as Lenny was subjected to, an artist of his caliber, working in conjunction with a legal mind of the resourcefulness of Sydney Irmas's, would have eventually found a way out of his dilemma. The problem was simply *Lenny*—who clasped the asp of persecution to his bosom and would not let go of it, even when its sting proved less than fatal.

He began to sink. Everyone who saw him during the fatal summer of '66 recalls how depressed and unresponsive he had become. He still maintained the outer semblance of his life, playing one last pair of dates at the Fillmore West—and almost driving Bill Graham to may-hem. He still got on the phone to New York and gave Judy Peabody dictation at five dollars a minute at 3 A.M. You could figure him to turn up at least once a week at Phil Spector's office on the Strip with a load of stuff to be Xeroxed, typed, and processed by the office staff. His routine with the chicks who came up to the house was, if anything, smoother than before. He had it down now to a fast one, two, three. He was the same old Lenny, right up to the end. But he was kaput.

The core of whatever made this human atom pile smolder wasn't cooking anymore. He was all bottled out. When faithful John would talk to him, Lenny would tell him the same shit he had told him the year before. He was still saying, "I got 'em! I got 'em!" But he couldn't get anything new. He was going around in circles. He was starting to drift into the past. He was back on heroin.

Honey was living at this time in Watts. Lenny always associated her with shit. Yet she had her scruples about going up on the hill with anything bad. She could be followed and nailed in the pad of a very notorious cat. So when Lenny would detect that she was high and ask for a little taste, Honey would say: "No! If you want it, get it someplace else. I don't want to be responsible."

One day, when Lenny scored through some couple that had come down to visit him from San Francisco, Honey recalls:

Lenny and I messed around for a while upstairs with them. Then we left them upstairs and we went downstairs. And I fixed again in the bathroom. And then Lenny was trying to fix, and he couldn't get a hit and it was taking so long, I left the bathroom. I went in the office and started messing around with the typewriter. He was in there an awful long time in the bathroom. So I went in to check him. He'd fixed and he was blue! Nodded out! So I got some ice cubes and put 'em down on his, ya know—prick. Tried to revive him. Put cold water on him. And then I had to yell upstairs to the other people! They came down. And he was too heavy for me to lift, he was too big! And we walked him around the pool for a long time and made him drink coffee. And somebody had some bennies, and I got some bennies down him with more coffee. And he finally came to. When he came to himself, he wanted to fix again. I told him I was gonna split, and that he's in no condition. I told him his health isn't the same. It isn't! I wasn't gonna 'cause he couldn't take it. He didn't do that much stuff! I told him, I wasn't gonna be up there with him *purple*! I said he came close to dying! And he said, he could handle it. He could shoot more stuff than me any day! And all this kind of stuff. I got kind of upset. I told him to stick with his speed. That I didn't want to be involved with him using stuff. That he wasn't strong enough. And I split!

At the end Lenny had all these morbid throw-away lines. "When I'm dead," he'd preface, or "After I'm gone." He was always alluding to death or talking about death or trying to feel his way over to the other side of the line. He had been getting into this death obsession ever since he went out that window in San Francisco. That event shook Lenny. It also branded a permanent mark upon his flesh. He was in such a hurry to cut the casts off his legs that he fucked up the whole healing process. John and Honey both remember how he went crazy one day and insisted that they bring him the tools to cut the plaster off his body.

"Lenny, don't you think you should wait?"

"Why? My legs are all right. I've got to get the casts off so they'll heal!"

An hour of pounding, sawing, chiseling, and prying with two pair of pliers and afterward, one leg was much smaller around and horribly discolored. John and Honey could see that it had been much too early to remove the casts.

"That's all right. It'll heal!" Lenny said, staring down at the mangled flesh before him. "It feels good to get the motherfuckers off!"

The left leg never did heal right. From the ankle to just above the knee it was always much smaller than the other leg. The ankle was grotesquely oversized, larger even than the calf of the leg. And the natural flesh tone never came back. It always remained a purplish-gray color. The color of a corpse.

Some time during that summer, a strange book turned up at the house. Nobody ever was able to figure where it came from. It was just the sort of volume that would appeal to a lot of spaced-out cats sitting way up high on top of Hollywood. The title was *The Road to Immortality: Being a Description of the Life Hereafter, with Evidence of the Survival of Human Personality*. A classic piece of spiritualism, the book records the trance writing of a minor Irish playwright, Geraldine Cummins. No less than fifty personalities voiced themselves through Miss Cummins's automatic writing. The most interesting of the lot was F. W. H. Myers, an English poet and essayist, who became a classical lecturer at Trinity College, Cambridge, in 1865 and who founded in 1882, with a number of other men of letters, the Society for Psychical Research. Myers died in January of 1901. Late in 1924, he suddenly broke into the consciousness of Geraldine Cummins while she was working with another woman by announcing his name and saying, "Good evening, ladies." During three successive visits in the years 1924–1925, 1927, and 1931, Miss Cummins transcribed Myers's voice in "scripts" that eventually extended to the length of 191 pages.

The Road to Immortality became Lenny's favorite book during his declining months. He was having a lot of pain that summer in his chest and back. Instead of going over to Dr. Romm and checking it out, he preferred to get high and loll on his bed with the light of the setting sun coming through the stained-glass cathedral panels that had been inserted in his bedroom windows, while listening to some chick like Sue Horowitz reading in a low soothing voice the words of the nineteenth-century English professor discoursing about the life after death. Lenny had one favorite passage which always made him exclaim with delight and wonder. Headed "Violent Death," its music sounded like this:

Sometimes the dead do not know that they are dead. This statement may seem incredible. Yet it is true in certain fairly rare cases.

Only the past history of the dead man can make clear this curious lack of apprehension of his state. If he passes through the gates of death bearing with him a passionate love of material possessions, he will, even after a fleeting glimpse of his discarnate kindred, tenaciously hold to the belief that he is still a man of flesh and blood, wandering, perhaps, on the hills in a mist, but still filled with the life of earth. He will passionately seek for his house, his money or whatever is his particular treasure, in the dark ways beyond death.

There are also certain others who linger thus in Hades, but not unhappily as a rule. I refer to certain young men of careless, animal and, occasionally, vicious life who die violent deaths. These poor fellows are suddenly wrenched from their bodies while still they are in the prime of manhood. They are not, in any sense, capable of grasping, for a while, the difference between earth life and the Afterlife. So they, too, remain in ignorance, and must remain in a kind of coma until the delicate etheric body had recovered from the shock of a too rapid severance from the earthly shape.

Twelve days before Lenny died, on Friday, July 22nd, he decided to slip over to the other side and see for himself what it would be like to be dead. His Golden Bough, his passport of safe passage and return, was a little tab of acid. Maury Hayden witnessed the trip.

He was giving himself a test, trying to anticipate his own death. It was purely an intellectual thing. What happened to Lenny on acid is what happens to me on marijuana: he would get to the point where he thought he was dying. I didn't understand all this the day he took the acid. All I knew was that I was talking with him and suddenly he was acting queer. I had just gotten a lead on a TV series. It was not a permanent thing, but they were going to rewrite the girl to come back seven times in the last thirteen shows of *Hey, Landlord*. I was pretending to be elated about it, but those things didn't mean anything to me at the time. In order to make death a truly comfortable thing for him, it had to be comfortable to me, too.

I just couldn't get through to him. So I said, "I don't know about tomorrow, but fuck you tonight, Lenny!" And I left.

By the time Maury got off the hill, Lenny Bruce was intensely alone. He was voyaging out toward the other world in that strange state of detachment that marks the mood of the acid tripper. Lenny was an anxious and guilty soul. His trip could not have been pleasant. When, the year before, he had taken off from a hill in the desert with Markland and Judnich, he had sung like a rabbi, *"Sh'ma Yisrael!"* Then he had solemnly implored them to wrap him up in a sheet like a corpse in its shroud. Death and rebirth. Dissolution and reconstitution. The familiar circuit of the acid trip.

While he was way out there, way up there on that sublimely isolated pinnacle of illumination, what could he have foreseen of the life after death? Did he picture the vague but comforting universe of emanations and shadows and "envelopes" pictured in *The Road to Immortality*? Or could he have caught a glimpse of his posthumous fame on earth? Lenny rarely speculated about what would happen after he was gone. About the most he ever said was a remark bitterly recollected by John: "Man, if anything ever happens to me, you're gonna see some vultures comin' down on this place. And the biggest vulture of all will be Sally. She'll come in here with *ten fingers on each hand*!" (John had that truth driven hard into his brain in the days following Lenny's death when Sally and her cronies swept through the house like a cyclone, sucking up everything that was loose and even digging the rose bushes out of the garden.)

What Lenny knew at the end—and for many years prior to his death—was that he was in the grip of something much bigger than himself. He was the hero of a myth not of his own making. He was simply its latest embodiment. Just as there were many hanged gods before Christ, there were many brilliantly inspired and desperately self-destructive heroes in the cult of the American Underground. Once Lenny committed himself to the jazz life, to the jazz myth, he was destined to the doom that awaits all such cometlike figures flashing across the American night. He never withheld himself from his fate. Never sought to deflect his destiny. He knew he was doomed as well as he knew his name. That was why he scoffed at the sentimentality of those who mourned a man like Joe Maini. Joe had died as Joe had lived. His whole existence was a game of Russian roulette. Lenny's life was no different.

What happens to the underground hero after he dies? He lies for a number of years in the cold, dark earth of oblivion. Then his cult begins to resurrect him. Men write articles and legends accumulate. Old records and tapes are dug out and played with devotional intensity. The reputation that may have been tarnished and tired at the time of death springs up with a vigor that no living artist can rival. Lenny had seen it happen with many men. He must have known that it would happen with him, but he could not have known the precise character of his own resurrection. Hip that alive he was a problem and dead he was a property, he wasn't hip to the strange ancestor worship of the youth generation.

He could never have foreseen that a casual photograph of him taken a couple of months before his death—a picture of him with his face ringed by a saintly beard and his eyes focused far off like a gazer at other worlds—would do more to assure his fame than all his thousands of hours on the stage, his hundreds of hours in court, his wild, crazy fabulous life. That little picture, blown up into a poster and stapled up in head shops from coast to coast was the beginning of the whole Lenny Bruce cult among modern youth.

Reduced again to the size of a paperback and stamped on the cover of a volume titled *The Essential Lenny Bruce,* that same picture helped to carry Lenny into thousands of pads and dorms and hangouts where he could never have penetrated by means of his own efforts, either live or on records. The real Lenny Bruce was a performer far beyond the modest capacities of the rock generation. His fast hipster delivery, his inside-dopester frame of reference, his essentially comic view of everything, including himself, precludes now, as it did when he died, any true and immediate appreciation of his art by boys and girls who grew up literally in another world. Lenny was perfectly right when he said he couldn't communicate with today's youth. But when his coruscating verbal solos are slowed down to the speed of a newspaper reader, when his ideas are chopped up into neat little categories like "Blacks," "Jews," and "Politics," and his whole character is transformed from that of the ultimate stand-up comic to that of the "tell-it-as-it-is" rapper and philosopher and hippie bullshit artist, Lenny Bruce suddenly becomes a lot more accessible to the socially critical and morally estranged youth generation.

If Lenny was made available to the kids in a paperback primer, he was delivered to their middle-class, middle-aged parents through a trashy, thrown-together musical comedy, *Lenny.* Not about Lenny Bruce but about what certain scheming operators assumed that the theater-party public believed Lenny was about, the show was a wretched travesty. Nor was it any better as a film starring Dustin Hoffman, who sentimentalized the hero to a putz.

The morning after Lenny's acid trip, Maury returned.

When he saw me, he threw his arms around me and said, "Oh, God! I've called you and called you! I love you! Oh God! I've hurt you so!" I looked out on the lights of Hollywood, and all I could see was a little glowing. I hated Lenny because he had died. To me he was already dead. I loved him and I felt sorry for him and I wanted to put my arms around him—but he had died. And I refused to become Honey to him. That's what he wanted me to do—to punish him. I told him that I didn't trust him anymore.

The next thing I knew we were in John's room. He was sitting on the rug, shooting up with some Meth. "What are you doing?" I said. "I'm hurting myself," he said, "because of what I did to you." Then he ran into the other room and threw up. When he came back, he picked up the bloody needle and told me to wash it out. I was still on acid, so I got so involved with playing with the blood. I didn't realize you could get a serious disease from a dirty needle. John came in and said, "Hey, baby, what are you doing?" He took the needle away from me.

Lili and I finally went to the beach, because that was the only permanent thing to look at, the ocean. I came back and as I walked in I heard Lenny ask John, "How 'bout that record I did with Phil Spector—is there anything going to happen with it?" "I'm sorry," said John, "the heat's too much on it." Lenny looked so dead, my heart died.

Then he went upstairs and made salami, spaghetti, frozen peas—all mixed together. I got nauseous and couldn't eat. He was hurt because he didn't cook for everyone. Then he kept trying to make jokes as to how he wasn't afraid to walk on shaky ground. I started to laugh at this tactic. Finally, he started begging me to go to bed with him. I decided to go back to my manager's. I got outside the house, and suddenly, I thought, "Fuck you, Maury! Forget yourself for a second! This is the most incredible crisis in the most important person's life you'll ever know. Go back and make it comfortable for him." I did. He and Lili and I slept together. Lili was completely asexual towards him—he never screwed her. That's why they were such good friends. Lili really loved me that night. I slept in between the two of them.

He wanted to make love to me, and I hated him for that because he really wasn't in his body. He said, "What are you feeling sorry for an old bum for?" He just wouldn't leave me alone. So I got out of bed and went into the other room because it was too crowded. He kept saying, "I love you. I'll do anything you want. I'll get on my knees." I said, "Don't you give that to me!" He wanted me to be Honey. . . . He wanted me to make him beg . . . to have him the way Honey had him was to have him not as a man but as a midget!

The Saturday before he died, Lenny taped a long funny bit as a radio commentator:

[Obscure voice sounds. Moans, groans. Radio voice-over] I'd like to tell you something about the personality of Alfred Hitchcock. He's a very vicious person and I worked with him on three series. Everybody will tell you he takes great delight spitting in your face. I'm seriously thinking of bringing charges against him. Actually, what he does when he does that—when he lowers his lip down and all that—well, when the camera cuts, he is known to have spit right in the director's face. A real hawker. Hhhhhhhhwwwwwwkkk! It's not funny at all. It's not funny and it's not nice. It's unkind. And just because he is Alfred Hitchcock, and just because he's who he is, you know, it doesn't buy him a goddamned cup of coffee in the Automat. Because anyone who would spit in someone's face, it's a cheap way of getting a laugh. And there's absolutely no excuse for it. Whatever pleasure he gets from it is not funny. And a joke is a joke, but that's just not humorous. He's a very unkind person and has hurt a lot of people—hurt their eyes especially. So . . . .

And while we're on the subject of stars, I'd like to give information, a seldom known fact—but important to the Christian people living out there—that Tony Curtis is in shock now. Are you ready now for a flash? His name is really Bernie Schwartz. I want to repeat that, too. Bernie, B-e-r-n-i-e S-c-h-w-a-r-t-z. Schwartz! He is obviously not a Curtis. A Curtis is never a Schwartz. A comedy team. Curtis and Schwartz—seen on the Louis Lomax Dinner Hour. February 17th, we're having Louis on our show, and we're going to pull his pants down and embarrass him and make him show his nana and everything—because he's very proper. Among other things on the agenda will be the f-u, you know, c- . . . I can't say the whole word.

That same Saturday night, Lenny manifested himself to Maury as a ghost.

We walked around the pool with our arms around each other. He looked in the window of his office, where a little light was burning. "That's where the man used to do his work," he said. Then he said, "Stay inside there and come out when I tell you to." He was wearing his white trousers and a heavy beard. He put himself right under the pool light coming down from the balcony. Then he called for me. When I came out, he looked like a spook. It was a misty night and all you could see in the light was a beard and white trousers. Like a statue with a halo.

The last Sunday on the hill was like a family reunion. Sally, Kitty, and Sue came in from the beach, all tanned and chattering gaily. Maury was on hand, as usual. Lenny was not feeling well, complaining of the pain in his chest. He was dressed in a shirt and slacks for a change— but he looked terrible. He and Sue got into a long rap because they hadn't seen each other for a week. At that time Sue had had her hair done and she looked great. So she called Lenny and said, "Do you have a camera?" When he came back from looking and said, "Yeah," she said, "Would you like to take some pictures of me?" Lenny started to laugh. Then he said, "Oh, God, I'm so tired. I just really don't want to do anything." Then, not wanting to seem harsh, he said, "What are you doing?" and invited her to the house. When she arrived, she found Lenny lying down. He was sick and he couldn't breathe. She asked him why he didn't see Dr. Romm, and Lenny said that he owed the doctor a lot of money. Sue told him to go and charge the visit to her, but Lenny was too proud to accept the offer.

The conversation then turned to death. Sue had just lost a very close friend, and she was preoccupied with the strangeness of the sensation. Lenny was also deep into the death mood; he told Sue to go downstairs and get *The Road to Immortality*. In the dark she read him his favorite passages from the book. He especially wanted to hear that part about the young men who are wrenched out of their bodies by sudden death. The word "wrench" appealed to him; it was the very English sort of word that his father might have used. When Sue went down the hill that night, she felt terribly sad. She feared that Lenny was going to die. It was his lungs, she was sure. He was dying of some terrible lung disease.

Now this afternoon at the house, they sat outside by the pool and Lenny made one of their oldest jokes. It was a line he used on those nights when he was urging Sue to stay up to all hours working with him on his legal business. "Just stay an extra hour," he would plead, "because I got it! I got it! After tonight, it's not going to be any more. I got the whole *answer to everything* tonight!" Or he would be searching for the ever-missing tape, and he'd say, "Oh, that one piece of tape . . . I just know it has the *answer to everything* on it!" It got to be a joke with them. The eternally elusive answer. On this soupy, lazy August afternoon, he told Sue quite earnestly that he had finally found the answer. She asked what it was. He went into a rap that she had heard months before. Lenny was going around in circles. It was sad-dening to hear. He started talking about the Speck case: the guy in Chicago who had climbed into a nurses' dormitory and killed seven out of eight nurses. Lenny had the answer to this one, too. Speck hadn't done it. It was the eighth girl, the surviving nurse. She was the murderess.

Sue grew so disturbed by the crazy character of Lenny's conver-sation that she did something she had never done before: she asked, "Lenny, are you using drugs? If you are, please don't be high tomorrow when you go to see your probation officer." She had never admonished him like that before; he was obviously troubled. He gave her this very weird look and said, "I'm not high now." "I know you're not," she hastily replied. Yet he kept on staring at her with that weird look in his eye, as much as to say, "How did you ever manage to see through me?" Haunted by that weird look, Sue left that day. She never saw Lenny again.

Shortly after Sue left, Maury was sitting outside at the pool when she heard Lenny calling from John's bathroom, "Where's Maury? Where's Maury?"

I went into the toilet, and he held a piece of silver foil in front of my face. He said, "Would you like some?" It was the first time he had ever done that.

At that point, —— came into the bathroom. I knew he'd called. He'd brought up $500 worth once before. Lenny said, "I want to buy. How much do I owe you?" —— said, "That's a lot . . . it's very strong!" Lenny said, "I don't care." "It's forty dollars," said ——, "but I'm telling you, Lenny, it's a lot." "I don't care, I want it!" said Lenny.

Finally, Sally came and yelled, "Lenny, I'm leaving!" "O.,K., Ma. I'm talking to Maury." He didn't even open the door.

We stayed in the bathroom a couple of hours until his high started to wear off. He wanted me to become Honey sometimes, or he would become Honey and was crucifying himself for having had that happen. [Tony arrives.] He thought I had eyes for Tony. I went upstairs to make him some Constant Comment and a cheese sandwich. Tony started to come on to me, and I was repulsed and embarrassed. He went in the other room, and then I didn't hear from him. I was afraid he fell asleep and would die. So I went in the bedroom and there he was naked. I turned and walked out.

I didn't say anything then to Lenny about Tony. Later at seven-thirty or eight, he was trying to transfer two tapes onto another tape, and it took him about two hours. When Lenny was coming down off heroin, you saw the cruelest part of him. Fortunately, I never let him intimidate me, ever. What I didn't like was what happened to me, that I went with it. He was always so proud that I could hurt him, he wanted me to hurt him. We were sitting there with Tony and I told him that Tony had come on to me, and Lenny said he'd sent him up there to test me.

He was also feeling guilty because the Usherette was coming over there that night with fruit and he didn't dig her. He dug her like I did. She was sweet.

Two and a half months before on a Friday night, he was in bed and I came back from rehearsal and he said, "I'm going to die this year. Two things I want to do first though. I want to finish the

trials." I knew from my father, who was very similar to Lenny,
that if he got uptight or upset about that, they got really uptight.
He wasn't just saying it for effect. He was saying to hear himself.
All I could say was, "Isn't there some way you can wait a year?"

Monday was August 1st, and on the first day of the month Lenny
had to report to his probation officer. Sally had reminded him of his
appointment the day before, joking: "I know you don't like your Jewish
mother taking you, but tomorrow's the first. I'll be here in the
morning."

"My God!" exclaimed Lenny. "I always forget." Next morning,
when Sally walked into the house, she found Lenny making some
strange preparations for his meeting with the law.

When I came, he was standing downstairs with a suit . . . standing
down at the gate. He's got a razor in his hand, and he's fraying
the sleeve. And he looked so funny, 'cause he never wore clothes.
He always wore those denims. And he wore a suit! It was an old
suit with an ascot. I laughed . . . and I wanted to cry. Did you
ever want to laugh and cry? But I would never cry in front of him.
　So I said, "What are you doing?" He said, "You know with
that conviction, I owe two hundred and fifty dollars, and I haven't
got the money, Ma." I said, "I know. So what are you going to
do?" He said, "I'm going down and plead poverty."
　The Usherette drove up—his little friend with the car. And she
said, "I'll take you, Lenny." I says, "O.K. See you later!"
　Well, twelve o'clock that night, laughing, I said: "How'd you
make out with the parole officer?" He says, "Ma, you wouldn't
believe it! He gave me ten dollars! And he cried, he felt so sorry
for me."

Later, that same Monday night, Lenny almost O.D.'d on sleeping
pills. Maury got very upset; and the next day, when she found him
sitting on the toilet fixing with some more of the stuff that —— had
brought, she warned him that he was "overdoing it." She recalls that
this was "the only time I ever told Lenny to cool it."
　By that evening, Lenny was stoned, but he was feeling funny.
Sitting in John's room with the Usherette and Lili and John, he made
his last tape. John had a new Sony tape recorder, and Lenny started
playing with the mike:

Testing the Sony dynamic microphone from three feet . . . testing
the Sony dynamic microphone from two feet . . . testing the new

psychic dynamophone from one feet . . . *tethatphatah* [Mouth on mike roaring gibberish that finally becomes a Samurai voice shouting] *Socking!* . . . *Socking!* . . . *Socking!* [Interspersed with loud, slurpy, sucking sounds]

After a burst of loud rock music, the sleepy, dopey voice of a zonked Lenny Bruce continues:

This is Night Line . . . for all you elderly drunks out there or pill-heads or people who want to talk about important things, like yourselves. Our show is pornography, and the reason we're announcing it is that we pornographers take fuckin' offense at you people who are offended at our humor. Our humor is very good humor, and if you don't like it—fuck you! How *dare* you be offended at our humor! *We're* offended at the fuckin' fact that you're offended—you cocksuckers! We're gonna pornographer our dick off. And we don't need fuckin' religion. We're gonna walk around with our dicks out. If you find any dick-out law, then you can fuck with us.

So he rambled, head heavy, lizard eyes blinking, through all his obsessive themes: narcotics, Maury, life after death, until he ran down like an exhausted spring and the tape rattled off the reel.

The last day of Lenny's life dawned no differently from any other that dismal summer. The first person to awake at the house was Maury Hayden. She had arrived late the night before. Finding Lenny about to retire with the Usherette, she had slept with Lili. She knew Lenny would be angry that she stayed overnight; hence she was eager to get out of the house before anyone awoke. An hour or more after her departure, roughly around noon, John Judnich arose, his mind focusing blearily on the audio equipment that he had to pack that day for shipment to Tim Hardin. About the same time that John began stirring in his equipment-stacked bedroom, the Usherette began poking around the upstairs kitchen. Discovering that there was nothing in the refrigerator for breakfast, she picked up the phone and dialed her sister. "Could you pick up some eggs and sausage and bring them up here? There's nothing to eat and I want to go out shopping."

While she was talking on the phone, Lenny slid back the glass door of the master bedroom and padded out on the balcony, wearing only blue jeans and tan suede desert boots. Stepping into Lili's room he said accusingly, "Maury slept here all night, didn't she?"

"Yeees."

"Well, I don't want that happening again," said Lenny. "I'm beginning to feel like a goddamned pimp!"

There was nothing that Lili could say.

Shambling into the kitchen, Lenny received the news that they were out of food with a shy grin.

"There's always Zip-Quix!" he laughed, hauling a box of ready-made cookie mix off the shelf. For the next ten minutes, he followed with absorption the printed directions for making cookie batter. Then, losing interest in the game, he wandered out into the hall and downstairs to his office, leaving the job of baking the cookies to the Usherette.

Kicking aside the wadded balls of legal paper on the floor of the office, he seated himself behind his desk and stared unseeingly at two open books: *Black's Law Dictionary* and Fricke's *Criminal Evidence.*

"Hey, what's happenin'?" smiled John Judnich, poking his head through the door.

"Hey, what's happenin'?" echoed Lenny mechanically, returning the greeting that had become their daily ritual.

John could see in a minute that Lenny was still down in the dumps. "How do you feel?"

"Ohhhhh!" Lenny groaned, picking at the sores on his bare chest. He didn't say any more. That moan told the whole story.

John was about to duck out the door again when Lenny looked up and said, "Do you know where I can get any shit?"

"My friends are your friends." John laughed. "What do you want me to do—*phone* for ya? Ah . . . I s'pose you could call——."

Lenny just sat there staring. What good would it do? He hadn't any bread. Lucky for him, he still had a taste stashed from Sunday.

John, sensing there was nothing to say, left the office and shortly afterward drove down from the hill on an errand. When he got back at two o'clock, he noticed a familiar car in the parking lot. The Usherette's sister had arrived, and the house was full of the smell of breakfast food.

A few minutes later, the Usherette came down the outside staircase carrying a tray loaded with a fat man's breakfast. She had fried eggs and simmered sausage, hashed-up potatoes, and buttered slices of toast. When she laid the savory meal on Lenny's desk, he grunted appreciatively and cranked another piece of legal-size paper into his typewriter.

A little before four, the Usherette prepared two glasses of tea for John and Lenny. Lili took the plastic glasses downstairs and gave one to John. Noticing that Lenny's door was closed, Lili was hesitating, wondering whether she should disturb him, when she heard a car pull up outside. It was John's buddy, big Bob Balliet. As he walked into the house, she handed him the tea. A half-hour later, John and Bob left to drive over to a doctor's office, where John was scheduled to have some blood tests.

Lili and the Usherette were upstairs at that moment discussing what the Usherette should buy at the store. "I'm going to go shopping now," she said to Lili. "Why don't you come? You know all the things that Lenny likes. Come with me now. You never leave the house!"

"Yes, I'm very nervous," said Lili. "I think it would be very good if I get out of the house."

So the two women went down the steps and got into the car and drove down the hill first to the Usherette's house and later to a big supermarket, where they bought a hundred dollars' worth of groceries. They didn't get back until eight-thirty that night.

Meanwhile, Judnich had gone off to the doctor worrying about the letter he had noticed in the mailbox as he came coasting down the driveway. It was a foreclosure notice; he could tell just by looking at the Home Savings and Loan envelope. It was a wonder they hadn't received it sooner. John had made a couple of payments on the house, but now they were definitely behind. "Shit!" John thought as he stared at the notice. This is really gonna pull Lenny's head down! He shoved the envelope back in the box and gunned his car down the hill.

At six o'clock John pulled into the parking lot again, having come back from the doctor with a little Band-Aid on his arm. Getting out of the car with Bob, he noticed the silence of the house.

"It's John, Lenny!" he yelled, using the prearranged signal that meant "I'm alone or with friends." There was no answer.

He walked through the downstairs apartment toward Lenny's office and pushed open the door. It was empty. The electric typewriter was running. A plate of hard-boiled eggs lay on some paper atop the desk. Water was still boiling on the pantry stove.

Figuring that Lenny had gone upstairs to get something, John walked back out of the house and mounted the staircase to the second-floor apartment followed by Bob Balliet. Together, they searched the rooms and found nothing. When John entered Lenny's bedroom and discovered it was empty, he instantly became apprehensive. Something was wrong. Signaling to Balliet, he tramped down the steps and entered the lower house a second time. Pausing in his own room to get his bearings, he decided to go back to the office and check the bathroom—Lenny's favorite retreat.

"Len?" he called tentatively, knocking on the closed door. Again, there was no answer.

John seized the grip and slid the door open. Lenny was lying

facedown on the floor, naked except for the jeans crowded down
around his boots. A spike was sticking out of his right arm. A blue
bathrobe sash was slung around his elbow. Obviously, he had toppled
forward while seated on the toilet. Instinctively John bent over and
grabbed the body. Hauling the enormous weight straight up, he
almost had Lenny on his feet when suddenly he slipped on the slimy
tile floor and went crashing over backward into the office. When he
opened his eyes, he was face to face with something he had never
faced before. Mucus was draining out of Lenny's nose. A strange glaze
had settled over Lenny's eyes. Lenny's body felt cold and stiff and
slippery. Flashing off every one of these signs: "Dead! . . . Dead! . . .
Dead!" Judnich suddenly unleashed a prolonged scream of horror:
"AAAAAAAAAAAAIIIIIIIIIIHHHHHHHHHHHHHHHH!!!!"

Bob Balliet came charging into the office on the run. "Oh! He's
gone, man," murmured Balliet, staring incredulously at the grusome
spectacle. Judnich jumped to his feet and picked the spike off the floor.
Laying it in the office sink, he ducked into the bathroom, snatched a
washcloth off the rail, soaked it under the tap, and came back to blot
away the blood from Lenny's needle-scarred arm. Picking up the blue
sash at one end, he threw it into a corner of the room. He seemed
intent on restoring the body to its normal condition.

"Oh, wow! Lenny!" Balliet moaned, shaking his head. "Why'd
you do it, man?" Then this big, bearded fellow turned around and
went upstairs, where he found a fleecy white blanket, which he brought
down and draped across the body as gently as you would a baby.

Judnich was slipping into shock as he pulled back a sliding glass
panel and escaped into the open air around the pool. Balliet stumbled
after him. For nearly a quarter of an hour the two men paced back
and forth from the yard to the kitchen, from the kitchen to the yard,
nearly oblivious of each other. Balliet kept pounding his fist against
his thigh and shaking his head. John was mumbling and talking out
loud to himself.

"Burnt it out in, like five *years*! Five years! Wheeew!"

When John finally recovered control of himself, he turned to Balliet
and said, "O.K. What are we gonna do, man?"

Without waiting for an answer, he suddenly strode into the house
and picked up the phone. The one thing he didn't want was a lot of
cops crawling all over the place. He dialed Sydney Irmas's home,
hoping that the lawyer would make arrangements to have the body
removed quietly. He got no answer. Then he dialed up Russell Bledsoe
at his office. Bledsoe had left for the day. Dialing Irmas again, at his
office, John left a message with the answering service. Finally, the
phone rang. Irmas was calling back.

John explained briefly what had happened. Irmas sounded like he didn't want to get involved. "Are you *sure* he's dead? . . . Are you sure he's *dead*?" he kept asking. John and Bob had both been medical corpsmen in the Army. They knew damn well Lenny was dead. Clapping his hand across the receiver, John burst out to Balliet: *"The motherfucker won't believe me!"* Irmas got the message. He mumbled, "I'll come by . . . I'll come over." Then he hung up.

John was now beginning to worry about Sally. He was afraid the news would give her a heart attack. Suddenly, it occurred to him that a guy he knew, Joe Overbeck, would be going that evening to the beach where Sally was living. Maybe Joe could break the news to her. John called him and the guy went completely to pieces on the phone. Disgusted, John hung up. Finally, he decided to call up Jo-Jo, who was always so tight with Sally. He could carry the message.

While John was waiting for Irmas, he went back and examined the bathroom carefully. He decided that there was something wrong about Lenny's death. It looked like an obvious O.D., but the bathroom didn't look like it always looked when Lenny fixed. There was no spoon, no cotton, no matches, no bloody mess from jacking the spike. Everything was much too neat and clean. John knew Lenny's shooting habits intimately—and this bathroom just didn't look right. Something strange had happened. Could someone have come up here and given Lenny a shot while the house was empty? Could someone have *killed* him? Lenny appeared to have been dead for a couple of hours. His limbs were so stiff that he might have been dead for three or four hours. Christ! Lenny could have died sitting on that crapper while the house was still full of people working and talking and laughing!

It was also puzzling that water was boiling on the stove and the IBM humming on the desk. John darted over to the machine and stared at the paper. He was reading Lenny's last words: "Conspiracy to interfere with the fourth amendment const . . ."

John's thoughts were suddenly interrupted by the noise of a car pulling into the parking lot. It was Sydney Irmas, dressed in a neat summer suit. "How are you?" he said, shaking hands. "I just got home from work when I got your message. Jesus Christ! What a shock!"

"He's in here, man," said John, leading him grimly to the body. "Jesus Christ!" muttered Irmas again, reaching down and pulling back the blanket. For one long moment the lawyer stood there, shaking his head sadly. Then he replaced the cover.

It was still light when the police came. First a black-and-white patrol car pulled into the lot. Two blue-uniformed officers came into the house and looked at the body. "Dead on arrival at 6:55," wrote Officer Don

Reed in his notebook. Just at that moment, an emergency rescue van came wailing up the driveway, disgorging two white-jacketed medical attendants. One of them sank to his knees beside the body and probed Lenny's chest with a stethoscope searching for signs of life. There were none, and the condition of the body made the fact of death unmistakable.

The next people to arrive were Frankie Ray, Jackie Gayle, and Jo-Jo D'Amore. John was beginning to get pretty uptight with this parade of visitors. When Jackie started offering dumb, unfeeling condolences—"Really rough! Huh, man!"—John slammed out of the house and retreated to the end of the property. There he struggled to regain control of his enraged feelings. One cop kept a wary eye on him, but there was no security until the plainclothes investigators arrived. Next thing John knew, the house had been sealed off by a police guard, and the parking lot was full of people trying to get into the house. Going over to the gate, he was told he would not be allowed to leave. Two uniformed patrolmen were checking the I.D.'s of the press and TV photographers who were entering the grounds two by two, like guys going to the race track. There was a lot of talking and joking. "Is this Lenny Bruce?" says one guy. "That *was* Lenny Bruce," yaks another. "Oh, that's brilliant, man!" sneers John. He decides to protest against this flock of vultures. Going up to the officers at the gate, he says: "Look, what right have you to allow all these strangers into this house? I don't know who these people are. They're trespassing. This is private property and I live here and I don't want them here!" Just at that moment, a photographer with a big movie camera on his shoulder makes some sort of wisecrack. John grabs the guy and is just about to throw him and his camera into the pool, when he is seized by the police.

"O.K., you! Get in here!" the cops say, hauling John into his end of the house.

"Fuck you!" snaps John.

"Watch your language!" warns the cop, shoving him into the room and ordering a guard posted at the door.

Next, the chief cop—a short, gray-haired detective who looks like a character on *Dragnet*—starts questioning John.

"Did anybody check you for marks yet?" the detective wants to know.

"No, you're the first guy I talked to. But if you want one," says John rolling up his sleeve, "I just came from the doctor."

Spotting the Band-Aid, the cop pulls it off and peers at the arm. Then he marches John out of the house and presents him to four other cops who are standing around in the gathering gloom. They all have a look at the arm while John keeps telling them: "Phone the doctor . . . phone the doctor!"

Sydney Irmas is standing by looking on helplessly as the police badger John. Finally he decides to call the doctor.

"What's the doctor's name, John?"

"Dr. Moss. 763-4407."

Irmas rings up the doctor—explains the situation and lets him talk to the police.

"I'm not on trial! Get away from me!" John is shouting at the cops. Finally the cops give up on him, and John goes over to the fence that rises steeply from the hill beside the highway. From 7:15 on, the radio has been broadcasting the news of Lenny's death, attributing it, prematurely, to an overdose of heroin. Sightseers by the dozen have driven up the hill. The whole street is blocked with cars and the parking lot is full of gaping strangers.

Frankie Ray hears one of the broadcasts. Before he takes off for the hill, he calls Sue Horowitz. She is working late at her job as a secretary for the producers of *The Hollywood Palace*, a television variety show.

"I guess you heard about Lenny, huh?"

"What?"

"He's dead."

"*You're kidding!* . . . What happened?"

"Well, you know."

"No, *what?*"

"Narcotics or something."

Sue immediately drives to the Singer Sewing Machine Center in Santa Monica, where she knows Kitty is taking her weekly sewing lesson. She waits in an anteroom until Sally arrives to collect the child.

The big smile on Sally's face as she walks into the room expresses her unexpected pleasure in seeing Sue. She has not heard the news.

Biting her lower lip, Sue leaps from her chair and grabs Sally's hand.

"Lenny's dead!" she says, blurting out the words.

Sally's face turns white. She drops her purse to the floor, stunned by the words.

"Oh, Sue!" she sighs, her lips tightening.

By the time Kitty has concluded her class and entered the room, the two quivering women are embracing each other in despair.

"What's the matter?" Kitty asks.

"Your father's sick," Sally replies, her voice breaking.

On the drive to the rented summer beach house, Sally is in the passenger's seat—sobbing to herself.

"I think if he's sick, we should definitely go up on the hill," Kitty calls out, from her perch in the back seat. Sally says nothing. "We should go up on the hill!" Kitty repeats.

Sue parks the car and enters the beach house, leaving Sally and Kitty alone. Suddenly she hears Kitty screaming hysterically. Sally has broken the news.

"I want my daddy," she screams, tears streaming down her cheeks as she runs into the house. "I want my daddy!"

Sally follows on her heels. The three of them sit despairingly on a bed, holding each other, wailing uncontrollably. Their tears are interrupted by a phone call from the police, officially informing Sally of the death and asking her to come to the house where the investigation is still in progress.

Up on the hill, Phil Spector was taking Lenny's death as hard as he could manage. Like everybody in L.A. that night, he had gotten the word over the radio. Instantly, he had dialed up his assistant, Danny Davis, and told him that they were taking off for the hill *at once!* Roaring up the serpentine curves of that deadly drive in a raging white Cadillac, Phil blasted his way into the parking lot and stormed past the officers at the gate. Stopping only when he had his winkle-pickers a scant six inches from Lenny's corpse, he began to shpritz all the surrounding officers with hate. "You killed him!"—that was the gist of everything he said, as he laid his weight on everybody in sight. Phil had always used Lenny as a get-off; that night he reached an apoplexy of psychodrama.

Finally, he'd had it with the body. Throwing an abrupt pull-out signal to Danny, he jumped into his huge white hog. Gunning his engine and burning his rubber, he screeched out of the lot and began to roar down the hill like a Stuka pilot screaming down onto the Maginot Line. Danny Davis broke into a cold sweat. He hadn't expected this! Phil was crazy! He was gonna go out with Lenny! They'd both be killed! The next curve! The next car! This is it!

"LENNNNNNNNNNNY!!! HOW COULD YA DO IT, MAN? HOW COULD YA DO IT! LENNNNNNNNNY!!!" The scream of Spector at the wheel mingled with the roar of the engine and the screech of the tires, as they rocketed down that dark and desperate track. Finally, Danny Davis gave up. He abandoned his life. Forced himself to lie back and stare helplessly at the madly jumbled windshield. By that time, the car had reached the Strip and darted off toward Spector's office.

Next morning, Danny was thanking whatever gods may be for sparing his life, when a police lieutenant walked up to his desk and introduced himself. Opening a manila envelope, he presented the astonished Davis with a sheaf of glossy 8 × 10s. They were the official pictures of Lenny Bruce lying dead on the bathroom floor. "I thought you might like to see these," said the officer. "They could make one helluva album cover! The price is five thousand dollars." Danny shrugged and picked up the phone. When he got Phil, he said: "There's a police lieutenant here with pictures of Lenny's body lying naked on the bathroom floor. He wants five thousand dollars for them. What should I do?" The snarling voice on the other end of the wire barked—*"Buy 'em!"*

The police spent nearly six hours examining the body, the house, and the people who had seen Lenny on his last day. At 8:30, Lili and the Usherette drove up to the house, their trunk and back seat loaded with groceries. When they saw the crowd at the gate and the police cars packed into the lot, they had no idea what was happening. Forcing their way through the sightseers, they identified themselves and were promptly ushered into the presence of the investigating detectives. Lili said that she had been living at the house for a week because she was broke, and she had never seen Lenny use any drugs. The Usherette said that she had been helping Lenny with his legal work and had spent the previous night with him. Asked if she had ever seen the deceased take pills or narcotics, she said she hadn't, but she had noticed syringes lying around the house.

When the coroner arrived and made his examination, the investigation was virtually complete. A hearse from the morgue was called and Lenny's body was removed at midnight. Sally was too shaken to go to the house. She couldn't bear the thought of looking at Lenny's dead body. Finally, she called and spoke with the coroner. She begged him to seal the office and post a guard on the property. Next day, she promised, she would come up and assume responsibility for everything.

When the police finished writing up their report that night, the case of Lenny Bruce was virtually closed. None of the investigators had the slightest doubt about what had killed Lenny. They were absolutely certain that it was an accidental overdose of narcotics. Their 1,500-word death report and the pictures they took of the body put the matter virtually beyond dispute. The pictures entailed a little cheating, of course. In the best-known picture, for example, Lenny is shown lying naked on his back with his feet pointing toward the toilet and his torso laid out on the pantry floor. Around his right wrist is coiled the bathrobe sash. Just beyond his limp right hand stands a white cardboard box—conspicuously propped against the baseboards—with the words "Asepto Syringes" clearly visible. The only objection to these props is that they were not part of the picture that greeted the

first investigators who examined Lenny's body. The sash had been
removed from Lenny's upper arm by John Judnich and thrown aside.
The syringe box was found by the police under the bathroom sink. Far
from providing confirmation of the manner in which Lenny died, these
props prove only that the police staged the photographs. The syringe
that belonged in the box shown in the picture was not even a hypodermic syringe. It was the large bulb device that had been used to
irrigate Lenny's arm the year before when he was recuperating from
gangrene.

John Judnich was inclined to believe that Lenny had been murdered because he found none of the litter in the bathroom that always
remained after Lenny's shoot-up scenes. The few drops of blood he
did observe, he carefully removed with a damp rag. The death report,
on the other hand, details almost every kind of evidence that can be
associated with illicit use of narcotics, from a bottle-cap "cooker" to
a box of partly used matches to a blood-filled syringe, matched by
many drops of blood on the floor. It even describes a gray packet of
white powder identical in appearance with heroin. Reading the following lines, what person familiar with the drug scene would hesitate
to ascribe Lenny's death to an accidental O.D.?

INVS. OBS. A BLUE CLOTH (VELVET) SASH OR TIE (APPROX. 20
INCHES LONG) ON FLOOR. ON A COUNTER ON THE NORTH WALL
OF THE DRESSING AREA INVEST. OBS. A SYRINGE WITH NEEDLE,
CONTAINING A RED SUBSTANCE RESEMBLING BLOOD. JUDNICH
ADVISED INVEST. THAT THE BLUE SASH AND THE SYRINGE WERE
THOSE THAT HE HAD DESCRIBED. THE SYRINGE WAS PICKED OFF
THE FLOOR BY HIM AND PLACED ON THE ABOVE COUNTER. THE
DECEASED BODY WAS EXAMINED AND INVEST. OBS. MUCUS IN
DECEASED NOSE. A SMALL AMOUNT OF BLOOD WAS OBS. ON UPPER
CHEST AND A BLOOD SMEAR INSIDE LEFT WRIST. OBS. NUMEROUS
NEEDLE MARKS ON BOTH ARMS. THE BATHROOM IS DESCRIBED AS
BEING APPROX. $5 \times 5'$ THE WESTERN PORTION CONTAINED AN
ENCLOSED BATHTUB SHOWER. THE EASTERN PORTION OF THE
BATHROOM CONTAINED CLOSET BOWL AND TANK ATTACHED TO
THE NORTH WALL. THE TOILET BOWL CONTAINED FECAL
MATTER. ON THE TANK LID INVEST. OBS. A RED BOTTLE CAP
SCORCHED AND SMOKE BLACKENED ON THE OUTSIDE BOTTOM.
THE CAP CONTAINED WHAT APPEARED TO BE A CRYSTALLINE
RESIDUE. ALONG SIDE THE CAP ON THE TANK LID THERE WAS A
SMALL MATCH BOX, CONTAINING ONE UNBURNT WOOD SAFETY
MATCH. ON THE BATHROOM FLOOR ADJACENT TO THE CLOSET
BOWL THERE WAS THREE BURNT WOODEN SAFETY MATCHES.

DIRECTLY SOUTH OF THE CLOSET BOWL ON THE FLOOR AND AP-
PROX. 1½′ FROM THE BOWL THERE WERE 10 TO 12 DROPS OF
BLOOD. FROM THE POSITION OF THE DECEASED BODY AT THE
TIME OF THE INVESTIGATION AND FROM THE DESCRIPTION OF
THE POSITION IN WHICH JUDNICH STATES HE FOUND DECEASED
IT IS OFFICERS' OPINION THAT DECEASED WAS SEATED ON THE
TOILET BOWL AND SLUMPED FORWARD TO THE FLOOR IN THE
POSITION AS DESCRIBED BY JUDNICH. DURING THE EXAMINATION
OF THE BATHROOM OFFICERS OBS. A GREY PIECE OF CLOTHING
UNDER DECEASED LEFT LEG AND BUTTOCK. DEPT. CORONERS
FLOWERS & VONDRA ARRIVED AT THE SCENE, EXAMINED
DECEASED AND REMOVED THE BODY. THE GREY PIECE OF CLOTH-
ING OBS. BY INVESTIGATORS UNDER DECEASED WAS FOUND TO
BE A MAN'S GREY SUIT COAT. THIS COAT WAS EXAMINED BY DEP.
VONDRA WHO FOUND IN THE POCKETS A SMALL METAL BOX CON-
TAINING SOME ORANGE CAPSULES RESEMBLING SECONAL AND
SOME OTHER PILLS NOT IDENTIFIED. ALSO FOUND IN THE COAT
POCKET WAS A BUNDLE MADE FROM GREY PAPER CONTAINING A
WHITE POWDER RESEMBLING HEROIN. A GENERAL SEARCH WAS
MADE OF THE ADJOINING OFFICE AREA AND UNDER A TYPE-
WRITER ON A DESK ALONG THE EAST WALL OF THE OFFICE OF-
FICERS FOUND A PRESCRIPTION BOTTLE, A PORTION OF THE LABEL
MISSING CONTAINING UNKNOWN NUMBER AND TYPE OF PILLS.
BY THIS BOTTLE OFFICERS ALSO FOUND A HYPE NEEDLE. THE
ABOVE-DESCRIBED PILLS, POWDER AND NARCO. PARAPHERNALIA
RETAINED BY DEPUTY CORONERS.

What is to be made of Judnich's vivid recollections of Lenny's
death scene and the contradictory account in the death report? The
only additional evidence of any value is that provided by the coroner's
autopsy in a document titled "Follow-Up Report" and dated August
16—thirteen days subsequent to Lenny's death. This report is the soul
of brevity. It reads:

> Toxological tests show death due to acute morphine poisoning.
> Due to the presence of narcotics paraphernalia found at the scene,
> etc., it is obvious deceased was administering a narcotics injection
> but did not intend to kill himself.

The unexpected finding of morphine poisoning may be understood in
two widely different senses. It is barely possible that Lenny did die of
an overdose of morphine, though there is absolutely no evidence that
he possessed such a drug. What is more likely is that the finding reflects

the perfunctory and superficial character of the toxocological test. The blood analysis that is conducted in cases of suspected narcotics poisoning proceeds through a number of steps of increasing refinement. The early steps determine whether the drug in question belongs to the morphine family. Once this fact is established, subsequent tests determine which morphine derivative was active in this particular case. With Lenny Bruce, the coroner apparently broke off the test series before he arrived at what would probably have been the final finding: heroin.

More important even than the discrepancy between the chemical analysis and the likeliest cause of Lenny's death is the conclusion that the deceased "did not intend to kill himself." The weight of that phrase could easily be missed by anyone who was not familiar with the police procedures of Los Angeles. By the time of Lenny's death, a practice had been adopted in any case of suspected suicide of conducting a thorough investigation—involving psychological as well as physical factors—concerning the manner of death as well as the circumstances preceding or contributing to the death. By finding that Lenny's death was clearly accidental, the coroner obviated any demand that the death be investigated further.

Had such an investigation been made, it would certainly have turned up voluminous evidence to support the idea that Lenny had *deliberately* killed himself. The evidence would have begun to accumulate from the day of Lenny's death, when the notice of foreclosure was delivered and discovered by John Judnich. The foreclosure notice was not in the mailbox when John checked it, and an intensive search of the house failed to turn it up. John believes Lenny read it and flushed it down the toilet.

Lenny Bruce had a profound involvement with his house; consequently, the thought of it being taken from him might well have precipitated suicidal longings that had been building in his mind for months, if not years. He had once told Lee Hill that the day "they" took the house, he would take his life. Even apart from such a disastrous loss, he was convinced that in any case he must soon die. He alluded frequently to his death and sought to prepare himself for this eventuality with his last two acid trips. In the final months of his life he had become chronically depressed, unresponsive, and apathetic. He was in constant pain, as well as $40,000 in debt. His legal mision was virtually accomplished; he had no desire to return to the stage. Neither his family nor his friends meant much to him; shortly before he died he told John Judnich that chicks didn't excite him any longer.

There were many other reasons why Lenny believed that his day was over. He was convinced that he could not communicate with the youth. He was also profoundly humiliated by his criminal conviction and his notoriety. Confronted by such bleak prospects in every direction, impelled by his sense of pride, egged on unconsciously to punish the people who had persecuted him, and convinced perhaps that he would become a posthumous martyr and saint, why shouldn't he have deliberately loaded an overdose into his syringe and simply jammed the spike into the most accessible vein, killing himself with a final ecstatic flash?

The strongest argument for suicide was that made by Tim Hardin in an interview that could not be used in the original edition of this biography because of legal constraints. Hardin and Lenny had both kicked in the summer of 1966 and were maintaining themselves on moderate doses that enabled them to do their work and live comfortably. Hardin was Lenny's supplier, providing him with a portion of the Mexican brown he received once a month from a Mexican customs official, who used to make the delivery in full uniform.

During this period, Lenny spoke often about suicide. He had decided that the best way to complete his life's work was to take his life. His thinking turned on the idea that the negative forces of society had focussed so intently upon him that if he ceased to be, these forces would be totally confounded and forced to disperse. Lenny had always thought about going out on dope. Now he exulted in the idea that, without suffering any pain himself, he could destroy his enemies with a single blow. Hardin agreed with Lenny and argued that the strategy had worked, for only a year after Lenny's death, the moral revolution of the sixties had triumphed.

Hardin made his last delivery on the day he took off for the Newport Folk Festival, which ran from July 21–24. He provided Lenny with a supply of heroin calculated to sustain him at his current level of two shots a day plus a special cache—equivalent to six times his normal dose—designed to assure his death. Hardin was convinced that his dope killed Lenny Bruce.

Hardin's leave-taking inspired Lenny to make a final gesture. Running out into the driveway, he thrust his shaving kit through the window of Hardin's car. "Here," he panted, "I won't be needing this anymore."

The argument against his having committed suicide is almost as compelling. It begins with the fact that Lenny loved life on any terms, and struggled to save himself right down to the end. Recognizing that he might die through an overdose, he had always given his companions detailed instructions on how to rescue him. Confronted on more than one occasion with deadly diseases, he had always fought back from his hospital bed and urged others, similarly ill, to do the same. "Don't cop out!" he shouted at any friend who lay close to death in a hospital. If Lenny had talked about suicide and thought about the best mode of killing himself, he had also said that he would never kill himself— Judnich remembers him saying this, even though John still regards Lenny's death as either suicide or murder. Though Lenny feared that he would soon die from natural causes, there was nothing basically wrong with his health. Nor had he actually completed the legal campaign for self-justification that he had stipulated to Maury as the one thing he desired to complete before his death. Surely, he was intelligent enough to realize that if he committed suicide by taking an overdose, he would not be qualifying himself as an American martyr but would be confirming the judgment of the police and the courts that had stigmatized him as a junkie. Even if life was gloomy at the age of forty, it was hardly over. He could work if he had to. He was still very attractive to women. If things got too bleak, he could always get off with a little chippie dose. Why should he sacrifice every future prospect of accomplishment and pleasure for a single moment of revenge?

Balancing these arguments back and forth—and taking into account the fact that Lenny had overdosed many times and been saved only because help was near—you find yourself wondering whether there is really an authentic distinction in a case like this between accidental and suicidal death. The fact is that by the fatal day, Lenny Bruce was lying on the narrow crack that divides the living from the dead. He was only marginally alive and he was facing the end. When he loaded that syringe, he might well have been motivated by the same attitude that prompted Joe Maini to put the gun to his head and crack, "Russian roulette anyone?" Does a man who really wants to live ignore the warning Joe received and squeeze the trigger? The deeper you look into lives like those of Joe and Lenny, the less do the conventional, virtually unexamined, categories of deliberate and accidental self-slaughter make sense.

The night of Lenny's death, all the TV stations in Los Angeles carried pictures, interviews, and stories about the notorious comedian. Most of the coverage was superficial but restrained. No network outlet would seek to exploit such a grimy event, but one local channel did break the rules of the business. It exposed some shocking and positively obscene footage of Lenny Bruce. The film begins somberly with shots of sightseers hanging around in the gloom outside the house. Then you get a glimpse of the interior, coming to focus briefly on Lenny's messy office and littered desk. Finally, for one brief moment, you glimpse the naked body lying on the floor. You see a fat, lardy-looking man stretched out on his back. As the camera catches the face, it shows a curious expression. It is hard to see on the screen, but if you examine the police picture, the expression is unmistakable. Lenny looks absolutely serene. Maybe even happy.

HOW THIS BOOK
WAS WRITTEN

Most biographers are fascinated first by their hero and afterward by his world. In the case of my relationship with Lenny Bruce, this familiar pattern was reversed. Years before I heard Lenny's name, I stumbled on his world: the fast-talking, pot-smoking, shtick-trading hipsters and hustlers who lent him his idiom, his rhythm, his taste in humor, and his typically cynical and jaundiced view of society. Lenny met this gang at Hanson's Drugstore; I met them on their home turf in Brooklyn during the years when I lived in Bensonhurst and taught at Brooklyn College. It was, in fact, one of my students who introduced me to this "element": George DeLeon—to whom this book is gratefully and affectionately dedicated. George worked in the shingle business with Rodney Dangerfield and Joe Ancis; he was himself a very funny man and a keen judge of comics. Most important, he was a comic guru who taught his disciples how to see, think, talk, and live according to the yoga of Funny! Without his tutelage and a great many years of comic fuguing, I should never have gotten so involved with Lenny Bruce nor understood half so well what Lenny was trying to say and do.

I finally got to see Lenny, at the Blue Angel in 1960, but several years elapsed before I actually met him. As soon as the first of the many articles I wrote about him appeared, we came together. He put me away with one of his elaborately collaged, obscenely captioned valentines, ringed round the words: "Best review I ever got!" I assumed he was impressed by the depth of my insights, the brilliance of my writing. What he really loved was the fact that I was a professor publishing in magazines like *Commentary* and *The New Leader*, which could crown him with the laurel of intellectual status. He was especially thrilled by my likening him to a shaman. Eventually he sucked me into his legal mania, making me his recruiting agent at Columbia University Law School. Many an afternoon I spent on the phone trying to sell him some young professor willing to devote himself to the cause. "No, man," Lenny would whine, "I need somebody with Supreme Court experience."

During Lenny's lifetime I never considered writing his biography. No one regarded him in those days as one of the seminal forces of modern American culture, nor did I have any special interest in his private doings. The information on which this book is built, therefore, is the product of posthumous inquiries, by both Lawrence Schiller and myself.

As I was about to sign a contract for this book in 1969, Larry came to me with the suggestion that we pool our resources for the making of what could prove to be the definitive biography. Larry had been at work on a book with another writer, Richard Warren Lewis, but that had not worked out, and now Larry wanted a new collaborator. So we made an arrangement in which I retained control of the composition of the book, while giving him credit for the massive journalism he contributed. There was no simple way of describing such an unusual collaboration, and so we adopted the formula which appears on the title page: "by Albert Goldman from the journalism of Lawrence Schiller."

Larry had become interested in Lenny after reading reports of his New York trial, but his real interest developed only after Lenny's death. Deeply involved with the subject of drugs (Larry was the first photo-journalist to publish a major story on the indiscriminate use of LSD—in *Life* magazine—and subsequently published a book on the same subject), he was prompted by the report that Lenny had died of an overdose and thereafter began an investigation into his last days. Within a few weeks, he became absorbed in Lenny's life—his family and friends, the judges and lawyers of his trials, the doctors and police officers concerned with his habit, the women who staffed his office and his bed, and the lady who knew Lenny better than anybody on earth, Honey. Larry made Honey his special project. He explored to the depths Honey's remarkable relationship with Lenny, which Larry believes produced the angry, embittered, wise, and brilliant comedian, who eventually walked out onstage and became Lenny Bruce. (The movie rights to Larry's material were sold to Marvin Worth of Columbia Pictures for the film based on the musical *Lenny*, which was made by Bob Fosse and starred Dustin Hoffman.)

Though the Schiller interviews, documents, and legal analyses gave me an enormous head start on the book, I found myself compelled to spend three more years in research before I actually began the writing. Fortunately, I uncovered three extraordinary informants—Kenny Hume, Richey Shackleton, and chic Eder—whose knowledge of Lenny and his milieu, combined with their great eagerness to be of help, allowed me to attempt the sustained close-ups which characterize this book.

The most prolonged of these close-ups is the first chapter, which is an attempt to provide the reader with a synoptic view of the subject's personality and lifestyle at the peak of his career. Nothing in this chapter is fictitious. Lenny's speeches are lifted from letters and interviews; the incidents all occurred in the years 1959–61, and all the facts come directly from interviews with intimates. Likewise, the passages that represent Lenny's thought processes are derived from his free-association monologues.

I wish to thank Richard Elman, the novelist, for his help in writing this chapter. Dick drew many of the scenes out of me onto a tape recorder and then rewrote several of the most important incidents, greatly improving on my original drafts. He also edited down to a single monologue material from three of the interviews which Schiller had conducted with Honey Bruce. Richard Warren Lewis also deserves credit and recognition for his narratives of Lenny's Chicago and West Coast trials, which I have adapted.

I also want to thank all the hundreds of other people who have contributed so generously to the fleshing out of Lenny's history. Though the information is theirs, I should emphasize that the interpretation is mine. I hope they will feel I have captured at least some part of the extraordinary power of Lenny Bruce's personality and the cathartic force of his art. In particular, I wish to thank my four loyal, gifted, and indefatigable editorial assistants—Sharon Thompson, Linda Lee, Mary Carr, and Holly Evarts—who aided me successively during the five years this undertaking consumed. Larry Schiller wishes especially to thank Sally Marr for "opening so many doors" and Honey Bruce for being so honest.

New York, 1974   —Albert Goldman

INDEX

Aaron's Hotel, Bruce's engagement
  at, 427, 429–31
Abrams, Joe, 156–57
Adams, Don, 252
Adams, Joey, 298
Addams, Charles, 252
Adderly, Cannonball, 272
agents, 122
Akerly, Ernest, 425
Alberta, Albertus, 29–30
"All Alone" (Bruce), 256, 258, 269
Allen, Steve, 32, 298
  Bruce on show of, 264–70
  on Bruce's style of comedy, 266–67
Allyn, David, 271–72
America (hotel), description of, 5–6
American Civil Liberties Union
  (ACLU), 224, 401
American Guild of Variety Artists
  (AGVA), 118, 329–30
Ancis, Joe, 40, 45, 50, 126–45, 643
  art interests of, 287–88
  Bruce influenced by, 131, 134, 136–
    139, 141–44, 158
  Bruce's break with, 143–44
  Bruce's relationship with, 129–30,
    134, 137, 142–45
  cleanliness phobias of, 132–33

comic style of, 126–30, 134–35,
  162, 287–88
crazy scenes created by, 134–36
distinctions between Bruce and,
  140–41
family of, 130, 132, 134
heritage of, 142
language use of, 138
lethargy of, 133
music enjoyed by, 133–34
native intelligence of, 137
physical appearance of, 132, 142
public performances of, 140–41
sexual fantasies of, 127–28, 136
Andre's, 432
Andros, George, 253
Ann's 440, 220, 224
  audiences of, 241
  Bruce's engagements at, 240–41,
    250
  description of, 240–41
Arthur Godfrey Talent Scouts, 27, 66,
  123, 232
Ashman, Charles R., 484
  Bruce's drug trials and, 486, 492,
    494, 496–98
  firing of, 497
Auerbach, Art, 377, 382–83

Australia:
    Bruce's engagements in, 426–33
    controversy over Bruce's perfor-
        mance in, 431–32
Axelrod, George:
    Bruce's contempt citation and, 411
    Bruce's obscenity trial and, 388–89,
        391–405

Babour, Sue, 226
Bailey, Pearl, 327–30
    Bruce's humiliation of, 328–29
Ball, Bobby, 24
Balliet, Bob, Bruce's death and, 629–
    631
Ballyhoo, 568
Banducci, Enrico, 294–96
Banks, Samuel V., 466–68, 475
Barnett, Samuel, 315, 319
Barton, Sandy:
    Bruce's acting career and, 116
    Bruce's romance with, 113–15
Basin Street West, *Lenny Bruce*
    filmed at, 592–93
Bateman, Howard, 425
Battista, O. A., 341
Beats:
    Ginsberg's position among, 525–26
    hipsters compared with, 229
    jazz and, 224–25
    police harassment of, 223–24
Bee, Tommy, 307
Behan, Brendan, 460
Belli, Melvin:
    Bruce's drug trials and, 448, 450–
        451, 461
    Bruce's obscenity trials and, 401–2,
        450
Bellwood, Peter, 481
Bendich, Albert:
    and Bruce's attempt to break with
        Fantasy, 423
    Bruce's contempt citation and, 411
    and Bruce's obscenity bust and trial,
        400–12, 462, 465, 479
Bennett, Alan, Bruce's London en-
    gagement and, 413–14
Berkowitz, Malcolm, Bruce's drug
    bust and, 371–72, 374–76, 384–
    385, 387–88
Berle, Milton, 120, 122
Berliner, Harry, 495

Berman, Shelley, 5
    Bruce's bits on, 19, 48
    Bruce's opinion of, 312
    Bruce's success and, 294, 297
    recordings of, 242
Bernstein, Barbara, Bruce's relation-
    ship with, 37–43
Bernstein, Brenda (pseudonym), 601–
    602
Berryman, John, 408
Beverly Hills, Calif., Bruce's obscenity
    busts and trial in, 449–51, 460–
    462, 464–66, 497, 552
Beyond the Fringe, 413–14, 416, 456
Bigarani, William, 223
Billboard, 321
Bishop, Danny, jibes aimed at, 152–
    153
Bishop, Joey, 122, 297–98
Black Leather Jacket, 105–6, 337
Black's Law Dictionary, 461–62
Blakey, Art, 470
Blasband, David, 372, 388, 521
Bledsoe, Russell, 257, 630
Block, Sherman, 447–49
    and Bruce's obscenity bust and trial,
        449, 464
Blue Angel:
    Bruce's engagements at, 3, 6, 19–
        20, 23, 30–32, 45–51, 321
    Bruce's negotiations for job at, 32–
        33
    opening night audience at, 45–51
Blume, Peter, 272
Bonder, Anthony, 367, 371
Bonus, Ben, 569–70
Borge, Victor, 120
Brennan, William, 542–43
Bright, Jack, 329–30
Brody, Samuel, 450
Brooke, Henry, 480–81
Brooklyn, U.S.S., Bruce's duty on,
    110–11, 114–15
Brooks, Mel, 46
Brother Matthias Foundation for Lep-
    ers scam, 73–74
Brown, Mr. and Mrs. Kenneth, 408
Bruce, Harriet "Honey" (wife), 16–
    17, 38, 55, 64–80, 164, 644
    ambitions of, 210–11
    Ancis and, 142–44
    attempts to kick drugs by, 294

black men dated by, 608
Bruce's act with, 71–75, 77
Bruce's ambivalence toward, 260
in Bruce's autobiography, 326, 337
Bruce's blind dates and, 61
and Bruce's care for daughter, 186–187
Bruce's courtship of, 68–70
Bruce's divorce from, 212
Bruce's drug busts and, 300, 303
Bruce's drug use and, 616–17
and Bruce's fall from hotel window, 579
Bruce's finances and, 21, 25
Bruce's first meeting with, 66–67
and Bruce's illnesses and injuries, 351–52, 617
and Bruce's involvement in movies, 157, 170
and Bruce's kidnapping of daughter, 206–7, 209
Bruce's love for, 65–70, 200, 258, 318–19
as Bruce's muse, 214, 244
Bruce's obscenity trials and, 398–400
Bruce's paranoia and, 493
Bruce's reunions with, 292–95, 314
Bruce's sexuality and, 21, 150
Bruce's Strip City engagement and, 148–49
Bruce's vacations with, 320, 326–28
Carson and, 246
childhood of, 64–65
Cobblestone engagement of, 159–60
Colony Club engagement of, 149
in custody battle, 211–13
dancing studied by, 73
drug bust of, 204–12
drugs used by, 65, 75, 77, 166–67, 182–83, 186, 201, 204, 293–94, 331–32, 617
Duffy's Gaities engagement and, 190–94, 197
in Europe, 331–32
finances of, 73, 77, 80, 210
first car of, 69
Francie and, 263, 291–92
freak parties and, 197, 199–200
frozen foods scheme of, 91
Hackett and, 143, 153
harem role of, 600, 602

Hayden and, 604–5, 609–10, 622, 625
illnesses and injuries of, 75, 151, 320, 331–33, 341
imprisonments of, 65, 68, 213, 244, 258–61
jealousy of, 150–51, 199–200
Maini and, 166
marital problems of, 80, 200–3, 205–12, 293, 305–6
physical appearance of, 36, 66–67, 150
pregnancies of, 65, 77–78, 80, 170, 183, 186, 332
probation violation of, 213
psychiatrists of, 314–15, 331, 341–42
Ray and, 312, 314
released from prison, 292–93
sexuality of, 66, 351–52
Shackleton and, 155, 341–42
singing act of, 70–72, 77
strip act of, 149
wedding of, 69–70
Bruce, Kathleen "Kitty" (daughter), 27, 204, 608, 611
birth of, 65, 78, 186
Carson and, 246–47
Duffy's Gaities engagements and, 190–91, 197
in Europe, 331–32
harem role of, 600–2
Hayden and, 605, 610
Honey Bruce's care for, 201, 331
Honey Bruce's imprisonment and, 258
and Honey Bruce's return from prison, 292
and Lenny and Honey Bruce's breaks, 202, 206, 209, 212
and Lenny and Honey Bruce's reunions, 314
Lenny Bruce's Australian engagement and, 429
Lenny Bruce's care for, 20, 55–57, 186–87, 216
Lenny Bruce's death and, 633–34
Lenny Bruce's drug use and, 65
Lenny Bruce's illnesses and, 351–352, 623
Lenny Bruce's kidnapping of, 206–207, 209–10

Bruce, Kathleen "Kitty" (*cont.*)
  Lenny Bruce's suit for custody of,
    210–13
Bruce, Lenny:
  acting career of, 116–17,
    157
  adolescent nature of, 34
  ambitions of, 264
  anger and rage of, 163, 214, 216–17,
    219, 284, 290, 335, 372
  anti-Semitism of, 87
  art of, 141, 230, 284
  attempts to kick drugs by, 290–91
  Balling Chicks of, 601–2
  battery charge against, 439, 448,
    460–61, 486
  bitterness of, 323
  blood obsession of, 343–44
  burglaries committed by, 185
  charm of, 10, 374
  childhood of, 28–29, 84–86, 89, 92–
    93, 99–106
  civil rights action planned by, 578–
    579, 587–88
  cleanliness phobias of, 17
  contempt citation against, 404, 411–
    412
  on creativity, 158
  creativity of, 274–75, 338–39
  criminal mentality of, 324–26
  critics enraged by, 321–22
  dancing studied by, 73
  death mask of, 287
  death obsession of, 617–20, 624–26
  death of, 620, 629–41, 644
  depressions of, 78, 125, 201, 493,
    616, 638
  diet of, 25, 539, 610
  dishonesty of, 183, 325
  doctors conned by, 10–12
  drug album of, 11–13
  drugs used by, 3–5, 7–13, 17–18,
    21, 23–27, 29, 35–36, 42–44, 53–
    55, 58–60, 65, 77, 138, 151, 166–
    167, 173, 176–82, 185, 200, 246,
    260–63, 284–87, 289–90, 316,
    318–19, 324–25, 333–37, 340,
    342–44, 346, 350, 353–55, 359–
    361, 386–87, 409–10, 418–19,
    428–29, 431, 433–34, 445, 469–
    470, 473, 482, 484–86, 489, 493,
    501, 539–41, 549–51, 557–59,

  578–83, 585, 588, 606, 611, 616–
    619, 621–22, 625–26, 639
  drug tests taken by, 338
  dry orgies of, 335
  education of, 14, 101, 103, 106, 108,
    110
  enthusiasm of, 27, 137, 171–73,
    292–93, 497
  exhibitionism of, 197–98
  fall from hotel window by, 576–82,
    592
  finances of, 5, 16, 20–21, 23–25, 32,
    73, 77, 148, 168, 205, 215–16,
    221–22, 274, 290, 315, 331, 361,
    423, 427–28, 461, 501, 584–85,
    596–97, 626, 638
  fist-fights of, 218
  forgiving nature of, 105
  generosity of, 24–25
  girlie magazines collected by, 14
  on happiness, 84
  harem of, 599–604, 606
  health kick of, 333–34
  heritage of, 14, 17, 36, 81–89, 119,
    141–42
  House on the Hill of, 39–41, 57,
    248, 315, 433, 461, 556–59, 585–
    587, 590, 598–99
  iconoclasm of, 322
  illnesses and injuries of, 7, 20, 90,
    200–2, 218, 320, 350–52, 366–67,
    433, 501, 505, 524–25, 535, 550–
    551, 576–85, 589, 617–18, 623–
    624, 638–40
  imagination of, 232–33, 277, 284
  importance of bathroom to, 17, 35–
    36
  information acquired by, 15–16
  insomnia of, 57–58
  jealousy of, 150, 200
  language use of, 138–39
  lethargy of, 157, 366
  life style of, 285–86, 418–19
  loneliness of, 103–4
  loquaciousness of, 103
  madness of, 563, 585, 598–99
  marital problems of, 80, 200–3,
    205–12, 293, 305–6
  masochism of, 99, 361
  maturing of, 115–16
  naked stage appearance of, 163–64,
    193

needle inventory of, 23–24
on overdosing, 53
panhandling arrest of, 74
paranoia of, 488–89, 491, 493–94,
   500–1, 506, 552, 572, 597–99
pedanticism of, 137
pharmacy of, 9–10
physical appearance of, 3–5, 11, 17,
   24, 29, 32, 36–37, 46–47, 60, 63,
   66, 90, 111, 115, 119–20, 124,
   142, 145, 161, 221, 251, 267, 270,
   344, 349–50, 366, 385, 451–52,
   454, 458, 464–65, 482, 485, 489,
   491, 535, 539, 574, 583, 587, 589,
   613, 641
as police informant, 207, 303–5
popularity of, 34–35, 44–45
practical jokes of, 42, 52–53, 152–
   153, 201–2, 217
pragmatism of, 530
press conferences of, 312–13, 385
provocativeness of, 323
psychiatric evaluations of, 492–95
radio enjoyed by, 103–4
reading enjoyed by, 14–15, 535–36
real name of, 65
rectum obsession of, 44
reputation of, 111, 151, 162, 218,
   235, 563, 611
romantic nature of, 68–69, 244–45
salesmanship skills of, 215
self-confidence of, 141, 323
self-image of, 15, 105–7
self-indulgent temperament of, 123
self-righteousness of, 182–83
sexuality of, 13–14, 17, 21, 30–31,
   34–35, 42, 58, 62, 150, 162, 196–
   200, 244–46, 291, 342–43, 603
as shaman, 462–63
shopping sprees of, 333–34
sophistication of, 271
spontaneity of, 78, 365
stage name selected by, 45
stagestruck personality of, 98, 115–
   116
stoicism of, 60
street gang of, 334–35
success of, 15, 91, 238–39, 294–95,
   297, 321, 620–21
suicidal thoughts of, 205, 207–8,
   550, 638–40
tantrums of, 163, 171

tape recordings made by, 24, 31,
   214, 561, 626–27
tattoo of, 7, 265
on tolerance, 336–37
turning point in career of, 214, 220
voyeurism of, 196–97
wardrobe of, 16–17, 23–24, 44, 60,
   63, 79, 119, 124, 404, 409
work ethic of, 36, 38
writing difficulties of, 39
Buccieri, Jules, 333
Buck, Pearl, 14, 96
Burris, Don Edgar, 497
Buttons, Red, 100, 124

Caen, Herb, 241
   Bruce's conflicts with, 295–97
   Bruce's friendship with, 247–48, 250
Caesar, Sid, 256
   comparisons between Bruce and,
      232, 235–38
   movie parodies of, 235–36
Cafe Au Go Go, Bruce's engagements
   at, 511, 514–17, 519–21, 594–95
Cahagan, Lawrence, 487
Callaghan, Jim, 432
Cantor, Eddie, 31
Carlin, George, 459
Carnegie Hall, Bruce's concerts at,
   346–49, 412, 422
Carson, Sheryl, 244–47
   Bruce attractive to, 244–45
   Bruce's relationship with, 244–47
Carter, Leland C., 486
Casey, George H., III, 410–11
Catskills, Bruce's routines in, 71–73
Cavanagh, Vincent, 497
Chamberlain, Wilt, 46–47
Un Chant d'Amour (Genet), 526
Chaplin, Charlie, 105–6, 116, 258,
   264, 502
Chicago, Ill.:
   Bruce's inability to get work in,
      510
   Bruce's obscenity bust and trial in,
      458–60, 465–79, 543
Clark, Ed, Bruce's assault of, 439,
   448, 486
Clary, Robert, 32
Claxton, Bill, 90, 589
Cleaver, Eldridge, 223
Cline, James L., 449

Cloister, 250–53
  Bruce's engagements at, 4, 251–53,
    261
Cobblestone Club:
  Bruce's engagements at, 158, 160–
    164, 188–89
  Bruce's musician friends at, 183–84
  description of, 158–59, 161–62
  Marr's engagements at, 159–60
Cochran, Francis A., 448, 450
Cohen, Esther, 24
Cohen, Mickey, 172
Colony Club, 149
comedy acts and bits:
  on Adolf Eichmann, 454–56
  of Ancis, 126–30, 134–35, 162,
    287–88
  animation of, 594
  on Arab pimps, 456–57
  in Australia, 430–31
  autobiographical, 316
  The Bavarian Mimic, 123–24
  "The Bride of Frankenstein," 72–73
  on being Jewish, 81, 83, 87
  at Blue Angel, 47–51
  on British narcotics program, 419
  and cabaret-theater revues, 255–58
  with campaign ribbons and medals,
    118
  on Cantor, 31
  in Catskills, 71–73
  "Chicken Flicker Skit," 83
  Christ and Moses, 339
  at Cloister, 251–53
  in concert, 316–17, 347–49
  on contents of backstage closets,
    457
  at Crescendo, 217, 338–39
  at Curran Theater, 397–400
  Custody, 452–53
  The Defiant Ones, 257
  at Den, 274, 282, 316
  dirty jokes, 151–52
  double-talk, 232
  on drugs, 191–92, 267, 316, 419
  The Drunkard, 238
  A Drunk There Was, 238
  at Duffy's Gaities, 190–97
  Father Flotsky's Triumph, 49–50,
    237–38, 243
  about Forest Lawn Cemetery, 256–
    257

  at Gate of Horn, 451–60
  The Glue Sniffer, 267
  about gym coach, 128–29
  on hookers' iceboxes, 63
  *How to Relax Your Colored Friends
    at Parties*, 50–51, 257, 321
  at hungry i, 295–96
  impressions, 122–25, 231–36, 238,
    277, 348
  insults, 457
  on intermarriage, 266
  at Jazz Workshop, 378–82, 389–92,
    394–96, 408–10
  The Jewish Mimic, 124
  Lawrence Welk's interview with
    jazzman, 230, 243, 250, 311
  The Lawrence Welk Story, 456
  in *Lenny Bruce*, 593
  Man with the Golden Arm take-off,
    191–92
  The March of High Fidelity, 243
  of Marr, 112–13
  on marriage break-ups, 268–69
  The Masked Man, 103–4, 234–35,
    594
  on mine disaster, 252–53
  about Miss Brown, 129
  about monsters, 72–73, 162
  movie parodies, 235–37
  Mr. First-Nighter, 45
  on obscenity, 139, 339, 378–81, 383,
    389–92, 394–400, 406, 409–10
  obscenity of, *see* obscenity busts and
    trials
  The Palladium, 275–85
  on patriotism, 453–54
  pissing-in-the-sink, 512–13
  political themes in, 226–28
  on racial prejudice, 47–48, 50–51,
    257, 321
  as radio commentator, 622–23
  on records, 241–44, 250
  at Red Hill Inn, 372–73
  Religions, Inc., 173, 239–41
  Rocket to Stardom put-on, 194–95,
    299
  of Sahl, 226–28
  sick jokes, 251–53
  on *Steve Allen Show*, 267–70
  on tattoos, 265
  with telephone, 195–96
  Tits 'n' Ass, 339

To Is a Preposition, Come Is a Verb, 139, 339, 380–81
The Tribunal, 98–99
at Troubadour, 447–49
on typical brotherhood films, 268
unstructured and vitriolic, 336
at Village Theater, 504–6, 511–14
What ifs, 19–20, 48–49, 127–28
"When I Cheat, I Always Tell My Wife," 452
The White-Collar Drunk, 49
comics:
impressionists and, 122–23
polished acts of, 123
Committee on Poetry, 526
Commonweal, 406
Coogan, Robert, Jr., 434–37
Cook, Peter:
and Bruce's expulsion from Britain, 480–81
Bruce's London engagement and, 413–14, 416–17
Cooney, James G., 497
Corey, Irwin, 511, 520
Crater, George, 336, 420
Creel, James R., Bruce's obscenity trial and, 524, 532, 536
Crescendo, Bruce's engagements at, 215–18, 235, 299, 301–3, 338–39
Crowther, Bosley, 546
Cummins, Geraldine, 618–20, 624
Cuneo, Officer, 223
Curran Theater, Bruce's concerts at, 207–8, 397–400
Curtis, Tony, 142

Dale, Alan, 124
D'Amore, Jo-Jo, 476, 487
Dance Hall Racket, 79–80
plot of, 156–57
Dangerfield, Rodney, 40–41, 45, 125, 136, 643
Davis, Danny, 597, 634–35
Davis, Sammy, Jr., 46–47
Dawson, LeRoy, 477
DeAlessi, Gene, 377
Dee, Ann, 220–22, 241
Bruce hired by, 221–22
Dee, Richard, 220–21
Deems, Mickey, 151
DeGrazia, Ed, Bruce's Supreme Court case and, 578–79

DeLeon, George, 643
DeLeon, Jack, 233
De Luca, Joe, 371
DeMarco, Rita, 100
DeMarco, Tony, 100
Demurs, Lowell, 412
Den, Bruce's engagements at, 143, 273–74, 282, 288, 290, 316
Dengler farm, Bruce's employment at, 108
Detroit News, 317
Devery, Nicholas, 431
DeWitt, George, 124
Ditman, Keith S., psychiatric evaluation of Bruce by, 492–94
Dodson, Daniel, 542, 546
Dolan, John, 523
Dracula Meets the Jews, 364
Drager, Judge, 465
Dream Follies, 155–56
drug busts and trials:
of Honey Bruce, 204–12
Lenny Bruce's cooperation in, 207, 303–5
in Los Angeles, 207, 299–305, 434–439, 448–51, 454, 460–61, 470–71, 477, 485–500, 610–15
in Miami, 483
in Philadelphia, 366–76, 384–88, 397
Playboy on, 502
Dubin, Marvin, 482
Duffy's Gaieties, 187–97
action at, 194
atmosphere of, 193–94
backstage scenes at, 196, 201
Bruce's engagements at, 189–97, 201–2, 209, 221, 235
description of, 188
Dulin, Judge, 461
Dunaway, Faye, 21, 481–82
Dunes Motel, Bruce's engagement at, 352–53

Eder, chic, 173–82, 249–50, 544–45
burglaries committed by, 174, 176
on drug dealers, 437
drugs used by, 175–79, 444–45
Fast Harry and, 176–82
Honey Bruce and, 208–9
Lenny Bruce's Australian engagement and, 427–29

Eder, chic (*cont.*)
  on Lenny Bruce's blood obsession,
    343–44
  Lenny Bruce's drug use and, 428–29
  Lenny Bruce's finances and, 427–28
  and Lenny Bruce's marital prob-
    lems, 208
  Lenny Bruce's relationship with, 174
  and Lenny Bruce's relationship with
    Horowitz, 484
  Lenny Bruce's Trolly-Ho engage-
    ment and, 507
  Lenny Bruce's wild romps with,
    439–47, 507–9
Ed Sullivan Show, 312
Ehrlich, Jake, 402–3
Eichmann, Adolf, Bruce's poem on,
  454–56
Elliott, Helen, 526
Elman, Richard, 645
El Patio, Bruce's engagements at,
  318–20
Enrico's, 222–23
Ernst, Morris, 521–22
Esquire, 322, 324, 350
Essential Lenny Bruce, The (Bruce),
  621
Establishment Club, The, Bruce's en-
  gagement at, 413–18

Fack's No. 2, Bruce's engagement at,
  253–55
Fanny Hill (Cleland), 543
Fantasy Records:
  Bruce's attempt to break with, 422–
    423
  Bruce's contract with, 315
  Bruce's recordings for, 241–44, 250,
    253–54, 298, 317
Fast Harry, 176–82, 249
Faux, Trevor, 491–92
Feiffer, Jules, 252, 531–33
Felker, Clay, 322
Ferlinghetti, Lawrence, 222–23, 241
  Bruce's obscenity trials and, 400–1
Fillmore West, 616
Finnerty, Bridey, 466
Fischer, John, 546–47
Fitzgerald, Barry, 231–32
Fitzpatrick, Emmett, 384
Flaming Creatures, 526
Fleet, Count, 374

Fleetfoot, 173
  filming and editing of, 168–71
Ford, Tommy, 124
Fort, Joel, 495–97
France, Jeanine, 190
Francie (pseudonym), 263, 306
  Bruce's relationship with, 288–92
  Bruce's telegram to, 288–89
  overdose taken by, 289–90
Francis, Arlene, 44
Frawley, Thomas P., 449
Friar, Buddy, 117
Fried, Seymour, 210–13, 218
  Bruce's obscenity trial and, 388–97,
    400, 402, 404–5, 412
Friedman, Don, 345–46, 352–53, 419,
  422–23
  Bruce's Village Theater concerts
    and, 501, 504–5, 511
Friefeld, Samuel, 465–66
Friendly, Henry, 573
Fromer, Gary, 185
  Duffy's Gaieties engagement of, 189
  Fast Harry and, 179–81
funny, meaning of word, 131

Gabel, Martin, 44
Gaillard, Slim, 225
Garbus, Martin, Bruce's obscenity
  trial and, 534–36, 542–43, 548–
    549, 559–60, 562, 572–74
Gardner, Harold, 483
Gate of Horn:
  Bruce's engagement at, 451–60
  recording of Bruce's performance
    at, 458, 473
Gavin, Jimmy, 604–5
Gayle, Jackie, 311, 584, 632
Geidt, Jeremy, 414, 417
Geiger, Don, 408
Gelb, Arthur, 406–7
Geller, Herb, 183, 185
  freak parties and, 198–99
Geller, Lorraine, 183–85
Geller Dramatic Workshop, 116
Genet, Jean, 526
Gibbs, Terry, 198
Gilbert, Sally, 247
Gilda, 220
Gillespie, Dizzy, 231
Gilman, Richard, Bruce's obscenity
  trial and, 533, 536–38, 541, 546

Ginsberg, Allen, 401–2
  Bruce's obscenity trial and, 525–26,
    528, 530–31
Glanville, Brian, 417–18
Gleason, Ralph J., 27, 241
  Bruce's friendship with, 247–48
  and Bruce's obscenity busts and
    trials, 382, 405–7, 503
Gold, Herb, 88, 382
Gold Diggers of 1933, 98
Golden, Harry, 142
Goldstein, Leonard, 153–54
Gonzalez, Babs, 225–26, 285
Goodwin, Don (pseudonym), 550–51
Gordon, Lee, 427, 429–32
Gordon, Max, 20, 23, 30, 255
  Bruce's negotiations with, 32–33
Gore, Thomas L., 495
Gottlieb, Lou, 241
  Bruce's autobiography and, 337
  Bruce's friendship with, 248
  Bruce's obscenity trials and, 407–8
  in Bruce's skits, 257
Graham, Bill, 616
Graham, John, 252
Graziano, Ray, 545
Great Britain, *see* London
Green, Abel, 322
Greene, Cecil, 36–37
Greene, Shecky, 46, 210, 257–58
  Bruce's insult contest with, 327, 330
Gregory, Dick, 579
Gross, Ezra, 359–60, 366
Grunwald, Henry, 297
Grush, Seymour, 57, 292, 428
  Bruce's drug use and, 290
  Bruce's finances and, 331
  Bruce's House on the Hill and, 39–
    41, 315
Gump, H. S., 174

Hackett, Buddy, 13, 46, 79, 219
  Ancis and, 126–27, 142, 144
  Bruce's break with, 143
  and Bruce's involvement in movies,
    153–54
  success of, 123, 125
Hall, Huntz, 306
Hanson's, 119–22, 124–25
Hardin, Tim, 604–7, 609, 627, 639
Harrell, Milton, 425–26
Harrington, Stephanie Gervis, 521

Harris, Davey, 125–26
Harris, William, 375
Hayden, Maury, 604–10
  Bruce's acid trip with, 619, 621–22
  Bruce's attraction to, 606–7
  Bruce's death and, 640
  Bruce's death obsession and, 619,
    625–26
  Bruce's illnesses and, 623
  Bruce's love for, 607–10, 622
  Bruce's marriage proposal to, 609–
    610
  Bruce's relationship with, 605–7,
    621–23
  on last day of Bruce's life, 627
Hays, Paul, 573
Hecht, Richard, 449
Heckler, Roy, 29, 272
Hefner, Hugh, 250, 473
  Bruce's autobiography and, 419–22
Hentoff, Nat, 27, 546, 570
  Bruce's obscenity trial and, 406–7
Hill, Bobby, 434
Hill, Everett "Lee":
  and Bruce's obsession with suicide,
    550, 638
  Bruce's performances taped by, 377
  Bruce's relationship with, 549–50
  drugs used by, 549–50, 580
"Hillbilly Lilly" (Bruce), 72
Himes, Bill, 168, 170–71
hipsters:
  Beats compared with, 229
  language of, 229–32
Hitler, Adolf, 258
Hoffman, Dustin, 621
Hogan, Frank S. Bruce's obscenity
    case and, 515–18, 541–42, 545–46
Holiday, Lynn, 185
Holmes, John Clellon, 229
Holtz, Lou, 274
Holzer, Sol, 262–63, 293
Honeytime, 79, 153
Hope, Bob, 120
Horn, Clayton:
  Bruce's contempt citation and, 404,
    411–12
  Bruce's obscenity trial and, 402–7,
    409–11
Horowitz, Sue:
  Bruce's death and, 633–34
  Bruce's drug trial and, 612

Horowitz, Sue (*cont.*)
  Bruce's illnesses and, 582–83, 618,
    623–24
  Bruce's last meeting with, 624–25
  Bruce's relationship with, 483–84,
    497
  harem role of, 600–1, 603, 606
  Hayden and, 606–7, 609
Howl (Ginsberg), 401–2
*How to Talk Dirty and Influence Peo-
    ple* (Bruce), 16, 139, 337–38, 349
  negotiations on publication of, 419–
    422
  serialization of, 83, 501–3
  Steuer's collaboration on, 33–34,
    323–26, 350, 419
Hughes, Charles N., 448
Hume, Kenny, 146–47, 285–89, 306
  Ancis and, 288
  drugs used by, 286–87, 289
  Francie and, 288–89
  Honey Bruce and, 292–94
  Lenny Bruce's drug use and, 290
  Lenny Bruce's illnesses and, 524–25
  Lenny Bruce's *Steve Allen Show* ap-
    pearances and, 265–69
  Lenny Bruce's TV pilot and, 261–63
  and *the World of Lenny Bruce*, 271
hungry i, 226
  Bruce's engagements at, 239, 294–
    297
  recordings made at, 275

International Talent Associates
    (I.T.A.), Bruce's proposal to,
    353, 355–59
Interviews of Our Times, 243
Irmas, Sidney, 616
  Bruce's death and, 630–31, 633
  Bruce's drug trial and, 497–500,
    611–12, 614–15
Isy's Supper Club, Bruce's engage-
    ment at, 424–25

Jacobellis decision, 542–43
Jacobs, Henry, 243
Jacobs, Phoebe, 340
Jacoby, Max, 255
Jaffee, Sol, 327
James, Billy, 54–55
jazz and jazz scene:
  Bruce on end of, 594–95

  Bruce's appreciation of, 134, 164,
    230, 243, 250, 311
  in San Francisco, 224–26
  slang of, 230–31
Jazz Workshop:
  Bruce's engagements at, 377–83
  Bruce's obscenity bust and, 382–83,
    389–92, 394–96, 405, 408–10
  Bruce's performances taped at, 377
Jollis, Merle Gaston (father-in-law),
    64
Jones, Philly Joe, 196
Jordan, Will, 124–25, 233–34
Judnich, John, 591, 597–600, 616
  background of, 557
  Bruce's acid trip with, 619
  Bruce's death and, 620, 629–33,
    636–38, 640
  Bruce's drug trial and, 611–12
  and Bruce's fall from hotel window,
    581
  Bruce's House on the Hill and, 557–
    559, 598–99
  and Bruce's illnesses and injuries,
    583, 617
  Bruce's last tape and, 626
  Bruce's Le Bistro engagement and,
    584–85
  Bruce's obscenity trial and, 572
  Bruce's paranoia and, 597–98
  Hayden and, 604–5, 622
  on last day of Bruce's life, 627–29
Junkie's Lament (Eder), 443–44

Kael, Pauline, 241
Kafka, Franz, 95, 615
Kalven, Harry:
  Bruce's drug trial and, 494
  and Bruce's obscenity busts and
    trials, 471, 473–74, 476–79, 536,
    543
Kamen, Milt, 46, 273
Karman, Harvey, 315, 331, 492
Kasten, Shelley, 250
Kaufman, Bob "Bomkauf," 223–24
Keaton, Buster, 6
Keiser, E. David, Bruce's drug case
    and, 371, 373, 375–76, 385, 397
Kennedy, Jacqueline, Bruce on, 513–
    514, 516, 561
Kennedy, John F., assassination of,
    500, 504–6, 513–14

Kerner, Otto, 477
Kerouac, Jack, 224–25, 229
Kesselring, Albert, 111
Kilgallen, Dorothy, Bruce's obscenity
    trial and, 543–44, 546, 548, 552–
    553
Kitchenberg, Carmen (uncle), 94, 96,
    105
Kitchenberg, Cheil (grandfather), 97–
    98
Knepper, Jimmy, 165–66
Knight, Gene, 321
Koga, George H., 447
Krask, Skip, 250
Krassner, Paul:
  Bruce's autobiography and, 419–22
  Bruce's illnesses and, 524–25
Kroll, Jack, 503
Kuh, Richard H., Bruce's obscenity
    case and, 514–15, 517–18, 529,
    532–33, 535–36, 538, 541, 543–
    546, 563, 568, 575

Landis, Benjamin, Bruce's drug trial
    and, 486–88, 611–15
Lane, Carol, 451
Lane, Robert, 516–17, 535
Lane, Terry:
  background of, 14
  with Bruce on New York City tour,
    25–31, 33–34
  Bruce's comedy bits and, 20
  Bruce's insomnia and, 58
  Bruce's relationship with, 4–9, 13–
    19, 21, 23–24, 35–38, 40–44, 52–
    55, 58–60
  business chores of, 17–18, 21, 23,
    36–37, 40–41
  drugs used by, 4, 8, 44–45, 53
  reading enjoyed by, 14–15
Last Mile, The, 116–17
Latangé, Henry, 73
Law Journal, 569
Lazar, Seymour, 292, 429, 433
  Bruce's drug case and, 451
  Bruce's obscenity case and, 450
  Miller's drug case and, 438
Leader, Maurice T., 478
Leather Jacket, 171
Le B, Bruce's engagements at, 482–83
Le Bistro, 426
  Bruce's engagements at, 584–85

Lefkowitz, Louis, 567
Lehrer, Tom, 252
Leifer, Woody, 243
Leigh, Janet, 142
Lenny, 84, 621
Lenny Bruce, 591–94
Lenny Bruce—American, 579
Lenny Bruce Is Out Again, 584
*Lenny Bruce Speaks for Profit—Tiny
    Tim Sings for Love*, 569–70
Leonard, Jack E., 122, 582
Leshin, Phil, 422
Leslie, Hubert "Hube the Cube," 226
Lesnick, Joel, 447
  Bruce's drug cases and, 299–305,
    434–36, 450–51, 454
  Bruce's relationship with, 304–5
  and Illinois fugitive warrant for
    Bruce, 478
Levinson, Arnold Brandeis, 17–24
  with Bruce on New York City tour,
    25–31, 33–34
  Bruce's relationship with, 18–23, 35,
    37–38, 40–44
  Bruce's sexuality and, 21
Levy, Garfield, Bruce's drug case and,
    372–74, 385–86
Levy, Lou, 164
Lewis, Fran, 341, 344
Lewis, Jerry, 120, 147
Lewis, Richard Warren, 644–45
Liddy, Judge, 70
Life, 229
Lindy's, 121–22
Lloyd, Mabel (mother-in-law), 209–10
Lo Fusello, Rocky, 187–89, 191–94,
    197, 313–14
London, England, 413–19
  Bruce's engagement in, 413–18
  Bruce's expulsion from, 479–82
  Bruce's offstage life in, 418–19
London, Ephraim:
  Bruce's difficulties with, 553–55,
    564
  Bruce's obscenity trial and, 523–24,
    530, 532–33, 535–37, 546, 548–
    549, 553–55, 560–62
  Bruce sued by, 560
London Observer, 415
Lopez, Benjamin, 434
Los Angeles, Calif.:
  Bruce's drug busts and trials in, 207,

Los Angeles, Calif. (*cont.*)
  299–305, 434–39, 448–51, 454,
  460–61, 470–71, 477, 485–500,
  610–15
  Bruce's inability to get work in, 510
Louise, Tina, 21
Loved One, The, 589–90
Lovers, The, 542
Lownes, Victor, III, 144, 418, 420
Luard, Nicholas:
  and Bruce's expulsion from Britain,
    480
  Bruce's London engagement and,
    413–14, 418
Lugosi, Bela, 186
Lum, Barbara, 332
Lyons, Herb, conflicts between Bruce
  and, 293, 297
Lyons, Ronnie, 569–70
  Tiny Tim and, 514–15

MacCambridge, Patrolman, 517
McDermott, Captain, Bruce's obscen-
  ity case and, 459, 472–73
McKeehan, Harry, 450
McKenna, Siobhan, 417
McKennson, William, 488
McLaughlin, June, 259
McQueen, Steve, 19
Magic Christian, The (Southern), 589
Magnuson, John:
  Lenny Bruce and, 591–94
  Mask Man and, 594
Mahoney, Phyllis, 585
Maidstone, 592
Mailer, Norman, 229, 592
Maini, Joe, 164–68, 184–86
  background of, 164–66
  burglaries committed by, 185–86
  death of, 545, 620, 640
  drugs used by, 164–67, 170, 177–78,
    185, 201
  Duffy's Gaities engagements of,
    189–194, 196
  exhibitionism of, 197–98
  Fast Harry and, 176–82
  freak parties and, 197–99
  Honey Bruce and, 294
  imprisonment of, 166
  and Lenny and Honey Bruce's vaca-
    tions, 327–28

  Lenny Bruce's custody case and,
    211–12
  at Lenny Bruce's dry orgies, 335
  and Lenny Bruce's involvement in
    movies, 168, 170
  Lenny Bruce's marital problems,
    208
  Lenny Bruce's relationship with,
    166–67
Maini, Sandra, 184–85
  freak parties and, 199
  Honey Bruce and, 294
"Major Bowes Hour," 118
Mandel, Jerry, 195
Mannes, Marya, Bruce's obscenity
  trial and, 546–48, 561
Mark, Loretta, 364
Mark, Sid:
  Bruce's drug case and, 366, 371, 374
  Bruce's friendship with, 363–66
Markland, Ted, 333, 335, 337, 339–
  340, 344
  Bruce's acid trip with, 619
  Bruce's recuperation and, 352
Marks, Burton:
  Bruce's battery trial and, 460–61
  Bruce's drug case and, 436–39,
    460–61
  Bruce's obscenity case and, 449,
    451, 460–62, 464–65
Marks, Jenny, 465
Marr, Sally (mother), 20, 27
  in act with Lenny and Honey Bruce,
    78–79
  apartment shared by Lenny Bruce
    and, 129–30
  Carson and, 246
  Cobblestone engagement of, 159–60
  dance studio of, 111–12
  dishonesty of, 98
  Duffy's Gaities engagements and,
    190
  finances of, 57
  harem role of, 600, 602
  Hayden and, 605, 610, 625
  Honey Bruce and, 208, 258, 293
  and Lenny and Honey Bruce's
    breaks, 202, 206, 209
  and Lenny and Honey Bruce's rela-
    tionship, 71, 73
  Lenny Bruce's acting career and,
    116

Lenny Bruce's Australian engagement and, 429
Lenny Bruce's childhood and, 28–
   29, 84–85, 99–102, 105
and Lenny Bruce's concerns about
   daughter, 55–57
Lenny Bruce's death and, 620, 631,
   633–35
Lenny Bruce's drug bust and, 300
and Lenny Bruce's fall from hotel
   window, 581–82
Lenny Bruce's illnesses and, 351–
   352, 25, 583, 623
and Lenny Bruce's involvement in
   movies, 106, 154–57, 159, 172–73
Lenny Bruce's Jewishness and, 84–
   85
and Lenny Bruce's kidnapping of
   daughter, 206–7, 210
Lenny Bruce's Naval career and,
   111–12, 115
Lenny Bruce's night club career
   and, 159
Lenny Bruce's obscenity case and,
   540
Lenny Bruce's paranoia and, 488
Lenny Bruce's probation officer
   and, 626
Lenny Bruce's relationship with,
   113–14
and Lenny Bruce's romance with
   Barton, 113–15
Lenny Bruce's show business career
   and, 117, 123–24, 220–21
odd jobs held by, 100, 174
pregnancies of, 96, 98
Ray and, 312
on Schneider, 90
Schneider divorced by, 98–99,
   103
Schneider's first meeting with, 93–
   94
Schneider's relationship with, 94,
   96–100
show business career of, 112–13
stagestruck personality of, 96–98,
   100
Viscarra's relationship with, 160–61
Marshall, John:
   Bruce's battery trial and, 486
   Bruce's drug case and, 470, 477,
      485–87, 489, 492–93
   and Illinois fugitive warrant for
      Bruce, 478
Marshall, Thurgood, 573
Martin, Whitey, 126
Mary Kaye Trio, 215
Mask Man, 594
Mason, Jackie, 575
Mason, Pamela, 315
Mathews, Jan, 554
Meader, Vaughn, 505
Mekas, Jonas, 518, 526
Melody, Tom, 202, 204–5
Memoirs of Hecate County (Wilson),
   516
Merton, Thomas, 454
Miami, Fla.:
   Bruce's drug bust in, 483
   Bruce's inability to get work in, 510
Miller, Arthur, 16
Miller, Eric, 50, 245, 305, 438–40
   Bruce's collaborations with, 320
   and Bruce's fall from hotel window,
      576–78, 580–81
   Bruce's relationship with, 249, 318,
      320
   in Bruce's skits, 257
   drug bust of, 438
Miller, Jonathan, 457–58,
   503.
   Bruce's London engagement and,
      413–16
Miller, Martin, 367
Millstein, Gilbert, 274
Milton, Burton, 112
   Bruce's show business career and,
      119, 124–25
Milwaukee, Wis., Bruce's engagement
   in, 339–40
Ming, Robert, 473, 476–77
Moe the Roller, 45
Moore, Donald Page, 465–66
Moore, Dudley, 413–14
Moore, Paul, 378
Morgan, Henry, 44
Mortimer, Lee, 124
Moses, Robert, 526
Moss, Dr., 633
Munnell, William A., Bruce's drug
   trial and, 495–97
Murphy, Frank, 168–71
Murphy, Tab, 386–87
Murray, Jan, 123

Murtagh, John M.:
  Bruce's injunction against, 564–66
  Bruce's obscenity trial and, 518,
    524, 532, 534, 537–38, 544, 547–
    549, 553–55, 559–66, 569, 574–75
Music Box, Bruce's concert at, 597
Myers, Charles, 369
Myers, F. W. H., 618

Navy, U.S.:
  boot camp in, 109–10
  Bruce's career in, 109–15
  Bruce's discharge from, 114
  Bruce's enlistment in, 107–11
  shock of being in, 109
NBC-TV, 218
Neimetz, David, 487
New Faces, 229
Newhart, Bob, 339
Newsweek, 5, 14, 84, 503, 533, 536
New York City:
  Bruce, Lane, and Levinson in, 25–
    31, 33–34
  Bruce's concerts in, 344–49, 412,
    419–20, 422, 500–1, 503–6, 511–
    514, 569–70
  Bruce's difficulty getting work in,
    510–11
  Bruce's life style in, 285–86
  Bruce's obscenity bust and trial in,
    514–49, 552–56, 559–75, 615–16
New York Daily News, 321
New Yorker, 414
New York Herald Tribune, 570
New York Journal-American, 321
New York Law Journal, 559
New York Society for the Suppression
  of Vice, 568
New York Times, 15, 274, 406, 528–29
Nichols and May, 252, 255, 273
Niebuhr, Reinhold, Bruce's obscenity
  trial and, 528–30
Norman, Gene, 338
  Bruce's drug bust and, 302–3
  Bruce's feud with, 215–16
Noro, Michael, 468–69, 475
Nye, Louis, 261

obscenity busts and trials:
  in Beverly Hills, 449–51, 460–62,
    464–66, 497, 552

  and Bruce's injunction against Mur-
    tagh, 564–66
  in Chicago, 458–60, 465–79, 543
  and circulation of petitions, 526–28
  in New York, 514–49, 552–56,
    559–75, 615–16
  Playboy on, 502–3
  press coverage of, 528–29, 531, 541
  in San Francisco, 382–83, 388–412,
    462, 464–66, 479, 588
  and transcript errors, 552, 560
O'Connor, Norman, 469
Off Broadway, Bruce's engagement at,
  549–50
Olwin, Derek, 204–5
O'Neal, William, 516–17
One Night Stand, Bruce's appearance
  on, 270–73
Orchid Room, Bruce's engagement at,
  202–3
Overbeck, Joe, 631

Parker, Charlie, 137, 231, 285
  and *Dracula Meets the Jews*, 364
  Maini's admiration for, 164–65, 189
  San Francisco Renaissance and, 224
Partisan Review, 457–58, 503
Paulakis, Vita "The Sculptor," 440–41
Peabody, Judy, 578, 616
  Bruce's acquaintance with, 570–71
  Bruce's obscenity trial and, 570–72
Peabody, Sam, 570–71
Perry, Albert, 367, 375
Peters, J. R., 495
Philadelphia, Pa.:
  Bruce's concerts in, 344, 350
  Bruce's drug bust and trial in, 366–
    376, 384–88, 397
Philadelphia Bulletin, 385
Phipps, Kenneth M., Bruce's obscen-
  ity trial and, 524, 532, 569
Pitchess, Peter J., 499
Playboy, 5, 14
  Bruce's autobiography and, 83,
    419–20, 501–3
  Bruce's Gate of Horn show and,
    458
Playboy Club, 144
Pollock, Jackson, 224
Polsky, Ned, 229
Portnoy's Complaint (Roth), 139–40
Post-Buckley Bill, 567–68

Potter, Daniel, Bruce's obscenity trial and, 546–47, 552
Powers, Gary, Bruce's bit on, 453–54
Prince, Dina, 148
Pully, B. S., 174

Raft, Tommy Moe, 66–67
Ray, Frankie, 201, 209–10, 217–20
  and Bruce's commercials, 311
  Bruce's death and, 632–33
  Bruce's relationship with, 306, 311–314
  in Bruce's skits, 257–58
  and Bruce's vacations with wife, 326–27
Realist, 419–20
Red Hill Inn, Bruce's engagements at, 362–63, 365, 372–73
Reed, Don, 631–32
Rembar, Charles, 569
Rennie, Michael, 148
Reporter, 407
Rexroth, Kenneth, 225
Reyes, Flip, 114
Ribback, Alan, 459–60
Richmond, Bill, 147
Rickles, Don, 220
Riot in Cell Block 9, 237
Rivera, Hector, 76
Riviera Theater, Bruce's concert at, 317
RKO Jefferson, 122
Road to Immortality, The (Cummins), 618–20, 624
Rocket Boy, 154, 159
Rogue, Bruce's negotiations with, 35
Roheim, Geza, 462
Romm, John David, 501, 581–84, 618, 624
Romney, Hugh, 602
Romney, Lili, 597
  Bruce's death and, 635
  Bruce's last tape and, 626
  harem role of, 601–3
  Hayden and, 622
  on last day of Bruce's life, 627–39
Roosevelt, Franklin D., 567–68
Rose, Jack, 307, 310
Rosenberg, Harold, 503
Rosenfeld, Maurice, Bruce's obscenity case and, 473, 476–77, 479
Ross, Deputy District Attorney, 465

Ross, Frank, 215
Rotenberg, Norman P., 11–12, 429, 435, 483
  Bruce's drug trial and, 493–95
Roth, Philip, 139–40
  Bruce's obscenity trial and, 531, 533–34
Rovinsky, Selma, Bruce's obscenity trial and, 559, 569–69, 572
Ruhe, Herbert S., Bruce's obscenity case and, 515, 523, 534–35
Russell, Lillian, 6
Russo, Lieutenant, 517
Ryan, James, Bruce's obscenity trial and, 389–93, 404–5
Ryan, Michael J.:
  and Bruce's obscenity bust and trial, 466–68, 471–77
  Bruce's telegrams to, 474–75
Ryder, Eddie, 147

Sahl, Mort, 222, 241–42
  background of, 226
  Bruce's opinion of, 312
  Bruce's success and, 294–95, 297
  comedy of, 226–28
  comparisons between Bruce and, 15, 228, 320
  information acquired by, 15
St. Louis Globe Democrat, 312
Sales, Grover:
  Bruce's friendship with, 249
  Bruce's obscenity trial and, 408
Sanders, Bob, 432
San Francisco, Calif.:
  Bruce's difficulty getting work in, 510–11
  Bruce's obscenity case in, 382–83, 388–412, 462, 464–66, 479, 588
  Bruce's success in, 238–39
  jazz in, 224–26
  poetry in, 225
  Renaissance of, 222–26
San Francisco Chronicle, 383, 403, 412
Santamaria, Mongo, 504–6
Sarod, Irving, 524, 584
Schaap, Dick, 570
Schaefer, Arthur, Bruce's obscenity trial and, 389, 391–94, 403
Schaeffer, Justice, Bruce's obscenity case and, 478–79
Schayer, Gerald, 449, 464

Schiller, Harry, 306
Schiller, Lawrence, 644–45
Schmidt, Howard, 439
Schneider, Dorothy Cohen (step-
    mother):
  and Lenny and Honey Bruce's mar-
    riage, 76–77
  Lenny Bruce's childhood and, 28,
    101–3
  and Lenny Bruce's enlistment in
    Navy, 107
  Marr compared with, 101
Schneider, Mark (uncle), 92, 103
Schneider, Myron "Mickey" (father),
    90–108, 209
  background of, 91–93
  in dealings with Honey Bruce, 91
  education of, 93, 99
  finances of, 102
  Hayden and, 607–8
  as Jewish mother, 94–96
  and Lenny and Honey Bruce's mar-
    riage, 76–77
  Lenny Bruce loved by, 104–5
  Lenny Bruce's break with, 77, 104–
    105, 116
  Lenny Bruce's childhood and, 28,
    86, 99–106
  Lenny Bruce's drug use and, 360
  and Lenny Bruce's enlistment in
    Navy, 107–8, 110
  Lenny Bruce's House on the Hill
    and, 315
  Lenny Bruce's Jewishness and, 86
  and Lenny Bruce's relationship with
    police, 305
  Lenny Bruce's reunions with, 115–
    116
  Marr divorced by, 98–99, 103
  Marr's first meeting with, 93–94
  Marr's relationship with, 94, 96–100
  physical appearance of, 76, 90, 97
  professional status of, 93
Schwartz, Allen, Bruce's obscenity
    trial and, 521–23, 540–41, 553,
    555
Shackleton, Richard, 184, 333–37,
    339–42
  drugs used by, 166, 334
  health kick of, 333–34
  Honey Bruce and, 155, 341–42
  Kitty Bruce and, 186

Lenny Bruce's arguments with, 323,
    350
  Lenny Bruce's autobiography and,
    337–38, 419
  Lenny Bruce's collaborations with,
    341, 344, 349
  at Lenny Bruce's dry orgies, 335
  and Lenny Bruce's involvement in
    movies, 154–55, 157, 168–69,
    171
  Lenny Bruce's recuperation and,
    352
  Lenny Bruce's relationship with, 155
Shaffron, Buddy, 173
Shapiro, Bennie, 257
Shay, Dorothy, 70
Shearing, George, 378
Sheldon, Jack, 184
  drugs used by, 201
  Duffy's Gaities engagements of,
    189, 193–94
  Rocket to Stardom put-on and, 194–
    195
Sheldon, Patty, 184
Sherman the Shutter, 187
Shorer, Mark, 241
show business, 117–26
  agents and, 122
  Bruce's analysis of, 45, 117–18,
    275–85, 339
  Bruce's break in, 123–24
  hangouts for people in, 119–22,
    124–26
  impressionists and, 122–25
Sick Humor of Lenny Bruce, The, 298
"Sick White Negro, The" (Miller),
    503
Silverstein, Shel, 602
Sims, Bennett, 317, 354–62
  on Bruce's act, 361–62
  Bruce's break with, 366
  Bruce's drug bust and, 368
  Bruce's drug use and, 360
  Bruce's I.T.A. proposal and, 355–
    359
  Bruce's relationship with, 354–55,
    359–61
  drugs used by, 360, 362, 366
Skelton, Red, 49
Slate, Henry, 219
Slate Brothers, Bruce's management
    at, 218–20

Sloate, Maynard, 146–49, 158, 183, 215, 217
Smith, Jack, 526
Smith, Julie Mae, 499
Sobel, Jack Nathan, 318, 353
  Bruce's appearances on *Steve Allen Show* and, 264
  Bruce's Australian engagement and, 426
  Bruce's autobiography and, 420–21
  Bruce's break with, 423–24
  Bruce's Den engagement and, 273
  Bruce's London engagement and, 413–14
  Bruce's obscenity trial and, 401–2
  Bruce's TV pilot and, 261
  Bruce's Village Theater concerts and, 511
  and *The World of Lenny Bruce*, 270
Solden, James, 390, 393–94
Solomon, Ella, 521, 548, 562
Solomon, Harold, 498
Solomon, Howard:
  Bruce's Cafe Au Go Go engagement and, 511
  obscenity bust and trial of, 520–23, 562, 575, 615–16
Soulman, 36–37
Southern, Terry, 344
  Bruce offered film role by, 589–90
  Bruce's relationship with, 588–91
  pranks played by Bruce and, 591
South Seas, Bruce's engagement at, 216
Speck, Joe, 489
Spectator, 418
Spector, Phil, 594–97, 616, 622
  background of, 595–96
  Bruce's death and, 634–35
  Bruce's relationship with, 594–97
Spellman, Cardinal, 526
Spivak, William, Jr., 433
Stamp Help Out (Bruce), 17, 171, 316, 344, 349–50, 356, 412
Statute 1140-A, 566–68, 574
Staunton, Ann, 168, 170
Stavers, Gloria, 342–43, 454
  Bruce's blind date with, 59–63
  postcards sent to Bruce by, 59
Stern, Bruce, 183
Steuer, Art, 322, 339
  background of, 324

Bruce's autobiography and, 33–34, 323–26, 350, 419
Steven Allen Show, Bruce's guest appearances on, 264–70
Storch, Larry, 125, 233
Strip City, 146–54
  Bruce's engagements at, 148–54, 157–58
  description of, 146–48
Strong, Frederick, 523
Sullivan, Ed, 233–34, 312, 575
Sultan, Arnie, 125
Supreme Court, U.S.:
  Bruce's civil rights case and, 578–579, 588
  obscenity rulings of, 542–43, 566
Swan, Bob, 168, 170
Swank, 459
Sylvester, Bob, 321

Tante, Judge, 470
Taylor, Elizabeth, 14, 266–67
Time, 4–5, 227, 297–98, 302, 513
Tiny Tim, 514–15, 525
  in planned concert with Bruce, 569–570
Town Hall, Bruce's concert at, 419–20
Tracy, Robert, 408
Trilling, Lionel, Bruce's obscenity trial and, 528–30
Trolley-Ho, Bruce's engagement at, 507
Trop, Jules, 483
Tropic of Cancer (Miller), 542
Troubadour:
  Bruce's engagement at, 447–49
  Bruce's obscenity bust at, 464
  disclaimer posted by, 447
Trout, Carl, Bruce busted by, 299–305
Truman, Harry, impressions of, 124
Tucker, Phil, 156, 168, 170
Tweed, A. R., 495
Twentieth-Century Fox, 153
Tynan, Kenneth, 530
  Bruce's London engagement and, 414, 416–18
Tyrrell, Arthur, 468, 475

Unicorn, Bruce's obscenity bust at, 464

Usherette, 602, 625–26
  Bruce's death and, 635
  on last day of Bruce's life, 627–29

Valentino, Rudolph, 97
Vancouver, Bruce's engagement in,
  424–26
Vancouver Sun, 424–26
Van den Haag, Ernest, Bruce's ob-
  scenity trial and, 546, 548
Variety, 124, 315, 321, 350, 355, 426
Village Theater:
  Bruce's concerts at, 500–1, 503–6,
  .511–14, 569–70
  fire bombing of, 500–1, 504, 506
Village Vanguard, Bruce's engage-
  ments at, 462–63
Village Voice, 521
Viscarra, Tony, 57
  Bruce's drug use and, 433–34
  Bruce's marital problems and, 202
  drug bust of, 434–37
  Duffy's Gaieties engagements and,
  190
  Hayden and, 625
  Marr's relationship with, 160–61

Walters, Isy, 424–25
Warner, Al, 217–18
Wasserman, Jack, 424–25
Watkins, Ralph, 340
Wayne, Seymour:
  Bruce's drug trial and, 488–92
  Bruce's paranoia and, 488–89, 491
Weaver, Helen, 526–27
Weaver, Pat, 264
Weeks, Jack, 173
Weiss, Max, 241–43, 331
Welk, Lawrence:
  Bruce's bits on, 230, 243, 250, 311,
  456
  Bruce's legal problems with, 249–50
Weston, Doug, 447
White, John Lee, 447

Bruce's drug case and, 435, 450,
  499–500, 612
narcotics charges against, 499–500,
  612
Williams, Tennessee, 16
Wilson, Edmund, 516
Winchell, Walter, 321
Winchester, Lem, 365
Winter Garden, Bruce's concert at,
  432
Winters, Jonathan, improvisations of,
  295
Wolfe, Tom, 595
Wollenberg, Albert, Jr.:
  on Bruce's drug use, 409–10
  Bruce's obscenity trial and, 403–4,
  406–11
*Wonderful Sick Evening with Lenny
  Bruce, A*, 258
World of Lenny Bruce, The, 270–73
Worth, Marvin, 123, 151
  Ancis and, 126, 142
Wyndon, Barbara, 430–31

Yaekel, Betty, 194
Yaekel, Bob, 194
Yanov, Jack, 511
Yarnell, David, 261
Young, Lester, 224, 229
Youngman, Henny, 122
Your Show of Shows, 236

Zaentz, Saul, 241–42, 422
Zaidins, Earle Warren, 422–23, 510
  and Bruce's expulsion from Britain,
  481–82
  Bruce's obscenity case and, 466–75
Zanuck, Darryl, 153–54
Zanuck, Richard, 154
Zapruder, Abraham, 513
Zawackis, John, 367
Zeidler, Marvin, 307
Zeidler & Zeidler, Bruce's commer-
  cials for, 306–11
Zucchini, Dr., 186